COLLECTED POEMS

Ted Hughes

COLLECTED POEMS

Edited by Paul Keegan

Farrar, Straus and Giroux / New York

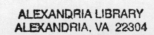

Farrar, Straus and Giroux
19 Union Square West, New York 10003

The Library of Congress has cataloged the hardcover edition as follows:
Hughes, Ted, 1930–
    [Poems]
    Collected poems / Ted Hughes.— 1st ed.
        p. cm.
    ISBN 0-374-12538-4 (hc : alk. paper)
    I. Title

PR6058.U37A17 2003
821'.914—dc22   2003059938

Paperback ISBN-13: 978-0-374-52965-9
Paperback ISBN-10: 0-374-52965-5

www.fsgbooks.com

1 3 5 7 9 10 8 6 4 2

Preface

'The page is printed.'

I

The present edition gathers in one volume the poetry published by Ted Hughes. It includes the familiar sequence of individual collections, from *The Hawk in the Rain* (1957) to *Birthday Letters* (1998), and takes account of a less familiar penumbra of broadsides, pamphlets and limited editions, published by numerous small presses and imprints during the same decades in which the official canon of his poetry was established with Faber and Faber. Hughes's engagement with small press publication extended to the co-ownership of actual presses, as a collaborative, even familial mode of literary production – and as an alternative to the protocols of trade publishing, according to which an author might be expected not to contribute to the design of a book, or choose its endpapers, or propose the typeface (declaring an abiding preference for blackest Bodoni) – all of which counted among Hughes's concerns.

During the 1970s, at the height of this engagement, much of Hughes's writing was initially published or collected by the Rainbow Press, an imprint owned by the poet and his sister Olwyn Hughes. ('The name of the press was related to an early plan – defeated by vagaries in the availability of materials – to have each smaller-format title bound in a different shade of leather so that the book spines would form a "rainbow" along the shelf.'*) Between 1979 and 1983, to take another example, the Morrigu Press – consisting of an Albion hand press contributed by Olwyn Hughes – published nearly twenty separate broadsides of individual poems by Hughes, all printed by his son Nicholas (a Blakean version of ownership of the means of production). Again, the Gehenna Press (*Paradise Lost*, I, 405: '. . . And black *Gehenna* call'd, the Type of Hell'), set up by his lifelong friend and collaborator Leonard Baskin, published the first broadside of a Hughes poem in 1959 – 'Pike', from *The Hawk in the Rain* – and equally published his very last volume of poetry, *Howls & Whispers*, 'during the

---

* Keith Sagar and Stephen Tabor (eds.), *Ted Hughes. A Bibliography. 2nd Edition. 1946–1995* (1998), p. 4

promising Spring of 1998', as the Gehenna colophon hopefully expressed it, just a few months before his death.

There was no Faber edition of *Howls & Whispers*, nor of several other private press volumes, notably *Recklings* (1967), *Orts* (1976), *A Primer of Birds* (1981), and *Capriccio* (1990). On the other hand, *Remains of Elmet*, *Spring Summer Autumn Winter* (*Season Songs*), *Prometheus On His Crag* and *Moortown Elegies* (*Moortown Diary*) began as limited editions and subsequently became Faber volumes. For Hughes these practices were complementary rather than opposed, and one of the roles of the small press was as a tiring room or rehearsal space. A constant small revisionary activity accompanied – or even defined – the sending out of poems into the world. On their first publication, in the sense of 'issued for sale to the public', many poems were already subject to post-publication revision. The *Collected Poems* must therefore reconcile two *systems* of publication within one chronology: the volumes which established Hughes's reputation – *The Hawk in the Rain*, *Lupercal*, *Wodwo*, *Crow*, *Cave Birds*, *Gaudete*, *River* and other collections – were accompanied or tugged into view by a hidden flotilla of smaller vessels, some of them fugitive, gaily coloured and strangely shaped. If the present edition, like the *Collected Poems* of any poet, ratifies a known body of work, it is also a display of fresh evidence: the poet encountered in these pages has yet to be fully assimilated.

In addition to the private press editions, many individual poems by Hughes first appeared in periodicals and as contributions to books. From the outset, and encouraged by his first wife Sylvia Plath, Hughes made extensive use of periodical publication prior to collecting poems in volume form. Later on, the private press to some extent replaced the intermediate role of the periodical, but throughout his career Hughes sent poems out to an eclectic and inclusive range of journals and magazines. Many of these – American or Australian as much as British – were short-lived, and many of the poems which appeared in their pages were never reprinted. The present edition has sought to include all (nearly one hundred and fifty) uncollected poems.

With the exception of the poems written for children, whose presence or absence is discussed below, the *Collected Poems* therefore includes the ensemble of the published poetry. Or rather, it includes *only* the poems which Hughes published (or which, in two relevant instances, were broadcast rather than printed). His manuscripts, now deposited in various collections – most importantly in the Robert W. Woodruff Library at Emory University, Atlanta – are voluminous for all aspects of the poetry and all stages of the career, but their collation must await the long-term project of a *Complete Poems*. For the present edition, pre-publication materials have not been consulted: no unpublished poems have been included in the text, and no manuscript drafts or variants for published poems have been recorded in the notes. The *Collected Poems* is an interim edition, restricted to the print history of the poetry.

II

Questions of structure inevitably arise, given the involutions of that history. On the one hand, the various kinds of publication – periodical, private press, trade – are accorded equal rights of inclusion. On the other hand a chronology must be established, and therefore a hierarchy. Hence the *Collected Poems* retains the familiar public shapes of Hughes's poetry – its volume-by-volume progress, from *The Hawk in the Rain* to *Birthday Letters* – as an overall structural principle: the sequence of Faber collections has been followed, as have their individual contents and ordering of poems. A slight exception has been made for *Crow*, which evolved through a succession of part-publications, and is here presented as a process which both preceded and followed the Faber edition.

Those private press volumes for which there were no subsequent Faber editions have been included in their entirety. However, where individual poems from these volumes appeared later on in Faber contexts, the *Collected Poems* follows suit: thus a poem from *A Primer of Birds* (1981) which reappears in *Wolfwatching* (1989) is placed with the latter collection, to reflect Hughes's intentions and to maintain the familiar contours of his poetry. The endnotes to each collection explain the local accommodations required in the interests of what might be called chronological advantage.

Sometimes the Faber collections themselves have more than one life. *Remains of Elmet* (1979) and *River* (1983) were considerably altered for their reissue in *Three Books* (1993). Since the *Collected Poems* has sought to include all of Hughes's printed poems – including poems subsequently omitted from the canon as it evolved – it has been decided to print the contents and follow the ordering of the original Faber editions, for reasons of chronology and of inclusiveness, while nevertheless offering the revised texts of individual poems (see the Note on the Text, page 1238). Likewise, the new poems which Hughes *added* to these two sequences in 1993 find their point of entry later on in the *Collected Poems*.

The attempt to shape a single chronology, while preserving the integrity of individual Faber collections, has dictated that uncollected poems be entered in groups between those collections – following Hughes's own policy when he inserted groupings of hitherto uncollected poems at various junctures in his *New Selected Poems* (1995). They are here entered by their dates of (first) publication, and the chronology of the edition is in all respects a chronology of publication. There is little evidence in Hughes's typescripts for dates of composition, and his tendency to engage simultaneously in different projects discourages attempts to date poems circumstantially by composition.

III

Hughes's collections are full of cross-pollination. Poems originally intended for *Crow* were finally published in *Cave Birds*; poems shared out between *Wodwo* and *Recklings* were first published together on the same pages of periodicals; the *Gaudete* epilogue poems have close affinities with *Orts*, and so on. On the one hand, from *Crow* onwards, Hughes worked predominantly with sequences (*Moortown Diary, Season Songs, Gaudete, Adam and the Sacred Nine, Cave Birds, Prometheus On His Crag, River, Remains of Elmet, Tales from Ovid, Birthday Letters*), the only thoroughgoing exception to which is *Wolfwatching*. On the other hand, the borders even of the sequence are permeable to a traffic in individual poems, as if the alternative modes of production at his disposal encouraged Hughes to take a provisional view of what might be termed the unrepeatability of the poem, and its supposed fixity of place.

Thus a well-known poem like 'A Dove' appears in *A Primer of Birds* (1981), and in *Season Songs* (1985), and in *Wolfwatching* (1989); individual poems from *The Hawk in the Rain, Lupercal* and *Wodwo* reappear three decades later in *Elmet* (1994); sometimes the same poem belongs equally in two collections (as opposed to putting in a guest appearance): 'Sheep' and 'March Morning Unlike Others' are integral both to *Moortown Diary* and to *Season Songs*, and are entered in both sequences in the present edition. This plurality of intentions means that editorially there are false friends throughout the work – the same poem under different titles, different poems under the same title – and that the fortunes of any individual poem are likely to be picaresque: 'Leaf Mould', to take one example, was first collected in *Remains of Elmet* (1979) under the title 'Hardcastle Crags'; it reappeared in the *TLS* in 1985, in heavily revised form but using the same title, and this version was then collected with further revisions in *Wolfwatching* (1989) under the new title of 'Leaf Mould'; after which it re-entered *Remains of Elmet* – in *Three Books* (1993) – and was reprinted in *Elmet* (1994) before coming to rest, with further small variations, in *New Selected Poems* (1995).

Hughes changed poems when he changed their places. Moreover these revisions were not usually incorporated into subsequent reprints of the collection in which the poem originally appeared. For example, the changes made to various *Wodwo* poems for their inclusion five years later in *Selected Poems 1957–1967* were never incorporated into subsequent reprints of *Wodwo*. The reader stands in an open and populous field, rather than on the path of a tidy self-replacement in which earlier versions are progressively disowned. Several texts of a Hughes poem often coexist in print, depending on whether it is encountered in its original setting, or in the changed context of a later collection, or in one of his several selections of his poetry (including those meta-selections, *Moortown* and *Elmet*), or even in one of his children's collections.

IV

Many of Hughes's poems were written 'within hearing' of children (as he remarked of the composition of *Season Songs*) and there was a traffic of poems between the collections for children and collections for adults. Thus *Moon-Bells*, published in the 'Chatto Poets for the Young' series in 1978, contains four poems subsequently folded into the *Moortown Elegies* sequence published later in that year. If *Season Songs* can be described as an anthology for adults of poems written for children, then the *Collected Animal Poems* (1994) is an anthology for children of poems many of which had previously appeared only in adult collections. Indicative of how open these borders became, or how difficult to close off, is the fact that twenty poems from the children's books *Under the North Star* and *What Is the Truth?* were originally included in *New Selected Poems* and removed by Hughes only at proof stage. The present edition includes *Season Songs*, and includes such children's poems as were published in Hughes's adult collections or selections. Poems beyond those bounds, and which seem written specifically for the hearing of children, have been excluded.

The solitude of Hughes's verse has sometimes been remarked upon, but much of his writing involved collaboration. His private press publications were collaborations, his revisions to poems are perhaps forms of self-collaboration, and some of his most individual sequences and utterances – *Remains of Elmet*, *Cave Birds*, *River* – were set in motion by or found their confirmation in the visual contributions of others, particularly Fay Godwin and Leonard Baskin. For reasons of space, the *Collected Poems* must exclude these visual dimensions. It likewise excludes Hughes's stage collaborations – the theatre works in verse, from *Seneca's Oedipus* (1968) to Euripides' *Alcestis* (1999) – and it excludes his verbal collaborations as a translator of poetry. Hughes was instrumental in founding the journal *Modern Poetry in Translation* (co-edited with Daniel Weissbort from 1965 until 1971) and he produced joint versions of contemporary European poets including Janos Pilinszky, Miroslav Holub, Yehuda Amichai and Marin Sorescu. These are omitted from the *Collected Poems*. On the other hand, *Tales from Ovid* – which grew directly out of the collaborative venture of *After Ovid* – is included in full, as are Hughes's own occasional non-dramatic verse translations (from Homer, or from *Sir Gawain and the Green Knight*, or from Pushkin).

The notes to the present edition, described in the Note on the Text (page 1238), are confined to such information as relates directly to the publication history of the poems and the decision to collect all of the published poetry. They retrace the moves and record the attendant variegations of text, if only in the atomised form of listed variants. Some contextual information is provided for individual poems, but their range of embedded reference (to an eclectic body of mythological and anthropological material, for example) is not addressed. Appendix One reproduces Hughes's own occasional remarks and explanations – prose prefaces, afterwords and notes – as included within his collections of poetry. The notes sometimes quote from written comments by Hughes, but rarely from the extensive sound archive of his comments on his poetry, made in broadcasts or in poetry readings and recordings. The latter are nevertheless a major resource for an understanding of the poetry, as are Hughes's occasional prose writings collected in *Winter Pollen*. The reader is referred to the indispensable bibliography compiled by Keith Sagar and Stephen Tabor (*op.cit.*).

Ted Hughes published a *New Selected Poems* in 1995, representing a relatively small proportion – perhaps one-fifth – of his published work. He left no organised and definitive text of his poetry, and would naturally have continued revisiting and revising what he had written. Making new poems was akin to making new habitats for old poems, and his writing possesses a characteristic copiousness of glance – backwards and forwards. Its organic interrelation transforms the frozen retrospect of a *Collected Poems* into an active instrument for reading the poetry.

Acknowledgements

I am grateful to Carol Hughes, who commissioned this volume, for her support and advice at all stages of its compilation. I would like variously to thank Simon Armitage, John Barnard, Lisa Baskin, Charles Boyle, Ron Costley, Jane Feaver, Roy Foster, David Harsent, Hugh Haughton, Seamus Heaney, Matthew Hollis, Karl Miller, Andrew Motion, Alice Oswald, Frank Pike, John Pitcher and Christopher Reid. I owe a particular debt to James Knapton, to Stephen Enniss and the staff of the Robert W. Woodruff Library at Emory University, and to the bibliographical labours of Keith Sagar and Stephen Tabor.

P.K.

Contents

UNCOLLECTED (1957–59)

LUPERCAL (1960)

from RECKLINGS (1966)

from WODWO (1967)

UNCOLLECTED (1977–78)

from ORTS (1978)

CAVE BIRDS (1978)

ADAM AND THE SACRED NINE (1979)

REMAINS OF ELMET (1979)

from RIVER (1983)

TALES FROM OVID (1997)

BIRTHDAY LETTERS (1998)

HOWLS & WHISPERS (1998)

EARLY POEMS AND JUVENILIA

Wild West

I'll tell you a tale of Carson McReared,
Who, south of the 49th was feared
Greater than any man ever before,
And men went in fear of his .44,
For he'd shoot the ears from any man
From Two-gun Ted to Desperate Dan.
His hoss's name was Diamond Ace
And he'd spit the teeth from a rattler's face,
He was 12 years old when he first ran wild
Because a teacher got him riled.
The sheriff and posse rode him into the hills,
'Cos he shot away the teacher's frills.
So he pulled his guns (his father's gift)
And as the sheriff drew, he gave him a lift
Over the edge of a cliff quite high,
With a .44 slug in either thigh.
Then he turned his guns on the sheriff's men
And shot 'em dead. Yeah, all the ten.
Then he saddled his hoss and rode away
To the land where Kinkaid the Marshal held sway.
'Twas in the street that the two first met,
And the sight of the bad man made Kinkaid sweat,
Then like a flash the two men went,
And Carson McReared the Terrible sent
A leaden slug weighing 200 grains
Slap into Kinkaid's squirming brains.
Then turning to his hoss he strode,
Leaving Kinkaid the Marshal dead in the road;
And all the town gaped with shock and fear,
Lest they should feel the burning sear
Of a rifled slug around their liver –
A thought which made the brave men shiver.
This check the President could not stand,
So he ordered the law with an iron hand
To encircle Carson with an armoured ring
And make him on a Redwood swing.
So 15 marshals and umpteen men
Hied them forth to Carson's den,
Carson McReared the terrible killer,
The man with a hide like an armadillo.

'Twas in Grand Canyon where they came to grips,
And with steely eyes and firm set lips
1,200 men on spirited hosses
Charged him regardless of all losses,
So Carson stood with his back to the wall,
Triggered his guns, and shot 'em all.
But alas! he too was shot to hell,
No more would he drink in the 'Southern Belle';
And knee deep in blood, where he had to paddle
Stood Diamond Ace, with an empty saddle.

Too Bad for Hell

Years ago across the bay,
You'll hear the folks in these parts say,
Came Whisky John with a pirate crew,
And rum in kegs for a thirsty few.
    'Twas dark, he came on the midnight tide,
Under the cliffs he slunk along,
For the revenue men had an open eye
When the moon was dark and the tides ran high,
And the revenue men heard a muffled song,
And they saw a shape on the midnight tide,
And they slapped a shell in its starboard side,
And the rum kegs burst and the ship went down;
Then they heard the captain in horror cry,
(Whisky John with the blood-red eye)
'Rum with water!   Holy Pete!
I can't die here where the rum's not neat!'
But the sea came up and he sank to drown.
    And each night since, the folks here say,
When a moon-dark tide runs in the bay,
You see their ship as it slinks along,
And hear through the night a terrible song,
Sung by the crew of the 'Smoky Crow'
As they sang the song many years ago:
    'We're the wicked crew of the "Smoky Crow"
And we lies in wait where the merchants go,
And we splinters up their bran' new barks,
And nails their captains to the mast,
And stows their rum in our holds below,

And slings their men where the sharks swim past,
And slings their women to the sharks,
And any that shout around alive
We bangs 'em down with our seventy-five,
    With a laugh Ha Ha for big bad men,
    And a smaller laugh for the smaller men.
But if ever we plunder on dry land
We bury our dead in stony ground,
Safe from the nails of the digging hound
That finds our dead if they lie in sand.
And all day long we sing and fight,
And drink and sing again all night,
And we never have time for a wink of sleep,
For we're the crew of the "Smoky Crow,"
With a Yo Ho Ho and Ho again,
For we are the worst of all bad men,
    And we sails the briny deep.
And this is our terrible smuggling song
That we sing at night and all night long,
    So long as the moon's not full.
And we keep our time with the fearful beat
Of the stamp and stamp of our pirate feet,
Or "Tree-heel" Tom's mahogany leg,
Or a pistol butt on a whisky keg,
    Or a bottle on a dead man's skull.
And to finish it off the man that's found
The liquor keg empty opens then
Another keg for the next time round,
    With a laugh Ha Ha for big bad men,
    And a smaller laugh for the smaller men.'
    Then the revenue gun in the night bangs out,
And you hear the drowning seamen shout,
And Whisky John through the clamour cry,
(Whisky John with the blood-red eye)
'Rum with water! Holy Pete!
I can't die here where the rum's not neat.'
But the voices sink where the bodies lie,
And the spray bursts over the sinful men.
And the sea is alone in the wind again.

The Recluse

... I soon must fire
This vampire from my mind, his dreams remember
The bones of an old feast somewhere.
'Unstilled Assegais' Book VI

'O lean dry man with your thin withered feet,
Feet like old rain-worn weasels, like old roots
Frost-warped and shrunken on the cold sea beach,
You have a sad world here:
Only the bitter windy rain and bareness of wet rock glistening;
Only the sand-choked marram, only their dead
Throats whispering always in despair:
Only the wild high phantom-drifting of the gulls,
Their slim wings wavering, crying through the mists –
Desolate voices over a desolate shore;
Only the lonely surf and its crumbling thunder,
Asking a question, telling its only secret in despair,
But no-one answers, no-one can understand,
Its eagerness is lost now in despair:
Only the sea; only the rain wind over the long wild beach;
Only those shell-grey ghouls in the wind lamenting.
(The otter comes here in the winter but even the shells are empty, –
At the mussel-pool's edge the heron's bones
Are white and fragile now, sobbing a thin sad dirge
Like some still harp in the salt-wind among the stones –
And the otter goes inland hungry)
O lean dry man with your thin withered feet,
Why do you sit alone where even the wind is sad?'
   And he rose from the wet black rocks with his old eyes burning
As though the stars were caught there, and his hair
Lived in the wind like weed in the wild sea tides.
   'Because the hours have robbed me, because the years
Have taken my joy with speed and left me only my despair;
And the moon wanes always and always the green leaf fades;
And petals are held by hours but hours pass swiftly,
Now I have only the thorn of all my days,
So I come to these shores where everything
Is futility and despair,
And I am happy here.'

Initiation

'Lady, let's dance.'
                    The seething Snake-Pit blares
Sick swirl and maddened frenzy, legs berserk
Fling out and stamp, hair whirling, eyes, mad jerk
Of glazed crazed faces reel their sudden stares,
Arms clutch and twist choked in the plunging mass:
The feeblest blood barbaric rages after
Wild and hysterical barbaric laughter
Of the loud unleashed cornet; as they pass,
With limbs possessed and lust-extorted cry,
They know the helplessness of insanity;
Hell-gripped musicians swaying, writhing over
Agonised rhythms, struggle, drag, torment
Hoarse screams from their reptilian instrument,
War-yell and sobbing moan – the Demon lover
Over his Demon love – the desperate crash
Of laboured cymbal and mad drums amok
Lash panic to the racing blood and lash
The cornet's wild cries skywards.
                                  'Have a Hock.
This dust comes from the rafters, see it when
The place gets properly filled up. Ready again?'

Here in the Green and Glimmering Gloom

Here in the green and glimmering gloom
We slumber, and our heads are laid,
In this sea-cave's most secret shade,
On couches soft with sea-flower's bloom,
For only dreams can dreams fulfil;
Far off now are ocean's storms;
Only the wandering mackerel gleams,
To lift our eyes, to soothe our dreams;
Wink through darkness wearily
Soft coral eyes, and the pale forms
Of those sad children, lost in dreams,
Stir dimly – these are seal-born, sea-
Born children here alone, alone,
Lulled by the century-laden moan

Of the sigh thronged slumbering sea,
Those moon-sick seas, tide-weary, moaning still.

Pastoral Symphony No. 1
Two Finger Arrangement

Far thunder of the coming sun; ablaze
At horizon that wild green rush bursts with the dawn;
Spring winds run in the valleys with the days,
The choking claw-down grip from their hearts torn
In a tossing flame of flowers their quick feet run;
While the white blizzards shriek in the North heaven,
In terror from the exulting season driven,
Ride their gray clanging seas out of the sun;
Polar eagle and owl scream, and retire
In their wrecked storms nurtured, dreading the warm light;
Dizzy with ecstasy for the warm light
Birds dance from the soaring sun, nurtured in fire,
Dazing the vales of the flowered time with songs:
And shall the song and dance of the singers go?
When from the sun's frenzy and cruel snow
That nurtured them, hung murderous in the wind,
The bearded ravens gather; sudden their throngs
Flock, blotting day, and swirling darkly and roaring, fall,
Bringing night.

The Little Boys and the Seasons

One came out of the wood. 'What a bit of a girl,'
The small boys cried, 'to drive my elder brother daft,
Tossing her petticoats under the bushes. O we know,
We know all about you: there's a story.
Well, we don't want your tinny birds with their noise,
And we don't want your soppy flowers with their smells,
And you can just take all that make-up off our garden,
And stop giving the animals ideas with your eyes.'
And she cried a cloud and all the children ran in.

10   One came out of the garden. A great woman.
The small boys muttered: 'This one's not much either.

She keeps my dad out till too late at night.
You can't get through the bushes for her great bosom
And her sweaty arms round you wherever you go.
The way she wears the sun is just gypsy.
And look how she leaves grownups lying about.'
Then they all sat down to stare her out with eyes
Hot as fever from hostility.

One came over the hill, bullying the wind,
Dragging the trees out of each other's arms, swearing   20
At first so that the children could hardly believe it. No one
Believed the children when they clapped he had come.
The weathercock would have crowed, but was in his hand,
The sun was in his haversack with hares,
Pheasants and singing birds all silent. Whereon
Parents pointed warningly to barometers.
But the small boys said: 'Wait till his friend gets here.'

Who came out of the sea, overturning the horses,
The hard captain, uniform over the hedges,
Drilling the air till it was threadbare, stamping   30
Up and down the fields with the nails in his boots
Till the cobbles of the fields were iron as nails.
Birds stood so stiff to attention it was death.
The sun was broken up for sabres. O he was a rough one.
And the little boys cried: 'Hurrah for the Jolly Roger,'
And ran out, merry as apples, to shoot each other
On landscapes of his icelocked battleships.

The Court-Tumbler and Satirist

'Scrambling after girls, bloodying his tusk,
Groping in the sweat halls for what he can get,
His fork in any hot dish, the two-backed beast
Spurring neck and neck with every slut,
Is how the blood of a true artist makes out,'

Cry all the princes; 'but to gambol in bells,
At which you strain as we at digestion sweat,
That from two or three of our wives may earn half smiles
(Which are rather to distinguish their profiles),
What art comes out of blood wretched as that?

9

Jingling trap-rhymes, rhyming us each a rat,
Rhymed in your kennel, with your aches at the rat-holes,
And your mouth on dirt, and yet you are paid for it
Like service.' Cuckolds! Little dreaming what
Acrobatic loins and leaping heels

This tumbler exercises to correct
The court's stiff cock strut. Each starchy beauty
Greedy to tumble and make her figure quick
Gets all that necessity can get from duty
Under that enviable accomplished back.

Song of the Sorry Lovers

At midnight in our rose garden a hyena laughed out loud.
'What peeping tom is that?' I whispered, imagining a tom-cat.
Whereat a wise woman out of my arms replied:
'Some dreadful face-eating animal there is that must be shot.'
I took up my man-killer, and the load was a man load.
O a lighter thing than the mice hear on the stair was my tread.
   The hot night was Spring.

I opened the door on the Spring night and in the garden stood.
Watching that crazy sky had made as many animals mad
As every rose in the garden turned the gaze of her burning head.
Blinded lovers side by side cried out of solitude.
The electric lick of the dark lifted the hackles of my blood,
And the roses and the lovers cried 'O hurry back to bed.'
   The hot night was Spring.

'What thing is in our garden?' enquired that loving lady above.
'There are sorry lovers spoiling, for their faces are off,
And that is such a misery, all the beasts of love
Laugh themselves mad against the moon and we must defend
   our life:
So rouse your animal faculties, or we cannot thrive,
Or grow to man and woman that acted husband and wife.'
   The hot night was Spring.

The Woman With Such High Heels She
Looked Dangerous

You would say the way she was painted was for the war-path,
And sure all sorts of corners stack her dead.
The way she comes at a man gives him no chances
To smile be suave and complicate a truce
And retire undefeated if disgraced.
When her blood beats its drum nobody dances.

Men become wolves, but a wolf has become a woman.
The light in her eyes slants hard and blue as hail.
And when the sun gets at her it is as if
A windy blue plume of fire from the earth raged upright,
Smelling of sulphur, the contaminations of the damned,
The refined fragile cosmetic of the dead.

She clings at your guarding arm as a grass-wisp weakly,
And then her eyes are timid as a hare's,
And her mouth merry as a robin on your finger.
O she is slick and silver as a whiting
To coax your delight as far as the dark, and there, friend, there
Darkness is the scabbard of her knife.

Poem

In clear Spring's high ice-breaking heaven, the snow-striped moors
Ring like goblets of blue crystal, and there, then, he climbs,
Above the simmering bird and water woods, watching the crows
Float out below him. Till he comes where the cramped
Tussocks creak in the sun, and the last drifts melt like sugar,
And the tear of the curlew turns its edge on silence
Over cemeteries of stone.

The hermit moor sheep, crazed by exposure to sun and moon
And the eye-concealing clouds, and the poised ambush of skylines,
In trance of clairvoyance living with the wind's shadow,
Fix him with magnifying unhuman attention: he looms
With clouds and skylines through the lens of emptiness
Into their watched world; and halts, his heart crouches and
    stares; alarmed,
He sits on a low rock.

Far out over the blue whale-herded horizons of the shires
Of heather, imagination ramped, but at once limps
Into his bosom like a scared dog; sortie for memories
Burrows downward and vanishes; fantasy clamps
Blank with desperation onto a cloud's figure:
He shivers, surrendering to the huge eye and the silence,
And the graveyard of stone.

But, with angry pride, sidesteps the spell, makes the sheep run
With a scream that cuts his throat – startled only for a second
To hear it coffin-stifled at a crag as sudden;
He stirs the corpse of a pool; sticks a rain-whitened ram's
Skull to stare from a cairn; kicks up grouse
Till every skyline's sentinelled with scolding cocks; comes
Valleyward whistling, never look back.

Scene Without An Act

Applaud this scene, cheer, stamp, but do not
Call an encore. How is it to be expressed –
The grace they have cannot be enough praised –
With which each speaks, smiles, profiles being smiled at –

Their attitudes, seeming more perilous
Than tight-rope-walkers' over Niagara
That for their shadows take your heart, yet are
Such nonchalant bravery your brow sweats pearls.

He and she – alas, alas – he
And she are in midst of the great love-scene.
Let your lip hang, set an idiot grin,
Let your eye deaden in a revery:

She pauses above him bird-quickly – they kiss
Briefly, agelessly, imponderably
As two stars either end of the night sky
Wink down each other's rays, once, then pass

On vague engagements of immortality.
How much, feel that, feel how great at that
Seas crashed behind the pecking lips, and beat
Over a world of deep sea sole a cry.

And yet they steady their bodies, and straight
Pour tea most delicately; each sits up
In a valuable frail chair to poise a cup –
Such love! It could be diplomatic hate!

You have paid for your seats, stare your moneysworth.
If either actor falsed a phrase or move
You'd see hell's flames make their live shapes their grave,
And drop like a spent match the flourishing earth.

If that pulse should tremble that gold
Dazzlingly bright cuff-link, – if that throat
Should other than to porcelain pitch its note –
God help our lovers! They would never grow old!

But the tailor's crease, the mercury finger poised
In air, the visor smile, make parade
Of an expert chivalry that risks no dead, –
Safe at world's smash and not even surprised!

It is late, leave, you with the wetted cheeks,
The best's done, but add wonder to your tear,
As you walk by houses where marriages snore,
How decorously the heart just not quite breaks.

And have no fear, though raging of that fear
Made excellence of the courage of their calm,
Nothing on that stage can come to harm,
Though well you guess both fire and flood strain there.

You had learned why the gestures of these lovers keep
Nonchalance and enigma, had you guessed
In what flaming red gulf their hearts lie lost,
Under what black wilderness of waters weep.

Bawdry Embraced

Great farmy whores, breasts bouncy more
Like buttocks, and with buttocks like
Two white sows jammed in a sty door,
Are no dunghills for Bawdry's cock.

No tigery tarts, with rubber backs,
Switches for tits and neon blood,

Hurdling the beds, their silk in shrieks,
Can ever come at Bawdrihood.

All iced-wedding-cakey dolls,
Molten in May's bubbly vat,
Gulped before their sugar cools
Sicken Bawdry's ostrich gut.

And the foxy slut who still
Scrubs at carrion with her brush,
Demuring down the marriage-aisle,
Can make bloody Bawdry blush.

Not in down-trousered slovenliness,
Nor vomitorial gluttony,
Bawdry's needle nakedness
Has this diamond in its eye:

Time was Tailfever struck this town.
    There was not one cramped street
But stroked itself to trembling curves
    When he glanced at it.

Tailfever was a bawdreur good,
    Raging delicate beast,
He trod this town a calendar
    To find his bawdriste.

Tom-catting over walls and tiles,
    His bared weapon blazed
As if a firedrake through the dark
    Dragged him by the waist.

The lily virgin at her prayer
    Who heard the roof shake
And ran to draw the blind, fell
    Deflowered at his look.

Till bright a day, and dark a day,
    His palate picked out
Of promiscuity's butchery
    Sweety Undercut.

Born bawdriste, in all England
    Never came better.

Heaven itself blazed in her bush.
   Tailfever got her.

From what dog's dish or crocodile's rotten
   Larder she had come
He questioned none: 'It is enough
   That she is and I am'.

They caught each other by the body
   And fell in a heap:
A cockerel there struck up a tread
   Like a cabman's whip.

And so they knit, knotted and wrought
   Braiding their ends in;
So fed their radiance to themselves
   They could not be seen.

And thereupon – a miracle!
   Each became a lens
So focussing creation's heat
   The other burst in flames.

Bawdry! Bawdry! Steadfastly
   Thy great protagonists
Died face to face, with bellies full,
   In the solar waste

Where there is neither skirt nor coat,
   And every ogling eye
Is a cold star to measure
   Their solitude by.

The Drowned Woman

Millionly-whored, without womb,
Her heart already rubbish,
Watching the garret death come,
This thirty year old miss

Walked in park pastoral
With bird and bee but no man
Where children were catching armsful
Of the untouched sun.

With plastic handbag, with mink fur,
A face sleep-haggard and sleep-puffed
Fresh-floured and daubed 'whore,'
This puppet was stuffed

With rags of beds and strangers'
Cast-offs, one cracked cup, a cough
That smoked and malingered.
But put a coin in her slot

This worn public lady
Would fountain a monologue,
Would statuesque and goddess a body,
Ladder Jacob a leg.

She plucked men's eyes from happy homes;
Hands grew in the empty dark
And hung like jewellery on her limbs,
Yet she came to this park

Not for the sun's forgetful look
Nor children running here and there;
On the mud bed of the lake
She found her comforter.

THE HAWK IN THE RAIN (1957)

The Hawk in the Rain

I drown in the drumming ploughland, I drag up
Heel after heel from the swallowing of the earth's mouth,
From clay that clutches my each step to the ankle
With the habit of the dogged grave, but the hawk

Effortlessly at height hangs his still eye.
His wings hold all creation in a weightless quiet,
Steady as a hallucination in the streaming air.
While banging wind kills these stubborn hedges,

Thumbs my eyes, throws my breath, tackles my heart,
And rain hacks my head to the bone, the hawk hangs
The diamond point of will that polestars
The sea drowner's endurance: and I,

Bloodily grabbed dazed last-moment-counting
Morsel in the earth's mouth, strain towards the master-
Fulcrum of violence where the hawk hangs still.
That maybe in his own time meets the weather

Coming the wrong way, suffers the air, hurled upside down,
Fall from his eye, the ponderous shires crash on him,
The horizon trap him; the round angelic eye
Smashed, mix his heart's blood with the mire of the land.

The Jaguar

The apes yawn and adore their fleas in the sun.
The parrots shriek as if they were on fire, or strut
Like cheap tarts to attract the stroller with the nut.
Fatigue with indolence, tiger and lion

Lie still as the sun. The boa-constrictor's coil
Is a fossil. Cage after cage seems empty, or
Stinks of sleepers from the breathing straw.
It might be painted on a nursery wall.

But who runs like the rest past these arrives
At a cage where the crowd stands, stares, mesmerized,
As a child at a dream, at a jaguar hurrying enraged
Through prison darkness after the drills of his eyes

10

On a short fierce fuse. Not in boredom –
The eye satisfied to be blind in fire,
By the bang of blood in the brain deaf the ear –
He spins from the bars, but there's no cage to him

More than to the visionary his cell:
His stride is wildernesses of freedom:
The world rolls under the long thrust of his heel.
Over the cage floor the horizons come.

Macaw and Little Miss

In a cage of wire-ribs
The size of a man's head, the macaw bristles in a staring
Combustion, suffers the stoking devils of his eyes.
In the old lady's parlour, where an aspidistra succumbs
To the musk of faded velvet, he hangs as in clear flames,
Like a torturer's iron instrument preparing
With dense slow shudderings of greens, yellows, blues,
Crimsoning into the barbs;

Or like the smouldering head that hung
In Killdevil's brass kitchen, in irons, who had been
Volcano swearing to vomit the world away in black ash,
And would, one day; or a fugitive aristocrat
From some thunderous mythological hierarchy, caught
By a little boy with a crust and a bent pin,
Or snare of horsehair set for a song-thrush,
And put in a cage to sing.

The old lady who feeds him seeds
Has a grand-daughter. The girl calls him 'Poor Polly', pokes fun;
'Jolly Mop.' But lies under every full moon,
The spun glass of her body bared and so gleam-still
Her brimming eyes do not tremble or spill
The dream where the warrior comes, lightning and iron,
Smashing and burning and rending towards her loin:
Deep into her pillow her silence pleads.

All day he stares at his furnace
With eyes red-raw, but when she comes they close.
'Polly. Pretty Poll', she cajoles, and rocks him gently.
She caresses, whispers kisses. The blue lids stay shut.

She strikes the cage in a tantrum and swirls out:
    Instantly beak, wings, talons crash
    The bars in conflagration and frenzy,
       And his shriek shakes the house.

The Thought-Fox

I imagine this midnight moment's forest:
Something else is alive
Beside the clock's loneliness
And this blank page where my fingers move.

Through the window I see no star:
Something more near
Though deeper within darkness
Is entering the loneliness:

Cold, delicately as the dark snow,
A fox's nose touches twig, leaf;
Two eyes serve a movement, that now
And again now, and now, and now

Sets neat prints into the snow
Between trees, and warily a lame
Shadow lags by stump and in hollow
Of a body that is bold to come

Across clearings, an eye,
A widening deepening greenness,
Brilliantly, concentratedly,
Coming about its own business

Till, with a sudden sharp hot stink of fox
It enters the dark hole of the head.
The window is starless still; the clock ticks,
The page is printed.

The Horses

I climbed through woods in the hour-before-dawn dark.
Evil air, a frost-making stillness,

Not a leaf, not a bird –
A world cast in frost. I came out above the wood

Where my breath left tortuous statues in the iron light.
But the valleys were draining the darkness

Till the moorline – blackening dregs of the brightening grey –
Halved the sky ahead. And I saw the horses:

Huge in the dense grey – ten together –
Megalith-still. They breathed, making no move,

With draped manes and tilted hind-hooves,
Making no sound.

I passed: not one snorted or jerked its head.
Grey silent fragments

Of a grey silent world.

I listened in emptiness on the moor-ridge.
The curlew's tear turned its edge on the silence.

Slowly detail leafed from the darkness. Then the sun
Orange, red, red erupted

Silently, and splitting to its core tore and flung cloud,
Shook the gulf open, showed blue,

And the big planets hanging –.
I turned

Stumbling in the fever of a dream, down towards
The dark woods, from the kindling tops,

And came to the horses.
                    There, still they stood,
But now steaming and glistening under the flow of light,

Their draped stone manes, their tilted hind-hooves
Stirring under a thaw while all around them

The frost showed its fires. But still they made no sound.
Not one snorted or stamped,

Their hung heads patient as the horizons,
High over valleys, in the red levelling rays –

In din of the crowded streets, going among the years, the faces,
May I still meet my memory in so lonely a place

Between the streams and the red clouds, hearing curlews,
Hearing the horizons endure.

Famous Poet

   Stare at the monster: remark
How difficult it is to define just what
Amounts to monstrosity in that
Very ordinary appearance. Neither thin nor fat,
   Hair between light and dark,

   And the general air
Of an apprentice – say, an apprentice house-
Painter amid an assembly of famous
Architects: the demeanour is of mouse,
   Yet is he monster.

   First scrutinize those eyes
For the spark, the effulgence: nothing. Nothing there
But the haggard stony exhaustion of a near-
Finished variety artist. He slumps in his chair
   Like a badly hurt man, half life-size.

   Is it his dreg-boozed inner demon
Still tankarding from tissue and follicle
The vital fire, the spirit electrical
That puts the gloss on a normal hearty male?
   Or is it women?

   The truth – bring it on
With black drapery, drums, and funeral tread
Like a great man's coffin – no, no, he is not dead
But in this truth surely half-buried:
   Once, the humiliation

   Of youth and obscurity,
The autoclave of heady ambition trapped,
The fermenting of a yeasty heart stopped –

Burst with such pyrotechnics the dull world gaped
    And 'Repeat that!' still they cry.

    But all his efforts to concoct
The old heroic bang from their money and praise,
From the parent's pointing finger and the child's amaze,
Even from the burning of his wreathed bays,
    Have left him wrecked: wrecked,

    And monstrous, so,
As a Stegosaurus, a lumbering obsolete
Arsenal of gigantic horn and plate
From a time when half the world still burned, set
    To blink behind bars at the zoo.

Song

O lady, when the tipped cup of the moon blessed you
You became soft fire with a cloud's grace;
The difficult stars swam for eyes in your face;
You stood, and your shadow was my place:
You turned, your shadow turned to ice
    O my lady.

O lady, when the sea caressed you
You were a marble of foam, but dumb.
When will the stone open its tomb?
When will the waves give over their foam?
You will not die, nor come home,
    O my lady.

O lady, when the wind kissed you
You made him music for you were a shaped shell.
I follow the waters and the wind still
Since my heart heard it and all to pieces fell
Which your lovers stole, meaning ill,
    O my lady.

O lady, consider when I shall have lost you
The moon's full hands, scattering waste,
The sea's hands, dark from the world's breast,
The world's decay where the wind's hands have passed,

And my head, worn out with love, at rest
In my hands, and my hands full of dust,
    O my lady.

Parlour-Piece

With love so like fire they dared not
Let it out into strawy small talk;
With love so like a flood they dared not
Let out a trickle lest the whole crack,

These two sat speechlessly:
Pale cool tea in tea-cups chaperoned
Stillness, silence, the eyes
Where fire and flood strained.

Secretary

If I should touch her she would shriek and weeping
Crawl off to nurse the terrible wound: all
Day like a starling under the bellies of bulls
She hurries among men, ducking, peeping,

Off in a whirl at the first move of a horn.
At dusk she scuttles down the gauntlet of lust
Like a clockwork mouse. Safe home at last
She mends socks with holes, shirts that are torn,

For father and brother, and a delicate supper cooks:
Goes to bed early, shuts out with the light
Her thirty years, and lies with buttocks tight,
Hiding her lovely eyes until day break.

Soliloquy

Whenever I am got under my gravestone,
Sending my flowers up to stare at the church-tower,
Gritting my teeth in the chill from the church-floor,
I shall praise God heartily, to see gone,

As I look round at old acquaintance there,
Complacency from the smirk of every man,
And every attitude showing its bone,
And every mouth confessing its crude shire;

But I shall thank God thrice heartily
To be lying beside women who grimace
Under the commitments of their flesh,
And not out of spite or vanity.

The Dove Breeder

Love struck into his life
Like a hawk into a dovecote.
What a cry went up!
Every gentle pedigree dove
Blindly clattered and beat,
And the mild-mannered dove-breeder
Shrieked at that raider.

He might well wring his hands
And let his tears drop:
He will win no more prizes
With fantails or pouters,
(After all these years
Through third, up through second places
Till they were all world beaters...)

Yet he soon dried his tears

Now he rides the morning mist
With a big-eyed hawk on his fist.

Billet-Doux

Here is the magniloquent truth –
His twelve bright brass bands
Diverted down mouseholes –
Walking the town with his head high
And naked as his breath.

I have looked far enough
If now I have found one who does
Not – hold that 'not' to the light –,
When I walk about in my blood and the air
Beside her, sweeten smiles, peep, cough,

Who sees straight through bogeyman,
The crammed cafés, the ten thousand
Books packed end to end, even my gross bulk,
To the fiery star coming for the eye itself,
And while she can grabs of them what she can.

Love you I do not say I do or might either.
I come to you enforcedly –
Love's a spoiled appetite for some delicacy –
I am driven to your bed and four walls
From bottomlessly breaking night –

If, dispropertied as I am
By the constellations staring me to less
Than what cold, rain and wind neglect,
I do not hold you closer and harder than love
By a desperation, show me no home.

A Modest Proposal

There is no better way to know us
Than as two wolves, come separately to a wood.
Now neither's able to sleep – even at a distance
Distracted by the soft competing pulse
Of the other; nor able to hunt – at every step
Looking backwards and sideways, warying to listen
For the other's slavering rush. Neither can make die
The painful burning of the coal in its heart
Till the other's body and the whole wood is its own.
Then it might sob contentment toward the moon.

Each in a thicket, rage hoarse in its labouring
Chest after a skirmish, licks the rents in its hide,
Eyes brighter than is natural under the leaves
(Where the wren, peeping round a leaf, shrieks out
To see a chink so terrifyingly open

Onto the red smelting of hatred) as each
Pictures a mad final satisfaction.

Suddenly they duck and peer.
                              And there rides by
The great lord from hunting. His embroidered
Cloak floats, the tail of his horse pours,
And at his stirrup the two great-eyed greyhounds
That day after day bring down the towering stag
Leap like one, making delighted sounds.

Incompatibilities

Desire's a vicious separator in spite
  Of its twisting women round men:
Cold-chisels two selfs single as it welds hot
  Iron of their separates to one.

Old Eden commonplace: something magnets
  And furnaces and with fierce
Hammer-blows the one body on the other knits
  Till the division disappears.

But desire outstrips those hands that a nothing fills,
10   It dives into the opposite eyes,
Plummets through blackouts of impassables
  For the star that lights the face,

Each body still straining to follow down
  The maelstrom dark of the other, their limbs flail
Flesh and beat upon
  The inane everywhere of its obstacle,

Each, each second, lonelier and further
  Falling alone through the endless
Without-world of the other, though both here
20   Twist so close they choke their cries.

September

We sit late, watching the dark slowly unfold:
No clock counts this.
When kisses are repeated and the arms hold
There is no telling where time is.

It is midsummer: the leaves hang big and still:
Behind the eye a star,
Under the silk of the wrist a sea, tell
Time is nowhere.

We stand; leaves have not timed the summer.
No clock now needs
Tell we have only what we remember:
Minutes uproaring with our heads

Like an unfortunate King's and his Queen's
When the senseless mob rules;
And quietly the trees casting their crowns
Into the pools.

Fallgrief's Girl-Friends

Not that she had no equal, not that she was
His before flesh was his or the world was;
Not that she had the especial excellence
To make her cat-indolence and shrew-mouth
Index to its humanity. Her looks
Were what a good friend would not comment on.
If he made flattery too particular,
Admiring her cookery or lipstick,
Her eyes reflected painfully. Yet not that
He pitied her: he did not pity her.   10

'Any woman born', he said, 'having
What any woman born cannot but have,
Has as much of the world as is worth more
Than wit or lucky looks can make worth more;
And I, having what I have as a man
Got without choice, and what I have chosen,
City and neighbour and work, am poor enough

29

To be more than bettered by a worst woman.
Whilst I am this muck of man in this
20 Muck of existence, I shall not seek more
Than a muck of a woman: wit and lucky looks
Were a ring disabling this pig-snout,
And a tin clasp on this diamond.'

By this he meant to break out of the dream
Where admiration's giddy mannequin
Leads every sense to motley; he meant to stand naked
Awake in the pitch dark where the animal runs,
Where the insects couple as they murder each other,
Where the fish outwait the water.

                              The chance changed him:
30 He has found a woman with such wit and looks
He can brag of her in every company.

Two Phases

I

You had to come
Calling my singularity,
In scorn,
Imprisonment.

It contained content
That, now, at liberty
In your generous embrace,
As once, in rich Rome,
Caractacus,
I mourn.

II

When the labour was for love
He did but touch at the tool
And holiday ran prodigal.

Now, stripped to the skin,
Can scarcely keep alive,
Sweats his stint out,
No better than a blind mole

That burrows for its lot
Of the flaming moon and sun
Down some black hole.

The Decay of Vanity

Now it is seven years since you were the Queen
That crowned me King; and six years since your ghost
Left your body cold in my arms as a stone.

Then for three years I did heart-brokenly
Embalm your remains; but after that
I let your eye shrink and your body dry,

And had forgotten whether you still hung here,
Or had gone, with all the old junk, out onto the heap
Where scraggy cockerels rake and stab and peer –

Till this man loomed up with your shrunken head.
He, I see, by the majesty in his stride,
Dreams he sweeps some great queen towards his bed,

Yet skulks by me, swagger as he dare:
This royal trophy, which, in a world of pride,
Makes him your King, makes him my scavenger.

Fair Choice

Fair choice? The appearance of the devil! Suave
Complicity with your vacillation
To your entire undoing! A midwife
Delivering darlings to your indecision –
Twins, quick in their cradle, loud as alive,

But rivalling eithers! Before choice's fairness
Humanized both, barbarously you might
Have made beast-death of the one a sacrifice
To the god-head of the other, and buried its right
Before it opened eyes to be emulous.

But now that your twins wail, are wide-eyed –
(Tugging between them some frivolous heirloom)
You must cold murder the one and force-feed

With your remorse the other and protect him from
The vengeful voluble ghost of the twin dead.

Or you must bend your dilemma-feebled spine
Under – as if nobly and under tons –
Rearing both fairly. The spilt blood be your own!
Your every glance shall see one of your twins
An Abel to the other's bloody Cain.

The Conversion of the Reverend Skinner

'Dare you reach so high, girl, from the gutter of the street?'
She slapped his cheek and turned his tongue right over:
'Your church has cursed me till I am black as it:
The devil has my preference forever.'
She spoke. An upstart gentleman
Flashed his golden palm to her and she ran.

But he lay there stretched full length in the gutter.
He swore to live on dog-licks for ten years.
'My pride has been the rotten heart of the matter.'
His eyes dwelt with the quick ankles of whores.
To mortify pride he hailed each one:
'This is the ditch to pitch abortions in.'

He stared up at the dark and he cursed that;
'As if my own heart were not bad enough,
But heaven itself must blacken with the rot!'
Then he saw the thin moon staggering through the rough
Wiping her wound. And he rose wild
And sought and blest only what was defiled.

Complaint

Aged Mother, Mary, even though – when that thing
Leaped hedge in the dark lane (or grabbed your heel
On the attic stair) by smell of man and coarse
Canvas he wore was disguised too well-ill
A scorching and dizzying blue apparition; –

Though that Jack Horner's hedge-scratched pig-splitting arm,
Grubbing his get among your lilies, was a comet

That plunged through the flowery whorl to your womb-root,
And grew a man's face on its burning head; –

Though no prompt thundercrack, no knave's remorse
Kneeling in the arch of lightning, fisting his guilt,
But the times quiet with God's satisfaction; –

Though you swallowed the honey of a parable,
No forced fistful of meat-and-potato fact –

History's grown gross-bellied, not bright-eyed.

Phaetons

Angrier, angrier, suddenly the near-madman
In mid-vehemence rolls back his eye
And lurches to his feet –

Under each sense the other four hurtle and thunder
Under the skull's front the horses of the sun

The gentle reader in his silent room
Loses the words in mid-sentence –

The world has burned away beneath his book
A tossing upside-down team drags him on fire
Among the monsters of the zodiac.

Egg-Head

   A leaf's otherness,
The whaled monstered sea-bottom, eagled peaks
And stars that hang over hurtling endlessness,
   With manslaughtering shocks

   Are let in on his sense:
So many a one has dared to be struck dead
Peeping through his fingers at the world's ends,
   Or at an ant's head.

But better defence
Than any militant pride are the freebooting crass
Veterans of survival and those champions
   Forgetfulness, madness.

  Brain in deft opacities,
Walled in translucencies, shuts out the world's knocking
With a welcome, and to wide-eyed deafnesses
   Of prudence lets it speak.

  Long the eggshell head's
Fragility rounds and resists receiving the flash
Of the sun, the bolt of the earth: and feeds
   On the yolk's dark and hush

  Of a helplessness coming
By feats of torpor, by circumventing sleights
Of stupefaction, juggleries of benumbing,
   By lucid sophistries of sight

  To a staturing 'I am',
To the upthrust affirmative head of a man.
Braggart-browed complacency in most calm
   Collusion with his own

  Dewdrop frailty
Must stop the looming mouth of the earth with a pin-
Point cipher, with a blank-stare courtesy
   Confront it and preen,

  Spurn it muck under
His foot-clutch, and, opposing his eye's flea-red
Fly-catching fervency to the whelm of the sun,
    Trumpet his own ear dead.

The Man Seeking Experience Enquires His Way of a Drop of Water

'This water droplet, charity of the air,
Out of the watched blue immensity –
(Where, where are the angels?) out of the draught in the door,
The Tuscarora, the cloud, the cup of tea,
The sweating victor and the decaying dead bird –
This droplet has travelled far and studied hard.

'Now clings on the cream paint of our kitchen wall.
Aged eye! This without heart-head-nerve lens
Which saw the first and earth-centering jewel
Spark upon darkness, behemoth bulk and lumber
Out of the instant flash, and man's hand
Hoist him upright, still hangs clear and round.

'Having studied a journey in the high
Cathedralled brain, the mole's ear, the fish's ice,
The abattoir of the tiger's artery,
The slum of the dog's bowel, and there is no place
His bright look has not bettered, and problem none
But he has brought it to solution.

'Venerable elder! Let us learn of you.
Read us a lesson, a plain lesson how
Experience has worn or made you anew,
That on this humble kitchen wall hang now,
O dew that condensed of the breath of the Word
On the mirror of the syllable of the Word.'

So he spoke, aloud, grandly, then stood
For an answer, knowing his own nature all
Droplet-kin, sisters and brothers of lymph and blood,
Listened for himself to speak for the drop's self.
This droplet was clear simple water still.
It no more responded than the hour-old child

Does to finger-toy or coy baby-talk,
But who lies long, long and frowningly
Unconscious under the shock of its own quick
After that first alone-in-creation cry
When into the mesh of sense, out of the dark,
Blundered the world-shouldering monstrous 'I'.

Meeting

   He smiles in a mirror, shrinking the whole
Sun-swung zodiac of light to a trinket shape
   On the rise of his eye: it is a role

In which he can fling a cape,
And outloom life like Faustus. But once when
On an empty mountain slope

A black goat clattered and ran
Towards him, and set forefeet firm on a rock
Above and looked down

A square-pupilled yellow-eyed look
The black devil head against the blue air,
What gigantic fingers took

Him up and on a bare
Palm turned him close under an eye
That was like a living hanging hemisphere

And watched his blood's gleam with a ray
Slow and cold and ferocious as a star
Till the goat clattered away.

Wind

This house has been far out at sea all night,
The woods crashing through darkness, the booming hills,
Winds stampeding the fields under the window
Floundering black astride and blinding wet

Till day rose; then under an orange sky
The hills had new places, and wind wielded
Blade-light, luminous and emerald,
Flexing like the lens of a mad eye.

At noon I scaled along the house-side as far as
The coal-house door. I dared once to look up –
Through the brunt wind that dented the balls of my eyes
The tent of the hills drummed and strained its guyrope,

The fields quivering, the skyline a grimace,
At any second to bang and vanish with a flap:
The wind flung a magpie away and a black-
Back gull bent like an iron bar slowly. The house

Rang like some fine green goblet in the note
That any second would shatter it. Now deep

In chairs, in front of the great fire, we grip
Our hearts and cannot entertain book, thought,

Or each other. We watch the fire blazing,
And feel the roots of the house move, but sit on,
Seeing the window tremble to come in,
Hearing the stones cry out under the horizons.

October Dawn

October is marigold, and yet
A glass half full of wine left out

To the dark heaven all night, by dawn
Has dreamed a premonition

Of ice across its eye as if
The ice-age had begun its heave.

The lawn overtrodden and strewn
From the night before, and the whistling green

Shrubbery are doomed. Ice
Has got its spearhead into place.

First a skin, delicately here
Restraining a ripple from the air;

Soon plate and rivet on pond and brook;
Then tons of chain and massive lock

To hold rivers. Then, sound by sight
Will Mammoth and Sabre-tooth celebrate

Reunion while a fist of cold
Squeezes the fire at the core of the world,

Squeezes the fire at the core of the heart,
And now it is about to start.

Roarers in a Ring

Snow fell as for Wenceslas.
  The moor foamed like a white
Running sea. A starved fox
  Stared at the inn light.

In the red gridded glare of peat,
  Faces sweating like hams,
Farmers roared their Christmas Eve
  Out of the low beams.

Good company kept a laugh in the air
  As if they tossed a ball
To top the skip of a devil that
  Struck at it with his tail,

Or struck at the man who held it long.
  They so tossed laughter up
You would have thought that if they did not
  Laugh, they must weep.

Therefore the ale went round and round.
  Their mouths flung wide
The cataract of a laugh, lest
  Silence drink blood.

And their eyes were screwed so tight,
  While their grand bellies shook –
O their flesh would drop to dust
  At the first sober look.

The air was new as a razor,
  The moor looked like the moon,
When they all went roaring homewards
  An hour before dawn.

Those living images of their deaths
  Better than with skill
Blindly and rowdily balanced
  Gently took their fall

While the world under their footsoles
  Went whirling still
Gay and forever, in the bottomless black
  Silence through which it fell.

Vampire

You hosts are almost glad he gate-crashed: see,
How his eyes brighten on the whisky, how his wit
Tumbles the company like a lightning stroke –
You marvel where he gets his energy from...

But that same instant, here, far underground,
This fusty carcass stirs its shroud and swells.

'Stop, stop, oh for God's sake, stop!' you shriek
As your tears run down, but he goes on and on
Mercilessly till you think your ribs must crack...

While this carcass's eyes grimace, stitched
In the cramp of an ordeal, and a squeeze of blood
Crawls like scorpions into its hair.

You plead, limp, dangling in his mad voice, till
With a sudden blood-spittling cough, he chokes: he leaves
Trembling, soon after. You slump back down in a chair
Cold as a leaf, your heart scarcely moving...

Deep under the city's deepest stone
This grinning sack is bursting with your blood.

Childbirth

When, on the bearing mother, death's
Door opened its furious inch,
Instant of struggling and blood,
The commonplace became so strange

There was not looking at table or chair:
Miracle struck out the brain
Of order and ordinary: bare
Onto the heart the earth dropped then

With whirling quarters, the axle cracked,
Through that miracle-breached bed
All the dead could have got back;
With shriek and heave and spout of blood

The huge-eyed looming horde from
Under the floor of the heart, that run

To the madman's eye-corner came
Deafening towards light, whereon

A child whimpered upon the bed,
Frowning ten-toed ten-fingered birth
Put the skull back about the head
Righted the stagger of the earth.

The Hag

The old story went that the cajoling hag
Fattened the pretty princess within a fence
Of barbs the spiders poked their eight eyes out in
Even, the points were so close, fattened her
With pastry pies and would not let her incline
One inch toward the threshold from the table
Lest she slip off the hag's dish and exchange
The hag's narrow intestine for the wide world.
And this hag had to lie in a certain way
At night lest the horrible angular black hatred
Poke through her side and surprise the pretty princess
Who was well-deceived by this posture of love.

Now here is an old hag, as I see,
Has got this story direly drastically wrong,
Who has dragged her pretty daughter home from college,
Who has locked up her pretty eyes in a brick house
And has sworn her pretty mouth shall rot like fruit
Before the world shall make a jam of it
To spread on every palate. And so saying,
She must lie perforce at night in a certain way
Lest the heart break through her side and burst the walls
And surprise her daughter with an extravagance
Of tearful love, who finds it easier
To resign her hope of a world wide with love,
And even to rot in the dark, but easier under
Nine bolts of spite than on one leash of love.

Law in the Country of the Cats

When two men meet for the first time in all
Eternity and outright hate each other,
Not as a beggar-man and a rich man,
Not as cuckold-maker and cuckold,
Not as bully and delicate boy, but
As dog and wolf because their blood before
They are aware has bristled into their hackles,
Because one has clubbed the other to death
With the bottle first broached to toast their transaction
And swears to God he went helpless black-out   10
While they were mixing smiles, facts have sacked
The oath of the pious witness who judged all men
As a one humble brotherhood of man.

When two men at first meeting hate each other
Even in passing, without words, in the street,
They are not likely to halt as if remembering
They once met somewhere, where in fact they met,
And discuss 'universal brotherhood',
'Love of humanity and each fellow-man',
Or 'the growing likelihood of perpetual peace',   20
But if, by chance, they do meet, so mistaking,
There will be that moment's horrible pause
As each looks into the gulf in the eye of the other,
Then a flash of violent incredible action,
Then one man letting his brains gently to the gutter,
And one man bursting into the police station
Crying: 'Let Justice be done. I did it, I.'

Invitation to the Dance

The condemned prisoner stirred, but could not stir:
Cold had shackled the blood-prints of the knout.
The light of his death's dawn put the dark out.
He lay, his lips numb to the frozen floor.
He dreamed some other prisoner was dragged out –
Nightmare of command in the dawn, and a shot.
The bestial gaoler's boot was at his ear.

Upon his sinews torturers had grown strong,
The inquisitor old against a tongue that could not,
Being torn out, plead even for death.
All bones were shattered, the whole body unstrung.
Horses, plunging apart towards North and South,
Tore his heart up by the shrieking root.
He was flung to the blow-fly and the dog's fang.

Pitched onto his mouth in a black ditch
All spring he heard the lovers rustle and sigh.
The sun stank. Rats worked at him secretly.
Rot and maggot stripped him stitch by stitch.
Yet still this dream engaged his vanity:
That could he get upright he would dance and cry
Shame on every shy or idle wretch.

The Casualty

Farmers in the fields, housewives behind steamed windows,
Watch the burning aircraft across the blue sky float,
As if a firefly and a spider fought,
Far above the trees, between the washing hung out.
They wait with interest for the evening news.

But already, in a brambled ditch, suddenly-smashed
Stems twitch. In the stubble a pheasant
Is craning every way in astonishment.
The hare that hops up, quizzical, hesitant,
10   Flattens ears and tears madly away and the wren warns.

Some, who saw fall, smoke beckons. They jostle above,
They peer down a sunbeam as if they expected there
A snake in the gloom of the brambles or a rare flower –
See the grave of dead leaves heave suddenly, hear
It was a man fell out of the air alive,

Hear now his groans and senses groping. They rip
The slum of weeds, leaves, barbed coils; they raise
A body that as the breeze touches it glows,
Branding their hands on his bones. Now that he has
20   No spine, against heaped sheaves they prop him up,

Arrange his limbs in order, open his eye,
Then stand, helpless as ghosts. In a scene
Melting in the August noon, the burned man
Bulks closer greater flesh and blood than their own,
As suddenly the heart's beat shakes his body and the eye

Widens childishly. Sympathies
Fasten to the blood like flies. Here's no heart's more
Open or large than a fist clenched, and in there
Holding close complacency its most dear
Unscratchable diamond. The tears of their eyes   30

Too tender to let break, start to the edge
Of such horror close as mourners can,
Greedy to share all that is undergone,
Grimace, gasp, gesture of death. Till they look down
On the handkerchief at which his eye stares up.

Bayonet Charge

Suddenly he awoke and was running – raw
In raw-seamed hot khaki, his sweat heavy,
Stumbling across a field of clods towards a green hedge
That dazzled with rifle fire, hearing
Bullets smacking the belly out of the air –
He lugged a rifle numb as a smashed arm;
The patriotic tear that had brimmed in his eye
Sweating like molten iron from the centre of his chest –

In bewilderment then he almost stopped –
In what cold clockwork of the stars and the nations
Was he the hand pointing that second? He was running
Like a man who has jumped up in the dark and runs
Listening between his footfalls for the reason
Of his still running, and his foot hung like
Statuary in mid-stride. Then the shot-slashed furrows

Threw up a yellow hare that rolled like a flame
And crawled in a threshing circle, its mouth wide
Open silent, its eyes standing out.
He plunged past with his bayonet toward the green hedge,
King, honour, human dignity, etcetera
Dropped like luxuries in a yelling alarm

To get out of that blue crackling air
His terror's touchy dynamite.

Griefs for Dead Soldiers

I

Mightiest, like some universal cataclysm,
Will be the unveiling of their cenotaph:
The crowds will stand struck, like the painting of a terror
Where the approaching planet, a half-day off,
Hangs huge above the thin skulls of the silenced birds;
Each move, each sound, a fresh-cut epitaph –
Monstrousness of the moment making the air stone.

Though thinly, the bugle will then cry,
The dead drum tap, and the feet of the columns
And the sergeant-major's voice blown about by the wind
Make these dead magnificent, their souls
Scrolled and supporting the sky, and the national sorrow,
Over the crowds that know of no other wound,
Permanent stupendous victory.

II

Secretest, tiniest, there, where the widow watches on the table
The telegram opening of its own accord
Inescapably and more terribly than any bomb
That dives to the cellar and lifts the house. The bared
Words shear the hawsers of love that now lash
Back in darkness, blinding and severing. To a world
Lonely as her skull and little as her heart

The doors and windows open like great gates to a hell.
Still she will carry cups from table to sink.
She cannot build her sorrow into a monument
And walk away from it. Closer than thinking
The dead man hangs around her neck, but never
Close enough to be touched, or thanked even,
For being all that remains in a world smashed.

Truest, and only just, here, where since
The battle passed the grass has sprung up
Surprisingly in the valleyful of dead men.
Under the blue sky heavy crow and black fly move.
Flowers bloom prettily to the edge of the mass grave
Where spades hack, and the diggers grunt and sweat.
Among the flowers the dead wait like brides

To surrender their limbs; thud of another body flung
Down, the jolted shape of a face, earth into the mouth –
Moment that could annihilate a watcher!
Cursing the sun that makes their work long
Or the black lively flies that bite their wrists,
The burial party works with a craftsman calm.
Weighing their grief by the ounce, and burying it.

Six Young Men

The celluloid of a photograph holds them well –
Six young men, familiar to their friends.
Four decades that have faded and ochre-tinged
This photograph have not wrinkled the faces or the hands.
Though their cocked hats are not now fashionable,
Their shoes shine. One imparts an intimate smile,
One chews a grass, one lowers his eyes, bashful,
One is ridiculous with cocky pride –
Six months after this picture they were all dead.

All are trimmed for a Sunday jaunt. I know   10
That bilberried bank, that thick tree, that black wall,
Which are there yet and not changed. From where these sit
You hear the water of seven streams fall
To the roarer in the bottom, and through all
The leafy valley a rumouring of air go.
Pictured here, their expressions listen yet,
And still that valley has not changed its sound
Though their faces are four decades under the ground.

This one was shot in an attack and lay
Calling in the wire, then this one, his best friend,   20

45

Went out to bring him in and was shot too;
And this one, the very moment he was warned
From potting at tin-cans in no-man's land,
Fell back dead with his rifle-sights shot away.
The rest, nobody knows what they came to,
But come to the worst they must have done, and held it
Closer than their hope; all were killed.

Here see a man's photograph,
The locket of a smile, turned overnight
Into the hospital of his mangled last
Agony and hours; see bundled in it
His mightier-than-a-man dead bulk and weight:
And on this one place which keeps him alive
(In his Sunday best) see fall war's worst
Thinkable flash and rending, onto his smile
Forty years rotting into soil.

That man's not more alive whom you confront
And shake by the hand, see hale, hear speak loud,
Than any of these six celluloid smiles are,
Nor prehistoric or fabulous beast more dead;
No thought so vivid as their smoking-blood:
To regard this photograph might well dement,
Such contradictory permanent horrors here
Smile from the single exposure and shoulder out
One's own body from its instant and heat.

Two Wise Generals

'Not as Black Douglas, bannered, trumpeted,
Who hacked for the casked heart flung to the enemy,
Letting the whole air flow breakneck with blood
Till he fell astride that handful, you and I

Come, two timid and ageing generals
To parley, and to divide the territory
Upon a map, and get honour, and by
This satisfaction part with regiments whole.'

They entered the lit tent, in no hurry to grab.
Apart in darkness twinkled their armies

Like two safe towns. Thus they drank, joked, waxed wise –
So heavily medalled never need fear stab.

The treaty sealed, lands allotted (and a good third
Stuffed down their tunic fronts' private estate)
They left the empty bottle. The tent-lamp out,
They lurched away in the knee-high mist, hearing the first bird,

Towards separate camps.
                        Now, one a late dew-moth
Eyes, as he sways, among the still tents. The other roars 'Guard!'
As a fox ducks from the silent parapet. Both
Have found their sleeping armies massacred.

The Ancient Heroes and the Bomber Pilot

With nothing to brag about but the size of their hearts,
Tearing boar-flesh and swilling ale,
A fermenting of huge-chested braggarts

Got nowhere by sitting still
To hear some timorous poet enlarge heroisms,
To suffer their veins stifle and swell –

Soon, far easier, imagination all flames,
In the white orbit of a sword,
Their chariot-wheels tumbling the necks of screams,

In a glory of hair and beard,
They thinned down their fat fulsome blood in war,
Replenishing both bed and board,

Making their own good news, restuffing their dear
Fame with fresh sacks-full of heads,
Roaring, burdened, back over the wet moor.

When archaeologists dig their remainder out –
Bits of bone, rust –
The grandeur of their wars humbles my thought.

Even though I can boast
The enemy capital will jump to a fume
At a turn of my wrist

And the huge earth be shaken in its frame –
I am pale.
When I imagine one of those warriors in the room

And hear his heart-beat burl
The centuries are a stopped clock; my heart
Is cold and small.

The Martyrdom of Bishop Farrar

Burned by Bloody Mary's men at Caermarthen. 'If I flinch from the
pain of the burning, believe not the doctrine that I have preached.'
(His words on being chained to the stake.)

Bloody Mary's venomous flames can curl;
They can shrivel sinew and char bone
Of foot, ankle, knee, and thigh, and boil
Bowels, and drop his heart a cinder down;
And her soldiers can cry, as they hurl
Logs in the red rush: 'This is her sermon.'

The sullen-jowled watching Welsh townspeople
Hear him crack in the fire's mouth; they see what
Black oozing twist of stuff bubbles the smell
That tars and retches their lungs: no pulpit
Of his ever held their eyes so still,
Never, as now his agony, his wit.

An ignorant means to establish ownership
Of his flock! Thus their shepherd she seized
And knotted him into this blazing shape
In their eyes, as if such could have cauterized
The trust they turned towards him, and branded on
Its stump her claim, to outlaw question.

So it might have been: seeing their exemplar
And teacher burned for his lessons to black bits,
Their silence might have disowned him to her,
And hung up what he had taught with their Welsh hats:
Who sees his blasphemous father struck by fire
From heaven, might well be heard to speak no oaths.

But the fire that struck here, come from Hell even,
Kindled little heavens in his words

As he fed his body to the flame alive.
Words which, before they will be dumbly spared,
Will burn their body and be tongued with fire
Make paltry folly of flesh and this world's air.

When they saw what annuities of hours
And comfortable blood he burned to get
His words a bare honouring in their ears,
The shrewd townsfolk pocketed them hot:
Stamp was not current but they rang and shone
As good gold as any queen's crown.

Gave all he had, and yet the bargain struck
To a merest farthing his whole agony,
His body's cold-kept miserdom of shrieks
He gave uncounted, while out of his eyes,
Out of his mouth, fire like a glory broke,
And smoke burned his sermons into the skies.

UNCOLLECTED (1957–59)

Letter

DEAR SIR,

I cannot say I hate your gut
More than you hate mine because it is plain
You are at your limit in not
Bursting towards me and blindly lashing out

Whenever I come in to watch you where
You bustle at your shop-counter, mince change,
Simper with madames, glare
Suddenly at me speechless when the shop is clear –

But your neat counter saves us; that and that high
Resistance conductor – what we exchange
In cash and goods: only eye and eye
Exchange in a flash a stunning headache blinklessly.

Last night I dreamed: a moon-vast meteorite
Had crashed down onto your shop and split the earth:
I came to, stumbling in ghastly light,
Suddenly you loomed lurching towards me with unhuman shout –

But how changed! Your body seared black, your eyes
Crazily, lidlessly staring,
Frightening my hatred with your cries,
Pointing to the desolated horizon and the swinging skies.

Quest

I know clearly, as at a shout, when the time
Comes I am to ride out into the darkened air
Down the deserted streets. Eyes, terrified and hidden,
Are a weight of watching on me that I must ignore
And a charge in the air, tingling and crackling bluely
From the points and edges of my weapons, and in my hair.
I shall never see the monster that I go to kill.

And how it is ever to be killed, or where it is,
No one knows, though men have ridden a thousand times
Against it as I now with my terror standing in my hair,
Hardly daring risk into my lungs this air the same
As carried the fire-belch and boistering of the thing's breath

Whose mere eye unlidded anywhere were a flame
To stir the marrow deep under most ignorant sleep.

I ride, with staring senses, but in
Complete blackness, knowing none of these faithful five
Clear to its coming till out of the blind-spot
Of the fitful sixth – crash on me the bellowing heaving
Tangle of a dragon all heads all jaws all fangs,
And though my weapons were lightning I am no longer alive.
My victory to raise this monster's shadow from my people

Shall be its trumpeting and clangorous flight
Over the moon's face to its white-hot icy crevasse
With fragments of my body dangling from its hundred mouths.

Constancy

The rivers are flowing, the air moving,
The landmark mountains are lasting: this persisting
Pig-headedness of the earth is not resisting
Time, but a rider astride it arriving.

The cloud of the mind climbs, declines,
The flowing of rivers a stay to its going,
The caress and press of the air sole knowing
Of its own being, and the mountain stones

Buttress awhile the cloud of the mind
As it leans to them. Braced against object
Body claims permanence like a muscle locked,
Never doubts that grip on ground;

But the mind's cloud is a coming and going
Of airs and dews that shape it and colour
And dusts floating, and for all its mountain pillow
Cannot affirm hardier being.

On every instant the earth arrives ...
Wide the feet brace, strong, as the hands
Haul against that massive careerer, but the mind's
Clouds are under its hooves.

Shells

Shells white, shells brown, sea-shells
Tumbled by sea, cry,
Swarm the foam's edge, twittering shoals,
A jostle of curiosity –
But they screech as the wave hauls,
Or, cast bare, gleam dry.

From that gigantic bed of the sea
Where darkness on Time
Begets pearl, monster and anemone
Only shells come
To chatter of emptiness, or lie
Lovely as dumb.

Gulls Aloft

Gulls are glanced from the lift
Of cliffing air
And left
Loitering in the descending drift,
Or tilt gradient and go
Down steep invisible clefts in the grain
Of air, blading against the blow,

Back-flip, wisp
Over the foam-galled green
Building seas, and they scissor
Tossed spray, shave sheen,
Wing-waltzing their shadows
Over the green hollows,

Or rise again in the wind's landward rush
And, hurdling the thundering bush,
With the stone wall flung in their faces,
Repeat their graces.

Snails

Out of earliest ooze, old
Even by sea-stone time,
Slimed as eels, wrinkled as whales,
And cold
As dogs' noses,
And slow, sap-slow,
Under their coiled cauls of shells
Snails
Climb
The roses

LUPERCAL (1960)

Things Present

All things being done or undone
As my hands adore or abandon –
Embody a now, erect a here
A bare-backed tramp and a ditch without fire

Cat or bread; and no shoes,
Honour, or hope, him – whose
Progenitors back to the sea-salt
Bride-bed to cradle assoiled

Honour of its shifty eyes, and hope
Of its shaky heart-beat, and step
By step got into stout shoes beneath
A roof treed to deflect death.

My sires had towers and great names,
And that their effort be brought to an edge
Honed their bodies away, dreams
The tramp in the sodden ditch.

Everyman's Odyssey

Telemachus, now to remember your coming of age.
Years your trust was open as the doors of your house
To the boisterous princes, all so phrasing your mother,
So cushioning the going of her feet with the glow of their eyes,
Who brought such trinkets, and hoisted the jugglers and the
    dancers
Onto the protesting trestles of your tables.

Your mother, white, a woe freezing a silence,
Parried long their impertinence with her shuttle,
And such after-banquet belching of adulation
Through your hoop and handball years. O Telemachus
Remember the day you saw the spears on the wall
And their great blades shook light at you like the sea.

If these memories move at all in your ghost
This last must open up a wound: recall that year
You sulked among the suitors – too big for their comfort
And yet too few for their fear. Your father's honour

Was a sword in the scabbard of your body you could not draw,
What patience you had a slow bird quartering the seas.

But avenge yourself on recalling that. I would hear
How the father arrives out of the bottom of the world.
I would see one of the beggars that brawl on my porch
Reach hands to the bow hardly to be strung by man –
I would see these gluttons, guests by grace of their numbers,
Flung through the doors with their bellies full of arrows.

Mayday on Holderness

This evening, motherly summer moves in the pond.
I look down into the decomposition of leaves –
The furnace door whirling with larvae.

                    From Hull's sunset smudge
Humber is melting eastward, my south skyline:
A loaded single vein, it drains
The effort of the inert North – Sheffield's ores,
Bog pools, dregs of toadstools, tributary
Graves, dunghills, kitchens, hospitals.
The unkillable North Sea swallows it all.
Insects, drunken, drop out of the air.
                           Birth-soils,
The sea-salts, scoured me, cortex and intestine,
To receive these remains.
As the incinerator, as the sun,
As the spider, I had a whole world in my hands.
Flowerlike, I loved nothing.
Dead and unborn are in God comfortable.
What a length of gut is growing and breathing –
This mute eater, biting through the mind's
Nursery floor, with eel and hyena and vulture,
With creepy-crawly and the root,
With the sea-worm, entering its birthright.

The stars make pietas. The owl announces its sanity.

The crow sleeps glutted and the stoat begins.
There are eye-guarded eggs in these hedgerows,
Hot haynests under the roots in burrows.
Couples at their pursuits are laughing in the lanes.

The North Sea lies soundless. Beneath it
Smoulder the wars: to heart-beats, bomb, bayonet.
'Mother, Mother!' cries the pierced helmet.
Cordite oozings of Gallipoli,

Curded to beastings, broached my palate,
The expressionless gaze of the leopard,
The coils of the sleeping anaconda,
The nightlong frenzy of shrews.

February

The wolf with its belly stitched full of big pebbles;
Nibelung wolves barbed like black pineforest
Against a red sky, over blue snow; or that long grin
Above the tucked coverlet – none suffice.

A photograph: the hairless, knuckled feet
Of the last wolf killed in Britain spoiled him for wolves:
The worst since has been so much mere Alsatian.
Now it is the dream cries 'Wolf!' where these feet

Print the moonlit doorstep, or run and run
Through the hush of parkland, bodiless, headless;   10
With small seeming of inconvenience
By day, too, pursue, siege all thought;

Bring him to an abrupt poring stop
Over engravings of gibbet-hung wolves,
As at a cage where the scraggy Spanish wolf
Danced, smiling, brown eyes doggily begging

A ball to be thrown. These feet, deprived,
Disdaining all that are caged, or storied, or pictured,
Through and throughout the true world search
For their vanished head, for the world   20

Vanished with the head, the teeth, the quick eyes –
Now, lest they choose his head,
Under severe moons he sits making
Wolf-masks, mouths clamped well onto the world.

Crow Hill

The farms are oozing craters in
Sheer sides under the sodden moors:
When it is not wind it is rain,
Neither of which will stop at doors:
One will damp beds and the other shake
Dreams beneath sleep it cannot break.

Between the weather and the rock
Farmers make a little heat;
Cows that sway a bony back,
Pigs upon delicate feet
Hold off the sky, trample the strength
That shall level these hills at length.

Buttoned from the blowing mist
Walk the ridges of ruined stone.
What humbles these hills has raised
The arrogance of blood and bone,
And thrown the hawk upon the wind,
And lit the fox in the dripping ground.

A Woman Unconscious

Russia and America circle each other;
Threats nudge an act that were without doubt
A melting of the mould in the mother,
Stones melting about the root,

The quick of the earth burned out:
The toil of all our ages a loss
With leaf and insect. Yet flitting thought
(Not to be thought ridiculous)

Shies from the world-cancelling black
Of its playing shadow: it has learned
That there's no trusting (trusting to luck)
Dates when the world's due to be burned;

That the future's no calamitous change
But a malingering of now,

Histories, towns, faces that no
Malice or accident much derange.

And though bomb be matched against bomb,
Though all mankind wince out and nothing endure –
Earth gone in an instant flare –
Did a lesser death come

Onto the white hospital bed
Where one, numb beyond her last of sense,
Closed her eyes on the world's evidence
And into pillows sunk her head.

Strawberry Hill

A stoat danced on the lawns here
To the music of the maskers;
Drinking the staring hare dry, bit
Through grammar and corset. They nailed to a door

The stoat with the sun in its belly,
But its red unmanageable life
Has licked the stylist out of their skulls,
Has sucked that age like an egg and gone off

Along ditches where flies and leaves
Overpower our tongues, got into some grave –
Not a dog to follow it down –
Emerges, thirsting, in far Asia, in Brixton.

Dick Straightup

Past eighty, but never in eighty years –
Eighty winters on the windy ridge
Of England – has he buttoned his shirt or his jacket.
He sits in the bar-room seat he has been
Polishing with his backside sixty-odd years
Where nobody else sits. White is his head,
But his cheek high, hale as when he emptied
Every Saturday the twelve-pint tankard at a tilt,
Swallowed the whole serving of thirty eggs,
And banged the big bass drum for Heptonstall –   10

With a hundred other great works, still talked of.
Age has stiffened him, but not dazed or bent,
The blue eye has come clear of time:
At a single pint, now, his memory sips slowly,
His belly strong as a tree bole.

He survives among hills, nourished by stone and height.
The dust of Achilles and Cuchulain
Itches in the palms of scholars; thin clerks exercise
In their bed-sitters at midnight, and the meat salesman can
20   Loft fully four hundred pounds. But this one,
With no more application than sitting,
And drinking, and singing, fell in the sleet, late,
Dammed the pouring gutter; and slept there; and, throughout
A night searched by shouts and lamps, froze,
Grew to the road with welts of ice. He was chipped out at dawn
Warm as a pie and snoring.

The gossip of men younger by forty years –
Loud in his company since he no longer says much –
Empties, refills and empties their glasses.
30   Or their strenuous silence places the dominoes
(That are old as the house) into patterns
Gone with the game; the darts that glint to the dartboard
Pin no remarkable instant. The young men sitting
Taste their beer as by imitation,
Borrow their words as by impertinence
Because he sits there so full of legend and life
Quiet as a man alone.

He lives with sixty and seventy years ago,
And of everything he knows three quarters is in the grave,
40   Or tumbled down, or vanished. To be understood
His words must tug up the bottom-most stones of this village,
This clutter of blackstone gulleys, peeping curtains,
And a graveyard bigger and deeper than the village
That sways in the tide of wind and rain some fifty
Miles off the Irish sea.
                The lamp above the pub-door
Wept yellow when he went out and the street
Of spinning darkness roared like a machine
As the wind applied itself. His upright walk,
His strong back, I commemorate now,

And his white blown head going out between a sky and an earth
That were bundled into placeless blackness, the one
Company of his mind.

   Obit.

Now, you are strong as the earth you have entered.

This is a birthplace picture. Green into blue
The hills run deep and limpid. The weasel's
Berry-eyed red lock-head, gripping the dream
That holds good, goes lost in the heaved calm

Of the earth you have entered.

Fourth of July

The hot shallows and seas we bring our blood from
Slowly dwindled; cooled
To sewage estuary, to trout-stocked tarn.
Even the Amazon's taxed and patrolled

To set laws by the few jaws –
Piranha and jaguar.
Columbus' huckstering breath
Blew inland through North America

Killing the last of the mammoths.
The right maps have no monsters.
Now the mind's wandering elementals,
Ousted from their traveller-told

Unapproachable islands,
From their heavens and their burning underworld,
Wait dully at the traffic crossing,
Or lean over headlines, taking nothing in.

A Dream of Horses

We were born grooms, in stable-straw we sleep still,
All our wealth horse-dung and the combings of horses,
And all we can talk about is what horses ail.

Out of the night that gulfed beyond the palace-gate
There shook hooves and hooves and hooves of horses:
Our horses battered their stalls; their eyes jerked white.

And we ran out, mice in our pockets and straw in our hair,
Into darkness that was avalanching to horses
And a quake of hooves. Our lantern's little orange flare

10   Made a round mask of our each sleep-dazed face,
Bodiless, or else bodied by horses
That whinnied and bit and cannoned the world from its place.

The tall palace was so white, the moon was so round,
Everything else this plunging of horses
To the rim of our eyes that strove for the shapes of the sound.

We crouched at our lantern, our bodies drank the din,
And we longed for a death trampled by such horses
As every grain of the earth had hooves and mane.

We must have fallen like drunkards into a dream
20   Of listening, lulled by the thunder of the horses.
We awoke stiff; broad day had come.

Out through the gate the unprinted desert stretched
To stone and scorpion; our stable-horses
Lay in their straw, in a hag-sweat, listless and wretched.

Now let us, tied, be quartered by these poor horses,
If but doomsday's flames be great horses,
The forever itself a circling of the hooves of horses.

Esther's Tomcat

Daylong this tomcat lies stretched flat
As an old rough mat, no mouth and no eyes.
Continual wars and wives are what
Have tattered his ears and battered his head.

Like a bundle of old rope and iron
Sleeps till blue dusk. Then reappear
His eyes, green as ringstones: he yawns wide red,
Fangs fine as a lady's needle and bright.

A tomcat sprang at a mounted knight,
Locked round his neck like a trap of hooks
While the knight rode fighting its clawing and bite.
After hundreds of years the stain's there

On the stone where he fell, dead of the tom:
That was at Barnborough. The tomcat still
Grallochs odd dogs on the quiet,
Will take the head clean off your simple pullet,

Is unkillable. From the dog's fury,
From gunshot fired point-blank he brings
His skin whole, and whole
From owlish moons of bekittenings

Among ashcans. He leaps and lightly
Walks upon sleep, his mind on the moon.
Nightly over the round world of men,
Over the roofs go his eyes and outcry.

Historian

As if the eye and the head
Were an underworld, all the dead
Come to garrulous quarters there,
Dignifying at a live ear

What befell. Each (his pride,
His downright lying vanity being
Disembodied from any twice-doing
That could prove, as from blood

That could blush) can brag
The decisive random of chance
Was concealed skill of his choice, license
Word breathed into a wig

To raze like Attila. Back and forth,
Vociferous as when they lived,
Infuriated still to be braved
Each by the rest, they protest their worth

And winnings of this world. Their graves
Have devoured tenure; perhaps something

Grafted to a warm bone's darkness lives
Of their effort, but to bring

Them to claim, still, clear gains
On times and bodies they have long lost
Takes a frivolous advocate. Or a live brain's
Envying to master and last.

Pennines in April

If this county were a sea (that is solid rock
Deeper than any sea) these hills heaving
Out of the east, mass behind mass, at this height
Hoisting heather and stones to the sky
Must burst upwards and topple into Lancashire.

Perhaps, as the earth turns, such ground-stresses
Do come rolling westward through the locked land.
Now, measuring the miles of silence
Your eye takes the strain: through

Landscapes gliding blue as water
Those barrellings of strength are heaving slowly and heave
To your feet and surf upwards
In a still, fiery air, hauling the imagination,
Carrying the larks upward.

Hawk Roosting

I sit in the top of the wood, my eyes closed.
Inaction, no falsifying dream
Between my hooked head and hooked feet:
Or in sleep rehearse perfect kills and eat.

The convenience of the high trees!
The air's buoyancy and the sun's ray
Are of advantage to me;
And the earth's face upward for my inspection.

My feet are locked upon the rough bark.
It took the whole of Creation

To produce my foot, my each feather:
Now I hold Creation in my foot

Or fly up, and revolve it all slowly –
I kill where I please because it is all mine.
There is no sophistry in my body:
My manners are tearing off heads –

The allotment of death.
For the one path of my flight is direct
Through the bones of the living.
No arguments assert my right:

The sun is behind me.
Nothing has changed since I began.
My eye has permitted no change.
I am going to keep things like this.

Nicholas Ferrer

Brought to bare trees, to spike and shard
Browned by cold, our birds
Breast a homing departure; on wings press
To correct earth's sure tilt into darkness

By a practical move – though they are more
Ignorant than their charted bones,
On lighthouse comforts beat out their brains,
In the Atlantic holes tire –

Toward an estranged sun. Rain-logged, wind-unroofed,
The manor farm hulked its last use
As landmark. The mice survived
All ownership, contested the house

With the owls, and toadstools
Heaved the black pavement of the kitchen. No
Signature but this threshold-held hollow
Remained of some vigorous souls

That had Englished for Elizabeth. Pigs and hay
Filled a church oozing manure mud
From the porch when Nicholas, with all his family,
Alit here, entering the shroud

Of weather and dissolution. That day on,
The farm, the church and Nicholas' frontal bone
Walled out a clouded world: he housekept
In fire of the martyrs: there the tree that crabbed

In Cromwell's belly as it bloomed in Rome
Burned down to the blue calm
They called God's look, and through years illumed
Their fingers on the bibles, and gleamed

From the eagle of brass.
                              Stones and grass
Have sealed our vows. Pig-sties, the earthen face
Drink November. And again the fire of God
Is under the shut heart, under the grave sod.

To Paint a Water Lily

A green level of lily leaves
Roofs the pond's chamber and paves

The flies' furious arena: study
These, the two minds of this lady.

First observe the air's dragonfly
That eats meat, that bullets by

Or stands in space to take aim;
Others as dangerous comb the hum

Under the trees. There are battle-shouts
And death-cries everywhere hereabouts

But inaudible, so the eyes praise
To see the colours of these flies

Rainbow their arcs, spark, or settle
Cooling like beads of molten metal

Through the spectrum. Think what worse
Is the pond-bed's matter of course;

Prehistoric bedragonned times
Crawl that darkness with Latin names,

Have evolved no improvements there,
Jaws for heads, the set stare,

Ignorant of age as of hour —
Now paint the long-necked lily-flower

Which, deep in both worlds, can be still
As a painting, trembling hardly at all

Though the dragonfly alight,
Whatever horror nudge her root.

Urn Burial

Born to these gentle stones and grass,
The whole of himself to himself:
Cheek by jowl in with the weasel;
Caesar no ghost but his passion.

An improvement on the eagle's hook,
The witty spider competitor,
Sets his word's strength against the rock,
No foot wrong in the dance figure —

So by manners, by music, to abash
The wretch of death that stands in his shoes:
The aping shape of earth — sure
Of its weight now as in future.

Of Cats

A heart constituted wholly of cats
(Even as the family nose derives)
From father and mother a child inherits,
And every cat gets fully nine lives.

Wildest cats, with scruff cats, queenly cats
(Crowned), they jig to violins; they go stately
Where a torched pageantry celebrates
A burial, or crowning (of a cat); or sing sweetly

At your ears and in harmony left with right
Till the moon bemoods: to the new, to the full,

Only look up: possessing night –
Cattic Bacchanal! A world of wild lamps and wauling,

A world gone to the cats, every cat of the heart out,
And darkness and light a cat upon a cat ——.
They have outwitted our nimblest wits.
One who, one night, sank a cat in a sack

With a stone to the canal-bottom
(Under the bridge, in the very belly of the black)
And hurried a mile home
Found that cat on the doorstep waiting for him.

So are we all held in utter mock by the cats.

Fire-Eater

Those stars are the fleshed forebears
Of these dark hills, bowed like labourers,

And of my blood.

The death of a gnat is a star's mouth: its skin,
Like Mary's or Semele's, thin

As the skin of fire:
A star fell on her, a sun devoured her.

My appetite is good
Now to manage both Orion and Dog

With a mouthful of earth, my staple.
Worm-sort, root-sort, going where it is profitable.

A star pierces the slug,

The tree is caught up in the constellations.
My skull burrows among antennae and fronds.

Acrobats

Among ropes and dark heights
Spot-lights sparkle those silver postures:
(The trapeze beginning to swing)
Casually they lean out

Over eyes opened deeper
Than the floored drop. Then fling
Out onto nothing, snap, jerk
Fulcrumed without fail
On axes immaterial as
Only geometry should use.

None below in the dumbstruck crowd
Thinks it else but miracle
That a man go somersaulting
(As might hardly be dared in the head)
Bodily out on space,
Gibboning, bird-vaulting
Out of all sedentary belief,
With unearthly access of grace,
Of ease: freer firmer world found
A hundred feet above ground.

The crowd, holding to their seats hard
Under the acrobats' hurtle and arc,
In their hearts miming that daring,
Are no longer assured
Of their body's nonchalant pride
Or of earth's firmness, bearing
Plunge of that high risk without
That flight; with only a dread
Crouching to get away from these
On its hands and knees.

The acrobats flashed
Above earth's ancient inertia,
Faltering of the will,
And the dullness of flesh –
In the dream's orbit; shone, soared,
Mocking vigil and ordeal,
And the prayer of long attempting
Body had endured
To break from a hard-held trembling seat
And soar at that height.

The Good Life

Nothing of profit to be got
So poor-bare to wind and to rain,
His spirit gone to patch his boot,
The hermit returned to the world again.

'Revelation's a burden not to be borne
Save by square-shouldered self-respect.'
But when that latter jaunted bedecked
His vanity was of apparent horn.

'Quiet enough at last I have won,
My body relieved of rag and of ache:
Only a plump, cuffed citizen
Gets enough quiet to hear God speak.'

Loud he prayed then; but late or early
Never a murmur came to his need
Save 'I'd be delighted!' and 'Yours sincerely',
And 'Thank you very much indeed!'

The Bull Moses

A hoist up and I could lean over
The upper edge of the high half-door,
My left foot ledged on the hinge, and look in at the byre's
Blaze of darkness: a sudden shut-eyed look
Backward into the head.
                    Blackness is depth
Beyond star. But the warm weight of his breathing,
The ammoniac reek of his litter, the hotly-tongued
Mash of his cud, steamed against me.
Then, slowly, as onto the mind's eye –
The brow like masonry, the deep-keeled neck:
Something come up there onto the brink of the gulf,
Hadn't heard of the world, too deep in itself to be called to,
Stood in sleep. He would swing his muzzle at a fly
But the square of sky where I hung, shouting, waving,
Was nothing to him; nothing of our light
Found any reflection in him.
                        Each dusk the farmer led him

Down to the pond to drink and smell the air,
And he took no pace but the farmer
Led him to take it, as if he knew nothing
Of the ages and continents of his fathers,
Shut, while he wombed, to a dark shed
And steps between his door and the duckpond;
The weight of the sun and the moon and the world hammered
To a ring of brass through his nostrils.

He would raise
His streaming muzzle and look out over the meadows,
But the grasses whispered nothing awake, the fetch
Of the distance drew nothing to momentum
In the locked black of his powers. He came strolling gently back,
Paused neither toward the pig-pens on his right,
Nor toward the cow-byres on his left: something
Deliberate in his leisure, some beheld future
Founding in his quiet.

I kept the door wide,
Closed it after him and pushed the bolt.

Cat and Mouse

On the sheep-cropped summit, under hot sun,
The mouse crouched, staring out the chance
It dared not take.

Time and a world
Too old to alter, the five mile prospect –
Woods, villages, farms – hummed its heat-heavy
Stupor of life.

Whether to two
Feet or four, how are prayers contracted!
Whether in God's eye or the eye of a cat.

View of a Pig

The pig lay on a barrow dead.
It weighed, they said, as much as three men.
Its eyes closed, pink white eyelashes.
Its trotters stuck straight out.

Such weight and thick pink bulk
Set in death seemed not just dead.
It was less than lifeless, further off.
It was like a sack of wheat.

I thumped it without feeling remorse.
One feels guilty insulting the dead,
Walking on graves. But this pig
Did not seem able to accuse.

It was too dead. Just so much
A poundage of lard and pork.
Its last dignity had entirely gone.
It was not a figure of fun.

Too dead now to pity.
To remember its life, din, stronghold
Of earthly pleasure as it had been,
Seemed a false effort, and off the point.

Too deadly factual. Its weight
Oppressed me – how could it be moved?
And the trouble of cutting it up!
The gash in its throat was shocking, but not pathetic.

Once I ran at a fair in the noise
To catch a greased piglet
That was faster and nimbler than a cat,
Its squeal was the rending of metal.

Pigs must have hot blood, they feel like ovens.
Their bite is worse than a horse's –
They chop a half-moon clean out.
They eat cinders, dead cats.

Distinctions and admirations such
As this one was long finished with.
I stared at it a long time. They were going to scald it,
Scald it and scour it like a doorstep.

The Retired Colonel

Who lived at the top end of our street
Was a Mafeking stereotype, ageing.
Came, face pulped scarlet with kept rage,
For air past our gate.
Barked at his dog knout and whipcrack
And cowerings of India: five or six wars
Stiffened in his reddened neck;
Brow bull-down for the stroke.

Wife dead, daughters gone, lived on
Honouring his own caricature.
Shot through the heart with whisky wore
The lurch like ancient courage, would not go down
While posterity's trash stood, held
His habits like a last stand, even
As if he had Victoria rolled
In a Union Jack in that stronghold.

And what if his sort should vanish?
The rabble starlings roar upon
Trafalgar. The man-eating British lion
By a pimply age brought down.
Here's his head mounted, though only in rhymes,
Beside the head of the last English
Wolf (those starved gloomy times!)
And the last sturgeon of Thames.

The Voyage

Without hope move my words and looks
Toward you, to claim
Neither known face nor held name –
Death-bed, book might keep those. The whole sea's

Accumulations and changes
Are the sea. The sea's elsewhere
Than surrenders to sand and rocks,
Other than men taste who drown out there.

Relic

I found this jawbone at the sea's edge:
There, crabs, dogfish, broken by the breakers or tossed
To flap for half an hour and turn to a crust
Continue the beginning. The deeps are cold:
In that darkness camaraderie does not hold:
Nothing touches but, clutching, devours. And the jaws,
Before they are satisfied or their stretched purpose
Slacken, go down jaws; go gnawn bare. Jaws
Eat and are finished and the jawbone comes to the beach:
This is the sea's achievement; with shells,
Vertebrae, claws, carapaces, skulls.

Time in the sea eats its tail, thrives, casts these
Indigestibles, the spars of purposes
That failed far from the surface. None grow rich
In the sea. This curved jawbone did not laugh
But gripped, gripped and is now a cenotaph.

Wilfred Owen's Photographs

When Parnell's Irish in the House
Pressed that the British Navy's cat-
O-nine-tails be abolished, what
Shut against them? It was
Neither Irish nor English nor of that
Decade, but of the species.

Predictably, Parliament
Squared against the motion. As soon
Let the old school tie be rent
Off their necks, and give thanks, as see gone
No shame but a monument –
Trafalgar not better known.

'To discontinue it were as much
As ship not powder and cannonballs
But brandy and women' (Laughter). Hearing which
A witty profound Irishman calls
For a 'cat' into the House, and sits to watch
The gentry fingering its stained tails.

Whereupon ...
                    quietly, unopposed,
The motion was passed.

An Otter

I

    Underwater eyes, an eel's
Oil of water body, neither fish nor beast is the otter:
  Four-legged yet water-gifted, to outfish fish;
    With webbed feet and long ruddering tail
    And a round head like an old tomcat.

    Brings the legend of himself
From before wars or burials, in spite of hounds and vermin-poles;
  Does not take root like the badger. Wanders, cries;
    Gallops along land he no longer belongs to;
    Re-enters the water by melting.   10

    Of neither water nor land. Seeking
Some world lost when first he dived, that he cannot come at since,
  Takes his changed body into the holes of lakes;
    As if blind, cleaves the stream's push till he licks
    The pebbles of the source; from sea

    To sea crosses in three nights
Like a king in hiding. Crying to the old shape of the starlit land,
  Over sunken farms where the bats go round,
    Without answer. Till light and birdsong come
    Walloping up roads with the milk wagon.   20

II

The hunt's lost him. Pads on mud,
Among sedges, nostrils a surface bead,
The otter remains, hours. The air,
Circling the globe, tainted and necessary,

Mingling tobacco-smoke, hounds and parsley,
Comes carefully to the sunk lungs.
So the self under the eye lies,
Attendant and withdrawn. The otter belongs

In double robbery and concealment –
From water that nourishes and drowns, and from land
That gave him his length and the mouth of the hound.
He keeps fat in the limpid integument

Reflections live on. The heart beats thick,
Big trout muscle out of the dead cold;
Blood is the belly of logic; he will lick
The fishbone bare. And can take stolen hold

On a bitch otter in a field full
Of nervous horses, but linger nowhere.
Yanked above hounds, reverts to nothing at all,
To this long pelt over the back of a chair.

Witches

Once was every woman the witch
To ride a weed the ragwort road:
Devil to do whatever she would:
Each rosebud, every old bitch.

Did they bargain their bodies or no?
Proprietary the devil that
Went horsing on their every thought
When they scowled the strong and lucky low.

Dancing in Ireland nightly, gone
To Norway (the ploughboy bridled),
Nightlong under the blackamoor spraddled,
Back beside their spouse by dawn

As if they had dreamed all. Did they dream it?
Oh, our science says they did.
It was all wishfully dreamed in bed.
Small psychology would unseam it.

Bitches still sulk, rosebuds blow,
And we are devilled. And though these weep
Over our harms, who's to know
Where their feet dance while their heads sleep?

November

The month of the drowned dog. After long rain the land
Was sodden as the bed of an ancient lake,
Treed with iron and birdless. In the sunk lane
The ditch – a seep silent all summer –

Made brown foam with a big voice: that, and my boots
On the lane's scrubbed stones, in the gulleyed leaves,
Against the hill's hanging silence;
Mist silvering the droplets on the bare thorns

Slower than the change of daylight.
In a let of the ditch a tramp was bundled asleep: 10
Face tucked down into beard, drawn in
Under his hair like a hedgehog's. I took him for dead,

But his stillness separated from the death
Of the rotting grass and the ground. A wind chilled,
And a fresh comfort tightened through him,
Each hand stuffed deeper into the other sleeve.

His ankles, bound with sacking and hairy band,
Rubbed each other, resettling. The wind hardened;
A puff shook a glittering from the thorns,
And again the rains' dragging grey columns   20

Smudged the farms. In a moment
The fields were jumping and smoking; the thorns
Quivered, riddled with the glassy verticals.
I stayed on under the welding cold

Watching the tramp's face glisten and the drops on his coat
Flash and darken. I thought what strong trust
Slept in him – as the trickling furrows slept,
And the thorn-roots in their grip on darkness;

And the buried stones, taking the weight of winter;
The hill where the hare crouched with clenched teeth.   30
Rain plastered the land till it was shining
Like hammered lead, and I ran, and in the rushing wood

Shuttered by a black oak leaned.
The keeper's gibbet had owls and hawks
By the neck, weasels, a gang of cats, crows:
Some, stiff, weightless, twirled like dry bark bits

In the drilling rain. Some still had their shape,
Had their pride with it; hung, chins on chests,
Patient to outwait these worst days that beat
40   Their crowns bare and dripped from their feet.

The Perfect Forms

Here is Socrates, born under Pisces,
Smiling, complacent as a phallus,
Or Buddha, whose one thought fills immensity:

Visage of Priapus: the undying tail-swinging
Stupidity of the donkey
That carries Christ. How carefully he nurses

This six-day abortion of the Absolute –
No better for the fosterings
Of fish, reptile and tree-leaper throughout

Their ages of Godforsaken darkness –
This monstrous-headed difficult child!
Of such is the kingdom of heaven.

Thrushes

Terrifying are the attent sleek thrushes on the lawn,
More coiled steel than living – a poised
Dark deadly eye, those delicate legs
Triggered to stirrings beyond sense – with a start, a bounce, a stab
Overtake the instant and drag out some writhing thing.
No indolent procrastinations and no yawning stares.
No sighs or head-scratchings. Nothing but bounce and stab
And a ravening second.

Is it their single-mind-sized skulls, or a trained
10   Body, or genius, or a nestful of brats
Gives their days this bullet and automatic
Purpose? Mozart's brain had it, and the shark's mouth
That hungers down the blood-smell even to a leak of its own
Side and devouring of itself: efficiency which
Strikes too streamlined for any doubt to pluck at it
Or obstruction deflect.

With a man it is otherwise. Heroisms on horseback,
Outstripping his desk-diary at a broad desk,
Carving at a tiny ivory ornament
For years: his act worships itself – while for him,   20
Though he bends to be blent in the prayer, how loud and
    above what
Furious spaces of fire do the distracting devils
Orgy and hosannah, under what wilderness
Of black silent waters weep.

Singers

The dregs of a long drinking sit late
Sinking far from their glasses, a grim
Unison not to be put out
By calendar more than by clock: they have come

To the lord who abducted the miller's daughter,
The farmer who killed his wife and a king –
One thrust. By Guinness, by mild, by bitter
Those stunned unspigotted heads sing,

Rightly too, the drunkenness of time:
For the words of all headache to come,
Of all gone, are on Dick, Jack, Dan,
And a curse on the age that loses the tune.

Bullfrog

With their lithe long strong legs
Some frogs are able
To thump upon double-
Bass strings though pond-water deadens and clogs.

But you, bullfrog, you pump out
Whole fogs full of horn – a threat
As of a liner looming. True
That, first hearing you
Disgorging your gouts of darkness like a wounded god,
Not utterly fantastical I expected
(As in some antique tale depicted)

A broken-down bull up to its belly in mud,
Sucking black swamp up, belching out black cloud

And a squall of gudgeon and lilies.
                                   A surprise,
To see you, a boy's prize,
No bigger than a rat – all dumb silence
In your little old woman hands.

Crag Jack's Apostasy

The churches, lord, all the dark churches
Stooped over my cradle once:
I came clear, but my god's down
Under the weight of all that stone:
Both my power and my luck since
Have kicked at the world and slept in ditches.

I do not desire to change my ways,
But now call continually
On you, god or not god, who
Come to my sleeping body through
The world under the world; pray
That I may see more than your eyes

In an animal's dreamed head; that I shall –
Waking, dragged suddenly
From a choir-shaken height
By the world, lord, and its dayfall –
Keep more than the memory
Of a wolf's head, of eagles' feet.

Pike

Pike, three inches long, perfect
Pike in all parts, green tigering the gold.
Killers from the egg: the malevolent aged grin.
They dance on the surface among the flies.

Or move, stunned by their own grandeur,
Over a bed of emerald, silhouette

Of submarine delicacy and horror.
A hundred feet long in their world.

In ponds, under the heat-struck lily pads –
Gloom of their stillness:
Logged on last year's black leaves, watching upwards.
Or hung in an amber cavern of weeds

The jaws' hooked clamp and fangs
Not to be changed at this date;
A life subdued to its instrument;
The gills kneading quietly, and the pectorals.

Three we kept behind glass,
Jungled in weed: three inches, four,
And four and a half: fed fry to them –
Suddenly there were two. Finally one

With a sag belly and the grin it was born with.
And indeed they spare nobody.
Two, six pounds each, over two feet long,
High and dry and dead in the willow-herb –

One jammed past its gills down the other's gullet:
The outside eye stared: as a vice locks –
The same iron in this eye
Though its film shrank in death.

A pond I fished, fifty yards across,
Whose lilies and muscular tench
Had outlasted every visible stone
Of the monastery that planted them –

Stilled legendary depth:
It was as deep as England. It held
Pike too immense to stir, so immense and old
That past nightfall I dared not cast

But silently cast and fished
With the hair frozen on my head
For what might move, for what eye might move.
The still splashes on the dark pond,

Owls hushing the floating woods
Frail on my ear against the dream

Darkness beneath night's darkness had freed,
That rose slowly towards me, watching.

Snowdrop

Now is the globe shrunk tight
Round the mouse's dulled wintering heart.
Weasel and crow, as if moulded in brass,
Move through an outer darkness
Not in their right minds,
With the other deaths. She, too, pursues her ends,
Brutal as the stars of this month,
Her pale head heavy as metal.

Sunstroke

Frightening the blood in its tunnel
The mowing machine ate at the field of grass.

My eyes had been glared dark. Through a red heat
The cradled guns, damascus, blued, flared –

At every stir sliding their molten embers
Into my head. Sleekly the clover

Bowed and flowed backward
Over the saw-set swimming blades

Till the blades bit – roots, stones, ripped into red –
Some baby's body smoking among the stalks.

Reek of paraffin oil and creosote
Swabbing my lungs doctored me back

Laid on a sack in the great-beamed engine-shed.
I drank at stone, at iron of plough and harrow;

Dulled in a pit, heard thick walls of rain
And voices in swaddled confinement near me

Warm as veins. I lay healing
Under the ragged length of a dog fox

That dangled head downward from one of the beams,
With eyes open, forepaws strained at a leap —

Also surprised by the rain.

Cleopatra to the Asp

The bright mirror I braved: the devil in it
Loved me like my soul, my soul:
Now that I seek myself in a serpent
My smile is fatal.

Nile moves in me; my thighs splay
Into the squalled Mediterranean;
My brain hides in that Abyssinia
Lost armies foundered towards.

Desert and river unwrinkle again.
Seeming to bring them the waters that make drunk
Caesar, Pompey, Antony I drank.
Now let the snake reign.

A half-deity out of Capricorn,
This rigid Augustus mounts
With his sword virginal indeed; and has shorn
Summarily the moon-horned river

From my bed. May the moon
Ruin him with virginity! Drink me, now, whole
With coiled Egypt's past; then from my delta
Swim like a fish toward Rome.

Lupercalia

I

The dog loved its churlish life,
Scraps, thefts. Its declined blood
An anarchy of mindless pride.
Nobody's pet, but good enough

To double with a bitch as poor.
It had bitten ears and little stone eyes,

A mouth like an incinerator.
It held man's reasonable ways

Between its teeth. Received death
Closed eyes and grinning mouth.

II

This woman's as from death's touch: a surviving
Barrenness: she abides; perfect,
But flung from the wheel of the living,
The past killed in her, the future plucked out.

The dead are indifferent underground.
Little the live may learn from them –
A sort of hair and bone wisdom,
A worn witchcraft accoutrement

Of proverbs. Now the brute's quick
Be tinder: old spark of the blood-heat
And not death's touch engross her bed,
Though that has stripped her stark indeed.

III

Goats, black, not angels, but
Bellies round as filled wine-skins
Slung under carcase bones.
Yet that's no brute light

And no merely mountain light –
Their eyes' golden element.
Rustle of their dry hooves, dry patter,
Wind in the oak-leaves; and their bent

Horns, stamp, sudden reared stare
Startle women. Spirit of the ivy,
Stink of goat, of a rank thriving,
O mountain listener.

IV

Over sand that the sun's burned out
Thudding feet of the powerful,
Their oiled bodies brass-bright
In a drift of dust. The earth's crammed full,

Its baked red bellying to the sky's
Electric blue. Their attitudes –
A theorem of flung effort, blades:
Nothing mortal falters their poise

Though wet with blood: the dog has blessed
Their fury. Fresh thongs of goat-skin   10
In their hands they go bounding past,
And deliberate welts have snatched her in

To the figure of racers. Maker of the world,
Hurrying the lit ghost of man
Age to age while the body hold,
Touch this frozen one.

UNCOLLECTED (1960–67)

A Fable

A man brought to his knees in the desert
Had a vision of our technological future –
And it was a city designed as an atom.
Mushrooms of glass, parabolas, spirals, these housed
The electronic brain, and the whole thing shuddered
Like a furnace against him
And his blackened mouth fell open.

There were no more houses modelled on skulls,
No four-footed vehicles
With eyes and with anus, roaring and stinking.
Because this was a home planned for the spirit –
A nuclear architecture
Sparking blue on a dust-speck.

Then he saw men moving in that city
As refractions rainbow through the snowflake –
These were disembarrassed of the lumber of guts,
The man-eating touchy parasite.
They lived on inoculations of light.
The lost man croaked, like a toad in a baking stone,

Interested only in water, water.

The Storm
from HOMER, *Odyssey*, Book V

And now Athene, daughter of Zeus, descended to change matters:
Reined back all blasts from their running and bound them
   in stillness.
Then called a smooth wind out of the North to flatten the
   mountainous water
Where the Zeus-born Odysseus laboured, and to help him to safety
With the Phaecians, those sea-farers.

Two nights and two days he floundered in massive seas
With the darkness of death breaking over and hollowing under.
Until, touched by the third dawn, all wind dropped of a sudden,
And in the airless after-calm
Craning around as the huge swell hoisted him upwards
He saw coast along the skyline. Then as children

See their father's life coming clear of the grip of an evil
That has stretched and drained him with agony long and binding,
And they rejoice that the gods have loosed him,
Odysseus exulted at his glimpse of the land and its trees,
And he drove through the waves to feel his feet upon earth.

But within hail of the land, heard sea rending on rock,
Eruption of the surge, whitening over the land-face,
Bundling everything in spray. No harbour fit for a ship and no inlet,
But thrust prows of crags and spines of reefs under hanging walls.

Then the heart of Odysseus shrank and he groaned:
'Against hope, Zeus gives this glance of the land,
And I have managed my body over the gulf
Only to find no way from the water. Offshore, horns of rock,
Surf bellowing and mauling around them,
Behind them, empty cliff going up
And the sea crowding in deeply. Nowhere foothold
To step from disaster, but, in attempting,
A surge would uproot me and shatter me on rock-edges,
Sluicing my whole trouble to nothing. And if I swim on further,
Seeking the sands of a bay where the sea goes in more peaceably
Some squall will whirl down and drag me,
For all my protesting, out into depths and the maws of
    ravenous fish,
Or a god fetch something monstrous up from the pit to attack me –
One of the horde that feed at the hand of Amphitrite;
And I know too well how the Earth-shaker detests me.'

A mounding wave heaved him from his deliberations,
Building beneath him it carried and crashed him onto the outworks.
There he would have been skinned in an instant
And the bones pestled within him,
But Owl-eyed Athene touched him. He plunged forward,
Both hands grasped rock, and he clung there groaning
As the mass ground over. So he survived it.
But, collapsing back, it stunned and tossed him far out into the sea.
Thickly as gravel crusting the suckers
Of some octopus plucked from its crevice
The rock tore flesh from his fingers.
And there wretched Odysseus, buried in the backwash welter,
Struggled with a death none had predicted
Till the Grey-eyed Athene found him.

Shouldering to air outside the surf and its wrack
He swam along watching the shore for a bay and quieter water.
Soon, off the mouth of a sweet river, saw landing,
Clear of rocks, and protected from the onset of open sea.
Feeling the shove of the current, he prayed in his heart to its god:
'Whoever you are, king, hear my prayers, for I come
Out of the sea's gape and Poseidon's anger.
The everlasting gods give ear to the prayer of a wanderer,
And a wanderer I come now, humbly to your waters,
After hard sufferings. Pity me, king, and take me into your care.'

Even as he spoke, the river stilled its momentum
And calming the chop of its waves and smoothing a path
Gathered the swimmer to safety. Now knees and thick arms folded:
His flesh swollen and his heart swamped by the seas
Odysseus slumped, unable to speak or move, and gulping at air
While sea-water belched from his mouth and nostrils.

Till his powers gathered and he stood. And unbinding the veil
  of the goddess,
Dropped it into the seaward river.
The weight of the current snatched it and in a moment Ino held it.
Then Odysseus turned from the river, kneeled in the reeds and
  kissing the earth
Groaned: 'What more misery now? and how shall a man get
  out of this?
What if I wait the night away, crouching here in the river-bottom?
Clamping frost and the saturating dews, sea-sodden as I am now,
Could be my death. And I know how bleakly
Wind before dawn comes off the water.

Or higher on the land, under the trees
And bedded in undergrowth, praying for the bone-chill
And fatigue to go from me, and praying for sleep to find me,
Maybe it will be the wild beasts that find me.'

Yet he took this last and climbed to a clump
Of trees in a clearing, near the water.
It was an olive and a wild olive knotting so densely one with the other

Neither the stroke of the naked sun
Nor wet sea-winds nor the needling rain could enter.
After his bitter ordeal, gladly royal Odysseus
Crept in under there and raked a bed wide

Where dead leaves were littered abundant enough
To warm two or three from the worst of winter.

Then he stretched out his body and heaped leaves over.
As one on a lonely farm and far from neighbours
Buries a live brand in black embers, preserving the seed of fire
Lest at need he be forced to go find fire elsewhere,
Odysseus hid under leaves. Then Athene ended his labours.
Covering his eyes, in sleep she released him.

Lines To A Newborn Baby

Your cries flash anguish and gutter:
Nothing exists, and you drop through darkness.

What could you recognise here? Though your mother's milk already
Toughens you and prepares you to share

The amazement of the baby mandrill
Crying out as the eyeteeth push through,

The helplessness of the poppy,
The lust of the worm that begins and ends in the earth.

There has been some trouble here, you will find.
A gallery of grisly ancestors

Waits in the schoolroom. Perhaps
You came expecting an Eden

Of perpetual fruit and kindness –
Easily credible after your nothingness.

You will find a world tossed into shape
Like a hatful of twisted lots; locked in shape

As if grown in iron: a stalagmite
Of history under the blood-drip.

Here the hand of the moment, casual
As some cloud touching a pond with reflection,

Grips the head of man as Judith
Gripped that one finished with free will

And the winner's leisure, that one
Finished with begging to differ.

Things being as they are, though only by a hair's breadth,
The brain-stuff is some safety.

Limpets, clamped, suck their salty tongues
Under the sea's explosions;

And the snail that spreads its edge so wonderingly
Presents, to a touch, an instant

Coiled caul shell of comprehension.
Soon, you will smile.

To F. R. At Six Months

I

You roam with my every move
Alert as the survivor
Drifting from the Arctic circle
Who tunes his radio's crackle
(Salt-sodden it is, and troubled
By the whole electrical globe)

Till it coughs and clears its throat
To word of salvation –
Intercom conversation
Of some Grimsby fleet
Bearing down, hurrying
To fill England with stale herring.

II

Though you have come to be called ours
The breadth of America and England generally
Water the roots that flower your eye.

This is the circulating earth, where all limbs
And features constrain their atoms
As the sea-cloud its droplets.

Meltings of the Himalayas, the Congo's
Load of Africa are among the magi
That crowd to your crib with their gifts.

How much is ours when it comes to being born and begetting?
Your Adam was the sun, your Eve the rock,
And the serpent water.

We search for likenesses in your eyes and mouth –
Your little jackets have more of a person about them.
You have dispossessed us.

Some star glared through. We lean
Over you like masks hung up unlit
After the performance.

Dully Gumption's College Courses

I SEMANTICS

Please sir, what was Charlie the First's bad luck?
Cromwell's stud bull got up out of the muck.

Please sir, what did the tossed court find in France?
Wigs full of rats and venomous elegance.

Please sir, what did the Restoration restore?
Clip-lipped fear of that great bull at the door.

How did the court manage the great bull then?
Spoke without nouns and never heard of it again.

Could they not smell it and see it there in position?
All pegged their noses, gazed in a glazed evasion.

Thus came language and manners to the ruling class:
Charles's stuffed head oracular under glass.

Now the bull learns that dead head's speech and glance,
And so England falls, finally, to France.

II POLITICAL SCIENCE

If every Chinaman's soul is a five-roomed flat in Europe
Every Westerner's soul is a Chinese whore.

III THEOLOGY

No, the serpent did not
Seduce Eve to the apple.

All that's simply
Corruption of the facts.

Adam ate the apple.
Eve ate Adam.
The serpent ate Eve.
This is the dark intestine.

The serpent, meanwhile,
Sleeps his meal off in Paradise –
Smiling to hear
God's querulous calling.

IV HUMANITIES

When Caesar clamped mankind in his money-mould,
With a cry of pain out flew the effeminate soul

And turned into vengeful Christ –
The first Romantic raging at the first Formalist

And like an amoeba multiplying himself with Pentecost.
So ever since we've had to take sides and everybody's lost,

By half.
Napoleon in St Petersburg beating out wretched Sonia's life;

Blue-black Sonia rising from the Mississippi, stamping a drum,
Uttering mind-darkening cries and fetching black blood up and
    calling on her kingdom come;

Sonia growing a small neat moustache
And flinging first Germany then all Europe into her furnace –

Half to pig-iron, half to ashes
Which blew into all the books and films as dumb girls with
    flower faces

Under which flower again there rages
The whorish dragon of the dark ages

Helmed with a modern capital and devouring
Virginal St George as a flower.

My Uncle's Wound

Not much remains of my uncle's Normandy.
The stones, but he'd signed none.
The grass is in its fortieth generation
And the skylines have moved subtly – pampered curves
Of a slut risen in the world.

Under the March washing wind
New wheat tugged and glistened.
We walked up a lane he had last marched up sick
With the black stench of dead men
And the beckoning of shell-burst and mile-off machine-gun –

He monologued the march he had come
Sleepwalking in the khaki familiar column,
Singing, but inwardly one silent eye
Seeing for the first time the crazed eyes of men
Once blown to pieces then reassembled

Hurriedly and healed with a cigarette –
The river of stretchers, bandages, crutches and blood
Oozing down from the trembling ridges
Where the twentieth century broke surface
And the machine guns transformed mathematics.

I was squeezing myself into the ditches
Reading my final moment off grassblades
Or the untroubled procedure of beetles,
Or else floating gingerly at head-height
My neck bare to the chill of an express track

Along which the vistas exchanged lightnings.
The fields, as they changed, were still finding dead men –
Richer dark patches in the pale watercolour wheat.
I scavenged for a memory, crumbs of rust or of bone
In one dead man's shadow of fertility.

But I found nothing and maybe they weren't dead men.
And when I looked at my uncle, to see in a glass
The landscape as it had been,
He had turned to a wandering bit of a dream.
It was a cold-eyed country, up and earning

Daily bread in a thoroughly wakened world.
He seemed certain only of the low wood
Bristling the ridge – in the first mist of bud –
Towards which we were walking and towards which
Long ago, he had started to run

Sketchily with some tentative others when
A bullet picked him up by the hip-bone
And laid him in a shell-hole. The sun
All the remainder of a day stared down
Into his wound. The war had gone

Away and left him alone
With a deliberate sniper who now signed
His brow with blood, and as that shrank him flat
Below the crater wall, bullet by bullet
Dug down after him and signed him again.

I wanted the exact spot – the earth-scar of that hole
Through which he bloodily crept into wealth and fatness.
I would have put in my wallet
One of the green-flagged thread-root wheat grains
Of his resurrection.

He'd lost touch – it was all 'Somewhere down there.'
Somewhere or other in time, somewhere in him.
As the world's mass kept those skylines so quiet
He became quiet
With his memories. But I know memory

As I know the blood-crammed dried out rabbit-coloured
Crumbs of soil that thicken this earth,
Or the blinding of the sun, or the green wheat blades
Sucking the crumbled soil
Into their glistenings.

The Road to Easington

Is there anything along this road, are there answers at the
    road's end?
For it to be suffering this waste passage
Murmuring, trying to add village to village –
(It remembers nothing, it has not the mind.)

The road is going, it concentrates, it is a craftsman
Proud of its job and of the traditions of its job –
Where is it going? Ahead is the North Sea. It goes on.
Ahead lie only dogfish and crab

Satisfied with their positions,
10   And the North Sea does without roads. The road goes
Bowing its head into the labour, it knows,
It has its master, it carries its commission.

And us? We are travelling on it as the fly travels
And by chance. Here come grim walls –
The road narrows. Faces streak white. The road rumbles –
An alarmed rhino dodging through bush tunnels –

Then fields flatten back in flight again.
A remote spire wilts off. Trees crumple and melt
Past in the slipstream. In a cold way, this road can exult,
20   It carries the news in its teeth, it has a grin –

Till the last roofs gleam gun-grey, the cold ebb's disclosure,
And suddenly the sea's breath and grey are everywhere
And its depth calling to the road – a grubby scrap-iron
North-Sea bastardy embittering the blood of the women,

Eating the men like lost anchors. The road does not care
That they need to be made happy, that they wait only for the road
To bring them envelopes,
That they need it to leave them as they are. What do they not need?

The road is not pausing for doorsteps
30   Or to lead time in a circle – whatever they are
People are the road's parasites and it does not attend.
The road is not interested in them and their way,

The road carries them its way, or they get off it, it is going to
    the end.

Sunday Evening

The sparrow whets
His stub weapon
And swites at a whistle –
Determined.

Everything prepares. The poplars, their leaves, their
Limp-necked spade-hands, feeling all round inside the air for
The comings and goings of apprehension.
Tree by tree they menace each other with the rumour –
Then stand trembling.

Nothing is ready, the sparrow curses, flings down
Things from the gutter.

While the sycamores are venturing to grow, to spread their
Nurseries of scissorwork, their huge webbed hands, and
    breathing deeply, preparing,

Their lizards spread enormous ruffs –

How much longer?

I have only to turn my head and the leaves crash, whole trees
Recoiling
On lolling springs – but at once, streaming they powerfully
Recover and are stilled
Like a football crowd at a near goal.
Then they lean their torn vast airless masks toward me –

Where?

The sparrow snaps all
His affairs shut in a
Tight case and goes off,
Furious.

I stand among puddles
Beneath these trees filling and brimming the air,
These staggering bouquets nobody knows how to accept.

Poem to Robert Graves Perhaps

The moon not to be named

Going over, clear of all poetry,
The exhauster of the poetical
Faculties of our race, surrendering nothing
Of her fourth day rights, ignores distance, deeds of property,
Hurtling on a leash of small permission, like a yo-yo,

A subjective Nirvana for the aggressor,

Ignorant of everything, being straightforward rock –
Haulage of gravities on it amount to no more
Than its curves do, as a responsive nervous system.
A calamity to be there, where there might as well be nothing!
And so ignorant, that to itself it might as well not be there.

Tomorrow the world will be back, hurrying you on into old age.

So why be disturbed, as if that were some bomb in orbit,
Precariously passing and passing, the juggling of no-brain.
Why lie awake, trying to focus that thing's helpless indifference
With your blood become phosphorous, your heart pounding its
    morse wastefully
Into the Universe in general

And your head in stone silence, listening for an echo.

On Westminster Bridge

A shattered army, Thames' filthy tonnage, tumbrils of carrion,
Not a beautiful spectacle
For the drinkers of history, or for me
Or my friends, this island's parallel issues.

Wordsworth's head went down here singing and the Isle Of
    Dogs ate it.
So now let us make our heads brass and proof,
O Thames
Plunder of your own defeat, O necessary sewer.

A woman somewhere upstream is washing the shirt of our
    future.
If you see her first she is powerless, full of blessings.
I have not seen her.
I see this disgorging of diseases, mud in a cupful,

And these refugees
Dragging the country down, without gesture or murmur, all
    heads bowed
In the lamentable press toward Atlantis
Under the bridges, with their attendant

Bladder dogs, their old corks and condoms ...
The swan-voiced Elgar's decomposing – Let us all go down to exult
Under the haddock's thumb, rejoice
Through the warped mouth of the flounder, let us labour with   20
   God on the beaches!

Daily in the scarfing water
The banners
Fouled
And bandaging the shamed
Nameless battalions draining
Out of a dead lion –
                        deliquescing
To an officiation of blowflies.

Nightly this dark, feminine agony
Stemming from the womb no older than ever it was.   30

After Lorca

The clock says 'When will it be morning?'
The sun says 'Noon hurt me.'
The river cries with its mouthful of mud
And the sea moves every way without moving.

Out of my ear grew a reed
Never touched by mouth.
Paper yellows, even without flame,
But in words carbon has already become diamond.

A supple river of mirrors I run on
Where great shadows rise to the glance,
Flowing all forward and bringing
The world through my reflection.

A voice like a ghost that is not
Rustle the dead in passage
Leaving the living chilled,
Wipe clear the pure glass of stone.

Wipe clear the pure stone of flesh.

A song tickling God's ear
Till he laughs and catches it with his hand.
A song with a man's face
That God holds up in his fingers.

Era of Giant Lizards

The stick insect sitting at his stillness
In the little lamp of his belly is an umbrella man
Lost among glittering traffic, and a white head quiet at a problem.

A toad is stone-motion, mould-pride, loam-song –
The jewel in his head is the wisdom of this.

Once I heard three notes of a nightingale in a dark wood.
The moon sailed. A pond shone. A fence waited.

A cry that momentarily threatened the earth
Gulped back into a bird the size of an oak-leaf.

Small Hours

The clock-face stares,
Its heart will betray it.

A creak stands on the landing, looking down.

The chairs have surrendered and are helpless.
The floor presses its face into the earth.

Bad News Good!

To act crow, you need not be black.
You only need the appetite,
And the mindless, gloating look
As you pull something's insides out.

The carrion crow that barks and goes
Over the house, disgorges ill-luck
Nowise created by the crows –
Gouts of death's abundant black.

A lady here, under crow-possession,
Will pluck out her evil tidings
From your eye's lightest confession,
Then flap off with the evidence bleeding.

Lately she tasted the satisfaction
Of seeing her crow-bodings kill
One brain where she set them in action,
But she did not then sit still

Since a sitting crow starves and
This real victim was too good
To lose to death. She hopped around
With torn fragments loud in blood.

And still into all sorts of heads
Jabs these grave incriminations –
Then regards with gloating beads
Her sudden eyehole excavations.

What of Iago, idiot, or revenge
There is in her, I do not know –
Lust to rend and to derange
Is the nature of a crow:

Messenger innocence of God's will,
Delivering the black of Hell –
Till every word that wounds be buried
Where it comes closest to kill.

Dice

1. TORTURE CHAMBER

Beyond any help now from the slugs under the rubbish
The roses close their eyes but cannot close their faces or their brains
As the sun re-enters refreshed.

2. ECLIPSE OF MOON-MAN

All white is black as charcoal,
All black is the eye's shadow flung from the gathering blaze in
    the head.

3. FIESTA

Through the limp hung leaves, frothing brown dog-heads, blue
  lance-heads,
Visored horse-heads, visored invisible faces –
Up and over a far ridge the rose skitters.

4. STATUE OF ATALANTA

The crouching madman in the stripped car cannot
Catch the standingest of stones
Without throwing it brains.

5. PORPOISES AT BRIGHTON

Out there they leap, and their black backs arch at the sun;
Plunged beneath dark spectacles, here they turn up their white
  bellies.

6. GUINNESS

I am a solitary drinking man because
I am in love with myself, who is a negress:
A secret smiling mirror, my glassful
Kisses me thickly through the meniscus.

7. DURST

Because earth was fire-gas in
Its preparations, and the father-fire retired
To diffidence of flints and coquetry
Of frigid jewellery, clay men groaned out and began
To wander about calling down lightning.

8. UPPER CODE

Turning the guns against these Africans and letting their black
  blood
I grow whiter and whiter.

O White Elite Lotus

Sheer as a bomb – still you are all veins.
Heart-muscle's moulded you.
Rage of heart-muscle, which is the dead, too, with their revenge.

Steel, glass – ghost
Of a predator's mid-air body conjured
Into a sort of bottle.

Flimsy-light, like a squid's funeral bone.
Or a surgical model
Of the uterus of The Great Mother of The Gods.

Out of this world! One more revelation
From the purply, grumbling cloud
And vulcanism of blood.

The killer whale's avalanching emergence
From the yawn
Of boredom this time.

Out of this world, and cruising at a hundred!
But alive, as even in blueprint you were alive,
Even as the little amoeba, flexing its lens,

Ranging in along a death-ray, is alive
With the eye that stares out through it.

What eye stares out through you?

You visor
Of a nature whose very abandoned bones
Will be an outpost of weapons.

Carol
(To the tune 'Once in Royal David's City')

Once an atom said to Mary
  God is weary of Mankind
Who has bulldozed all Creation
  With the iron of his mind.
    Heaven's absence cannot mend him,
    So we stand arrayed to end him.

Mary wept, remembering Jesus
  And the hour that he was slain.
Still in each man's face she looked at
  She could see the cross of pain.
    'Surely man is worth God's keeping
    While there lives but one man weeping.

'Mental pride, that halved the angels,
  Plunges man through night, alone.
While the fires of his falling
  Burn his children to the bone.
    Tell to God again how man
    Pays in men the price of man.'

So the atom flew to Heaven
  And in stillness Heaven heard
What a solitary confinement
  Is man's deafness to the Word:
    What an agony of thinking,
    In what death-cell silence sinking.

Then God touched the little atom
  And the altered heavens cried:
'What was Danger shall be Beauty
  And the atom be man's bride;
    And the frailty of her defenses
    Bring man's iron to its senses.'

Warm Moors

The moorline fumes like a pane of ice held up to the thawing blue.
And the lark, that toad of the roots,
Begins under the ear's moist threshold.

Then out and up, the lung's deep muscle
Building the stair, lifting stone
By stone a stair up the air, taking his time

To score the face of every stone as he sings
With a scoring and scribbling chisel,
This is the way the lark climbs into the sun –

Till your eye's gossamer snaps and your hearing floats back
   widely to earth.

After which the sky lies blank open
Without wings, and the earth is a folded clod.
Only the sun goes silently and endlessly on with the lark's song.

Folk-Lore

The voice
Travelling so powerfully through the floor here
Shakes us,
And shakes others dead sixty year

Up into a roomful of laughter, spittled jaws
Heavy on the clock's perspective,
Gaping in air, in favour with the whole
Convention of the visible heavens.

He was big. He is shrunk down, twisted down
To a rheumatoid idol, a collector's find
Of eternity's tough equipment.
Eighty, with the tilted eyes of a demon.

A historian of more than stones
Or the simple enclosures of landscape
Have an eye for,
He smells out the old spark of graves,

Raises again, not noticeably corrupted,
An eye's force and flare-up,
Words that stapled kicking thicknesses
Of air and instant, ghosts from his buttoned guts,

Plucking those dead people from underground
With a gesture
As if he had snatched the tongue from our heads, but livelier,
And at once found nothing between his fingers –

While we rock with simple laughter.

Gibraltar

Empire has rotted back,
Like a man-eater
After its aeon of terror, to one fang.

Apes on their last legs –
Rearguard of insolence –
Snapping at peanuts and defecating.

The heirloom garrison's sold as a curio
With a flare of Spanish hands
And a two-way smile, wafer of insult,

Served in carefully-chipped English.
The taxi-driver talking broken American
Has this rock in his palm.

When the next Empire noses this way
Let it sniff here.

Birdsong

First, love is a little bird
That sings in the orchard blossoms
I think it is a wren
It sings in the brambles and out of the wall
It sings out of the wall.

Then love is a fine falcon
Soaring O soaring, brother of the Archer
Or it rests inside the sun
While the whole earth kneels
        kneels
While the whole earth kneels.

Love becomes a cruel leopard
And its voice rips through the locks
A black bagful of emeralds
It leaps to the woods with the crying body
It leaps with the crying body.

Love becomes a nightly owl
All the night it dooms in your ear

All the day it hides in the wood
Gripping skulls in its talons
                talons   ,
Gripping skulls in its talons

And then love is a madonna
Deep, deep the river of her peace
And drowned are the floating hands
That did not even wave goodbye
That did not even wave goodbye.

But love like a circus returns
The elephants stand on their heads
Small eye and huge anus
And the tigers offer their gullets
                gullets
The tigers offer their gullets.

And love is careful stretcher
For an angel, newly fallen,
With a wound as wide as the world
Where a man dare hardly breathe
                breathe
Where a man dare hardly breathe.

And love is a tourniquet
And the tourniquet a garotte
O love is a song from the lifer's cell
By day it is breaking the stones
                stones
By day it is breaking the stones.

Till love becomes a crow
Upon a desolation
The crow makes a drum
The crow begins to dance
                dance
The crow begins to dance.

There is nothing else
The crow has gone mad
Upon a desolation
It drums and it dances
                dances
Upon a desolation.

While the clouds above
Roll their great bodies together
And maybe it is love moves them   .
They do not have to live
        live
They do not have to live.

Plum Blossom

Not the snail's river of itself
Nor a man's mental den of no departure
But all night
The shadows of these riders trampling the street-lamps.

The plum tree has battled the whole way
Up the hard road of the roots, its mouth full of stones.
The buds of the plum tree are scarred veterans
Full of last words, the old saws of zero.

But the plum-blossoms open
Volcanoes of frailty –
Mouths without hunger but to utter
Love, love to each other.

Neither the granite, hewn, bag-breasted Sheilas,
With their knees hauled back,
Pulling themselves big-fingered wide-open,
Presenting the voice in their bellies

Or the dog-heads of infernal darkness
Gripped into grinning gargoyle stone
Shall protect the time-blackened Cathedrals
From the plum-blossom.

Past, present, future –
Luckless snow-crystals
In the silent laughter
Of these raw barbarians, these burning hairy mouths.

The Last Migration

So God died. And a new god
With narrowed eyes,
Carrying the Word reversed,
Gazed across the earth.

Which was cluttered with unbelievables.

There stood the Irish Elk,
A ponderous machinery of pain,
A purposeless castle of gristle,
Above a frosty hollow of heather
On a sea of empty skylines.
How had the sea, that throws crabs up, thrown this up?
Had those antlers fallen from a star?
Had those eyes come from the moon?
It stooped drinking where snow-water puddled among stones.
It hoisted its head, as in a daze,
And clattered to some other draughty standing place
With its absurd furniture and snow-proof eyelids,
Staring around without comprehension,
Like an error from timelessness,
Twitching its ears, browsing a little, shivering.
The narrowed eye, the God, spoke,
Calling the Elk back.
And the scene was amended
As that furniture collapsed, and those eyes accepted the verdict
Like a hero's, without change of expression,
As the Elk's blood smoked, pulled back through the tiny hole
Of God's eye-pupil.
It lasted a few minutes and the Elk was unravelled.
The waters of Elk had gone.
Only the hooves and antlers remained for a while, among the
    stones and heather roots
Where they did not belong,
Among the world-weather and the insects.

God turned his gaze slowly,
And the Aurochs dropped to its knees, astounded,
Meeting His eye.
And He called back the Aurochs.
It struggled to rise, it wanted to charge,

It thought He was only a man,
But had already begun to leave the earth, spiralling
Clockwise weightlessly
Into God's mesmerism,
Leaving shuddering haunches and the huge horns jammed
    across the doorway of the earth.

Then God called to the doves.
And the Passenger Pigeons,
The foliage of a continent's fatness,
Whirled up, darkening the old heaven,
And came whirling down
Into the vortex and rifling
Of the Word.
They dived in under the eyebrow.
Their lineage, like a whip, cracked to an end
Leaving a few breast-feathers floating.

But God looked out beyond them,
And the peaceful blood of the buffaloes recoiled.
And God called in the buffalo.
And the Great Lakes on the hoof
Quaked, began to converge
Toward the sudden hole in the centre,
Draining, with a tumbling final thunder,
Through the rifled bore,
And at that bottleneck of bellowing and pain
For lasting seconds the hooves dug in,
The tongue reached stiffly into air
As the bellow clawed out for a hold behind the skylines,
And the eye gripped at the slipping expanses,
The near soil-crumbs, the last grass
Around the rim of the terrible black hole
Which was the eye-pupil
Of the God of the Steady Gaze.

And God saw everything He had unmade and Behold
It was what He wanted.
And then God spoke to the whole world,
And right around the world, the waters trembled
And began to move ...

The Burning of the Brothel

'Pounding the pulpit and foaming
  Against the inviting eleven
Apertures of the rabidly-homing
  Devil into his heaven –
Flesh of a woman or man –
  Comes to no good these days:
My congregation's gone
  Into Hell on its knees,'
      Muttered the Reverend Bladderwrack
      And poured another and tossed it back.

God knows how he came to the place.
  Madame Owlmount's brothel
Opened its door in his face
  As he fought up the steps with his bottle.
Tolerant man as he was,
  A queue at a brother door
Would put God's wrath in an ass
  To kick out every whore:
      'Lechery I love not, but
      For the Lord God I'll marry the lot.'

As he swung his John Jameson bottle,
  From the windows up the house front
The whores were lowing like cattle
  To hear the heads that went:
You could not have ducked from his blows
  Save with such a duck
You would have buried your nose
  To the eyes in a pavement crack.
      All the whores hallooed his approach
      And vowed to meet him with his match.

'Here comes a man times fifty,'
  They cried, and caught those wretches
Then bedded, and with hefty
  Crutch-holds and half-hitches
Rubbished them into the street,
  Their singlets round their ears,
The windows wide open for that,
  Then the whores crowded the stairs:

Madame Owlmount smiled him in
Then slammed the door on the town.

Bloodied, Bladdewrack stood,
    The bottle-neck in his hand,
His back to the bolts, but the rude
    Fingers of whores wound
Every inch of his every
    Member as if they meant
His body a braille breviary:
    'Blindly have we sinned!'
        'My lost sheep,' he cried, with tears.
        The wolves' grins split their ears.

Loud on the door from the street
    Customer's privilege
Banged a hundred fists and feet:
    Projectiles of that grudge
Brought windows showering in,
    And the whole street's air,
By the mob's black lung drawn,
    Roared like a tunnel fire,
        More shook that house, to every bed,
        Than ever fornication did.

Inside was worse even than that:
    A fox chopped among hounds
Or a flung-among-terriers rat,
    Under those whores' hands
Bladderwrack whirled to rags.
    Then they danced on him all,
Tits whipping and spinning their wigs:
    His blood shot up the wall.
        But he clenched a hymn-book in his teeth
        And mouth-organned aloud his faith.

Katie Padompa snagged him
    By the mouth with hers
And onto her drubbed bed dragged him.
    It was not weeks or hours –
Within five seconds he struck:
    High with righteous ire
Stood blood in Bladderwrack
    And the Holy Fire.

'God help us !' startled Katie cried,
'How long have you kept this hid?'

Then Bladderwrack began
  His sermon, the motor it was
Of a drill that thundered on stone
  (Somewhere Katie's cries)
'You have cast to work for the devil.
  I have a devil here
Shall sweat you of your evil –
  Here is a poker-player
      Shall so raise you at your games
      You shall quit, though you forfeit limbs.'

Whores that had crowded the room
  To applaud that ordination
Saw what buffalo groom
  Mounted the cow in question:
They stood, shriek at half-cock,
  As he whipped her like an egg
For aphrodisiac
  To manage the next hag:
      Then they fled loud through the corridors –
      Pity it was to hear those whores!

Bladderwrack in full cry
  Came frogging after them,
Left Katie impatiently,
  Not noticing the flame
That under her buttocks was glowing
  With little randy sparks,
And Katie was past knowing.
  He flapped his bible blacks
      And overhauled, at the top of the stair,
      Bella Balloomop by her blue hair.

None now dared watch him exact
  That Christian penalty.
Some frantically packed,
  Some naked as your eye
Except for a blanket or gown
  Panicked into the streets
Where now the worst half of the town
  Clamoured for their rights,

Accepting gladly the sudden swarms
Of wailing whores into their arms.

Meanwhile Katie's bed
  Was blazing like a pyre.
Katie stood nine feet red
  Flame like a vision whore:
Then Bella Balloomop under
  Bladderwrack's awful stroke
Saw miracle and wonder
  Through wall and ceiling break:
    Still, like a salamander man,
    Furnaced in fire he rutted on.

From the clasp of a constable,
  Though deep in a doorway,
Madame Owlmount gave a yell:
  Every eye straightway
A single mirror stare
  Repictured the bawdy house
Windows picturing fire,
  Till the roof collapsed with a crash,
    And flames that seemed volcanoeing
    Out of Hell from the gap flung.

The fire-engine jammed in the crowd
  By now jammed in themselves.
'This is a fire,' the fireman said,
  'Is not burning by halves.
Some tinder and combustible
  Substance...' 'Shame on your mouth!'
The Madame cried, 'The joint's crammed full
  Of live and lovely youth.'
    And sure enough, the flames shot up
    As if the darkness must cry 'Rape!'

Some that were still half-packed,
  Half-dressed, half-choked, lay
Half-out of the windows and shrieked
  'The stairs have burned away!'
And 'Save us from Bladderwrack!'
  While Bladderwrack's silhouette
Rose horned and black at their back
  Like Lucifer the Great,

And if they did not leap for their lives
He forked them down like barley sheaves.

From window to window he paced.
    They saw him from the street.
Their eyes saucered amaze
    To see him live in that.
Not a whore was remaining.
    The fire with its roots in the cellar
That stem up the house was straining
    To a night full of leaf and flower
        Bore him, gesticulating psalms,
        Through spaces of those purgèd rooms.

A miserable drizzle came on.
    The crowd it crept away.
The flame died on the black stone
    An hour before day.
The husk of the brothel reeked.
    At first light, in rain,
Firemen peered and poked.
    But not one charred bone
        Remained of the furious body that
        Bladderwrack's great soul had quit.

And what of the whores of the house?
    Where had they laid their heads?
Some had caught the first bus.
    Others were warm in beds
While gleeful bachelors tiptoed
    With hot tea to their sides.
Some remained concubines for good,
    Some few became brides.
        But high in Heaven smiles Bladderwrack.
        May the Lord God send us his luck.

To W. H. Auden

As to the limestone upland
Cradle of their water,
The trout, the fatter,
Should, should –

As hikers and cross-country anglers
Who have cached their car,
To the cartographer
Certainly, certainly –

As the riddled boy in the dust
To lofty Apollo's son
In grubby Paddington
Lives to, lives to –

As the tapeworms feasting
Blind as gods,
To the cat's gut
Dumbly, dumbly –

We who, as Tobias
Found in the great fish, found
Saturn and Mercury joined
In you, to you

Give thanks, give thanks.

from RECKLINGS (1966)

On the Slope

Having taken her slowly by surprise
For eighty years
The hills have won, their ring is closed.

The field-walls float their pattern
Over her eye
Whether she looks outward or inward.

Nothing added, nothing taken away.
Year after year the trout in the pools
Grow heavy and vanish without ever emerging.

Foxglove and harebell neither protest nor hope
By the steep slope where she climbs.
Out of nothing she grew here simply

Also suffering to be merely flowerlike

But with the stone agony growing in her joints
And eyes dimming with losses, widening for losses.

Water

On moors where people get lost and die of air
On heights where the goat's stomach fails

In gorges where the toad lives on starlight
In deserts where the bone comes through the camel's nostril

On seas where the white bear gives up and dies of water
In depths where only the shark's tooth resists

At altitudes where the eagle would explode
Through falls of air where men become bombs

At the poles where zero is the sole hearth
Water is not lost, is snug, is at home –

Sometimes with its wife, stone –
An open-armed host, of poor cheer.

Fishing at Dawn

Captured by dumb orders of herbage.
Much buried root-eaten blood
Is exhaled in part as night-fog.

Freed, but not from their deadness,
Now ploughed-in roundheads
Conform with mastodon and wart-hog.

Girls in plenty – risen virginity
Of many a tough, smoked hag
That wearied the neighbourhood.

God yawns onto the black water.

There aches through my dull head
The bellowing of the maggot.

Dully Gumption's Addendum

At his begetting a Welsh adder
Declaiming in Ayrshire against Divine Kings
With the jewel of Ireland under its skullbone
Entered his mother and for nine months

The ghost confronted her in doorways.
She suckled him in an unlit crevice of country
Where words grew out of the ground freakishly
With a sort of Neanderthal slouch.

England in that day lay under the head of the dead god king
Cromwell cut from the country body but could not bury or silence:
It moved with a kind of maggot.
These maggots were all words stuffed with dead godly kingliness.

The maggots multiplied, spilling into the shires.
Each maggot wore a crown like a basilisk
And the bumpkin English took them for the words of god-sent law.
So these maggots bit deep into the brains of the bumpkin English.

Englishman after Englishman fell eaten to a mummy skin
Around a man-weight maggot and stiffened
To a chrysalis from which a black fly in no time
Flew up into the rotten face of the kingdom.

At grammar school this remorseless strain of maggot
Behind greying disciplinarian masks
Of Addison of Gladstone and of Arnold
Ate into his brain, ate into his brain.

They took up house in there, they pronounced for him,
They peered from the gnawn-out eyesockets, they budged him
Southwards and southwards, Oxford and Cambridge,
And his body bundled behind like a lopped earthworm's.

The colleges stooped over him and night after night thereafter
He dreamed the morphine of his Anglicising:
Dreamed his tongue uprooted, dreamed his body drawn and
    quartered
High over England and saw Thames go crawling from the
    fragments –

And fell, and lay his own gravestone, which went on all night
Carving itself in lordly and imperturbable English.
So he woke numbed. So came of age, like a cheese, mouldering
To England's expectations.

Now this chrysalis twitches into his thirties,
The fly hardening in him that will soon one sunrise
Pop eyes into the open and go up
From the husk of his mother earth with a cloud

Of loyal Trafalgar black starlings
And the morning flocks blackening the nostrils
Mouth and eyes of London where it
Leans so low over England.

Guinness

I am a solitary drinking man because
I am in love with myself, who is a negress:
A secret, smiling mirror, my glassful
Kisses me thickly through the meniscus.

Flanders

Dead eyes, blurred by hard rain,
Mouths that grin into mud and
Puddles unwinding heavy crimson.

Still they hear nothing of peace.
They remain locked in the problem.
The young clover cannot distract them

Keats

Once I heard three notes of a nightingale in a dark wood.

The moon lay open, wide and bright, like a pond.
The brimming moon looked through me and I could not move.

A cry that momentarily threatened the earth
Gulped back into a bird the size of an oak-leaf.

Beech Tree

The beech-bole is an angel of the earth. A torso sooted and silvery,
Twisting muscular upwards
To the whirlwind of light, as a menhir to its own might.

Blind with God. And like a bursting sea
The shoulders of a girl.
A soldier in a frozen coat, living by rote.

And like an old, mossed hunter, sucking the bones
Of all speculation. On its leashes
Fly owls and astronomers' skulls.

Toll

These are the aged who hide their sadness
And deaths in rinds of bacon and are inherited by flies;
These are the children multiplied every morning
With the harvest of hen-eggs; these are the suburbs
Bearing their cargo of people under the skylines

As the Gulf Stream bears its populations
Without voice without diminution
Without birth-pangs or death-pangs, with only abundance
Into the bellies of Europe.

Memory

The morass is bulging and aborting –
Mother, mother, mother, what am I?

Hands of light, hands of light
Wash the writhing darkness.

Mother, the eel in the well is eating the moon!

If I stop my heart and hold my breath

The needle will thread itself.
Daring the no-man quiet of my no-being

A mouse buds at the washboarding. A nose
Of ginger spider weaves its hairs toward me.

Claws trickle onto my palm.
An ounce pins itself there,

Nose wavering to investigate me.
Am I a mouse's remembrance?

I start, and it bounces past its shadow
Into my mother's shoe

Which twists out.
                    I fly up flustered
Into the winter of a near elm.

Heatwave

Between Westminster and sunstruck St Paul's
The desert has entered the flea's belly.

Like shut-eyed, half-submerged Nile bulls
The buildings tremble with breath.

The mirage of river is so real
Bodies drift in it, and human rubbish.

The main thing is the silence.
There are no charts for the silence.

Men can't penetrate it. Till sundown
Releases its leopard

Over the roofs, and women are suddenly
Everywhere, and the walker's bones

Melt in the coughing of great cats.

Fallen Eve

My mouth is the despair of God
Formed only for men.

The serpent remains earthen, brutishly-veined,
Rooted in crevices, living on flies and men –

The serpent that should have strangled me
And then eaten itself.

I sing, stamping the gruelling drum-beat
To renew fallen men.

Love is weak to protect as webs.

In April my body begins to frighten me
And my sleep fills with weeping –

Again and again the forced grave of men.

The Toughest

I

The eye was a masterful horseman
Hardened, proud and fierce.
He reined in the listening tremors of the earth,
He spurred its humped blindness.

But the sky-collapse of lightning
The earth flopping in violet like a fish jerked from its element

Drove the eye squirming into the skull –

It survived
Where a church-tower did not.

The eye reappeared, close to orange lichens.

While the ears ranged far off
Where the laughter of great outer darkness threatened to close
    its teeth on the skull
And the mouth chewed lumps of sun that were melting the brains.

II

To be sober in sober company, with the water in the cup
And the great seas negotiating their statuary confines,
The lucid moon, and the Great Outer Darkness

Which is the same as the small inner darkness

After huge weepings
And vanishing of islands
To watch

Because nothing else can watch

Leading
A ghost
Of query, alone, to a

Doubtful haunting –

Reading the empty chart that the stars are
Under the hopeful light of the leaf

Thaw

Who'll read off the pulsings of thaw? Who'll calibrate
Combustion of the maniac's nerve? Or appraise
The damp straw's prayer to the sunrise?

In the fever ward, pillows grow deeper –
The Universe thickens to numbness, fumbled
By the huge lips of a phantom.

But already lambs totter out, and are apt.
And the Almighty's crept into snowdrops, where He'll be believed.

The star-litter is all that's left
Of his broken barometer.

The swollen statistics of anguish
Are jumbled and lost in the voices of water.

Plum-Blossom

I

The plum-tree has battled the whole way
Up the hard road of the roots, its mouth full of stones.
The buds of the plum tree are scarred veterans
Full of last words, the old saws of zero.

But the plum-blossoms open
Volcanoes of frailty
Mouths without hunger but to utter
Love, love to each other.

II

The baboon in the zoo
Shows me its multicoloured arse
Meaning it wants to be friendly.
It looks over its shoulder
With narrow glittering eyes
Like an Egyptian priestess.
We are both in a world
Where the dirt is God.

III

Inside the head of a cat
Under the bones, the brains, the blood-tissue,
Bone of the bone and brain of the brain,
Blood of the blood and tissue of the tissue,
Is God's head, with eyes open.
And under that my own head, with wide eyes.
And under that the head of a cat, with eyes
Smiling and closed.

Public Bar T.V.

That glass, bubble-bodied, dream-foetus of shadow-pallor,
Which will never enter life,
Looms like the negative
Of a clumsy, weary and ageing man's failure.

Men that have been bending all their lives
In the one dim lamp of a pension
To lift their needs, relax as in graves,
Lifeless but for the eye-gleams of attention.

They haze and sip, like a mountain-range in the dew.
These are the Giant Stupids.
They are grimy to the spinal fluid
As if they slept nightly in the earth.

Mankind floats up the air in a peephole cloud —
That's moonland!
They can't comprehend. They undergo it like death.
They swallow all its drizzling nothings, like the mild earth.

As Woman's Weeping

After the bloody dead-end
Evaporation of souls
Comes a slow sift from the stars
Of prams and nurses and giggles
                              a secret laughter

And the washing on the line in the city
Is flagging the lovers on in the deep fields
Waved by a wind
That swells from the gulf
                        as woman's weeping

Death is not failure and cease
But clean back to a fresh start
Laying the original wide open
Like a bitch on heat
                    a secret laughter

Then the earth-splitting
Havoc of birth, enters conquering

And to conquer,
As woman's weeping
                    a secret laughter

Trees

I whispered to the holly....
There was a rustle of answer – dark,
Dark, dark, a gleamer recoiling tensely backward
Into a closing nest of shattered weapons,
Like a squid into clouds of protection.
I plucked a spiny leaf. Nothing protested.
Glints twitched, watched me.

I whispered to the birch....
My breath crept up into a world of shudderings.
Was she veiled?
Herself her own fountain
She pretended to be absent from it, or to be becoming air
Filtering herself from her fingertips,
Till her bole paled, like a reflection on water,
And I felt the touch of my own ghostliness –

I moved on, looking neither way,
Trying to hear
The outcry that must go with all
Those upflung maidenly gestures, that arrested humpback rout
Stumbling in blackberries and bracken –

Silence.

Trees, it is your own strangeness, in the dank wood,
Makes me so horrifying
I dare not hear my own footfall.

A Colonial

A face of searchlight, lamp off, glass jarred opaque
Eyes of asbestos in a cold country
Spectacles of protection
The crash-goggles of monosyllabic impacts

'Where is the British Museum?'

Like a cactus in desert, concentrating
On roots and prickles, he faded
As in failing light
Shoulders of parade-ground in the bomb-light
Shoulders braced under a bubble
Shoulders noble under the yoke of no plough
Spine long after summer
Spine upright by presumption, that forgets itself
Spine by sleight of balance
Spine by connivance with the sidelong head
Spine in despite of the feet's grief
Waist of echo, waist of aftermath
Waist insistent
Waist without navel
Waist ducking into the pelvis
As under skylines
Occupied with the animal routine

Of getting over the ground at all costs

Don Giovanni

Your shapely tongue, your whipstock back,
Keep your end up very well.
But the cold plot, and the colder action,
Weigh to the gravity of hell.

Such a stricture and shrinkage of offering
Cramps to physical heart-stiffening.
A fly-wheel zoomed free, your ravening
Is the trajectory of your suffering.

Now you have only a kind of rape,
Desperate as a cliff-leap,
Upon a body you must first kill,
For your death-cell final appeal.

Who's at the door? Blind, and dumb,
Who's in the room? You are your own
Guest of annihilating stone,
Invited a lifetime, now come.

A Match

Spluttering near out, before it touches the moors,
You start, threatened by your own tears.
But not your skin, not doors, not borders
Will be proof against your foraging
Through everything unhuman or human
To savour and own the dimensions of woman
As water does those of water.
                                    But the river
Is a prayer to its own waters
Where the circulation of our world is pouring
In stillness –
Everyone's peace, no less your own peace.
No movement but rooted willows.

Out of bedrock your blood's operation
Carves your eyes clear not so quickly
As your mouth dips deeper
Into the massed darkness.

Small Events

The old man's blood had spoken the word: 'Enough'.
Now nobody had the heart to see him go on.
His photographs were a cold mercy, there on the mantel.
So his mouth became a buttonhole and his limbs became
    wrapped iron.

Towards dying his eyes looked just above the things he looked at.
They were the poor rearguard on the beach
And turned, watering, with all his hope, from the smoke
To the sea for the Saviour

Who is useful only in life.

So, under a tree a tree-creeper, on dead grass sleeping –
It was blind, its eyes matte as blood-lice
Feeding on a raw face of disease.
I set it on dry grass, and its head fell forward, it died

Into what must have cupped it kindly.

And a grey, aged mouse, humped shivering
On the bare path, under November drizzle –
A frail parcel, delivered in damaging mail and still unclaimed,
Its contents no longer of use to anybody.

I picked it up. It was looking neither outward nor inward.
The tremendous music of its atoms
Trembled it on my fingers. As I watched it, it died.
A grey, mangy mouse, and seamed with ancient scars,

Whose blood had said: 'Sleep'.

So this year a swift's embryo, cracked too early from its fallen egg –
There, among mineral fragments,
The blind blood stirred,
Freed,

And, mystified, sank into hopeful sleep.

To be a Girl's Diary

Crumbling, glanced into
By strange smiles, in a saleroom,
Where the dust is of eyes and hearts, in proportion,
As well as of old shoes, meteors, and dung ...

To be an heirloom spoon, blackening
Among roots in a thorn-hedge, forgetful
Of flavours as of tongues,
Fleeting towards heavenly dispersal,
Walked by spiders ...

Nightfall collects the stars
Only in a manner of speaking.

Everything is inheriting everything.

Stealing Trout on a May Morning

I park the car half in the ditch and switch off and sit.
The hot astonishment of my engine's arrival
Sinks through 5 a.m. silence and frost.
At the end of a long gash

An atrocity through the lace of first light
I sit with the reeking instrument.
I am on delicate business.
I want the steel to be cold instantly
And myself secreted three fields away
And the farms, back under their blankets, supposing a plane passed.

Because this is no wilderness you can just rip into.
Every leaf is plump and well-married,
Every grain of soil of known lineage, well-connected.
And the gardens are like brides fallen asleep
Before their weddings have properly begun.
The orchards are the hushed maids, fresh from convent . . .
It is too hushed, something improper is going to happen.
It is too ghostly proper, all sorts of liveried listenings
Tiptoe along the lanes and peer over hedges.

I listen for the eyes jerked open on pillows,
Their dreams washed with sudden ugly petroleum.
They need only look out at a sheep.
Every sheep within two miles
Is nailing me accurately down
With its hellishly-shaven starved-priest expression.

I emerge. The air, after all, has forgotten everything.
The sugared spindles and wings of grass
Are etched on great goblets. A pigeon falls into space.
The earth is coming quietly and darkly up from a great depth,
Still under the surface. I am unknown,
But nothing is surprised. The tarmac of the road
Is velvet with sleep, the hills are out cold.
A new earth still in its wrappers
Of gauze and cellophane,
The frost from the storage still on its edges,
My privilege to poke and sniff.
The sheep are not much more than the primroses.
And the river there, amazed with itself,
Flexing and trying its lights
And unused fish, that are rising
And sinking for the sheer novelty
As the sun melts the hill's spine and the spilled light
Flows through their gills . . .

My mind sinks, rising and sinking,
And the opening arms of the sky forget me
Into the buried tunnel of hazels. There
My boot dangles down, till a thing black and sudden
Savages it, and the river is heaping under,
Alive and malevolent,
A coiling glider of shock, the space-black 50
Draining off the night-moor, under the hazels . . .
But I drop and stand square in it, against it,
Then it is river again, washing its soul,
Its stones, its weeds, its fish, its gravels
And the rooty mouths of the hazels clear
Of the discolourings bled in
Off ploughlands and lanes . . .

At first, I can hardly look at it –
The riding tables, the corrugated
Shanty roofs tightening 60
To braids, boilings where boulders throw up
Gestures of explosion, black splitting everywhere
To drowning skirts of whiteness, a slither of mirrors
Under the wading hazels. Here it is shallow,
Ropes my knees, lobbing fake boomerangs,
A drowned woman loving each ankle,
But I'm heavier and I wade with them upstream,
Flashing my blue minnow
Up the open throats of water
And across through the side of the rush 70
Of alligator escaping along there
Under the beards of the hazels, and I slice
The wild nape-hair off the bald bulges,
Till the tightrope of my first footholds
Tangles away downstream
And my bootsoles move as to magnets.

Soon I deepen. And now I meet the piling mob
Of voices and hurriers coming towards me
And tumbling past me. I press through a panic . . .
This headlong river is a rout 80
Of tumbrils and gun-carriages, rags and metal,
All the funeral woe-drag of some overnight disaster
Mixed with planets, electrical storms and darkness
On a mapless moorland of granite,

Trailing past me with all its frights, its eyes
With what they have seen and still see,
They drag the flag off my head, a dark insistence
Tearing the spirits from my mind's edge and from under ...

90 To yank me clear takes the sudden, strong spine
Of one of the river's real members –
Thoroughly made of dew, lightning and granite
Very slowly over four years. A trout, a foot long,
Lifting its head in a shawl of water,
Fins banked stiff like a trireme
It forces the final curve wide, getting
A long look at me. So much for the horror
It has changed places.
                                    Now I am a man in a painting
(Under the mangy, stuffed head of a fox)
Painted about 1905
100 Where the river steams and the frost relaxes
On the pear-blossoms. The brassy wood-pigeons
Bubble their colourful voices, and the sun
Rises upon a world well-tried and old.

Humanities

When Caesar clamped mankind in his money-mould
With a cry of pain out flew the effeminate soul

And turned into vengeful Christ –
The first Romantic raging at the first Formalist

And like an amoeba multiplying himself with Pentecost.
So ever since we've had to take sides and everybody's lost,

By half.
Napoleon in St Petersburg beating out wretched Sonia's life;

Blue-black Sonia rising from the Mississippi, stamping a drum,
Uttering mind-darkening cries and fetching black blood up and
      calling on her kingdom come;

Sonia growing a small neat moustache
And flinging first Germany then all Europe into her furnace –

Half to pig-iron, half to ashes
Which blew into all the books and films as dumb girls with
    flower faces

Under which flower again there rages
The whorish dragon of the dark ages

Helmed with a modern capital and devouring
Virginal St George as a flower.

Tutorial

Like a propped skull,
His humour is mediaeval.

What are all those tomes? Tomb-boards
Pressing the drying remains of men.
He brings some out, we stew them up to a dark amber and
    sit sipping.

He is fat, this burst bearskin, but his mind is an electric mantis
Plucking the heads and legs off words, the homunculi.
I am thin but I can hardly move my bulk, I go round and round
    numbly under the ice of the North Pole.

This scholar dribbling tea
Onto his tie, straining pipe-gargle   10
Through the wharfe-weed that ennobles

The mask of enquiry, advancing into the depths like a harbour,
Like a sphynx cliff,
Like the papery skull of a fish

Lodged in dune sand, with a few straws,
Rifled by dry cold.
His words

Twitch and rustle, twitch
And rustle.
The scarred world looks through their gaps.   20

I listen
With bleak eyeholes.

Poltergeist

When the colliers of Kingswood began to sing
What bright angel crossed the gulf.

Wesley riding the wet roads of England,
What jealous woman leaned and longed.

When Saul called up Samuel
The spirits thought it was the resurrection.

Blake leapt from the cradle,
The ghoul married Keats.

Napoleon mounted on Robespierre
Rode up through the hole in Louis' shoulders.

And America rose from all fours,
George falling on his head.

Last Lines

My blood goes now, and the starry city
Struggles every minute more sogged and
Helpless like a gnat in it. The nurses
Waver at the glass and make silent mouths
As their ark founders – but I ignore
Inflexibly and am God uncreating
All things during my minutes. Blood slides
From me, the limbs for the first time
Slipping unrecognizably naked
And lit out of me, their one garment, as I crumple –
I thought me them and their pride. Blood clings
As it leaves. The loaded vampire I have been
All this time and fed on this heart and reared
From birth is moulting me, collecting
Now its last belongings, clinging but leaving
Slowly my brazen face silvering
Into vapours – finally, as a sigh, exhaling
My whole body, as a parting
Smile faint and thoughtful beyond

The Lake

Better disguised than the leaf-insect,

A sort of subtler armadillo,
The lake turns with me as I walk.

Snuffles at my feet for what I might drop or kick up,
Sucks and slobbers the stones, snorts through its lips

Into broken glass, smacks its chops.
It has eaten several my size

Without developing a preference —
Prompt, with a splash, to whatever I offer.

It ruffles in its wallow, or lies sunning,
Digesting old senseless bicycles

And a few shoes. The fish down there
Do not know they have been swallowed

Any more than the girl out there, who over the stern of a rowboat
Tests its depth with her reflection.

Yet how the outlet fears it!

                              — dragging it out,
Black and yellow, a maniac eel,

Battering it to death with sticks and stones.

Unknown Soldier

A gleam in a whisky head became a command.
Out of the opaque bubbling of England
The officer's face was a crystal. This refracted
The gleam and turned it to mathematics.

The sergeant thickened, stiffened to a body
Around the officer's aired word.
The ordinary privates stood in a herd.
They only had to hear and get ready.

This one, drugged with a hangover from
The draughts of courage they drank at home

Dozed a little in a hopeful suppose.
Anything to avoid a fuss.

To luck he had already surrendered.
If life was going to play foul
It could have the game, see if he cared.
Going with his mates was a goal meanwhile.

Until the brain that stands to right
Could find a rightful argument,
The monkey body didn't mind –
Finding plenty to imitate.

His life hung on a silk thread
Around his neck, with his name inscribed –
A good luck charm, to joke about,
A superstition – inherited.

Obscure was the command from the start
That took a bullet's spiritual arc
From the officer's throat through darkness
To jolt a mound of dirt.

from WODWO (1967)

Sumwhyle wyth wormeʒ he werreʒ, and wyth wolves als,
Sumwhyle wyth wodwos, þat woned in þe knarreʒ,
Boþe wyth bulleʒ and bereʒ, and boreʒ oþerquyle,
And etayneʒ, þat hym anelede of þe heʒe felle.

Sir Gawayn and Þe Grene Knyʒt, lines 720–723

Part I

Thistles

Against the rubber tongues of cows and the hoeing hands of men
Thistles spike the summer air
Or crackle open under a blue-black pressure.

Every one a revengeful burst
Of resurrection, a grasped fistful
Of splintered weapons and Icelandic frost thrust up

From the underground stain of a decayed Viking.
They are like pale hair and the gutturals of dialects.
Every one manages a plume of blood.

Then they grow grey, like men.
Mown down, it is a feud. Their sons appear,
Stiff with weapons, fighting back over the same ground.

Still Life

Outcrop stone is miserly

With the wind. Hoarding its nothings,
Letting wind run through its fingers,
It pretends to be dead of lack.
Even its grimace is empty,
Warted with quartz pebbles from the sea's womb.

It thinks it pays no rent,
Expansive in the sun's summerly reckoning.
Under rain, it gleams exultation blackly
As if receiving interest.
Similarly, it bears the snow well.

Wakeful and missing little and landmarking
The fly-like dance of the planets,
The landscape moving in sleep,
It expects to be in at the finish.
Being ignorant of this other, this harebell,

That trembles, as under threats of death,
In the summer turf's heat-rise,
And in which – filling veins
Any known name of blue would bruise
Out of existence – sleeps, recovering,

The maker of the sea.

Her Husband

Comes home dull with coal-dust deliberately
To grime the sink and foul towels and let her
Learn with scrubbing brush and scrubbing board
The stubborn character of money.

And let her learn through what kind of dust
He has earned his thirst and the right to quench it
And what sweat he has exchanged for his money
And the blood-weight of money. He'll humble her

With new light on her obligations.
The fried, woody chips, kept warm two hours in the oven,
Are only part of her answer.
Hearing the rest, he slams them to the fire back

And is away round the house-end singing
'Come back to Sorrento' in a voice
Of resounding corrugated iron.
Her back has bunched into a hump as an insult.

For they will have their rights.
Their jurors are to be assembled
From the little crumbs of soot. Their brief
Goes straight up to heaven and nothing more is heard of it.

Cadenza

The violinist's shadow vanishes.

The husk of a grasshopper
Sucks a remote cyclone and rises.

The full, bared throat of a woman walking water,
The loaded estuary of the dead.

And I am the cargo
Of a coffin attended by swallows.

And I am the water
Bearing the coffin that will not be silent.

The clouds are full of surgery and collisions   10
But the coffin escapes – as a black diamond,

A ruby brimming blood,
An emerald beating its shores,

The sea lifts swallow wings and flings
A summer lake open,

Sips and bewilders its reflection,
Till the whole sky dives shut like a burned land back to its spark –

A bat with a ghost in its mouth
Struck at by lightnings of silence –

Blue with sweat, the violinist   20
Crashes into the orchestra, which explodes.

Ghost Crabs

At nightfall, as the sea darkens,
A depth darkness thickens, mustering from the gulfs and the
     submarine badlands,
To the sea's edge. To begin with
It looks like rocks uncovering, mangling their pallor.
Gradually the labouring of the tide
Falls back from its productions,
Its power slips back from glistening nacelles, and they are crabs.
Giant crabs, under flat skulls, staring inland
Like a packed trench of helmets.
Ghosts, they are ghost-crabs.   10
They emerge
An invisible disgorging of the sea's cold
Over the man who strolls along the sands.
They spill inland, into the smoking purple
Of our woods and towns – a bristling surge

Of tall and staggering spectres
Gliding like shocks through water.
Our walls, our bodies, are no problem to them.
Their hungers are homing elsewhere.
20   We cannot see them or turn our minds from them.
Their bubbling mouths, their eyes
In a slow mineral fury
Press through our nothingness where we sprawl on beds,
Or sit in rooms. Our dreams are ruffled maybe,
Or we jerk awake to the world of possessions
With a gasp, in a sweat burst, brains jamming blind
Into the bulb-light. Sometimes, for minutes, a sliding
Staring
Thickness of silence
30   Presses between us. These crabs own this world.
All night, around us or through us,
They stalk each other, they fasten on to each other,
They mount each other, they tear each other to pieces,
They utterly exhaust each other.
They are the powers of this world.
We are their bacteria,
Dying their lives and living their deaths.
At dawn, they sidle back under the sea's edge.
They are the turmoil of history, the convulsion
40   In the roots of blood, in the cycles of concurrence.
To them, our cluttered countries are empty battleground.
All day they recuperate under the sea.
Their singing is like a thin sea-wind flexing in the rocks of
   a headland,
Where only crabs listen.

They are God's only toys.

Boom

And faces at the glutted shop-windows
Gaze into the bottomless well
Of wishes

Like rearlights away up the long road
Toward an earth-melting dawn
Of the same thing, but staler.

More More More
Meaning Air Water Life
Cry the mouths

That are filling with burning ashes.

Ludwig's Death Mask

Words for his ugly mug his
Naked exhibitions at windows shaking a
Fist at the gapers, his whalish appetite
For cold douches and changing lodgings.

Words for his black-mouth derisive
Engulfing in laughter the sweet-eyed attendance
Of aesthetes spreading their marzipan amazement
Over his music and nibbling it amazedly off.

But no words for the loyal
Formations of angels which attended
All this in misunderstanding and
Despair and finally grimly as Shakespeare

Caused himself flee seventeen feet down
Through the church-floor into dumb earth touched
His ears dead to continue complete
In union with the communion of angels.

Second Glance at a Jaguar

Skinful of bowls he bowls them,
The hip going in and out of joint, dropping the spine
With the urgency of his hurry
Like a cat going along under thrown stones, under cover,
Glancing sideways, running
Under his spine. A terrible, stump-legged waddle
Like a thick Aztec disemboweller,
Club-swinging, trying to grind some square
Socket between his hind legs round,
Carrying his head like a brazier of spilling embers,   10
And the black bit of his mouth, he takes it
Between his back teeth, he has to wear his skin out,

He swipes a lap at the water-trough as he turns,
Swivelling the ball of his heel on the polished spot,
Showing his belly like a butterfly.
At every stride he has to turn a corner
In himself and correct it. His head
Is like the worn down stump of another whole jaguar,
His body is just the engine shoving it forward,
Lifting the air up and shoving on under,
The weight of his fangs hanging the mouth open,
Bottom jaw combing the ground. A gorged look,
Gangster, club-tail lumped along behind gracelessly,
He's wearing himself to heavy ovals,
Muttering some mantra, some drum-song of murder
To keep his rage brightening, making his skin
Intolerable, spurred by the rosettes, the Cain-brands,
Wearing the spots off from the inside,
Rounding some revenge. Going like a prayer-wheel,
The head dragging forward, the body keeping up,
The hind legs lagging. He coils, he flourishes
The blackjack tail as if looking for a target,
Hurrying through the underworld, soundless.

Public Bar T.V.

On a flaked ridge of the desert

Outriders have found foul water. They say nothing;
With the cactus and the petrified tree
Crouch numbed by a wind howling all
Visible horizons equally empty.

The wind brings dust and nothing
Of the wives, the children, the grandmothers
With the ancestral bones, who months ago
Left the last river,

Coming at the pace of oxen.

Fern

Here is the fern's frond, unfurling a gesture,
Like a conductor whose music will now be pause
And the one note of silence
To which the whole earth dances gravely.

The mouse's ear unfurls its trust,
The spider takes up her bequest,
And the retina
Reins the creation with a bridle of water.

And, among them, the fern
Dances gravely, like the plume
Of a warrior returning, under the low hills,

Into his own kingdom.

A Wind Flashes the Grass

Leaves pour blackly across.
We cling to the earth, with glistening eyes, pierced afresh
   by the tree's cry.

And the incomprehensible cry
From the boughs, in the wind
Sets us listening for below words,
Meanings that will not part from the rock.

The trees thunder in unison, on a gloomy afternoon,
And the ploughman grows anxious, his tractor becomes terrible,
As his memory litters downwind
And the shadow of his bones tosses darkly on the air.

The trees suddenly storm to a stop, in a hush
Against the sky, where the field ends.
They crowd there shuddering
And wary, like horses bewildered by lightning.

The stirring of their twigs against the dark, travelling sky
Is the oracle of the earth.

They too are afraid they too are momentary
Streams rivers of shadow

A Vegetarian

Fearful of the hare with the manners of a lady,
Of the sow's loaded side and the boar's brown fang,

Fearful of the bull's tongue snaring and rending,
And of the sheep's jaw moving without mercy,

Tripped on Eternity's stone threshold.

                              Staring into the emptiness,
Unable to move, he hears the hounds of the grass.

Sugar Loaf

The trickle cutting from the hill-crown
Whorls to a pure pool here, with a whisp trout like a spirit.
The water is wild as alcohol –
Distilling from the fibres of the blue wind.
Reeds, nude and tufted, shiver as they wade.

I see the whole huge hill in the small pool's stomach.

This will be serious for the hill.
It suspects nothing.
Crammed with darkness, the dull, trusting giant
Leans, as over a crystal, over the water
Where his future is forming.

Bowled Over

By kiss of death, bullet on brow,
No more life can overpower
That first infatuation, world cannot
Ever be harder or clearer or come
Closer than when it arrived there

Spinning its patched fields, churches
Trees where nightingales sang in broad daylight
And vast flaring blue skirts of seas –
Then sudden insubordination
Of boredom and sleep

When the eyes could not find their keys
Or the neck remember what mother whispered
Or the body stand to its word.

Desertion in the face of a bullet!

Buried without honours.

Wino

Grape is my mulatto mother
In this frozen whited country. Her veined interior
Hangs hot open for me to re-enter
The blood-coloured glasshouse against which the stone world
Thins to a dew and steams off –
Diluting neither my blood cupful
Nor its black undercurrent. I swell in there, soaking.
Till the grape for sheer surfeit of me
Vomits me up. I'm found
Feeble as a babe, but renewed.

Logos

God gives the blinding pentagram of His power
For the frail mantle of a person
To be moulded onto. So if they come
This unlikely far, and against such odds –
   the perfect strength is God's.

And if the family features mount yet another
Opportune, doomed bid
To grapple to everlasting
Their freehold of life –
   it is by God's leave.

Creation convulses in nightmare. And awaking
Suddenly tastes the nightmare moving   10
Still in its mouth
And spits it kicking out, with a swinish cry –
   which is God's first cry.

Like that cry within the sea,
A mumbling over and over
Of ancient law, the phrasing falling to pieces
Garbled among shell-shards and gravels,
   the truths falling to pieces,

The sea pulling everything to pieces
Except its killers, alert and shapely.
And within seconds the new-born baby is lamenting
That it ever lived –
   God is a good fellow, but His mother's against Him.

Reveille

No, the serpent was not
One of God's ordinary creatures.
Where did he creep from,
This legless land-swimmer with a purpose?

Adam and lovely Eve
Deep in the first dream
Each the everlasting
Holy One of the other

Woke with cries of pain.
Each clutched a throbbing wound –
A sudden, cruel bite.
The serpent's head, small and still,

Smiled under the lilies.
Behind him, his coils
Had crushed all Eden's orchards.
And out beyond Eden

The black, thickening river of his body
Glittered in giant loops
Around desert mountains and away
Over the ashes of the future.

The Rescue

That's what we live on: thinking of their rescue
And fitting our future to it. You have to see it:
First, the dry smudge above the sea-line,
Then the slow growth of a shipful of strangers
Into this existence. White bows, the white bow-wave
Cleaving the nightmare, slicing it open,
Letting in reality. Then all the sailors white
As maggots waving at the rail. Then their shouting –
Faintly at first, as you can think
The crowd coming with Christ sounded   10
To Lazarus in his cave.
Then the ship's horn giving blast after blast out
Announcing the end of the island. Then the rowboat.
I fancy I saw it happen. The five were standing
In the shallows with the deathly sea
Lipping their knees and the rattle of oar-locks
Shaking the sand out of their brain-cells,
The flash of wet oars slashing their eyes back alive –
All the time the long white liner anchoring the world
Just out there, crowded and watching.   20
Then there came a moment in the eternity of this island
When the rowboat's bows bit into the beach
And the lovely greetings and chatter scattered –
This is wrong.
          The five never moved.
They just stood sucked empty
As grasses by this island's silence. And the crew
Helped them into the boat not speaking
Knowing the sound of a voice from the world
Might grab too cheery-clumsy
Into their powdery nerves. Then they rowed off   30
Toward the shining ship with carefully
Hushed oars dipping and squeaking. And the five sat all the time
Like mummies with their bandages lifted off –
While the ship's dazzling side brimmed up the sky
And leaned over, pouring faces.

Stations

I

Suddenly his poor body
Had its drowsy mind no longer
For insulation.

Before the funeral service foundered
The lifeboat coffin had shaken to pieces
And the great stars were swimming through where he had been.

For a while

The stalk of the tulip at the door that had outlived him,
And his jacket, and his wife, and his last pillow
Clung to each other.

II

I can understand the haggard eyes
Of the old

Dry wrecks

Broken by seas of which they could drink nothing.

III

They have sunk into deeper service. They have gone down
To labour with God on the beaches. They fatten
Under the haddock's thumb. They rejoice
Through the warped mouth of the flounder

And are nowhere they are not here I know nothing
Cries the poulterer's hare hanging
Upside down above the pavement
Staring into a bloody bag. Not here

Cry the eyes from the depths

Of the mirror's seamless sand.

IV

You are a wild look – out of an egg
Laid by your absence.

In the great Emptiness you sit complacent,
Blackbird in wet snow.

If you could make only one comparison –
Your condition is miserable, you would give up.

But you, from the start, surrender to total Emptiness,
Then leave everything to it.

Absence. It is your own
Absence

Weeps its respite through your accomplished music,
Wraps its cloak dark about your feeding.

V

Whether you say it, think it, know it
Or not, it happens, it happens as
Over rails over
The neck the wheels leave
The head with its vocabulary useless,
Among the flogged plantains.

The Green Wolf

My neighbour moves less and less, attempts less.
If his right hand still moves, it is a farewell
Already days posthumous.

But the left hand seems to freeze,
And the left leg with its crude plumbing;
And the left half jaw and the left eyelid and the words all the
    huge cries

Frozen in his brain his tongue cannot unfreeze –
While somewhere through a dark heaven
The dark bloodclot moves in.

I watch it approaching but I cannot fear it.   10
The punctual evening star,
Worse, the warm hawthorn blossoms, their foam,

Their palls of deathly perfume,
Worst of all the beanflower
Badged with jet like the ear of the tiger

Unmake and remake me. That star
And that flower and that flower
And living mouth and living mouth all

One smouldering annihilation
Of old brains, old bowels, old bodies
In the scarves of dew, the wet hair of nightfall.

The Bear

In the huge, wide-open, sleeping-eye of the mountain
The bear is the gleam in the pupil
Ready to awake
And instantly focus.

The bear is glueing
Beginning to end
With glue from people's bones
In his sleep.

The bear is digging
In his sleep
Through the wall of the Universe
With a man's femur.

The bear is a well
Too deep to glitter
Where your shout
Is being digested.

The bear is a river
Where people bending to drink
See their dead selves.

The bear sleeps
In a kingdom of walls
In a web of rivers.

He is the ferryman
To dead land.

His price is everything.

Part III

Theology

No, the serpent did not
Seduce Eve to the apple.
All that's simply
Corruption of the facts.

Adam ate the apple.
Eve ate Adam.
The serpent ate Eve.
This is the dark intestine.

The serpent, meanwhile,
Sleeps his meal off in Paradise –
Smiling to hear
God's querulous calling.

Gog

I

I woke to a shout: 'I am Alpha and Omega.'
Rocks and a few trees trembled
Deep in their own country.
I ran and an absence bounded beside me.

The dog's god is a scrap dropped from the table.
The mouse's saviour is a ripe wheat grain.
Hearing the Messiah cry
My mouth widens in adoration.

How fat are the lichens!
They cushion themselves on the silence.   10
The air wants for nothing.
The dust, too, is replete.

What was my error? My skull has sealed it out.
My great bones are massed in me.
They pound on the earth, my song excites them.
I do not look at the rocks and trees, I am frightened of what
  they see.

I listen to the song jarring my mouth
Where the skull-rooted teeth are in possession.
I am massive on earth. My feetbones beat on the earth
20 Over the sounds of motherly weeping...

Afterwards I drink at a pool quietly.
The horizon bears the rocks and trees away into twilight.
I lie down. I become darkness.

Darkness that all night sings and circles stamping.

II

The sun erupts. The moon is deader than a skull.
The grass-head waves day and night and will never know it exists.
The stones are as they were. And the creatures of earth
Are mere rainfall rivulets, in flood or empty paths.
The atoms of saints' brains are swollen with the vast bubble
  of nothing.
Everywhere the dust is in power.

Then whose
Are these
Eyes,
      eyes and
10 Dance of wants,
Of offering?

Sun and moon, death and death,
Grass and stones, their quick peoples, and the bright particles
Death and death and death

Her mirrors.

III

Out through the dark archway of earth, under the ancient lintel
  overwritten with roots,
Out between the granite jambs, gallops the hooded horseman
  of iron.

Out of the wound-gash in the earth, the horseman mounts,
  shaking his plumes clear of dark soil.
Out of the blood-dark womb, gallops bowed the horseman of iron.
The blood-crossed Knight, the Holy Warrior, hooded with
  iron, the seraph of the bleak edge.
Gallops along the world's ridge in moonlight.

Through slits of iron his eyes search for the softness of the
  throat, the navel, the armpit, the groin.
Bring him clear of the flung web and the coil that vaults from
  the dust.

Through slits of iron, his eyes have found the helm of the
  enemy, the grail,
The womb-wall of the dream that crouches there, greedier than
  a foetus,
Suckling at the root-blood of the origins, the salt-milk drug of
  the mothers.

Shield him from the dipped glance, flying in half light, that
  tangles the heels,
The grooved kiss that swamps the eyes with darkness.
Bring him to the ruled slab, the octaves of order,
The law and mercy of number. Lift him
Out of the octopus maw and the eight lunatic limbs
Of the rocking, sinking cradle.

The unborn child beats on the womb-wall.
He will need to be strong
To follow his weapons towards the light.
Unlike Coriolanus, follow the blades right through Rome

And right through the smile
That is the judge's fury
That is the wailing child
That is the ribboned gift
That is the starved adder
That is the kiss in the dream
That is the nightmare pillow
That is the seal of resemblances
That is illusion
That is illusion

The rider of iron, on the horse shod with vaginas of iron,
Gallops over the womb that makes no claim, that is of stone.

His weapons glitter under the lights of heaven.
He follows his compass, the lance-blade, the gunsight, out
Against the fanged grail and tireless mouth
Whose cry breaks his sleep
Whose coil is under his ribs
Whose smile is in the belly of woman
Whose satiation is in the grave.

Out under the blood-dark archway, gallops bowed the
horseman of iron.

Kreutzer Sonata

Now you have stabbed her good
A flower of unknown colour appallingly
Blackened by your surplus of bile
Blooms wetly on her dress.

'Your mystery! Your mystery!...'
All facts, with all absence of facts,
Exhale as the wound there
Drinks its roots and breathes them to nothing.

Vile copulation! Vile! – etcetera.
But now your dagger has outdone everybody's.
Say goodbye, for your wife's sweet flesh goes off,
Booty of the envious spirit's assault.

A sacrifice, not a murder.
One hundred and forty pounds
Of excellent devil, for God.
She tormented Ah demented you

With that fat lizard Trukachevsky,
That fiddling, leering penis.
Yet why should you castrate yourself
To be rid of them both?

Now you have stabbed her good
Trukachevsky is cut off
From any further operation on you.
And she can find nobody else.

Rest in peace, Tolstoy!
It must have taken supernatural greed
To need to corner all the meat in the world,
Even from your own hunger.

Out

I THE DREAM TIME

My father sat in his chair recovering
From the four-year mastication by gunfire and mud,
Body buffeted wordless, estranged by long soaking
In the colours of mutilation.
                              His outer perforations
Were valiantly healed, but he and the hearth-fire, its blood-flicker
On biscuit-bowl and piano and table leg,
Moved into strong and stronger possession
Of minute after minute, as the clock's tiny cog
Laboured and on the thread of his listening
Dragged him bodily from under   10
The mortised four-year strata of dead Englishmen
He belonged with. He felt his limbs clearing
With every slight, gingerish movement. While I, small and four,
Lay on the carpet as his luckless double,
His memory's buried, immovable anchor,
Among jawbones and blown-off boots, tree-stumps, shellcases
    and craters,
Under rain that goes on drumming its rods and thickening
Its kingdom, which the sun has abandoned, and where nobody
Can ever again move from shelter.

II

The dead man in his cave beginning to sweat;
The melting bronze visor of flesh
Of the mother in the baby-furnace –
Nobody believes, it
Could be nothing, all
Undergo smiling at
The lulling of blood in
Their ears, their ears, their ears, their eyes
Are only drops of water and even the dead man suddenly

Sits up and sneezes – Atishoo!
Then the nurse wraps him up, smiling,
And, though faintly, the mother is smiling,
And it's just another baby.

As after being blasted to bits
The reassembled infantryman
Tentatively totters out, gazing around with the eyes
Of an exhausted clerk.

III REMEMBRANCE DAY

The poppy is a wound, the poppy is the mouth
Of the grave, maybe of the womb searching –

A canvas-beauty puppet on a wire
Today whoring everywhere. It is years since I wore one.

It is more years
The shrapnel that shattered my father's paybook

Gripped me, and all his dead
Gripped him to a time

He no more than they could outgrow, but, cast into one, like iron,
Hung deeper than refreshing of ploughs

In the woe-dark under my mother's eye –
One anchor

Holding my juvenile neck bowed to the dunkings of the
    Atlantic.

So goodbye to that bloody-minded flower.

You dead bury your dead.
Goodbye to the cenotaphs on my mother's breasts.

Goodbye to all the remaindered charms of my father's survival.

Let England close. Let the green sea-anemone close.

New Moon in January

A splinter, flicked
Into the wide eyeball,
Severs its warning.

The head, severed while staring,
Felt nothing, only
Tilted slightly.

O lone
Eyelash on the darkening
Stripe of blood, O sail of death!

Frozen
In ether
Unearthly

Shelley's faint-shriek
Trying to thaw while zero
Itself loses consciousness.

The Warriors of the North

Bringing their frozen swords, their salt-bleached eyes, their
   salt-bleached hair,
The snow's stupefied anvils in rows,
Bringing their envy,
The slow ships feelered Southward, snails over the steep sheen
   of the water-globe.

Thawed at the red and black disgorging of abbeys,
The bountiful, cleft casks,
The fluttered bowels of the women of dead burghers,
And the elaborate, patient gold of the Gaels.

To no end
But this timely expenditure of themselves,
A cash-down, beforehand revenge, with extra,
For the gruelling relapse and prolongueur of their blood

Into the iron arteries of Calvin.

Karma

When the world-quaking tears were dropped
At Dresden at Buchenwald
Earth spewed up the bones of the Irish.

Queen Victoria refused the blame
For the Emperors of Chou herding their rubbish
Into battle roped together.

The seven lamented millions of Zion
Rose musically through the frozen mouths
Of Russia's snowed-under millions.

They perch, as harps,
Over the slaves whose singing blood still flows
Through the Atlantic and up the Mississippi

And up the jugular
Smoulderingly
Skywriting across the cortex

That the heart, a gulping mask, demands, demands
Appeasement
For its bloody possessor.

And a hundred and fifty million years of hunger
Killing gratefully as breathing
Moulded the heart and the mouth

That cry for milk
From the breast
Of the mother

Of the God
Of the world
Made of Blood.

They have gone into dumber service. They have gone down
To labour with God on the beaches. They fatten
Under the haddock's thumb. They rejoice
Through the warped mouth of the flounder.

They have melted like my childhood under earth's motherly curve
And are nowhere they are not here I know nothing
Cries the poulterer's hare hanging
Upside down above the pavement
Staring into a bloody bag Not here

Cry the eyes from the depths

Of the mirror's seamless sand.

Song of a Rat

I THE RAT'S DANCE

The rat is in the trap, it is in the trap,
And attacking heaven and earth with a mouthful of screeches
    like torn tin,

An effective gag.
When it stops screeching, it pants

And cannot think
'This has no face, it must be God' or

'No answer is also an answer.'
Iron jaws, strong as the whole earth

Are stealing its backbone
For a crumpling of the Universe with screechings,

For supplanting every human brain inside its skull with a
    rat-body that knots and unknots,
A rat that goes on screeching,

Trying to uproot itself into each escaping screech,
But its long fangs bar that exit –

The incisors bared to the night spaces, threatening the constellations,
The glitterers in the black, to keep off,

Keep their distance,
While it works this out.

The rat understands suddenly. It bows and is still,
With a little beseeching of blood on its nose-end.

II THE RAT'S VISION

The rat hears the wind saying something in the straw
And the night-fields that have come up to the fence, leaning
    their silence,
The widowed land
With its trees that know how to cry

The rat sees the farm bulk of beam and stone
Wobbling like reflection on water.
The wind is pushing from the gulf

Through the old barbed wire in through the trenched gateway,
    past the gates of the ear, deep into the worked design of days,

Breathes onto the solitary snow crystal

The rat screeches
And 'Do not go' cry the dandelions, from their heads of folly
And 'Do not go' cry the yard cinders, who have no future, only
    their infernal aftermath
And 'Do not go' cries the cracked trough by the gate, fatalist of
    starlight and zero

'Stay' says the arrangement of stars

Forcing the rat's head down into godhead.

III THE RAT'S FLIGHT

The heaven shudders, a flame unrolled like a whip,
And the stars jolt in their sockets.
And the sleep-souls of eggs
Wince under the shot of shadow −

That was the Shadow of the Rat
Crossing into power
Never to be buried

The horned Shadow of the Rat
Casting here by the door
A bloody gift for the dogs

While it supplants Hell.

Heptonstall

Black village of gravestones.
Skull of an idiot
Whose dreams die back
Where they were born.

Skull of a sheep
Whose meat melts
Under its own rafters.
Only the flies leave it.

Skull of a bird,
The great geographies
Drained to sutures
Of cracked windowsills.

Life tries.

Death tries.

The stone tries.

Only the rain never tires.

Ballad from a Fairy Tale

I stood in a dark valley
And I saw, down the dark valley,
Halifax boiling in silver
A moon disintegrating
In a fury of ghostly brilliance

And climbing out, in a glare of snow,
Pounding to smoke a lake of silver
A swan the size of a city
A slow, colossal power
Far too heavy for the air
Writhing slowly upwards
It came beating towards me
Low over Hathershelf
In a storm of pouring light

And it was no swan
It was a white angel
Leaning into her flight
Gigantic above the moor
Which glowed redly beneath her
An angel of smoking snow
With bare, lovely feet
Her long dress fluttering at her ankles
And silent, immense wingbeat.
'Mother,' I cried, 'O Mother,
I have seen an angel

Will it be a blessing?'
But my mother's answer
Even now I dare not write.

And still the angel lit the valley
And all the moors to the south
Flying toward the West
Slowly, not fading,
And strangest of all
Wearing no halo
But a strange square of satin
I could not understand it
A rippling brim of satin
That fluttered its fringed edges
In the wind of her flying.
Then this enormous beauty
Passed under the rough hilltop
Opposite the house
Where my father was born
Where my grandmother died.
It passed from my sight
And the valley was dark.
And it had been a vision.
That was long ago.

When I next saw
That fringed square of satin
I could have reached and touched it
But I was standing in a valley
Deeper than any dream.
And again it passed from my sight
And sank beneath the hilltop
Opposite the other.

And through my mother's answer
I saw all I had dreaded
But with its meaning doubled.
And the valley was dark.

Skylarks

I

The lark begins to go up
Like a warning
As if the globe were uneasy –

Barrel-chested for heights,
Like an Indian of the high Andes,

A whippet head, barbed like a hunting arrow,

But leaden
With muscle
For the struggle
Against
Earth's centre.

And leaden
For ballast
In the rocketing storms of the breath.

Leaden
Like a bullet
To supplant
Life from its centre.

II

Crueller than owl or eagle

A towered bird, shot through the crested head
With the command, Not die

But climb

Climb

Sing

Obedient as to death a dead thing.

III

I suppose you just gape and let your gaspings
Rip in and out through your voicebox
O lark

And sing inwards as well as outwards
Like a breaker of ocean milling the shingle
                                        O lark

O song, incomprehensibly both ways –
Joy! Help! Joy! Help!
                        O lark

   IV

You stop to rest, far up, you teeter
Over the drop

But not stopping singing

Resting only for a second

Dropping just a little

Then up and up and up

Like a mouse with drowning fur
Bobbing and bobbing at the well-wall

Lamenting, mounting a little –

But the sun will not take notice
And the earth's centre smiles.

   V

My idleness curdles
Seeing the lark labour near its cloud
Scrambling
In a nightmare difficulty
Up through the nothing

Its feathers thrash, its heart must be drumming like a motor,
As if it were too late, too late

Dithering in ether
Its song whirls faster and faster
And the sun whirls
The lark is evaporating
Till my eye's gossamer snaps
                        and my hearing floats back widely to earth

After which the sky lies blank open
Without wings, and the earth is a folded clod.

Only the sun goes silently and endlessly on with the lark's song.

VI

All the dreary Sunday morning
Heaven is a madhouse
With the voices and frenzies of the larks,

Squealing and gibbering and cursing

Heads flung back, as I see them,
Wings almost torn off backwards – far up

Like sacrifices set floating
The cruel earth's offerings

The mad earth's missionaries.

VII

Like those flailing flames
The lift from the fling of a bonfire
Claws dangling full of what they feed on

The larks carry their tongues to the last atom
Battering and battering their last sparks out at the limit –
So it's a relief, a cool breeze
When they've had enough, when they're burned out
And the sun's sucked them empty
And the earth gives them the O.K.

And they relax, drifting with changed notes

Dip and float, not quite sure if they may
Then they are sure and they stoop

And maybe the whole agony was for this

The plummeting dead drop

With long cutting screams buckling like razors

But just before they plunge into the earth

They flare and glide off low over grass, then up
To land on a wall-top, crest up,

Weightless,
Paid-up,
Alert,

Conscience perfect.

VIII

Manacled with blood,
Cuchulain listened bowed,
Strapped to his pillar (not to die prone)
Hearing the far crow
Guiding the near lark nearer
With its blind song

'That some sorry little wight more feeble and misguided than thyself
Take thy head
Thine ear
And thy life's career from thee.'

Mountains

I am a fly if these are not stones,
If these are not stones, they are a finger –

Finger, shoulder, eye.
The air comes and goes over them as if attentively.

They were there yesterday and the world before yesterday,
Content with the inheritance,

Having no need to labour, only to possess the days,
Only to possess their power and their presence,

Smiling on the distance, their faces lit with the peace
Of the father's will and testament,

Wearing flowers in their hair, decorating their limbs
With the agony of love and the agony of fear and the agony
    of death.

You Drive in a Circle

Slowly a hundred miles through the powerful rain.

Your clothes are towelled with sweat and the car-glass sweats,
And there is a smell of damp dog.
Rain-sog is rotting your shoes to paper.

Over old hairy moors, a dark Arctic depth, cresting under rain,
Where the road topples, plunging with its crazed rigging
Like a rackety iron tanker

Into a lunge of spray, emerges again –
Through hard rendings of water,
Drowned eyes at the melting windshield,

Out above the swamped moor-wallows, the mist-gulfs of
   no-thinking.
Down in there are the sheep, rooted like sponges,
Chewing and digesting and undeterred.

What could they lose, however utterly they drowned?
Already sodden as they are with the world, like fossils.
And what is not the world is God, a starry comforter of
   good blood.

Where are you heading? Everything is already here.
Your hardest look cannot anchor out among these rocks, your
   coming days cannot anchor among these torn clouds that
   cannot anchor.

Your destination waits where you left it.

Wings

I M. SARTRE CONSIDERS CURRENT AFFAIRS

Humped, at his huge broken wing of shadow,
He regrows the world inside his skull, like the spectre of a flower.

His eyes are imprisoned in the fact
That his hands have sunk to the status of flies.

With skull-grins, the earth's populations
Drift off over graves, like the fumes of a rained-out campfire.

He yawns, tilting an extinct eyeball
To the fly asleep on the lampshade.

Yet his heart pounds on undeterred....

The skull-splitting polyp of his brain, on its tiny root,
Lolls out over him ironically:

Angels, it whispers, are metaphors, in man's image,
For the amoeba's exhilarations.

He sits on, in the twice-darkened room,
Pondering on the carrion-eating skate,

And on its wings, lifted, white, like an angel's,
And on those cupid lips in its deathly belly,

And on the sea, this tongue in his ear, licking the last of pages.

II KAFKA

And he is an owl
He is an owl, 'Man' tattooed in his armpit
Under the broken wing
(Stunned by the wall of glare, he fell here)
Under the broken wing of huge shadow that twitches across
    the floor.

He is a man in hopeless feathers.

III EINSTEIN PLAYS BACH

And finally he has fallen. And the great shattered wing
Of shadow is across the floor.
His memory is lifting what it can manage
Of the two worlds, and a few words.

The tired mask of folds, the eyes in mourning,
The sadness of the monkeys in their cage –
Star peering at star through the walls
Of a cage full of nothing.

And no quails tumbling
From the cloud. And no manna
For angels.
Only the pillar of fire contracting its strength into a star-mote.

Now the sargasso of a single sandgrain
Would come sweeter than the brook from the rock
To a mouth
Blasted with star-vapour.

A robin glimpsed him walking, – that was exciting!
But the tears he almost shed went away,
A cloud no bigger than his hand,
A cramped wreath of lightnings, that could not find the earth.

He bows in prayer over music, as over a well.
But it is the cauldron of the atom.
And it is the Eye of God in the whirlwind.
It is a furnace, storming with flames.

It is a burned-out bottomless eye-socket
Crawling with flies
In fugues
And he prays

'Mother! Mother!
                    O mother

Send me love.'

                    But the flies

The flies rise in a cloud.

Pibroch

The sea cries with its meaningless voice
Treating alike its dead and its living,
Probably bored with the appearance of heaven
After so many millions of nights without sleep,
Without purpose, without self-deception.

Stone likewise. A pebble is imprisoned
Like nothing in the Universe.
Created for black sleep. Or growing
Conscious of the sun's red spot occasionally,
Then dreaming it is the foetus of God.   10

Over the stone rushes the wind
Able to mingle with nothing,

Like the hearing of the blind stone itself.
Or turns, as if the stone's mind came feeling
A fantasy of directions.

Drinking the sea and eating the rock
A tree struggles to make leaves —
An old woman fallen from space
Unprepared for these conditions.
She hangs on, because her mind's gone completely.

Minute after minute, aeon after aeon,
Nothing lets up or develops.
And this is neither a bad variant nor a tryout.
This is where the staring angels go through.
This is where all the stars bow down.

The Howling of Wolves

Is without world.

What are they dragging up and out on their long leashes of sound
That dissolve in the mid-air silence?

Then crying of a baby, in this forest of starving silences,
Brings the wolves running.
Tuning of a viola, in this forest delicate as an owl's ear,
Brings the wolves running — brings the steel traps clashing
   and slavering,
The steel furred to keep it from cracking in the cold,
The eyes that never learn how it has come about
That they must live like this,

That they must live

Innocence crept into minerals.

The wind sweeps through and the hunched wolf shivers.
It howls you cannot say whether out of agony or joy.

The earth is under its tongue,
A dead weight of darkness, trying to see through its eyes.
The wolf is living for the earth.
But the wolf is small, it comprehends little.

It goes to and fro, trailing its haunches and whimpering horribly.

It must feed its fur.

The night snows stars and the earth creaks.

Gnat-Psalm

When the gnats dance at evening
Scribbling on the air, sparring sparely,
Scrambling their crazy lexicon,
Shuffling their dumb Cabala,
Under leaf shadow

Leaves only leaves
Between them and the broad swipes of the sun
Leaves muffling the dusty stabs of the late sun
From their frail eyes and crepuscular temperaments

Dancing   10
Dancing
Writing on the air, rubbing out everything they write
Jerking their letters into knots, into tangles
Everybody everybody else's yoyo

Immense magnets fighting around a centre

Not writing and not fighting but singing
That the cycles of this Universe are no matter
That they are not afraid of the sun
That the one sun is too near
It blasts their song, which is of all the suns   20
That they are their own sun
Their own brimming over
At large in the nothing
Their wings blurring the blaze
Singing

That they are the nails
In the dancing hands and feet of the gnat-god
That they hear the wind suffering
Through the grass
And the evening tree suffering   30

The wind bowing with long cat-gut cries
And the long roads of dust

Dancing in the wind
The wind's dance, the death-dance, entering the mountain
And the cow dung villages huddling to dust

But not the gnats, their agility
Has outleaped that threshold
And hangs them a little above the claws of the grass
Dancing
40   Dancing
In the glove shadows of the sycamore

A dance never to be altered
A dance giving their bodies to be burned

And their mummy faces will never be used

Their little bearded faces
Weaving and bobbing on the nothing
Shaken in the air, shaken, shaken
And their feet dangling like the feet of victims

O little Hasids
50   Ridden to death by your own bodies
Riding your bodies to death
You are the angels of the only heaven!

And God is an Almighty Gnat!
You are the greatest of all the galaxies!
My hands fly in the air, they are follies
My tongue hangs up in the leaves
My thoughts have crept into crannies

Your dancing

Your dancing

60   Rolls my staring skull slowly away into outer space.

Full Moon and Little Frieda

A cool small evening shrunk to a dog bark and the clank of a bucket –

And you listening.
A spider's web, tense for the dew's touch.
A pail lifted, still and brimming – mirror
To tempt a first star to a tremor.

Cows are going home in the lane there, looping the hedges with
    their warm wreaths of breath –
A dark river of blood, many boulders,
Balancing unspilled milk.

'Moon!' you cry suddenly, 'Moon! Moon!'

The moon has stepped back like an artist gazing amazed at a work

That points at him amazed.

Wodwo

What am I? Nosing here, turning leaves over
Following a faint stain on the air to the river's edge
I enter water. What am I to split
The glassy grain of water looking upward I see the bed
Of the river above me upside down very clear
What am I doing here in mid-air? Why do I find
this frog so interesting as I inspect its most secret
interior and make it my own? Do these weeds
know me and name me to each other have they
seen me before, do I fit in their world? I seem
separate from the ground and not rooted but dropped
out of nothing casually I've no threads
fastening me to anything I can go anywhere
I seem to have been given the freedom
of this place what am I then? And picking
bits of bark off this rotten stump gives me
no pleasure and it's no use so why do I do it
me and doing that have coincided very queerly
But what shall I be called am I the first
have I an owner what shape am I what
shape am I am I huge if I go
to the end on this way past these trees and past these trees
till I get tired that's touching one wall of me
for the moment if I sit still how everything
stops to watch me I suppose I am the exact centre
but there's all this what is it roots
roots roots roots and here's the water
again very queer but I'll go on looking

UNCOLLECTED (1967–70)

Scapegoats and Rabies

I A HAUNTING

Soldiers are marching singing down the lane

They get their abandon
From the fixed eyes of girls, from their own
Armed anonymity
And from having finally paid up
All life might demand. They get
Their heroic loom
From the statue stare of old women,
From the trembling chins of old men,
From the napes and bow legs of toddlers,   10
From the absolute steel
Of their automatic rifles, and the lizard spread
Of their own fingers, and from their bird stride.
They get their facelessness
From the blank, deep meadows and the muddling streams
And the hill's eyeless outlook,
The babel of gravestones, the mouldering
Of letters and citations
On rubbish dumps. They get the drumming engine
Of their boots   20
From their hearts,
From their eyeless, earless hearts,
Their brainless hearts. And their bravery
From the dead millions of ghosts
Marching in their boots, cumbering their bodies,
Staring from under their brows, concentrating
Toward a repeat performance. And their hopelessness
From the millions of the future
Marching in their boots, blindfold and riddled,
Rotten heads on their singing shoulders,   30
The blown-off right hand swinging to the stride
Of the stump-scorched and blown-off legs
Helpless in the terrible engine of the boots.

The soldiers go singing down the deep lane
Wraiths into the bombardment of afternoon sunlight,
Whelmed under the flashing onslaught of the barley,
Strangled in the drift of honeysuckle.

Their bodiless voices rally on the slope and again
In the far woods

40 Then settle like dust
Under the ancient burden of the hill.

II THE MASCOT

Somewhere behind the lines, over the map,
The General's face hangs in the dark, like a lantern.

Every shell that bursts
Blows it momentarily out, and he has to light it.

Every bullet that bangs off
Goes in at one of his ears and out at the other.

Every attack every rout
Storms through that face, like a flood through a footbridge.

Every new-dead ghost
10 Comes to that worn-out blood for its death-ration.

Every remotest curse, weighted with a bloodclot,
Enters that ear like a blowfly.

Knives, forks, spoons divide his brains.
The supporting earth, and the night around him,

Smoulder like the slow, curing fire
Of a Javanese head-shrinker.

Nothing remains of the *tête d'armée* but the skin –
A dangling parchment lantern

Slowly revolving to right, revolving to left,

20 Trembling a little with the incessant pounding,

Over the map, empty in the ring of light.

III WIT'S END

The General commits his emptiness to God.

And in place of his eyes
Crystal balls
Roll with visions.

And his voice rises
From the dead fragments of men

A Frankenstein
A tank
A ghost
Roaming the impossible   10
Raising the hair on men's heads.

His hand
Has swept the battlefield flat as a sheet of foolscap.
He writes:

I AM A LANTERN
            IN THE HAND
                        OF A BLIND PEOPLE

IV TWO MINUTES' SILENCE

The soldier's boots, beautifully bulled,
Are graves
On the assembly line
Rolls Royces
Opera boxes
Double beds
Safes
With big smiles and laced-up eyes

His stockings
Are his own intestines   10
Cut into lengths –
They wear better and are
Nobody else's loss,
So he needn't charge diffidently

His battledress
Is Swanwhite's undies
Punch and Judy curtains
The Queen's pajamas
The Conjuror's hankie

The flapping sheet   20
Of the shithouse phantom

His helmet
Is a Ministry pisspot

His rifle
Is a Thames turd

And away downwind he runs, over no man's land,
In a shouting flight
From his own stink

Into the mushroom forest

30   Watched from the crowded walls.

V THE RED CARPET

So the leaves trembled.

He leaned for a moment
Into the head-on leaden blast of ghost
From death's doorway
Then fell forward, under his equipment.
But though the jungle morass has gripped him to the knees
His outflung left hand clawed and got a hold
On Notting Hill
His brow banged hard down once then settled gently
10   Onto Hampstead Heath
The thumb of his twisted, smashed right hand
Settled in numb snugness
Across the great doorway of St Paul's
His lips oozed soft words and blood bubbles
Into the Chalk Farm railway cutting
Westminster knuckled his riddled chest
His belt-buckle broke Clapham
His knees his knees were dissolving in the ebb of the Channel
And there he lay alive
20   His body full of lights, the restaurants seethed,
He groaned in the pushing of traffic that would not end
The girls strolled and their perfumes gargled in his throat
And in the holes in his chest
And though he could not lift his eyes to the streetlights
And though he could not stir either hand
He knew in that last stride, that last
Ten thousand league effort, and even off balance,
He had made it home. And he called –

Into mud.

Again the leaves trembled.   30

Splinters flew off Big Ben.

from Three Legends

II

How deeply the stone slept
There can be no measurement.

The stone slept, and the roots of the oak
Were a brief dream of silly ogres.

The stone slept, though towers through a maze of cities
Hunted it in its sleep and it could not move.

The stone slept, though men thundered
At its doors with iron.

Though heaven prised
At its doors with ice.

Though the wind, insatiable mosquito,
Fed at it.

But time rocked it, sang to it.
Time would not surrender the stone.

The stone slept.

Suddenly the stone opened its eyes.
Crow blinked at the world.

III

Black had swallowed, the sun –
Loved it, gloated, delighted,
Closed its eyes.

Black held the trees, though they lived,
They were like cemetery statues
In an eclipse

Black held the stream, it ran vividly
But black as the blood
In the locks of the heart.

Black held the house-ridges.
It held the roads, the hills,
The floors of lakes, the flies under the leaves.

The sun blazed, black has burst like a balloon,
And the leaves trembled, discovered
In appalling light.

Shadows of grass-heads deepened engraved
On the doomsday skin
Of the Universe.

Ordinary dawn.

And crouching
Among the hurtling spears of the dew

The collison of flowers and blood
The crow's eye widened

Like an emblem on a tattered banner

Like the eye of Adam
When a hand jerked him out of clay, by the hair.

T.V. On

And the ashes gust, hands, faces, crumble,
Shouts and explosions batter the limits
And a Jew-burning music blares.
At intervals it talks to me reasonably
Then the flames whiten.
                              It has eaten
Pretty nearly the whole world.
I feed it without moving.
And I see the Arctic circle collapse
With its peculiar people, quivering embers,
In a conflagration and after-glow
Of commentary.
The Amazon capitulates into the vortex
Of the chimney gullet.

Africa stripped of all its beasts and peoples
Trembles in the incinerating mouth.
Japan and China flip like pages
Up its draught, with twisted faces.
Sun and moon, the bottom of the Pacific,
The praying mantis and the husks of Egypt
All chewed up with chat,
The camera's salivations,
As if douched with petroleum.
They writhe in the crucible.

The great, the gifted, the outstandingly odd,
The gangsters and the virtuoso creepers,
They enter one by one with their gab-baggage
And stand looking around sheepishly at the strangeness
Just like those Jews who had not heard
Where it was they had arrived
On such a sunny day,
Protesting as politely as
A dignity requires, but they're going,
Soon as seen they are all flames
And charry shadows, fumes and evanescence,
Flickering out in a vacuum,
Gone with their gulped back words and bitten tongues.

And I keep on stoking it with myself –
There go my guts and nerves, too,
Like an amoeba being electrocuted,
Disintegrating in glare
Behind the furnace glass
Surrendering its spectres,
A killed brain spooling off its rubbish,
And I cannot move

My shoes are too heavy
As if I were no longer in them,
Trousers, shirt, coat, all too heavy,
My body too inaccessibly heavy.
My strength has all gone into the white core,
Into that drumming crematorium.
Those are my ashes snowing.

Only my dreams escape through the door –
They will unearth Eden!
And repopulate it!
But their faces are burned off
Their eyes are empty holes
Their mouths cry without sound
They stagger on burned anklebones
Through a cinder substitute
An ashen simulacrum, a fossil of char,
Which was once the only world.

Gagged with their dream, they cry
Consumed to fundamental potash,
The new ghosts, passing over,
A tremor of ESP detectors,
The whispering medium's sweat –

And stumbling on into the negative
Crying Too late Too late inaudibly
And woe woe woe
Cannot blame Hitler or Evil.

The Brother's Dream

In a blue, deadly brilliance, a parched madness of rock, of dust
And a pounding ache of blood
I go upward
            In a mountain world of fear
And leathery grass.
Of pine-trees, blasted like gibbets,
Holding out fistfuls of needles, bunched at the branch-end,
Bristling, still as coral.
A mountain is lifting me into terror.
With a clatter of little stones
I climb out onto eternity.
My shadow trails with me.
I have come here of my own will.
My voice is ready for any cries needed.
Like a grave, the cave-hole is watching,
In appalling quiet.
               I stand, part of the stillness –
Not the alert lizard's trigger stillness.

Stillness of some skulls, lying in the open.
And a lilac scent of rottenness
Hanging, like a veil, over the retina.
And a scream going on and on, too fierce for the ear-nerve,
Too deep in the air's stillness.
The masked hills trying to tell me, straining their stillness.
Flies meander in and out of the cave.
They settle on the sunny rocks to clean their wrists and behind
   their heads.

They settle on my shirt.
The rocks, that stare through the end,
Stare deep into me
With their final faces.
I am very frail, almost nothing.
Not here, yet here. A moment ago, not here.
Suddenly shouting into the cave: 'Come out!'
And 'Come out! Come out!' the echo
Brightens the hills like a bombflash.
Somewhere under the ground, the bear is at home.
The brain, flickering, quicker than any of these flies;
The bunched talons, contented;
The fangs, in their own kingdom,
And the happy blood –
The black well
Too deep to glitter
Where my shout, that clangs among open mountains,
Is already being digested.

For the pine-trees,
And for the sprawled hills, pasturing their shadows,
It is ordinary morning.

But the bear is filling the cave-mouth.
Its aimed gullet, point-blank, blasting
Into my face, the risen bear
Walks to embrace me,
With a scream like a weapon
Twisting into my midriff,
The rib-roofed gape measuring at my head,
And I see black lips, the widening curtains of saliva,
The small eyes brown and wet and full of evil
Locked in a fever of annihilation,

Lifted talons spread out like dungforks
Reaching to drag the sky down
Over my eyes, the bear crashes its mass
Onto me like a conifer

And at that moment I grip it.
I push away those eyes, the maniacs,
And the ripsaw scream,
The hatred like agony,
The jaws like a ghastly injury, widening, widening –

I grip it with my left hand by the shag
And cordage of its gullet and I hold it
At my locked arms length and with my dagger
In this other hand I rip it up
From the belly – up, up, up
I rip it. I am a steel madman.
The bear's scream is sawing at my brains
But I rip upward till the heart-muscle
Kicks at the dagger haft.
And I have opened a river.
And the bear slides from me like a robe
I have cut the cords of. I wade
Out of the daze.
                          A long while I stand
Like a man awakening.
                          The rocks
Wait for me, landmarks
Back to enormous mountain silence.

Time tries to move.
                          I watch blood
Crawling to touch my boot, slowly, blindly
Tasting the dust.

And the treetops stir.
The bluetits are busy and inquisitive.

But the rocks, and the engraved hills, are altered.
Their incomprehensible faces stare at me
With a new fear.

I come back down through the fir-trees
To my companions and the eyes of the dogs
That were afraid to come with me.

I'm bloody as a Caesarian babe – not my blood.
I send them up to strip the carcass.
I sleep, exhausted.

Dog Days on the Black Sea

The world hangs like a bead of perspiration
In the writer's eyebrow.
He slogs on in his space-ditch
Under a straw sombrero of culture.

The earth's on heat – all day the fever is a glittering
Creep of cars towards the beaches. There the lizards
Sprawl like a massacre, or lurch from towels
To plunge into the surf of prehistory.

Day long and the thunderhead will not grow!
The writer has to lift enough world, by weight,
And before dark, to balance all
Those soft-bellied baskers with the oiled eyes...

While the land weighs towards evening, like a big rose,
And the harvest leans, heavy and still.

And thunder-blue, flickering, the swallow
Toils to bundle the whole burden of summer
Into loops of air,
Under and over, fleeing and fleeing –

Voice struggling away ahead for relief
From the ache of its body –
A boomerang shadow
Across cushioned meadows, and under woods,

Touching the river slow as honey, and up
And turning
Returning, a pendulum of crying shadow –

The writer's sweat drops. He stares hopelessly.

?

Why should Time be a road?
Why should tomorrow be a destination?
Why should yesterday be another country?

Everything is in the scales
And every second weighs
Exactly everything – as I can see

With my see-saw brains.

Crowquill

Where there is nothing

The crow's feather falls spinning

A hoar-frost of sun and bristling
Galactic encrustations
Whiten along its edges

Still the feather falls

And winds stir over it, a
Breeding of space bacteria
Rejoicing and multiplying

Still the crowfeather goes on falling

Mountains rib and hump and
lift heads and stare out
From the dorsal spine itself

And still the feather falls

Rivers peer from its scales and
Creep to seas
And the rain prospers

And that feather goes on falling

And the five coloured leopard
Drops from a tree near the river
A toad splits out of a pebble

The feather is still falling

While rhinos erupt from brambles
And the butterfly eddies in
And the mouse sits up, amazed by its place

The feather is falling and falling

And people clasp each other close
With their froglike hands, inside houses
And look out of the windows at

The emptiness through which the feather falls

Like a wand

That has swallowed its wizard.

Ballad of Bauble-head

He woke where the sleepers are upright,
Wide-eyed, but worldless –
A kaleidoscope of the world's jigsaw
Shaken like a rattle
To the crying of a child with a beard or a long tooth,
A King Lear running in space, like a mad dog
With the globe tied to its tail . . .

So, till the heart says Stop,
Or a knife rules him off,
Or snow in the woods finds him like a frog,
Or a truck ignores his sulk
And flattens his struts like a toy,
Or a bomb reminds his nursery
Of the rule of the elements,
Or he forgets to eat and his strength absconds
Like a mother driven as mad,
And the worms
Tear his Insurance Card to bits,
And the rains
Melt his tower of sugar
And the dogs start at his hands and feet while he just goes on
    laughing madly,

And his cynical Napoleon
And all his red Indians

Hardening in strength, extinguish into the remote future
That notch in the stony skyline
The size of a star
Where the stones

Have split in the cold
And the hare's foot
Rested a moment in fear, and went on,
And a little water collects.

Crow's Feast

Between banked computers Crow
Pecked out an operator's eyes
And pulled out his intestines
And gorged on his sweetbreads, saying 'I'm glad.
It does not matter any more. I'm glad
All this has not become redundant.

Everything God does not want is mine.'

A Crow Hymn

Flame works at the sun, the sun at the earth
The moon works at the sea the sea
Works at the moon and works at the earth
And the wind at the sea and the earth
And the seasons work at all life
And the sun works at all life
The earth works at all life

And all life works at death

The queen ant works at eggs
The maneater works at its own life
The mosquito works at its own life
Life works at life using men and women

Atoms work at the flame that works at the sun
That works at the seasons and the winds
And the sea and the earth
And men and women who work at life and at death

The leaves working at life and at death
The viper working at life and at death
And the blowfly and the labour
Of wedding bells and the hungry man
Working at life and at death
Are not busier than the stars

All are parts of a strange engine
Flying through space, with the power of all the suns

A huge insect, towards marriage

Song of Woe

Once upon a time
There was a person
Wretched in every vein —
His heart pumped woe.
Trying to run it clear
His heart pumped only more muddy woe.
He looked at his hands, and they were woe.
His legs there, long, bony and remote
Like the legs of a stag in wet brambles,
They also were woe.
His shirt over the chair at night
Was like a curtain over the finale
Of all things.

He walked out onto a field
And the trees were grief —
Cemetery non-beings.
The clouds bore their burdens of grief
Into non-being.
The flowers
The birds, the spiders
Staring into space like sacrifices
Clung with madman's grip
To the great wheel of woe.

So he flung them out among the stars —
Trees, toppling clouds, birds and insects,
He was rid of them.
He flung away the field and its grass,

The whole grievous funeral,
His clothes and their house,
And sat naked on the naked earth
And his mouth filled his eye filled
With the same muddy woe.

So he abandoned himself, his body, his blood –
He left it all lying on the earth
And held himself resolute
As the earth rolled slowly away
Smaller and smaller away
Into non-being.

And there at last he had it
As his woe struggled out of him
With a terrific cry

Staring after the earth
And stood out there in front of him,
His howling transfigured double.

And he was rid of it.
And he wept with relief,
With joy, laughing, he wept –

And at last, tear by tear,
Something came clear.

Existential Song

Once upon a time
There was a person
Running for his life.
This was his fate.
It was a hard fate.
But Fate is Fate.
He had to keep running.

He began to wonder about Fate
And running for dear life.
Who? Why?
And was he nothing
But some dummy hare on a racetrack?

At last he made up his mind.
He was nobody's fool.
It would take guts
But yes he could do it.
Yes yes he could stop.
Agony! Agony
Was the wrenching
Of himself from his running.
Vast! And sudden
The stillness
In the empty middle of the desert.

There he stood – stopped.
And since he couldn't see anybody
To North or to West or to East or to South
He raised his fists
Laughing in awful joy
And shook them at the Universe

And his fists fell off
And his arms fell off
He staggered and his legs fell off

It was too late for him to realize
That this was the dogs tearing him to pieces
That he was, in fact, nothing
But a dummy hare on a racetrack

And life was being lived only by the dogs.

A Lucky Folly

Crow heard the maiden screaming – and here came the dragon.
He fantasied building a rocket and getting out fast –
Not a hope.
O for a castle – battlements. A pinnacle prison.
Too late. The dragon surrounded him like a seaquake
And the maiden cried lamentably.
Crow cut holes in his nose. He fingered this flute,
Dancing, with an occasional kick at his drum.

The dragon was dumbfounded – he was manic
For music. He began to grin.

He too began to dance. And in horror and awe
The maiden danced with him, incredulous.
'O do not stop,' she whispered, 'O do not stop.'
So the three danced – and Crow dared not stop –

To the creaking beak pipe and the kicked drum.

But, at last, Crow's puff ran out and he stopped.
The maiden paled.
But the dragon wept. The dragon licked Crow's foot,
He slobbered Crow's fingers –
'More, more' he cried, and 'Be my god.'

Fighting for Jerusalem

The man who seems to be dead

With Buddha in his smile
With Jesus in his stretched out arms
With Mahomet in his humbled forehead

With his feet in hell
With his hands in heaven
With his back to the earth

Is escorted
To his eternal reward
By singing legions

Of what seem to be flies

This Game of Chess

This Game of Chess is played for Love.
Father, Son and Holy Ghost
Question and ponder their next, cold move.
The nightmare game seems almost lost.
What hill is this? Is it a hill
Or the crown of a skull?
What is that conflagration? Sun? Moon?
A Supernova? Or a Heavenly bundle?
Whose are these heads? The three Fates
Of a single life? Or two Guardians

And a single soul?
One soul and its two Angels,
The good and the bad? Or the doppelgangers
Of a god and two thieves
Come too early?

                   Or three Kings
Searching on their thrones
In the Nativity snow? Or three Furies
Already on the hill, hungry
Conjured out of the astral
On their earthly cubes, calling in the snow:
We have heard the birth-cry. We can see
His reflection in Heaven,
We can smell the blood. We are ready,
Where is He?
Who shall win this Game of Chess?
The Trinity are blinded by
The Triple Face of a Goddess
And a Goddess and a Goddess.

[CROW]

That Moment

When the pistol muzzle oozing blue vapour
Was lifted away
Like a cigarette lifted from an ashtray

And the only face left in the world
Lay broken
Between hands that relaxed, being too late

And the trees closed forever
And the streets closed forever

And the body lay on the gravel
Of the abandoned world
Among abandoned utilities
Exposed to infinity forever

Crow had to start searching for something to eat.

King of Carrion

His palace is of skulls.

His crown is the last splinters
Of the vessel of life.

His throne is the scaffold of bones, the hanged thing's
Rack and final stretcher.

His robe is the black of the last blood.

His kingdom is empty –

The empty world, from which the last cry
Flapped hugely, hopelessly away
Into the blindness and dumbness and deafness of the gulf

Returning, shrunk, silent

To reign over silence.

Crow and the Birds

When the eagle soared clear through a dawn distilling of emerald
When the curlew trawled in seadusk through a chime of wineglasses
When the swallow swooped through a woman's song in a cavern
And the swift flicked through the breath of a violet

When the owl sailed clear of tomorrow's conscience
And the sparrow preened himself of yesterday's promise
And the heron laboured clear of the Bessemer upglare
And the bluetit zipped clear of lace panties
And the woodpecker drummed clear of the rotovator and
     the rose-farm
And the peewit tumbled clear of the laundromat

While the bullfinch plumped in the apple bud
And the goldfinch bulbed in the sun
And the wryneck crooked in the moon
And the dipper peered from the dewball

Crow spraddled head-down in the beach-garbage, guzzling a
     dropped ice-cream.

Crow's Last Stand

Burning
          burning
                    burning
                              there was finally something
The sun could not burn, that it had rendered
Everything down to – a final obstacle
Against which it raged and charred

And rages and chars

Limpid among the glaring furnace clinkers
The pulsing blue tongues and the red and the yellow
The green lickings of the conflagration

Limpid and black –

Crow's eye-pupil, in the tower of its scorched fort.

Crow's First Lesson

God tried to teach Crow how to talk.
'Love,' said God. 'Say, Love.'
Crow gaped, and the white shark crashed into the sea
And went rolling downwards, discovering its own depth.

'No, no,' said God. 'Say Love. Now try it. LOVE.'
Crow gaped, and a bluefly, a tsetse, a mosquito
Zoomed out and down
To their sundry flesh-pots.

'A final try,' said God. 'Now, LOVE.'
Crow convulsed, gaped, retched and
Man's bodiless prodigious head
Bulbed out onto the earth, with swivelling eyes,
Jabbering protest –

And Crow retched again, before God could stop him.
And woman's vulva dropped over man's neck and tightened.
The two struggled together on the grass.
God struggled to part them, cursed, wept –

Crow flew guiltily off.

A Kill

Flogged lame with legs
Shot through the head with balled brains
Shot blind with eyes
Nailed down by his own ribs
Strangled just short of his last gasp
By his own windpipe
Clubbed unconscious by his own heart

Seeing his life stab through him, a dream flash
As he drowned in his own blood

Dragged under by the weight of his guts

Uttering a bowel-emptying cry which was his roots tearing out
Of the bedrock atom
Gaping his mouth and letting the cry rip through him as at
  a distance

And smashed into the rubbish of the ground

He managed to hear, faint and far – 'It's a boy!'

Then everything went black

Notes for a Little Play

First – the sun coming closer, growing by the minute.
Next – clothes torn off.
Without a goodbye
Faces and eyes evaporate.
Brains evaporate.
Hands arms legs feet head and neck
Chest and belly vanish
With all the rubbish of the earth.

And the flame fills all space.
The demolition is total
Except for two strange items remaining in the flames –
Two survivors, moving in the flames blindly.

Mutations – at home in the nuclear glare.

Horrors – hairy and slobbery, glossy and raw.

They sniff towards each other in the emptiness.

They fasten together. They seem to be eating each other.

But they are not eating each other.

They do not know what else to do.

They have begun to dance a strange dance.

And this is the marriage of these simple creatures –
Celebrated here, in the darkness of the sun,

Without guest or God.

A Grin

There was this hidden grin.
It wanted a permanent home. It tried faces
In their forgetful moments, the face for instance
Of a woman pushing a baby out between her legs
But that didn't last long the face
Of a man so preoccupied
With the flying steel in the instant
Of the car-crash he left his face
To itself that was even shorter, the face
Of a machine-gunner a long burst not long enough and
The face of a steeplejack the second
Before he hit the paving, the faces
Of two lovers in the seconds
They got so far into each other they forgot
Each other completely that was O.K.
But none of it lasted.

So the grin tried the face
Of somebody lost in sobbing
A murderer's face and the racking moments
Of the man smashing everything
He could reach and had strength to smash
Before he went beyond his body.

It tried the face
In the electric chair to get a tenure
In eternal death, but that too relaxed.

The grin
Sank back, temporarily nonplussed,
Into the skull.

The Battle of Osfrontalis

Words came with Life Insurance policies –
Crow feigned dead.
Words came with warrants to conscript him –
Crow feigned mad.
Words came with blank cheques –
He drew Minnie Mice on them.

Words came with Aladdin's lamp –
He sold it and bought a pie.
Words came in the likeness of vaginas in a row –
He called in his friends.
Words came in the likeness of a wreathed vagina pouring
    out Handel –
He gave it to the museum.
Words came with barrels of wine –
He let them go sour and pickled his onions.

Crow whistled.

Words attacked him with the glottal bomb –
He wasn't listening.
Words surrounded and over-ran him with light aspirates –
He was dozing.
Words infiltrated guerrilla labials –
Crow clapped his beak, scratched it.
Words swamped him with consonantal masses –
Crow took a sip of water and thanked heaven.

Words retreated, suddenly afraid
Into the skull of a dead jester
Taking the whole world with them –

But the world did not notice.

And Crow yawned – long ago
He had picked that skull empty.

Crow Tyrannosaurus

Creation quaked voices –
It was a cortege
Of mourning and lament
Crow could hear and he looked around fearfully.

The swift's body fled past
Pulsating
With insects
And their anguish, all it had eaten.

The cat's body writhed
Gagging   10
A tunnel
Of incoming death-struggles, sorrow on sorrow.

And the dog was a bulging filterbag
Of all the deaths it had gulped for the flesh and the bones.
It could not digest their screeching finales.
Its shapeless cry was a blort of all those voices.

Even man he was a walking
Abattoir
Of innocents –
His brain incinerating their outcry.   20

Crow thought 'Alas
Alas ought I
To stop eating
And try to become the light?'

But his eye saw a grub. And his head, trapsprung, stabbed.
And he listened
And he heard
Weeping

Grubs   grubs   He stabbed   he stabbed
Weeping   30
Weeping

Weeping he walked and stabbed

Thus came the eye's
                    roundness
                                the ear's
                                    deafness.

A Childish Prank

Man's and woman's bodies lay without souls,
Dully gaping, foolishly staring, inert
On the flowers of Eden.
God pondered.

The problem was so great, it dragged him asleep.

Crow laughed.
He bit the Worm, God's only son,
Into two writhing halves.

He stuffed into man the tail half
With the wounded end hanging out.

He stuffed the head half headfirst into woman
And it crept in deeper and up
To peer out through her eyes
Calling its tail-half to join up quickly, quickly
Because O it was painful.

Man awoke being dragged across the grass.
Woman awoke to see him coming.
Neither knew what had happened.

God went on sleeping.

Crow went on laughing.

Carnival

Once again Crow lifted his head
And saw his bones in the void
He saw his eyes in paperback
He saw his guts in Schopenhauer's spectacle case
He saw his blood spattered
Across Beethoven's score
He saw his brains splashed like a custard pie
Jung had lobbed at Freud
He saw his skin still bandaged on the cross

And in fact it was worse there were details

Only his vomit in the grass
Lay innocent, under the dewy dawn
Where the doors leaned all ways like gravestones

He writhed he lashed himself free and out –
A whipcrack viper out of the spluttering bush

Not the snake either but the snake too late
The spectre of a snake screaming the spectre of a scream

The flailing blueprint of a planarian

Blind into the glare, black into the black

While the wind harrowed the oakleaves and the bleak lakes
   glittered.

from CROW:
FROM THE LIFE AND SONGS OF THE CROW (1970)

Two Legends

I

Black was the without eye
Black the within tongue
Black was the heart
Black the liver, black the lungs
Unable to suck in light
Black the blood in its loud tunnel
Black the bowels packed in furnace
Black too the muscles
Striving to pull out into the light
Black the nerves, black the brain
With its tombed visions
Black also the soul, the huge stammer
Of the cry that, swelling, could not
Pronounce its sun.

II

Black is the wet otter's head, lifted.
Black is the rock, plunging in foam.
Black is the gall lying on the bed of the blood.

Black is the earth-globe, one inch under,
An egg of blackness
Where sun and moon alternate their weathers

To hatch a crow, a black rainbow
Bent in emptiness
                    over emptiness

But flying

Lineage

In the beginning was Scream
Who begat Blood
Who begat Eye
Who begat Fear
Who begat Wing
Who begat Bone
Who begat Granite
Who begat Violet
Who begat Guitar
10 Who begat Sweat
Who begat Adam
Who begat Mary
Who begat God
Who begat Nothing
Who begat Never
Never Never Never

Who begat Crow

Screaming for Blood
Grubs, crusts
20 Anything

Trembling featherless elbows in the nest's filth

Examination at the Womb-door

Who owns these scrawny little feet? *Death.*
Who owns this bristly scorched-looking face? *Death.*
Who owns these still-working lungs? *Death.*
Who owns this utility coat of muscles? *Death.*
Who owns these unspeakable guts? *Death.*
Who owns these questionable brains? *Death.*
All this messy blood? *Death.*
These minimum-efficiency eyes? *Death.*
This wicked little tongue? *Death.*
This occasional wakefulness? *Death.*

Given, stolen, or held pending trial?
Held.

Who owns the whole rainy, stony earth?   *Death.*
Who owns all of space?   *Death.*

Who is stronger than hope?   *Death.*
Who is stronger than the will?   *Death.*
Stronger than love?   *Death.*
Stronger than life?   *Death.*

But who is stronger than death?

                              Me, evidently.

Pass, Crow.

Crow and Mama

When Crow cried his mother's ear
Scorched to a stump.

When he laughed she wept
Blood her breasts her palms her brow all wept blood.

He tried a step, then a step, and again a step –
Every one scarred her face for ever.

When he burst out in rage
She fell back with an awful gash and a fearful cry.

When he stopped she closed on him like a book
On a bookmark, he had to get going.

He jumped into the car the towrope
Was around her neck he jumped out.

He jumped into the plane but her body was jammed in the jet –
There was a great row, the flight was cancelled.

He jumped into the rocket and its trajectory
Drilled clean through her heart he kept on

And it was cosy in the rocket, he could not see much
But he peered out through the portholes at Creation

And saw the stars millions of miles away
And saw the future and the universe

Opening and opening
And kept on and slept and at last

Crashed on the moon awoke and crawled out
Under his mother's buttocks.

The Door

Out under the sun stands a body.
It is growth of the solid world.

It is part of the world's earthen wall.
The earth's plants – such as the genitals
And the flowerless navel
Live in its crevices.
Also, some of the earth's creatures – such as the mouth.
All are rooted in earth, or eat earth, earthy,
Thickening the wall.

Only there is a doorway in the wall –
A black doorway:
The eye's pupil.

Through that doorway came Crow.

Flying from sun to sun, he found this home.

Crow Alights

Crow saw the herded mountains, steaming in the morning.
And he saw the sea
Dark-spined, with the whole earth in its coils.
He saw the stars, fuming away into the black, mushrooms of
    the nothing forest, clouding their spores, the virus of God.

And he shivered with the horror of Creation.

In the hallucination of the horror
He saw this shoe, with no sole, rain-sodden,
Lying on a moor.
And there was this garbage can, bottom rusted away,
A playing place for the wind, in a waste of puddles.

There was this coat, in the dark cupboard, in the silent room, in
   the silent house.
There was this face, smoking its cigarette between the dusk
   window and the fire's embers.

Near the face, this hand, motionless.

Near the hand, this cup.

Crow blinked.   He blinked.   Nothing faded.

He stared at the evidence.

Nothing escaped him. (Nothing could escape.)

Crow Hears Fate Knock on the Door

Crow looked at the world, mountainously heaped.
He looked at the heavens, littering away
Beyond every limit.
He looked in front of his feet at the little stream
Chugging on like an auxiliary motor
Fastened to this infinite engine.

He imagined the whole engineering
Of its assembly, repairs and maintenance –
And felt helpless.

He plucked grass-heads and gazed into them
Waiting for first instructions.
He studied a stone from the stream.
He found a dead mole and slowly he took it apart
Then stared at the gobbets, feeling helpless.
He walked, he walked
Letting the translucent starry spaces
Blow in his ear cluelessly.

Yet the prophecy inside him, like a grimace,
Was I WILL MEASURE IT ALL AND OWN IT ALL
AND I WILL BE INSIDE IT
AS INSIDE MY OWN LAUGHTER
AND NOT STARING OUT AT IT THROUGH WALLS
OF MY EYE'S COLD QUARANTINE
FROM A BURIED CELL OF BLOODY BLACKNESS –

This prophecy was inside him, like a steel spring

Slowly rending the vital fibres.

Crow's Account of the Battle

There was this terrific battle.
The noise was as much
As the limits of possible noise could take.
There were screams higher groans deeper
Than any ear could hold.
Many eardrums burst and some walls
Collapsed to escape the noise.
Everything struggled on its way
Through this tearing deafness
10   As through a torrent in a dark cave.

The cartridges were banging off, as planned,
The fingers were keeping things going
According to excitement and orders.
The unhurt eyes were full of deadliness.
The bullets pursued their courses
Through clods of stone, earth and skin,
Through intestines, pocket-books, brains, hair, teeth
According to Universal laws.
And mouths cried 'Mamma'
20   From sudden traps of calculus,
Theorems wrenched men in two,
Shock-severed eyes watched blood
Squandering as from a drain-pipe
Into the blanks between stars.
Faces slammed down into clay
As for the making of a life-mask
Knew that even on the sun's surface
They could not be learning more or more to the point.
Reality was giving its lesson,
30   Its mishmash of scripture and physics,
With here, brains in hands, for example,
And there, legs in a treetop.

There was no escape except into death.
And still it went on – it outlasted

Many prayers, many a proved watch,
Many bodies in excellent trim,
Till the explosives ran out
And sheer weariness supervened
And what was left looked round at what was left.

Then everybody wept,   40
Or sat, too exhausted to weep,
Or lay, too hurt to weep.
And when the smoke cleared it became clear
This had happened too often before
And was going to happen too often in future
And happened too easily
Bones were too like lath and twigs
Blood was too like water
Cries were too like silence
The most terrible grimaces too like footprints in mud   50
And shooting somebody through the midriff
Was too like striking a match
Too like potting a snooker ball
Too like tearing up a bill
Blasting the whole world to bits
Was too like slamming a door
Too like dropping in a chair
Exhausted with rage
Too like being blown to bits yourself
Which happened too easily   60
With too like no consequences.

So the survivors stayed.
And the earth and the sky stayed.
Everything took the blame.

Not a leaf flinched, nobody smiled.

The Black Beast

Where is the Black Beast?
Crow, like an owl, swivelled his head.
Where is the Black Beast?
Crow hid in its bed, to ambush it.
Where is the Black Beast?

Crow sat in its chair, telling loud lies against the Black Beast.
Where is it?
Crow shouted after midnight, pounding the wall with a last.
Where is the Black Beast?
Crow split his enemy's skull to the pineal gland.
Where is the Black Beast?

Crow crucified a frog under a microscope, he peered into the
    brain of a dogfish.
Where is the Black Beast?

Crow roasted the earth to a clinker, he charged into space –
Where is the Black Beast?

The silences of space decamped, space flitted in every direction –
Where is the Black Beast?

Crow flailed immensely through the vacuum, he screeched after
    the disappearing stars –
Where is it? Where is the Black Beast?

Crow Communes

'Well,' said Crow, 'What first?'
God, exhausted with Creation, snored.
'Which way?' said Crow, 'Which way first?'
God's shoulder was the mountain on which Crow sat.
'Come,' said Crow, 'Let's discuss the situation.'
God lay, agape, a great carcase.

Crow tore off a mouthful and swallowed.

'Will this cipher divulge itself to digestion
Under hearing beyond understanding?'

(That was the first jest.)

Yet, it's true, he suddenly felt much stronger.

Crow, the hierophant, humped, impenetrable.

Half-illumined. Speechless.

(Appalled.)

Crow's Account of St George

He sees everything in the Universe
Is a track of numbers racing towards an answer.
With delirious joy, with nimble balance
He rides those racing tracks. He makes a silence.
He refrigerates an emptiness,
Decreates all to outer space,
Then unpicks numbers. The great stones fall open.
With the faintest breath
He melts cephalopods and sorts raw numbers
Out of their dregs. With tweezers of number
He picks the gluey heart out of an inaudibly squeaking cell –
He hears something. He turns –
A demon, dripping ordure, is grinning in the doorway.
It vanishes. He concentrates –
With a knife-edge of numbers
He cuts the heart cleanly in two. He shivers –
Looks up. A demon with a face flat as a snail
Or the underface of a shark, is grinning at him
Through the window. It vanishes. Confused,
Shaken, he aims his attention –
Finding the core of the heart is a nest of numbers.
His heart begins to pound, his hand trembles.
Something grabs at his arm. He turns. A bird-head,
Bald, lizard-eyed, the size of a football, on two staggering bird-legs
Gapes at him all the seams and pleats of its throat,
Clutching at the carpet with horny feet,
Threatens. He lifts a chair – fear lifts him –
He smashes the egg-shell object to a blood-rag,
A lumping sprawl, he tramples the bubbling mess.
The shark-face is screaming in the doorway
Opening its fangs. The chair again –
He splits that face and beats the chair to pieces
On the writhing unbreakably tough horror
Till it lies still. Now with a shriek
An object four times bigger than the others –
A belly-ball of hair, with crab-legs, eyeless,
Jabs its pincers into his face,
Its belly opens – a horrible oven of fangs,
The claws are clawing to drag him towards it.

He snatches from its mount on the wall a sword,
A ceremonial Japanese decapitator,
And as hacking a path through thicket he scatters
The lopped segments, the opposition collapses.
He stands trousered in blood and log-splits
The lolling body, bifurcates it
Top to bottom, kicks away the entrails –
Steps out of the blood-wallow. Recovers –

Drops the sword and runs dumb-faced from the house
Where his wife and children lie in their blood.

A Disaster

There came news of a word.
Crow saw it killing men. He ate well.
He saw it bulldozing
Whole cities to rubble. Again he ate well.
He saw its excreta poisoning seas.
He became watchful.
He saw its breath burning whole lands
To dusty char.
He flew clear and peered.

10   The word oozed its way, all mouth,
Earless, eyeless.
He saw it sucking the cities
Like the nipples of a sow
Drinking out all the people
Till there were none left,
All digested inside the word.

Ravenous, the word tried its great lips
On the earth's bulge, like a giant lamprey –
There it started to suck.

20   But its effort weakened.
It could digest nothing but people.
So there it shrank, wrinkling weaker,
Puddling
Like a collapsing mushroom.
Finally, a drying salty lake.

Its era was over.
All that remained of it a brittle desert
Dazzling with the bones of earth's people

Where Crow walked and mused.

Crow's Theology

Crow realised God loved him –
Otherwise, he would have dropped dead.
So that was proved.
Crow reclined, marvelling, on his heart-beat.

And he realised that God spoke Crow –
Just existing was His revelation.

But what
Loved the stones and spoke stone?
They seemed to exist too.
And what spoke that strange silence
After his clamour of caws faded?

And what loved the shot-pellets
That dribbled from those strung-up mummifying crows?
What spoke the silence of lead?

Crow realised there were two Gods –

One of them much bigger than the other
Loving his enemies
And having all the weapons.

Crow's Fall

When Crow was white he decided the sun was too white.
He decided it glared much too whitely.
He decided to attack it and defeat it.

He got his strength flush and in full glitter.
He clawed and fluffed his rage up.
He aimed his beak direct at the sun's centre.

He laughed himself to the centre of himself

And attacked.

At his battle cry trees grew suddenly old,
Shadows flattened.

But the sun brightened –
It brightened, and Crow returned charred black.

He opened his mouth but what came out was charred black.

'Up there,' he managed,
'Where white is black and black is white, I won.'

Criminal Ballad

There was a man and when he was born
A woman fell between the ship and the jetty
At a heave from the moon and the sun
Her pleading cries were humbled out
And when he sucked
And fastened greedily at the hot supply
An old lady's head sank sideways, her lips relaxed
Drained of fuel, she became a mere mask
Reflected in half-empty brown bottles
And the eyes of relatives
That were little circles in blind skin
And when he ran and got his toy squealing with delight
An old man pulled from under the crush of metal
Gazed towards the nearby polished shoes
And slowly forgot the deaths in Homer
The sparrowfall natural economy
Of the dark simple curtain
And when he clasped his first love belly to belly
The yellow woman started to bellow
On the floor, and the husband stared
Through an anaesthetized mask
And felt the cardboard of his body
And when he walked in his garden and saw his children
Bouncing among the dogs and balls
He could not hear their silly songs and the barking
For machine guns
And a screaming and laughing in the cell
Which had got tangled in the air with his hearing

And he could not turn towards the house
Because the woman of complete pain rolling in flame   30
Was calling to him all the time
From the empty goldfish pond
And when he began to shout to defend his hearing
And shake his vision to splinters
His hands covered with blood suddenly
And now he ran from the children and ran through the house
Holding his bloody hands clear of everything
And ran along the road and into the wood
And under the leaves he sat weeping

And under the leaves he sat weeping   40

Till he began to laugh

Crow on the Beach

Hearing shingle explode, seeing it skip,
Crow sucked his tongue.
Seeing sea-grey mash a mountain of itself
Crow tightened his goose-pimples.
Feeling spray from the sea's root nothinged on his crest
Crow's toes gripped the wet pebbles.
When the smell of the whale's den, the gulfing of the crab's
    last prayer,
Gimletted in his nostril
He grasped he was on earth.
                        He knew he grasped
Something fleeting
Of the sea's ogreish outcry and convulsion.
He knew he was the wrong listener unwanted
To understand or help –

His utmost gaping of brain in his tiny skull
Was just enough to wonder, about the sea,

What could be hurting so much?

Oedipus Crow

Mummies stormed his torn insides
With their bandages and embalming honey.
He contorted clear, he vomited empty –
He flew.

A gravestone fell on his foot
And took root –
He bit through the bone and he fled.

The water-spirit in the happy valley
Twined his brains with primroses, dogroses,
Pulling his mouth down to the wet humus –
With a howl he left what she held.

And he ran, cheered by the sound of his foot and its echo
And by the watch on his wrist

One-legged, gutless and brainless, the rag of himself –

So Death tripped him easy
And held him up with a laugh, only just alive.

And his watch galloped away in a cloud of corpse-dust.

Crow dangled from his one claw – corrected.

A warning.

Crow's Vanity

Looking close in the evil mirror Crow saw
Mistings of civilizations   towers   gardens
Battles he wiped the glass   but there came

Mistings of skyscrapers   webs of cities
Steaming the glass he wiped it   there came

Spread of swampferns fronded on the mistings
A trickling spider   he wiped the glass   he peered

For a glimpse of the usual grinning face

But it was no good he was breathing too heavy
And too hot   and space was too cold

And here came the misty ballerinas
The burning gulfs   the hanging gardens   it was eerie

A Horrible Religious Error

When the serpent emerged, earth-bowel brown,
From the hatched atom
With its alibi self twisted around it

Lifting a long neck
And balancing that deaf and mineral stare
The sphinx of the final fact

And flexing on that double flameflicker tongue
A syllable like the rustling of the spheres

God's grimace writhed, a leaf in the furnace

And man's and woman's knees melted, they collapsed
Their neck-muscles melted, their brows bumped the ground
Their tears evacuated visibly
They whispered 'Your will is our peace.'

But Crow only peered.
                    Then took a step or two forward,
Grabbed this creature by the slackskin nape,

Beat the hell out of it, and ate it.

Crow Tries the Media

He wanted to sing about her

He didn't want comparisons with the earth or anything to do
   with it
Oversold like detergents
He did not even want words
Waving their long tails in public
With their prostitute's exclamations

He wanted to sing very clear

But this tank had been parked on his voice
And his throat was nipped between the Roman Emperor's
    finger and thumb
Like the neck of a linnet
While King Kong in person
Held the loop of his blood like a garotte
And tycoons gambled his glands away in a fog of cigar smoke

He shuddered out of himself he got so naked
When he touched her breast it hurt him

He wanted to sing to her soul simply

But still Manhattan weighed on his eyelid

He looked at the corner of her eye
His tongue moved like a poisoned estuary

He touched the smiling corner of her mouth
His voice reverberated like the slow millstone of London
Raising a filthy haze,
                              her shape dimmed.

Crow's Nerve Fails

Crow, feeling his brain slip,
Finds his every feather the fossil of a murder.

Who murdered all these?
These living dead, that root in his nerves and his blood
Till he is visibly black?

How can he fly from his feathers?
And why have they homed on him?

Is he the archive of their accusations?
Or their ghostly purpose, their pining vengeance?
Or their unforgiven prisoner?

He cannot be forgiven.

His prison is the earth. Clothed in his conviction,
Trying to remember his crimes

Heavily he flies.

In Laughter

Cars collide and erupt luggage and babies
In laughter
The steamer upends and goes under saluting like a stuntman
In laughter
The nosediving aircraft concludes with a boom
In laughter
People's arms and legs fly off and fly on again
In laughter
The haggard mask on the bed rediscovers its pang
In laughter, in laughter   10
The meteorite crashes
With extraordinary ill-luck on the pram

The ears and eyes are bundled up
Are folded up in the hair,
Wrapped in the carpet, the wallpaper, tied with the lampflex
Only the teeth work on
And the heart, dancing on in its open cave
Helpless on the strings of laughter

While the tears are nickel-plated and come through doors
    with a bang

And the wails stun with fear   20
And the bones
Jump from the torment flesh has to stay for

Stagger some distance and fall in full view

Still laughter scampers around on centipede boots
Still it runs all over on caterpillar tread
And rolls back onto the mattress, legs in the air

But it's only human

And finally it's had enough – enough!
And slowly sits up, exhausted,
And slowly starts to fasten buttons,   30
With long pauses,

Like somebody the police have come for.

Crow Frowns

Is he his own strength?
What is its signature?
Or is he a key, cold-feeling
To the fingers of prayer?

He is a prayer-wheel, his heart hums.
His eating is the wind –
Its patient power of appeal.
His footprints assail infinity

With signatures: We are here, we are here.
He is the long waiting for something
To use him for some everything
Having so carefully made him

Of nothing.

Magical Dangers

Crow thought of a palace –
Its lintel crashed on him, his bones were found.

Crow thought of a fast car –
It plucked his spine out, and left him empty and armless.

Crow thought of the wind's freedom –
And his eyes evaporated, the wind whistled over the Turkish
   Saddle.

Crow thought of a wage –
And it choked him, it was cut unspoiled from his dead stomach.

Crow thought of the soft and warm that is long remembered –
It blindfolded him with silk, it gangplanked him into a volcano.

Crow thought of intelligence –
It turned the key against him and he tore at its fruitless bars.

Crow thought of nature's stupor –
And an oak tree grew out of his ear.

A row of his black children sat in the top.
They flew off.

Crow
Never again moved.

Robin Song

I am the hunted king
   Of the frost and big icicles
      And the bogey cold
      With its wind boots.

I am the uncrowned
   Of the rainworld
      Hunted by lightning and thunder
      And rivers.

I am the lost child
   Of the wind
      Who goes through me looking for something else
      Who can't recognize me though I cry.

I am the maker
   Of the world
      That rolls to crush
      And silence my knowledge.

Conjuring in Heaven

So finally there was nothing.
It was put inside nothing.
Nothing was added to it
And to prove it didn't exist
Squashed flat as nothing with nothing.

Chopped up with a nothing
Shaken in a nothing
Turned completely inside out
And scattered over nothing –
So everybody saw that it was nothing
And that nothing more could be done with it

And so it was dropped. Prolonged applause in Heaven.

It hit the ground and broke open –
There lay Crow, cataleptic.

Crow Goes Hunting

Crow
Decided to try words.

He imagined some words for the job, a lovely pack –
Clear-eyed, resounding, well-trained,
With strong teeth.
You could not find a better bred lot.

He pointed out the hare and away went the words
Resounding.
Crow was Crow without fail, but what is a hare?

10   It converted itself to a concrete bunker.
The words circled protesting, resounding.

Crow turned the words into bombs – they blasted the bunker.
The bits of bunker flew up – a flock of starlings.

Crow turned the words into shotguns, they shot down the starlings.
The falling starlings turned to a cloudburst.

Crow turned the words into a reservoir, collecting the water.
The water turned into an earthquake, swallowing the reservoir.

The earthquake turned into a hare and leaped for the hill
Having eaten Crow's words.

20   Crow gazed after the bounding hare
Speechless with admiration.

Owl's Song

He sang
How the swan blanched forever
How the wolf threw away its telltale heart
And the stars dropped their pretence
The air gave up appearances
Water went deliberately numb

The rock surrendered its last hope
And cold died beyond knowledge

He sang
How everything had nothing more to lose

Then sat still with fear

Seeing the clawtrack of star
Hearing the wingbeat of rock

And his own singing

Crow's Undersong

She cannot come all the way

She comes as far as water no further

She comes with the birth push
Into eyelashes into nipples the fingertips
She comes as far as blood and to the tips of hair
She comes to the fringe of voice
She stays
Even after life even among the bones

She comes singing she cannot manage an instrument
She comes too cold afraid of clothes
And too slow with eyes wincing frightened
When she looks into wheels

She comes sluttish she cannot keep house
She can just keep clean
She cannot count she cannot last

She comes dumb she cannot manage words
She brings petals in their nectar fruits in their plush
She brings a cloak of feathers an animal rainbow
She brings her favourite furs and these are her speeches

She has come amorous it is all she has come for

If there had been no hope she would not have come

And there would have been no crying in the city

(There would have been no city)

Crow's Elephant Totem Song

Once upon a time
God made this Elephant.
Then it was delicate and small
It was not freakish at all
Or melancholy

The Hyenas sang in the scrub: You are beautiful –
They showed their scorched heads and grinning expressions
Like the half-rotted stumps of amputations –
We envy your grace
Waltzing through the thorny growth
O take us with you to the Land of Peaceful
O ageless eyes of innocence and kindliness
Lift us from the furnaces
And furies of our blackened faces
Within these hells we writhe
Shut in behind the bars of our teeth
In hourly battle with a death
The size of the earth
Having the strength of the earth.

So the Hyenas ran under the Elephant's tail
As like a lithe and rubber oval
He strolled gladly around inside his ease
But he was not God no it was not his
To correct the damned
In rage in madness then they lit their mouths
They tore out his entrails
They divided him among their several hells
To cry all his separate pieces
Swallowed and inflamed
Amidst paradings of infernal laughter.

At the Resurrection
The Elephant got himself together with correction
Deadfall feet and toothproof body and bulldozing bones
And completely altered brains
Behind aged eyes, that were wicked and wise.

So through the orange blaze and blue shadow
Of the afterlife, effortless and immense,
The Elephant goes his own way, a walking sixth sense,

238 [CROW]

And opposite and parallel
The sleepless Hyenas go   40
Along a leafless skyline trembling like an oven roof
With a whipped run
Their shame-flags tucked hard down
Over the gutsacks
Crammed with putrefying laughter
Blotched black with the leakage and seepings
And they sing: 'Ours is the land
Of loveliness and beautiful
Is the putrid mouth of the leopard
And the graves of fever   50
Because it is all we have –'
And they vomit their laughter.

And the Elephant sings deep in the forest-maze
About a star of deathless and painless peace
But no astronomer can find where it is.

Dawn's Rose

Is melting an old frost moon.

Agony under agony, the quiet of dust,
And a crow talking to stony skylines.

Desolate is the crow's puckered cry
As an old woman's mouth
When the eyelids have finished
And the hills continue.

A cry
Wordless
As the newborn baby's grieving
On the steely scales.

As the dull gunshot and its after-râle
Among conifers, in rainy twilight.

Or the suddenly dropped, heavily dropped
Star of blood on the fat leaf.

Crow's Playmates

Lonely Crow created the gods for playmates –
But the mountain god tore free

And Crow fell back from the wall-face of mountains
By which he was so much lessened.

The river-god subtracted the rivers
From his living liquids.

God after god – and each tore from him
Its lodging place and its power.

Crow straggled, limply bedraggled his remnant.
He was his own leftover, the spat-out scrag.

He was what his brain could make nothing of.

So the least, least-living object extant
Wandered over his deathless greatness

Lonelier than ever.

Crowego

Crow followed Ulysses till he turned
As a worm, which Crow ate.

Grappling with Hercules' two puff-adders
He strangled in error Dejanira.

The gold melted out of Hercules' ashes
Is an electrode in Crow's brain.

Drinking Beowulf's blood, and wrapped in his hide,
Crow communes with poltergeists out of old ponds.

His wings are the stiff back of his only book,
Himself the only page – of solid ink.

So he gazes into the quag of the past
Like a gypsy into the crystal of the future,

Like a leopard into a fat land.

The Smile

Began under the groan of the oldest forest
It ran through the clouds, a third light
And it ran through the skin of the earth

It came circling the earth
Like the lifted bow
Of a wave's submarine running
Tossing the willows, and swelling the elm-tops
Looking for its occasion

But people were prepared
They met it
With visor smiles, mirrors of ricochet
With smiles that stole a bone
And smiles that went off with a mouthful of blood
And smiles that left poison in a numb place
Or doubled up
Covering a getaway

But the smile was too vast, it outflanked all
It was too tiny it slipped between the atoms
So that the steel screeched open
Like a gutted rabbit, the skin was nothing
Then the pavement and the air and the light
Confined all the jumping blood
No better than a paper bag
People were running with bandages
But the world was a draughty gap
The whole creation
Was just a broken gutter pipe

And there was the unlucky person's eye
Pinned under its brow
Widening for the darkness behind it
Which kept right on getting wider, darker
As if the soul were not working

And at that very moment the smile arrived

And the crowd, shoving to get a glimpse of a man's soul
Stripped to its last shame,
Met this smile
That rose through his torn roots

Touching his lips, altering his eyes
And for a moment
Mending everything

Before it swept out and away across the earth.

Crow Improvises

There was this man
Who took the sun in one hand, a leaf in the other –
The spark that jumped burned out his name.
So he took his lavender-bag ancestors under one arm
And his twisting dog under the other –
The spark that flash-thumped fused his watch of all things,
And left a black orifice instead of a time-sense.
So he took the battle of the Somme in one hand
And a sleeping tablet in the other –
The spark that blasted blew the valves of his laugh.
So he took the humane-killed skull of a horse in one hand
And a baby's fairy-bait molar in the other –
The spark that banged burned out his weeper.
So he leaned one hand on a gravestone
With his jolly roger in the other –
The spark that clouted cloaked him all in Iguana.
So he rested a dead vole in one hand
And grasped Relativity in the other –
The spark that gored through gouged out his wordage.
So in one hand he caught a girl's laugh – all there was of it,
In the other a seven-year honeymoon – all that he remembered –
The spark that crashed through coked up his gonads.
So in one hand he held a sham-dead spider,
With the other he reached for the bible –
The spark that thunderbolted blanched his every whisker.

So he took his birth-sneeze in one hand
And his death-chill in the other
And let the spark scour him to ashes.

And so the smile not even Leonardo
Could have fathomed
Flew off into the air, the rubbish heap of laughter
Screams, discretions, indiscretions etcetera.

Crowcolour

Crow was so much blacker
Than the moon's shadow
He had stars.

He was as much blacker
Than any negro
As a negro's eye-pupil.

Even, like the sun,
Blacker
Than any blindness.

Crow's Battle Fury

When the patient, shining with pain,
Suddenly pales,
Crow makes a noise suspiciously like laughter.

Seeing the night-city, on the earth's blue bulge,
Trembling its tambourine,
He bellows laughter till the tears come.

Remembering the painted masks and the looming of the balloons
Of the pinpricked dead
He rolls on the ground helpless.

And he sees his remote feet and he chokes he   10
Holds his aching sides –
He can hardly bear it.

One of his eyes sinks into his skull, tiny as a pin,
One opens, a gaping dish of pupils,
His temple-veins gnarl, each like the pulsing head of a
    month-old baby,
His heels double to the front,
His lips lift off his cheekbone, his heart and his liver fly in
    his throat,
Blood blasts from the crown of his head in a column –

Such as cannot be in this world.

A hair's breadth out of the world   20

He comes forward a step,
                    and a step,
                              and a step –

Crow Blacker than Ever

When God, disgusted with man,
Turned towards Heaven,
And man, disgusted with God,
Turned towards Eve,
Things looked like falling apart.

But Crow   Crow
Crow nailed them together,
Nailing Heaven and earth together –

So man cried, but with God's voice.
And God bled, but with man's blood.

Then Heaven and earth creaked at the joint
Which became gangrenous and stank –
A horror beyond redemption.

The agony did not diminish.

Man could not be man nor God God.

The agony

Grew.

Crow

Grinned

Crying: 'This is my Creation,'

Flying the black flag of himself.

Revenge Fable

There was a person
Could not get rid of his mother
As if he were her topmost twig.
So he pounded and hacked at her

With numbers and equations and laws
Which he invented and called truth.
He investigated, incriminated
And penalized her, like Tolstoy,
Forbidding, screaming and condemning,
Going for her with a knife,
Obliterating her with disgusts
Bulldozers and detergents
Requisitions and central heating
Rifles and whisky and bored sleep.

With all her babes in her arms, in ghostly weepings,
She died.

His head fell off like a leaf.

A Bedtime Story

Once upon a time there was a person
Almost a person

Somehow he could not quite see
Somehow he could not quite hear
He could not quite think
Somehow his body, for instance,
Was intermittent

He could see the bread he cut
He could see the letters of words he read
He could see the wrinkles on handskin he looked at   10
Or one eye of a person
Or an ear, or a foot, or the other foot
But somehow he could not quite see

Nevertheless the Grand Canyon spread wide open
Like a surgical operation for him
But somehow he had only half a face there
And somehow his legs were missing at the time
And though somebody was talking he could not hear
Though luckily his camera worked O.K.
The sea-bed lifted its privacy   20
And showed its most hidden fish-thing
He stared he groped to feel

But his hands were funny hooves just at the crucial moment
And though his eyes worked
Half his head was jellyfish, nothing could connect
And the photographs were blurred
A great battleship broke in two with a boom
As if to welcome his glance
An earthquake shook a city onto its people
Just before he got there
With his rubber eye his clockwork ear
And the most beautiful girls
Laid their faces on his pillow staring him out
But somehow his eyes were in the wrong way round
He laughed he whispered but somehow he could not hear
He gripped and clawed but somehow his fingers would not catch
Somehow he was a tar-baby
Somehow somebody was pouring his brains into a bottle
Somehow he was already too late
And was a pile of pieces under a blanket
And when the seamonster surfaced and stared at the rowboat
Somehow his eyes failed to click
And when he saw the man's head cleft with a hatchet
Somehow staring blank swallowed his entire face
Just at the crucial moment
Then disgorged it again whole
As if nothing had happened

So he just went and ate what he could
And did what he could
And grabbed what he could
And saw what he could

Then sat down to write his autobiography

But somehow his arms were just bits of stick
Somehow his guts were an old watch-chain
Somehow his feet were two old postcards
Somehow his head was a broken windowpane

'I give up,' he said. He gave up.

Creation had failed again.

Crow's Song of Himself

When God hammered Crow
He made gold
When God roasted Crow in the sun
He made diamond
When God crushed Crow under weights
He made alcohol
When God tore Crow to pieces
He made money
When God blew Crow up
He made day
When God hung Crow on a tree
He made fruit
When God buried Crow in the earth
He made man
When God tried to chop Crow in two
He made woman
When God said: 'You win, Crow,'
He made the Redeemer.

When God went off in despair
Crow stropped his beak and started in on the two thieves.

Crow Sickened

His illness was something could not vomit him up.

Unwinding the world like a ball of wool
Found the last end tied round his own finger.

Decided to get death, but whatever
Walked into his ambush
Was always his own body.

Where is this somebody who has me under?

He dived, he journeyed, challenging, climbed and with a glare
Of hair on end finally met fear.

His eyes sealed up with shock, refusing to see.

With all his strength he struck. He felt the blow.

Horrified, he fell.

Song for a Phallus

There was a boy was Oedipus
   Stuck in his Mammy's belly
His Daddy'd walled the exit up
   He was a horrible fella
                       Mamma   Mamma

You stay in there his Daddy cried
   Because a Dickybird
Has told the world when you get born
   You'll treat me like a turd
                       Mamma   Mamma

His Mammy swelled and wept and swelled
   With a bang he busted out
His Daddy stropped his hacker
   When he heard that baby shout
                       Mamma   Mamma

O do not chop his winkle off
   His Mammy cried with horror
Think of the joy will come of it
   Tomorrer and tomorrer
                       Mamma   Mamma

But Daddy had the word from God
   He took that howling brat
He tied its legs in crooked knots
   And threw it to the cat
                       Mamma   Mamma

But Oedipus he had the luck
   For when he hit the ground
He bounced up like a jackinabox
   And knocked his Daddy down
                       Mamma   Mamma

He hit his Daddy such a whack
   Stone dead his Daddy fell
His cry went straight to God above
   His ghost it went to Hell
                       Mamma   Mamma

The Dickybird came to Oedipus
   You murderous little sod
The Sphinx will bite your bollocks off
   This order comes from God
                 Mamma   Mamma

The Sphinx she waved her legs at him
   And opened wide her maw
Oedipus stood stiff and wept
   At the dreadful thing he saw
                 Mamma   Mamma

He stood there on his crooked leg
   The Sphinx began to bawl
Four legs three legs two legs one leg
   Who goes on them all
                 Mamma   Mamma

Oedipus took an axe and split
   The Sphinx from top to bottom
The answers aren't in me, he cried
   Maybe your guts have got em
                 Mamma   Mamma

And out there came ten thousand ghosts
   All in their rotten bodies
Crying, You will never know
   What a cruel bastard God is
                 Mamma   Mamma

Next came out his Daddy dead
   And shrieked about the place
He stabs his Mammy in the guts
   And smiles into her face
                 Mamma   Mamma

Then out his Mammy came herself
   The blood poured from her bucket
What you can't understand, she cried
   You sleep on it or sing to it
                 Mamma   Mamma

Oedipus raised his axe again
   The World is dark, he cried

The World is dark one inch ahead
  What's on the other side?

                              Mamma   Mamma

He split his Mammy like a melon
  He was drenched with gore
He found himself curled up inside
  As if he had never been bore

                              Mamma   Mamma

Apple Tragedy

So on the seventh day
The serpent rested.
God came up to him.
'I've invented a new game,' he said.

The serpent stared in surprise
At this interloper.
But God said: 'You see this apple?
I squeeze it and look – Cider.'

The serpent had a good drink
And curled up into a questionmark.
Adam drank and said: 'Be my god.'
Eve drank and opened her legs

And called to the cockeyed serpent
And gave him a wild time.
God ran and told Adam
Who in drunken rage tried to hang himself in the orchard.

The serpent tried to explain, crying 'Stop'
But drink was splitting his syllable
And Eve started screeching: 'Rape! Rape!'
And stamping on his head.

Now whenever the snake appears she screeches
'Here it comes again! Help! O help!'
Then Adam smashes a chair on its head,
And God says: 'I am well pleased'

And everything goes to hell.

Crow Paints Himself into a Chinese Mural

The grass camps in its tussock
With its spears and banners, at nightfall.

A ghost comes
With the circumspect ribs of a tank
Crumpled to wet cardboard
And all the crew grinning out
As out of a wedding photo
Scorched, black-edged, in wet ashes –

My thin shoesoles tremble,
And the sulphur-blast passes, the fright-glare.   10
And the people scamper past, coughing and stumbling.
(The picture blurred, for even the eye trembles)
The trees cough and shake,
And the great lizards go galloping past, heads high,
And horses breaking to freedom.
The soil cracks between tussock and tussock
Between my feet, as a mouth trying to speak,
The mortuary heart and guts of the globe
Trying to speak, against gravity,
The still-warm, stopped brain of a just-dead god   20
Trying to speak
Against its thickening death,
The mauled, blood-plastered, bodiless head of a planet
Trying to speak,
Lopped before birth
Rolled off into space, with mouth smashed
And tongue still moving
To find mother, among the stars and the blood-spittle,
Trying to cry –
And a blackbird sitting in the plum tree   30
Shakes and shakes its voice.

And I too am a ghost. I am the ghost
Of a great general, silent at my chess.
A thousand years have gone over
As I finger one piece.

The dusk waits.

The spears, the banners, wait.

Crow and the Sea

He tried ignoring the sea
But it was bigger than death, just as it was bigger than life.

He tried talking to the sea
But his brain shuttered and his eyes winced from it as from
    open flame.

He tried sympathy for the sea
But it shouldered him off – as a dead thing shoulders you off.

He tried hating the sea
But instantly felt like a scrutty dry rabbit-dropping on the
    windy cliff.

He tried just being in the same world as the sea
But his lungs were not deep enough

And his cheery blood banged off it
Like a water-drop off a hot stove.

Finally

He turned his back and he marched away from the sea

As a crucified man cannot move.

Truth Kills Everybody

So Crow found Proteus – steaming in the sun.
Stinking with sea-bottom growths
Like the plug of the earth's sump-outlet.
There he lay – belching quakily.

Crow pounced and buried his talons –

And it was the famous bulging Achilles – but he held him
The oesophagus of a staring shark – but he held it
A wreath of lashing mambas – but he held it

It was a naked powerline, 2000 volts –
He stood aside, watching his body go blue
As he held it and held it

It was a screeching woman and he had her by the throat –
He held it

A gone steering wheel bouncing towards a cliff edge –
He held it

A trunk of jewels dragging into a black depth – he held it

The ankle of a rising, fiery angel – he held it

Christ's hot pounding heart – he held it

The earth, shrunk to the size of a hand grenade

And he held it he held it and held it and   20

BANG!

He was blasted to nothing.

Crow and Stone

Crow was nimble but had to be careful
Of his eyes, the two dewdrops.
Stone, champion of the globe, lumbered towards him.

No point in detailing a battle
Where stone battered itself featureless
While Crow grew perforce nimbler.

The subnormal arena of space, agog,
Cheered these gladiators many aeons.
Still their struggle resounds.

But by now the stone is a dust – flying in vain,
And Crow has become a monster – his mere eyeblink
Holding the very globe in terror.

And still he who never has been killed
Croaks helplessly
And is only just born.

Fragment of an Ancient Tablet

Above – the well-known lips, delicately downed.
Below – beard between thighs.

Above – her brow, the notable casket of gems.
Below – the belly with its blood-knot.

Above – many a painful frown.
Below – the ticking bomb of the future.

Above – her perfect teeth, with the hint of a fang at the corner.
Below – the millstones of two worlds.

Above – a word and a sigh.
Below – gouts of blood and babies.

Above – the face, shaped like a perfect heart.
Below – the heart's torn face.

Snake Hymn

The snake in the garden
If it was not God
It was the gliding
And push of Adam's blood.

The blood in Adam's body
That slid into Eve
Was the everlasting thing
Adam swore was love.

The blood in Eve's body
That slid from her womb –
Knotted on the cross
It had no name.

Nothing else has happened.
The love that cannot die
Sheds the million faces
And skin of agony

To hang, an empty husk.
Still no suffering

Darkens the garden
Or the snake's song.

Lovesong

He loved her and she loved him
His kisses sucked out her whole past and future or tried to
He had no other appetite
She bit him she gnawed him she sucked
She wanted him complete inside her
Safe and sure forever and ever
Their little cries fluttered into the curtains

Her eyes wanted nothing to get away
Her looks nailed down his hands his wrists his elbows
He gripped her hard so that life   10
Should not drag her from that moment
He wanted all future to cease
He wanted to topple with his arms round her
Off that moment's brink and into nothing
Or everlasting or whatever there was
Her embrace was an immense press
To print him into her bones
His smiles were the garrets of a fairy palace
Where the real world would never come
Her smiles were spider bites   20
So he would lie still till she felt hungry
His words were occupying armies
Her laughs were an assassin's attempts
His looks were bullets daggers of revenge
Her glances were ghosts in the corner with horrible secrets
His whispers were whips and jackboots
Her kisses were lawyers steadily writing
His caresses were the last hooks of a castaway
Her love-tricks were the grinding of locks
And their deep cries crawled over the floors   30
Like an animal dragging a great trap

His promises were the surgeon's gag
Her promises took the top off his skull
She would get a brooch made of it
His vows pulled out all her sinews

He showed her how to make a love-knot
Her vows put his eyes in formalin
At the back of her secret drawer
Their screams stuck in the wall

Their heads fell apart into sleep like the two halves
Of a lopped melon, but love is hard to stop

In their entwined sleep they exchanged arms and legs
In their dreams their brains took each other hostage

In the morning they wore each other's face

Glimpse

'O leaves,' Crow sang, trembling, 'O leaves –'

The touch of a leaf's edge at his throat
Guillotined further comment.

                          Nevertheless
Speechless he continued to stare at the leaves

Through the god's head instantly substituted.

Two Eskimo Songs

I FLEEING FROM ETERNITY

Man came running faceless over earth
Eyeless and mouthless baldface he ran

He knew he trod the stone of death
He knew he was a ghost it was all he knew.

    Feeling a million years under stones
    He found a slug
                  but the lightning struck it
    It fumed to a scorched halo on his numbed palm.

    Feeling a million years under stones
    He found a trout
                  but a white hot frost fell
    From the exhaust of a star the fish frittered to crystals.

Feeling a million years under stones
He found a mouse
                        but a sigh of time
Breathed it to crumbs of knuckles.

He got a sharp rock he gashed holes in his face
Through the blood and pain he looked at the earth.

He gashed again deeper and through the blood and pain
He screeched at the lightning, at the frost, and at time.

Then, lying among the bones on the cemetery earth,
He saw a woman singing out of her belly.

He gave her eyes and a mouth, in exchange for the song.
She wept blood, she cried pain.

The pain and the blood were life. But the man laughed –

The song was worth it.

The woman felt cheated.

II HOW WATER BEGAN TO PLAY

Water wanted to live
It went to the sun it came weeping back
Water wanted to live
It went to the trees they burned it came weeping back
They rotted it came weeping back
Water wanted to live
It went to the flowers they crumpled it came weeping back
It wanted to live
It went to the womb it met blood
It came weeping back
It went to the womb it met knife
It came weeping back
It went to the womb it met maggot and rottenness
It came weeping back it wanted to die

It went to time it went through the stone door
It came weeping back
It went searching through all space for nothingness
It came weeping back it wanted to die

Till it had no weeping left

It lay at the bottom of all things

Utterly worn out   utterly clear

Littleblood

O littleblood, hiding from the mountains in the mountains
Wounded by stars and leaking shadow
Eating the medical earth.

O littleblood, little boneless little skinless
Ploughing with a linnet's carcase
Reaping the wind and threshing the stones.

O littleblood, drumming in a cow's skull
Dancing with a gnat's feet
With an elephant's nose with a crocodile's tail.

Grown so wise grown so terrible
Sucking death's mouldy tits.

Sit on my finger, sing in my ear, O littleblood.

from CROW WAKES (1971)

Crow Wakes

I had exploded, a bombcloud, lob-headed, my huge fingers
Came feeling over the fields, like shadows.
I became smaller than water, I stained into the soilcrumble.
I became smaller.
My eyes fell out of my head and into an atom.
My right leg stood in the room raving at me like a dog.
I tried to stifle its bloody mouth with a towel
But it ran on ahead. I stumbled after it
A long way and came to a contraption like a trap
Baited with human intestines.
A stone drummed and an eye watched me out of a cat's anus.
I swam upstream, cleansed, in the snow-water, upstream.
Till I grew tired and turned over. I slept.
When I woke I could hear voices, many voices.

It was my bones all chattering together
At the high-tide mark, bedded in rubble, littered among shells
And gull feathers.
                    And the breastbone was crying:
'I begat a million and murdered a million:
I was a leopard.' And 'No, no, no, no,
We were a fine woman,' a rib cried.
'No, we were swine, we had devils, and the axe halved us,'
The pelvis was shouting. And the bones of the feet
And the bones of the hands fought: 'We were alligators,
We dragged some beauties under, we did not let go.'
And, 'We were suffering oxen,' and 'I was a surgeon,'
And 'We were a stinking clot of ectoplasm that suffocated a nun
Then lay for years in a cobbler's cellar.'
The teeth sang and the vertebrae were screeching
Something incomprehensible.
                            I tried to creep away —
I got up and ran. I tried to get up and run
But they saw me. 'It's him, it's him again. Get him.'
They came howling after me and I ran.
A freezing hand caught hold of me by the hair
And lifted me off my feet and set me high
Over the whole earth on a blazing star
Called

Bones

Bones is a crazy pony.
Moon-white — star-mad.
All skull and skeleton.

Her hooves pound. The sleeper awakes with a cry.

Who has broken her in?
Who has mounted her and come back
Or kept her?

She lifts under them, the snaking crest of a bullwhip.

Hero by hero they go —
Grimly get astride
And their hair lifts.

She laughs, smelling the battle – their cry comes back.

Who can live her life?
Every effort to hold her or turn her falls off her
Like rotten harness.

Their smashed faces come back, the wallets and the watches.

And this is the stunted foal of the earth –
She that kicks the cot
To flinders and is off.

Amulet

Inside the wolf's fang, the mountain of heather.
Inside the mountain of heather, the wolf's fur.
Inside the wolf's fur, the ragged forest.
Inside the ragged forest, the wolf's foot.
Inside the wolf's foot, the stony horizon.
Inside the stony horizon, the wolf's tongue.
Inside the wolf's tongue, the doe's tears.
Inside the doe's tears, the frozen swamp.
Inside the frozen swamp, the wolf's blood.
Inside the wolf's blood, the snow wind.
Inside the snow wind, the wolf's eye.
Inside the wolf's eye, the North star.
Inside the North star, the wolf's fang.

In the Land of the Lion

He lived in a painting, well-framed.
There the colour red raved its worst
But was after all only paint.
Black threw its lightnings, a shock,
But only so far as the frame's edge.
Gold opened its eye
But only seemed to see –
It never saw the jailor's key,
The can-opener that fed him.
So there he was content.
And there the rainfall

Became its precedents,
And there the tears
Were really bad government not tears,
And there the bloody accident
Was lack of planning not frailty of bone,
And there the kiss
Involved itself deeply with God's mother and daughter.
And the whole thing stood frontispiece to a book
Which was in turn a masterpiece,
The work of a lifetime.

Somewhere among those pages
A pansy, faded, frail as a fly's wing,
Marked the passage he was once coming to
When something precious happened –
Forgotten. What? Forgotten.
The pansy
Has nothing to do with the words it has stained.
There is simply no clue, no connection.

And this book flies in space
Unopened,
A parenthesis
Like a bullet-hole into which a person's whole life vanished –

Though if it fell on a city
Somebody might get hurt
And it would have to be burned
Or at least get kicked aside.

The pansy hasn't a hope.

I See a Bear

Growing out of a bulb in wet soil licks its black tip
With a pink tongue its little eyes
Open and see a present an enormous bulging mystery package
Over which it walks sniffing at seams
Digging at the wrapping overjoyed holding the joy off sniffing
    and scratching
Teasing itself with scrapings and lickings and the thought of it
And little sips of the ecstasy of it

O bear do not open your package
Sit on your backside and sunburn your belly
It is all there it has actually arrived
No matter how long you dawdle it cannot get away
Shamble about lazily laze there in the admiration of it
With all the insects it's attracted all going crazy
And those others the squirrel with its pop-eyed amazement
The deer with its pop-eyed incredulity
The weasel pop-eyed with envy and trickery
All going mad for a share wave them off laze
Yawn and grin let your heart thump happily
Warm your shining cheek fur in the morning sun

You have got it everything for nothing

Bedtime Anecdote

There was a man
Who got up from a bed that was no bed
Who pulled on his clothes that were no clothes
(A million years whistling in his ear)
And he pulled on shoes that were no shoes
Carefully jerking the laces tight – and tighter
To walk over floors that were no floor
Down stairs that were no stairs
Past pictures that were no pictures
10   To pause
To remember and forget the night's dreams that were no dreams

And there was the cloud, primeval, the prophet;
There was the rain, its secret writing, the water-kernel
Of the tables of the sun;
And there was the light with its loose rant;
There were the birch trees, insisting and urging.
And the wind, reproach upon reproach.
At the table he cupped his eyes in his hands
As if to say grace

20   Avoiding his reflection in the mirror
Huddled to read news that was no news
(A million years revolving on his stomach)
He entered the circulation of his life

But stopped reading feeling the weight of his hand
In the hand that was no hand
And he did not know what to do or where to begin
To live the day that was no day

And Brighton was a picture
The British Museum was a picture
The battleship off Flamborough was a picture   30
And the drum-music the ice in the glass the mouths
Stretched open in laughter
That was no laughter
Were what was left of a picture

In a book
Under a monsoon downpour
In a ruinous mountain hut

From which years ago his body was lifted by a leopard.

Song against the White Owl

The white owl got its proof weapons –
Bequests of its victims.

And it got those eyes that look beyond life
From fluorescence of old corpses,

It snatched its bones as it could
From the burnings of blizzard.

Death loaned it a belly.
It wears a face it found on the sea.

Twisting sinews of last breaths
It bent these oddments together.

With a ghostly needle of screech
It sewed a coat of the snow –

From the knobbed and staring ice
Wringing blood and fat.

O stare Owl stare
Through your glacier wall
At a fatal terrain
Of weeping snow and the leaf of the birch

Where I spoon your soul from a bowl
And my song steams.

The Ship

Keep your foot off this ship, keep your foot off it.
Or come in your soul only. And only on tiptoe.
    Wrap your feet in polythene.
    Don't bring your fear or your fingers.
    Leave your mouth and your lungs or you'll know what I mean.
    You'll be pressganged for the voyage
To the kingdom of Maggot.

Keep your foot well off this ship.
It's a prison hulk. The prisoners are in irons
    With galaxies and snowflakes, waiting for the verdict.
    Not a sigh can be heard, not a tear noticed.
    And if you scream then that goes down
    As evidence against you and overboard
Go your clothes and your snapshots.

So keep your foot right off this ship –
It is the ship of death. It has its cargo
    And its crew – which are invisible devils
    With no other hooks or holds on your hopes
    But a cancer, or their claws in your kidneys –
    The owner's gang, bored and become monstrous
On their endless to and fro between here and the otherworld.

Here is the dear old lady with the bluefaced skull
She looks like some latest propaganda for Asiatic dysentery.
    She waves her arms shrunk to the shanks of a sheep.
    She's arguing with the Angel of Death in person.
    He has already impatiently started to eat her
    Under the blankets listening to all that she says
Without interrupting.

Don't bother lifting the blanket.
Regard these faces under their careful hair,
    Staring speechless off their pillows they stare through their chatter
    At their visitors propped like pictures.
    It's a space-ship, crashed from some other dimension

Into this one of stone, time and iron
And words dead of shock.

For this is the gallant ship of mutilations
And cries too huge for the ear
    That leave your amazement just numb
    And evaporate your prayers like a too-near and oncoming sun.
    So just let your brain give up and stare back empty
    At eyes that are simply raw holes and full
Of nothing but blood and bacteria.

Then get off this ship, get off it
The latest cargo of mistakes is about to move away –
    The latest purge of the luckless
    Lightens you to go back to cleaning your teeth.
    So go back.
    Or be dragged back from your bag of nerves, beyond your
        last howls
Into the Paradise of the crew.

Lullaby

Baby bawled for Mama – skull savaged it,
Death-hunger anger, the kissless trap-clamp.
Baby bawled for Mama – skeleton skelped it,
Clash of crockery knuckles, the shatter-bottle bones.
Baby bawled for Mama – grave grinned, gripped it,
Windowgap teeth and a flagfloor tongue,
Crawled toward the cupboard, Baby bawled for Mama.

Mama came, with her bull nostrils
Mama came, a feather on a stick
Mama came, in the skin of a weasel

Bestrid the thing, between her thighs she trapped it, throttled it
Till the snake-face gaped O became Beauty.
She twisted its deceits, it promised the earth.
And the skeleton pledged its hundred year strength.
And the skull's jaws opened. She loosed it, released it.

Delivered it.

Baby bawled for Mama.

Snow Song

In the beginning of beginning
A sea of blood: it heaved under hair.
Stamped hooves, hoisted antlers.
Ran. Firstman caught it. Flayed it.
Bit into its heart. It was a bear
Running roaring. He caught it. Flayed it.
Bit into its heart. It was a salmon
Slipping through walls of water. He caught it
Ate its heart. But spared its eggs.

Night: bones and dung.
He scraped the blood off his muscles.
Faced upwards. Slept.
Floated his ghost clear of bloody fingers
Hung it on the stars.
Mother Of All Things – she washed it.
He awoke with a new knife.

The Red Fox was afraid: he feared for his hide.
He bit the Elk: it became a dead tree at the earth's edge.
He bit the salmon: it sank anchor
To sea mud.
He bit the bear it slept a snarl
Of stony roots.

In skin too small for his bones
With a twist of rotten grass in his gut
Firstman wept.
And the Mother Of All Things wept.
And the Fox laughed under the earth.

Then the Mother Of All Things swelled and the bloodsea split
Its plenty for man's hunger.
But the Fox gripped shut her belly.
He seemed to be licking a stone.
His fangs gripped shut her belly.
He seemed to be crunching a tomtit
Or gnawing at a piece of old leather.
So his teeth spittled and the grip grinned
And nothing could be born.

And so, Firstman wept on his rock of hunger
And the Mother Of All Things wept.
Her tears fell. Only her tears fell. Nothing could be born.
Only the tears fell, freezing as they fell

Faltering over the earth
Herding towards Firstman 'We love you, we love you.'

They licked at his mouth. They nuzzled his eyes.
They nestled into his hands.

But the Fox grinned in heaven.

Man's cry sharpened. The snow deepened.

The Contender

There was this man and he was the strongest
Of the strong.
He gritted his teeth like a cliff.
Though his body was sweeling away like a torrent on a cliff
Smoking towards dark gorges
There he nailed himself with nails of nothing

All the women in the world could not move him
They came their mouths deformed against stone
They came and their tears salted his nail-holes
Only adding their embitterment
To his effort
He abandoned his grin to them his grimace
In his face upwards body he lay face downwards
As a dead man adamant

His sandals could not move him they burst their thongs
And rotted from his fixture
All the men in the world could not move him
They wore at him with their shadows and little sounds
Their arguments were a relief
Like heather flowers
His belt could not endure the siege – it burst
And lay broken
He grinned
Little children came in chorus to move him
But he glanced at them out of his eye-corners

Over the edge of his grin
And they lost their courage for life

Oak forests came and went with the hawk's wing
Mountains rose and fell
He lay crucified with all his strength
On the earth
Grinning towards the sun
Through the tiny holes of his eyes
And towards the moon
And towards the whole paraphernalia of the heavens
Through the seams of his face
With the strings of his lips
Grinning through his atoms and decay
Grinning into the black
Into the ringing nothing
Through the bones of his teeth

Sometimes with eyes closed

In his senseless trial of strength.

from POEMS [WITH RUTH FAINLIGHT AND
    ALAN SILLITOE] (1971)

Genesis of Evil

When Adam relaxed
And Heaven closed for the day
Eve began again
With what her little snake, her familiar,
Had whispered while she slept.

Every day Adam could hardly wait
For Heaven to close
And the next instalment
Of the snake's bloody love-thriller
From Eve's lovely lips.

When God heard about this from Michael
He came creeping close, in the form of a mouse,
And listened –

It was there, hidden in the bush,
That He became blind with Jealousy.

Crow's Song about England

Once upon a time there was a girl
Who tried to give her mouth
It was snatched from her and her face slapped
She tried to give her eyes
They were knocked to the floor the furniture crushed them
She tried to give her breasts
They were cut from her and canned
She tried to give her cunt
It was produced in open court she was sentenced

She stole everything back

She was mad with pain she humped into a beast
She changed sex he came back

Where he saw her mouth he stabbed with a knife
Where he saw her eyes he stabbed likewise
Where he saw her breasts her cunt he stabbed

He was sentenced

He escaped lobotomised he changed sex
Shrunk to a little girl she came back

She tried to keep her mouth
It was snatched from her and her face slapped
She tried to keep her eyes
They were knocked to the floor the furniture crushed them
She tried to keep her breasts
They were cut from her and canned
She tried to keep her cunt
It was produced in open court she was sentenced

She did life

Crow's Courtship

Crow got impatient knocking on God's door.
'Hurry up with my bride,' he cried, 'For the years are passing.'
He could see old women going in by the cartload
He could hear the furnace thundering
In the flues of heaven
As God forged the body of his bride
Out of the carcases of hags.
'Silence,' shouted God, 'You are interrupting
The Great Work. Only get away and be patient.'

Crow shuffled at the door, hummed a little.
He stared down onto the hills of orchards –
Then stood sweating, transfixed by fantasy.

Before he was aware he was battering on God's door,
'Hurry up with my bride, for the years are passing.'
The hags' bodies though they were dead and red-hot
Screeched under the hammers of God,
Laminations of hag –
Millionfold in the blade of the bride's body.
'Get away,' shouted God, 'You are ruining the work.
Will you get away and be patient.'

Crow knotted his arms, his breast was a sweltering boil
Of the pain of impatience –

He kicked open the door. God roared into tears.

Crow stared wooden eyed at the heap of ashes.

'The worst moment!' God wept, 'The worst moment!'

Crow's Song about God

Somebody is sitting
Under the gatepost of heaven
Under the lintel
On which are written the words: 'Forbidden to the living'
A knot of eyes, eyeholes, lifeless, the life-shape
A rooty old oak-stump, aground in the ooze
Of some putrid estuary,
Snaggy with amputations,

His fingernails broken and bitten,
His hair vestigial and purposeless, his toenails useless
    and deformed,
His blood filtering between
In the coils of his body, like the leech life
In a slime and ochre pond
Under the smouldering collapse of a town dump,
His brain a hacked ache, a dull flint,
His solar plexus crimped in his gut, hard,
A plastic carnation
In a gutter puddle
Outside the registry office –
Somebody
Sitting under the gatepost of heaven

Head fallen forward
Like the nipped head of somebody strung up to a lamp-post
With a cheese-wire, or an electric flex,
Or with his own belt,
Trousers round his ankles,
Face gutted with shadows, like a village gutted with bombs,
Weeping plasma,
Weeping whisky,
Weeping egg-white,
He has been choked with raw steak it hangs black over his chin,
Somebody
Propped in the gateway of heaven
Clinging to the tick of his watch
Under a dream muddled as vomit
That he cannot vomit, he cannot wake up to vomit,
He only lifts his head and lolls it back
Against the gatepost of heaven

Like a broken sunflower
Eyesockets empty
Stomach laid open
To the inspection of the stars
The operation unfinished
(The doctors ran off, there was some other emergency)
Sweat cooling on his temples
Hands hanging – what would be the use now
Of lifting them?
They hang

Clumps of bloodclot, varicose and useless
As afterbirths –

But God sees nothing of this person
His eyes occupied with His own terror
As He mutters
My Saviour is coming,
He is coming, who does not fear death,
He shares his skin with it,
He gives it his cigarettes,
He cuts up its food, he feeds it like a baby,
He keeps it warm he cherishes it
In the desolations of space,
He dresses it up in his best, he calls it his life –

He is coming.

Crow the Just

Crow jeered at – only his own death.
Crow spat at – only his own death.
He spread rumours – only about his own death.
He robbed – only his own death.
He knocked down and kicked – only his own death.
He vowed revenge – only on his own death.
He tricked – only his own death.
He murdered – only his own death.
He ate – only his own death.

This is how he kept his conscience so pure
He was black

(Blacker

Than the eyepupils

Of the gunbarrels.)

UNCOLLECTED (1971–73)

The Space-Egg was Sailing

When the Universe attacked it.
Suns collided, burst and evaporated
    And the egg sailed out of the vapour.

Fire attacked it
And iron surrendered all its nodes and cores
    The egg sailed away over the heavy surface

Water attacked it
And mountains kneeled to seas
    The egg bobbed clear on the ripples

Earth attacked it
The world writhed like a grimace
    The egg sat like a fly.

Life attacked it, yes, a crow
A crow gobbled that fly
    And the egg dropped from the crow's egg-duct

A jay ate the egg and beetles ate the jay
And a crow ate the beetles
    And the egg dropped from the crow's egg-duct.

Then there was a silence in heaven –

Sun and moon stopped struggling, the elements were hushed,
The trees disentangled their antlers

And the white owl and the weasel
And the wild dog came to a standstill

Volcanoes stopped, seas stopped, waterfalls stopped,
The clock stopped – like a conductor, arms raised

And Crow stepped into the open.

With a scream of rage, everything attacked

Crow took to his wings
                        singing

    When God hammered Crow
    He made gold
    When God roasted Crow in the sun
    He made diamond

When God crushed Crow under weights
He made alcohol
When God tore Crow to pieces
He made money
When God blew Crow up
He made day
When God hung Crow on a tree
He made fruit
When God buried Crow in the earth
He made man
When God tried to chop Crow in two
He made woman
When God said: 'You win, Crow'
He made the Redeemer.

When God went off in despair
Crow stropped his beak and started in on the two thieves.

'In the little girl's angel gaze'

In the little girl's angel gaze
Crow lost every feather
In the little boy's wondering eyes
Crow's bones splintered

In the little girl's passion
Crow's bowels fell in the dust
In the little boy's rosy cheeks
Crow became an unrecognizable rag

Crow got under the brambles, capitulated
To nothingness eyes closed
Let those infant feet pound through the Universe

The New World

I

It is not too long you'll be straddling the rocket,
My children,
The rocket that will carry you far
To crash you on to an unknown star.

It's a long, long time, little children,
With the moon in your mouth
Riding the bones
Of Eohippus
Over the craters
Into the sunset.

2

When the star was on her face
I held her by the hair
Higher than the moon
She cleared the gate of bone.

We rode into the land of light
Where trees beat their boughs
As at the birthroom midnight window
The dead make hopeless mouths.

All the earth's light was our cloak
We wrapped ourselves. We left
Naked to night the frosty mud
The bare twigs, and the shores.

3

A star stands on her forehead.
In her moving hands
She has cupped the moon.
Her smile says it does not burn.

The earth has been woven
Its animals and flowers
And that is her dress.
It is under her dress
You must seek the sun.

Emptiness of space
Makes her the only Island
Where I can live.

This is the new world.
These are its seven wonders.

4

I said goodbye to earth
I stepped into the wind
Which entered the tunnel of fire
Beneath the mountain of water.
I arrived at light
Where I was shadowless,
I saw the snowflake crucified
On the nails of nothing.

I heard the atoms praying
To enter his kingdom,
To be broken like bread
On a warm sill, and to weep.

5

The street was empty and stone
Like the Himalayas.
The moon was like a low door,
In half sleep I stepped through it.
The stair toppled niagara
I rose floating with the dust.
The room was like a grave
I was the one life left on earth.
The bed was like a star
Like a soul, a singing.
I reached, I groped
Through all of dark space.

I fell asleep
Shaken with laughter of foxes
Who had put something in my hand.

Centuries, centuries later
I woke.

The ice age leaned on the window.

6

Where did we go?
I cannot find us.

Only a tie, draped on the sun.
Only a shoe, dangling on the moon.

We did not land on a star.
Where did we go?

I roam the corridors of space
But the black between the stars

Is like the honeymooner's door,
Locked night and day.

An Alchemy

War in the egg
          Lustig the Moor
Aaron began it
          When Salt Tamora
In full blush of Lucretia
          Dawned on Leontes
Icicle Angelo
          Died Adonis' agony
Butchered by Richard
          The lineal Boar
Who darkened darkness
          With ravishing strides
And an Ass's horn
          To gore Titania
Queen of Fays
          For a pound of blood
Stinging Prince Hal
          To Portia's answer
Who defrocked
          Moses' Serpent
On the Hebrew Tree
          Anathalamia
Collapsed as Falstaff
          In the Boar's Head
The Knight of Venus
          After his Feast
Under Herne's acorns,
          Belated as bloated

A mushroom Caesar
                    The wounds of Rome
Mouthing prophesy
                    From which flittered
A mourning dove

Ancestral her sorcery
                    Helena the Healer
Diana her owl side
                    Outwitted Angelo
Who walled up Ophelia
                    She wept to Othello
Willow Willow
                    As he lopped his rivals
A Fortinbras steeled
                    To close with Gertrude
Who Came again

Desdemona rising
                    The Nun of Vienna
From killing her swine
                    The ring-dove's advent
Hamlet's muse
                    Hamlet's madness
Soused by Tempest
                    To Venus's Island
With her weird sisters
                    The blue Hag Hecate
Deflecting the dagger
                    With some rough magic
Into the Sanctum
                    Of Saintly Duncan
Double Macbeth
                    The crown's contagion
Drawn by the blade of Tarquin
                    Cordelia guiding
Blinded Gloucester
                    Cutting to the brain
Then Lear saw nine-fold
                    The under-crown lightning

The Boar's Moons mangling

                    His sainted flesh

Lear Furens

He snapped its fang

                It was Regan's body

He plucked out Goneril

                  Still it gored him

His third effort it vanished

                      And it had been his nothing

It had been his Joy

                His truth beyond telling

In a warm body

              Rock-dove of Aphrodite

Leaving a feather only

That Timon damned with gold

That carried Coriolanus

                  Crushed from Caesar

It was Old Nile's Serpent

                    Moon-browed Isis

Bride and Mother

              Mourning a Rome

Leontes banished

              Lear redivivus

Phoenix-Posthumous

                Found breath in Marina

Redeemed all Tempest

                His kiss of life

Stirred the Turtle

              Of the waters of amnios

The lunar cauldron

Then black Venus

              double tongued

Swine-uddered Sycorax

                Lilith the night-crow

Slid from the Tree

Released the Rainbow
                    Breasted Dove
With a leaf of light
                    Miranda with a miracle
To Adam Adonis

And sank
            In the crucible
                        Tiamat
                                    The Mother
The Scales
            The Coil
                    Of the Matter
                                Deeper
Then ever plummet
                    With Prospero's bones
And the sounding Book

PROMETHEUS ON HIS CRAG (1973)

1

His voice felt out the way. 'I am' he said

'Returning,' he said, and 'Now I am
Feeling into my body,' and 'Something is strange –

Something is altered.' And he paused
Just within darkness, just within numbness.
He let his mouth-mask far off

Loll in the light.
'What has happened to me, what has altered?'
He whispered and he lay frightened –

Letting his veins venture for him
Feeling his ice-burned lungs gulp huge clarity
Letting his laborious chest lift him

Like the wingbeats of an eagle
                              and
                                    'Am I an eagle?'

2

Prometheus On His Crag

Relaxes
In the fact that it has happened.

The blue wedge through his breastbone, into the rock,
Unadjusted by vision or prayer – so.

His eyes, brainless police.
His brain, simple as an eye.

Nevertheless, now he exults – like an eagle

In the broadening vastness, the reddening dawn
Of the fact

That cannot be otherwise
And could not have been otherwise,

And never can be otherwise.

And now, for the first time
                    relaxing
                              helpless

The Titan feels his strength.

3

Prometheus On His Crag

Pestered by birds roosting and defecating,
The chattering static of the wind-honed summit,
The clusterers to heaven, the sun-darkeners –

Shouted a world's end shout.
Then the swallow folded its barbs and fell,
The dove's bubble of fluorescence burst,

Nightingale and cuckoo
Plunged into padded forests where the woodpecker
Eyes bleached insane

Howled laughter into dead holes.
The birds became what birds have ever since been,
Scratching, probing, peering for a lost world –

A world of holy, happy notions shattered
By the shout
That brought Prometheus peace

And woke the vulture.

4

Prometheus On His Crag

Spotted the vulture coming out of the sun
The moment it edged clear of the world's edge.

There was nothing for him to do
As it splayed him open from breastbone to crotch
But peruse its feathers.

Black, bold and plain were those headline letters.
Do you want to know what they said?
Each one said the same:

'Today is a fresh start
Torn up by its roots
As I tear the liver from your body.'

5

Prometheus On His Crag

Dreamed he had burst the sun's mass
And emerged mortal. He raised his earth-soaked head
Like a new-born calf. A skirl of cold air

Joggled the flowers.

And the exploded heavens peeled away
Into a mess of glare – the star-head rivets,
The hook-faced majesties of revelation

Writhed maelstrom-molten back
Into the heart's jar
That clapped again shut

On grasshopper silence.
                    He had resolved God
As a cow swallows its afterbirth.

But over the dark earth escaped
The infant's bottomless cry, the mother's lament,
The father's curse.

6

Prometheus On His Crag

Has bitten his prophetic tongue off.
Mountains gargoyle the earth
And the sea retches bile.

The thoughts that basted sweat down his flushed features
And carved his body in a freezing ecstasy
Like a last supper, are dead as Harakhty.

Heaven funnels its punishment
Into a heart that beats ostrich
Into a brain horoscoped cretaceous.

Below, among car-bumpers and shopping baskets,
A monkey of voice, shuffling Tarot
For corpses and embryos, quotes Ecclesiastes

To the clock that talks backward.

7

Prometheus

Arrested half-way from heaven
And slung between heaven and earth

Swallowed what he had stolen.

Chains hungered. These chains were roots
Reaching from frozen earth.
They sank searching into his flesh
Interrogating the bones.

And the sun, plundered and furious,
Planted its vulture.

So the sun bloomed, as it drank him,
Earth purpled its crocus.

So he flowered
Flowers of a numb bliss, a forlorn freedom –

Groanings of the sun, sighs of the earth –

Gathered by withering men.

8

Prometheus On His Crag

Lay astonished all his preparations
For his humanity
Were disablements he lay disabled

He knew he could not walk he did not
Know how he could not crawl
He could not move he was a prisoner

Was he new born was he wounded fatal
An invalid new born healing
Bone fractures alert alarmed death numbness

Was this stone his grave this cradle
Nothingness nothingness over him over him
Whose mouth and eyes? A mother another

Prisoner a jailor? He spoke it was a scream

9

Now I know I never shall

Be let stir.
The man I fashioned and the god I fashioned
Dare not let me stir.

This leakage of cry these face-ripples
Calculated for me – for mountain water
Dammed to powerless stillness.

What secret stays
Stilled under my stillness?
Not even I know.

Only he knows – that bird, that
Filthy-gleeful emissary and
The hieroglyph he makes of my entrails

Is all he tells.

10

Prometheus On His Crag

Began to admire the vulture
It knew what it was doing

It went on doing it
Swallowing not only his liver
But managing also to digest its guilt

And hang itself again just under the sun
Like a heavenly weighing scales
Balancing the gift of life

And the cost of the gift
Without a tremor
As if both were nothing.

11

Prometheus On His Crag

Tried to recall his night's dream –

Where wrists and ankles were anchored, in safe harbour,
And two cosmic pythons, the Sea and the Sky,

Fought for the earth – a single jewel of power.
And the hammer-splayed head of the spike through his chest
Was a swallowtail butterfly, just trembling,

And neither wrist nor ankle must move –
And he dared hardly look at the butterfly,
Hardly dared breathe for the pain of joy

As it lasted and lasted –
                         a world
Where his liver healed to being his liver.

But now he woke to a world where the sun was the sun,
Iron iron,
              sea sea,
                    sky sky,
                         the vulture the vulture.

12

Prometheus On His Crag

Had begun to sing
A little before dawn
A song to his wounds.

The sun signalled him red through his closed eyelids
The vulture rustled
And the smoulder of man rose from the cities.

But he went on singing –
A pure
Unfaltering morphine

Drugging the whole earth with bliss.

13

Prometheus On His Crag

Heard the cry of the wombs.
He had invented them.
Then stolen the holy fire, and hidden it in them.

It seemed to him
The wombs drummed like furnaces
And that men were being fed into the wombs.

And it seemed
Babies were being dragged crying pitifully
Out of the wombs.

And it seemed
That the vulture was the revenge of the wombs
To show him what it was like,

That his chains would last, and the vulture would awake him,
As long as there were wombs
Even if that were forever,

And that he had already invented too much.

14

Prometheus On His Crag

Sees the wind
Whip all things to whip all things
The light whips the water the water whips the light

And men and women are whipped
By invisible tongues
They claw and tear and labour forward

Or cower cornered under the whipping
They whip their animals and their engines
To get them from under the whips

They lift their faces and look all round
For their master and tormentor
When they collapse to curl inwards

They are like cut plants and blind
Already beyond pain or fear
Even the snails are whipped

The swifts too screaming to outstrip the whip
Even as if being were a whipping

Even the earth leaping

Like a great ungainly top

15

Prometheus On His Crag

Had such an advantageous prospect
He could see, even as he slept,
The aeons revolving.

He could see, centre of every aeon,
Like the grit in its pearl,
Himself sealed on his rock.

Between the aeons – dark nothing. But he could see
Himself wading escaping through dark nothing
From aeon to aeon, prophesying Freedom –

It was his soul's sleepwalking and he dreamed it.
Only waking when the vulture woke him
In a new aeon
                    to the old chains
                                    and the old agony.

16

Prometheus On His Crag

Too far from his people to tell them
Suffers out his sentence
For having robbed earth of clay and heaven of fire.

He yields his own entrails
A daily premium
To the winged Death In Life, to keep it from men.

He lays himself down in his chains
On the Mountain,
                    under Heaven
                            as THE PAYMENT –
Too far from his people to tell them

Now they owe nothing.

17

No God – only wind on the flower.

No chains – only sinews, nerves, bones.
And no vulture – only a flame

A word
A bitten-out gobbet of sun

Buried behind the navel, unutterable.
The vital, immortal wound.

One nuclear syllable, bleeding silence.

18

The character neglected in this icon

Is not moon-head Io, or the hornet
That drove her through the limits.
It is not the vulture

With its solar digestion.
Is not even Epimetheus the twin
Who got away, in the end, with the heaven-sent girl.

Is not even the girl
With her gift pot, and its solitary hope.
Is not even the Almighty Presence

Of Everything.
The figure overlooked in this fable
Is the tiny trickle of lizard

Listening near the ear of Prometheus,
Whispering – at his each in-rip of breath,
Even as the vulture buried its head –

'Lucky, you are so lucky to be human!'

19

Prometheus On His Crag

Shouts and his words
Go off in every direction
Like birds

Like startled birds
They cry the way they fly away
Start up others which follow

For words are the birds of everything –
So soon
Everything is on the wing and gone

So speech starts hopefully to hold
Pieces of the wordy earth together
But pops to space-silence and space-cold

Emptied by words
Scattered and gone.
                  And the mouth shuts
Savagely on a mouthful

Of space-fright which makes the ears ring.

20

Prometheus On His Crag

Pondered the vulture. Was this bird
His unborn half-self, some hyena
Afterbirth, some lump of his mother?

Or was it his condemned human ballast –
His dying and his death, torn daily
From his immortality?

Or his blowtorch godhead
Puncturing those horrendous holes
In his human limits?   10

Was it his prophetic familiar?
The Knowledge, pebble-eyed,
Of the fates to be suffered in his image?

Was it the flapping, tattered hole –
The nothing door
Of his entry, draughting through him?

Or was it atomic law –
Was Life his transgression?
Was he the punished criminal aberration?

Was it the fire he had stolen?   20
Nowhere to go and now his pet,
And only him to feed on?

Or the supernatural spirit itself
That he had stolen from,
Now stealing from him the natural flesh?

Or was it the earth's enlightenment –
Was he an uninitiated infant
Mutilated towards alignment?

Or was it his anti-self –
30 The him-shaped vacuum
In unbeing, pulling to empty him?

Or was it, after all, the Helper
Coming again to pick at the crucial knot
Of all his bonds...?

Image after image. Image after image. As the vulture
Circled

Circled.

21

His mother covers her eyes.
The mountain splits its sweetness.
The blue fig splits its magma.

And the cry bulges.
And the veiny mire
Bubbles scalded.

The mountain is uttering
Blood and again blood.
Puddled, blotched newsprint.

With crocus evangels.
The mountain is flowering
A gleaming man.

And the cloudy bird
Tearing the shell
Midwifes the upfalling crib of flames.

And Prometheus eases free.
He sways to his stature.
And balances. And treads

On the dusty peacock film where the world floats.

UNCOLLECTED (1974–75)

Welcombe

Under the last fling of upward orange
The west doors of cloud standing open
The still-quivering furnace

A bullock of cooling black bronze
Stands on a holly-dark emerald
That is crumbling to granite embers.

His banner is apple-blossom.

Milk and blood are frail
In the shivering wind off the sea.

Exits

'We believers shall get away to God
That much earlier if the bomb drops!' rejoices
Our parson to the old women's faces
That are cold and folded, like plucked dead hens' arses.

In many a corner tonight
The rat chews off its paw
And dedicates the other three
To getting away out of it joyfully.

A sudden pinky-blue scowling glistener
The baby balloons out of its mother –
Splitting the tissue of all time, and the tarmac too
Like a mushroom, O genii of the atom.

The Lamentable History of the Human Calf

O there was a maiden, a maiden, a maiden
And she was a knock-out.
Will you be my bride, I sighed, I cried, I was ready to die.
And she replied, what did she reply?

'Give me your nose, for a kiss' she sighed. 'It's a fair pawn!'
  So I sliced off my nose
And she fed it to her puppy.

Lady, are you satisfied?

'O give me your ears, to share my fears, in the night, in my bed,
     where nobody hears, my darling!'
So I sliced off my ears
And she fed them to her puppy.

'Now let me have your legs, lest they carry you far,
     O my darling, far from my side," she cried.
So I chopped off my legs and she gave them to her puppy.

Lady, are you happy?

'O I want your heart, your heart, your heart, will it never be
     mine? Let me hold it,' she cried.
So I sliced me wide, and I ripped out the part
And she fed it to her puppy.

Lady, are you satisfied?

'O give me your liver, or I'll leave you forever.
Give me your tongue, your tongue, your tongue
Lest it whisper to another.
Give me your lungs that hurt you with their sighs,'
She cried.
With tears of love, with tears of love, I hacked out those dainties
And she fed them to her puppy.

Lady, are you satisfied?

'O give me your eyes, your rolling eyes,
That splash me with their tears, that go roving after others.
And give me your brains, that give you such pains
With doubting of my love, with doubting of my love.
And give me your arms, that all night long when you're far
     from my side they'll clasp me, clasp me'
And she cried, 'I'll be your bride!'
So I tore out my eyes and I gouged out my brains and I sawed off
     my arms and I gave them to my darling
And she fed them to her puppy.

Lady, are you satisfied?

'No, give me your skin, that holds you in,
O pour out your blood in a bowl and let me drink it, be mine.
O slice off your flesh and I'll nibble your bones, my darling!'

So I dragged off my skin and I brimmed it with my blood and I
   rolled up my flesh and I basketted my bones and I laid them
   at her door and she cried and she cried

Puppy, puppy, puppy.

Lady, I said, though I'm nothing but a soul, I have paid down
   the price, now come to be my bride.
But the puppy had grown, the puppy was a dog, was a big fat
   bitch, and my darling wept

'Take my dog,' she wept, 'O take it.
You are only a soul, how can we now be married?
So take my dog for this dog it is my soul,
I give you my soul!' And she gave me her dog.

Lady are you satisfied?

Now I live with a bitch an old sour bitch now I live with a bitch
   a bitch a bitch so I live with a bitch an old sour bitch and
   there was a maiden a maiden a maiden...

from SPRING SUMMER AUTUMN WINTER

Hunting the Summer

The fleeing summer! The fleeing summer!
   I got up at dawn,
   In the still, frail dawn
To hunt her and heard the swift's quiver of arrows
      Rattle as she twisted fleeing
         Flying asleep.

The ghostly summer! The ghostly summer!
   Deep was the lane,
   The tarmac velvet,
Banks of cow-parsley brimmed night's creamy stillness,
      Gypsy fox-gloves slept eyes open,
         A field-ghost lingered.

The hot-headed summer! The thoughtless summer!
   A hill in the noon,
   Man-high thistles,

Bullocks that knotted their tails in tight letters
   Bounded rodeo and their roars ripped
      Hanging woodland.

The secret summer! The hiding summer!
   She was sweating a bit
   And a bit too plump
Scarlet she flopped under sycamores panting
      Saying that the butterflies just
         Gave her a headache.

The foxy summer! The swift sly summer!
   On into evening
   I tracked her way
By barley that bowed it and dogrose that littered it,
      Honeysuckle oozing sweetness
         Stopped me dizzied.

Late in the evening I stood by the pond.
Huge was the carp that heaved among big lilies
And sank again, like a whole chest of treasure.
How shall I catch her, the beautiful summer!

I stared at the pond, I stared at the pond
Till the sun slid from my fingertips.
The sun sank under a golden field
And the moon climbed up my back.

The Defenders

With the apple in his strength,
And the Quince, his wise adviser,
And the pear his thoughtful brother,
With the blackberry and his thorn,
So ready to shed his blood,
And the plum with his stony bone,
With the wheat in his millions,
The barley and the rye
We shall hold our own
Against all winter's armour.

With the pumpkin in reserve
The turnip and the marrow

We shall hold our fire.
We shall go guerrilla
Asleep among the squirrels.
Over open ground we'll go
In the likeness of a Crow.
When the gale comes we shall claw it
With a claw like a tree,
Then we'll hide down in the roots.
Or in a fox's footprints
Escape across the snow.

And nightly underground
We'll prepare the secret hero,
The little honey bee,
Whose drum, when it begins,
Will bring back all the blossom
And sink the iceberg winter
In the bottom of the sea.

SEASON SONGS (1976)

A March Calf

Right from the start he is dressed in his best – his blacks and
   his whites.
Little Fauntleroy – quiffed and glossy,
A Sunday suit, a wedding natty get-up,
Standing in dunged straw

Under cobwebby beams, near the mud wall,
Half of him legs,
Shining-eyed, requiring nothing more
But that mother's milk come back often.

Everything else is in order, just as it is.
Let the summer skies hold off, for the moment.   10
This is just as he wants it.
A little at a time, of each new thing, is best.

Too much and too sudden is too frightening –
When I block the light, a bulk from space,
To let him in to his mother for a suck,
He bolts a yard or two, then freezes,

Staring from every hair in all directions,
Ready for the worst, shut up in his hopeful religion,
A little syllogism
With a wet blue-reddish muzzle, for God's thumb.   20

You see all his hopes bustling
As he reaches between the worn rails towards
The topheavy oven of his mother.
He trembles to grow, stretching his curl-tip tongue –

What did cattle ever find here
To make this dear little fellow
So eager to prepare himself?
He is already in the race, and quivering to win –

His new purpled eyeball swivel-jerks
In the elbowing push of his plans.   30
Hungry people are getting hungrier,
Butchers developing expertise and markets,

But he just wobbles his tail – and glistens
Within his dapper profile
Unaware of how his whole lineage
Has been tied up.

He shivers for feel of the world licking his side.
He is like an ember – one glow
Of lighting himself up
With the fuel of himself, breathing and brightening.

Soon he'll plunge out, to scatter his seething joy,
To be present at the grass,
To be free on the surface of such a wideness,
To find himself himself. To stand. To moo.

The River in March

Now the river is rich, but her voice is low.
It is her Mighty Majesty the sea
Travelling among the villages incognito.

Now the river is poor. No song, just a thin mad whisper.
The winter floods have ruined her.
She squats between draggled banks, fingering her rags
    and rubbish.

And now the river is rich. A deep choir.
It is the lofty clouds, that work in heaven,
Going on their holiday to the sea.

The river is poor again. All her bones are showing.
Through a dry wig of bleached flotsam she peers up ashamed
From her slum of sticks.

Now the river is rich, collecting shawls and minerals.
Rain brought fatness, but she takes ninety-nine percent
Leaving the fields just one percent to survive on.

And now she is poor. Now she is East wind sick.
She huddles in holes and corners. The brassy sun gives her
    a headache.
She has lost all her fish. And she shivers.

But now once more she is rich. She is viewing her lands.
A hoard of king-cups spills from her folds, it blazes, it cannot
    be hidden.
A salmon, a sow of solid silver,

Bulges to glimpse it.

March Morning Unlike Others

Blue haze. Bees hanging in air at the hive-mouth.
Crawling in prone stupor of sun
On the hive-lip. Snowdrops. Two buzzards,
Still-wings, each
Magnetised to the other,
Float orbits.
Cattle standing warm. Lit, happy stillness.
A raven, under the hill,
Coughing among bare oaks.
Aircraft, elated, splitting blue.
Leisure to stand. The knee-deep mud at the trough
Stiffening. Lambs freed to be foolish.

The earth invalid, dropsied, bruised, wheeled
Out into the sun,
After the frightful operation.
She lies back, wounds undressed to the sun,
To be healed,
Sheltered from the sneapy chill creeping North wind,
Leans back, eyes closed, exhausted, smiling
Into the sun. Perhaps dozing a little.
While we sit, and smile, and wait, and know
She is not going to die.

Spring Nature Notes

I

The sun lies mild and still on the yard stones.

The clue is a solitary daffodil – the first.

And the whole air struggling in soft excitements
Like a woman hurrying into her silks.
Birds everywhere zipping and unzipping
Changing their minds, in soft excitements,
Warming their wings and trying their voices.

The trees still spindle bare.

Beyond them, from the warmed blue hills
An exhilaration swirls upward, like a huge fish.

As under a waterfall, in the bustling pool.

Over the whole land
Spring thunders down in brilliant silence.

II

An oak tree on the first day of April
Is as bare as the same oak in December
But it looks completely different.

Now it bristles, it is a giant brazier
Of invisible glare, an invisible sun.
The oak tree's soul has returned and flames its strength.
You feel those rays – even though you can't see them
They touch you.

(Just as you feel touched, and turn round
To meet eyes staring straight at the back of your head.)

III

A spurt of daffodils, stiff, quivering –
Plumes, blades, creases, Guardsmen
At attention

Like sentinels at the tomb of a great queen.
(Not like what they are – the advance guard
Of a drunken slovenly army

Which will leave this whole place wrecked.)

IV

The crocuses are too naked. Space shakes them.
They remind you the North Sky is one vast hole
With black space blowing out of it
And that you too are being worn thin
By the blowing atoms of decomposed stars.

Down the moonbeams come hares
Hobbling on their square wheels.
What space has left, the hares eat.

What the hares do not want
Looks next morning like the leavings of picnickers   10
Who were kidnapped by a fright from space.

The crocus bulb stays hidden – veteran
Of terrors beyond man.

V

Spring bulges the hills.
The bare trees creak and shift.
Some buds have burst in tatters –
Like firework stubs.

But winter's lean bullocks
Only pretend to eat
The grass that will not come.

Then they bound like lambs, they twist in the air
They bounce their half tons of elastic
When the bale of hay breaks open.   10

They gambol from heap to heap,
Finally stand happy chewing their beards
Of last summer's dusty whiskers.

VI

With arms swinging, a tremendous skater
On the flimsy ice of space,
The earth leans into its curve –

Thrilled to the core, some flies have waded out
An inch onto my window, to stand on the sky
And try their buzz.

April Birthday

When your birthday brings the world under your window
      And the song-thrush sings wet-throated in the dew
And aconite and primrose are unsticking the wrappers
      Of the package that has come today for you

            Lambs bounce out and stand astonished
            Puss willow pushes among bare branches
            Sooty hawthorns shiver into emerald

                        And a new air
                  Nuzzles the sugary
                  Buds of the chestnut. A groundswell and a stir
                  Billows the silvered
                  Violet silks
                  Of the south – a tenderness
                  Lifting through all the
                  Gently-breasted
                  Counties of England.

When the swallow snips the string that holds the world in
      And the ring-dove claps and nearly loops the loop
You just can't count everything that follows in a tumble
      Like a whole circus tumbling through a hoop

            Grass in a mesh of all flowers floundering
            Sizzling leaves and blossoms bombing
            Nestlings hissing and groggy-legged insects

                        And the trees
                  Stagger, they stronger
                  Brace their boles and biceps under
                  The load of gift. And the hills float

        Light as bubble glass
        On the smoke-blue evening

    And rabbits are bobbing everywhere, and a thrush   30
    Rings coolly in a far corner. A shiver of green
    Strokes the darkening slope as the land
    Begins her labour.

Icecrust and Snowflake

I

A polished glancing. A blue frost-bright dawn.

And the ox's hoof-quag mire
At the ice-cumbered trough has so far protected
A primrose.

And the wild mares, in the moor hollow,
Stand stupid with bliss
Among the first velvet-petalled foal-flowers.

They are weeping for joy in a wind

That blows through the flint of the ox's horn.

II

The North Wind brought you too late

To the iron bar, rusted sodden
In the red soil.

The salmon weightless
In the flag of depth
Green as engine oil.

A snowflake in April
That touched, that registered
Was felt.

Solitary signal
Of a storm too late to get in

Past the iron bar's leaf

Through the window
Of the salmon's egg
With its eager eye.

Deceptions

The oak is a railway station.
Wait there for the spring.
Will it stop for you?
The famous express blurs through –
Where is it going?
Leaving all the oak's fronds in a blush and agitation –

       Nor will you catch it at the ash.

The March hare brings the spring
For you personally.
He is too drunk to deliver it.
He loses it on some hare-brained folly –
Now you will never recover it.
All year he will be fleeing and flattening his ears and fleeing –

       Eluding your fury.

With the cherry bloom for her fancy dress
Spring is giving a party –
And we have been invited.
We've just arrived, all excited,
When she rushes out past us weeping, tattered and dirty –
Wind and rain are wrecking the place

       And we can only go home.

Spring will marry you. A promise!
Cuckoo brings the message: May.
O new clothes! O get your house ready!
Expectation keeps you starry.
But at which church and on what day?
All month you sit waiting, and in June you know that it's off.

       And the cuckoo has started to laugh.

Swifts

Fifteenth of May. Cherry blossom. The swifts
Materialise at the tip of a long scream
Of needle. 'Look! They're back! Look!' And they're gone
On a steep

Controlled scream of skid
Round the house-end and away under the cherries.
   Gone.
Suddenly flickering in sky summit, three or four together,
Gnat-whisp frail, and hover-searching, and listening

For air-chills – are they too early? With a bowing   10
Power-thrust to left, then to right, then a flicker they
Tilt into a slide, a tremble for balance,
Then a lashing down disappearance

Behind elms.
           They've made it again,
Which means the globe's still working, the Creation's
Still waking refreshed, our summer's
Still all to come –
         And here they are, here they are again
Erupting across yard stones
Shrapnel-scatter terror. Frog-gapers,
Speedway goggles, international mobsters –   20

A bolas of three or four wire screams
Jockeying across each other
On their switchback wheel of death.
They swat past, hard-fletched,

Veer on the hard air, toss up over the roof,
And are gone again. Their mole-dark labouring,
Their lunatic limber scramming frenzy
And their whirling blades

Sparkle out into blue –
         Not ours any more.
Rats ransacked their nests so now they shun us.   30

Round luckier houses now
They crowd their evening dirt-track meetings,

Racing their discords, screaming as if speed-burned,
Head-height, clipping the doorway
With their leaden velocity and their butterfly lightness,
Their too much power, their arrow-thwack into the eaves.

Every year a first-fling, nearly-flying
Misfit flopped in our yard,
Groggily somersaulting to get airborne.
He bat-crawled on his tiny useless feet, tangling his flails

Like a broken toy, and shrieking thinly
Till I tossed him up – then suddenly he flowed away under
His bowed shoulders of enormous swimming power,
Slid away along levels wobbling

On the fine wire they have reduced life to,
And crashed among the raspberries.
Then followed fiery hospital hours
In a kitchen. The moustached goblin savage

Nested in a scarf. The bright blank
Blind, like an angel, to my meat-crumbs and flies.
Then eyelids resting. Wasted clingers curled.
The inevitable balsa death.

                    Finally burial
For the husk
Of my little Apollo –

The charred scream
Folded in its huge power.

Mackerel Song

While others sing the mackerel's armour
His stub scissor head and his big blurred eye
And the flimsy savagery of his onset
I sing his simple hunger.

While others sing the mackerel's swagger
His miniature ocelot oil-green stripings

And his torpedo solidity of thump
I sing his gormless plenty.

While others sing the mackerel's fury
The belly-tug lightning-trickle of his evasions
And the wrist-thick muscle of his last word
I sing his loyal come-back.

While others sing the mackerel's acquaintance
The soap of phosphorus he lathers on your fingers
The midget gut and the tropical racer's torso
I sing his scorched sweetness.

While others sing the mackerel's demise
His ultimatum to be cooked instantly
And the shock of his decay announcement
I sing how he makes the rich summer seas

A million times richer

With the gift of his millions.

Hay

The grass is happy
To run like a sea, to be glossed like a mink's fur
By polishing wind.
Her heart is the weather.
She loves nobody
    Least of all the farmer who leans on the gate.

The grass is happy
When the June sun roasts the foxgloves in the hedges.
She comes into her flower.
She lifts her skirts.
It does not concern her
    The pondering farmer has begun to hope.

The grass is happy
To open her scents, like a dress, through the county,
Drugging light hearts
To heavy betrothals
And next April's Fools,
    While pensioners puzzle where life went so airily.

The grass is happy
When the spinner tumbles her, she silvers and she sweetens.
Plain as a castle
The hare looks for home
And the dusty farmer
    For a hand-shaped cloud and a yellow evening.

Happy the grass
To be wooed by the farmer, who wins her and brings her to
    church in her beauty,
Bride of the Island.
Luckless the long-drawn
Aeons of Eden
    Before he came to mow.

Sheep

I

The sheep has stopped crying.
All morning in her wire-mesh compound
On the lawn, she has been crying
For her vanished lamb. Yesterday they came.
Then her lamb could stand, in a fashion,
And make some tiptoe cringing steps.
Now he has disappeared.
He was only half the proper size,
And his cry was wrong. It was not
A dry little hard bleat, a baby-cry
Over a flat tongue, it was human,
It was a despairing human smooth Oh!
Like no lamb I ever heard. Its hindlegs
Cowered in under its lumped spine,
Its feeble hips leaned towards
Its shoulders for support. Its stubby
White wool pyramid head, on a tottery neck,
Had sad and defeated eyes, pinched, pathetic,
Too small, and it cried all the time
Oh! Oh! staggering towards
Its alert, baffled, stamping, storming mother
Who feared our intentions. He was too weak
To find her teats, or to nuzzle up in under,

He hadn't the gumption. He was fully
Occupied just standing, then shuffling
Towards where she'd removed to. She knew
He wasn't right, she couldn't
Make him out. Then his rough-curl legs,
So stoutly built, and hooved
With real quality tips,
Just got in the way, like a loose bundle
Of firewood he was cursed to manage,
Too heavy for him, lending sometimes
Some support, but no strength, no real help.
When we sat his mother on her tail, he mouthed her teat,
Slobbered a little, but after a minute
Lost aim and interest, his muzzle wandered,
He was managing a difficulty
Much more urgent and important. By evening
He could not stand. It was not
That he could not thrive, he was born
With everything but the will –
That can be deformed, just like a limb.
Death was more interesting to him.
Life could not get his attention.
So he died, with the yellow birth-mucus
Still in his cardigan.
He did not survive a warm summer night.
Now his mother has started crying again.
The wind is oceanic in the elms
And the blossom is all set.

    II

What is it this time the dark barn again
Where men jerk me off my feet
And shout over me with murder voices
And do something painful to somewhere on my body

Why am I grabbed by the leg and dragged from my friends
Where I was hidden safe though it was hot
Why am I dragged into the light and whirled onto my back
Why am I sat up on my rear end with my legs splayed

A man grips me helpless his knees grip me helpless
What is that buzzer what is it coming

Buzzing like a big fierce insect on a long tangling of snake
What is the man doing to me with his buzzing thing

That I cannot see he is pressing it into me
I surrender I let my legs kick I let myself be killed

I let him hoist me about he twists me flat
In a leverage of arms and legs my neck pinned under his ankle

While he does something dreadful down the whole length of my belly
My little teats stand helpless and terrified as he buzzes around them

Poor old ewe! She peers around from her ridiculous position.
Cool intelligent eyes, of grey-banded agate and amber,

Eyes deep and clear with feeling and understanding
While her monster hooves dangle helpless
And a groan like no bleat vibrates in her squashed windpipe
And the cutter buzzes at her groin and her fleece piles away

Now it buzzes at her throat and she emerges whitely
More and more grotesquely female and nude
Paunchy and skinny, while her old rug, with its foul tassels
Heaps from her as a foam-stiff, foam-soft, yoke-yellow robe

Numbed all over she suddenly feels much lighter
She feels herself free, her legs are her own and she scrambles up
Waiting for that grapple of hands to fling her down again
She stands in the opened arch of his knees she is facing a
    bright doorway

With a real bleat to comfort the lamb in herself
She trots across the threshold and makes one high clearing bound
To break from the cramp of her fright
And surprised by her new lightness and delighted

She trots away, noble-nosed, her pride unsmirched.
Her greasy winter-weight stays coiled on the foul floor, for
    somebody else to bother about.
She has a beautiful wet green brand on her bobbing brand-new
    backside,
She baas, she has come off best.

III

The mothers have come back
From the shearing, and behind the hedge

The woe of sheep is like a battlefield
In the evening, when the fighting is over,
And the cold begins, and the dew falls,
And bowed women move with water.
Mother mother mother the lambs
Are crying, and the mothers are crying.
Nothing can resist that probe, that cry
Of a lamb for its mother, or an ewe's crying
For its lamb. The lambs cannot find
Their mothers among those shorn strangers.
A half-hour they have lamented,
Shaking their voices in desperation.
Bald brutal-voiced mothers braying out,
Flat-tongued lambs chopping off hopelessness.
Their hearts are in panic, their bodies
Are a mess of woe, woe they cry,
They mingle their trouble, a music
Of worse and worse distress, a worse entangling,
They hurry out little notes
With all their strength, cries searching this way and that.
The mothers force out sudden despair, blaaa!
On restless feet, with wild heads.

Their anguish goes on and on, in the June heat.
Only slowly their hurt dies, cry by cry,
As they fit themselves to what has happened.

Apple Dumps

After the fiesta, the beauty-contests, the drunken wrestling
Of the blossom
Come some small ugly swellings, the dwarfish truths
Of the prizes.

After blushing and confetti, the breeze-blown bridesmaids, the
    shadowed snapshots
Of the trees in bloom
Come the gruelling knuckles, and the cracked housemaid's hands,
The workworn morning plainness of apples.

Unearthly was the hope, the wet star melting the gland,
Staggering the offer –

But pawky the real returns, not easy to see,
Dull and leaf-green, hidden, still-bitter, and hard.

The orchard flared wings, like a new heaven, a dawn-lipped
    apocalypse
Kissing the sleeper –
The apples emerge, in the sun's black shade, among stricken trees,
A straggle of survivors, nearly all ailing.

Work and Play

The swallow of summer, she toils all summer,
A blue-dark knot of glittering voltage,
A whiplash swimmer, a fish of the air.
    But the serpent of cars that crawls through the dust
    In shimmering exhaust
    Searching to slake
    Its fever in ocean
    Will play and be idle or else it will bust.

The swallow of summer, the barbed harpoon,
She flings from the furnace, a rainbow of purples,
Dips her glow in the pond and is perfect.
    But the serpent of cars that collapsed at the beach
    Disgorges its organs
    A scamper of colours
    Which roll like tomatoes
    Nude as tomatoes
    With sand in their creases
    To cringe in the sparkle of rollers and screech.

The swallow of summer, the seamstress of summer,
She scissors the blue into shapes and she sews it,
She draws a long thread and she knots it at corners.
    But the holiday people
    Are laid out like wounded
    Flat as in ovens
    Roasting and basting
    With faces of torment as space burns them blue
    Their heads are transistors
    Their teeth grit on sand grains
    Their lost kids are squalling

While man-eating flies
Jab electric shock needles but what can they do?

They can climb in their cars with raw bodies, raw faces
    And start up the serpent
    And headache it homeward
    A car full of squabbles
    And sobbing and stickiness
    With sand in their crannies
    Inhaling petroleum
    That pours from the foxgloves
    While the evening swallow
The swallow of summer, cartwheeling through crimson,
Touches the honey-slow river and turning
Returns to the hand stretched from under the eaves –
A boomerang of rejoicing shadow.

The Harvest Moon

The flame-red moon, the harvest moon,
Rolls along the hills, gently bouncing,
A vast balloon,
Till it takes off, and sinks upward
To lie in the bottom of the sky, like a gold doubloon.

The harvest moon has come,
Booming softly through heaven, like a bassoon.
And earth replies all night, like a deep drum.

So people can't sleep,
So they go out where elms and oak trees keep
A kneeling vigil, in a religious hush.
The harvest moon has come!

And all the moonlit cows and all the sheep
Stare up at her petrified, while she swells
Filling heaven, as if red hot, and sailing
Closer and closer like the end of the world

Till the gold fields of stiff wheat
Cry 'We are ripe, reap us!' and the rivers
Sweat from the melting hills.

The Golden Boy

In March he was buried
    And nobody cried
Buried in the dirt
    Nobody protested
Where grubs and insects
    That nobody knows
With outer-space faces
    That nobody loves
Can make him their feast
    As if nobody cared.

But the Lord's mother
    Full of her love
Found him underground
    And wrapped him with love
As if he were her baby
    Her own born love
She nursed him with miracles
    And starry love
And he began to live
    And to thrive on her love

He grew night and day
    And his murderers were glad
He grew like a fire
    And his murderers were happy
He grew lithe and tall
    And his murderers were joyful
He toiled in the fields
    And his murderers cared for him
He grew a gold beard
    And his murderers laughed.

With terrible steel
    They slew him in the furrow
With terrible steel
    They beat his bones from him
With terrible steel
    They ground him to powder
They baked him in ovens
    They sliced him on tables

They ate him they ate him
    They ate him they ate him

Thanking the Lord
Thanking the Wheat
Thanking the Bread
For bringing them Life
Today and Tomorrow
Out of the dirt.

Autumn

Leaves

Who's killed the leaves?
Me, says the apple, I've killed them all.
Fat as a bomb or a cannonball
I've killed the leaves.

Who sees them drop?
Me, says the pear, they will leave me all bare
So all the people can point and stare.
I see them drop.

Who'll catch their blood?
Me, me, me, says the marrow, the marrow.   10
I'll get so rotund that they'll need a wheelbarrow.
I'll catch their blood.

Who'll make their shroud?
Me, says the swallow, there's just time enough
Before I must pack all my spools and be off.
I'll make their shroud.

Who'll dig their grave?
Me, says the river, with the power of the clouds
A brown deep grave I'll dig under my floods.
I'll dig their grave.   20

Who'll be their parson?
Me, says the Crow, for it is well-known
I study the bible right down to the bone.
I'll be their parson.

Who'll be chief mourner?
Me, says the wind, I will cry through the grass
The people will pale and go cold when I pass.
I'll be chief mourner.

Who'll carry the coffin?
30 Me, says the sunset, the whole world will weep
To see me lower it into the deep.
I'll carry the coffin.

Who'll sing a psalm?
Me, says the tractor, with my gear grinding glottle
I'll plough up the stubble and sing through my throttle.
I'll sing the psalm.

Who'll toll the bell?
Me, says the robin, my song in October
Will tell the still gardens the leaves are over.
40 I'll toll the bell.

Autumn Nature Notes

I

The Laburnum top is silent, quite still
In the afternoon yellow September sunlight,
A few leaves yellowing, all its seeds fallen.

Till the goldfinch comes, with a twitching chirrup,
A suddenness, a startlement, at a branch-end.
Then sleek as a lizard, and alert, and abrupt
She enters the thickness, and a machine starts up
Of chitterings, and a tremor of wings, and trillings –
The whole tree trembles and thrills.
10 It is the engine of her family.
She stokes it full, then flirts out to a branch-end
Showing her barred face identity mask

Then with eerie delicate whistle-chirrup whisperings
She launches away, towards the infinite

And the laburnum subsides to empty.

The sun finally tolerable.
The sunflowers tired out, like old gardeners.
Cabbage-white butterflies eddying
In the still pool of what is left to them.
The buddleia's last cones of lilac intoxicant
Crusted with Peacock butterflies and Red Admirals.

A raven, orbiting elm-high, lazily,
Two cronks to each circuit.
Sky sprinkled with forked martins
Swallows glittering their voices.   10

Now a cooler push, rocking the mesh of soft-edged shadows.

So we sit on the earth which is warmed
And sweetened and ripened
By the furnace
On which the door has just about closed.

III

The chestnut splits its padded cell.
It opens an African eye.

A cabinet-maker, an old master
In the root of things, has done it again.

Its slippery gloss is a swoon,
A peek over the edge into – what?

Down the well-shaft of swirly grain,
Past the generous hands that lifted the May-lamps,

Into the Fairytale of a royal tree
That does not know about conkers   10

Or the war-games of boys.
Invisible though he is, this plump mare

Bears a tall armoured rider towards
The mirk-forest of rooty earth.

He rides to fight the North corner.
He must win a sunbeam princess

From the cloud castle of the rains.
If he fails, evil faces,

Jaws without eyes, will tear him to pieces.
10   If he succeeds, and has the luck

To snatch his crown from the dragon
Which resembles a slug

He will reign over our garden
For two hundred years.

IV

When the Elm was full
When it heaved and all its tautnesses drummed
Like a full-sail ship

It was just how I felt.
Waist-deep, I ploughed through the lands,
I leaned at horizons, I bore down on strange harbours.

As the sea is a sail-ship's root
So the globe was mine.
When the swell lifted the crow from the Elm-top
10   Both Poles were my home, they rocked me and supplied me.

But now the Elm is still
All its frame bare
Its leaves are a carpet for the cabbages

And it stands engulfed in the peculiar golden light
With which Eternity's flash
Photographed the sudden cock pheasant –

Engine whinneying, the fire-ball bird clatters up,
Shuddering full-throttle
Its three tongued tail-tip writhing

20   And the Elm stands, astonished, wet with light,

And I stand, dazzled to my bones, blinded.

V

Through all the orchard's boughs
A honey-colour stillness, a hurrying stealth,
A quiet migration of all that can escape now.

Under ripe apples, a snapshot album is smouldering.

With a bare twig,
Glow-dazed, I coax its stubborn feathers.
A gold furred flame. A blue tremor of the air.

The fleshless faces dissolve, one by one,
As they peel open. Blackenings shrivel
To grey flutter. The clump's core hardens. Everything   10

Has to be gone through. Every corpuscle
And its gleam. Everything must go.
My heels squeeze wet mulch, and my crouch aches.

A wind-swell lifts through the oak.
Scorch-scathed, crisping, a fleeing bonfire
Hisses in invisible flames – and the flame-roar.

An alarmed blackbird, lean, alert, scolds
The everywhere slow exposure – flees, returns.

VI

Water-wobbling blue-sky-puddled October.
The distance microscopic, the ditches brilliant.
Flowers so low-powered and fractional
They are not in any book.

I walk on high fields feeling the bustle
Of the million earth-folk at their fair.
Fieldfares early, exciting foreigners.
A woodpigeon pressing over, important as a policeman.

A far Bang! Then Bang! and a litter of echoes –
Country pleasures. The farmer's guest,   10
In U.S. combat green, will be trampling brambles,
Waving his gun like a paddle.

I thought I'd brushed with a neighbour –
Fox-reek, a warm web, rich as creosote,
Draping the last watery blackberries –
But it was the funeral service.

Two nights he has lain, patient in his position,
Puckered under the first dews of being earth,

Crumpled like dead bracken. His reek will cling
20   To his remains till spring.

Then I shall steal his fangs, and wear them, and honour them.

VII

Three pale foxglove lamp-mantles, in full flare
Among gritty burned-out spires of old foxgloves
Under needling sleet, in a crossing squall.

This last week, a baby hand of blossom
Among corroded leaves, over windfall apples.

Every apple a festival of small slugs

Probably thinking their good time had just started.

So the old year, tired,
Smiles over his tools, fondling them a little,
10   As he puts them away.

VIII

Oceanic windy dawn.
Shapes grab at the window.
Ravens go head over heels.
The flood has scoured the sky.

No going on deck today.
I see, through the submerged window,
That the quince tree, which yesterday
Still clung to a black leaf, has lost it.

The Seven Sorrows

The first sorrow of autumn
Is the slow goodbye
Of the garden who stands so long in the evening –
A brown poppy head,
The stalk of a lily,
And still cannot go.

The second sorrow
Is the empty feet

Of the pheasant who hangs from a hook with his brothers.
The woodland of gold
Is folded in feathers
With its head in a bag.

And the third sorrow
Is the slow goodbye
Of the sun who has gathered the birds and who gathers
The minutes of evening,
The golden and holy
Ground of the picture.

The fourth sorrow
Is the pond gone black
Ruined and sunken the city of water –
The beetle's palace,
The catacombs
Of the dragonfly.

And the fifth sorrow
Is the slow goodbye
Of the woodland that quietly breaks up its camp.
One day it's gone.
It has left only litter –
Firewood, tentpoles.

And the sixth sorrow
Is the fox's sorrow
The joy of the huntsman, the joy of the hounds,
The hooves that pound
Till earth closes her ear
To the fox's prayer.

And the seventh sorrow
Is the slow goodbye
Of the face with its wrinkles that looks through the window
As the year packs up
Like a tatty fairground
That came for the children.

A Cranefly in September

She is struggling through grass-mesh – not flying,
Her wide-winged, stiff, weightless basket-work of limbs
Rocking, like an antique wain, a top-heavy ceremonial cart
Across mountain summits
(Not planing over water, dipping her tail)
But blundering with long strides, long reachings, reelings
And ginger-glistening wings
From collision to collision.
Aimless in no particular direction,
Just exerting her last to escape out of the overwhelming
Of whatever it is, legs, grass,
The garden, the county, the country, the world –

Sometimes she rests long minutes in the grass forest
Like a fairytale hero, only a marvel can help her.
She cannot fathom the mystery of this forest
In which, for instance, this giant watches –
The giant who knows she cannot be helped in any way.

Her jointed bamboo fuselage,
Her lobster shoulders, and her face
Like a pinhead dragon, with its tender moustache,
And the simple colourless church windows of her wings
Will come to an end, in mid-search, quite soon.
Everything about her, every perfected vestment
Is already superfluous.
The monstrous excess of her legs and curly feet
Are a problem beyond her.
The calculus of glucose and chitin inadequate
To plot her through the infinities of the stems.

The frayed apple leaves, the grunting raven, the defunct tractor
Sunk in nettles, wait with their multiplications
Like other galaxies.
The sky's Northward September procession, the vast soft armistice,
Like an Empire on the move,
Abandons her, tinily embattled
With her cumbering limbs and cumbered brain.

There Came a Day

There came a day that caught the summer
Wrung its neck
Plucked it
And ate it.

Now what shall I do with the trees?
The day said, the day said.
Strip them bare, strip them bare.
Let's see what is really there.

And what shall I do with the sun?
The day said, the day said.
Roll him away till he's cold and small.
He'll come back rested if he comes back at all.

And what shall I do with the birds?
The day said, the day said.
The birds I've frightened, let them flit,
I'll hang out pork for the brave tomtit.

And what shall I do with the seed?
The day said, the day said.
Bury it deep, see what it's worth.
See if it can stand the earth.

What shall I do with the people?
The day said, the day said.
Stuff them with apple and blackberry pie –
They'll love me then till the day they die.

There came this day and he was autumn.
His mouth was wide
And red as a sunset.
His tail was an icicle.

The Stag

While the rain fell on the November woodland shoulder of Exmoor
While the traffic jam along the road honked and shouted
Because the farmers were parking wherever they could
And scrambling to the bank-top to stare through the tree-fringe

Which was leafless,
The stag ran through his private forest.

While the rain drummed on the roofs of the parked cars
And the kids inside cried and daubed their chocolate and fought
And mothers and aunts and grandmothers
Were a tangle of undoing sandwiches and screwed-round
    gossiping heads
Steaming up the windows,
The stag loped through his favourite valley.

While the blue horsemen down in the boggy meadow
Sodden nearly black, on sodden horses,
Spaced as at a military parade,
Moved a few paces to the right and a few to the left and felt
    rather foolish
Looking at the brown impassable river,
The stag came over the last hill of Exmoor.

While everybody high-kneed it to the bank-top all along the road
Where steady men in oilskins were stationed at binoculars,
And the horsemen by the river galloped anxiously this way
    and that
And the cry of hounds came tumbling invisibly with their echoes
    down through the draggle of trees,
Swinging across the wall of dark woodland,
The stag dropped into a strange country.

And turned at the river
Hearing the hound-pack smash the undergrowth, hearing the
    bell-note
Of the voice that carried all the others,
Then while his limbs all cried different directions to his lungs,
    which only wanted to rest,
The blue horsemen on the bank opposite
Pulled aside the camouflage of their terrible planet.

And the stag doubled back weeping and looking for home up a
    valley and down a valley
While the strange trees struck at him and the brambles lashed him,
And the strange earth came galloping after him carrying the
    loll–tongued hounds to fling all over him
And his heart became just a club beating his ribs and his own
    hooves shouted with hounds' voices,

And the crowd on the road got back into their cars
Wet-through and disappointed.

Two Horses

I

Earth heaved, splitting. Towers
Reared out. I emerged
Behind horses, updragging with oaken twists
Swaying castles of elastic

My fortifications moved on the sky
The ploughshare my visor
Crowned by wind burn, ploughing my kingdom

Instated by the sun's sway
The fortunes of war, a famished people
Corn barons.   10

II

I advanced
Under the November sooty gold heaven
Among angling gulls

Behind those earth-swaying buttocks
Their roil and gleam, as in a dark wind
And the smoky foliage of their labour
Their tree-strength

Hauling earth's betrothal
From an underworld, with crocus glints
A purplish cloak-flap   20
The click hooves flicking
Hot circles flashing back at me lightly

Shaggy forest giants, gentle in harness
Their roots tearing and snapping
They were themselves the creaking boughs and the burden
Of earth's fleshiest ripeness, her damson tightest
Her sweetest

Earth splayed her thighs, she lay back.

III

The coulter slid effortless
The furrow's polished face, with a hiss
Coiling aside, a bow-wave that settled
Beside the poisonous brown river
As I stumbled deeper.
                         Hour after hour
The tall sweat-sleeked buttocks
Mill-wheels heavily revolving
Slackness to tautness, stretch and quiver – the vein-mapped
Watery quake-weight
In their slapping traces, drawing me deeper

Into the muffled daze and toil of their flames
Their black tails slashing sideways
The occasional purring snort

The stubble's brassy whisper
The mineral raw earth smell, the town-wind of sulphur
The knotted worms, sheared by light
The everlasting war behind the shoulder
The old ploughman still young

Furrow by furrow darkening toward summer.

IV

A shout – and the dream broke, against the thorns of the headland.
Chins back, backing
Trampling sideways, a jangling of brisk metals
High-kneed, levered by cries
The plough hard over –

They had jerked awake
Into urgent seconds
Now they trod deep water, champing foam
Where were they suddenly?
                         And suddenly they knew

Like turning in a bed, and settling to sleep
The share sank

With a hard sigh, the furrow-slice sprawled over

And they bowed again to their worship.

V

The last friendly angels
Lifting their knees out of the earth, their clay-balled fetlocks
Heads down praying

And lifting me with them, into their furnace

I walked in their flames

Their long silk faces, shag-haired as old sheepdogs
Their brown eyes, like prehistoric mothers
Their mouse-belly mouths, their wire-spring whiskers
Sudden yellow teeth of the nightmare and skull

Wading the earth's wealth   10
In a steam of dung and sweat, to soft horse-talk

Nodding and slow in their power, climbing the sky

On the crumbling edge.

Winter

The Warrior of Winter

He met the star his enemy
    They fought the woods leafless.
He gripped his enemy.
    They trampled fields to quag.
His enemy was stronger.
    A star fought against him.

He fought his losing fight
    Up to the neck in the river.
Grimly he fought in gateways,
    He struggled among stones.   10
He left his strength in puddles.
    The star grew stronger.

Rising and falling
    He blundered against houses.
He gurgled for life in ditches.
    Clouds mopped his great wounds.

His shattered weapons glittered.
　　The star gazed down.

Wounded and prisoner
　　He slept on rotten sacking.
He gnawed bare stalks and turnip tops
　　In the goose's field.
The sick sheep froze beside him.
　　The star was his guard.

With bones like frozen plumbing
　　He lay in the blue morning.
His teeth locked in his head
　　Like the trap-frozen fox.
But he rejoiced a tear in the sun.
　　Like buds his dressings softened.

20

30

Christmas Card

You have anti-freeze in the car, yes,
　　But the shivering stars wade deeper.
Your scarf's tucked in under your buttons,
　　But a dry snow ticks through the stubble.
Your knee-boots gleam in the fashion,
　　But the moon must stay

　　　　And stamp and cry
　　　　As the holly the holly
　　　　Hots its reds.

Electric blanket to comfort your bedtime
　　The river no longer feels its stones.
Your windows are steamed by dumpling laughter
　　The snowplough's buried on the drifted moor.
Carols shake your television
　　And nothing moves on the road but the wind

　　　　Hither and thither
　　　　The wind and three
　　　　Starving sheep.

Redwings from Norway rattle at the clouds
　　But comfortless sneezers puddle in pubs.
The robin looks in at the kitchen window

10

20

But all care huddles to hearths and kettles.
The sun lobs one wet snowball feebly
  Grim and blue

    The dusk of the coombe
    And the swamp woodland
    Sinks with the wren.

See old lips go purple and old brows go paler.
  The stiff crow drops in the midnight silence.
Sneezes grow coughs and coughs grow painful.
  The vixen yells in the midnight garden.
You wake with the shakes and watch your breathing
  Smoke in the moonlight – silent, silent.

    Your anklebone
    And your anklebone
    Lie big in the bed.

December River

After the brown harvest of rains, express lights
Are riding behind bare poles.

As the flood clears to cider and shrinks a little,
Leaves spinning and toiling in the underboil,
I go to find salmon.

A frost-fragility hangs.
Duck-eggshell emptiness, bare to the space-freeze.
Jupiter crucified and painful. Vapour-trails keen as incisions.

Blackly
Crusty tricorne sycamore leaves are tick-tocking down
To hit the water with a hard tiny crash.

From under the slag-smoke west
The molten river comes, bulging,
With its skin of lights.

Too late now to see much
I wade into the unfolding metals.

This vein from the sky is the sea-spirit's pathway.

Here all year salmon have been their own secret.
They were the heavy slipperiness in the green oils.

20   The steady name – unfathomable –
In the underbrow stare-darkness.

They leapfrogged the river's fifty-mile ladder
With love-madness for strength,
Weightlifting through all its chimneys of tonnage

And came to their never-never land – to these
Gutters the breadth of a tin bath.
And dissolved

Into holes of obviousness. Anchored in strongholds
Of a total absence. Became
30   The transparency of their own windows.

So, day in day out, this whole summer
I offered all I had for a touch of their wealth –
I found only endlessly empty water.

But I go now, in near-darkness,
Frost, and close to Christmas, and am admitted
To glance down and see, right at my heel,
A foot under, where backwater mills rubbish,
Like a bleached hag laid out – the hooked gape
And gargoyle lobster-claw grab

40   Of a dead salmon, and its white shirt-button eye.

That grimace
Of getting right through to the end and beyond it –
That helm
So marvellously engineered

Discarded, an empty stencil.
A negative, pale
In the dreggy swirlings
Of earth's already beginning mastication.

I freed it, I wanted to get it
50   Wedged properly mine
While the moment still held open.

As I lifted its child-heavy rubbery bulk
Marbled crimson like an old woman's fire-baked thigh

The shallows below lifted
A broad bow-wave lifted and came frowning
Straight towards me, setting the whole pool rocking,

And slid under smoothness into the trench at my feet.

Into the grave of steel
Which it could still buckle.

New Year Song

Now there comes
  The Christmas rose
    But that is eerie
               too like a ghost
    Too like a creature
               preserved under glass
    A blind white fish
               from an underground lake
    Too like last year's widow
               at a window
               And the worst cold's to come.

Now there comes
  The tight-vest lamb
    With its wriggle eel tail
               and its wintry eye
    With its ice-age mammoth
               unconcern
    Letting the aeon
               seconds go by
    With its little peg hooves
               to dot the snow
    Following its mother
               into worse cold and worse
               And the worst cold's to come.

Now there come
  The weak-neck snowdrops
    Bouncing like fountains
               and they stop you, they make you
    Take a deep breath
               make your heart shake you

10

Such a too much of a gift
                         for such a mean time
     Nobody knows
                    how to accept them
     All you can do
                   is gaze at them baffled
                   And the worst cold's to come.

And now there comes
  The brittle crocus
     To be nibbled by the starving hares
                         to be broken by snow
     Now comes the aconite
                   purpled by cold
     A song comes into
                   the storm-cock's fancy
     And the robin and the wren
                   they rejoice like each other
In an hour of sunlight
                   for something important
                         Though the worst cold's to come.

Snow and Snow

Snow is sometimes a she, a soft one.
   Her kiss on your cheek, her finger on your sleeve
In early December, on a warm evening,
   And you turn to meet her, saying 'It's snowing!'
       But it is not. And nobody's there.
       Empty and calm is the air.

Sometimes the snow is a he, a sly one.
   Weakly he signs the dry stone with a damp spot.
Waifish he floats and touches the pond and is not.
Treacherous-beggarly he falters, and taps at the window.
       A little longer he clings to the grass-blade tip
       Getting his grip.

Then how she leans, how furry foxwrap she nestles
   The sky with her warm, and the earth with her softness.
How her lit crowding fairytales sink through the space-silence
   To build her palace, till it twinkles in starlight –

Too frail for a foot
  Or a crumb of soot.

Then how his muffled armies move in all night
  And we wake and every road is blockaded   20
Every hill taken and every farm occupied
  And the white glare of his tents is on the ceiling.
    And all that dull blue day and on into the gloaming
    We have to watch more coming.

Then everything in the rubbish-heaped world
  Is a bridesmaid at her miracle.
Dunghills and crumbly dark old barns are bowed in the chapel
  of her sparkle,
    The gruesome boggy cellars of the wood
    Are a wedding of lace   30
    Now taking place.

The Warm and the Cold

Freezing dusk is closing
  Like a slow trap of steel
On trees and roads and hills and all
  That can no longer feel.
    But the carp is in its depth
      Like a planet in its heaven.
    And the badger in its bedding
      Like a loaf in the oven.
    And the butterfly in its mummy
      Like a viol in its case.   10
    And the owl in its feathers
      Like a doll in its lace.

Freezing dusk has tightened
  Like a nut screwed tight
On the starry aeroplane
  Of the soaring night.
    But the trout is in its hole
      Like a chuckle in a sleeper.
    The hare strays down the highway
      Like a root going deeper.   20
    The snail is dry in the outhouse

Like a seed in a sunflower.
The owl is pale on the gatepost
Like a clock on its tower.

Moonlight freezes the shaggy world
Like a mammoth of ice –
The past and the future
Are the jaws of a steel vice.
But the cod is in the tide-rip
Like a key in a purse.
The deer are on the bare-blown hill
Like smiles on a nurse.
The flies are behind the plaster
Like the lost score of a jig.
Sparrows are in the ivy-clump
Like money in a pig.

Such a frost
The flimsy moon
Hast lost her wits.

A star falls.

The sweating farmers
Turn in their sleep
Like oxen on spits.

UNCOLLECTED (1976–77)

He called

Near the door, under the square of light.

Only a fly
Landed on his lip.

He tried to feel death. He dreamed a person
Numbed in icy petroleum

Burning, and in the nest of flames
Becoming a huge cockroach –
A thing
That slowly raised a claw to point at him.

He tried to feel life.
He drew aside the curtain of a dead sparrow's eye
That could once lift the head off him, like a chloroform –
It stared dull and worthless.

He shouted
As if mountains had spoken.
                              As if he stood
In the mountainous after-silence
Hearing his voice crumble.

The whole earth
Had turned in its bed
To the wall.

Eclipse

For half an hour, through a magnifying glass,
I've watched the spiders making love undisturbed,
Ignorant of the voyeur, horribly happy.

First in the lower left-hand corner of the window
I saw an average spider stirring. There
In a midden of carcases, the shambles
Of insects dried in their colours,
A trophy den of uniforms, reds, greens,
Yellow-striped and detached wing-frails, last year's
Leavings, parched a winter, scentless – heads,   10
Bodices, corsets, leg-shells, a crumble of shards

In a museum of dust and neglect, there
In the crevice, concealed by corpses in their old wrappings,
A spider has come to live. She has spun
An untidy nearly invisible
Floss of strands, a few aimless angles
Camouflaged as the grey dirt of the rain-stains
On the glass. I saw her moving. Then a smaller,
Just as ginger, similar all over,
Only smaller. He had suddenly appeared.

Upside down, she was doing a gentle
Sinister dance. All legs clinging
Except for those leading two, which tapped on the web,
Trembling it, I thought, like a fly, to attract
The immobile, upside-down male, near the frame,
Only an inch from her. He moved away,
Turning ready to flee, I guessed. Maybe
Fearful of her intentions and appetites:
Doubting. But her power, focussing,
Making no error after the millions of years
Perfecting this art, turned him round
At a distance of two inches, and hung him
Upside down, head under, belly towards her.
Motionless, except for a faint
And just-detectable throb of his hair-leg tips.
She came closer, upside down, gently,
And enmeshed his forelegs in hers.

So, I imagined, here is the famous murder.
I got closer to watch. Something
Difficult to understand, difficult
To properly observe was going on.
Her two hands seemed swollen, like tiny crab-claws.
Those two nippers she folds up under her nose
To bring things to her pincers, they were moving,
Glistening. He convulsed now and again.
Her abdomen pod twitched – spasmed slightly
Little mean ecstasies. Was she pulling him to pieces?
Something much more delicate, a much more
Delicate agreement was in process.
Under his abdomen he had a nozzle –
Presumably his lumpy little cock,
Just as ginger as the rest of him, a teat,

An infinitesimal nipple. Probably
Under a microscope it is tooled and designed
Like some micro-device in a space rocket.
To me it looked crude and simple. Far from simple,
Though, were her palps, her boxing-glove nippers –
They were like the mechanical hands
That manipulate radio-active matter
On the other side of safe screen glass.   60
But hideously dexterous. She reached out one,
I cannot imagine how she saw to do it,
And brought monkey-fingers from under her crab-nippers
And grasped his nipple cock. As soon as she had it
A bubble of glisteny clear glue
Ballooned up from her nipper, the size of her head,
Then shrank back, and as it shrank back
She wrenched her grip off his cock
As if it had locked there, and doubled her fistful
Of shining wet to her jaw-pincers   70
And rubbed her mouth and underskin with it,
Six, seven stiff rubs, while her abdomen twitched,
Her tail-tip flirted, and he hung passive.
Then out came her other clutcher, on its elbow,
And grabbed his bud, and the gloy-thick bubble
Swelled above her claws, a red spur flicked
Inside it, and he jerked in his ropes.
Then the bubble shrank and she twisted it off
And brought it back to stuff her face-place
With whatever it was. Very still,   80
Except for those stealths and those twitchings
They hung upside down, face to face,
Holding forelegs. It was still obscure
Just what was going on. It went on.
Half an hour. Finally she backed off.
He hung like a dead spider, just as he'd hung
All the time she'd dealt with him.
I thought it must be over. So now, I thought,
I see the murder. I could imagine now
If he stirred she'd think he was a fly,   90
And she'd be feeling ravenous. And so far
She'd shown small excitement about him
With all that concentration on his attachment,
As if he upside down were just the table

Holding the delicacy. She moved off.
Aimlessly awhile she moved round,
Till I realized she was concentrating
On a V of dusty white, a delta
Of floss that seemed just fuzz. Then I could see
100   How she danced her belly low in the V.
I saw her fitting, with accurate whisker-fine feet,
Blobs of glue to the fibres, and sticking others
To thicken and deepen the V, and knot its juncture.
Then she danced in place, belly down, on this –
Suddenly got up and hung herself
Over the V. Sitting in the cup of the V
Was a tiny blob of new whiteness.
A first egg? Already? Then very carefully
She dabbed at the blob, and worked more woolly fibres
110   Into the V, to either side of it,
Diminishing it as she dabbed. I could see
I was watching mighty nature
In a purposeful mood, but not what she worked at.
Soon, the little shapeless dot of white
Was a dreg of speck, and she left it. She returned
Towards her male, who hung still in position.
She paused and laboriously cleaned her hands,
Wringing them in her pincers. And suddenly
With a swift, miraculously-accurate snatch
120   Took something from her mouth, and dumped it
On an outermost cross-strand of web –
A tiny scrap of white – refuse, I thought,
From their lovemaking. So I stopped watching.
Ten minutes later they were at it again.
Now they have vanished. I have scrutinized
The whole rubbish tip of carcases
And the window-frame crannies beneath it.
They are hidden. Is she devouring him now?
Or are there still some days of bliss to come
130   Before he joins her antiques. They are hidden
Probably together in the fusty dark,
Holding forearms, listening to the rain, rejoicing
As the sun's edge, behind the clouds,
Comes clear of our shadow.

Pets

A dark November night, late. The back door wide.
Beyond the doorway, the step off into space.
On the threshold, looking out,
With foxy-furry tail lifted, a kitten.
Somewhere out there, a badger, our lodger,
A stripe-faced rusher at cats, a grim savager,
Is crunching the bones and meat of a hare
Left out for her nightly emergence
From under the outhouses.

The kitten flirts his tail, arches his back –   10
All his hairs are inquisitive.
Dare he go for a pee?
Something is moving there, just in dark.
A prowling lump. Grows. A tabby tom.
And the battered master of the house
After a month at sea, comes through the doorway.

Recovered from his nearly fatal mauling,
Two, probably three pounds heavier
Since that last time he dragged in for help.
He deigns to recognise me   20
With his criminal eyes, his deformed voice.
Then poises, head lowered, muscle-bound,
Like a bull for the judges,
A thick Devon bull,
Sniffing the celebration of sardines.

Green Mother

I am the pillow where angels come for the sleeper.

Grey-long-eyed and silvery-limbed, a tremor, a girl, strong-fingered
With the washed voice of a thrush,
Glistening wet – the angel of the ash

A toppling tower of gargoyles and ogres –
With a voice of splitting, a sulphur-glare
And a numbness
The angel of the oak lifts his trophy

Slow and charred from the furnace, in red-oiled strength,
Crippled with overcoming, the angel of the yew
Cradles the molten dove, which is his voice.

Every flower sends an angel.

And the worm leans down –
A forgiving God.

And you shall climb with the angels
Of the insects – the trembling hosts of light
The chivalry of sun and moon
On the field of the leaf.

And from heaven to heaven
You shall enter the heaven of the birds – the trumpets
The heaven of the beasts – who labour in the foundations
The heaven of the fish – banners in the long flame
Of the beginning

Many heavens, none of them fallen.

Do not think I am the stone of the grave.

I pillow the face of everliving.

Lie down – rejoice!
                    among roots, among mouths.

[Caprichos]

Who lives in my skin with me?
Who takes me
For his one opportunity?
Who ignores
Everything I properly am
To be what I am not more freely?

Who sleeps
Most of my days as if he were defunct?
Who is it gets up wild
Just where I sink down most carefully calm?
Who belongs
Like a conger eel in a night-storm sea
Where I am lost?

Who corrupts me
Borrows me with a laugh
Strips off my ugliness
Then savagely gets so much more out of me
Than I can
And gives me myself back
Unrecognisable?

Refuses all explanation or comment
Just laughs

Sets the sun, sets the dogs
Laughing at me

*

If the mouth could properly open
If the ear could only unplug itself
If the eyes could only split their blinds and peep through finally

If the leverage of the arms
Could get a proper purchase
And if the feet could move in the right direction

If the head could get upright and the body upright
If the whole body would only balance

If the skin would cover and take messages
And do its job properly

If the heart would just stay in place
Just concentrate and apply itself steadily

If only that shadow there, out there in front of me
Were my shadow, obeying me, some proof

If only the words coming from this throat
Were my words

*

When dawn lifts the eyelid behind the eyelid
A night knowledge

Sinks to the roots of hair
To the seed of bone-marrow

A gravity pulls down the dark knowledge
A black hole gravity

A swallowing galaxy absence
Pulls against the ridges of hair

The faint peaks of blood
Pulls the smile sad.

So light yawns her dumb salivas
Dragging the whole face into a web of slow earth roots.

This is the baby-scream. This is the real sun.
This is what lifts the ribs through the breast

A keel older than the Himalayas.

*

Nevertheless rejoice
Rejoice rejoice

This is the shriek out of scissors
Two hundred feet above ground

The surgery overture, the heron's grace
Vomited between blades

Likewise the famished adoration
Smoking from the trachea
And from the altar of the fat and the lean
Past a malodorous tongue

With the actual absolution of all hurt
In hydrochloric acids

The heron alights – folding a whole sky
The heron stalks – up to the knees in soul
Up to the crest in shimmering equipoise

Singing:
In the nothingness of man I delight and of all being.

from GAUDETE (1977)

[The Epilogue Poems]

What will you make of half a man
Half a face
A ripped edge

His one-eyed waking
Is the shorn sleep of aftermath

His vigour
The bone-deformity of consequences

His talents
The deprivations of escape

How will you correct
The veteran of negatives
And the survivor of cease?

＊

I hear your congregations at their rapture

Cries from birds, long ago perfect
And from the awkward gullets of beasts
That will not chill into syntax.

And I hear speech, the bossed Neanderthal brow-ridge
Gone into beetling talk
The Java Man's bone grinders sublimed into chat.

Words buckle the voice in tighter, closer
Under the midriff
Till the cry rots, and speech

Is a fistula

Eking and deferring
Like a stupid or a crafty doctor
With his year after year
Of sanguinary nostrums
Of almosts and their tomorrows

Through a lifetime of fees.

＊

Who are you?

The spider clamps the bluefly – whose death panic
Becomes sudden soulful absorption.

A stoat throbs at the nape of the lumped rabbit
Who watches the skylines fixedly.

Photographs of people – open-mouthed
In the gust of being shot and falling

And you grab me
So the blood jumps into my teeth

And 'Quick!' you whisper, 'O quick!'
And 'Now! Now! Now!'

Now what?

That I hear the age of the earth?

That I feel
My mother lift me up from between her legs?

*

At the top of my soul
A box of dolls.

In the middle of my soul
A circus of gods.

At the bottom of my soul
The usual mess of squabblers.

In front of me
A useful-looking world, a thrilling weapon.

Behind me
A cave

Inside the cave, some female groaning
In labour –

Or in hunger –

Or in fear, or sick, or forsaken –

Or –

At this point, I feel the sun's strength.
I take a few still-aimless happy steps.

*

The lark sizzles in my ear
Like a fuse –

A prickling fever
A flush of the swelling earth –

When you touch his grains, who shall stay?

Over the lark's crested tongue
Under the lark's crested head
A prophecy

From the core of the blue peace

From the sapphire's flaw

From the sun's blinding dust

*

I watched a wise beetle
Walking about inside my body

I saw a tree
Grow inward from my navel

Hawks clashed their courtship
Between my ears.

Slowly I filled up with the whole world.
Only one thing stayed outside me, in the glare.

You beckoned.

*

In a world where all is temporary
And must pass for its opposite

The trousseau of the apple
Came by violence into my possession.

I neglected to come to degree of nature
In the patience of things.

I forestalled God –

I assailed his daughter.

Now I lie at the road's edge.
People come and go.

Dogs watch me.

＊

Collision with the earth has finally come –
How far can I fall?

A kelp, adrift
In my feeding substance

A mountain
Rooted in stone of heaven

A sea
Full of moon-ghost, with mangling waters

Dust on my head
Helpless to fit the pieces of water
A needle of many Norths

Ark of blood
Which is the magic baggage old men open
And find useless, at the great moment of need

Error on error
Perfumed
With a ribbon of fury

＊

Trying to be a leaf
In your kingdom
For a moment I am a leaf
And your fullness comes

And I reel back
Into my face and hands

Like the electrocuted man
Banged from his burst straps

＊

I heard the screech, sudden –
Its steel was right inside my skull

It scraped all round, inside it
Like the abortionist's knife.

My blood lashed and writhed on its knot –
Its skin is so thin, and so blind,
And earth is so huge, so hard, wild
And so nearly nothing
And so final with its gravity stone –

My legs, though, were already galloping to help
The woman who wore a split lopsided mask –

That was how the comedy began.

Before I got to her – it was ended
And the curtain came down.

But now, suddenly,
Again the curtain goes up.

This is no longer the play.

The mask is off.

*

Once I said lightly
Even if the worst happens
We can't fall off the earth.

And again I said
No matter what fire cooks us
We shall be still in the pan together.

And words twice as stupid.
Truly hell heard me.

She fell into the earth
And I was devoured.

*

Music, that eats people
That transfixes them
On its thorns, like a shrike
To cut up at leisure

Or licks them all over carefully gently
Like a tiger

Before leaving nothing but the hair of the head
And the soles of the feet

Is the maneater
On your leash.

But all it finds of me, when it picks me up

Is what you have
Already
Emptied and rejected.

*

The rain comes again
A tightening, a prickling in
On the soft-rotten gatepost.

But the stars
Are sunbathing
On the shores
Of the sea whose waves

Pile in from your approach
An unearthly woman wading shorewards
With me in your arms

The grey in my hair.

*

This is the maneater's skull.
These brows were the Arc de Triomphe
To the gullet.

The deaf adder of appetite
Coiled under. It spied through these nacelles
Ignorant of death.

And the whole assemblage flowed hungering through the long ways.
Its cry
Quieted the valleys.

It was looking for me.

I was looking for you.

You were looking for me.

*

I see the oak's bride in the oak's grasp.

Nuptials among prehistoric insects
The tremulous convulsion
The inching hydra strength
Among frilled lizards
Dropping twigs, and acorns, and leaves.

The oak is in bliss
Its roots
Lift arms that are a supplication
Crippled with stigmata
Like the sea-carved cliffs earth lifts
Loaded with dumb, uttering effigies
The oak seems to die and to be dead
In its love-act.

As I lie under it

In a brown leaf nostalgia

An acorn stupor.

*

She rides the earth
On an ass, on a lion.
She rides the heavens
On a great white bull.

She is an apple.
Whoever plucks her
Nails his heart
To the leafless tree.

*

The huntsmen, on top of their swaying horse-towers,
Faces raw as butcher's blocks, are angry.
They have lost their fox.

They have lost most of their hounds.
I can't help.

The one I hunt
The one
I shall rend to pieces

Whose blood I shall dab on your cheek

Is under my coat.

*

A primrose petal's edge
Cuts the vision like laser.

And the eye of a hare
Strips the interrogator naked
Of all but some skin of terror –
A starry frost.

Who is this?
She reveals herself, and is veiled.
Somebody

Something grips by the nape
And bangs the brow, as against a wall
Against the untouchable veils

Of the hole which is bottomless

Till blood drips from the mouth.

*

Waving goodbye, from your banked hospital bed,
Waving, weeping, smiling, flushed
It happened
You knocked the world off, like a flower-vase.

It was the third time. And it smashed.

I turned
I bowed
In the morgue I kissed
Your temple's refrigerated glazed
As rained-on graveyard marble, my
Lips queasy, heart non-existent

And straightened
Into sun-darkness

Like a pillar over Athens

Defunct

In the blinding metropolis of cameras.

*

I said goodbye to earth
I stepped into the wind
Which entered the tunnel of fire
Beneath the mountain of water

I arrived at light
Where I was shadowless
I saw the snowflake crucified
Upon the nails of nothing

I heard the atoms praying
To enter his kingdom
To be broken like bread
On a dark sill, and to bleed.

*

The swallow – rebuilding –
Collects the lot
From the sow's wallow.

But what I did only shifted the dust about.
And what crossed my mind
Crossed into outer space.

And for all rumours of me read obituary.
What there truly remains of me
Is that very thing – my absence.

So how will you gather me?

I saw my keeper
Sitting in the sun –

If you can catch that, you are the falcon of falcons.

*

The night wind, muscled with rain,
Is going to tug out
The trees like corks –

Just as in the dream –
A voice quaking lit heaven
The stone tower flies.

A night
To scamper naked
To the dry den

Where one who would have devoured me is driven off

By a wolf.

⁎

The viper fell from the sun
Jerked and lay in the road's dust,
Started horribly to move, as I watched it.

A radiant goose dropped from a fire-quake heaven,
Slammed on to earth beside me
So hard, it bounced me off my feet.

Something dazzling crashed on the hill field,
Elk-antlered, golden-limbed, a glowing mass
That started to get up.

I stirred, like a discarded foetus,
Already grey-haired,
In a blowing of bright particles.

A hand out of a hot cloud
Held me its thumb to suck.

Lifted me to the dug that grew
Out of the brow of a lioness.

⁎

A doctor extracted
From my blood its tusk

Excavated
The mountain-root from my body

Excised
The seven-seas' spring from under my eye-tooth

Emptied my skull
Of clouds and stars

Pounded up what was left
Dried it and lit it and read by its flame
A story to his child

About a God
Who ripped his mother's womb
And entered it, with a sword and a torch

To find a father.

*

The coffin, spurred by its screws,
Took a wrong turning.

The earth can't balance its load
Even to start.

The creaking heavens
Will never get there.

As for me
All I have

For an axle

Is your needle
Through my brains.

*

The grass-blade is not without
The loyalty that never was beheld.

And the blackbird
Sleeking from common anything and worm-dirt
Balances a precarious banner
Gold on black, terror and exultation.

The grim badger with armorial mask
Biting spade-steel, teeth and jaw-strake shattered,

Draws that final shuddering battle cry
Out of its backbone.

Me too,
Let me be one of your warriors.

Let your home
Be my home. Your people
My people.

        *

Churches topple
Like the temples before them.

The reverberations of worship
Seem to help
Collapse such erections.

In all that time
The river
Has deepened its defile
Has been its own purification

Between your breasts

Between your thighs

        *

I know well
You are not infallible

I know how your huge your unmanageable
Mass of bronze hair shrank to a twist
As thin as a silk scarf, on your skull,
And how your pony's eye darkened larger

Holding too lucidly the deep glimpse
After the humane killer

And I had to lift your hand for you

While your chin sank to your chest
With the sheer weariness
Of taking away from everybody
Your envied beauty, your much-desired beauty

Your hardly-used beauty

Of lifting away yourself
From yourself

And weeping with the ache of the effort

        *

The sun, like a cold kiss in the street —
A mere disc token of you.

Moon — a smear
Of your salivas, cold, cooling.

Bite. Again, bite.

*

Sometimes it comes, a gloomy flap of lightning,
Like the flushed gossip
With the tale that kills

Sometimes it strengthens very slowly
What is already here —
A tree darkening the house.

The saviour
From these veils of wrinkle and shawls of ache

Like the sun
Which is itself cloudless and leafless

Was always here, is always as she was.

*

Having first given away pleasure —
Which is hard —
What is there left to give?
There is pain.

Pain is hardest of all.
It cannot really be given.

It can only be paid down
Equal, exactly,
To what can be no part of falsehood.

This payment is that purchase.

*

Looking for her form
I find only a fern.

Where she should be waiting in the flesh
Stands a sycamore with weeping letters.

I have a memorial too.

Where I lay in space
Is the print of the earth which trampled me

Like a bunch of grapes.

Now I am being drunk
By a singing drunkard.

*

A man hangs on
To a bare handful of hair.

A woman hangs on
To a bare handful of flesh.

Who is it
Reaches both hands into the drop

Letting flesh and hair
Follow if they can?

*

When the still-soft eyelid sank again
Over the stare
Still bright as if alive

The chiselled threshold
Without a murmur
Ground the soul's kernel

Till blood welled.

And your granite –
Anointed –
Woke.

Stirred.

*

The sea grieves all night long.
The wall is past groaning.
The field has given up –
It can't care any more.

Even the tree
Waits like an old man
Who has seen his whole family murdered.

Horrible world

Where I let in again –
As if for the first time –
The untouched joy.

*

Hearing your moan echo, I chill. I shiver.

I know
You can't stay with those trees.

I know
The river is only fabled to be orphan.

I know
The flowers also look for you, and die looking.

Just as the sun returns every day
As if owned.

Like me
These are neither your brides, nor your grooms.

Each of us is nothing
But the fleeting warm pressure

Of your footfall

As you pace
Your cage of freedom.

*

Faces lift out of the earth
Moistly-lidded, and gazing unfocussed
Like babies new born.

And with cries like the half-cry
Of a near-fatally wounded person
Not yet fallen, but already unconscious.

And these are the ones
Who are trying to tell
Your name.

From age to age
Nothing bequeathed
But a gagged yell

A clutchful of sod

And libraries
Of convalescence.

*

I skin the skin
Take the eye from the eye
Extract the entrails from the entrails

I scrape the flesh from the flesh
Pluck the heart
From the heart
Drain away the blood from the blood

Boil the bones till nothing is left
But the bones

I pour away the sludge of brains
Leaving simply the brains

Soak it all
In the crushed-out oil of the life

Eat

Eat

*

What steel was it the river poured
Horizontally
Into the sky's evening throat –

Put out the sun.

The steel man, in his fluttering purples,
Is lifted from the mould's fragments.

I breathe on him

Terrors race over his skin.

He almost lives

Who dare meet you.

*

Calves harshly parted from their mamas
Stumble through all the hedges in the country
Hither thither crying day and night
Till their throats will only grunt and whistle.

After some days, a stupor sadness
Collects them again in their field.
They will never stray any more.
From now on, they only want each other.

So much for calves.
As for the tiger
He lies still
Like left luggage

He is roaming the earth light, unseen.

He is safe.

Heaven and hell have both adopted him.

*

A bang – a burning –
I opened my eyes
In a vale crumbling with echoes.

A solitary dove
Cries in the tree – I cannot bear it.

From this centre
It wearies the compass.

Am I killed?
Or am I searching?

Is this the rainbow silking my body?

Which wings are these?

*

The dead man lies, marching here and there
In the battle for life, without moving.

He prays he will escape for what comes after.
At least that he'll escape. So he lies still.

But it arrives
Invisible as a bullet
And the dead man flings up his arms
With a cry
Incomprehensible in every language

And from that moment
He never stops trying to dance, trying to sing
And maybe he dances and sings

Because you kissed him.

If you miss him, he stays dead
Among the inescapable facts.

     *

Every day the world gets simply
Bigger and bigger
And smaller and smaller

Every day the world gets more
And more beautiful

And uglier and uglier.

Your comings get closer.
Your goings get worse.

     *

Your tree – your oak
A glare

Of black upward lightning, a wriggling grab
Momentary
Under the crumbling of stars.

A guard, a dancer
At the pure well of leaf.

Agony in the garden. Annunciation
Of clay, water and the sunlight.
They thunder under its roof.
Its agony is its temple.

Waist-deep, the black oak is dancing
And my eyes pause
On the centuries of its instant
As gnats
Try to winter in its wrinkles.

The seas are thirsting
Towards the oak.

The oak is flying
Astride the earth.

   *

Glare out of just crumpled grass –
Blinded, I blink.

Glare out of muddled clouds –
I go in.

Glare out of house-gloom –
I close my eyes.

And the darkness too is aflame.

So you have come and gone again
With my skin.

UNCOLLECTED (1977–78)

He Gets Up in Dark Dawn

To misted stillness.
First thrush splutters and chips at the thick light.
Suddenly the room leaps, blue-lit. Was it lightning?
Then the crumplings and the bamboo splittings
In echoey heaven-corridors, of close thunder.

He listens for the rain and it starts.
Taptap on the roof. The birds too,
Gurgling and exercising their highest and their lowest
And all the twisting stairs from one to the other,
Singing in dark holds of young leaves and unopened blossoms,   10
Not knowing who lives in the house, or who has lived,
Or what year this is, or what century this is.

Through thick vapour swaddle
Violet lightning shakes its shutters
And thunder trundles its drums from the highest attic
Of heaven to the lowest, furthest basement.
He stands in the open door and cannot go fishing.

He sits hearing his kettle. Lightning again
Tosses the kitchen, the birds bustle their voices
Squibby-damp, echoless, but not daunted   20
Out in the nodding, dripping, flickering, blue garden.
The thunder splits and lets its domes collapse.
Ginger, his cat, tenses and rises listening
To the step by step approach of the thunder

As if ghosts were creaking all over the house.
His head sleeks very slender, with ears
That want both to prick listening and to flatten.
Thunder unloads its last stamping arrival
As the lights jump in and out – the sky is falling –
He flattens –   30

His master explains with quiet, meaningless words.

Unknown Warrior

At curious eyes
He was conscripted

At sly fingers
He was equipped

At aimed perfume
He was armed

At bowel-churning glance
He received orders

At curl behind ear
He put on the helmet of dread

At sea-bottom mouth
He entered the trench and saw wounds

At lightly-disguised throat
He lay all night, on trembling earth

At sudden breasts
He went over the top

At wild thighs
He fell and rose again wet

At open belly
Battle-fury took his mind from him

At Mons
He found his monument

After the Grim Diagnosis

He just laughed the same – as after
A near-miss mishap
At the rifle-club. After the first operation,
The flame-scar between his eyes, from forehead
To nostril, he just clowned
A comical face. And the shops, and his pals, and his job
Told him nothing had altered. He only had
His old silly self. Then for a year, daily,
His body grew more and more grave.

It was searching for its speech.
But he just shrugged, and chuckled T.V.

Suddenly he tired.
He lay down. Visibly his body
Began translating him with difficulty
Into its meanings. It took
A long time.
Hideous effort.
Finally
It spoke.

And the whole countryside flew up like a scared bird.
His darling Jensen, his wife and kids, his firm's
Near world-monopoly, and all his friend's voices
Just flew away with earth and heaven in a blur

From the puff of breath
Left hanging
Where there had been a crematorium.

1952–77

A Nation's a soul.
A Soul is a Wheel
With a Crown for a Hub
To keep it whole.

A Solstice

Drip-tree stillness. Spring-feeling elation
Of mid-morning oxygen. There is a yeasty simmering
Over the land – all compass points are trembling,
Bristling with starlings, hordes out of Siberia,
Bubbly and hopeful.

We stand in the mist-rawness
Of the sodden earth. Four days to Christmas.
We can hear the grass seeping.
                              Now a wraith-smoke
Writhes up from a far field, condenses

On a frieze of goblin hedge-oaks, sizzling
Like power-pylons in mist.

We ease our way into this landscape.
Casual midnightish draughts, in the soaking stillness.
Itch of starlings is everywhere.
                                        The gun
Is old, rust-ugly, single-barrelled, borrowed
For a taste of English sport. And you have come
From eighteen years Australian estrangement
And twelve thousand miles in thin air
To walk again on the small hills of the West,
In the ruby and emerald lights, the leaf-wet oils
Of your memory's masterpiece.
                                        Hedge-sparrows
Needle the bramble-mass undergrowth
With their weepy warnings.
                                        You have the gun.
We harden our eyes. We are alert.
The gun-muzzle is sniffing. And the broad land
Tautens into wilder, nervier contrasts
Of living and unliving. Our eyes feather over it
As over a touchy detonator.

Bootprints between the ranks of baby barley
Heel and toe we go
Narrowed behind the broad gaze of the gun
Down the long woodside. I am your dog.

Now I get into the wood. I push parallel
And slightly ahead of you – the idea
Is to flush something for the gun's amusement.
I go delicate. I don't want to panic
My listeners into a crouch–freeze.
I want them to keep their initiative
And slip away, confident, impudent,
Out across your front.
                                        Pigeons, too far,
Burst up from under the touch
Of our furthest listenings. A bramble
Claws across my knee, and a blackbird
Five yards off explodes its booby-trap
Shattering wetly

Black and yellow alarm-dazzlings, and a long string
Of fireworks down the wood. It settles
To a hacking chatter and that blade-ringing –
Like a flint on an axe-head.
                                        I wait.
That startled me too.   50
I know I am a Gulliver now
Tied by my every slightest move
To a thousand fears. But I move –
And a jay, invisibly somewhere safe,
Starts pretending to tear itself in half
From the mouth backward. With three screams
It scares itself to silence.
                                        The whole wood
Has hidden in the wood. Its mossy tunnels
Seem to age as we listen. A raven
Dabs a single charcoal toad-croak   60
Into the finished picture.

                                        I come out
To join you in the field. We need a new plan
To surprise something.
                                        But as I come over the wire
You are pointing, silent.
I look. One hundred yards
Down the woodside, somebody
Is watching us.

A strangely dark fox
Motionless in his robe of office
Is watching us. It is a shock.   70

Too deep in the magic wood, suddenly
We meet the magician.
                                        Then he's away –
A slender figurine, dark and witchy,
A rocking nose-down lollop, and the load of tail
Floating behind him, over the swell of faint corn
Into the long arm of woodland opposite.

The gun does nothing. But we gaze after
Like men who have been given a secret sign.
We are studying the changed expression

80   Of that straggle of scrub and poor trees
      Which is now the disguise of a fox.

      And the gun is thinking. The gun
      Is working its hunter's magic.
      It is transforming us, there in the dull mist,
      To two suits of cold armour –
      Empty of all but a strange new humming,
      A mosquito of primaeval excitements.

      And as we start to walk out over the field
      The gun smiles.

90   The fox will be under brambles.
      He has set up all his antennae,
      His dials are glowing and quivering,
      Every hair adjusts itself
      To our coming.

                            Will he wait in the copse
      Till we've made our move, as if this were a game
      He is interested to play?
      Or has he gone through and away over further fields,
      Or down and into the blueish mass and secrecy
      Of the main wood?

100   Under a fat oak, where the sparse copse
      Joins the main wood, you lean in ambush.

      Well out in the field, talking to air
      Like quiet cogs, I stroll to the top of the strip –
      Then pierce it, clumsy as a bullock, a careless trampling
      Like purposeless machinery, towards you,
      Noisy enough for you to know
      Where not to point your blind gun.

      Somewhere between us
      The fox is inspecting me, magnified.
110   And now I tangle all his fears with a silence,
      Then a sudden abrupt advance, then again silence,
      Then a random change of direction –

      And almost immediately –
      Almost before I've decided we are serious –
      The blast wall hits me, the gun bang bursts

Like a paper bag in my face,
The whole day bursts like a paper bag –

But a new world is created instantly
With no visible change.

I pause. I call. You do not answer.   120
Everything is just as it had been.
The corroded blackberry leaves,
The crooked naked trees, fingering sky
Are all the usual careful shapes
Of the usual silence.

I go forward. And now I see you,
As if you had missed,
Leaning against your tree, casual.

But between us, on the tussocky ground,
Somebody is struggling with something.   130

An elegant gentleman, beautifully dressed,
Is struggling there, tangled with something,
And biting at something
With his flashing mouth. It is himself
He is tangled with. I come close
As if I might be of help.
But there is no way out.
It is himself he is biting,
Bending his head far back, and trying
To bite his shoulder. He has no time for me.   140
Blood beneath him is spoiling
The magnificent sooted russet
Of his overcoat, and the flawless laundering
Of his shirt. He is desperate
To get himself up on his feet,
And if he could catch the broken pain
In his teeth, and pull it out of his shoulder,
He still has some hope, because
The long brown grass is the same
As it was before, and the trees   150
Have not changed in any way,
And the sky continues the same –

It is doing the impossible deliberately
To set the gun-muzzle at his chest

And funnel that sky-bursting bang
Through a sudden blue pit in his fur
Into the earth beneath him.

He cannot believe it has happened.

His chin sinks forward, and he half-closes his mouth
160   In a smile
Of ultimate bitterness,
And half closes his eyes
In a fineness beyond pain –

And it is a dead fox in the dank woodland.
And you stand over him
Meeting your first real Ancient Briton
In eighteen years.
And I stand awake – as one wakes
From what feels like a cracking blow on the head.

170   That second shot has ruined his skin.
We chop his tail off
Thick and long as a forearm, and black.
Then bundle him and his velvet legs
His bag of useless jewels,
The phenomenal technology inside his head,
Into a hole, under a bulldozed stump,
Like picnic rubbish. There the memory ends.

We must have walked away.

New Foal

Yesterday he was nowhere to be found
In the skies or under the skies.

Suddenly he's here – a warm heap
Of ashes and embers, fondled by small draughts.

A star dived from outer space – flared
And burned out in the straw.
Now something is stirring in the smoulder.
We call it a foal.

Still stunned
10   He has no idea where he is.

His eyes, dew-dusky, explore gloom walls and a glare doorspace.
Is this the world?
It puzzles him. It is a great numbness.

He pulls himself together, getting used to the weight of things
And to that tall horse nudging him, and to this straw.

He rests
From the first blank shock of light, the empty daze
Of the questions –
What has happened? What am I?

His ears keep on asking, gingerly.   20

But his legs are impatient,
Recovering from so long being nothing
They are restless with ideas, they start to try a few out,
Angling this way and that,
Feeling for leverage, learning fast –

And suddenly he's up

And stretching – a giant hand
Strokes him from nose to heel
Perfecting his outline, as he tightens
The knot of himself.   30
                          Now he comes teetering
Over the weird earth. His nose
Downy and magnetic, draws him, incredulous,
Towards his mother. And the world is warm
And careful and gentle. Touch by touch
Everything fits him together.

Soon he'll be almost a horse.
He wants only to be Horse,
Pretending each day more and more Horse
Till he's perfect Horse. Then unearthly Horse
Will surge through him, weightless, a spinning of flame   40
Under sudden gusts,

It will coil his eyeball and his heel
In a single terror – like the awe
Between lightning and thunderclap.

And curve his neck, like a sea-monster emerging
Among foam,

And fling the new moons through his stormy banner,
And the full moons and the dark moons.

Wycoller Hall

Such long ago see-saw of fortunes
Such toiling of sword-edge and saddle
So much dispossession repossession
Such juggling of Bishops and Kings
So many crucial oaths
So much outward blood and inward joy

So much forgetting of cries
So much determination so much money
So many tons of stone
So many oaks and sawyers and dust
So much energy staring at slant rain
Collapsing into the hill

Such spreading of farms so many tenants
So many couriers so much reckoning
Such coming and going of horses so many horses
Such study of dynasties and tithes
Such studied intermixture of bloods
Such tennis of heraldic emblems

So many generations of leaves
Such flitting of Queens so much re-arming
Such splitting of oak such tread of scripture
Such vigilance of portraits
So much repairing of roofs
Such steely clash of young voices
And old voices, so many feasts
So much merriment between lit faces
So much argument of deeds and holdings

So many years of wedded satisfaction
So many departures, solemn departures
Excited departures, dutiful departures
Such sudden returns, dreaded returns

Such joyful returns, so many returns
Such perpetual returning, so many hooves

So many hopes, so much laughter
So many births
So much sudden punishment by God
So much bitter logic of God
So much sword-length of God
So much blood, such speech-hardening
So many hooves

So much relaxing of memory
So many visitors, so many sunny breakfasts
So much noise of children so many coaches
So much news so many new gowns

So many funerals
So much weeping, so many decisions
So many mornings at the mirror
So much effort
So many years of rain-smoke dimming the hill
Such shrinkage of lands
So many lonely winters of ailment
Hearing the trees and the flood river

So many hours of prayer
So much worship of the old house

So much stubborn history in the old dark house
So much seasoning of old darkening stone
So much safety inside the dark stone
Of the old house, so many lit evenings
So many footfalls listening to themselves
Through the echoing beauty of the old house
Such furious hooves such hatred
Such screams
So many documents

Such vintage of pain

Drained finally to the dregs
Tumbled stones and a dry emptiness

The cup shattered

from ORTS (1978)

1

The fallen oak sleeps under the bog
Assuming new centuries
Of black strength.

It is nursing a hope
Of being disinterred in some good age
And lovingly carved into a hard body
For the goddess of oaks.

It does not care
That the sun will split it with light.

The acorn, in its nightmare of pigs,
Has no less of a hope.

The leaf-skeleton, lifted away by autumn,
Inconsequential as the wings of a crane-fly,
Has a hope.

2

Let that one shrink into place
Camouflaged and doggo
Under his eye-wall
Like an over-looked lizard.

Let the madman thrash in his pram
And the fool harden his opinion
And the man of bile
Deify his will,

And that one, the eagle-nosed, the broad-handed
Be above the battle – i.e. lie
Carcase under it, cheek turned
To the propitiation of the blow-fly.

Let you keep one world nearer the world
Simple as those puffball rabbits
Who multiply themselves, in abandon and joy

For what seem to be foxes.

3

The Queen of Egypt
Sent me a swallow
From beyond the last lighthouse star

Out of some atom's Africa
A swallow
Flutter-falling down here onto my chest
Too bloodied and weary, where it huddled,

To remember its errand.

4

You have come down from the clouds
From the sea, from the earlier
Dew of the earth.

Better than oxygen to me.

You run you pool your smiles your glancings
And are full of pictures of the greenery
Weirdly whorled, a world of clear wonders.

Waiting for nothing pirouetting at obstacles.

Till your deepest quiet is a circling
Collecting egg-pebbles, tops of dandelions,
Revolving your next rush, your ringing break-out.

5

Skin
Made out of the company of grass.

Grass pricked it
In its language
Smelling fellow earth, but somehow nervous.

Skin tightened
Suppressing its reflex
Shudder of dawn —

Thinking, it is beginning, just fingerings
At my knots,
Then will come rippings, and drenchings of
                                    world-light

And my naked joy
Will be lifted out with shouts of joy –

And if that is the end of me
Let it be the end of me.

6

Air

Nosed the new burrow of flesh
Where something alive hid.

The ear, like a sand-lion,
Twitched to capture the air.

The air, no matter what it held,
Could not satisfy the ear.

And the dumb ear could not cry out
Its secret.

The air, doting but neuter,
Brought everything it found.

The ear, closer and closer to despair
Humoured this trinket love.

While the wound without cure
Raged and starved.

7

At some juncture the adult dies
And shells off

The soft parts, heart and vitals,
Get a new skin, or perish.

The naked hunter, the soul-gambler,
Bleating like a calf

Summons the man-eater of a thousand men.
Sometimes it comes.

Whoever wins
He will be wearing its skin.

A sage
Or royally insane.

8

So much going on
Round the apple tree.

A door swinging gently, creak-soft,
To the congregation of airs.

A doorway, with movements, incense, voices
Beyond it.

The tree-creeper inches up, abrupt inches,
Clockwork expert,

Accepting fat offerings
From the steady face of dark flame, so steady,
The furnace's flame-surface

So naked, slender
A shiverer, a girl tree

A god's
Vertical altar.

9

Huge global trouble all to earn
Money to dress up
To go out to eat.

After the fishbone,
After the meat-sauce cooled and glued to the plate,
After the unsatisfactory coffee

A cigarette prolongs the after-comfort,
The yawning deprivation
Into anaesthesia.

Smoke-haze, laughter,
To sit on, bored and tired,
Clinging together with words

Is only human

As the fly-leg in the spider's web

Is all that can be found of the fly.

14

Sunday bells
Dangle their mouths
Down the body's well

Acrobat laughter
Fling their skirts
And gambol their leg-joints

Fat cast-iron
Can-can angels
Pound me to dust.

The Sunday bells
Jam their mouths
In the head's light –

But you have bolted.

You flee, you flee
Helpless as grass.

Iron hounds
Tumble across country

Soon lost
In your wide lands

15

The volcano
Stifles in its landmark of cinders.

The brain
In its city dump of scrap iron.

Both confuse
Their rebirth and being blown to bits.

The cinders leak sulphur.

The scrap-iron pins up a condemned god.

17

The white shark
With its strength of madness

The mutt-faced hyena
Trailing its half-dance

The rat
With its file

The gull, vomiting its laughter
And gulping it in again
Like intestines hanging from the mouth

– the thorn
With its petals.

18

Eye went out to hunt you.
It vanished.

Nostril mounted a search party.
It vanished.

Ear followed the trail.
No more was heard of it.

Hands, heavily armed, combed the whole country.
Returned empty.

Now mouth
Sits in the tree of silence

Over cry
Tethered as bait.

Cry just cries.

19

He sickened
For that one's lecherous pallor.   He sickened
For that one's elvish sideglance – dainty
As the skull of a weasel.

He sickened for that one's long smoothness
And her flanks lithe as a fish.   He sickened
For that one's long dugs
Her oil-silk underthigh.   He sickened

For that one's yellow wolf rankness, her vulturous maw.

For that one's cool salivas
Like the root of a bluebell
He sickened.   He sickened

For that one's dirty feet in sandals
For that one's crazy yells and claws
For this one's this and that one's that

As the blacktongued explorer, gibbering prayers,
Gulps the hoofprint.

21

Searching, I am confronted again
By the tottering masks of the chestnut.

A subterrene laughter of annulment.
The earth's own visage thrust through my torn thinkings.

Strip off all such!
Let me come
Blind against bare.

That third, the Creation, will end us two
Unless we twist together quickly

A knot of the one iron
Of non-existence.

24

The buzzard mews –
A soaring parabola
That flares and is swirled off
On the flood-wind, above the tree-thunder.

Airs pouring and piling everywhere
Over the year's threshold
Where the bare ash-poles clash.

Your passenger or your skiff?

Tossed at a loss, no more mooring
Than a last year's leaf –

Again the rocket lobbing the safety rope
To the surge-clogged hull
Drops short into the welter –

I am still visible, though.

26

Where shall I put my hand?
Where shall I put my head?
What shall I do with my legs?
I don't understand myself.

All this machinery
Is just lumber
Till you start work.

And when you start –
In no time, it produces
A new world.
Hurry, hurry, my love, my love,
I rest, I rust.

Soon enough I start falling to pieces.

27

Words bring wet lumps of earth
Sometimes a whiff of smoke
Sometimes blood and hair
Sometimes they peg their noses.

A fox's mask flayed from its skull
Annihilated by its own toughness
Redolent with fat
Suffering the face of emptiness –

Whatever is laid on an altar
Has to wait.

28

Sitting under the downpour
Of the dead poet's lament for a burned people
I forgot for an hour

This other people
Who eat dung
Who dangle in torture silence
Beyond the last gasp
Sometimes seeming to smile
Who dig their own graves, who simply wait

Through the long numbness of their exile

From the places where they stand.

29

They brought you a lit-up flying city –
You let it fly away to the moon.

They brought you a magic hat,
You could put your hands in and just wish –
A whole lifetime of wishes was in there for you.
You left it for the birds to nest in.

You only wanted back your only toy –
Your battered naked old doll.

And when they tried to keep it from you
You went crazy.

They thought you were a half-wit.

30

The mother of the tree
Is a tree.

And a tree
Is the tree's daughter.

The mother of horses are horses.
Horses are the daughters of horses.

So it comes to be
That the sun's daughter
Is the mother of the sun.

So the thrones of things
Keep words
For catspaws and fools.

31

If searching can't find you

Show me that corner
Where I can sit, your prisoner,
Till you come.

As my blood, waiting for food – its god,
Is a prisoner in my darkness,
And cannot thrive anywhere else.

As a fig-tree, burdened with figs,
In its trench of rubble
Is a prisoner.

32

Before I was born, you were a spirit.

When I got into this graveyard
I started my search.
Everywhere I unearthed you

Stuck in marriage, like a decaying tooth
In an imbecile's mouth.

33

Where you wait

Everything is waiting.
The tree stilled in tree – swells in waiting.
The river stilled in flow – in away-flow push.

Even the birds, here and gone –
The sparrowhawk, bolt out of the oak-tree
Slamming the crying dipper
Down through the water-hatch

To hold its breath in bubble-cellar safety

Are waiting.

34

Stilled at his drink
Old, in his body's deadfall.
His body fills the whole stage.

Spirit has all evaporated
Coolly as alcohol

From the bulbous blue weldings
Of his knuckles, from his whiskery eyesockets.
Illusion
Cannot raise the energy.

General closure
Has confessed him.

Throat of primordial Iguana
Brain of dried herbs.

He sits – idol of some extinct religion.
The dust worships his feet.

He stares
Into – some wateriness.

Jilted
For the last time.

37

Your eyes are poor,
Your mind over-preoccupied,
Your heart given wholly elsewhere.

Why did you make me
Support me this long and this far
Just to forget me now?

To let my words
Beat air like wings of those flies
Which live only one hour?

Tell me
Is your silence your deafness in a great din –
In a bell, a gigantic bell

Its voice too huge too all-inclusive
For my hearing

And which holds you, too, dazed and deafened?

38

Better, happier, to stay clear of the pure
Water of the source

Drink it and your throat is cleansed
But you can drink nothing else

Drink it and your head is cleared
But the world smells of decay

Drink it and your face is altered
Like one returned from a long journey

Except that you never return
Your body returns, your eyes with their colour

Hungry for company, famished for a kiss
Famished especially for the kiss

But you – the you you have to die with – stays
Stone of the stone hill where the water

Brims so pure it is tasteless.

40

After years of methodical, daily,
Laborious, deliberate
Building up muscles
Comes a day
The slightest effort starts everything trembling.

After a lifetime's patient
Wearing the eyes out
And the brain-cells
The library is sold.

Body and mind, you see,
Get nowhere.

You will have to carry something

O lady.

41

Like the future oak invisible
In the warp of soil and rock.

Like the drunken weddings of peace
In the trench-struggle

Like tomorrow morning's marvellous stag
On today's field of picnickers

This planetary rawness,
This mangling of frenzy
And exhaustion, of aimless elation
And stone-dullness

That empties me every instant

Pulses your fullness.

42

The bulging oak is not as old
As the crooked tree of blood
In the body of the girl
Who marvels at it.

The tree, too, knows its owner.

When she walked away the history oak
That leaned over immortal water
Fell in a flurry of shadows
Ghosting away downstream.

43

A cry is coming closer

Like a child coming up the road
Leaves blood somewhere
Keeps staggering bones together

Has lost all the jigsaw of words
Searches round cloud comes out at teeth
Will be revenged on the walls

Shrinks itself into dust
Hangs onto an angel that keeps crashing further up the road
Bores its head into the road

Grows enraged grows huge has swallowed the sun gags
Is amazed, tries to surface, recovers
Eats eats earth, earth cry gulps too much like salt water
Lifts eyes like little gutted animals
Lifts mouth broken with dirt
But has found itself, is tightly in its own hand

Will not be denied

Is coming home, is happy

Slowly opens its ocean

44

He did all that he thought he wanted to do
He had what people called luck
And opportunities
Which he took.

He had what was called love
So much such a weight of it
The axle broke
On the cart of everything that was not love.

In the end
He found he had been learning a language
In school.
Now he comes to the land where it is spoken.

And he understands nothing. And he is dumb.

45

Why do you take such nervy shape to become
A victim, so violin-like?

The Inquisitors have caught you.
Now you are under the discretion

Of their fingers and smiles.
'Where do you come from?'

You cannot speak their tongue.
You can only cry wordlessly

Crying sideways
From the eyes of men, to the shut doors

Of the dust-grains. Shaking the dust

Of the wrong world.

46

You have made me careless.
There is a callous
Of jumping into a volcano.

At the top of the hill
The furnace flue
Rolls out unconcern.

Inside the hill
Lashed with rods
The joyful singers
Fracture with their sweat
Red-hot stones.

These are not people.
Their initiation
Was inhuman cruelty.
Each one has murdered
The poor fool he was.

You scare me.

48

Does it matter how long
A stone glows in the fire?
In an hour it will be cold.

Does it matter how much
I want to pour myself
Into your goblet?
The bottle's form is of hard glass.

Like a man walking in the park
I stand in court.

Like a judge
You sentence me to you for life.

Like an explorer
I search the highest peaks for the source
At the centre of the earth.

And there, at the highest of the high,
I shall have to find it.

49

The salmon's egg winters the gouging floods
Among giants and gods, hammers and anvils,
The protecting pebbles.

Its chances are quite slight.

As the humanising skull
Weathers the glaciations
Among blades and club-axes.

Its chances are nearly nil.

Their only hope – your help.

Stay with me.
And stay me.

50

Your touch jerks me –

As a fish jerked into air makes nothing
Of the suddenly opened world

The gape of earth's face
Reclaiming all bones and flesh.

Your touch opens the dead to life
Like the great plains
Photographed slow black with buffalo

The horizons
Their earth-quake millstone, their circling dust hung dance

In a flash glare –

Held as long as the breath lasts –

That shuts on gravel and sparrow silence.

51

Churches darken like scabs
Over wounds
I bring from a war
In my mother's belly –

The leaves, like my words
Are content to stay near,
Amusing me,
But their ways can never be my ways.

They can talk, they can sing, dance –
Or simply lean
In their warrior metals
Watching the late sky lose colour.

But I
Still lie on the battlefield
Where you move, with water.

52

As often as I affirm
I illume
A midnight match and am
A sniper aiming.

Till now I hear
'Is', 'am', or 'are'
As the last round
Of a last stand.

And 'I do'
As the doomed charge
Of a hurt leopard
That might have recovered.

So do not deny
So say nothing
So my love
Flourish like life.

53

In the zoo
The animals are imprisoned
For life.
Misery of concrete and steel.
It is worse
That they can't feel guilty.
Bafflement

Stares from every mirror
Whichever escapes, ten to one

Will be killed.

Now you have opened the door –

What?

54

The engine under the car-bonnet
Works, works, works –
It never reaches you.

The factories utter
Artefacts of perfect intention –
You accept none.

The listening of all heads, and their message,
The web of world they service,
Do not catch one tremor of your nearness.

Is the world of men
A dead end?
Correct the direction finder.

Let me find you
Without losing the water, or the air, or the fire,

Or the earth.

55

By the splitting, spilling, fly-crazing
Honeypot buds

By the calf's drunken eye
As he butts his mammy's hot udder
With milk-plastered face, the milk unspooling
From his foamy muzzle as he pauses
To weigh up the watcher

By the hills of such mass
Of such poise it is unthinkable
And they seem moored at a haze-thought

You steppingstone from nothingness

Across the shoreless

56

The cat, craning over the long grass,
Helplessly alert
As the needle trembles for North

Was getting nowhere
Waiting for the vole to unfreeze
Its concealment.

Till I strolled past, scattering general alarm.
Just so, the world strolled past, unthinking,
And in my to-fro distraction

You snatched me up and you carry me off
To cry –
As the dangling vole morses its fear –

All that remains of resistance.

57

The cut stone
Is that much lost to the mountain.
It stands thereafter, like a horse,
In harness of human manipulation.

And the horse, staring hatefully over the hedge,
Has diminished the horse
By one horse.

At what shade of theft
Did man and woman steal
Man and woman

From the work they were born for

And hide them?

60

Twisted mouths
Can still tell what hurts.

False faces
Can still declare their wants.

The dumb
Can drive their appeal to the head.

Everywhere there is something
Not to be doubted.

Even in me, a column of doubts
As a column of midges is of midges,

Is something not to be doubted.

61

A wild drop flies in space –

With appearance on it of lands, of clouds.
Actually, with cities and peoples.
The people are reading newspapers,
Nodding their heads towards each other
Hurrying in opposite directions
And lying staring at windows –

All know they have lost you.
And you have lost them.
That drop is your tear for what you have lost.

It is populated spookily
Like a crystal ball
By your heart-broken idea
Of what you search for,

For what you hope, still, somewhere, to find.

62

He sits grinning, he blurts laughter
Sits on shiftless
Listening any old chat
And comical gossip giggle

Bulldozers pushing
Away slowly ahead away
The cemetery mask of mind

As your hand pushes aside the chickweed
And you see yourself
Bending from the sky behind you

To sip.

CAVE BIRDS (1978)

An Alchemical Cave Drama

The Scream

There was the sun on the wall – my childhood's
Nursery picture. And there my gravestone
Shared my dreams, and ate and drank with me happily.

All day the hawk perfected its craftsmanship
And even through the night the miracle persisted.

Mountains lazed in their smoky camp.
Worms in the ground were doing a good job.

Flesh of bronze, stirred with a bronze thirst,
Like a newborn baby at the breast,
Slept in the sun's mercy.   10

And the inane weights of iron
That come suddenly crashing into people, out of nowhere,
Only made me feel brave and creaturely.

When I saw little rabbits with their heads crushed on roads
I knew I rode the wheel of the galaxy.

Calves' heads all dew-bristled with blood on counters
Grinned like masks where sun and moon danced.

And my mate with his face sewn up
Where they'd opened it to take something out
Lifted a hand –   20

He smiled, in half-coma,
A stone temple smile.

Then I, too, opened my mouth to praise –

But a silence wedged my gullet.

Like an obsidian dagger, dry, jag-edged,
A silent lump of volcanic glass,

The scream
Vomited itself.

The Summoner

Spectral, gigantified,
Protozoic, blood-eating.

The carapace
Of foreclosure.

The cuticle
Of final arrest.

Among crinkling of oak-leaves – an effulgence,
Occasionally glimpsed.

Shadow stark on the wall, all night long,
From the street-light. A sigh.

Evidence, rinds and empties,
That he also ate here.

Before dawn, your soul, sliding back,
Beholds his bronze image, grotesque on the bed.

You grow to recognize the identity
Of your protector.

Sooner or later –
The grip.

After the First Fright

I sat up and took stock of my options.
I argued my way out of every thought anybody could think
But not out of the stopping and starting
Catherine wheel in my belly.
The disputation went beyond me too quickly.
When I said: 'Civilization',
He began to chop off his fingers and mourn.
When I said: 'Sanity and again Sanity and above all Sanity',
He disembowelled himself with a cross-shaped cut.
I stopped trying to say anything.
But then when he began to snore in his death-struggle
The guilt came.
And when they covered his face I went cold.

The Interrogator

Small hope now for the stare-boned mule of man
Lumped on the badlands, at his concrete shadow.

This bird is the sun's keyhole.
The sun spies through her. Through her

He ransacks the camouflage of hunger.

Investigation
By grapnel.

Some angered righteous questions
Agitate her craw.

The blood-louse   10
Of ether.

With her prehensile goad of interrogation
Her eye on the probe

Her olfactory X-ray
She ruffles the light that chills the startled eyeball.

Later, a dripping bagful of evidence
Under her humped robe,

She sweeps back, a spread-fingered Efreet,
Into the courts of the afterlife.

She Seemed So Considerate

And everything had become so hideous
My solemn friends sat twice as solemn
My jokey friends joked and joked

But their heads were sweating decay,
Like dead things I'd left in a bag
And had forgotten to get rid of.

I bit the back of my hand
And sniffed mortification.

Then the bird came.
She said: 'Your world has died.'   10
It sounded dramatic.

But my potted pet fern, the one fellow spirit I still cherished,
It actually had withered.

As if Life had decided to desert me.
As if it saw more hope for itself elsewhere.

Then this winged being embraced me saying:
'Look up at the sun. I am the one creature
Who never harmed any living thing.'

I was glad to shut my eyes, and be held.
20   Whether dead or unborn, I did not care.

The Judge

The pondering body of the law teeters across
A web-glistening geometry.

Lolling, he receives and transmits
Cosmic equipoise.

The offal-sack of everything that is not
The Absolute on to whose throne he lowers his buttocks.

Clowning, half-imbecile,
A Nero of the unalterable.

His gluttony
10   Is a strange one – his leavings are guilt and sentence.

Hung with precedents as with obsolete armour
His banqueting court is as airy as any idea.

At all hours he comes wobbling out
To fatten on the appeal of those who have fouled

His tarred and starry web.

Or squats listening
To his digestion and the solar silence.

The Plaintiff

These are the wings and beak of light!

This is your moon of pain – and the wise night-bird
Your smile's shadow.

This bird
Is the life-divining bush of your desert.

The heavy-fruited, burning tree
Of your darkness.

How you have nursed her!

Her feathers are leaves, the leaves tongues,
The mouths wounds, the tongues flames   10

The feet
Roots

Buried in your chest, a humbling weight
That will not let you breathe.

Your heart's winged flower
Come to supplant you.

In These Fading Moments I Wanted to Say

How close I come to flame
Just watching sticky flies play

How I cry unutterable outcry
Reading the newspaper that smells of stale refuse

How I just let the excess delight
Spill out of my eyes, as I walk along

How imbecile innocent I am

So some perfect stranger's maiming
Numbs me in freezing petroleum
And lights it, and lets me char to the spine   10

Even the dusty dead sparrow's eye
Lifts the head off me – like a chloroform

But she was murmuring: 'Right from the start, my life
Has been a cold business of mountains and their snow
Of rivers and their mud

Yes there were always smiles and one will do a lot
To be near one's friends
But after the bye-byes, even while the door was closing, even
    while the lips still moved
The scree had not ceased to slip and trickle
20   The snow-melt was cutting deeper
Through its anaesthetic
The brown bulging swirls, where the snowflakes vanished into
    themselves
Had lost every reflection.'

The whole earth
Had turned in its bed
To the wall.

The Executioner

Fills up
Sun, moon, stars, he fills them up

With his hemlock –
They darken

He fills up the evening and the morning, they darken
He fills up the sea

He comes in under the blind filled-up heaven
Across the lightless filled-up face of water

He fills up the rivers he fills up the roads, like tentacles
10   He fills up the streams and the paths, like veins

The tap drips darkness darkness
Sticks to the soles of your feet

He fills up the mirror, he fills up the cup
He fills up your thoughts to the brims of your eyes

You just see he is filling the eyes of your friends
And now lifting your hand you touch at your eyes

Which he has completely filled up
You touch him

You have no idea what has happened
To what is no longer yours   20

It feels like the world
Before your eyes ever opened

The Accused

Confesses his body –
The gripful of daggers.

And confesses his skin – the bedaubed, begauded
Eagle-dancer.

His heart –
The soul-stuffed despot.

His stomach –
The corpse-eating god.

And his hard life-lust – the blind
Swan of insemination.   10

And his hard brain – sacred assassin.

On a flame-horned mountain-stone, in the sun's disc,
He heaps them all up, for the judgement.

So there his atoms are annealed, as in X-rays,
Of their blood-aberration –

His mudded body, lord of middens, like an ore,

To rainbowed clinker and a beatitude

First, the Doubtful Charts of Skin

Came into my hands – I set out.

After some harmless, irrelevant marvels
And much boredom at sea

Came the wrecked landfall, sharp rocks, hands and knees
Then the small and large intestine, in their wet cave.
These gave me pause.

Then came the web of veins
Where I hung so long
For the giant spider's pleasure, twitching in the darkest corner.

10   Finally
After the skull-hill of visions and the battle in the valley of screams

After the islands of women

I came to loose bones
On a heathery moor, and a roofless church.

Wild horses, with blowing tails and manes,
Standing among tombs.

And a fallen menhir, my name carved into it,
And an epitaph:
'Under this rock, he found weapons.'

The Knight

Has conquered. He has surrendered everything.

Now he kneels. He is offering up his victory.
Unlacing his steel.

In front of him are the common wild stones of the earth –

The first and last altar
On to which he lowers his spoils.

And that is right. He has conquered in earth's name.
Committing these trophies

To the small madness of roots, to the mineral stasis
10   And to rain.

An unearthly cry goes up.
The Universes squabble over him –

Here a bone, there a rag.
His sacrifice is perfect. He reserves nothing.

Skylines tug him apart, winds drink him,
Earth itself unravels him from beneath —

His submission is flawless.

Blueflies lift off his beauty.
Beetles and ants officiate

Pestering him with instructions.   20
His patience grows only more vast.

His eyes darken bolder in their vigil
As the chapel crumbles.

His spine survives its religion,
The texts moulder —

The quaint courtly language
Of wingbones and talons.

And already
Nothing remains of the warrior but his weapons

And his gaze.   30
Blades, shafts, unstrung bows — and the skull's beauty
Wrapped in the rags of his banner.
He is himself his banner and its rags.

As hour by hour the sun
Deepens its revelation.

Something was Happening

While I strolled
Where a leaf or two still tapped like bluetits

I met thin, webby rain
And thought: 'Ought I to turn back, or keep going?'
Her heart stopped beating, that second.

As I hung up my coat and went through into the kitchen
And peeled a flake off the turkey's hulk, and stood vacantly
    munching
Her sister got the call from the hospital
And gasped out the screech.

In the fifteen seconds
I was scrubbing at my nails and glancing up through the window
She began to burn.

Some, who had been close, walked away
Because it was beyond help now.

They did not stay to see
Her body trying to sit up, her face unrecognizable
With the effort
Of trying to be heard,
Trying to tell
How it went on getting worse and worse –

And when I saw the quince in April tufted again with emerald,
And knew – again everything had got past me
The leather of my shoes
Continued to gleam
The silence of the furniture
Registered nothing

The earth, right to its furthest rims, ignored me.

Only the snow-burned eagle-hunter
Beating himself to keep warm
And bowing towards his trap
Started singing

(Two, three, four thousand years off key).

The Gatekeeper

A reflective sphynx.
A two-headed questioner.

First, a question –
The simple fork in the road.

You seem to choose. It is a formality.
Already yourself has confessed yourself.

All those sweatings and grinnings are redundant.
The candidate is stripped.

So much fear – its weight oozes from you.
No matter, it was upholstering ease,

It was insulation
From this stranger who wails out your name

Then drops, hugging the bare ground
Where everything is too late.

Remorse, promises, a monkey chitter
Blurting from every orifice.

Your cry is like a gasp from a turned corpse
As everything comes back. And a wingspread

Thumps you with its claws. And an eagle
Is flying   20

To drop you into a bog or carry you to eagles.

A Flayed Crow in the Hall of Judgement

All darkness comes together, rounding an egg.
Darkness in which there is now nothing.

A blot has knocked me down. It clogs me.
A globe of blot, a drop of unbeing.

Nothingness came close and breathed on me – a frost
A shawl of annihilation curls me up like a shrimpish foetus.

I rise beyond height – I fall past falling.
I float on a nowhere
As mist-balls float, and as stars.

A condensation, a gleam simplification   10
Of all that pertained.
This cry alone struggles in its tissues.

Where am I going? What will come to me here?
Is this everlasting? Is it
Stoppage and the start of nothing?

Or am I under attention?
Do purposeful cares incubate me?
Am I the self of some spore

In this white of death blackness,
This yoke of afterlife?   20
What feathers shall I have? What is my weakness

Good for? Great fear
Rests on the thing I am, as a feather on a hand.

I shall not fight
Against whatever is allotted to me.

My soul skinned, and my soul-skin pinned out
A mat for my judges.

The Baptist

Enfolds you, as in arms, in winding waters
A swathing of balm

A mummy bandaging
Of all your body's puckering hurts

In the circulation of sea.
A whale of furtherance

Cruises through the Arctic of stone,
Bearing you blindfold and gagged

So you dissolve, in the cool wholesome salts
Like a hard-cornered grief

An iceberg of loss
Shrinking towards the equator

A seed under snow

In its armour.

Only a Little Sleep, a Little Slumber

And suddenly you
Have not a word to say for yourself.

Only a little knife, a small incision,
A snickety nick in the brain
And you drop off, like a polyp.

Only a crumb of fungus,
A pulp of mouldy tinder
And you flare, fluttering, black out like a firework.

Who are you, in the nest among the bones?
You are the shyest bird among birds.   10

'I am the last of my kind.'

A Green Mother

Why are you afraid?
In the house of the dead are many cradles.
The earth is a busy hive of heavens.
This is one lottery that cannot be lost.

Here is the heaven of the tree:
Angels will come to collect you.
And here are the heavens of the flowers:
These are an ever-living bliss, a pulsing, a bliss in sleep.

And here is the heaven of the worm –
A forgiving God.   10
Little of you will be rejected –
Which the angels of the flowers will gladly collect.

And here is the heaven of insects.
From all these you may climb
To the heavens of the birds, the heavens of the beasts, and of the fish.

These are only some heavens
Not all within your choice.
There are also the heavens
Of your persuasion.
Your candle prayers have congealed an angel, a star –   20
A city of religions
Like a city of hotels, a holiday city.
There too I am your guide.
In none of these is the aftertaste of death
Pronounced poor. This earth is the sweetness
Of all the heavens. It is Heaven's mother.

The grave is her breast, her nipple in its dark aura.
Her milk is unending life.

                    You shall see
How tenderly she wipes her child's face clean

Of the bitumen of blood and the smoke of tears.   30

431

As I Came, I Saw a Wood

Where trees craned in dirt, clutching at the sky
Like savages photographed in the middle of a ritual
Birds danced among them and animals took part
Insects too and around their feet flowers

And time was not present none ever stopped
Or left anything old or reached any new thing
Everything moved in an excitement that seemed permanent

They were so ecstatic
I could go in among them, touch them, even break pieces off them
Pluck up flowers, without disturbing them in the least.
The birds simply flew wide, but were not for one moment distracted
From the performance of their feathers and eyes.
And the animals the same, though they avoided me
They did so with holy steps and never paused
In the glow of fur which was their absolution in sanctity

And their obedience, I could see that.

I saw I stood in a paradise of tremblings

At the crowded crossroads of all the heavens
The festival of all the religions

But a voice, a bell of cracked iron
Jarred in my skull

Summoning me to prayer

To eat flesh and drink blood.

A Riddle

Who am I?

Just as you are my father
I am your bride.

As your speech sharpened
My silence widened.

As your laughter fitted itself
My dumbness stretched its mouth wider

As you made good progress
I was torn up and dragged

As you defended yourself   10
I collected your blows, I was knocked backward

As you dodged
I caught in full

As you counter-attacked
I was under your feet

As you saved yourself
I was lost

And so, when you arrived empty,
I gathered up all you had and left you

Now as you abandon yourself to your death   20
I hold your life

Just as surely as you are my father
I shall deliver you

My firstborn
Into a changed, unchangeable world
Of wind and of sun, of rock and water
To cry.

The Scapegoat

The beautiful thing beckoned, big-haunched he loped,
Swagged with wealth, full-organed he tottered,

His sweetnesses dribbled,
His fever misted, he wanted to sob,

His cry starved watering,
Shudderings bone-juddered his hot weakness.

The frilled lizard of cavort
Ran in his wheel like a man, burned by breath.

The baboon of panoply
Jumped at the sky-rump of a greasy rainbow.   10

The flag of the crotch, his glistenings tapered to touch,
Furled and unfurled, in chill draughts of sun.

The comedian
Of the leap out of the body and back in again.

Gargled a mandrake oath
In a sputter of unborn spirits, a huddle of oracles.

The joker
That the confederate pack has to defer to

Gambled and lost the whole body –
An I.O.U. signed by posterity, a smear on the light.

The champion of the swoon
Lolls his bauble head, a puppet, a zombie

And the lord of immortality is a carcase of opals,
A goat of testaments, a wine-skin of riddance,

A slaking of thistles.

After There was Nothing Came a Woman

Whose face has arrived at her mirror
Via the vulture's gullet
And the droppings of the wild dog, and she remembers it
Massaging her brow with cream

Whose breasts have come about
By long toil of earthworms
After many failures, but they are here now
And she protects them with silk

Her bones
Are as they are because they cannot escape anything
They hang as if in space
The targets of every bombardment

She found her belly
In a clockwork pool, wound by the winding and unwinding sea
First it was her toy, then she found its use
She curtains it with a flowered frock
It makes her eyes shine

She looks at the grass trembling among the worn stones

Having about as much comprehension as a lamb
Who stares at everything simultaneously   20
With ant-like head and soldierly bearing

She had made it but only just, just –

The Guide

When everything that can fall has fallen
Something rises.
And leaving here, and evading there
And that, and this, is my headway.

Where the snow glare blinded you
I start.
Where the snow mama cuddled you warm
I fly up. I lift you.

Tumbling worlds
Open my way   10

And you cling.

And we go

Into the wind. The flame-wind – a red wind
And a black wind. The red wind comes
To empty you. And the black wind, the longest wind
The headwind

To scour you.

Then the non-wind, a least breath,
Fills you from easy sources.

I am the needle   20

Magnetic
A tremor

The searcher
The finder

His Legs Ran About

Till they seemed to trip and trap
Her legs in a single tangle

His arms lifted things, felt through dark rooms, at last with
    their hands
Caught her arms
And lay down enwoven at last at last

His chest pushed until it came against
Her breast at the end of everything

His navel fitted over her navel as closely as possible
Like a mirror face down flat on a mirror

And so when every part
Like a bull pressing towards its cows, not to be stayed
Like a calf seeking its mama
Like a desert staggerer, among his hallucinations
Finding the hoof-churned hole

Finally got what it needed, and grew still, and closed its eyes

Then such truth and greatness descended

As over a new grave, when the mourners have gone
And the stars come out
And the earth, bristling and raw, tiny and lost
Resumes its search

Rushing through the vast astonishment.

Walking Bare

What is left is just what my life bought me
The gem of myself.
A bare certainty, without confection.
Through this blowtorch light little enough

But enough.
The stones do not cease to support me.
Valleys unfold their invitations.
A progress beyond assay, breath by breath.

I rest just at my weight.
Movement is still patient with me –   10
Lightness beyond lightness releasing me further.

And the mountains of torment and mica
Pass me by.

Ampler skylines lift wider wings
Of simpler light.

The blood-worn cries have hardened
To moisteners for my mouth.

Hurrying worlds of voices, on other errands,
Traffic through me, ignore me.

A one gravity keeps touching me.   20

For I am the appointed planet
Extinct in an emptiness

But a spark in the inhalation
Of the corolla that sweeps me.

Bride and Groom Lie Hidden for Three Days

She gives him his eyes, she found them
Among some rubble, among some beetles

He gives her her skin
He just seemed to pull it down out of the air and lay it over her
She weeps with fearfulness and astonishment

She has found his hands for him, and fitted them freshly at the wrists
They are amazed at themselves, they go feeling all over her

He has assembled her spine, he cleaned each piece carefully
And sets them in perfect order
A superhuman puzzle but he is inspired   10
She leans back twisting this way and that, using it and
   laughing, incredulous

Now she has brought his feet, she is connecting them
So that his whole body lights up

And he has fashioned her new hips
With all fittings complete and with newly wound coils, all
   shiningly oiled
He is polishing every part, he himself can hardly believe it

They keep taking each other to the sun, they find they can easily
To test each new thing at each new step

And now she smooths over him the plates of his skull
So that the joints are invisible
And now he connects her throat, her breasts and the pit of
   her stomach
With a single wire

She gives him his teeth, tying their roots to the centrepin of his body

He sets the little circlets on her fingertips

She stitches his body here and there with steely purple silk

He oils the delicate cogs of her mouth

She inlays with deep-cut scrolls the nape of his neck

He sinks into place the inside of her thighs

So, gasping with joy, with cries of wonderment
Like two gods of mud
Sprawling in the dirt, but with infinite care

They bring each other to perfection.

The Owl Flower

Big terror descends.

A drumming glare, a flickering face of flames.

Something writhes apart into a signal,
Fiendish, a filament of incandescence.

As it were a hair.

In the maelstrom's eye,
In the core of the brimming heaven-blossom,
Under the tightening whorl of plumes, a mote
Scalds in dews.

A leaf of the earth   10
Applies to it, a cooling health.

A coffin spins in the torque.
Wounds flush with sap, headful of pollen,
Wet with nectar
The dead one stirs.

A mummy grain is cracking its grimace
In the cauldron of tongues.

The ship of flowers
Nudges the wharf of skin.

The egg-stone   20
Bursts among broody petals –

And a staggering thing
Fired with rainbows, raw with cringing heat,

Blinks at the source.

The Risen

He stands, filling the doorway
In the shell of earth.

He lifts wings, he leaves the remains of something,
A mess of offal, muddled as an afterbirth.

His each wingbeat – a convict's release.
What he carries will be plenty.

He slips behind the world's brow
As music escapes its skull, its clock and its skyline.

Under his sudden shadow, flames cry out among thickets.
When he soars, his shape   10

Is a cross, eaten by light,
On the Creator's face.

He shifts world weirdly as sunspots
Emerge as earthquakes.

A burning unconsumed,
A whirling tree –

Where he alights
A skin sloughs from a leafless apocalypse.

On his lens
20   Each atom engraves with a diamond.

In the wind-fondled crucible of his splendour
The dirt becomes God.

But when will he land
On a man's wrist.

Finale

At the end of the ritual
                up comes a goblin.

ADAM AND THE SACRED NINE (1979)

The Song

Did not want the air
Or the distant sky

The song
Did not want the hill-slope from which it echoed

Did not want the leaves
Through which its vibrations ran

Did not want the stones whose indifference
It nevertheless ruffled

Did not want the water

The song did not want its own mouth
Was careless of its own throat
Of the lungs and veins
From which it poured

The song made of joy
Searched, even like a lament

For what did not exist

Pouring out over the empty grave
Of what was not yet born

Adam

Lay defeated, low as water.

Too little lifted from mud
He dreamed the tower of light.

Of a piece with puddles
He dreamed flying echelons of steel.

Rigged only with twigs
He dreamed advancement of bulldozers and cranes.

Wrapped in peach-skin and bruise
He dreamed the religion of the diamond body.

His dream played with him, like a giant tabby.
Like a bitten black-wet mouse, even his morse had ceased.

Open as a leafless bush to wind and rain
He shook and he wept, he creaked and shivered.

Awake!

Awake!   said the flint-faced bird, Awake! Arise!
Get up!   said the harpoon-shaped fish
We were depending on you

Get up!   said the weasel, Or you're no brother
Your weepy look is shaming me, rusting me

Get up!   hissed the thorn leaf
Don't discourage the hosts, they are all watching
Get up!   said the thistle
Do you need to be told how?

Ah God!   said the ant, If we had your strength
Get up!   Get up!   Get up!

All this time his cry

Was a breeze happening to dry grass

And his cry
Was starry wind
Having nothing at all to do with him, just passing

His cry was random atoms
Lamenting a lost gamble

His cry
Was sun-grief
Battering itself
Against the memorial stone of the globe

He had retreated

To the last redoubt of bone.

His skeleton glittered in its hanger of emptiness.
Like the Southern Cross.

The final trophy, the antlers of utter fall,
And one of the elementals – eternal.

Except that a voice sat in his bones.

Beyond birth-pang and the maggot, in the bright sky-crack
    of listening,
A bone star, he trembled.

And the Falcon came

The gunmetal feathers
Of would not be put aside, would not falter.

The wing-knuckles
Of dividing the mountain, of hurling the world away behind him.

With the bullet-brow
Of burying himself head-first and ahead
Of his delicate bones, into the target
Collision.

The talons
Of a first, last, single blow
Of grasping complete the crux of rays.

With the tooled bill
Of plucking out the ghost
And feeding it to his eye-flame

Of stripping down the loose, hot flutter of earth
To its component parts
For the reconstitution of Falcon.

With the eye
Of explosion of Falcon.

The Skylark came

With its effort hooked to the sun, a swinging ladder

With its song
A labour of its whole body
Thatching the sun with bird-joy

To keep off the rains of weariness
The snows of extinction

With its labour
Of a useless excess, lifting what can only fall

With its crest
Which it intends to put on the sun

Which it meanwhile wears itself
So earth can be crested

With its song
Erected between dark and dark

The lark that lives and dies
In the service of its crest.

The Wild Duck

                    got up with a cry

Shook off her Arctic swaddling

Pitched from the tower of the North Wind
And came spanking across water

The wild duck, fracturing egg-zero,
Left her mother the snow in her shawl of stars
Abandoned her father the black wind in his beard of stars

Got up out of the ooze before dawn

Now hangs her whispering arrival
Between earth-glitter and heaven-glitter

Calling softly to the fixed lakes

As earth gets up in the frosty dark, at the back of the Pole Star
And flies into dew
Through the precarious crack of light

Quacking Wake Wake

The Swift comes the swift

Casts aside the two-arm two-leg article –
The pain instrument
Flesh and soft entrails and nerves, and is off.

Hurls itself as if again beyond where it fell among roofs
Out through the lightning-split in the great oak of light

One wing below mineral limit
One wing above dream and number

Shears between life and death

Whiskery snarl-gape already gone ahead
The eyes in possession ahead

Screams guess its trajectory
Meteorite puncturing the veils of worlds

Whipcrack, the ear's glimpse
Is the smudge it leaves

Hunting the winged mote of death into the sun's retina
Picking the nymph of life
Off the mirror of the lake of atoms

Till the Swift
Who falls out of the blindness, swims up
From the molten, rejoins itself

Shadow to shadow – resumes proof, nests
Papery ashes
Of the uncontainable burning.

The Unknown Wren

Hidden in Wren, sings only Wren. He sings.
World-proof Wren
In thunderlight, at wrestling daybreak. Wren unalterable
In the wind-buffed wood.

Wren is here, but nearly out of control –
A blur of throbbings –
Electrocution by the god of wrens –
A battle-frenzy, a transfiguration –

447

Wren is singing in the wet bush.
His song sings him, every feather is a tongue
He is a song-ball of tongues –
The head squatted back, the pin-beak stretching to swallow the sky

And the wings quiver-lifting, as in death-rapture
Every feather a wing beating,
Wren is singing Wren – Wren of Wrens!
While his feet knot to a twig.

Imminent death only makes the wren more Wren-like
As harder sunlight, and realler earth-light.
Wren reigns! Wren is in power!
Under his upstart tail.

And when Wren sleeps even the star-drape heavens are a dream
Earth is just a bowl of ideas.

But now the lifted sun and the drenched woods rejoice with
    trembling –

WREN OF WRENS!

And Owl

Floats, a masked soul listening for death.
Death listening for a soul.
Small mouths and their incriminations are suspended.
Only the centre moves.

Constellations stand in awe. And the trees very still, the fields
    very still
As the Owl becalms deeper
To stillness.
Two eyes, fixed in the heart of heaven.

Nothing is neglected, in the Owl's stare.
The womb opens and the cry comes
And the shadow of the creature
Circumscribes its fate. And the Owl

Screams, again ripping the bandages off
Because of the shape of its throat, as if it were a torture
Because of the shape of its face, as if it were a prison
Because of the shape of its talons, as if they were inescapable.

Heaven screams. Earth screams. Heaven eats. Earth is eaten.

And earth eats and heaven is eaten.

The Dove Came

Her breast big with rainbows
She was knocked down

The dove came, her wings clapped lightning
That scattered like twigs
She was knocked down

The dove came, her voice of thunder
A piling heaven of silver and violet
She was knocked down

She gave the flesh of her breast, and they ate her
She gave the milk of her blood, they drank her

The dove came again, a sun-blinding

And ear could no longer hear

Mouth was a disembowelled bird
Where the tongue tried to stir like a heart

And the dove alit
In the body of thorns.

Now deep in the dense body of thorns
A soft thunder
Nests her rainbows.

The Crow came to Adam

And lifted his eyelid
And whispered in his ear

Who has heard the Crow's love-whisper?
Or the Crow's news?

Adam woke.

And the Phoenix has come

Its voice
Is the blade of the desert, a fighting of light
Its voice dangles glittering
In the soft valley of dew

Its voice flies flaming and dripping flame
Slowly across the dusty sky
Its voice burns in a rich heap
Of mountains that seem to melt

Its feathers shake from the eye
Its ashes smoke from the breath

Flesh trembles
The altar of its death and its birth

Where it descends
Where it offers itself up

And naked the newborn
Laughs in the blaze

Light

Eased eyes open, showed leaves.

Eyes, laughing and childish
Ran among flowers of leaves
And looked at light's bridge
Which led from leaf, upward, and back down to leaf.

Eyes, uncertain
Tested each semblance.
Light seemed to smile.

Eyes ran to the limit
To the last leaf
To the least vein of the least flower-leaf.

Light smiled
And smiled and smiled.

Eyes
Darkened

Afraid suddenly
That this was all there was to it.

Bud-tipped twig

Touched nipple.
The tree recoiled, aloof, still wintry.

Feathery grass-plume touches
Stroked across nipple
And the grass fled, shrinking, queerly far off.

Brambles by chance clawed breast
Sprang off, and reached quietly elsewhere
Still green-tender, otherworldly.

Clouds tumbled their godly beds
Drawing a vast coldness
Over the breast.

The sea, preoccupied with moon and sun
With earth's centre, with its own substance and the laws of waves
Made the breast feel lost.

Breast lifted its simple face
To the sun.
The first beggar.

Unable to see
Or to hear
Or to cry.

The sole of a foot

Pressed to world-rock, flat
Warm

With its human map
Tough-skinned, for this meeting
Comfortable

The first acquaintance of the rock-surface
Since it was star-blaze,
The first host, greeting it, gladdened

With even, gentle squeeze
Grateful
To the rock, saying

I am no wing
To tread emptiness.
I was made

For you.

REMAINS OF ELMET (1979)

The Dark River

Six years into her posthumous life
My uncle raises my mother's face. He says
Yes, he would love a cup of tea.

Her memory still intact, still good
Under his baldness.
Her hands a little plumper, trembling more
Chatter his cup in its saucer.

Keeping their last eighty years alive and attached to me.
Keeping their strange depths alive and attached to me.

And now he restores his prime   10
Exercising everything that happened,
As his body tries to renew its cells –

Empty air, hijacked in the larynx
To fly a dream, populated with glimpses –

And the smoky valley never closes,
The womb that bore him, chimney behind chimney,
Horizons herded – behind encircling horizons,
A happy hell, the arguing, immortal dead,
The hymns rising past farms.

So he has brought me my last inheritance: 20
Archaeology of the mouth: the home fire's embers,
Fluff, breath-frail, from under the looms of Egypt.
Funeral treasures that crumble at the touch of day –
The huge fish, the prize of a lifetime,
Exhausted at the surface, the eye staring up at me,
But on such a frayed, fraying hair-fineness –

Any moment now, a last kick –
And the dark river will fold it away.

Abel Cross, Crimsworth Dene

Where the Mothers
Gallop their souls

Where the howlings of heaven
Pour down on to earth

Looking for bodies
Of birds, animals, people

A happiness starts up, secret and wild,
Like a lark-song just out of hearing
Hidden in the wind

A silent evil joy
Like a star-broken stone
Who knows nothing more can happen to it
In its cradle-grave.

Hardcastle Crags

'Think often of the silent valley, for the god lives there.'
But here the leaf-loam silence
Is old siftings of sewing machines and shuttles,
And the silence of ant-warfare on pine-needles
Is like the silence of clogs over cobbles,
And the beech-tree solemnities
Muffle much cordite.

In a deep gorge under palaeolithic moorland
Meditation of conifers, a hide-out of elation,
Is a grave of echoes.
Name-lists off cenotaphs tangle here to mystify
The voice of the dilapidated river
And picnickers who paddle in the fringes of fear.
Far above, mown fields escape like wings.

But happiness is now broken water at the bottom of a precipice
Where the red squirrel drops shavings from a branch-end of survival
And beech-roots repair a population
Of fox and badger. And the air-stir releases
The love-murmurs of a generation of slaves
Whose bones melted in Asia Minor.

Lumb Chimneys

Days are chucked out at night.
The huge labour of leaf is simply thrown away.
Great yesterdays are left lying.

Nose upwind, the slogging world
Cannot look aside or backward.

Brave dreams and their mortgaged walls are let rot in the rain.
The dear flesh is finally too much.
Heirloom bones are dumped into wet holes.
And spirit does what it can to save itself alone.

Nothing really cares. But soil deepens.   10

And the nettle venoms into place
Like a cynical old woman in the food-queue.
The bramble grabs for the air
Like a baby burrowing into the breast.
And the sycamore, cut through at the neck,
Grows five or six heads, depraved with life.

Before these chimneys can flower again
They must fall into the only future, into earth.

Two Trees at Top Withens

Open to huge light
Wind-shepherds
Play the reeds of desolation.

Dragged out of the furnace
They rose and staggered some way.
It was God, they knew.

Now hills bear them through visions
From emptiness to brighter emptiness
With music and with silence.

Startled people look up
With sheep's heads
Then go on eating.

Stanbury Moor

These grasses of light
Which think they are alone in the world

These stones of darkness
Which have a world to themselves

This water of light and darkness
Which hardly savours Creation

And this wind
Which has enough just to exist

Are not

10   A poor family huddled at a poor gleam

Or words in any phrase

Or wolf-beings in a hungry waiting

Or neighbours in a constellation

They are
The armour of bric-à-brac
To which your soul's caddis
Clings with all its courage.

Moors

Are a stage
For the performance of heaven.
Any audience is incidental.

A chess-world of top-heavy Kings and Queens
Circling in stilted majesty
Tremble the bog-cotton
Under the sweep of their robes.

Fools in sunny motley tumble across,
A laughter – fading in full view
10   To grass-tips tapping at stones.

The witch-brew boiling in the sky-vat
Spins electrical terrors
In the eyes of sheep.

Fleeing wraith-lovers twist and collapse
In death-pact languor
To bedew harebells
On the spoil-heaps of quarries.

Wounded champions lurch out of sunset
To gurgle their last gleams into potholes.

Shattered, bowed armies, huddling leaderless 20
Escape from a world
Where snipe work late.

The Trance of Light

The upturned face of this land
The mad singing in the hills
The prophetic mouth of the rain

That fell asleep

Under migraine of headscarves and clatter
Of clog-irons and looms
And gutter-water and clog-irons
And clog-irons and biblical texts

Stretches awake, out of Revelations
And returns to itself.

Chapels, chimneys, vanish in the brightening

And the hills walk out on the hills
The rain talks to its gods
The light, opening younger, fresher wings
Holds this land up again like an offering

Heavy with the dream of a people.

West Laithe Cobbles

It is all
Happening to the sun.

The fallen sun
Is in the hands of water.

There are gulleys gouged in cold hills
By the sufferings of water

And gulleys
Cut in the cold fire

By the worn-out water of women
And the lost rivers of men.

Long Screams

Dark voices.
Swift weapons.

What rummaging of light
At the end of the world.

Unending bleeding.
Deaths left over.
The dead piled in cairns
Over the dead.
Everywhere dead things for monuments
Of the dead.

And now this whole scene, like a mother,
Lifts a cry
Right to the source of it all.

A solitary cry.

She has made a curlew.

Curlews

I

They lift
Out of the maternal watery blue lines

Stripped of all but their cry
Some twists of near-inedible sinew

They slough off
The robes of bilberry blue
The cloud-stained bogland

They veer up and eddy away over
The stone horns

They trail a long, dangling, falling aim
Across water

Lancing their voices
Through the skin of this light

Drinking the nameless and naked
Through trembling bills.

II

Curlews in April
Hang their harps over the misty valleys

A wobbling water-call
A wet-footed god of the horizons

New moons sink into the heather
And full golden moons

Bulge over spent walls.

Walls at Alcomden

It set out —
Splendours burst against its brow
Broke over its shoulders.
The hills heeled, meeting the blast of space.

The stone rigging was strong.
Exhilarated men
Cupped hands and shouted to each other
And grew stronger riding the first winters.

The great adventure had begun —
Even the grass
Agreed and came with them,
And crops and cattle —

No survivors.
Here is the hulk, every rib shattered.

A few crazed sheep
Pulling its weeds
On a shore of cloud.

Walls

What callussed speech rubbed its edges
Soft and hard again and soft
Again fitting these syllables

To the long swell of land, in the long
Press of weather? Eyes that closed
To gaze at grass-points and gritty chippings.

Spines that wore into a bowed
Enslavement, the small freedom of raising
Endless memorials to the labour

Buried in them. Faces
Lifted at the day's end
Like the palms of the hands

To cool in the slow fire of sleep.
A slow fire of wind
Has erased their bodies and names.

Their lives went into the enclosures
Like manure. Embraced these slopes
Like summer cloud-shadows. Left

This harvest of long cemeteries.

First, Mills

                         and steep wet cobbles
Then cenotaphs.

First, football pitches, crown greens
Then the bottomless wound of the railway station
That bled this valley to death.

The fatal wound. And faces whitening
At the windows. Even the hair whitened

The whole land was quietly drained.
Everything became very quiet.

Then the hills were requisitioned
For gravemounds.

The towns and the villages were sacked.

Everything fell wetly to bits
In the memory
And along the sides of the streets.

Over this trench
A sky like an empty helmet
With a hole in it.

And now – two minutes silence
In the childhood of earth.

Hill-Stone was Content

To be cut, to be carted
And fixed in its new place.

It let itself be conscripted
Into mills. And it stayed in position
Defending this slavery against all.

It forgot its wild roots
Its earth-song
In cement and the drum-song of looms.

And inside the mills mankind
With bodies that came and went
Stayed in position, fixed, like the stones
Trembling in the song of the looms.

And they too became four-cornered, stony

In their long, darkening, dwindling stand
Against the guerrilla patience
Of the soft hill-water.

Mill Ruins

One morning
The shuttle's spirit failed to come back
(Japan had trapped it
In a reconstructed loom
Cribbed from smiling fools in Todmorden).

Cloth rotted, in spite of the nursing.
Its great humming abbeys became tombs.

And the children
Of rock and water and a draughty absence
Of everything else
Roaming for leftovers

Smashed all that would smash
What would not smash they burned
What would not burn

They levered loose and toppled down hillsides.

Then trailed away homeward aimlessly
Like the earliest
Homeless Norsemen.

Wild Rock

                    Tamed rock.
Millstone-grit – a soul-grinding sandstone.

Roof-of-the-world-ridge wind
And rain, and rain.

Heaven – the face of a quarry.
Oak-leaves of hammered copper, as in Cranach.
Grass greening on acid.

Wind. Cold. A permanent weight
To be braced under. And rain.

A people fixed
Staring at fleeces, blown like blown flames.

A people converting their stony ideas
To woollen weave, thick worsteds, dense fustians

Between their bones and the four trembling quarters.

The Sheep Went on Being Dead

Under the Heights Road, under crucified oaks
Among slovenly bracken
In the broken spine of a fallen land.

Happy work-hum of the valley mills
Stifled the shouting above looms
Which were too sunk in the pit anyway
To share the air-stir ironically
With the sheep's crumble of doll's curls and calcium.

It was a headache
To see earth such a fierce magnet
Of death. And how the sheep's baggage
Flattened and tried to scatter, getting flatter
Deepening into that power
And indrag of wet stony death.

Time sweetens
The melting corpses of farms
The hills' skulls peeled by the dragging climate –
The arthritic remains
Of what had been a single strength
Tumbled apart, forgetting each other –

The throb of the mills and the crying of lambs
Like shouting in Flanders
Muffled away
In white curls
And memorial knuckles

Under hikers' heels.

The Big Animal of Rock

Is kneeling
In the cemetery of its ancestors.

In its home
Among its pious offspring
Of root and leaf.

In its homeland
Among a solemn kin
Who visit each other in heaven and earth.

Here

At the Festival of Unending
In the fleshly faith
Of the Mourning Mother
Who eats her children

The cantor
The rock,
Sings.

Tree

A priest from a different land
Fulminated
Against heather, black stones, blown water.

Excommunicated the clouds
Damned the wind
Cast the bog pools into outer darkness
Smote the horizons
With the jawbone of emptiness

Till he ran out of breath –

In that teetering moment
Of lungs empty
When only his eye-water protected him
He saw
Heaven and earth moving.

And words left him.
Mind left him. God left him.

Bowed –
The lightning conductor
Of a maiming glimpse – the new prophet –

Under unending interrogation by wind   20
Tortured by huge scaldings of light
Tried to confess all but could not
Bleed a word

Stripped to his root-letter, cruciform
Contorted
Tried to tell all

Through crooking of elbows
Twitching of finger-ends.

Finally
Resigned   30
To be dumb.

Lets what happens to him simply happen.

Heather

The upper millstone heaven
Grinds the heather's face hard and small.
Heather only toughens.

And out of a mica sterility
That nobody else wants
Thickens a nectar
Keen as adder venom.

A wind from the end of the sky
Buffs and curries the grizzly bear-dark pelt
Of long skylines
Browsing in innocence
Through their lasting purple aeons.

Heather is listening
Past hikers, gunshots, picnickers

For the star-drift
Of the returning ice.

No news here
But the crumbling outcrop voices
Of grouse.

A sea of bees, meanwhile, mapped by the sun.

Alcomden

Rock has not learned
Valleys are not aware
Heather and bog-cotton fit themselves
Into their snugness, vision sealed

And faces of people that appear
Moist-eyed, confronting the whole work

With cries that wince out
Just as they shape and tear clear

The whispery husk bones of faces

Are ground into fineness of light
By a weight
And shadowy violence
Of blind skylines revolving numbly

Ignorant in ignorant air

Remains Of Elmet

Death-struggle of the glacier
Enlarged the long gullet of Calder
Down which its corpse vanished.

Farms came, stony masticators
Of generations that ate each other
To nothing inside them.

The sunk mill-towns were cemeteries
Digesting utterly
All with whom they swelled.

Now, coil behind coil,
A wind-parched ache,
An absence, famished and staring,
Admits tourists

To pick among crumbling, loose molars
And empty sockets.

There Come Days to the Hills

Of armadas about to set out –
Fresh mediaeval paintwork
Dragons on mainsails
A shouting throughout heaven

The moorlines cast off ropes, heaving their sides
Patched with harbour reflections
Turn into the light, nosing the distance
Strain in position, fluttering pennants

And the light itself leans taut
Tacking overtaking returning
Urgent and important

Everywhere exhilarated water

Even the sheep, standing windslapped
High in rigging
Look heroic

Every flashing face gazes westward –

Shackleton Hill

Dead farms, dead leaves
Cling to the long
Branch of world.

Stars sway the tree
Whose roots
Tighten on an atom.

The birds beautiful-eyed, with soft cries,
The cattle of heaven,
Visit

And vanish.

When Men Got to the Summit

Light words forsook them.
They filled with heavy silence.

Houses came to support them,
But the hard, foursquare scriptures fractured
And the cracks filled with soft rheumatism.

Streets bent to the task
Of holding it all up
Bracing themselves, taking the strain
Till their vertebrae slipped.

The hills went on gently
Shaking their sieve.

Nevertheless, for some giddy moments
A television
Blinked from the wolf's lookout.

Churn-Milk Joan

A lonely stone
Afloat in the stone heavings of emptiness
Keeps telling her tale. Foxes killed her.

You take the coins out of the hollow in the top of it.
Put your own in. Foxes killed her here.
Why just here? Why not five yards that way?
A squared column, planted by careful labour.

Sun cannot ease it, though the moors grow warm.

Foxes killed her, and her milk spilled.

Or they did not. And it did not. Maybe

10

Farmers brought their milk this far, and cottagers
From the top of Luddenden valley left cash
In the stone's crown, probably in vinegar,
And the farmers left their change. Relic of The Plague.

Churn-milk *jamb*. And Joan did not come trudging
Through the long swoon of moorland
With her sodden feet, her nipped face.
Neither snow nor foxes made her lie down
While they did whatever they wanted.

The negative of the skylines is blank.   20

Only a word wrenched. Then the pain came,
And her mouth opened.
                        And now all of us,
Even this stone, have to be memorials
Of her futile stumbling and screams
And awful little death.

Grouse-Butts

Where all the lines embrace and lie down
Roofless hovels of turf, tapped by harebells,
Weather humbler.

In a world bare of men
They are soothing as ruins
Where the stones roam again free.

But inside each one, under sods, nests
Of spent cartridge-cases
Are acrid with life.
Those dead-looking fumaroles are forts.   10

Monkish cells, communal, strung-out, solitary,
The front-line emplacements of a war nearly religious –
Dedicated to the worship
Of costly, beautiful guns.

A religion too arcane
For the grouse who grew up to trust their kingdom
And its practical landmarks.

I see a hill beyond a hill beyond a hill
Cries the hen-bird, with imperious eyes,
To her bottle-necked brood.

I see a day beyond a day beyond a day beyond a day
Cries the cock.

Too late, heads high and wings low
They curve in from heaven –
With a crash they pitch through stained glass
And drop onto a cold altar

Two hundred miles away.

The Weasels We Smoked out of the Bank

Ran along the rowan branch, a whole family,
Furious with ill-contained lightning
Over the ferny falls of clattering coolant.

After the time-long Creation
Of this hill-sculpture, this prone, horizon-long
Limb-jumble of near-female

The wild gentle god of everywhereness
Worships her, in a lark-rapture silence.

But the demons who did all the labouring
Run in and out of her holes

Crackling with redundant energy.

High Sea-Light

Pearl-robe
Of earth's grit

Heaven glows through
Into the streams
Into gulping mouths

Into a world
Of busy dark atoms
Inside the live wreathed stone

Of light worn warm by a wonder.

Bridestones

Scorched-looking, unhewn – a hill-top chapel.
Actually a crown of outcrop rock –
Earth's heart-bone laid bare.

Crowding congregation of skies.
Tense congregation of hills.
You do nothing casual here.

The wedding stones
Are electrified with whispers.

And marriage is nailed down
By this slender-necked, heavy-headed   10
Black exclamation mark
Of rock.

And you go
With the wreath of weather
The wreath of horizons
The wreath of constellations
Over your shoulders.

And from now on
The sun
Can always touch you   20
With the shadow of this finger.

From now on
The moon can always lift your skull
On to this perch, to clean it.

Wadsworth Moor

Where the millstone of sky
Grinds light and shadow so purple-fine

And has ground it so long

Grinding the skin off earth
Earth bleeds her raw true darkness

A land naked now as a wound
That the sun swabs and dabs

Where the miles of agony are numbness
And harebell and heather a euphoria

Spring-Dusk

                              – a frost-frail
Amethyst.

An iron earth sinking,
Frozen in its wounds.

A snipe
Knowing it has to move fast
Hurtles upwards and downwards

Drumming in the high dark – witchdoctor

Climbing and diving

Drawing the new
Needle of moon
Down

Gently

Into its eggs.

Football at Slack

Between plunging valleys, on a bareback of hill
Men in bunting colours
Bounced, and their blown ball bounced.

The blown ball jumped, and the merry-coloured men
Spouted like water to head it.
The ball blew away downwind –

The rubbery men bounced after it.
The ball jumped up and out and hung on the wind
Over a gulf of treetops.
Then they all shouted together, and the ball blew back.

Winds from fiery holes in heaven
Piled the hills darkening around them
To awe them. The glare light
Mixed its mad oils and threw glooms.
Then the rain lowered a steel press.

Hair plastered, they all just trod water
To puddle glitter. And their shouts bobbed up
Coming fine and thin, washed and happy

While the humped world sank foundering
And the valleys blued unthinkable
Under depth of Atlantic depression –

But the wingers leapt, they bicycled in air
And the goalie flew horizontal

And once again a golden holocaust
Lifted the cloud's edge, to watch them.

Sunstruck

The freedom of Saturday afternoons
Starched to cricket dazzle, nagged at a theorem –
Shaggy valley parapets
Pending like thunder, narrowing the spin-bowler's angle.

The click, disconnected, might have escaped –
A six! And the ball slammed flat!
And the bat in flinders! The heart soaring!
And everybody jumping up and running –

Fleeing after the ball, stampeding
Through that sudden hole in Saturday – but
Already clapped into hands and the trap-shout
The ball jerked back to the stumper on its elastic.

Everything collapsed that bit deeper
Towards Monday.

Misery of the brassy sycamores!
Misery of the swans and the hard ripple!

Then again Yes Yes a wild YES –
The bat flashed round the neck in a tight coil,
The stretched shout snatching for the North Sea –
20   But it fell far short, even of Midgley.

And the legs running for dear life, twinkling white
In the cage of wickets
Were cornered again by the ball, pinned to the crease,
Tethered to the green and white pavilion.

Cross-eyed, mid-stump, sun-descending headache!
Brains sewn into the ball's hide
Hammering at four corners of abstraction
And caught and flung back, and caught, and again caught

To be bounced on baked earth, to be clubbed
30   Toward the wage-mirage sparkle of mills
Toward Lord Savile's heather
Toward the veto of the poisonous Calder.

Till the eyes, glad of anything, dropped
From the bails
Into the bottom of a teacup,
To sandwich crusts for the canal cygnets.

The bowler had flogged himself to a dishclout.
And the burned batsmen returned, with changed faces,
'Like men returned from a far journey,'
40   Under the long glare walls of evening

To the cool sheet and the black slot of home.

Willow-Herb

The canal sunning slack ripples,
Rusts, useless.

Black chimneys, lopped stump-low for safety,
Sprout willow-herb.

Down the Egyptian walls
The voices trickled

Into gleam-black stagnation.

Something that was fingers and
Slavery and religious, reflects sky.

Stone softens. Obsolete despair
Smiles this toothless and senile

Mauve-pink flower.

The Canal's Drowning Black

Bred wild leopards – among the pale depth fungus.
Loach. Torpid, ginger-bearded, secret
Prehistory of the canal's masonry,
With little cupid mouths.

Five inches huge!
On the slime-brink, over bridge reflections,
I teetered. Then a ringing, skull-jolt stamp
And their beards flowered sudden anemones

All down the sunken cliff. A mad-house thrill –
The stonework's tiny eyes, two feet, three feet,   10
Four feet down into my reflection
Watched for my next move.

Their schooldays were over.
Peeping man was no part of their knowledge.
So when a monkey god, a Martian
Tickled their underchins with his net rim

They snaked out and over the net rim easy
Back into the oligocene –
Only restrained by a mesh of kitchen curtain.
Then flopped out of their ocean-shifting aeons   20

Into a two pound jam-jar
On a windowsill
Blackened with acid rain fall-out
From Manchester's rotten lung.

Next morning, Mount Zion's
Cowled, Satanic Majesty behind me
I lobbed – one by one – high through the air
The stiff, pouting, failed, paled new moons

Back into their Paradise and mine.

The Long Tunnel Ceiling

Of the main road canal bridge
Cradled black stalactite reflections.
That was the place for dark loach!

At the far end, the Moderna blanket factory
And the bushy mask of Hathershelf above it
Peered in through the cell-window.

Lorries from Bradford, baled with plump and towering
Wools and cotton met, above my head,
Lorries from Rochdale, and ground past each other
10   Making that cavern of air and water tremble –

Suddenly a crash!
The long gleam-ponderous watery echo shattered.

And at last it had begun!
That could only have been a brick from the ceiling!
The bridge was starting to collapse!

But the canal swallowed its scare,
The heavy mirror reglassed itself,
And the black arch gazed up at the black arch.

Till a brick
20   Rose through its eruption – hung massive
Then slammed back with a shock and a shattering.

An ingot!
Holy of holies! A treasure!
A trout
Nearly as long as my arm, solid
Molten pig of many a bronze loach!

There he lay – lazy – a free lord,
Ignoring me. Caressing, dismissing

The eastward easing traffic of drift,
Master of the Pennine Pass!

Found in some thin glitter among mean sandstone,
High under ferns, high up near sour heather,

Brought down on a midnight cloudburst
In a shake-up of heaven and the hills
When the streams burst with zig-zags and explosions

A seed
Of the wild god now flowering for me
Such a tigerish, dark, breathing lily
Between the tyres, under the tortured axles.

Under the World's Wild Rims

Five hundred glass skylights, a double row,
Watched me, across the canal,
Halfway to school.

A thousand green skylights
Guarded a sacked tomb.

In submarine twilight, boots hushed
Ankle-deep through volcanic talc
Kicking up magical steel objects
For futuristic knobkerries.

Lifelines poured into wagepackets
Had leaked a warm horror, like Pompeii,
Into that worn-out, silent dust.

Vandal plumes of willow-herb
Desecrated the mounds –
Wild encampments, over crude fires
Converting the work-rich scrap to what they could eat.

Gradually five hundred skylights
Came within range. Five hundred stones
Gave my school-going purpose. One by one
Five hundred sunbeams fell on the horns of the flowers.

Two

Two stepped down out of the morning star,
The grouse glowed, they were stolen embers.
The dew split colour.
And a cupped hand brimmed with cock-crows.

Two came down with long shadows
Between the dawn's fingers
With the swinging bodies of hares
And snipe robbed of their jewels.

The stream spoke an oracle of unending,
The sun spread a land at their feet.

Two dropped from the woods that hung in the sky
Bringing the scorched feet of carrion crows.
And the war opened –
                              a sudden yelling
Ricocheted among huddled roof-tops.

The guide flew up from the pathway.

The other swayed.

The feather fell from his head.
The drum stopped in his hand.
The song died in his mouth.

Mount Zion

Blackness
Was a building blocking the moon.
Its wall – my first world-direction –
Mount Zion's gravestone slab.

Above the kitchen window, that uplifted mass
Was a deadfall –
Darkening the sun of every day
Right to the eleventh hour.

Marched in under, gripped by elders
Like a jibbing calf
I knew what was coming.
The convicting holy eyes, the convulsed Moses mouthings –

Mouths that God had burnt with the breath of Moriah.
They were terrified too.
A mesmerized commissariat,
They terrified me, but they terrified each other.
And Christ was only a naked bleeding worm
Who had given up the ghost.

Women bleak as Sunday rose-gardens
Or crumpling to puff-pastry, and cobwebbed with deaths.   20
Men in their prison-yard, at attention,
Exercising their cowed, shaven souls.
Lips stretching saliva, eyes fixed like the eyes
Of cockerels hung by the legs,
As the bottomless cry
Beat itself numb again against Wesley's foundation stone.

Alarm shouts at dusk!
A cricket had rigged up its music
In a crack of Mount Zion wall.
A cricket! The news awful, the shouts awful, at dusk –   30
Like the bear-alarm, at dusk, among smoky tents –
What was a cricket? How big is a cricket?

Long after I'd been smothered in bed
I could hear them
Riving at the religious stonework
With their furious chisels and screwdrivers.

The Ancient Briton Lay under His Rock

Under the oaks, the polished leaves of Sunday.

He was happy no longer existing
Happy being nursery school history
A few vague words
A stump of local folk-lore.

A whorl in our ignorance.

That valley needed him, dead in his cave-mouth,
Bedded on bones of cave-bear, sabre-tooth.
We needed him. The Mighty Hunter.

We dug for him. We dug to be sure.   10

Stinging brows, Sunday after Sunday.
Iron levers.

We needed that waft from the cave
The dawn dew-chilling of emergence,
The hunting grounds untouched all around us.

Meanwhile his pig-headed rock existed.
A slab of time, it surely did exist.
Loyal to the day, it did not cease to exist.

As we dug it waddled and squirmed deeper.
As we dug, slowly, a good half ton,
It escaped us, taking its treasure down.

And lay beyond us, looking up at us

Labouring in the prison
Of our eyes, our sun, our Sunday bells.

Rhododendrons

Dripped a chill virulence
Into my nape –
Rubberized prison-wear of suppression!

Guarding and guarded by
The Council's black
Forbidding forbidden stones.

The policeman's protected leaf!

Detestable evergreen sterility!
Over dead acid gardens
Where blue widows, shrined in Sunday, shrank

To arthritic clockwork,
Yapped like terriers and shook sticks from doorways
Vast and black and proper as museums.

Cenotaphs and the moor-silence!
Rhododendrons and rain!
It is all one. It is over.

Evergloom of official titivation –
Uniform at the reservoir, and the chapel,
And the graveyard park,

Ugly as a brass-band in India.

Crown Point Pensioners

Old faces, old roots.
Indigenous memories.
Flat caps, polished knobs
On favoured sticks.

Under the blue, widening morning and the high lark.

The map of their days, like the chart of an old board-game,
Spreads crumpled below them.
Their yarning shifts over it, this way and that,
Occupying the blanks.

Attuned to each other, like the strings of a harp,   10
They are making mesmerizing music,
Each one bowed at his dried bony profile, as at a harp.
Singers of a lost kingdom.

Moor-water toils in the valley.

An America-bound jet, on its chalky thread,
Dozes in the dusty burning dome.

Their vowels furl downwind, on air like silk.

For Billy Holt

The longships got this far. Then
Anchored in nose and chin.

Badlands where outcast and outlaw
Fortified the hill-knowle's long outlook.

A far, veiled gaze of quietly
Homicidal appraisal.

A poverty
That cut rock lumps for words.

Requisitioned rain, then more rain,
For walls and roof.

Enfolding arms of sour hills
For company.

Blood in the veins
For amusement.

A graveyard
For homeland.

Heptonstall

            – old man
Of the hills, propped out for air
On his wet bench –
Lets his memories leak.

He no longer calls the time of day
Across to Stoodley, soured on that opposite ridge.
And Stoodley has turned his back
On the Museum silence.

He ignores Blackstone Edge –
A huddle of wet stones and damp smokes
Decrepit under sunsets.

He no longer asks
Whether Pecket under the East Wind
Is still living.

He raises no hand
Towards Hathershelf. He knows
The day has passed
For reunion with ancestors.

He knows
Midgley will never return.

The mantel clock ticks in the lonely parlour
On the Heights Road, where the face
Blue with arthritic stasis
And heart good for nothing now
Lies deep in the chair-back, angled

From the window-skylines,
Letting time moan its amnesia
Through the telegraph wires

As the fragments
Of the broken circle of the hills   30
Drift apart.

The Beacon

You claw the door. Rain
Crashes the black taut glass.

Lights in foundering valleys, in the gulf,
Splinter from their sockets.

Lights
Over conversation and telly and dishes
In graves full of eternal silence.

Lights
Of the wolf's wraith
That cannot any longer on all these hills
Find her pelt.

While the world rolls in rain
Like a stone inside surf.

Emily Brontë

The wind on Crow Hill was her darling.
His fierce, high tale in her ear was her secret.
But his kiss was fatal.

Through her dark Paradise ran
The stream she loved too well
That bit her breast.

The shaggy sodden king of that kingdom
Followed through the wall
And lay on her love-sick bed.

The curlew trod in her womb.

The stone swelled under her heart.

Her death is a baby-cry on the moor.

Haworth Parsonage

Infatuated stones.

Hills seeming to strain
And cry out
In labour.

Three weird sisters.

Imbecile silence
Of a stone god
Cut into gravestones.

The brother
Who tasted the cauldron of thunder
Electrocuted.

A house
Emptied and scarred black.

In a land
Emptied and scarred black.

Top Withens

Pioneer hope squared stones
And laid these roof slabs, and wore a way to them.

How young that world was!
The hills full of savage promise.

And the news kept coming
Of America's slow surrender – a wilderness
Blooming with cattle, and wheat, and oil, and cities.

The dream's fort held out –
Stones blackening with dogged purpose.
But at the dead end of a wrong direction.

And the skylines, howling, closed in –

Now it is all over.

The wind swings withered scalps of souls
In the trees that stood for men

And the swift glooms of purple
Are swabbing the human shape from the freed stones.

The Sluttiest Sheep in England

      that never
Get their back ends docked. Who
Doctors their wormy coughs? Maggots
Bring them down in quarry dead ends
And the fluke reigns.

They get by
On the hill subsidy. Splash-black faces
Of psychotic mashams, possessed
By their demonic agates. They clatter
Over worthless moraines, tossing   10
Their Ancient Briton draggle-tassel sheepskins
Or pose, in the rain-smoke, like warriors –

Eyes of the first water
Stare from perfunctory near-bald
Skulls of iguana
Like eyes trapped in helmets –

This lightning-broken huddle of summits
This god-of-what-nobody-wants

Has sent what he uses for angels
To watch you.   20

Auction at Stanbury

On a hillside, part farm, part stone rubble
Shitty bony cattle disconsolate
Rotten and shattered gear

Farmers resembling the gear, the animals
Resembling the strewn walls, the shabby slopes

Shivery Pakistanis
Wind pressing the whole scene towards ice

Thin black men wrapped in bits of Bradford
Waiting for a goat to come up

Widdop

Where there was nothing
Somebody put a frightened lake.

Where there was nothing
Stony shoulders
Broadened to support it.

A wind from between the stars
Swam down to sniff at the trembling.

Trees, holding hands, eyes closed,
Acted at world.

Some heath-grass crept close, in fear.

Nothing else
Except when a gull blows through

A rip in the fabric

Out of nothingness into nothingness

Light Falls through Itself

Loses most of itself
And all its possessions.

Falls naked
Into poverty grass, poverty stone,
Poverty thin water.

Sees, sudden-close,
The smoking breath of a poor cow
Standing in thin mud.

Sees skylines blue far
Trembling like flames flattened under wind.

Wind without hindrance
Blows on the threadbare light
And through it.

Light creeps in grass
And cries
And shivers.

In April

The black stones
Bear blueish delicate milk,

A soft animal of peace
Has come a million years
With shoulders of pre-dawn
And shaggy belly

Has got up from under the glacier
And now lies openly sunning
Huge bones and space-weathered hide

Healing and sweetening
Stretched out full-length for miles –
With eyes half-closed, in a quiet cat-ecstasy.

The Word that Space Breathes

Through tumbled walls

Is accompanied
By lost jawbones of men
And lost fingerbones of women
In the chapel of cloud

And the walled, horizon-woven choir
Of old cares
Darkening back to heather

The huge music
Of sightlines
From every step of the slopes

The Messiah
Of opened rock.

Heptonstall Old Church

A great bird landed here.

Its song drew men out of rock,
Living men out of bog and heather.

Its song put a light in the valleys
And harness on the long moors.

Its song brought a crystal from space
And set it in men's heads.

Then the bird died.

Its giant bones
Blackened and became a mystery.

The crystal in men's heads
Blackened and fell to pieces.

The valleys went out.
The moorland broke loose.

Tick Tock Tick Tock

Peter Pan's days of pendulum
Cut at the valley groove.

Tick Tock Tick Tock
Everlasting play bled the whole unstoppable Calder
And incinerated itself happily
From a hundred mill chimneys.

Tick Tock Summer Summer
Summer Summer.
And the hills unalterable and the old women unalterable.
And the ageless boy
Among the pulsing wounds of Red Admirals.

Somebody else acted Peter Pan.
I swallowed an alarm clock

And over the school playground's macadam
Crawled from prehistory towards him

Tick Tock Tick Tock the crocodile.

Cock-Crows

I stood on a dark summit, among dark summits –
Tidal dawn splitting heaven from earth,
The oyster
Opening to taste gold.

And I heard the cock-crows kindling in the valley
Under the mist –
They were sleepy,
Bubbling deep in the valley cauldron.

Then one or two tossed clear, like soft rockets
And sank back again dimming.   10

Then soaring harder, brighter, higher
Tearing the mist,
Bubble-glistenings flung up and bursting to light
Brightening the undercloud,
The fire-crests of the cocks – the sickle shouts,
Challenge against challenge, answer to answer,
Hooking higher,
Clambering up the sky as they melted,
Hanging smouldering from the night's fringes.

Till the whole valley brimmed with cock-crows,   20
A magical soft mixture boiling over,
Spilling and sparkling into other valleys

Lobbed-up horse-shoes of glow-swollen metal
From sheds in back-gardens, hen-cotes, farms
Sinking back mistily

Till the last spark died, and embers paled

And the sun climbed into its wet sack
For the day's work

While the dark rims hardened
Over the smoke of towns, from holes in earth.   30

Heptonstall Cemetery

Wind slams across the tops.
The spray cuts upward.

You claw your way
Over a giant beating wing.

And Thomas and Walter and Edith
Are living feathers

Esther and Sylvia
Living feathers

Where all the horizons lift wings
A family of dark swans

And go beating low through storm-silver
Toward the Atlantic.

The Angel

In my dream I saw something disastrous.

The full moon had crashed on to Halifax.
Black Halifax boiled in phosphorus.
Halifax was an erupting crater.

The flames seemed to labour. Then a tolling glare
Heaved itself out and writhed upwards –
And it was a swan the size of a city!

Far too heavy for the air, it pounded towards me,
Low over Hathershelf.

And it was no swan.

It was an angel made of smoking snow.
Her long dress fluttered about her ankles,
Her bare feet just cleared the moor beneath her
Which glowed like the night-cloud over Sheffield.

Mother, I cried, O Mother, there is an angel –
Is it a blessing? Then my mother's answer
Turned that beauty suddenly to terror.
I watched for the angel to fade and be impossible.

But the huge beauty would not fade.
She was cast in burning metal. Her halo
Was an enigmatic square of satin
Rippling its fringed edges like a flounder.

I could make no sense of that strange head-dress.

Till this immense omen, with wings rigid,
Sank out of my sight, behind Stoodley,
Under the moor, and left my darkness empty.

When I next saw that strange square of satin
I reached out and touched it.

When next I stood where I stood in my dream
Those words of my mother,
Joined with earth and engraved in rock,
Were under my feet.

UNCOLLECTED (1979)

Irish Elk

Here stood the Irish Elk
In its castle of gristle
Its machinery of pain
Staring around, under its absurd furniture.

It browsed a little, it shivered,
Then clattered to some other draughty standing place,
Improbably balanced
On the sea of skylines.

The geography was amended.
The Elk's ceremony became redundant.
That eye accepted the verdict
Like a hero, without change of expression.

The mystery of Elk was unravelled.

The waters of Elk have gone.

The bog-cotton drank them.

And now the memorial of Elk
Is the harebell

Feeding downwind.

Barley

Barley grain is like seeds of gold bullion.
When you turn a heap with a shovel it pours
With the heavy magic of wealth.
Every grain is a sleeping princess –
Her kingdom is still to come.
She sleeps with sealed lips.
Each grain is like a mouth sealed
Or an eye sealed.
In each mouth the whole bible of barley.
In each eye, the whole sun of barley.
From each single grain, given time,
You could feed the earth.

You treat them rough, dump them into the drill,
Churn them up with a winter supply

Of fertiliser, and steer out onto the tilth
Trailing your wake of grains.

When the field's finished, fresh-damp,
Its stillness is no longer stillness.
The coverlet has been drawn tight again
But now over breathing and dreams.
And water is already bustling to sponge the newcomers.
And the soil, the ancient nurse,
Is assembling everything they will need.
And the angel of earth
Is flying through the field, kissing each one awake.
But it is a hard nursery.
Night and day all through winter huddling naked
They have to listen to pitiless lessons
Of the freezing constellations
And the rain. If it were not for the sun
Who visits them daily, briefly,
To pray with them, they would lose hope
And give up. With him
They recite the Lord's prayer
And sing a psalm. And sometimes at night
When the moon haunts their field and stares down
Into their beds
They sing a psalm softly together
To keep up their courage.

Once their first leaf shivers they sing less
And start working. They cannot miss a day.
They have to get the whole thing right.
Employed by the earth, employed by the sky,
Employed by barley, to be barley.
And now they begin to show their family beauty.
They come charging over the field, under the wind, like warriors—
'Terrible as an army with banners',
Barbaric, tireless, Amazon battalions.

And that's how they win their kingdom.
Then they put on gold, for their coronation.
Each one barbed, feathered, a lithe weapon,
Puts on the crown of her kingdom.
Then the whole fieldful of queens
Swirls in a dance

With their invisible partner, the wind,
Like a single dancer.

That is how barley inherits the kingdom of barley.

A Lamb in the Storm

But the world is brave.
Eyes squeezed tight shut, she plunges.
Surf goes over the house, dust-bin lids fly.

Ears of owls, hairfine electronics
Are jammed with the sky-disaster.
They anchor their cork-weights, clamped hungry
To trees that struggle to save themselves.

The world's brow
Plunges into blindness and deafness –
Farms and villages cling.

Chunks of the wreck reel past.

But the world
Just about finished,
Stripped and stunned, keeps her battered direction –

She knows who it is, still alive out there,
That castaway voice
Where heaven breaks up in the darkness.

The Rose

Unconcerned with men's writings,
In a dingy corner of her room
Flames to its petal-fringe, and no further,
Keeping perfect propriety,
Its petals not a lyrical cry, like the anguished lily,
But a muffled thunder of perturbation,
A coloratura of openings, beckonings,
The simple, cool eyes, the core hectic.
Miniature admirers with black legs disport themselves.
Your picture floats, logical, illogical,
With flames, with undies, without drapery,

Wide open, your secret averted
As the sharp-nosed critic, the puritan
Rejects the excess of your silks,
And your abandon, like the needlessness of a parrot,
Mountain behind mountain, dawn beyond dawn.

In the Black Chapel

In the black chapel, a shut stone.
In the shut stone, a humming absence.
In the humming absence, a big-eyed feather.
In the big-eyed feather, a thousand songs.

In ten hundred songs, one furious king.
In the furious king, a forked riddle.
In the forked riddle, a blood-soft bird.
In the blood-soft bird, a proud bride.

In the proud bride, a bright chapel.

MOORTOWN DIARY (1979)

Rain

Rain. Floods. Frost. And after frost, rain.
Dull roof-drumming. Wraith-rain pulsing across purple-bare woods
Like light across heaved water. Sleet in it.
And the poor fields, miserable tents of their hedges.
Mist-rain off-world. Hills wallowing
In and out of a grey or silvery dissolution. A farm gleaming,
Then all dull in the near drumming. At field-corners
Brown water backing and brimming in grass.
Toads hop across rain-hammered roads. Every mutilated leaf there
Looks like a frog or a rained-out mouse. Cattle
Wait under blackened backs. We drive post-holes.
They half fill with water before the post goes in.
Mud-water spurts as the iron bar slam-burns
The oak stake-head dry. Cows
Tamed on the waste mudded like a rugby field
Stand and watch, come very close for company
In the rain that goes on and on, and gets colder.
They sniff the wire, sniff the tractor, watch. The hedges
Are straggles of gap. A few haws. Every half-ton cow
Sinks to the fetlock at every sliding stride.
They are ruining their field and they know it.
They look out sideways from under their brows which are
Their only shelter. The sunk scrubby wood
Is a pulverised wreck, rain riddles its holes
To the drowned roots. A pheasant looking black
In his waterproofs, bends at his job in the stubble.
The mid-afternoon dusk soaks into
The soaked thickets. Nothing protects them.
The fox corpses lie beaten to their bare bones,
Skin beaten off, brains and bowels beaten out.
Nothing but their blueprint bones last in the rain,
Sodden soft. Round their hay racks, calves
Stand in a shine of mud. The gateways
Are deep obstacles of mud. The calves look up, through
    plastered forelocks,
Without moving. Nowhere they can go
Is less uncomfortable. The brimming world
And the pouring sky are the only places
For them to be. Fieldfares squeal over, sodden
Toward the sodden wood. A raven,

Cursing monotonously, goes over fast
And vanishes in rain-mist. Magpies
Shake themselves hopelessly, hop in the spatter. Misery.
Surviving green of ferns and brambles is tumbled
Like an abandoned scrapyard. The calves
Wait deep beneath their spines. Cows roar
Then hang their noses to the mud.
Snipe go over, invisible in the dusk,
With their squelching cries.

4 December 1973

Dehorning

Bad-tempered bullying bunch, the horned cows
Among the unhorned. Feared, spoilt.
Cantankerous at the hay, at assemblies, at crowded
Yard operations. Knowing their horn-tips' position
To a fraction, every other cow knowing it too,
Like their own tenderness. Horning of bellies, hair-tufting
Of horn-tips. Handy levers. But
Off with the horns.
So there they all are in the yard –
The pick of the bullies, churning each other
Like thick fish in a bucket, churning their mud.
One by one, into the cage of the crush: the needle,
A roar not like a cow – more like a tiger,
Blast of air down a cavern, and long, long
Beginning in pain and ending in terror – then the next.
The needle between the horn and the eye, so deep
Your gut squirms for the eyeball twisting
In its pink-white fastenings of tissue. This side and that.
Then the first one anaesthetised, back in the crush.
The bulldog pincers in the septum, stretched full strength,
The horn levered right over, the chin pulled round
With the pincers, the mouth drooling, the eye
Like a live eye caught in a pan, like the eye of a fish
Imprisoned in air. Then the cheese cutter
Of braided wire, and stainless steel peg handles,
Aligned on the hair-bedded root of the horn, then leaning
Backward full weight, pull-punching backwards,

Left right left right and the blood leaks
Down over the cheekbone, the wire bites
And buzzes, the ammonia horn-burn smokes
And the cow groans, roars shapelessly, hurls
Its half-ton commotion in the tight cage. Our faces
Grimace like faces in the dentist's chair. The horn
Rocks from its roots, the wire pulls through
The last hinge of hair, the horn is heavy and free,
And a water-pistol jet of blood
Rains over the one who holds it – a needle jet
From the white-rasped and bloody skull-crater. Then tweezers
Twiddle the artery nozzle, knotting it enough,
And purple antiseptic squirts a cuttlefish cloud over it.
Then the other side the same. We collect
A heap of horns. The floor of the crush
Is a trampled puddle of scarlet. The purple-crowned cattle,
The bullies, with suddenly no horns to fear,
Start ramming and wrestling. Maybe their heads
Are still anaesthetised. A new order
Among the hornless. The bitchy high-headed
Straight-back brindle, with her Spanish bull trot,
And her head-shaking snorting advance and her crazy spirit,
Will have to get maternal. What she's lost
In weapons, she'll have to make up for in tits.
But they've all lost one third of their beauty.

14 May 1974

Poor birds

In the boggy copse. Blue
Dusk presses into their skulls
Electrodes of stars. All night
Clinging to sodden twigs, with twiggy claws,
They dream the featherless, ravenous
Machinery of heaven. At dawn, fevered,
They flee to the field. All day
They try to get some proper sleep without
Losing sight of the grass. Panics
Fling them from hill to hill. They search everywhere
For the safety that sleeps

Everywhere in the closed faces
Of stones.

10 December 1973

Feeding out-wintering cattle at twilight

The wind is inside the hill.
The wood is a struggle – like a wood
Struggling through a wood. A panic
Only just holds off – every gust
Breaches the sky-walls and it seems, this time,
The whole sea of air will pour through,
The thunder will take deep hold, roots
Will have to come out, every loose thing
Will have to lift and go. And the cows, dark lumps of dusk
10   Stand waiting, like nails in a tin roof.
For the crucial moment, taking the strain
In their stirring stillness. As if their hooves
Held their field in place, held the hill
To its trembling shape. Night-thickness
Purples in the turmoil, making
Everything more alarming. Unidentifiable, tiny
Birds go past like elf-bolts.
Battling the hay-bales from me, the cows
Jostle and crush, like hulls blown from their moorings
20   And piling at the jetty. The wind
Has got inside their wintry buffalo skins,
Their wild woolly bulk-heads, their fierce, joyful breathings
And the reckless strength of their necks.
What do they care, their hooves
Are knee-deep in porridge of earth –
The hay blows luminous tatters from their chewings,
A fiery loss, frittering downwind,
Snatched away over the near edge
Where the world becomes water
30   Thundering like a flood-river at night.
They grunt happily, half-dissolved
On their steep, hurtling brink, as I flounder back
Towards headlights.

17 February 1974

Foxhunt

Two days after Xmas, near noon, as I listen
The hounds behind the hill
Are changing ground, a cloud of excitements,
Their voices like rusty, reluctant
Rolling stock being shunted. The hunt
Has tripped over a fox
At the threshold of the village. A crow in the fir
Is inspecting his nesting site, and he expostulates
At the indecent din. A blackbird
Starts up its cat-alarm. The grey-cloud mugginess   10
Of the year in its pit trying to muster
Enough energy to start opening again
Roars distantly. Everything sodden. The fox
Is flying, taking his first lesson
From the idiot pack-noise, the puppyish whine-yelps
Curling up like hounds' tails, and the gruff military barkers:
A machine with only two products:
Dog-shit and dead foxes. Lorry engines
As usual modulating on the main street hill
Complicate the air, and the fox runs in a suburb   20
Of indifferent civilized noises. Now the yelpings
Enrich their brocade, thickening closer
In the maze of wind-currents. The orchards
And the hedges stand in coma. The pastures
Have got off so far lightly, are firm, cattle
Still nose hopefully, as if spring might be here
Missing out winter. Big lambs
Are organizing their gangs in gateways. The fox
Hangs his silver tongue in the world of noise
Over his spattering paws. Will he run   30
Till his muscles suddenly turn to iron,
Till blood froths his mouth as his lungs tatter,
Till his feet are raw blood-sticks and his tail
Trails thin as a rat's? Or will he
Make a mistake, jump the wrong way, jump right
Into the hound's mouth? As I write this down
He runs still fresh, with all his chances before him.

27 December 1975

New Year exhilaration

On the third day
Finds its proper weather. Pressure
Climbing and the hard blue sky
Scoured by gales. The world's being
Swept clean. Twigs that can't cling
Go flying, last leaves ripped off
Bowl along roads like daring mice. Imagine
The new moon hightide sea under this
Rolling of air-weights. Exhilaration
Lashes everything. Windows flash,
White houses dazzle, fields glow red.
Seas pour in over the land, invisible maelstroms
Set the house-joints creaking. Every twig-end
Writes its circles and the earth
Is massaged with roots. The powers of hills
Hold their bright faces in the wind-shine.
The hills are being honed. The river
Thunders like a factory, its weirs
Are tremendous engines. People
Walk precariously, the whole landscape
Is imperilled, like a tarpaulin
With the wind under it. 'It nearly
Blew me up the chymbley!' And a laugh
Blows away like a hat.

3 January 1975

Struggle

We had been expecting her to calve
And there she was, just after dawn, down.
Private, behind bushed hedge-cuttings, in a low rough corner.
The walk towards her was like a walk into danger,
Caught by her first calf, the small-boned black and white heifer
Having a bad time. She lifted her head,
She reached for us with a wild, flinging look
And flopped flat again. There was the calf,
White-faced, lion-coloured, enormous, trapped
Round the waist by his mother's purpled elastic,

His heavy long forelegs limply bent in a not-yet-inherited gallop,
His head curving up and back, pushing for the udder
Which had not yet appeared, his nose scratched and reddened
By an ill-placed clump of bitten-off rushes,
His fur dried as if he had been
Half-born for hours, as he probably had.
Then we heaved on his forelegs,
And on his neck, and half-born he mooed
Protesting about everything. Then bending him down,
Between her legs, and sliding a hand   20
Into the hot tunnel, trying to ease
His sharp hip-bones past her pelvis,
Then twisting him down, so you expected
His spine to slip its sockets,
And one hauling his legs, and one embracing his wet waist
Like pulling somebody anyhow from a bog,
And one with hands easing his hips past the corners
Of his tunnel mother, till something gave.
The cow flung her head and lifted her upper hind leg
With every heave and something gave   30
Almost a click —
And his scrubbed wet enormous flanks came sliding out,
Coloured ready for the light his incredibly long hind legs
From the loose red flapping sack-mouth
Followed by a gush of colours, a mess
Of puddled tissues and jellies.
He mooed feebly and lay like a pieta Christ
In the cold easterly daylight. We dragged him
Under his mother's nose, her stretched-out exhausted head,
So she could get to know him with lickings.   40
They lay face to face like two mortally wounded duellists.
We stood back, letting the strength flow towards them.
We gave her a drink, we gave her hay. The calf
Started his convalescence
From the gruelling journey. All day he lay
Overpowered by limpness and weight.
We poured his mother's milk into him
But he had not strength to swallow.
He made a few clumsy throat gulps, then lay
Mastering just breathing.   50
We took him inside. We tucked him up
In front of a stove, and tried to pour

509

Warm milk and whisky down his throat and not into his lungs.
But his eye just lay suffering the monstrous weight of his head,
The impossible job of his marvellous huge limbs.
He could not make it. He died called Struggle.
Son of Patience.

17 April 1974

Bringing in new couples

Wind out of freezing Europe. A mean snow
Fiery cold. Ewes caked crusty with snow,
Their new hot lambs wet trembling
And crying on trampled patches, under the hedge –
Twenty miles of open lower landscape
Blows into their wetness. The field smokes and writhes
Burning like a moor with snow-fumes.
Lambs nestling to make themselves comfortable
While the ewe nudges and nibbles at them
And the numbing snow-wind blows on the blood tatters
At her breached back-end.
The moor a grey sea-shape. The wood
Thick-fingered density, a worked wall of whiteness.
The old sea-roar, sheep-shout, lamb-wail.
Redwings needling invisible. A fright
Smoking among trees, the hedges blocked.
Lifting of ice-heavy ewes, trampling anxieties
As they follow their wide-legged tall lambs,
Tripods craning to cry bewildered.
We coax the mothers to follow their babies
And they do follow, running back
In sudden convinced panic to the patch
Where the lamb had been born, dreading
She must have been deceived away from it
By crafty wolvish humans, then coming again
Defenceless to the bleat she's attuned to
And recognizing her own – a familiar
Detail in the meaningless shape-mass
Of human arms, legs, body-clothes – her lamb on the white earth
Held by those hands. Then vanishing again
Lifted. Then only the disembodied cry

Going with the human, while she runs in a circle
On the leash of the cry. While the wind
Presses outer space into the grass
And alarms wrens deep in brambles
With hissing fragments of stars.

16 February 1975

Snow smoking as the fields boil

The bull weeps.
The trough solidifies.
The cock pheasant has forgotten his daughters.
The fox crosses mid-field, careless of acquittal.
Twigs cannot pay the interest.
The farm-roofs sink in the welter again, like a whale's fluke.
Sheep fade humbly.
The owl cries early, breaking parole,
With icicles darkening witness.

8 February 1975

Tractor

The tractor stands frozen – an agony
To think of. All night
Snow packed its open entrails. Now a head-pincering gale,
A spill of molten ice, smoking snow,
Pours into its steel.
At white heat of numbness it stands
In the aimed hosing of ground-level fieriness.

It defies flesh and won't start.
Hands are like wounds already
Inside armour gloves, and feet are unbelievable
As if the toe-nails were all just torn off.
I stare at it in hatred. Beyond it
The copse hisses – capitulates miserably
In the fleeing, failing light. Starlings,
A dirtier sleetier snow, blow smokily, unendingly, over
Towards plantations eastward.

All the time the tractor is sinking
Through the degrees, deepening
Into its hell of ice.

The starter lever
Cracks its action, like a snapping knuckle.
The battery is alive – but like a lamb
Trying to nudge its solid-frozen mother –
While the seat claims my buttock-bones, bites
With the space-cold of earth, which it has joined
In one solid lump.

I squirt commercial sure-fire
Down the black throat – it just coughs.
It ridicules me – a trap of iron stupidity
I've stepped into. I drive the battery
As if I were hammering and hammering
The frozen arrangement to pieces with a hammer
And it jabbers laughing pain-crying mockingly
Into happy life.

And stands
Shuddering itself full of heat, seeming to enlarge slowly
Like a demon demonstrating
A more-than-usually-complete materialisation –
Suddenly it jerks from its solidarity
With the concrete, and lurches towards a stanchion
Bursting with superhuman well-being and abandon
Shouting Where Where?

Worse iron is waiting. Power-lift kneels,
Levers awake imprisoned deadweight,
Shackle-pins bedded in cast-iron cow-shit.
The blind and vibrating condemned obedience
Of iron to the cruelty of iron,
Wheels screeched out of their night-locks –

Fingers
Among the tormented
Tonnage and burning of iron

Eyes
Weeping in the wind of chloroform

And the tractor, streaming with sweat,
Raging and trembling and rejoicing.

31 January 1976

Roe-deer

In the dawn-dirty light, in the biggest snow of the year
Two blue-dark deer stood in the road, alerted.

They had happened into my dimension
The moment I was arriving just there.

They planted their two or three years of secret deerhood
Clear on my snow-screen vision of the abnormal

And hesitated in the all-way disintegration
And stared at me. And so for some lasting seconds

I could think the deer were waiting for me
To remember the password and sign   10

That the curtain had blown aside for a moment
And there where the trees were no longer trees, nor the road a road

The deer had come for me.

Then they ducked through the hedge, and upright they rode their legs
Away downhill over a snow-lonely field

Towards tree dark – finally
Seeming to eddy and glide and fly away up

Into the boil of big flakes.
The snow took them and soon their nearby hoofprints as well

Revising its dawn inspiration   20
Back to the ordinary.

13 February 1973

Couples under cover

The ewes are in the shed
Under clapping wings of corrugated iron
Where entering rays of snow cut horizontal

513

Fiery and radio-active, a star-dust.
The oaks outside, half-digested
With a writhing white fire-snow off the hill-field
Burning to frails of charcoal
Roar blind, and swing blindly, a hill-top
Helpless self-defence. Snow
Is erasing them, whitening blanks
Against a dirty whiteness. The new jolly lambs
Are pleased with their nursery. A few cavorts
Keep trying their hind-legs – up and a twist,
So they stagger back to balance, bewildered
By the life that's working at them. Heads, safer,
Home in on udders, under-groin hot flesh-tent,
Hide eyes in muggy snugness. The ewes can't settle,
Heads bony and ratty with anxiety,
Keyed to every wind-shift, light-footed
To leap clear when the hill-top
Starts to peel off, or those tortured tree-oceans
Come blundering through the old stonework.
They don't appreciate the comfort.
They'd as soon be in midfield suffering
The twenty mile snow-gale of unprotection,
Ice-balls anaesthetising their back-end blood-tatters,
Watching and worrying while a lamb grows stranger –
A rumpy-humped skinned-looking rabbit
Whose hunger no longer works.
                                        One day
Of slightly unnatural natural comfort, and the lambs
Will toss out into the snow, imperishable
Like trawlers, bobbing in gangs, while the world
Welters unconscious into whiteness.

4 March 1974

Surprise

Looking at cows in their high-roofy roomy
Windy home, mid-afternoon idling,
Late winter, near spring, the fields not greening,
The wind North-East and sickening, the hay
Shrinking, the year growing. The parapets

Of toppled hay, the broken walls of hay,
The debris of hay. The peace of cattle
Mid-afternoon, cud-munching, eyelids lowered.
The deep platform of dung. Looking at cows
Sharing their trance, it was an anomalous
Blue plastic apron I noticed
Hitched under the tail of one cow
That went on munching, with angling ears. A glistening
Hanging sheet of blue-black. I thought
Of aprons over ewes' back-ends
To keep the ram out till it's timely. I thought
Of surgical aprons to keep cleanliness
Under the shit-fall. Crazily far thoughts
Proposed themselves as natural, and I almost
Looked away. Suddenly
The apron slithered, and a whole calf's
Buttocks and hind-legs – whose head and forefeet
Had been hidden from me by another cow –
Toppled out of its mother, and collapsed on the ground.
Leisurely, as she might be leisurely curious,
She turned, pulling her streamers of blood-tissue
Away from this lumpish jetsam. She nosed it
Where it lay like a still-birth in its tissues.
She began to nibble and lick. The jelly
Shook its head and nosed the air. She gave it
The short small swallowed moo-grunts hungry cows
Give when they stand suddenly among plenty.

   21 March 1975

Last night

She would not leave her dead twins. The whole flock
Went on into the next field, over the hill,
But she stayed with her corpses. We took one
And left one to keep her happy.
The North wind brought the worst cold
Of this winter. Before dawn
It shifted a little and wetter. First light, the mist
Was like a nail in the head. She had gone through
Into the next field, but still lingered

Within close crying of her lamb, who lay now
Without eyes, already entrails pulled out
Between his legs. She cried for him to follow,
Now she felt so much lighter. As she cried
The two rams came bobbing over the hill,
The greyface and the blackface.
                                        They came straight on,
Noses stretching forward as if they were being pulled
By nose-rings. They milled merrily round her,
Fitting their awkward bodies to the requirement
That was calling, and that they could not resist
Or properly understand yet. Confusion of smells
And excitements. She ran off. They followed.
The greyface squared back and bounced his brow
Off the head of the surprised blackface, who stopped.
The greyface hurried on and now she followed.
He was leading her away and she followed.
She had stopped crying to her silent lamb.
The blackface caught them up on the steepness.
The greyface shouldered her away, drew back
Six or seven paces, dragging his forelegs, then curling his head.
He bounded forward and the other met him.
The blackface stood sideways. Then the greyface
Hurried to huddle with her. She hurried nibbling,
Making up for all she'd missed with her crying.
Then blackface came again. The two jostled her,
Both trying to mount her simultaneously
As she ran between them and under them
Hurrying to nibble further.
They drew back and bounced and collided again.
The greyface turned away as if
He'd done something quite slight but necessary
And mounted her as she nibbled. There he stayed.
The blackface ran at her and, baffled, paused.
Searched where to attack to get her for himself.
The greyface withdrew and flopped off,
And she ran on nibbling. The two rams
Turned to stare at me.
Two or three lambs wobbled in the cold.

10 March 1975

Ravens

As we came through the gate to look at the few new lambs
On the skyline of lawn smoothness,
A raven bundled itself into air from midfield
And slid away under hard glistenings, low and guilty.
Sheep nibbling, kneeling to nibble the reluctant nibbled grass.
Sheep staring, their jaws pausing to think, then chewing again,
Then pausing. Over there a new lamb
Just getting up, bumping its mother's nose
As she nibbles the sugar coating off it
While the tattered banners of her triumph swing and drip from
    her rear-end.
She sneezes and a glim of water flashes from her rear-end.
She sneezes again and again, till she's emptied.
She carries on investigating her new present and seeing how
    it works.
Over here is something else. But you are still interested
In that new one, and its new spark of voice,
And its tininess.
Now over here, where the raven was,
Is what interests you next. Born dead,
Twisted like a scarf, a lamb of an hour or two,
Its insides, the various jellies and crimsons and transparencies
And threads and tissues pulled out
In straight lines, like tent ropes
From its upward belly opened like a lamb-wool slipper,
The fine anatomy of silvery ribs on display and the cavity,
The head also emptied through the eye-sockets,
The woolly limbs swathed in birth-yolk and impossible
To tell now which in all this field of quietly nibbling sheep
Was its mother. I explain
That it died being born. We should have been here, to help it.
So it died being born. 'And did it cry?' you cry.
I pick up the dangling greasy weight by the hooves soft as
    dogs' pads
That had trodden only womb-water
And its raven-drawn strings dangle and trail,
Its loose head joggles, and 'Did it cry?' you cry again.
Its two-fingered feet splay in their skin between the pressures
Of my fingers and thumb. And there is another,
Just born, all black, splaying its tripod, inching its new points

Towards its mother, and testing the note
It finds in its mouth. But you have eyes now
Only for the tattered bundle of throwaway lamb.
'Did it cry?' you keep asking, in a three-year-old field-wide
Piercing persistence. 'Oh yes' I say 'it cried.'

Though this one was lucky insofar
As it made the attempt into a warm wind
And its first day of death was blue and warm
The magpies gone quiet with domestic happiness
And skylarks not worrying about anything
And the blackthorn budding confidently
And the skyline of hills, after millions of hard years,
Sitting soft.

    15 April 1974

February 17th

A lamb could not get born. Ice wind
Out of a downpour dishclout sunrise. The mother
Lay on the mudded slope. Harried, she got up
And the blackish lump bobbed at her back-end
Under her tail. After some hard galloping,
Some manoeuvring, much flapping of the backward
Lump head of the lamb looking out,
I caught her with a rope. Laid her, head uphill
And examined the lamb. A blood-ball swollen
10   Tight in its black felt, its mouth gap
Squashed crooked, tongue stuck out, black-purple,
Strangled by its mother. I felt inside,
Past the noose of mother-flesh, into the slippery
Muscled tunnel, fingering for a hoof,
Right back to the port-hole of the pelvis.
But there was no hoof. He had stuck his head out too early
And his feet could not follow. He should have
Felt his way, tip-toe, his toes
Tucked up under his nose
20   For a safe landing. So I kneeled wrestling
With her groans. No hand could squeeze past
The lamb's neck into her interior
To hook a knee. I roped that baby head

And hauled till she cried out and tried
To get up and I saw it was useless. I went
Two miles for the injection and a razor.
Sliced the lamb's throat-strings, levered with a knife
Between the vertebrae and brought the head off
To stare at its mother, its pipes sitting in the mud
With all earth for a body. Then pushed   30
The neck-stump right back in, and as I pushed
She pushed. She pushed crying and I pushed gasping.
And the strength
Of the birth push and the push of my thumb
Against that wobbly vertebra were deadlock,
A to-fro futility. Till I forced
A hand past and got a knee. Then like
Pulling myself to the ceiling with one finger
Hooked in a loop, timing my effort
To her birth push groans, I pulled against   40
The corpse that would not come. Till it came.
And after it the long, sudden, yolk-yellow
Parcel of life
In a smoking slither of oils and soups and syrups –
And the body lay born, beside the hacked-off head.

   17 February 1974

March morning unlike others

Blue haze. Bees hanging in air at the hive-mouth.
Crawling in prone stupor of sun
On the hive-lip. Snowdrops. Two buzzards,
Still-wings, each
Magnetized to the other,
Float orbits.
Cattle standing warm. Lit, happy stillness.
A raven, under the hill,
Coughing among bare oaks.
Aircraft, elated, splitting blue.
Leisure to stand. The knee-deep mud at the trough
Stiffening. Lambs freed to be foolish.

The earth invalid, dropsied, bruised, wheeled
Out into the sun,

After the frightful operation.
She lies back, wounds undressed to the sun,
To be healed,
Sheltered from the sneapy chill creeping North wind,
Leans back, eyes closed, exhausted, smiling
Into the sun. Perhaps dozing a little.
While we sit, and smile, and wait, and know
She is not going to die.

    15 March 1974

Turning out

Turned the cows out two days ago.
Mailed with dung, a rattling armour,
They lunged into the light,
Kneeling with writhing necks they
Demolished a hill of soil, horning and
Scouring their skull-tops. They hurried
Their udders and their stateliness
Towards the new pasture. The calves lagged, lost,
Remembering only where they'd come from,
Where they'd been born and had mothers. Again
And again they galloped back to the empty pens,
Gazing and mooing and listening. Wearier, wearier –
Finally they'd be driven to their mothers,
Startling back at gates, nosing a nettle
As it might be a snake. Then
Finding their field of mothers and simple grass,
With eyes behind and sideways they ventured
Into the flings and headlong, breakthrough
Gallops toward freedom, high tails riding
The wonderful new rockinghorse, and circling
Back to the reassuring udders, the flung
Sniffs and rough lickings. The comforting
Indifference and contentment, which
They settled to be part of.

    3 May 1975

She has come to pass

A whole day
Leaning on the sale-ring gates
Among the peninsula's living gargoyles,
The weathered visors
Of the labourers at earth's furnace
Of the soil's glow and the wind's flash,
Hearing the auctioneer's
Epic appraisal

Of some indigenous cattle, as if
This were the soul's timely masterpiece.
Comparing buttocks, anxious for birth-dates,
Apportioning credit for the calf,
Finally climaxing her blood-pressure
In a table-tennis to-fro strife

Of guineas by twenties for a bull
All of three quarters of a ton
Of peace and ability, not to say
Beauty, and to lose it, after all,
And to retire, relieved she had lost it, so,
As from a job well done.

30 May 1974

Birth of Rainbow

This morning blue vast clarity of March sky
But a blustery violence of air, and a soaked overnight
Newpainted look to the world. The wind coming
Off the snowed moor in the South, razorish,
Heavy-bladed and head-cutting, off snow-powdered ridges.
Flooded ruts shook. Hoof-puddles flashed. A daisy
Mud-plastered unmixed its head from the mud.
The black and white cow, on the highest crest of the round ridge,
Stood under the end of a rainbow.
Head down licking something, full in the painful wind   10
That the pouring haze of the rainbow ignored.
She was licking her gawky black calf
Collapsed wet-fresh from the womb, blinking his eyes

In the low morning dazzling washed sun.
Black, wet as a collie from a river, as she licked him,
Finding his smells, learning his particularity.
A flag of bloody tissue hung from her back-end
Spreading and shining, pink-fleshed and raw, it flapped and coiled
In the unsparing wind. She positioned herself, uneasy
20   As we approached, nervous small footwork
On the hoof-ploughed drowned sod of the ruined field.
She made uneasy low noises, and her calf too
With his staring whites, mooed the full clear calf-note
Pure as woodwind, and tried to get up,
Tried to get his cantilever front legs
In operation, lifted his shoulders, hoisted to his knees,
Then hoisted his back end and lurched forward
On his knees and crumpling ankles, sliding in the mud
And collapsing plastered. She went on licking him.
30   She started eating the banner of thin raw flesh that
Spinnakered from her rear. We left her to it.
Blobbed antiseptic on to the sodden blood-dangle
Of his muddy birth-cord, and left her
Inspecting the new smell. The whole South West
Was black as nightfall.
Trailing squall-smokes hung over the moor leaning
And whitening towards us, then the world blurred
And disappeared in forty-five degree hail
And a gate-jerking blast. We got to cover.
40   Left to God the calf and his mother.

19 March 1974

Orf

Because his nose and face were one festering sore
That no treatment persuaded, month after month,
And his feet four sores, the same,
Which could only stand and no more,

Because his sickness was converting his growth
Simply to strengthening sickness
While his breath wheezed through a mask of flies
No stuff could rid him of

I shot the lamb.
I shot him while he was looking the other way.
I shot him between the ears.

He lay down.
His machinery adjusted itself
And his blood escaped, without loyalty.

But the lamb-life in my care
Left him where he lay, and stood up in front of me

Asking to be banished,
Asking for permission to be extinct,
For permission to wait, at least,

Inside my head
In the radioactive space
From which the meteorite had removed his body.

3 July 1976

Happy calf

Mother is worried, her low, short moos
Question what's going on. But her calf
Is quite happy, resting on his elbows,
With his wrists folded under, and his precious hind legs
Brought up beside him, his little hooves
Of hardly-used yellow-soled black.
She looms up, to reassure him with heavy lickings.
He wishes she'd go away. He's meditating
Black as a mole and as velvety,
With a white face-mask, and a pink parting,
With black tear-patches, but long
Glamorous white eyelashes. A mild narrowing
Of his eyes, as he lies, testing each breath
For its peculiar flavour of being alive.
Such a pink muzzle, but a black dap
Where he just touched his mother's blackness
With a tentative sniff. He is all quiet
While his mother worries to and fro, grazes a little,
Then looks back, a shapely mass
Against the South sky and the low frieze of hills,

And moos questioning warning. He just stays,
Head slightly tilted, in the mild illness
Of being quite contented, and patient
With all the busyness inside him, the growing
Getting under way. The wind from the North
Marching the high silvery floor of clouds
Trembles the grass-stalks near him. His head wobbles
Infinitesimally in the pulse of his life.
A buttercup leans on his velvet hip.
He folds his head back little by breathed little
Till it rests on his shoulder, his nose on his ankle,
And he sleeps. Only his ears stay awake.

14 May 1975

Coming down through Somerset

I flash-glimpsed in the headlights – the high moment
Of driving through England – a killed badger
Sprawled with helpless legs. Yet again
Manoeuvred lane-ends, retracked, waited
Out of decency for headlights to die,
Lifted by one warm hindleg in the world-night
A slain badger. August dust-heat. Beautiful,
Beautiful, warm, secret beast. Bedded him
Passenger, bleeding from the nose. Brought him close
Into my life. Now he lies on the beam
Torn from a great building. Beam waiting two years
To be built into new building. Summer coat
Not worth skinning off him. His skeleton – for the future.
Fangs, handsome concealed. Flies, drumming,
Bejewel his transit. Heatwave ushers him hourly
Towards his underworlds. A grim day of flies
And sunbathing. Get rid of that badger.
A night of shrunk rivers, glowing pastures,
Sea-trout shouldering up through trickles. Then the sun again
Waking like a torn-out eye. How strangely
He stays on into the dawn – how quiet
The dark bear-claws, the long frost-tipped guard hairs!
Get rid of that badger today.
And already the flies.

More passionate, bringing their friends. I don't want
To bury and waste him. Or skin him (it is too late).
Or hack off his head and boil it
To liberate his masterpiece skull. I want him
To stay as he is. Sooty gloss-throated,
With his perfect face. Paws so tired,
Power-body relegated. I want him
To stop time. His strength staying, bulky,
Blocking time. His rankness, his bristling wildness,
His thrillingly painted face.
A badger on my moment of life.
Not years ago, like the others, but now.
I stand
Watching his stillness, like an iron nail
Driven, flush to the head,
Into a yew post. Something has to stay.

   8 August 1975

Little red twin

Sister of little black twin,
Is sick. Scour. Granny, their mother,
For a change from pampering the herd's growthiest bullock,
Has this year preferred a pretty pair

Of miniature sisters. But her power-milk
Has overdone this baby's digestion who now,
Wobbly-legged, lags behind the migrations
From field-corner to corner. Her licked white face

Is still bravely calf-like, and does not
Comprehend the non-participation
Of her back-legs, or that huge drag-magnet
Of reluctance to move. Oh, she is sick!

She squirts yellow soup and waits.
Blue Dartmoor waits. The oak by the trough
Swirls its heat-wave shadow-skirt so slowly
It's half a day's sleep. Little red twin

Has to get her body here and there
On only quarter power. Now, one eighth power.

Examiners conclude, solemn,
She might not make it. Scour

Has drained her. She parches, dry-nosed.
We force-feed her with medical powder mix.
We brim her with pints of glucose water.
Her eyes are just plum softness, they thought

She'd come to be a cow. Dark-lovely
Eyes to attract protection. White eyelashes
To fringe her beauty that bit more perfect –
They have to go along with her failing.

And now after a day in the upper eighties
There she lies dead. The disc-harrow –
An intelligence test for perverse
Animal suicides – presented its puzzle,

And somehow she got her hind legs between bars
And fell as if cleverly forward, and locked
Where no mother could help her. There she lay
Up to eight hours, under the sun's weight.

As if to be sick-weak to the point of collapse
Had not been enough. Yet she's alive!

Extricated, slack as if limp dead,
But her eyes are watching. Her legs
Probably numb as dead. Her bleat
Worn to nothing. Just enough strength left

To keep her heart working, and her eye
Knowing and moist. Her mother
Had given her up and gone off. Now she comes back,
Clacks her ear tag, tack tack, on her horn,

Watches in still close-up, while we
Pump more glucose water down her daughter's
Helpless glug-glug. Sundown polishes the hay.
Propped on her crumpled legs, her sunk fire

Only just in. Now some sacks across her,
To keep in the power of the glucose
Through night's bare-space leakage. The minutes
Will come one by one, with little draughts,
And feel at her, and feel her ears for warmth,

And reckon up her chances, all night
Without any comfort. We leave her
To her ancestors, who should have prepared her

For worse than this. The smell of the mown hay
Mixed by moonlight with driftings of honeysuckle
And dog-roses and foxgloves, and all
The warmed spices of earth
In the safe casket of stars and velvet

Did bring her to morning. And now she will live.

1 June 1975

Teaching a dumb calf

She came in reluctant. The dark shed
Was too webby with reminiscences, none pleasant,
And she would not go in. She swung away
Rolled her tug belly in the oily sway of her legs.
Deep and straw-foul the mud. Leakage green
From earlier occupants, fermenting. I tried
To lift her calf in ahead of her, a stocky red block,
And she pacific drove her head at me
Light-nimble as a fist, bullied me off,
And swung away, calling her picky-footed boy
And pulling for the open field, the far beeches
In their fly-green emerald leaf of a day.
We shooed and shouted her back, and I tried again
Pulling the calf from among her legs, but it collapsed
Its hind legs and lay doggo, in the abominable mud,
And her twisting hard head, heavier than a shoulder,
Butted me off. And again she swung away.
Then I picked her calf up bodily and went in.
Little piggy eyes, she followed me. Then I roped her,
And drew her to the head of the stall, tightened her
Hard to the oak pillar, with her nose in the hay-rack,
And she choke-bellowed query comfort to herself.
He was trying to suck – but lacked the savvy.
He didn't get his nape down dipped enough,
Or his nose craning tongue upward enough
Under her tight hard bag of stiff teats each

The size of a labrador's muzzle. They were too big.
He nuzzled slobbering at their fat sides
But couldn't bring one in. They were dripping,
And as he excited them they started squirting.
I fumbled one into his mouth – I had to hold it,
Stuffing its slippery muscle into his suction,
His rim-teeth and working tongue. He preferred
The edge of my milk-lathered hand, easier dimension,
But he got going finally, all his new
Machinery learning suddenly, and she stilled,
Mooing indignity, rolling her red rims,
Till the happy warm peace gathered them
Into its ancient statue.

15 May 1975

Last load

Baled hay out in a field
Five miles from home. Barometer falling.
A muffler of still cloud padding the stillness.
The day after day of blue scorch up to yesterday,
The heavens of dazzling iron, that seemed unalterable,
Hard now to remember.

Now, tractor bounding along lanes, among echoes,
The trailer bouncing, all its iron shouting
Under sag-heavy leaves
That seem ready to drip with stillness.
Cheek in the air alert for the first speck.

You feel sure the rain's already started –
But for the tractor's din you'd hear it hushing
In all the leaves. But still not one drop
On your face or arm. You can't believe it.
Then hoicking bales, as if at a contest. Leaping
On and off the tractor as at a rodeo.

Hurling the bales higher. The loader on top
Dodging like a monkey. The fifth layer full
Then a teetering sixth. Then for a seventh
A row down the middle. And if a bale topples

You feel you've lost those seconds forever.
Then roping it all tight, like a hard loaf.

Then fast as you dare, watching the sky
And watching the load, and feeling the air darken
With wet electricity,
The load foaming through leaves, and wallowing
Like a tug-boat meeting the open sea –
The tractor's front wheels rearing up, as you race,
And pawing the air. Then all hands   30
Pitching the bales off, in under a roof,
Anyhow, then back for the last load.

And now as you dash through the green light
You see between dark trees
On all the little emerald hills
The desperate loading, under the blue cloud.

Your sweat tracks through your dust, your shirt flaps chill,
And bales multiply out of each other
All down the shorn field ahead.
The faster you fling them up, the more there are of them –   40
Till suddenly the field's grey empty. It's finished.

And a tobacco reek breaks in your nostrils
As the rain begins
Softly and vertically silver, the whole sky softly
Falling into the stubble all round you

The trees shake out their masses, joyful,
Drinking the downpour.
The hills pearled, the whole distance drinking
And the earth-smell warm and thick as smoke

And you go, and over the whole land   50
Like singing heard across evening water
The tall loads are swaying towards their barns
Down the deep lanes.

   20 June 1975

While she chews sideways

He gently noses the high point of her rear-end
Then lower and on each side of the tail,
Then flattens one ear, and gazes away, then decidedly
    turns, wheels,
And moves in on the pink-eyed long-horned grey.
He sniffs the length of her spine, arching slightly
And shitting a tumble-thud shit as he does so.
Now he's testy.
He takes a push at the crazy galloway with the laid back ears.
Now strolling away from them all, his aim at the corner gate.
He is scratching himself on the fence, his vibration
Travels the length of the wire.
His barrel bulk is a bit ugly.
As bulls go he's no beauty.
His balls swing in their sock, one side idle.
His skin is utility white, shit-patched,
Pink sinewed at the groin, and the dewlap nearly naked.
A feathery long permed bush of silky white tail –
It hangs straight like a bell rope
From the power-strake of his spine.
He eats steadily, not a cow in the field is open,
His gristly pinkish head, like a shaved blood-hound,
Jerking at the grass.
Overmuch muscle on the thighs, jerk-weight settling
Of each foot, as he eats forward.
His dangle tassel swings, his whole mind
Anchored to it and now dormant.
He's feeding disgustedly, impatiently, carelessly.
His nudity is a bit disgusting. Overmuscled
And a bit shameful, like an overdeveloped body-builder.
He has a juvenile look, a delinquent eye
Very unlikeable as he lifts his nostrils
And his upper lip, to test a newcomer.
Today none of that mooning around after cows,
That trundling obedience, like a trailer. None of the cows
Have any power today, and he's stopped looking.
He lays his head sideways, and worries the grass,
Keeping his intake steady.

15 September 1973

Sheep

The sheep has stopped crying.
All morning in her wire-mesh compound
On the lawn, she has been crying
For her vanished lamb. Yesterday they came.
Then her lamb could stand, in a fashion,
And make some tiptoe cringing steps.
Now he has disappeared.
He was only half the proper size.
And his cry was wrong. It was not
A dry little hard bleat, a baby-cry
Over a flat tongue, it was human,
It was a despairing human smooth Oh!
Like no lamb I ever heard. Its hindlegs
Cowered in under its lumped spine,
Its feeble hips leaned towards
Its shoulders for support. Its stubby
White wool pyramid head, on a tottery neck,
Had sad and defeated eyes, pinched, pathetic,
Too small, and it cried all the time
Oh! Oh! staggering towards
Its alert, baffled, stamping, storming mother
Who feared our intentions. He was too weak
To find her teats, or to nuzzle up in under,
He hadn't the gumption. He was fully
Occupied just standing, then shuffling
Towards where she'd removed to. She knew
He wasn't right, she couldn't
Make him out. Then his rough-curl legs,
So stoutly built, and hooved
With real quality tips,
Just got in the way, like a loose bundle
Of firewood he was cursed to manage,
Too heavy for him, lending sometimes
Some support, but no strength, no real help.
When we sat his mother on her tail, he mouthed her teat,
Slobbered a little, but after a minute
Lost aim and interest, his muzzle wandered,
He was managing a difficulty

Much more urgent and important. By evening
He could not stand. It was not
That he could not thrive, he was born
With everything but the will –
That can be deformed, just like a limb.
Death was more interesting to him.
Life could not get his attention.
So he died, with the yellow birth-mucus
Still in his cardigan.
He did not survive a warm summer night.
Now his mother has started crying again.
The wind is oceanic in the elms
And the blossom is all set.

    20 May 1974

    II

The mothers have come back
From the shearing, and behind the hedge
The woe of sheep is like a battlefield
In the evening, when the fighting is over,
And the cold begins, and the dew falls,
And bowed women move with water.
Mother Mother Mother the lambs
Are crying, and the mothers are crying.
Nothing can resist that probe, that cry
Of a lamb for its mother, or a ewe's crying
For its lamb. The lambs cannot find
Their mothers among those shorn strangers.
A half-hour they have lamented,
Shaking their voices in desperation.
Bald brutal-voiced mothers braying out,
Flat-tongued lambs chopping off hopelessness
Their hearts are in panic, their bodies
Are a mess of woe, woe they cry,
They mingle their trouble, a music
Of worse and worse distress, a worse entangling,
They hurry out little notes
With all their strength, cries searching this way and that.
The mothers force out sudden despair, blaaa!
On restless feet, with wild heads.

Their anguish goes on and on, in the June heat.
Only slowly their hurt dies, cry by cry,
As they fit themselves to what has happened.

  4 June 1976

The day he died

Was the silkiest day of the young year,
The first reconnaissance of the real spring,
The first confidence of the sun.

That was yesterday. Last night, frost.
And as hard as any of all winter.
Mars and Saturn and the Moon dangling in a bunch
On the hard, littered sky.
Today is Valentine's day.

Earth toast-crisp. The snowdrops battered.
Thrushes spluttering. Pigeons gingerly
Rubbing their voices together, in stinging cold.
Crows creaking, and clumsily
Cracking loose.

The bright fields look dazed.
Their expression is changed.
They have been somewhere awful
And come back without him.

The trustful cattle, with frost on their backs,
Waiting for hay, waiting for warmth,
Stand in a new emptiness.

From now on the land
Will have to manage without him.
But it hesitates, in this slow realisation of light,
Childlike, too naked, in a frail sun,
With roots cut
And a great blank in its memory.

A monument

Your burrowing, gasping struggle
In the knee-deep mud of the copse ditch
Where you cleared, with bill-hook and slasher,
A path for the wire, the boundary deterrent,
That memorable downpour last-ditch hand to hand battle
With the grip of the swamped blue clay, to and fro,
The wallowing weight of the wire-roll,
Your raincoat in tatters, face fixed at full effort,
And the to-fro lurching under posts and tools and pile-driver,
While the rain glittered all the sapling purple birches
And clothing deadened to sheet lead,
That appalling stubbornness of the plan, among thorns,
Will remain as a monument, hidden
Under tightening undergrowth
Deep under the roadside's car-glimpsed May beauty,
To be discovered by some future owner
As a wire tensed through impassable thicket,
A rusting limit, where cattle, pushing unlikely,
Query for two minutes, at most,
In their useful life.
And that is where I remember you,
Skullraked with thorns, sodden, tireless,
Hauling bedded feet free, floundering away
To check alignments, returning, hammering the staple
Into the soaked stake-oak, a careful tattoo
Precise to the tenth of an inch,
Under December downpour, mid-afternoon
Dark as twilight, using your life up.

The formal auctioneer

Is trying to sell cattle. He is like a man
Walking noisily through a copse
Where nothing will be flushed. All eyes watch.
The weathered, rooty, bushy pile of faces,
A snaggle of faces
Like pulled-out and heaped-up old moots,
The natural root archives
Of mid-Devon's mud-lane annals,

Watch and hide inside themselves
Absorbing the figures like weather,
Or if they bid, bid invisibly, visit
The bidding like night-foxes,
Slink in and out of bidding
As if they were no such fools
To be caught interested in anything,
Escaping a bidding with the secret
Celebration of a bargain, a straight gain
And that much now in hand.

When you were among them
Hidden in your own bidding, you stood tall,
A tree with two knot-eyes, immovable,
A root among roots, without leaf,
Buying a bullock, with the eye-gesture
Of a poker-player
Dead-panning his hand. Deep-root weathering
The heat-wave of a bargain.

A memory

Your bony white bowed back, in a singlet,
Powerful as a horse,
Bowed over an upturned sheep
Shearing under the East chill through-door draught
In the cave-dark barn, sweating and freezing –
Flame-crimson face, drum-guttural African curses
As you bundled the sheep
Like tying some oversize, overweight, spilling bale
Through its adjustments of position

The attached cigarette, bent at its glow
Preserving its pride of ash
Through all your suddenly savage, suddenly gentle
Masterings of the animal

You were like a collier, a face-worker
In a dark hole of obstacle
Heedless of your own surfaces
Inching by main strength into the solid hour,

Bald, arch-wrinkled, weathered dome bowed
Over your cigarette comfort

Till you stretched erect through a groan
Letting a peeled sheep leap free

Then nipped the bud of stub from your lips
And with glove-huge, grease-glistening carefulness
Lit another at it

Now you have to push

Your hands
Lumpish roots of earth cunning
So wrinkle-scarred, such tomes
Of what has been collecting centuries
At the bottom of so many lanes
Where roofs huddle smoking, and cattle
Trample the ripeness

Now you have to push your face
So tool-worn, so land-weathered,
This patch of ancient, familiar locale,
Your careful little moustache,
Your gangly long broad Masai figure
Which you decked so dapperly to dances,
Your hawser and lever strength
Which you used, so recklessly,
Like a tractor, guaranteed unbreakable

Now you have to push it all –
Just as you loved to push the piled live hedge-boughs –
Into a gathering blaze

And as you loved to linger late into the twilight,
Coaxing the last knuckle embers,
Now you have to stay
Right on, into total darkness

Hands

Your hands were strange – huge.
A farmer's joke: 'still got your bloody great hands!'
You used them with as little regard
As old iron tools – as if their creased, glossed, crocodile leather
Were nerveless, like an African's footsoles.

When the barbed wire, tightening hum-rigid,
Snapped and leaped through your grip
You flailed your fingers like a caned boy, and laughed:
'Barbarous wire!' then just ignored them
As the half-inch deep, cross-hand rips dried.   10

And when your grasp nosed bullocks, prising their mouths wide,
So they dropped to their knees
I understood again
How the world of half-ton hooves, and horns,
And hides heedless as oaken-boarding, comes to be manageable.

Hands more of a piece with your tractor
Than with their own nerves,
Having no more compunction than dung-forks,
But suave as warm oil inside the wombs of ewes,
And monkey delicate   20

At that cigarette
Which glowed patiently through all your labours
Nursing the one in your lung
To such strength, it squeezed your strength to water
And stopped you.

Your hands lie folded, estranged from all they have done
And as they have never been, and startling –
So slender, so taper, so white,
Your mother's hands suddenly in your hands –
In that final strangeness of elegance.   30

from EARTH-NUMB (1979)

Earth-numb

Dawn – a smouldering fume of dry frost.
Sky-edge of red-hot iron.
Daffodils motionless – some fizzled out.
The birds – earth-brim simmering.
Sycamore buds unsticking – the leaf out-crumpling, purplish.

The pheasant cock's glare-cry. Jupiter ruffling softly.

Hunting salmon. And hunted
And haunted by apparitions from tombs
Under the smoothing tons of dead element
In the river's black canyons.   10

The lure is a prayer. And my searching –
Like the slow sun.
A prayer, like a flower opening.
A surgeon operating
On an open heart, with needles –

And bang! the river grabs at me

A mouth-flash, an electrocuting malice
Like a trap, trying to rip life off me –
And the river stiffens alive,
The black hole thumps, the whole river hauls   20
And I have one.

A piling voltage hums, jamming me stiff –
Something terrified and terrifying
Gleam-surges to and fro through me
From the river to the sky, from the sky into the river

Uprooting dark bedrock, shatters it in air,
Cartwheels across me, slices thudding through me
As if I were the current –
Till the fright flows all one way down the line

And a ghost grows solid, a hoverer,   30
A lizard green slither, banner heavy –

Then the wagging stone pebble head
Trying to think on shallows –

Then the steel spectre of purples
From the forge of water
Gagging on emptiness

As the eyes of incredulity
Fix their death-exposure of the celandine and the cloud.

That girl

Promised by her looks, is saving up
To buy a maxi-coat.
It will not keep her warm.
She does not want
It to keep her warm. She wants it
To hurry her
Down that lane – which her wanted money
Conceals like a bank
Of flowers, and at the end of which,
When all the flowers have gone,
She will lie naked on the bottom-most weave of life
No better than a bacterium

But as joyful
And as coddled and supplied
By grateful nature
By young mother nature
By old father nature, too,
Hairy old man.

Here is the Cathedral

                              And here
Under the West Front Saints' crumbling features
The Roman Garrison bath-house is being unearthed
Out of the dried blood of the redland marl –
Splayed, bleeding in rain, like an accident,
Gaped-at, photographed, commented-on, and coddled
With waterproofs. Nobody knows what to think of it.

And here are plague burials, incidentals
Surprised by the excavation –

Amber skeletons in their wedding chambers,   10
Touching couples, modest husbands and wives,
Dazzled awake by this sudden rude afterlife,
Cleaned with toothbrushes tenderly as hurt mouths,
Fleshless handbones folded over stomachs
Which no longer exist, and for faces
Clods of rained-on breccia –
                    And here
Under the tarmac brink, under headlamp chromes
Of Peugeots, Toyotas, Volkswagens, Jaguars, Saabs,
Spades have hacked an eight-foot vertical cliff
Through mediaeval solid bone-dump, skull-caps   20
Carried about by dogs, rib-struts, limb-strakes
Littering the redland mud, like trampled laths
At a demolition. And this is the House of the Dead,
Open to everybody.

              And here is the door
Of the Cathedral. Going in out of the rain
I met a dark figure in the doorway:

Shuffling on rotten feet in rotten shoes
The whuffling wino with simplified face
Outsize R.A.F. greatcoat, trailing tatters,
Dragged lower by the black unlabelled bottle   30
In his pocket, was asking for something. A whimper.
A paw red as if sore, oily and creased,
Muffled some request.

              Cash for renovations –
A cup of tea and a sandwich.

My first tenpenny piece conjured voices.
All my loose change shattered the heights –
And two furious ones, with sparkling faces,
With fierce heavenly eyes, with Sunday suits,
Arrived in a glare of question.
              One swayed
Crushing me with new worlds of consideration,   40
With angelic mouthfuls of sociology,
The other, pink-scrubbed, brass-eyed, Christian Knight,
Was butting at the wino with his chest,
Impeccable godly fists clenched at his seams
At attention, like a police horse at a crowd,

He bumped the faceless mop of boy-black hair,
The dwarf-swollen nose, the coat on two shabby boots –

'How many times do you have to be told – out!
We've told you, haven't we? You do know, don't you?
Then out! Get out! Get out and stay out!'

Huddling mouse in his cloth,
Goblin aboriginal under his hair mop
Shuffled and tottered out.
       Flushed with the work
Glistening righteousness and staring image
Wrathful commissionaires
Whisked back into the heights
Among columns and arches –

Leaving me an expendable tortoise
Of the war in Heaven.
       Between masks
In rictus of sanctity, and the glossed slabs
Of the defunct.
     With whispers
Draining down from the roots of the hair – OUT
OUT OUT OUT

Postcard from Torquay

He gazed round, the tall young German at the jetty,
With a few words
That sounded like English so lordly
It was incomprehensible. It was actually *echt Deutsch*.

Under one hand, the uptilting stern of his glass yacht.
In the other, the dainty, quivering wind-vane
Like a conductor's baton. He paused.
His two companions, almost English

In their woolly gloom, demoralised Bavarians,
Brother and bespectacled dull sister,
Hating England,
Humped by the brilliant yacht like too much baggage.

He narrowed heron-pale eyes
In the spanking mid-morning Sunday wind

That bounced off the July sea, and panicked bunting
And slapped shots out of the stacked deckchairs.

He poised, in the wobbly mirror
Of the snapping puddles
And the curl-mouthed glances of the rabble English,
Gazed over the sea's heroic bulge,   20

Then stalked off
In his minimal continental sportswear,
Commandant – at home
On the first morning of Occupation –

To arrange, with lofty carrying words,
His costly yacht's descent
Into that swell of tourist effluent
And holiday turds.

Old age gets up

Stirs its ashes and embers, its burnt sticks

An eye powdered over, half-melted and solid again
Ponders
Ideas that collapse
At the first touch of attention

The light at the window, so square and so same
So full-strong as ever, the window-frame
A scaffold in space, for eyes to lean on

Supporting the body, shaped to its old work
Making small movements in grey air
Numbed from the blurred accident
Of having lived, the fatal, real injury
Under the amnesia

Something tries to save itself – searches
For defences – but words evade
Like flies with their own notions

Old age slowly gets dressed
Heavily dosed with death's night
Sits on the bed's edge

Pulls its pieces together
Loosely tucks in its shirt
Pulls the clouds of star-gas together

Leans on the door-frame, breathing heavily
Creaks toward the bathroom

Nefertiti

Sits in the bar-corner – being bought
Halves by the shouting, giggling, market-tipsy
Farmers who squabble to pay –

She hunches, to deepen
Her giddy cleavage and hang properly
The surrealist shocking masterpiece
Of her make-up.

She can't breathe a word
That wouldn't short out
The trip-wire menace
Of her precariously-angled
Knees and wrist. Gorgeous, delicate,
Sipping insect,
With eyelids and lips
Machined to the millionth.

She gets her weird power
In the abattoir. All day you hear
The sheep wailing in religious terror,
The cattle collapsing to pour out
Their five gallons of blood onto concrete,
Pigs flinging their legs apart with screams

For the dividing steel
Of her pen in the office.

A Motorbike

We had a motorbike all through the war
In an outhouse – thunder, flight, disruption
Cramped in rust, under washing, abashed, outclassed
By the Brens, the Bombs, the Bazookas elsewhere.

The war ended, the explosions stopped.
The men surrendered their weapons
And hung around limply.
Peace took them all prisoner.
They were herded into their home towns.
A horrible privation began   10
Of working a life up out of the avenues
And the holiday resorts and the dance-halls.

Then the morning bus was as bad as any labour truck,
The foreman, the boss, as bad as the S.S.
And the ends of the street and the bends of the road
And the shallowness of the shops and the shallowness of the beer
And the sameness of the next town
Were as bad as electrified barbed wire.
The shrunk-back war ached in their testicles
And England dwindled to the size of a dog-track.   20

So there came this quiet young man
And he bought our motorbike for twelve pounds.
And he got it going, with difficulty.
He kicked it into life – it erupted
Out of the six year sleep, and he was delighted.

A week later, astride it, before dawn,
A misty frosty morning,
He escaped

Into a telegraph pole
On the long straight west of Swinton.   30

Deaf School

The deaf children were monkey-nimble, fish-tremulous and sudden.
Their faces were alert and simple
Like faces of little animals, small night lemurs caught in the
    flash-light.
They lacked a dimension,
They lacked a subtle wavering aura of sound and responses
    to sound.
The whole body was removed
From the vibration of air, they lived through the eyes,
The clear simple look, the instant full attention.
Their selves were not woven into a voice
Which was woven into a face
Hearing itself, its own public and audience,
An apparition in camouflage, an assertion in doubt –
Their selves were hidden, and their faces looked out of hiding.
What they spoke with was a machine,
A manipulation of fingers, a control-panel of gestures
Out there in the alien space
Separated from them –

Their unused faces were simple lenses of watchfulness
Simple pools of earnest watchfulness

Their bodies were like their hands
Nimbler than bodies, like the hammers of a piano,
A puppet agility, a simple mechanical action
A blankness of hieroglyph
A stylised lettering
Spelling out approximate signals

While the self looked through, out of the face of simple concealment
A face not merely deaf, a face in darkness, a face unaware,
A face that was simply the front skin of the self concealed
    and separate

Photostomias

A small, predatory, luminous fish of the great deeps.

I

Through roofless Gulf-cellars
Hungers a galaxy.

Through black obsidian
A fossil ghost craves.

A feast, charged with lights,
Searching for guests.

Here is the radiant host.
Nobody loves him.

He is just what he looks like – a calculus
Woven by atoms on a lost warp of sunlight.   10

Quiet little Einstein
Of outer darkness.

His formula final – an illumination
Of fangs, a baleful perspective

Of the gravity
With which this Universe shall consume itself.

At the sunken window of the world
He peers in.

II

Volcanic, meteoric ooze
Opens an eye – lights up.

Apotheosis – Buddha-faced, the tiger
In his robe of flames.
                    And no further
From belief's numb finger
Than the drab-jacketted
Glow-worm beetle, in a spooky lane,
On a wet evening.
                    The Peacock butterfly, pulsing
On a September thistle-top

Is just as surely a hole
In what was likely.

Star-hardened, over this scene,
The miserly heather-flower, with his lamp,
Leans from the atom.

                        Blossoms
Pushing from under blossoms –
From the one wound's
Depth of congealments and healing.

Earth is gulping the same
Opium as the heart.

III

Creation's hammer
Anvil of Nothing

A spark
A larval

Insect-frail
Gadget of spectrum hunger fury

A prisoner
A prison

Eros, dumbstruck, starving, staring
From a space-computer –

Glassy digits
Bottomless zero

Jehova – mucous and phosphorescence
In the camera's glare –

A decalogue
A rainbow.

The Lovepet

Was it an animal was it a bird?
She stroked it. He spoke to it softly.
She made her voice its happy forest.

He brought it out with sugarlump smiles.
Soon it was licking their kisses.

She gave it the strings of her voice which it swallowed
He gave it the blood of his face it grew eager
She gave it the liquorice of her mouth it began to thrive
He opened the aniseed of his future
And it bit and gulped, grew vicious, snatched
The focus of his eyes
She gave it the steadiness of her hand
He gave it the strength of his spine it ate everything

It began to cry what could they give it
They gave it their calendars it bolted their diaries
They gave it their sleep it gobbled their dreams
Even while they slept
It ate their bodyskin and the muscle beneath
They gave it vows its teeth clashed its starvation
Through every word they uttered

It found snakes under the floor it ate them
It found a spider horror
In their palms and ate it

They gave it double smiles and blank silence
It chewed holes in their carpets
They gave it logic
It ate the colour of their hair
They gave it every argument that would come
They gave it shouting and yelling they meant it
It ate the faces of their children
They gave it their photograph albums they gave it their records
It ate the colour of the sun
They gave it a thousand letters they gave it money
It ate their future complete it waited for them
Staring and starving
They gave it screams it had gone too far
It ate into their brains
It ate the roof
It ate lonely stone it ate wind crying famine
It went furiously off

They wept they called it back it could have everything
It stripped out their nerves chewed chewed flavourless

It bit at their numb bodies they did not resist
It bit into their blank brains they hardly knew

It moved bellowing
Through a ruin of starlight and crockery

It drew slowly off they could not move

It went far away they could not speak

Second Birth

When he crept back, searching for
The womb-doorway, remorseful,
It was an ugly grave
Fallen in on bleached sticks.

For flesh
It had dry bleached weeds over dry stones
Of a dried-up river.

Well it was a revelation to meet
Mother Death, a smack on the nose-end
That inverted all his ideas.

There is nothing to be done
About what a head becomes
After years in wild earth.

And there is nowhere else to look for it.
And if what it says now
Can't be understood
Nothing else can speak for it.

Such words
Can only be swallowed, like stones,
And voided, or carried for life,
Or died of.

Song of Longsight

No came from the earth
The egg Yes grew at No's nucleus
The egg hatched and No came out

Wet with Yes
And the voice of the No-bird was Yes

The No-bird reversed itself on a spike
Yes was now its ghost
Yes flew into a cliff-crack, like a rock-dove
So the No of Earth
Had to give birth and it was Yes

Yes was sick with No
Surgeons cut and found a star No
Which rose above earth, as her sign
A star like a sword, with downward point
Yes recovered

Living in uplooking fear and knowing
That whatever he begot on his kind
Could only be No
That whatever he conceived in his own heart
Could only be No
And there was nothing he could do or become
Which would not be No

The laws of space and matter are bitter

Life Is Trying to Be Life

Death also is trying to be life.
Death is in the sperm like the ancient mariner
With his horrible tale.

Death mews in the blankets – is it a kitten?
It plays with dolls but cannot get interested.
It stares at the windowlight and cannot make it out.
It wears baby clothes and is patient.
It learns to talk, watching the others' mouths.
It laughs and shouts and listens to itself numbly.

It stares at people's faces   10
And sees their skin like a strange moon, and stares at the grass
In its position just as yesterday.
And stares at its fingers and hears: 'Look at that child!'
Death is a changeling
Tortured by daisy chains and Sunday bells

It is dragged about like a broken doll
By little girls playing at mothers and funerals.
Death only wants to be life. It cannot quite manage.

Weeping it is weeping to be life
20   As for a mother it cannot remember.

Death and Death and Death, it whispers
With eyes closed, trying to feel life

Like the shout in joy
Like the glare in lightning
That empties the lonely oak.
                    And that is the death
In the antlers of the Irish Elk. It is the death
In the cave-wife's needle of bone. Yet it still is not death –

Or in the shark's fang which is a monument
Of its lament
30   On a headland of life.

A Citrine Glimpse

I

It was slender but

The chance flashed startling – a glance
A footfall

And stones leapt in their prison
Clay cried out in its chains
Bedrock, in its little-ease, cried with silent open mouth

The sun watched through bars, stilled
Like one tortured too long
But the air
10   Wept for its long hopelessness and for joy
Water fell down where it laboured
And worshipped full length, and leaped

He is alive
He who will free us all
He who will give us new limbs and eyes

It will not be much longer only days
He will lift us
We shall be in his arms, our fingers will touch the soul

And we shall enter the great beauty

We shall leap over each other, with him and his mate   20
Through the ecstasy flame

We shall sing through real mouths

For joy

The earth shook

II

He had hardly stepped

When he heard the water crying
He stared at it it continued to cry
And sob under naked shoulders

He stepped again
And the swamp quaked and a cry came
All the length of the reeds
A groan stifled and a silence worse

He stepped again
And stony words deep under his feet jabbered   10
He listened
As if he were empty sky listening
The stony words tore their throats and deepened on into a
    hard agony
Beyond hearing, a silence that numbed

He stepped
And the moon in the bottom of the sea
Was a shriek, a gouging
The sea was like the hands and the hair
Of the moon
Whose shriek brought blood into the mouth   20
And was the dumbness of blood
And was the blackness of moonlight

Too late to flee
He hung
A nerve torn from the root of the tongue

The wind breathed on his rawness a word

And a wolf cried in its deformity

FOUR TALES TOLD BY AN IDIOT

I

I woke in the bed of the Rains

Of the fat sobbing one, the overflowing

Whose elephant madness
And rickets and dysentery and deprivation

Dropped on me like a krait
In a cellar of fruit-machines

And held me in an amazon boggy fastness
Whose performance of misty bellowing

Acted the digesting a carven temple
In which I was the basalt stump of some god.

I escaped, in a malarial sweat,
To a worse chamber.

2

I was tied to a stake, in a tectite desert,
By lion-eyes

Who so focussed the sun, with her glassy body,
She roasted my inmost marrow, my inmost ghost

Giving my skin no more than a slight flush.

Then she poured me water.

And so distorted the moon
She could grind my skull, not in the dimension of illusion,

With huge stones of illusion.

Then she gave me bread.

Then dragged the spinal cord out of me downward
Like a white hot wire –

This she swallowed and became incandescent.

And lay down in front of me with my shadow.
The sun set, and they vanished together.

3

Night-wind, a freedom
That wanted me, took me

Shook doors, and left shapes of me leaning there
Shook windows, which kept a faint print of me

Twitched gates, left a habit of me to squeak out in those hinges
Shook trees, where twists of me still tangle

Swayed flowers, and much of me withered there later
Swept grass, the impress will not altogether release me

Stirred papers, wisps of me stayed snagged in hooked letters
Stirred garments, which motes of me will never be out of

Stirred river, which subtracted me from my reflection
Stirred fire, which shed me numb-frozen

On a cinder of heaven.

4

That star
Will blow your hand off

That star
Will scramble your brains and your nerves

That star
Will frazzle your skin off

That star
Will turn everybody yellow and stinking

That star
Will scorch everything dead fumed to its blueprint

That star
Will make the earth melt

That star ... and so on.

And they surround us. And far into infinity.
These are the armies of the night.
There is no escape.
Not one of them is good, or friendly, or corruptible.

One chance remains: KEEP ON DIGGING THAT HOLE

KEEP ON DIGGING AWAY AT THAT HOLE

Actaeon

He looked at her but he could not see her face.
He could see her hair of course, it was a sort of furniture.
Like his own. He had paid for it.
He could see the useful gadgets of her hands. Which produced
    food naturally.

And he could hear her voice
Which was a comfortable wallpaper.
You can get used to anything.
But he could not see her face.

He did not understand the great danger.

The jigsaw parts of her face, still loose in their box,
Began to spin.
Began to break out.
Openly they became zig-zagging hounds.
Their hunger rang on the hills.
Soon they were out of control.

But the blank of his face
Just went on staring at her
Talking carpet talking hooverdust.

And just went on staring at her
As he was torn to pieces.
Those hounds tore him to pieces.
All the leaves and petals of his body were utterly scattered.

And still his face-blank went on
Staring, seeing nothing, feeling nothing

And still his voice went on, decorating the floor

Even though life had ceased.

SEVEN DUNGEON SONGS

1 *The Wolf*

Gazed down at the babe.
The beast's gangrenous breath
Clouded the tabula rasa.

The wolf was wounded in the jaw.
The blood dripped
On to the babe's hands.
The babe reached towards the pretty creature,
Laughing a baby laugh,
A soft-brained laugh.

The wolf
Picked up the babe and ran among the stars.

The wolf's eye was icy with pain
And milk dripped from its tits.

The baby's cry
Echoed among the precipices.

2

Dead, she became space-earth
Broken to pieces.
Plants nursed her death, unearthed her goodness.

But her murderer, mad-innocent
Sucked at her offspring, reckless of blood,
Consecrating them in fire, muttering
It is good to be God.

He used familiar hands
Incriminating many,

And he borrowed mouths, leaving names
Being himself nothing

But a tiger's sigh, a wolf's music
A song on a lonely road

What it is
Risen out of mud, fallen from space
That stares through a face.

   3

Face was necessary – I found face.
Hands – I found hands.

I found shoulders, I found legs
I found all bits and pieces.

We were me, and lay quiet.
I got us all of a piece, and we lay quiet.

We just lay.
Sunlight had prepared a wide place

And we lay there.
Air nursed us.

We recuperated.
While maggots blackened to seeds, and blood warmed its stone.

Only still something
Stared at me and screamed

Stood over me, black across the sun,
And mourned me, and would not help me get up.

   4

The earth locked out the light,
Blocking the light, like a door locked.
But a crack of light

Between sky and earth, was enough.
He called it, Earth's halo.

And the lizard spread of his fingers
Reached for it.

He called it, The leakage of air
Into this suffocation of earth.

And the gills of his rib-cage
Gulped to get more of it.

His lips pressed to its coolness
Like an eye to a crack.

He lay like the already-dead

Tasting the tears
Of the wind-shaken and weeping
Tree of light.

5

I walk
Unwind with activity of legs
The tangled ball
Which was once the orderly circuit of my body

Some night in the womb
All my veins and capillaries were taken out
By some evil will
And knotted in a great ball and stuffed back inside me

Now I rush to and fro
I try to attach a raw broken end
To some steady place, then back away
I look for people with clever fingers
Who might undo me

The horrible ball just comes
People's fingers snarl it worse

I hurl myself
To jerk out the knot
Or snap it

And come up short

So dangle and dance
The dance of unbeing

6

The oracle
Had nothing to say

The crevasse
Was silent.

And the eyes of the witnesses,
The human eyes, jammed in flesh,
Which seemed to know, in their silence,
Were graves
Of silence.

And the tall rock of the sacred place,
An instrument, among stars,
Of the final music,
The final justice,
Was silent.

A bird cried out in the sky
As if the great crystal of silence
Suddenly split across.

But the rubbly dust at my feet
Could not utter
What it was humbled to.

And the great crystal of light
Healed, as before,
And was silent.

7

If mouth could open its cliff
If ear could unfold from this strata
If eyes could split their rock and peep out finally

If hands of mountain-fold
Could get a proper purchase
If feet of fossil could lift

If head of lakewater and weather
If body of horizon
If whole body and balancing head

If skin of grass could take messages
And do its job properly

If spine of earth-foetus
Could unfurl

If man-shadow out there moved to my moves

The speech that works air
Might speak me

A Knock at the door

                         You open the door
And you step back
From a sheltering bulk. A tumblesky wet January
Mid-morning. Close, tall, in-leaning
Hairiness of a creature, darkness of a person –

A bristling of wet-rotten woods, mould-neglect, night-weather,
A hurt wildness stands there for help
And is saying something. Wild lumpy coat,
Greasy face-folds and sly eyes and a bandit abruptness,
Speech nearly not speech   10
Ducking under speech, asking for money
As if not asking. Huge storm-sky strangeness

And desperation. He knows he stands
In a shatter of your expectations. He waits for you
To feel through to his being alive.
He wants to flee. His cornered wildness
Dodges about in his eyes
That try to hide inside themselves, and his head jerks up
Trying to fit back together odd bits of dignity,
And he goes on, muttering, nodding, signalling O.K. O.K.   20

Till you register: Money.

You give him bread, plastered with butter and piled with marmalade,
And stand watching him cram it into his mouth –
His wet, red, agile mouth
In the swollen collapsed face.
His grimed forefinger cocked.

A black column of frayed coat, belted with string,
Has surfaced for help.
Stares into the house-depth past you
30   Stranger than a snow-covered starving stag.

Munches, wipes his fingers on his coat, and wipes his mouth
With the black-creased red palm.
A smile works his rubbery face
Like a hand working into a big glove.
His eyes wobble at you
Then an assault of launched eloquence
Like a sudden flooding of gratitude –
But you can't decode it.
He is extricating from his ponderous coat a topless bean-can.
40   *Spot o' tea in this ere, surr, if it's possible –*

A prayer to be invisible,
Eyes flickering towards the road as if casually
He dips his lips to the scalding can's metal and sucks
Coolingly, hurriedly,
And now it comes again (the tossed-empty can back in his pocket)
In a slither of thanks and salutes and shoulder-squarings
And sparring, feinting, dagger-stab glances
From the dissolved blue eyes
And the cornered mouse panic trying to slip into the house
        past you –

50   MONEY!

Anaesthetic for the big body,
Its glistening full veins, its pumping organs,
Its great nerves to the eyes,
Unmanageable parcel of baggy pain
With its dry-sore brains, its tied rawness –

You give him your pocketful and he buries it without a glance
And he's gone
60   Under his shoulder hunch, with hiding hands
And feet pretending no hurry
Under spattering and sneezing trees, over shining cobbles

To fall within two hundred yards
Dead-drunk in the church, to lie
Blowing, as if in post-operational shock,
Abandoned to space,

A lolling polyp of sweaty life, wrapped in its Guy Fawkes rags
Bristling face-patch awry.

ORTS

1 *Each new moment my eyes*

Open to the candidate
For being –
          but my brain closes
Exhausted, staled and appalled

But beyond that something opens
Arms
       like a host who has been
Watching the clock to the point
Of despair
             and like a swan launching
Into misty sunrise –

Convulsion of wings, snake-headed
Uncoilings, conflagration of waters

2 *Are they children*

                    or senile?
A touch
And words scatter from him
Him, him and still more him
Like seeds
From Jumping Jack Balsam

And from the sealed, limestone, rockface lip
A drip

And from the lightning-humped oak, out of its lumpen
blazonry
Of burst mouths
Its gargoyle vaginas and old brain-wounds

A leaf – a leaf – a leaf

3 *For weights of blood*

Granite farms.
For swaying breaths
Granite bridges.

For a watering eye
Granite walls
Granite headstones
For what is lost

For what adheres
To the lips' stir
As to the granite
A hand's shadow.

Granite oblations
Propped on the summit
For faceless presence ·
By soft-hand absence.

5 *In the M5 restaurant*

Our sad coats assemble at the counter

The tyre face pasty
The neon of plaster flesh
With little inexplicable eyes
Holding a dish with two buns

Symbolic food
Eaten by symbolic faces
Symbolic eating movements

The road drumming in the wall, drumming in the head

The road going nowhere and everywhere

My freedom evidently
Is to feed my life
Into a carburettor

Petroleum has burned away all
But a still-throbbing column
Of carbon-monoxide and lead.

I attempt a firmer embodiment
With illusory coffee
And a gluey quasi-pie.

6 *Poets*

Crowd the horizons, poised, wings
Lifted in elation, vast
Armadas of illusion
Waiting for a puff.

Or they dawn, singing birds – all
Mating calls
Battle bluff
And crazy feathers.

Or disappear
Into the grass-blade atom – one flare
Annihilating the world
To the big-eyed, simple light that fled

When the first word lumped out of the flint.

7 *Grosse Fuge*

Rouses in its cave
Under faint peaks of light

Flares abrupt at the sun's edge, dipping again
This side of the disc
Now coming low out of the glare

Coming under skylines
Under seas, under liquid corn
Snaking among poppies

Soft arrival pressing the roof of ghost
Creaking of old foundations
The ear cracking like a dry twig

Heavy craving weight
Of eyes on your nape
Unadjusted to world

Huge inching through hair, through veins
Tightening stealth of blood
Breath in the tunnel of spine

And the maneater
Opens its mouth and the music
Sinks its claw
Into your skull, a single note

Picks you up by the small of the back, weightless
Vaults into space, dangling your limbs

Devours you leisurely among litter of stars
Digests you into its horrible joy
This is the tiger of heaven

Hoists people out of their clothes

Leaves its dark track across the octaves

8 *Lucretia*

The buttercup lifts her wing-cases
From between the claws
Of the retracting glacier.

Still she shakes out, on her crane stilt,
With her green core of tough subsistence,
Venturing over the bog.

So Lucretia has overtaken Englishness
The angler golden to the knees
The steeple at anchor on the river of honey

Just as she did the trekking weight of the mammoth
That jolted her cup
And set her pollens smoking.

9 *The Cathedral*

                       for all its defiance
Of the demolisher
Is ghost only.

As the coral island
Is the communal ghost of the corals.

As the jawbone
Goes on monumentally grinning
Over the spirit of temporal profit.

You too are a ghost –
The mountain, no less than the cat of the mountain –
Susceptible to a breath.

I too am a ghost
Where the airiest words

Move like ploughs,
                    like bullets
                              and like chains.

10 *Pan*

Flowers open pits of allure.
The beast's glance makes the ghost faint.

Invitation in the bird's throat, a gobletful,
Wet mouth and hot under-softness
Where the heart struggles at the surface.
Abandonment of water, long openings,
Dishevelled silks, and nakedness of what resists nothing.

The painful stiff grace of insects
Making the stones ache.

So early earth, in stifled convulsion,
With bellowings, with gasps,
Roots torn up,
With life gushing from the body in relief
As eye widens against eye,
With death in hot bracken and birth under catkins

Yields her daughters.

11 *Speech out of shadow*

Not your eyes, but what they disguise

Not your skin, with just that texture and light
But what uses it as cosmetic

Not your nose – to be or not to be beautiful
But what it is the spy for

Not your mouth, not your lips, not their adjustments
But the maker of the digestive tract

Not your breasts
Because they are diversion and deferment

Not your sexual parts, your proffered rewards
Which are in the nature of a flower
Technically treacherous

Not the webs of your voice, your poise, your tempo
Your drug of a million micro-signals

But the purpose.

The unearthly stone in the sun.

The glare
Of the falcon, behind its hood

Tamed now
To its own mystifications

And the fingerings of men.

12 *Everything is waiting*

The tree stilled in tree – swells in waiting.
The river stilled in flow – in away-flow push.

Even the birds, here and gone –
The sparrowhawk, bolt out of the oak-tree
Slamming the crying dipper
Down through the water-hatch

To hold its breath in bubble-cellar safety –

Are waiting.

14 *Flight from Egypt*

He stole immortality
From the sleeping sun's disarray
Like moisture from the eye-corner.

He stole beauty
From the sun's windy mirror.
He stole the laws
Like a hair from the beard of light.
He stole music
From the shell of the sun's ear.

He stole the cloak of joy
From the wall.

The slender daughter of the sun embraced him.

Together they fled, into darkness,
On the only beast available –

The ugliest of the ugly. And she fell off.

15 *Beeches, leafless*

                              and lean hills
Muscle earth's grip on the core.

Cities, oceans, each thing anchors it
To the anchor of itself.

Yet it is weak. Weak

And unreal. Look –

              Dusk
Exorcises it, without effort.
And the whole globe flits, bat-like,

From this bright unaltered, unaltering place
Where you sit in final fear, and you,
And you still not daring to look up

Only waiting for me to touch you

And tell you again, 'It's going to be O.K.'

16 *Look back*

See how he waves goodbye
Gingerly fathoming his own smile
See how he goes on waving

While the numbness grows in from his nails and hair
The ignorance from the platform and the soles of his shoes
The unknowing from the weave of his coat

The blindness from the bones of his face
The blindness of his skin
While the girdered deadness grows down from the station dome

Till nothing is there
But his shape in its clothes
Noticed by nobody in particular

Walking tinily out of the station

17 *Buzz in the window*

                                    Buzz frantic
And prolonged. Fly down near the corner,
The cemetery den. A big blue-fly
Is trying to drag a plough, too deep
In earth too stony, immovable. Then the fly
Buzzing its full revs forward, budges backward.
Clings. Deadlock.
The spider has gripped its anus. Slender talons
Test the blue armour gently, the head
Buried in the big game. He tugs
Tigerish, half the size of his prey. A pounding
Glory-time for the spider. For the other
A darkening summary of some circumstances
In the window-corner, with a dead bee,
Wing-petals, husks of insect-armour, a brambled
Glade of dusty web. It buzzes less
As the drug argues deeper and deeper.
In fluttery soundless tremors it tries to keep
A hold on the air. The North sky
Moves northward. The blossom is clinging
To its hopes, re-furnishing the constant

Of ignorant life. The blue-fly,
Without changing expression, only adjusting
Its leg-stance, as if to more comfort,
Undergoes ultimate ghastliness. Finally agrees to it.
The spider tugs, retreating. The fly
Is going to let it do everything. Something is stuck.
The fly is fouled in web. Intelligence, the spider,
Comes round to look and patiently, joyfully,
Starts cutting the mesh. Frees it. Returns
To the haul – homeward in that exhausted ecstasy
The loaded hunters of the Pleistocene
Never recorded either.

18 *Lumb*

At the bottom of the Arctic sea, they say.

Or 'Terrible as an army with banners.'

If I wait, I am a castle
Built with blocks of pain.

If I set out
A kayak stitched with pain.

19 *The express*

                         with a bang
Lays its stationary blur
Of exploding stasis five seconds
Across our eyes where we loll

Blurred broader on benches.
It rivets ear-holes, wind-tunnels
The world into a fleeing
Panic of atoms

Lifts the long trembling platform
To the dimension brink
Of disintegration. Wrenches
A whole dull covering off

Whips it away, claps it
Into its vanishing, amputated
Rear-end, with a fireworks
Of blue and yellow, in under

Its black iron rockers ...
                         That is how
You nearly arrived.
                    Already gone
Leaving silence mangled
And the flayed soul
Settling among steely gleams and cinders.

20 *T.V. off*

He hears lithe trees and last leaves swatting the glass –

Staring into flames, through the grille of age
Like a late fish, face clothed with fungus,
Keeping its mouth upstream.

Remorseful for what nobody any longer suffers
Nostalgic for what he would not give twopence to see back
Hopeful for what he will not miss when it fails

Who lay a night and a day and a night and a day
Golden-haired, while his friend beside him
Attending a small hole in his brow
Ripened black.

21 *Ophiuchos*

That face, real-skinned as iron.
Those tears, like scars.
Other faces also apply, with distortions.

Hands reach spreading fingers
With barbed neighbour-raising screams

Body with raw mouth
The soul torn from the body

Cigarettes no working anaesthetic
Careful kindness no tool in the tray
All sense the wrong shape and inflammable

Sleep horror waking worse horror

Only fire inexhaustible

Fining the marital metal

22 Funeral

Twice a day
The brain-flaying ratchet of the storm-cock
Announces the hawk here
With his implements.

Then for some minutes every bird in the neighbourhood tolling
    the alarm

Then a silence –
The odd starling crossing
Like a convict escaping,
The odd blackbird
Hurtling to better hiding, low.

And for the next half-hour
A prison-state curfew execution silence, horrific.
Maybe a hedge-sparrow weeping – peep, peep.

Somewhere the hawk's face patiently
Disentangles the fluff belly
Yellow-gape, stub-tail throstling
From inside its pin-feathers.

But now, suddenly, the cool, funeral bell.

Bill Fowkes, publican
Of the Ring Of Bells
Is meeting the King of the Dead.

Too deep in age and diabetes
For illusion,
With his gangrenous foot
He lay awake three weeks of nights
Hearing his black Great Dane announce him.

And at last he is being received – in person,
Bodily, irrecoverably,
As if torn to pieces.

The leaves have a stunned, elated look.

23 *Children*

                              new to the blood
Whose hot push has surpassed
The sabretooth
Never doubt their rights of conquest.

Their voices, under the leaf-dazzle
An occupying army
A foreign tongue
Loud in their idleness and power.

Figures in the flaming of hell
A joy beyond good and evil
Breaking their toys.

Soon they'll sleep where they struck.
They'll leave behind
A man like a licked skull
A gravestone woman, their playthings.

24 *Prospero and Sycorax*

She knows, like Ophelia,
The task has swallowed him.
She knows, like George's dragon,
Her screams have closed his helmet.

She knows, like Jocasta,
It is over.
He prefers
Blindness.

She knows, like Cordelia,
He is not himself now,
And what speaks through him must be discounted –
Though it will be the end of them both.

She knows, like God,
He has found
Something
Easier to live with –

. His death, and her death.

25 *Before-dawn twilight, a sky dry as talc*

The horizons
Bubbling with bird voices

The blackbird arrives a yard away, in a black terror
And explodes off
As if searching for a way out
Of a world it has just been flung into.

The shrews, that have never seen man, are whizzing everywhere.

Who is that tall lady walking on our lawn?

The star in the sky is safe.

The owl on the telegraph pole
Warm and dry and twice his right size
Scratches his ear.

Under the stones are the woodlice, your friends.

Tiger-psalm

The tiger kills hungry. The machine-guns
Talk, talk, talk across their Acropolis.
The tiger
Kills expertly, with anaesthetic hand.
The machine-guns
Carry on arguing in heaven
Where numbers have no ears, where there is no blood.
The tiger
Kills frugally, after close inspection of the map.
The machine-guns shake their heads,   10
They go on chattering statistics.
The tiger kills by thunderbolt:

God of her own salvation.
The machine-guns
Proclaim the Absolute, according to morse,
In a code of bangs and holes that makes men frown.
The tiger
Kills with beautiful colours in her face,
Like a flower painted on a banner.
20 The machine-guns
Are not interested.
They laugh. They are not interested. They speak and
Their tongues burn soul-blue, haloed with ashes,
Puncturing the illusion.
The tiger
Kills and licks her victim all over carefully.
The machine-guns
Leave a crust of blood hanging on the nails
In an orchard of scrap-iron.
30 The tiger
Kills
With the strength of five tigers, kills exalted.
The machine-guns
Permit themselves a snigger. They eliminate the error
With a to-fro dialectic
And the point proved stop speaking.
The tiger
Kills like the fall of a cliff, one-sinewed with the earth,
Himalayas under eyelid, Ganges under fur –

40 Does not kill.

Does not kill. The tiger blesses with a fang.
The tiger does not kill but opens a path
Neither of Life nor of Death:
The tiger within the tiger:
The Tiger of the Earth.
                    O Tiger!
O Sister of the Viper!
                    O Beast in Blossom!

The stone

Has not yet been cut.
It is too heavy already
For consideration. Its edges
Are so super-real, already,
And at this distance,
They cut real cuts in the unreal
Stuff of just thinking. So I leave it.
Somewhere it is.
Soon it will come.
I shall not carry it. With horrible life
It will transport its face, with sure strength,
To sit over mine, wherever I look,
Instead of hers.
It will even have across its brow
Her name.

Somewhere it is coming to the end
Of its million million years –
Which have worn her out.
It is coming to the beginning
Of her million million million years
Which will wear out it.

Because she will never move now
Till it is worn out.
She will not move now
Till everything is worn out.

STAINED GLASS

1 *The Virgin*

Was silent

She was so silent
The clock stopped, at a sheer brink.

So silent
The stars pressed in on her ear-drum
Like children's noses at a window.

A silent
Carving in a never-trodden cavern.

So silent
The Creator woke, sweating fear

And saw her face stretching like a sphincter
Round a swelling cry.

Drop by drop

Like bodiless footsteps

Blood was collecting beneath her.

2 *The Womb*

Ponders
In its dark tree

Like a crucifix, still empty –
Dreaming rituals of moon-religions.

Dream after fruitless dream

Stains the feet of that tree
With salty drops of pain.

Between the fullness of its root
And the emptiness of its arms

It swells
A bud of hunger.

It blooms
A splitting sweetness.

It sings, through its flower
A silent lament

For the dark world
Hanging on its dark tree.

3 *The Virgin Knight*

How did she prepare?

What salt was her shield?
What lime was her spur?
What phosphorus her visor?

What sigh was her sword?
What strand of mucus her baldric?
What lust her charger?

What month's blood was her gauntlets?
What placenta her breastplate?
What sperm her helm?

What secret weapon, what *gae bulga*
Did she hide with a goat-skin?

Her lance was her naked waist
Her oath – a wetness

Her battle-cry
The silence between
Systole and diastole

Her heraldry a lily

And as she rode out

The hills quaked
The sea cried in fear
Incredulous
The stars trembled

A God

Pain was pulled down over his eyes like a fool's hat.
They pressed electrodes of pain through the parietals.

He was helpless as a lamb
Which cannot be born
Whose head hangs under its mother's anus.

Pain was stabbed through his palm, at the crutch of the M,
Made of iron, from earth's core.

From that pain he hung,
As if he were being weighed.
The cleverness of his fingers availed him
As the bullock's hooves, in the offal bin,
Avail the severed head
Hanging from its galvanised hook.

Pain was hooked through his foot.
From that pain, too, he hung
As on display.
His patience had meaning only for him
Like the sanguine upside-down grin
Of a hanging half-pig.

There, hanging,
He accepted the pain beneath his ribs
Because he could no more escape it
Than the poulterer's hanging hare,
Hidden behind eyes growing concave,
Can escape
What has replaced its belly.

He could not understand what had happened.

Or what he had become.

UNCOLLECTED (1980–81)

Unfinished Mystery

Enter Hamlet, stabbed, no longer baffled,
Stepping across his mother, drowned in a pearl,
Carrying lifeless Ophelia. Now enter

Stabbed Othello, enlightened at last,
From his cistern of toad-genderings, bearing
Suffocated Desdemona. Now enter

Headless Macbeth, regicide killed in him,
Stepping from the cauldron of sisters
Bearing his cold Queen. Now enter

Crack-brained Lear, finally freed
From the foam-lipped vortex of his daughters,
Carrying strangled Cordelia. Now enter

Prospero smiling. Rolls up the magic island
And wakes out of being.

         Enter Oliver
Milton – carrying under his arm
His own head, helmed, stake-pierced, and blind.

A crowned monkey picks its nose on his neck-stump.

Delilah, with bitumen cries,
Limbs blazing, bears Blake in the Mills of Hell.

Do not Pick up the Telephone

That plastic Buddha jars out a Karate screech

Before the soft words with their spores
The cosmetic breath of the gravestone

Death invented the phone it looks like the altar of death
Do not worship the telephone
It drags its worshippers into actual graves
With a variety of devices, through a variety of disguised voices

Sit godless when you hear the religious wail of the telephone

Do not think your house is a hide-out it is a telephone
Do not think you walk your own road, you walk down a telephone

Do not think you sleep in the hand of God you sleep in the
    mouthpiece of a telephone
Do not think your future is yours it waits upon a telephone
Do not think your thoughts are your own thoughts they are the
    toys of the telephone
Do not think these days are days they are the sacrificial priests
    of the telephone
The secret police of the telephone

O phone get out of my house
You are a bad god
Go and whisper on some other pillow
Do not lift your snake head in my house
Do not bite any more beautiful people

You plastic crab
Why is your oracle always the same in the end?
What rake-off for you from the cemeteries?

Your silences are as bad
When you are needed, dumb with the malice of the clairvoyant
    insane
The stars whisper together in your breathing
World's emptiness oceans in your mouthpiece
Stupidly your string dangles into the abysses
Plastic you are then stone a broken box of letters
And you cannot utter
Lies or truth, only the evil one
Makes you tremble with sudden appetite to see somebody undone

Blackening electrical connections
To where death bleaches its crystals
You swell and you writhe
You open your Buddha gape
You screech at the root of the house

Do not pick up the detonator of the telephone
A flame from the last day will come lashing out of the telephone
A dead body will fall out of the telephone

Do not pick up the telephone

Lily

Dragonflower.
Ice-flame fontanelle plume
Of the Virgin –

The spine coarsening on upwards
The leaves centipede and sinister
For swarming up the body

For stiffening out the gorged soul
Ribs
Fish and perfunctory

To lift the flared cheekbones, the mouthings
Of the hydra-face.
Core-abstract

Shameless and craving
Of cunt-flesh –
The splitting grin and the burst gape-scream

Infernal, anointed.
A torturer's wrought-iron
Brand of office.

And life cannot peel naked enough
Hurt cannot open deep enough
To quench it.

Sky Furnace

Earth rolls
Into the sky furnace.
The ore awakes
To trumpets of bright metal.

Aurora Borealis
Shakes out wings
Treads the quivering and the molten
With mud webs.

An eye has opened in the egg.
A caught star struggles in the iris.

The moon's broken shell, ashen,
Drifts off.

The winds of space cry out
Over human sleep
Through outstretched throats
Unearthly words
                  and drop a mud feather.

Fort

I climb the nameless tump.
'Iron Age.'
Pyramid of oak-leaves.

Nothing is left really. Not even foundations or ditches.
No teeth. No crocks. No legend. Nobody's dug.
Everything it amounted to is here.

Brimming airy fullness. Empty
Tomb glamour. What happened?
Magnetic enigma.

Because this ivy insists: 'I was disturbed.'
And the new oak-leaves
Gorged again with vintage atoms, flush.

And the map: Castle.
In wrought Gothic.
Bald as a slingstone pebble.

Air stirs the hill's roots. I peer out
Across the river
Through a trembling rigging of leaf.

I re-open the former perspectives,
Lend my retina to whatever ghost –
Underswell scenarios annul each other.

Only one thing is sure: this fortress
Turned out to be a mere goblet –
Fragile as any eye. What impact

Spilled the dreams from their mouths? These brambles
Say the whole garrison agreed
To leaf-mould. Did a few bubbling cries

Wobble as far as the skyline? Two thousand
Years dropped, lightly, from the lift
Of a heron's wing. The river

Carted away the blood. Peace. Peace.

Maybe, like the sun's controlled disaster
Which could be melting the eyeball
But yields only this haze pollen of light,
It is all still going on inside molecules,
History screaming in its sleep –
                                        Eyeholes
Listen. This summit is sacred
To a coven of crows. Crypts, excavated by badgers,
Resurrect badgers. Wild garlic. Fantasy.
Timber valued by the cubic foot. The farmer
Lets his ejected cartridge cases lie.

I come away with a shrew's skull –
Frail – a seed-husk –
Vessel of the orgy and the aftertaste.

Fishing the Estuary

Among smashed crockery rocks of jet,
            on a collapsed shelf,
I study the brimming estuary,
            dawn tinting its porcelain.
A heron, silhouetted and stealthy, here before me,
            is now discarded.
It circled, cranking rusty abuse,
            like an unwanted porter.

I got up too early, dreams still daze me,
            condemned
To the priorities of myself,
            my eyes just ajar,
My attention just open
            on its over-loose hinge,

A snake-stripe of scum upriver-centre
        processions quaintly.

The sea is pushing.
            Blueish clouds fracture
Pinky golden honey-light.
            And the human world is shut.
These piling, racing whorls of silence
        floor a wide vision.
The town's sewage snaking upstream,
        flitter-fry in the water-fringe.

The world, which suffers so much,
        is its own culprit.
I question with a flung lure this comfortless
        and doubtfully clean scene.
Salmon answer with a drastic shatter
        of their windows.
Ravens, crows, curlews convene,
        declaiming for me my lonely privilege.

It is true my bait comes back in
        draped with frills unspeakably sordid.
But here the filth of what has managed
        to become the world
Is also a part
        of a stainless perfection.
I cast out hopelessly
        sleepily persistent.

[PUBLICATIONS OF THE MORRIGU PRESS, 1979–80]

Wolf

The Iron Wolf, the Iron Wolf

Stands on the world with jagged fur.
The rusty Moon rolls through the sky.
The iron river cannot stir.
The iron wind leaks out a cry

Caught in the barbed and iron wood.
The Iron Wolf runs over the snow
Looking for a speck of blood.
Only the Iron Wolf shall know

The iron of his fate.
He lifts his nose and moans,
Licks the world clean as a plate
And leaves his own bones.

Puma

God put the Cougar on the Mountain
To be the organist
Of the cathedral-shaped echoes.

Her screams play the hollow cliffs, the brinks
And the abyss.
Her music amazes the acoustics.

She lifts the icy shivering summit
Of her screech
And climbs it, looking for her Maker.

A crazy-gaze priestess of caverns –
All night she tries to break into heaven
With a song like a missile, while the Moon frosts her face.

All day afterwards, worn out,
She sleeps in the sun.

Sometimes – half-melted
In the sheet-flame silence –
Opens one jewel.

Brooktrout

The Brooktrout, superb as a matador,
Sways invisible there
In water empty as air.

The Brooktrout leaps, gorgeous as a jaguar,
But dropping back into swift glass
Resumes clear nothingness.

The numb-cold current's brain-wave is lightning –
No good shouting: 'Look!'
It vanished as it struck.

You can catch Brooktrout, a goggling gewgaw –
But never the flash God made
Drawing the river's blade.

Eagle

Big wings dawns dark.
The sun is hunting.
Thunder collects, under granite eyebrows.

The horizons are ravenous.
The dark mountain has an electric eye.
The sun lowers its meat-hook.

His spread fingers measure a heaven, then a heaven.
His ancestors worship only him,
And his children's children cry to him alone.

His trapeze is a continent.
The sun is looking for fuel
With the gaze of a guillotine.

And already the white hare crouches at the sacrifice,
Already the fawn stumbles to offer itself up,
And the wolf-cub weeps to be chosen.

The huddle-shawled lightning-faced warrior
Stamps his shaggy-trousered dance
On an altar of blood.

Mosquito

To get into life
Mosquito died many deaths.

The slow millstone of polar ice, turned by the galaxy,
Only polished her egg.

Sub-zero, bulging all its mountain-power,
Failed to fracture her bubble.

The lake that squeezed her kneeled,
Tightened to granite – splintering quartz teeth,
But only sharpened her needle.

Till the strain was too much, even for Earth.

The stars drew off, trembling.
The mountains sat back, sweating.

The lake burst.

Mosquito

Flew up singing, over the broken waters –
A little haze of wings, a midget sun.

THREE RIVER POEMS

Catadrome

Where does the river come from?
And the eel, the night-mind of water –
The river within the river and opposite –
The night-nerve of water?

Not from the earth's remembering mire
Not from the air's whim
Not from the brimming sun. Where from?

From the bottom of the nothing pool
Sargasso of God
Out of the empty spiral of stars

A glimmering person

Caddis

Struggle-drudge – with the ideas of a crocodile
And the physique of a foetus.

Absurd mudlark – living your hovel's life –
Yourself your own worst obstacle.

Lugging Castle Paranoia
Through that moonland, like a train off its track,

Under the river's hurricane.
You should have been a crab. It's no good.

Trout in March are crammed
With the debris of your hopeful redoubts.

Wasp-face, orphaned and a waif too early,
Improvising – with inaudible war-cries –

This Herculean makeshift, hoisting your house,
You can nip my finger but

You are still a baby.
Your alfresco Samurai suit of straws,

Your Nibelungen mail of agates, affirms
Only fantasies of fear and famine.

Hurry up. Join the love-orgy
Up here among leaves, in the light rain,

Under a flimsy tent of dusky wings.

Visitation

All night the river's twists
Bit each other's tails, in happy play.

Suddenly a dark other
Twisted among them.

And a cry, half sky, half bird,
Slithered over roots.
                    A star

Fleetingly etched it.
                    Dawn
Puzzles a sunk branch under deep tremblings.

Nettles will not tell.
                    Who shall say
That the river
Crawled out of the river, and whistled,
And was answered by another river?

A strange tree
Is the water of life –

Sheds these pad-clusters on mud-margins
One dawn in a year, her eeriest flower.

from A PRIMER OF BIRDS (1981)

For Leonard and Lisa

He casts off the weight of space
Like patience

Disguised with life
He advances inevitably
As if squeezed
Into the death-corner

An electric thrill – a cactus flower
Among moon-rubble

An ultrasonic cry,
A tiger-yawn
Of amnesia

A mighty god
Wraps his hunger for the whole earth
In a shawl of feathers

Signs the sun in Hebrew
And flies in his sleep.

Cuckoo

Cuckoo's first cry, in light April,
Taps at the cool, suspended, ponderous jar
Of maiden blood
Like a finger-tip at a barometer.

That first ribald whoop, as a stolen kiss
Sets the diary trembling.
The orchard flushes. The hairy copse grows faint
With bluebells.

Sudden popping up of a lolling Priapus –
Hooha! Hooha!   10
Dizzying Milkymaids with innuendo.

Cuckoo jinks in – dowses his hawk-fright crucifix
Over the nest-bird's eye
And leaves his shadow in the egg.

Then his cry flees guilty – woodland to woodland,
Hunted by itself, all day dodging
The dropped double that dogs it.

O Orphan of Orphans! O moon-witted
Ill-bred dud-hawk!
20   Cavorting on pylons, you and your witchy moll!

With heartless blow on blow all afternoon
He opens hair-fine fractures through the heirloom
Chinaware hearts of spinsters in rose-cottages.

Then comes ducking under gates, pursued by a husband.
Or, invisibly, stately, through the blue shire
Trawls a vista-shimmering shawl of echo.

Later, the pair of them sit hiccoughing,
Chuckling, syncopating, translating
That lewd loopy shout

30   Into a ghoulish
Double-act, stuttering
Gag about baby-murder.

Swans

Washed in Arctic,
Return to their ballroom of glass
Still in the grip of the wizard,

With the jewel stuck in their throats.

Each one still condemned
To meditate all day on her mirror
Hypnotised with awe.

Each swan glued in her reflection
Airy
As the water-caught plume of a swan.

Each snowdrop lyrical daughter possessed
By the coil
Of a black and scowling serpent –

Dipping her eyes into subzero darkness,
Searching the dregs of old lakes
For her lost music.

Then they all writhe up the air,
A hard-hooved onset of cavalry –
Harp the iceberg wall with soft fingers.

Or drift, at evening, far out
Beyond islands, where the burning levels
Spill into the sun

And the snowflake of their enchantment melts.

Buzzard

Big hands, big thumbs, broad workaday hands
Darkened with working the land
Kneading the contours, squeezing out rats and rabbits.

Most of the day elongates a telephone pole
With his lighthouse lookout and swivel noddle.

O beggared eagle! O down-and-out falcon!
Mooning and ambling along hedgerow levels,
Forbidden the sun's glittering ascent –

As if you were sentenced to pick blackberries
At Easter, searching so fearful-careful,
So hopeless-careless, rag-wings, ragged trousers.

Too low-born for the peregrine's trapeze, too dopey
For the sparrowhawk's jet controls –
Where's the high dream when you rode circles

Mewing near the sun
Into your mirror-self – something unearthly
Lowering from heaven towards you?

Buzzard sits in mid-field, in mild sunlight,
Listening to tangled tales, by mole and by bee,
And by soft-headed dandelion.

When he treads, by chance, on a baby rabbit
He looks like an old woman
Trying to get her knickers off.

In the end he lumbers away
To find some other buzzard, maybe older,
To show him how.

Black-back Gull

Tide sighs and turns over. The black-back gull
Capers from his yoga-sleep
On the far sand-shine. Reality touched him.

The brain-flaying sea-storm's
Old brain wakes up. You see a sun-splinter crystal,
Sharpening clear, lift off inland.

Sea can stay, lazy, sipping
Among mussels. The black-backed gull mounts earth
And crests inland, over his eyes depth,

Bending against wind with the mask-stiff
Solemnity of a mouth
God is trying to speak through.

From a sunken echo-tomb of iron
All the drowned
Gargle over his tongue –

Water, stone, wind, almost spoke.

Dispersing, he whisps frailly along
The sand-hills. Opens the lamb's parcel,
Finds a caring home

For the cow's afterbirth. Collects
What has slipped from human finger-bones
Into the town dump.

The sea's wings, black-backed,
Caress the earth. And a cliff-wheel of wind
Is the fairground

Where a salt god laughs. Vomits his laughter
And gulps it back in. Laughs it and gulps it –
Like intestines hanging from the mouth.

Snipe

You are soaked with the cold rain –
Like a pelt in tanning liquor.
The moor's swollen waterbelly
Swags and quivers, ready to burst at a step.

Suddenly
Some scrap of dried fabric rips
Itself up
From the marsh-quake, scattering. A soft

Explosion of twilight
In the eyes, with a spinning fragment
Somewhere. Nearly lost, wing-flash

Stab-trying escape routes, wincing
From each, ducking under
And flinging up over –

Bowed head, jockey shoulders
Climbing headlong
As if hurled downwards –

A mote in the watery eye of the moor –

Hits cloud and
Skis down the far rain wall

Slashes a wet rent
In the rain-dusk
Twisting out sideways –

            rushes his alarm
Back to the ice-age.

          The downpour helmet
Tightens on your skull, riddling the pools,
Washing the standing stones and fallen shales
With empty nightfall.

A Swallow

Has slipped through a fracture in the snow-sheet
Which is still our sky —

She flicks past, ahead of her name,
Twinkling away out over the lake.

Reaching this way and that way, with her scissors,
Snipping midges
Trout are still too numb and sunken to stir for.

Sahara clay ovens, at mirage heat,
Glazed her blues, and still she is hot.

10   She wearied of snatching clegs off the lugs of buffaloes
And of lassooing the flirt-flags of gazelles.

They told her the North was one giant snowball
Rolling South. She did not believe them.
So she exchanged the starry chart of Columbus
For a beggar's bowl of mud.

Setting her compass-tremor tail-needles
She harpooned a wind
That wallowed in the ocean,
Working her barbs deeper
20   Through that twisting mass she came —

Did she close her eyes and trust in God?
No, she saw lighthouses
Streaming in chaos
Like sparks from a chimney —
She had fixed her instruments on home.

And now, suddenly, into a blanch-tree stillness
A silence of celandines,
A fringing and stupor of frost
She bursts, weightless —
                    to anchor
30   On eggs frail as frost.

There she goes, flung taut on her leash,
Her eyes at her mouth-corners,
Water-skiing out across a wind
That wrecks great flakes against windscreens.

Sparrow

The strike drags on. With the other idle hands
He draws dole. The sun is a dusty cinder.
Gold-haze afternoon muffles their shouts
Scuffling over a tossed coin, on the allotments.

Shut in his elder bush, he's a drab artist –
He chisels a pebble,
Or swites and scrapes at a stub-whistle
With a worn little pen-knife.

Suddenly flings it all down, furious,
And joins the gang-scrimmage.
A flustery hen-bird with her knickers torn
Tries to escape through the rhubarb.

Pin-legged urchin, he's patient.
He bathes in smoke. He towels in soot,
And with his prematurely-aged hungry street-cry
Sells his consumptive sister.

Or he swirls to the stackyard –
A thrown handful of him and his family –
Seed and chaff together –
The country air is good. It carves him afresh

Out of a ripely-grained chunk of dark oak.

Or he rests, face of a senile mouse,
Odysseus just back, penniless,
Burned out with African adventure,
Picking up how to beg.

The Hen

The Hen
Worships the dust. She finds God everywhere.
Everywhere she finds his jewels.
And she does not care
What the cabbage thinks.

She has forgotten flight
Because she has interpreted happily

Her recurrent dream
Of clashing cleavers, of hot ovens,
10   And of the little pen-knife blade
Splitting her palate.
She flaps her wings, like shallow egg-baskets,
To show her contempt
For those who live on escape
And a future of empty sky.

She rakes, with noble, tireless foot,
The treasury of the dirt,
And clucks with the mechanical alarm clock
She chose instead of song
20   When the Creator
Separated the Workers and the Singers.

With her eye on reward
She tilts her head religiously
At the most practical angle
Which reveals to her
That the fox is a country superstition,
That her eggs have made man her slave
And that the heavens, for all their threatening,
Have not yet fallen.

30   And she is stern. Her eye is fierce – blood
(That weakness) is punished instantly.
She is a hard bronze of uprightness.
And indulges herself in nothing
Except to swoon a little, a delicious slight swoon,
One eye closed, just before sleep,
Conjuring the odour of tarragon.

Mallard

Gloom-glossy wind
Ransacking summer's end.

Crammed, churned leaf-mass.
The river's shutters clatter.

Myself mixed with it – gusty skeleton,
Scarecrow blown
Inside out, clinging to my straws –

Horizons rolling up. A space-witch
Mussel-blue, in a fling of foul skirts

Gapes a light-streak –

I squint up and vertigo
Has unbalanced the clouds, slithering everything

Into a sack.
                        As a dark horse – sudden
Little elf-horse – bolts for freedom.

Gallops out of the river
Flashes white chevrons, climbs

The avalanche of leaves, flickering pennons,
Whinnies overhead –
                        and is
Snatched away by a huge hand.

Evening Thrush

Beyond a twilight of limes and willows
The church craftsman is still busy –
Switing idols,
Rough pre-Goidelic gods and goddesses,
Out of old bits of churchyard yew.

Suddenly flinging
Everything off, head-up, flame-naked,
Plunges shuddering into the creator –

Then comes plodding back, with a limp, over cobbles.

That was a virtuoso's joke.   10

Now, serious, stretched full height, he aims
At the zenith. He situates a note
Right on the source of light.

Sews a seamless garment, simultaneously
Hurls javelins of dew
Three in air together, catches them.

Explains a studied theorem of sober practicality.

Cool-eyed,
Gossips in a mundane code of splutters
20 With Venus and Jupiter.
                              Listens –
Motionless, intent astronomer.

Suddenly launches a soul –

The first roses hang in a yoke stupor.
Globe after globe rolls out
Through his fluteful of dew –

The tree-stacks ride out on the widening arc.

Alone and darkening
At the altar of a star
With his sword through his throat
30 The thrush of clay goes on arguing
Over the graves.

O thrush,
If that really is you, behind the leaf-screen,
Who is this –

Worn-headed, on the lawn's grass, after sunset,
Humped, voiceless, turdus, imprisoned
As a long-distance lorry-driver, dazed

With the pop and static and unending
Of worms and wife and kids?

Magpie

The licensed clown – chak chak!
With no proper part in the play –
Puts his remark in each scene.

Standing on presage, in duplicate, in triplicate,
A laundered puffball,
A sky-skiff, with his one oar.

At every picture's edge, on the top twig,
He watches. He dozes. Working for Fate.
Quick-eyed Mercury, the go-between –

A rattling laugh at the world's blind weight,
A pilfering gleam on its oversights –
These are his perks.

In his whites, his innocence of colour,
In his blacks, infra and ultra,
He struts across the tragic rainbow.

Between caterpillar and diamond.

Shrike

The talons close amicably
Round the accused
And her pipe of cry.

The dispute is appeased
In a ruffling of comfort,
A cleaning of face-knives.

Shrike, painted for war
And recognition
Digests his fame.

His law, lunar and songless,
Rounds his gaze, a two-lidded eclipse
Of crater silence.

One end of the world!

The suns' justice.

A jury of cadavers.

Starlings Have Come

A horde out of sub-Arctic Asia
Darkening nightfall, a faint sky-roar
Of pressure on the ear.

More thicken the vortex, gloomier.

A bacteria cyclone, a writhing of imps
Issuing from a hole in the horizon
Topples and blackens a whole farm.

Now a close-up seething of fleas.
                      And now a silence –
The doom-panic mob listens, for a second.
Then, with a soft boom, they wrap you
Into their mind-warp, assembling a nightmare sky-wheel
Of escape – a Niagara
Of upward rumbling wings – that collapses again

In an unmanageable weight
Of neurotic atoms.
                  They're the subconscious
Of the Smart-Alec, all slick hair and Adam's apple,
Sunday chimney starling.
                This Elizabethan songster,
Italianate, in damask, emblematic,
Trembles his ruff, pierces the Maytime
With his perfected whistle
Of a falling bomb – or frenzies himself
Into a Gothic, dishevelled madness,
Chattering his skeleton, sucking his brains,
Gargling his blood through a tin flute –
                      Ah, Shepster!
Suddenly such a bare dagger of listening!

Next thing – down at the bread
Screeching like a cat
Limber and saurian on your hind legs,

Tumbling the sparrows with a drop kick –

A Satanic hoodlum, a cross-eyed boss,
Black body crammed with hot rubies
And Anthrax under your nails.

Bullfinch

A mournful note, a crying note
A single tin-whistle half-note, insistent
Echoed by another

Slightly bluer with a brief distance
In March, in the draughty dripping orchard.

And again and again – and the echo prompt.
Bullfinch is melancholy.

Bullfinch wants us to feel a cold air, a shivery sadness
And to pity him in his need,
In the poverty start of the year, the hungry end,
Too early
In his Persian plum-plush wedding regalia
Above bleak virginal daffodils.

He wants us to feel protective
At least for as long as it takes him
To strip every tree of its bud-blossom –

To pack a summerful of apple power
Under his flaming shirt.

Wren

Who owns
Each tail-feather barred like a falcon?
He does – that freckled inspector

Of the woodland's vaults. Burglar
Alarm of the undergrowth. King
Of the lowest hovel of winter bramble.

The wren is a nervous wreck
Since he saw the sun from the back of an eagle.
He prefers to creep. If he can't creep

He'll whirr trickle-low as his shadow –
Brief as a mouse's bounce from safety to safety.
Even the ermine snow-flake's nose can't start him –

When the thicket's drifted, a shrouded corpse,
He's in under there, ticking,
Not as a last pulse, but a new life waiting.

Lonely keeper of the gold
In the tumbled cleave.
A bird out of Merlin's ear.

Silent watcher. Suddenly
Singing, like a martyr on fire,
Glossolalia.

Treecreeper

On the tree-bole a zig-zag upward rivulet
Is a dodgy bird, a midget ace,
Busy as a shrew, moth-modest as lichen.

Inchmeal medical examination
Of the tree's skin. Snap-shot micro-scanner
And a bill of instant hypodermic.

He's unzipping the tree-bole
For deeper scrutiny. It sticks. It jerks.
No microbe dare be, nor bubble spider.

All the trees are waiting – pale, undressed –
So he can't dawdle. He jabs, dabs, checks essentials,
Magnet-safe on undersides, then swings

In a blur of tiny machinery
To the next patient's foot, and trickles upward
Murmuring 'Good, good!' and 'Good, good!'

Into the huge satisfying mass of work.

Nightingale

This crack-brained African priest creates his own temple ruins
With his cry, with his sacred blade
Rending the veils, opening the throb of God.

Pale Spaniard, your throat thick with death,
Your blood is out of date. The lilac bush
Is no longer the Lord's torture chamber.

Let rip! Sing the score of the stars,
Crash your timbrel hung with negative particles,
Twang the bone guitar of protein!

Your lightning and thunderclap night-voice
Shuts back, with gaggings and splutters,
Into a nun's illuminated book.

And by day you do not exist.

The Moorhen

Might not notice you.
She's policing the water-bugs
In her municipal uniform.

A watchful clockwork
Jerks her head ahead, to inspect ahead
At each deep tread
Of her giant ooze-treading clawspread.

Her undertail flirts, jerk by jerk,
A chevron blaze, her functionary flash,
And the blood-orange badge or bleb
On her helmet neb
Lets the transgressing water-skeeter know
The arresting face, the stabbing body-blow
Is official.

Her legs are still primeval –
Toy-grotesque
As when she – thistledown, black, tip-toe –
Scampered across the picture-skin of water.

Lumpier now, she sprint-strides into flight
Across stepping-stones of slapped circles

Then dangles her drape of webs below her
Like a hawthorn fly, till she hoicks up
Clear over the bulrush plumes, and crash-drops

Into her off-duty nervous collapse.

Pheasant

Rama, in a horned blood-mask,
As a reptile of bronze leaves,
Steps from a shivering furnace.

Already the whole cloak of landscape
With flame-soft clashings
Trails after his fashion.

This is the incineration of the year.
In the sun's open door,
On a leafless black branch,

The Pheasant
Ruffles his burning book.

Darkens into a deep tapestry
Hung from Orion
Where the Dog's tongue smokes twilight
And gun barrels blue brittle as frost.

With his inlaid head in the East
The pheasant cools
Among the day's embers
On the finger of Lord Buddha – in Great Peace

Where the fox's icicles
Melt into moon,
And the poachers' sulphur
Suffers only in an opposite mirror –

Upside down, with gape in a bag of blood,
Among goblin pigs' ears
At a disembowelled trance-dancing
Of hare-priests.

Phoenix

The funny Phoenix
Is no Sphynx
Rotting forever
In Egypt's stinks.

When his sun sets
He does not sulk
And sink in sands
His deathless bulk

But blazing in perfume
Like the morn
He eats himself roasted
And is reborn.

UNCOLLECTED (1981–83)

Cows

There's a ruined holy city
In the herd of lying-down cud-chewing cows –
Noses raised, eyes nearly closed
They are fragments of temples – even their outlines

Still at an angle unearthly,
As if a ray from heaven still rested across their brows,
As if they felt it, a last ray.

When they come, swinging their ballast, bowing
As if they dragged slow loads slightly uphill,
There's a dance in the swaying walk of cows

With their long dancers' necks, to left and to right,
And that slight outfling of hooves – a slow dance-step,
Bodies of oil,
Dancers coming from hard labour in the fields.

And there's a flare of wide skirts when they swirl
On such exact feet
With the ankles of tall dancers

In under the girders and asbestos.

Drove six or so high miles

      in downpour dark and moor-road inconsequence.
Descended to the pub on the hill's brink, on a notion,
A granny-knot of nostalgia, twenty years older,
My expectations vacuous, to kill a half-hour.

Stupor of transfiguration! My memory flipped
In the near-sheer car park formerly raw moorland.
The locked wheels clung there, over the half-mile drop.
Rain reappeared. We plunged plastered
Into a submarine disco, the bump of the beat,
The jolly bouncers demanding 50p in a purple glow.
The whacking swipe of fluorescents sluiced us to skeletons.
We somnambulated across empty gulfs of glare and gloom
Among a few phosphorous fragments of nymphs

Jagged down stairs of old stone into a steadier century
And found oxygen of comparative quiet in the bar –
A sin-sleazy tatty film-set, paraffin-stove West Riding Las Vegas,
And a big sadly sitting Alsatian with afflicted ears
And the beer chemically reconstituted from the outhouse piss
And the poor sod behind the bar not knowing the name of the
    town at the bottom of the nose-dive-exit hill.

River of Dialectics

Thin questionings through thick lips:
That's water, socratic.

                    Not the dark
Pupil of a fish-eyed Creator.
Just clear. A query, solving, simple.
Through clear comes great light. The needle
Clothing the world, remaining naked.

Maybe there are some old grannies,
Archaic boulders, in shawls of river,
Unpicking woolly worn-out heavens,

The wigs and cast-offs of absconded gods

Re-weaving the coat of aureole
The many-coloured

For the favoured children.

That is how trout
Come to move, holy, in the dawn's mouth:

The images of gold
Whose shadows darken these pools.

Sing the Rat

Sing the hole's plume, the rafter's cockade
Who melts from the eye-corner, the soft squealer
Pointed at both ends, who chews through lead

Sing the scholarly meek face
Of the penniless rat

Who studies all night
To inherit the house

Sing the riff-raff of the roof-space, who dance till dawn
Sluts in silk, sharpers with sleek moustaches
Dancing the cog-roll, the belly-bounce, the trundle

Sing the tireless hands
Of the hardworking rat
Who demolishes the crust, and does not fail
To sign the spilt flour

The rat, the rat, the ratatatat
The house's poltergeist, shaped like a shuttle
Who longs to join the family

Sing his bright face, cross-eyed with eagerness
His pin-fingers, that seem too small for the job
Sing his split nose, that looks so sore
O sing his fearless ears, the listener in the wall

Let him jump on your head, let him cling there
Save him from sticks and stones

Sing the rat so poor he thrives on poison
Who has nothing to give to the trap, though it gapes for a year
Except his children
Who prays only to the ferret
'Forget me' and to the terrier
'In every thousand of me, spare two'

Sing him

Who stuffs his velvet purse, in hurry and fear
With the memory of the fork,
The reflections of the spoon, the hope of the knives

Who woos his wife with caperings, who thinks deep

Who is the slave of two fangs

O sing
The long-tailed grey worry of the night-hours
Who always watches and waits
Like a wart on the nose
Even while you snore

O sing
Little Jesus in the wilderness
Carrying the sins of the house
Into every dish, the hated one

O sing
Scupper-tyke, whip-lobber
Smutty-guts, pot-goblin
Garret-whacker, rick-lark
Sump-swab, cupboard-adder
Bobby-robin, knacker-knocker
Sneak-nicker, sprinty-dinty
Pintle-bum

Giant Dream of Elephants

                              The sleep
They enlarge, and move without breaking,
Gathers the eyes in. They carry
With ease all your slowness. Heads
Modelled with intelligent aptitude,
Three loll together. Huge dung-balls
Wrinkled and disintegrating. They sway,
Humming inaudibly in unison.
The trunk is coiled and tucked in,
Or wanders extended, rising, travelling
With a lifted neck. Handle or spout,
They rock their nightmare animated teapot
Full of dark Indian dregs. The hedgehog eye
Is intent on the ground, full of enquiry,
None too bothered about the body
Protected by its vastness, its far-flung
Barren continent, its deserts and caves
Wrinkled into sterility and numbness.

Ceaseless swinging investigation of heads,
And a foreleg out reaching, a mighty sucker
Lifting the earth into a safety
And foot-rest under it, then sliding the whole
Balance gently onto the fresh
Footsole platform. Holding their silence
In the dance of elephant stateliness,

Burdened with too much god-head,
Too much kingdom. At the same time,
Their old beggarly trash-bin-emptying patience,
Hanging around, disreputable and hairy,
In somebody else's pants. Faces full
Of difficult wrinkled problems
While they chew and spit out husks.
Skin for long-lasting and hard-travelling,
Bags of a hard traveller,
Hold-alls for an investigation of earth,
Lumpy with wisdom and useless
Odd-ends of information, loose
With experience. Elastic sacks
Of protoplasmic innocence,
Peeping out through the trunk's end. Outcrops
Of earth, moving embassies
From the rocky clay, making enquiries,
Establishing relations, ready
To sink away into silence
Like the side of a hill. A booming
Goes with them, deep gongs
Round their dancing hips, their swirling faces
As they pivot on oil. Great ideas
Toil in their granite, nudging them slowly
Into human likeness. They are towers
Of watching shadow. Islands
Of prehistoric volcanoes, mountains of tufa,
The boulder's short cut
To clowning and eating and crossing
From skyline to skyline. A huge mind
Moves with a fly's controls
And antennae. The ghostly tonnage
Operates by its hairs, and listens
By leanings and anglings.

       Who's this? An old gaffer
Bow-legged coming uphill and moving
In his sandwich-boards. Advance, a top speed
Drifting flight, in slow motion,
His forelegs stretching forwards and down
To fasten their sucker-hold, ears elated,
The African bull. Balances on the rim

To stretch his hoover out
To mop up the crop and nip up
Lost peanuts from underfoot.
Huge smile and skull caverns. Huge grin
And clownish underlip, he heaves
And bounces away, balloon-slow
And balloon-softly, returns to hay
And concrete and serious elephance.

Remembering Teheran

How it hung
In the electrical loom
Of the Himalayas – I remember
The spectre of a rose.

All day the flag on the military camp flowed South.

In the Shah's Evin Motel
The Manageress – a thunderhead Atossa –
Wept on her bed
Or struck awe. Tragic Persian
10   Quaked her bosom – precarious balloons of water –
But still nothing worked.

Everything hung on a prayer, in the hanging dust.

With a splash of keys
She ripped through the lock, filled my room, sulphurous,
With plumbers –
Twelve-year-olds, kneeling to fathom
A pipeless tap sunk in a blank block wall.

*

I had a funny moment
Beside the dried-up river of boulders. A huddle of families
20   Were piling mulberries into wide bowls, under limp, dusty trees.
All the big males, in their white shirts,
Drifted out towards me, hands hanging –

I could see the bad connections sparking inside their heads

As I picked my way among thistles
Between dead-drop wells – open man-holes
Parched as snake-dens –

Later, three stoned-looking Mercedes,
Splitting with arms and faces, surfed past me
Warily over a bumpy sea of talc,
The uncials on their number-plates like fragments of scorpions.   30

    *

I imagined all Persia
As a sacred scroll, humbled to powder
By the God-conducting script on it –
The lightning serifs of Zoroaster –
The primal cursive.

    *

Goats, in charred rags,
Eyes and skulls
Adapted to sunstroke, woke me
Sunbathing among the moon-clinker.
When one of them slowly straightened into a goat-herd   40
I knew I was in the wrong century
And wrongly dressed.

All around me stood
The tense, abnormal thistles, desert fanatics;
Politicos, in their zinc-blue combat issue;

Three-dimensional crystal theorems
For an optimum impaling of the given air;
Arsenals of pragmatic ideas –

I retreated to the motel terrace, to loll there
And watch the officers half a mile away, exercising their   50
   obsolete horses.

A bleaching sun, cobalt-cored,
Played with the magnetic field of the mountains.

And prehistoric giant ants, outriders, long-shadowed,
Cast in radiation-proof metals,
Galloped through the land, lightly and unhindered,
Stormed my coffee-saucer, drinking the stain –

At sunset
The army flag rested for a few minutes
Then began to flow North.

    *

60   I found a living thread of water
Dangling from a pipe. A snake-tongue flicker.
An incognito whisper.
It must have leaked and smuggled itself, somehow,
From the high Mother of Snows, halfway up the sky.
It wriggled these last inches to ease
A garden of pot-pourri, in a tindery shade of peach-boughs,
And played there, a fuse crackling softly –

As the whole city
Sank in the muffled drumming
70   Of a subterranean furnace.

And over it
The desert's bloom of dust, the petroleum smog, the transistor
    commotion
Thickened a pinky-purple thunderlight.

The pollen of the thousands of years of voices
Murmurous, radio-active, rubbing to flash-point –

    *

Scintillating through the migraine
The world-authority on Islamic Art
Sipped at a spoonful of yoghurt
And smiling at our smiles described his dancing
80   Among self-beheaded dancers who went on dancing with their heads
(But only God, he said, can create a language).

Journalists proffered, on platters of silence,
Split noses, and sliced-off ears and lips –

    *

Chastened, I listened. Then for the belly-dancer
(Who would not dance on my table, would not kiss me
Through her veil, spoke to me only
Through the mouth
Of her demon-mask
Warrior drummer)

I composed a bouquet – a tropic, effulgent
Puff of publicity, in the style of Attar,

And saw myself translated by the drummer
Into her liquid
Lashing shadow, those arabesques of God,

That thorny fount.

90

The Great Irish Pike

The pike has been condemned.
The Virgin, dipping her lily in the lough, decreed it.
This is no precinct for anything fishy
That revives the underhang of the Dragon.

He fell asleep in Job.
He woke in The Book of Vermin.

And in the Courts of Beauty-care and Cosmetics
His picture is pinned up – as the criminal norm.
No trial for those eyes. No appeal
For that mouth. And flesh of such length,
So gilled, so slimed, is *flagrante delicto*.

Nursery trout bore witness in falsetto.
Shameless hatchery smolts
United their plea with the helpless and oppressed.
And the pretty rudd
Cast themselves as the allotted
Mediaeval maidens.

Whenever the pike tried to protest
The show of his fangs emptied the hearing.

Therefore the vibrato of Sunday bells
Atomised him
In the straitened souls of our grandmothers.

The water-colourist of human progress
Is painting the ponds afresh,
The rivers and the loughs, without him.

627

Even the deft snake of Freud
Invested him, religiously,
For nightmare returns only.

Can he still be said to exist?

Between the mud bed sown with bronze daggers and gold fibulae
And the crannog reeds guarded by ornamental herons

The pike in his cell

Only survives till the hired German beheads him
And strings his skull, with twelve others,
Along the gunnel of a Shannon cruiser,

Or nails it, on a plaque,
Over the resurrection of Valhalla.

Thomas the Rhymer's Song

When you are old enough to love,
You'll be taken prisoner,
By the blossom of apple and pear,
In the pink shade of the cherry.
The feathery grass, and the garden seat,
And the sweet blackbird and all your other torturers,
Will make merry,
With the poor heart in your breast,
As they did with others in the past,
When you are old enough to love.

When you are old enough to love,
Beware of the chestnut's smouldering flowers,
Its great glove leaves,
And its flowers.

The hanging mask of the chestnut will undo your body like a parcel,
And give it to somebody else,
On the path growing greyly beneath it,
As a present, and a toy.

Thomas was walking in the fume of the thorn,
When out of the orchard smiling came,
A Lady with a knife of flame,
Oh there he met love's pain!

As she stripped the flesh from his bones,
And nailed his heart to a tree,
Where it shall ever be,
Where it shall ever be!

Madly Singing in the Mountains
For John Montague

The water-skeeter is old. As the sunlight
That microscopes the quartzes
In his quarried, water-walking body
Is old.

The whole crooked river is old. And the land
It lies down with is as old. The rocks
That it quarrels with, that quarrel with it,
That it embraces, that embrace it
Are as old.

                        This marriage is old.

Old are the elvers. Old are all ephemerids
That will float away sealed flat as fossils
In the water-skin tomorrow.

The river and her family are so old
They have lost their way in our age.
Time has given up trying to find them.

Here in their first childhood, wrinkled ancients,
They sun themselves
Or roam in the weather
Still singing the songs time can't touch.

To Be Harry

Whatever you hung onto it has all
Abandoned you, quite faithless. Nothing has changed.

Even your poems – careless of how you died
They will now take up a strenuous career.
(The true book of your silence was burned with you.)
They will have the suspect air

Of talkative survivors –
They will tell all that happened, and more, except
How, in your worst moments, they failed you, and forsook you.

One thing has changed. Though it tries not to change,
The space inside our heads – the theatre
Where for a whole day you were surely happy
As the corpse of Oz,
Under flowers, sunk in a coffin, alive,
Round and round on the Circle Line, to music –
This has changed.

Everything has stopped. It is dark.
The audience has left.
Your great eye, unchanged
(Narcissus, inverted in his pool),
Goes on rehearsing, alone,
That last curtain of your last moment –

(Lying in a garden, alone,
Eyelids apart, alive, the last moment,
Noticing leaves – then eyelids closing together –)

Trying to get it right, just how it felt

Mice Are Funny Little Creatures

                                                you nearly don't see them
Getting out so fast under the sacks more like a bird's shadow
Amazing living like that on fearful lightning
Funny too how they smell like lions did you ever smell lions in a zoo?
You see one come tottering out
When maybe you're just sitting quiet and he'll come right out
With his nose-end wriggling investigating
Every speck of air he seems to be – high on his trembly legs
Very long legs really and his queer little pink hands
Little monkey's hands very human I always think
And his wiry bent tail high up there behind him
Wavering about he looks to be on a tight-rope

Then he finds something and starts trembling over it
His nibbling is an all over trembling, his whole body
Trembles as if he were starving and couldn't wait

But it's really listening, he's listening for danger – so sensitive
He's trembling it's like a tenderness
So many things can hurt him
And his ears thin as warm wax you've squeezed between your
    finger and thumb
Always remind me of an elephant's ears
A bit shapeless and his long face really like an elephant
If he had a trunk he'd be a tiny elephant exact
At least his face would and his tail being a kind of trunk at the
    wrong end
And his feet being so opposite to great elephant's feet
Help remind you of elephants altogether he really is like an elephant
Except his size of course but that reminds you of elephants too
Because it's the opposite end of the animals
Like they say extremes meet I can understand
Why mice frighten elephants but they're dear little things
I don't mind what they nibble

Weasels at Work

Every creature in its own way
Mistakes the weasel
For somebody else – too late.

The weasel's white chest
Is the dainty pinafore of the waitress
Who brings the field-vole knife and fork.

The weasel's black ripe eyes
Brim with a heady elderberry wine
That makes the rat drunk.

The weasel's fully-fashioned coat,
Lion-colour, wins her admittance
To the club of snobby goslings.

When the weasel dances her belly dance
Brainless young buck rabbits
Simpering, go weak at the knees.

When the weasel laughs
Even the mole sees the joke
And rolls in the aisles, helpless.

*

His face is a furry lizard's face, but prettier.

Only the weasel
Is wick as a weasel.
Whipping whisk

Of a grim cook. And a lit trail
Of gunpowder, he fizzes
Towards a shocking stop.

His tail jaunts along for the laughs.

His grandfather, to keep him active,
Buried the family jewels
Under some rabbit's ear.

Tyrannosaur — miniaturised
To slip through every loop-hole
In the laws of rats and mice.

Terrorist
Of the eggs —

Over the rim of the thrush's nest
The weasel's face, bright as the evening star,
Brings night.

Fly Inspects

Fly
Is the Sanitary Inspector. He detects every speck
With his Geiger counter.
Detects it, then inspects it
Through his multiple spectacles. You see him everywhere
Bent over his microscope.

He costs nothing, needs no special attention,
Just gets on with the job, totting up the dirt.

All he needs is a lick of sugar
Maybe a dab of meat –
Which is fuel for his apparatus.
We never miss what he asks for. He can manage
With so little you can't even tell
Whether he's taken it.

In his black boiler suit, with his gas-mask,
His oxygen pack,
His crampons,
He can get anywhere, explore any wreckage,
Find the lost –

Whatever dies – just leave it to him.
He'll move in with his team of gentle undertakers,
In their pneumatic protective clothing, afraid of nothing,
Little white Michelin men,
They hoover up the rot, the stink, and the goo.
He'll leave you the bones and the feathers – souvenirs
Dry-clean as dead sticks in the summer dust.
Panicky people misunderstand him –
Blitz at him with nerve-gas puff-guns,
Blot him up with swatters.

He knows he gets filthy
He knows his job is dangerous, wading in the drains
Under cows' tails, in pigs' eye-corners
And between the leaky, broken toes
Of the farm buildings –
He too has to cope with the microbes.
He too wishes he had some other job.

But this is his duty.
Just let him be. Let him rest on the wall there,
Washing the back of his neck. This is his rest-minute

Once he's clean, he's a gem.

A freshly-barbered Sultan, royally armoured
In dusky rainbow metals.

A knight on a dark horse.

Swallows

What The Schoolmaster Said:

She flicks past, ahead of her name,
Twinkling away out over the lake.

Reaching this way and that way, with her scissors,
Snipping midges
Trout are too numb and sunken to stir for.

Sahara clay ovens, at mirage heat,
Glazed her blues, and still she is hot.

She wearied of snatching clegs off the lugs of buffaloes
And of lassooing the flirt-flags of gazelles.

They told her the North was one giant snowball
Rolling South. She did not believe them.
She exchanged the starry chart of Columbus
For a beggar's bowl of mud.

Did she close her eyes and trust in God?
No, she saw lighthouses
Streaming in chaos
Like sparks from a chymney –

She had fixed her instruments on home.

So now, suddenly, into a blanch-tree stillness,
A silence of celandines,
A fringing and stupor of frost
She bursts, weightless –

                                and anchors

On eggs frail as frost.

There she goes, flung taut on her leash,
Her eyes at her mouth-corners,
Water-skiing out across a wind
That wrecks great flakes against windscreens.

What The Farmer's Wife Said:

It's the loveliest thing about swallows,
The moment they come,
The moment they dip in, and are suddenly there.

For months you just never thought about them
Then suddenly you see one swimming maybe out there
Over our bare tossing orchard, in a slattery April blow,
Probably among big sloppy snowflakes.

And there it is – the first swallow,
Flung and frail, like a midge caught in the waterskin
On the weir's brink – and straightaway you lose it.
You just got a glimpse of whisker and frailty

Then there's nothing but jostled daffodils, like the girls running
    in from a downpour
Shrieking and giggling and shivering
And the puckered primrose posies, and the wet grit.
It's only a moment, only a flicker, easy to miss –

That first swallow just swinging in your eye-corner
Like a mote in the wind-smart,
A swallow pinned on a roller of air that roars and snatches it away

Out of sight, and booms in the bare wood

And you know there'll be colder nights yet
And worse days and you think
'If he's here, there must be flies for him'
And you think of the flies and their thin limbs in that cold.

What The Vicar Said:

I agree
There's nothing verminous, or pestilential, about swallows.
Swallows are the aristocrats
The thoroughbreds of summer.
Still, there is something sinister about them.
I think it's their futuristic design.
The whole evolution of aircraft
Has been to resemble swallows more and more closely.
None of that propellor-blur, ponderous, biplane business
Of partridges and pheasants,
Or even the spitfire heroics of hawks.
When I was a boy I remember
Their shapes always alarmed me, slightly,
With the thought of the wars to come,
The speed beyond sound, the molten forms.
You might say

They have a chirruppy, chicken-sweet expression
With goo-goo starlet wide-apart eyes,
And their bills seem tiny, almost retroussé cute –
In fact, the whole face opens
Like a jet engine.

And before this, they solved the problem, did they not,
Of the harpoon.

from RIVER (1983)

The Morning before Christmas

Buds fur-gloved with frost. Everything had come to a standstill
In a brand new stillness.
The river-trees, in a blue haze,
Were fractured domes of spun ghost.
Wheel-ruts frost-fixed. Mid-morning, slowly
The sun pushed dark spokes of melt and sparkle
Across the fields of hoar. And the river steamed –
Flint-olive.
        By the salmon-ladder at the weir –
The sluice cut, the board exit lifted –
The cage drained slowly. A dead cock fish
Hung its head into the leaf-dregs. Another
Sunk on its side, seemed to pincer-lock
The cage wire with its kipe. Already
They were slinging the dead out, rigid in the net,
Great, lolling lilies of fungus, irreplaceable –
Eggs rotten in them, milt rotten. Nothing
So raggy dead offal as a dead
Salmon in its wedding finery. So
After their freakish luck in the lottery –
Their five thousand to one against survival –
Dead within days of marriage. Three, four, five.

Then a hen fish – ten pounds – lurching alive.
Rough grip and her head in an armpit.
Now the thumb and finger kneading her belly.
The frost-smoking sun embellishes her beauty,
Her red-black love-paints, her helpless, noble mask.
Suddenly eggs
Squirt in a liquid loosening – spatter
Into the kitchen bowl. A long, deep-kneading
Oily massage – again and again. Then the fish
Drop-slung, head down, ponderous jerk-shake, and up
For another milking. And now, gentler,
An artful, back-of-the-fingers, cheek-stroke-dainty
Feathering along her flank sets the eggs spurting –
She tries to writhe and shiver a real mating.
The pink mess deepens in the bowl, and her belly
Starts to bag empty. Still there's more. Amazing
Finally the wealth of eggs. Then a cock –

Brindled black and crimson, with big, precious spots
Like a jeweller's trout – gapes his hook
And releases a milk-jet of sperm
Under a skilful thumb, into the treasure.
A little is plenty. He goes back into the net
And into the river – to wait
For his next violation. A stirring
Now of eggs and milt, to a vital broth.
Then they're set aside. Another hen-fish
Comes wagging weakly from the prison.
Four fish only, forty-odd thousand eggs.
The hard frosts this last week
Brought the fish on, ripened them, but killed
Five with sudden death-bloom. Six
Kicking strong, clean, green, unripe, refuse
To yield an egg to the handling. They go
Free above the weir – gloom-flag dissolve
Under the whorled, sliding, morning-smoking
Flat of the pool above. With luck
In natural times, those six, with luck,
In five years, with great luck, might make nine.

That's how four kitchen plastic bowls
Employ eight grown men and keep them solemn.
Precarious obstetrics. First, the eggs clot,
Then loosen. Then, lovingly, the rinsings,
The lavings, the drainings, the rewashings –
A few eggs trundle clear and vanish
Into the white crash of the weir.
                                        A world
Wrought in wet, heavy gold. Treasure-solid.
That morning
Dazzle-stamped every cell in my body
With its melting edge, its lime-bitter brightness.

A flood pond, inch-iced, held the moment of a fox
In touch-melted and refrozen dot-prints.

Japanese River Tales

I

Tonight
From the swaddled village, down the padded lane
Snow is hurrying
To the tryst, is touching
At her hair, at her raiment
Glint-slippered
Over the stubble,
                              naked under
Her light robe, jewels
In her hair, in her ears, at her bare throat
Dark eye-flash
                              twigs and brambles
Catch at her
                    as she lifts
The raggy curtains
Of the river's hovel, and plunges
Into his grasping bed.

II

The lithe river rejoices all morning
In his juicy bride – the snow princess
Who peeped from clouds, and chose him,
                              and descended.

The tale goes on
With glittery laughter of immortals
Shaking the alders –
In the end a drowsy after-bliss
Blue-hazes the long valley. High gulls
Look down on the flash
And languor of suppled shoulders
Bedded in her ermine.
                              Night
Lifts off the illusion. Lifts
The beauty from her skull. The sockets, in fact,
Are root-arches – empty
To ashes of stars. Her kiss
Grips through the full throat and locks

On the dislodged vertebrae.
                              Her talons
Lengthened by moonlight, numb open
The long belly of blood.
                              And the river
Is a gutter of death,
A spill of glitters
                    dangling from her grasp
As she flies
Through the shatter of space and
Out of being.

Flesh of Light

From a core-flash, from a thunder-silence
In the sun – something has fallen.
It crawls in glair, among heather-topped stones.

Cattle stumble into it. Lift muzzles
Unspooling the glimmer.
Dark bodies dense with boiling light.

Something new-born crawls, a phosphorescence
Illuminates the underleaves of stolid
Oak and the quivering iris. Eyes of ova

10   Round and swell with the waters of hunger,
Hesitate and ease
Into focus, magnetised by light

In these coils of aura. You peer down
Into a self reflected, a spectre.
This is the sun's oiled snake, dangling, fallen,

The medicinal, mercury creature
Sheathed with the garb, in all its rainbow scales,
That it sheds

And refreshes, spasming and whispering.
20   Spinal cord of the prone, adoring land,
Rapt

To the roots of the sea,
To the blossoming
Of the sea.

New Year

Snow falls on the salmon redds. Painful

To think of the river tonight – suffering itself.
I imagine a Caesarian,
The wound's hapless mouth, a vital loss
Under the taut mask, on the heaped bed.

The silent to-fro hurrying of nurses,
The bowed stillness of surgeons,
A trickling in the hush. The intent steel
Stitching the frothing womb, in its raw hole.

And walking in the morning in the blue glare of the ward
I shall feel in my head the anaesthetic,
The stiff gauze, the congealments. I shall see
The gouged patient sunk in her trough of coma –

The lank, dying fish. But not the ticking egg.

Whiteness

Walks the river at dawn.

The thorn-tree hiding its thorns
With too much and too fleshy perfume.

Thin water. Uneasy ghost.
Whorls clotted with petals.

Trout, like a hidden man's cough,
Slash under dripping roots.

Heron. Clang
Coiling its snake in heavy hurry
Hoists away, yanked away   10

Ceases to ponder the cuneiform
Under glass

Huge owl-lump of dawn
With wrong fittings, a parasol broken
Tumbles up into strong sky

Banks precariously, risks a look
A writhing unmade bedstead

Sets the blade between its shoulders
And hang-falls
Down a long aim

Dangles its reeds

Till it can see its own pale eyes

Suddenly shakes off cumbersome cloud
To anchor, tall,
An open question.

Now only the river nags to be elsewhere.

Four March Watercolours

I

Earth is just unsettling
Her first faint scents.
                  My shadow, soft-edged,
On drying, pale sand, among baby nettles,
Where floodwater whorled and sowed it.
                            The blue
Is a daze of bubbly fire – naked
Ushering and nursing of electricity
With caressings of air. Earth,
Mud-stained, stands in sparkling beggary.
                                  Bergs of old snow-drifts
Still stubborn in shadows.
                        The river
Acts fishless. It is
Fully occupied with its callisthenics,
Its twistings and self-wrestlings. The pool by the concrete buttress
Has just repaired its intricate engine,
Now revs it full-bore, underground,
Under my footsole. Tries to split the foundations,

Running in, testing and testing.
                              Spring is over there.
Tits exciting the dour oak. Cows soften their calls
Into the far, crumble-soft calling
Of ewes. The land hangs, tremulous.
It pays full attention to each crow-caw,
Turning full-face to the entering, widening,
Flame-cored, burrowing havoc of a jet. Wild, stumpy daffodils
Shiver under the shock wave.

II

Nearly a warmth
Edging this wind.
                    A skylark, solitary
Glittering high out
Over the buoyant up-boil – a spice-particle
From the tumbled-out, hump-backed,
Bursting bales of river.
                        Spring
Just hesitates. She can't quite
Say what she feels yet. She's numb and pale.
But she's here, and looking at everything – first morning
Of real convalescence.
                        The river's hard at it,
Tries and tries to wash and revive
A bedraggle of dirty bones. Primitive, radical
Engine of earth's renewal. A solution
Of all dead ends – an all-out evacuation
To the sea. All debts
Of wings and fronds, of eyes, nectar, roots, hearts
Returning, cancelled, to solvency –
Back to the sea's big re-think.
                        While the fieldful of novelty lambs
Suns and sprawls, mid-morning,
High-headed, happy, supposing
Here is a goodness that will stay forever.
A bluetit de-rusts its ratchet. We trees,
We tall ones, sunning, somewhat mutilated,
Inured by one more winter
To this muddy, heedless earth, and to our scaly
Provisional bodies, relax,

Enjoy the fraternity of survival,
Even a hope of new leaf.

III

The river
Concentrates its work. Its wheels churn.
Foam at the pool-tail blazes tawny – thrashing
Tight blown flames.
Bleeding the valley older.
                              An inch of snow
Whitened last night and the world
Slipped back under. This morning
Touch-precarious snow
Fledged all complexities of trees
And perfected fields. By noon
The earth's absorbed it.
                              An ewe,
Steep-spined, is lowering herself
To the power-coils
Of the river's bulge, to replenish her udder.
And a big-thumbed buzzard swirls
To a stall
Over the wood-top opposite, mewing, now settling
Heavy with domestic purpose.
                              Clouds lift anchors. The world
Tries its weights. All these branches are jammed
Solid with confidences. A market of gossip.
A spider has found me.

IV

The river-epic
Rehearses itself. Embellishes afresh and afresh
Each detail. Baroque superabundance.
Earth-mouth brimming. But the snow-melt
Is an invisible restraint. If there are salmon
Under it all, they are in coma. They are stones
Lodged among stones, sealed as fossils
Under the grained pressure. I look down onto the pour
Of melted chocolate. They look up
At a guttering lamp
Through a sand-storm boil of silt

That scratches their lidless eyes,
Fumes from their gill-petals. They have to toil,
Trapped face-workers, in their holes of position
Under the mountain of water.
               Up here
A lightness breathes, a morning-sleep lightness –
A glow on the closed eyelids
· Or seen through the wet cracks of eyelashes
A crammed and jostly pushing
Of crow-tended, buzzard-adjusted
Germination. Now only hour after hour
Of the sweating, speechless labour of trees –

And the long ropes of light
Hauling the river's cargo
The oldest commerce.

Dee

The hills locked in snow
Have locked up their springs. The shining paps
That nurse the river's plumpness
Are locked up.
And the North Star is frozen in its lock.

The expenditure of swift purity
Nevertheless goes on. But so thinly,
So meanly, and from such stale cellars
No fish will face it.
Somewhere the salmon have turned back into the sea.

So this is the majesty of the April Dee
When the snowdrops, pert and apart,
Domes of ice-light, deviants
From a world preoccupied with water,
Hurt into perfection, steal a summer
Out of the old, river-worried
Carcase of winter.

Nothing else dare or can
Pilfer from the shrunk, steely procession.

Nevertheless, the lit queenliness of snow hills,
The high, frozen bosom, wears this river
Like a peculiarly fine jewel.

The Merry Mink

                    – the Arctic Indian's
Black bagful of hunter's medicine –
Now has to shift for himself.

Since he's here, he's decided to like it.
Now it is my turn, he says,
To enjoy my pelt uselessly.

I am the Mighty Northern Night, he says,
In my folktale form.
See, I leave my stars at the river's brim.

10   Little Black Thundercloud, lost from his mythology,
A-boil with lightnings
He can't get rid of. He romps through the ramsons

(Each one like a constellation), topples into the river,
Jolly goblin, realist–optimist
(Even his trapped, drowned snake-head grins)

As if he were deathless. Bobs up
Ruffed with a tough primeval glee. Crams trout, nine together,
Into his bank-hole – his freezer –

Where they rot in three days. Makes love
20   Eight hours at a go.
                    My doings and my pelt,
He says, are a Platonic idea
Where I live with God.

Salmon-taking Times

After a routing flood-storm, the river
Was a sounder of loud muddy pigs
Flushed out of hillsides. Tumbling hooligans
They jammed the old bends. Diabolical muscle,

Piglets, tusky boars, possessed, huge sows
Piling in the narrows.

> I stayed clear. 'Swine
Bees and women cannot be turned.'

> But after
The warm shower
That just hazed and softened the daffodil buds   10
And clotted the primroses, a gauze
Struggles tenderly in the delighted current –
Clambers wetly on stones, and the river emerges
In glistenings, and gossamer, bridal veils,
And hovers over itself – there is a wedding
Delicacy –

> so delicate
I touch it and its beauty-frailty crumples
To a smear of wet, a strengthless wreckage
Of dissolving membranes – and the air is ringing.

It is like a religious moment, slightly dazing.   20

It is like a shower of petals of eglantine.

Under the Hill of Centurions

The river is in a resurrection fever.
Now at Easter you find them
Up in the pool's throat, and in the very jugular
Where the stickle pulses under grasses –

Cock minnows!

They have abandoned contemplation and prayer in the pool's crypt.

There they are, packed all together,
In an inch of seething light.

A stag-party, all bridegrooms, all in their panoply –

Red-breasted as if they bled, their Roman
Bottle-glass greened bodies silked with black

In the clatter of the light loom of water
All singing and

649

Toiling together,
Wreathing their metals
Into the warp and weft of the lit water –

I imagine their song,
Deep-chested, striving, solemn.

A wrestling tress of kingfisher colour,
Steely jostlings, a washed mass of brilliants

Labouring at earth
In the wheel of light –

Ghostly rinsings
A struggle of spirits.

A Cormorant

Here before me, snake-head
My waders weigh seven pounds.

My Barbour jacket, mainly necessary
For its pockets, is proof

Against the sky at my back. My bag
Sags with lures and hunter's medicine enough

For a year in the Pleistocene.
My hat, of use only

If this May relapses to March,
Embarrasses me, and my net, long as myself,

Optimistic, awkward, infatuated
With every twig-snag and fence-barb

Will slowly ruin the day. I paddle
Precariously on slimed shale,

And infiltrate twenty yards
Of gluey and magnetised spider-gleam

Into the elbowing dense jostle-traffic
Of the river's tunnel, and pray

With futuristic, archaic under-breath
So that some fish, telepathically overpowered,

Will attach its incomprehension
To the bauble I offer to space in general.

The cormorant eyes me, beak uptilted,
Body snake-low – sea-serpentish.

He's thinking: 'Will that stump
Stay a stump just while I dive?' He dives.

He sheds everything from his tail end
Except fish-action, becomes fish,

Disappears from bird,
Dissolving himself   30

Into fish, so dissolving fish naturally
Into himself. Re-emerges, gorged,

Himself as he was, and escapes me.
Leaves me high and dry in my space-armour,

A deep-sea diver in two inches of water.

Stump Pool in April

Crack willows in their first pale eclosion
Of emerald. The long pool
Is seething with oily lights. Deep labour
Embodied under filmy spanglings. Oxygen
Boils in its throat, and the new limbs
Flex and loosen. It keeps
Making the effort to burst its glistenings
With sinewy bulgings, gluey splittings
All down its living length.

                The river is trying
To rise out of the river.   10
              April
Has set its lights working. Its limp wings
Crease in their folds, hump and convulse
To lift out over the daffodils.
                The soft strokings
Of south wind keep touching all its membranes
Into spasming torments. It knows
The time has come for it to alter

And to fly, and to fasten – in wedlock –
With the hill-wood waiting high there, flushed
In her bridal veil of haze-violet.

Go Fishing

Join water, wade in underbeing
Let brain mist into moist earth
Ghost loosen away downstream
Gulp river and gravity

Lose words
Cease
Be assumed into glistenings of lymph
As if creation were a wound
As if this flow were all plasm healing

10   Be supplanted by mud and leaves and pebbles
By sudden rainbow monster-structures
That materialize in suspension gulping
And dematerialize under pressure of the eye

Be cleft by the sliding prow
Displaced by the hull of light and shadow

Dissolved in earth-wave, the soft sun-shock,
Dismembered in sun-melt

Become translucent – one untangling drift
Of water-mesh, and a weight of earth-taste light
20   Mangled by wing-shadows
Everything circling and flowing and hover-still

Crawl out over roots, new and nameless
Search for face, harden into limbs

Let the world come back, like a white hospital
Busy with urgency words

Try to speak and nearly succeed
Heal into time and other people

Milesian Encounter on the Sligachan

for Hilary and Simon

'Up in the pools,' they'd said, and 'Two miles upstream.'

Something sinister about bogland rivers.

And a shock –

after the two miles of tumblequag, of Ice-Age hairiness,
crusty, quaking cadaver and me lurching over it in elation
like a daddy-long-legs –

after crooked little clatterbrook and again clatterbrook (a
hurry of shallow grey light so distilled it looked like acid) –

and after the wobbly levels of a razor-edged, blood-smeared
grass, the flood-sucked swabs of bog-cotton, the dusty calico   10
rip-up of snipe –

under those petrified scapulae, vertebrae, horn-skulls the
Cuillins (asylum of eagles) that were blue-silvered like
wrinkled baking foil in the blue noon that day, and
tremulous –

early August, in a hot lateness (only three hours before my
boat), a glimpse of my watch and suddenly

up to my hip in a suck-hole then on again teetering over the
broken-necked heath-bobs a good half-hour and me melting
in my combined fuel of toil and clobber suddenly   20

The shock.
The sheer cavern of current piling silence
Under my feet.

So lonely-drowning deep, so drowned-hair silent
So clear
Cleansing the body cavity of the underbog.

Such a brilliant cut-glass interior
Sliding under me

And I felt a little bit giddy
Ghostly   30
As I fished the long pool-tail
Peering into that superabundance of spirit.

And now where were they, my fellow aliens from prehistory?
Those peculiar eyes
So like mine, but fixed at zero,
Pressing in from outer darkness
Eyes of aimed sperm and of egg on their errand,
Looking for immortality
In the lap of a broken volcano, in the furrow of a lost glacier,
Those shuttles of love-shadow?

Only humbler beings waved at me –
Weeds grazing the bottom, idling their tails.

Till the last pool –
A broad, coiling whorl, a deep ear
Of pondering amber,
Greenish and precious like a preservative,
With a ram's skull sunk there – magnified, a Medusa,
Funereal, phosphorescent, a lamp
Ten feet under the whisky.

I heard this pool whisper a warning.

I tickled its leading edges with temptation.
I stroked its throat with a whisker.
I licked the moulded hollows
Of its collarbones
Where the depth, now underbank opposite,
Pulsed up from contained excitements –

Eerie how you know when it's coming –
So I felt it now, my blood
Prickling and thickening, altering
With an ushering-in of chills, a weird onset
As if mountains were pushing mountains higher
Behind me, to crowd over my shoulder –

Then the pool lifted a travelling bulge
And grabbed the tip of my heart-nerve, and crashed,

Trying to wrench it from me, and again
Lifted a flash of arm for leverage
And it was a Gruagach of the Sligachan!
Some Boggart up from a crack in the granite!

A Glaistig out of the skull!
                         − what was it gave me
Such a supernatural, beautiful fright   70

And let go, and sank disembodied
Into the eye-pupil darkness?

Only a little salmon.
                    Salmo salar
The loveliest, left-behind, most-longed-for ogress
Of the Palaeolithic
Watched me through her time-warped judas-hole
In the ruinous castle of Skye

As I faded from the light of reality.

Ophelia

Where the pool unfurls its undercloud −
There she goes.

And through and through
The kneading tumble and the water-hammer.

If a trout leaps into air, it is not for a breather.
It has to drop back immediately

Into this peculiar engine
That made it, and keeps it going,

And that works it to death −
                         there she goes

Darkfish, finger to her lips,
Staringly into the afterworld.

Creation of Fishes

All day
Sun burned among his burning brood
As all night
Moon flamed and her offspring spangled.

Under the Moon and her family
The souls of earthlings tried to hide in the sea.
Under the Sun and his family
Earth gaped: tongue and root shrivelled.

Said Moon to Sun: 'Our children are too much
For this Creation. In their flame-beauty
They are too intolerably beautiful.
If the world is to live, they must be quenched.'

Sun and Moon, solemn,
Gathered their children into a sack, to drown them.

Noble Sun, tear-blind, plucked his darlings.
Subtle Moon gathered glossy pebbles.
Both emptied their sack into the rivers.

Enraged, the hoodwinked Sun stared down, bereft.
Smiling, the Moon sloped away with her family.

The raving Sun fished up his loveliest daughter
To set her again beside him, in heaven,
But she spasmed, and stiffened, in a torture of colours.

He fished up his fieriest son who leaped
In agony from his hands, and plunged under.

He fished up his quickest, youngest daughter –
With dumb lips, with rigid working eye
She died in his fingers.

Flaring, his children fled through the river glooms.

Fingers dripping, the Sun wept in heaven.

Smiling, the Moon hid.

River Barrow

The light cools. Sun going down clear
Red-molten glass-blob, into green ember crumble
Of hill trees, over the Barrow
Where the flushed ash-grey sky lies perfect.

A skull tower is a nameless tomb. We sprawl
Rods out, giant grasshopper antennae, listening

For the bream-shoal to engage us.
                              The current
Hauls its foam-line feed-lane
Along under the far bank – a furrow
Driving through heavy wealth,
Dragging a syrupy strength, a down-roping
Of the living honey.
                    It's an ancient thirst
Savouring all this, at the day's end,
Soaking it all up, through every membrane,
As if the whole body were a craving mouth,
As if a hunted ghost were drinking – sud-flecks
Grass-bits and omens
Fixed in the glass.
                  Trees inverted
Even in this sliding place are perfect.
All evil suspended. Flies
Teem over my hands, twanging their codes
In and out of my ear's beam. Future, past,
Reading each other in the water mirror
Barely tremble the thick nerve.
                              Heavy belly
Of river, solid mystery
With a living vein. Odd trout
Flash-plop, curdle the molten,
Rive a wound in the smooth healing.
Over the now pink-lit ballroom glass
Tiny sedge-flies partner their shadows.

A wobbly, wavering balance of light
Mercury precarious in its sac
Leans to the weir's edge, spilling. Dog-bark stillness.
A wood-pigeon is buffing the far edges
Of the smoothing peace.
                      Great weight
Resting effortless on the weightless.
A cow's moo moves through the complex
Of internestled metals, a moon-spasm
Through interfolded underseas. I lie here,
Half-unearthed, an old sword in its scabbard,
Happy to moulder. Only the river moves.

Feet prickling in my tight-sock gumboots,
Hair itching with midges, blood easy
As this river. Honeysuckle
Pouring its horns of plenty over us
From the thickets behind.
                                    A big fish,
Bream-roll or evening salmon, crashes
A crater of suds, and the river widens.

A long-armed spider readjusts his gunsights
Between glumes of over-leaning river-grass.

Midge bites itching and swelling.

The West Dart

It spills from the Milky Way, spiked with light,
It fuses the flash-gripped earth –

The spicy torrent, that seems to be water
Which is spirit and blood.

A violet glance of lightning
Melts the granite to live glass,
Pours it into the mould of quick moor-water

A trout swipes its flank at the thundercloud

A shatter of crowns, a tumbling out of goblets

Where the slag of world crumbles cooling
In thunders and rainy portents.

Strangers

Dawn. The river thins.
The combed-out coiffure at the pool-tail
Brightens thinly.
The slung pool's long hammock still flat out.

The sea-trout, a salt flotilla, at anchor,
Substanceless, flame-shadowed,
Hang in a near emptiness of sunlight.

There they actually are, under homebody oaks,
Close to teddybear sheep, near purple loose-strife –

Space-helms bowed in preoccupation,   10
Only a slight riffling of their tail-ailerons
Corrective of drift,
Gills easing.

And the pool's toiled rampart roots,
The cavorting of new heifers, water-skeeters
On their abacus, even the slow claim
Of the buzzard's hand
Merely decorate a heaven
Where the sea-trout, fixed and pouring,
Lean in the speed of light.   20
                            And make nothing
Of the strafed hogweed sentry skeletons,
Nothing of the sun, so openly aiming down.

Thistle-floss bowls over them. First, lost leaves
Feel over them with blind shadows.

The sea-trout, upstaring, in trance,
Absorb everything and forget it
Into a blank of bliss.

And this is the real samadhi – worldless, levitated.

Till, bulging, a man-shape
Wobbles their firmament.   30
                            Now see the holy ones
Shrink their auras, slim, sink, focus, prepare
To scram like trout.

After Moonless Midnight

I waded, deepening, and the fish
Listened for me. They watched my each move
Through their magical skins. In the stillness
Their eyes waited, furious with gold brightness,
Their gills moved. And in their thick sides
The power waited. And in their torpedo
Concentration, their mouth-aimed intent,
Their savagery waited, and their explosion.

They waited for me. The whole river
Listened to me, and, blind,
Invisibly watched me. And held me deeper
With its blind, invisible hands.
'We've got him,' it whispered, 'We've got him.'

An August Salmon

Upstream and downstream, the river's closed.
Summer wastes in the pools.
A sunken calendar unfurls,
Fruit ripening as the petals rot.

A holed-up gangster,
He dozes, his head on the same stone,
Gazing towards the skylight,
Waiting for time to run out on him.

Alone, in a cellar of ash-roots,
The bridegroom, mortally wounded
By love and destiny,
Features deforming with deferment.

His beauty bleeding invisibly
From every lift of his gills.

He gulps, awkward in his ponderous regalia,
But his eye stays rapt,
Elephantine, Arctic –
A god, on earth for the first time,
With the clock of love and death in his body.

Four feet under weightless, premature leaf-crisps
Stuck in the sliding sky. Sometimes
A wind wags a bramble up there.

The pulsing tiny trout, so separately fated,
Glue themselves to the stones near him.

His tail-frond, the life-root,
Fondling the poor flow, stays him
On the torpedo launch of his poise –
Sleeked ice, a smear of being
Over his anchor shadow.

Monkish, caressed
He kneels. He bows
Into the ceaseless gift
That unwinds the spool of his strength.

Dusk narrows too quickly. Manic-depressive
Unspent, poltergeist anti-gravity
Spins him in his pit, levitates him
Through a fountain of plate glass,

Reveals his dragonised head,
The March-flank's ice-floe soul-flash
Rotted to a muddy net of bruise,
Flings his coil at the remainder of light –

Red-black and nearly unrecognisable,
He drops back, helpless with weight,
Tries to shake loose the riveted skull
And its ghoul decor –

                              sinks to the bed
Of his wedding cell, the coma waiting
For execution and death
In the skirts of his bride.

The Vintage of River is Unending

Grape-heavy woods ripen darkening
The sweetness.

Tight with golden light
The hills have been gathered.

Granite weights of sun.
Tread of burning days.

Unending river
Swells from the press
To gladden men.

Night Arrival of Sea-Trout

Honeysuckle hanging her fangs.
Foxglove rearing her open belly.
Dogrose touching the membrane.

Through the dew's mist, the oak's mass
Comes plunging, tossing dark antlers.

Then a shattering
Of the river's hole, where something leaps out –

An upside-down, buried heaven
Snarls, moon-mouthed, and shivers.

Summer dripping stars, biting at the nape.
Lobworms coupling in saliva.
Earth singing under her breath.

And out in the hard corn a horned god
Running and leaping
With a bat in his drum.

The Kingfisher

The Kingfisher perches. He studies.

Escaped from the jeweller's opium
X-rays the river's toppling
Tangle of glooms.

Now he's vanished – into vibrations.
A sudden electric wire, jarred rigid,
Snaps – with a blue flare.

He has left his needle buried in your ear.

Oafish oaks, kneeling, bend over
Dragging with their reflections
For the sunken stones. The Kingfisher
Erupts through the mirror, beak full of ingots,

And is away – cutting the one straight line
Of the raggle-taggle tumbledown river
With a diamond –

Leaves a rainbow splinter sticking in your eye.

Through him, God, whizzing in the sun,
Glimpses the angler.

Through him, God
Marries a pit   20
Of fishy mire.

        And look! He's
– gone again.
        Spark, sapphire, refracted
From beyond water
Shivering the spine of the river.

That Morning

We came where the salmon were so many
So steady, so spaced, so far-aimed
On their inner map, England could add

Only the sooty twilight of South Yorkshire
Hung with the drumming drift of Lancasters
Till the world had seemed capsizing slowly.

Solemn to stand there in the pollen light
Waist-deep in wild salmon swaying massed
As from the hand of God. There the body

Separated, golden and imperishable,   10
From its doubting thought – a spirit-beacon
Lit by the power of the salmon

That came on, came on, and kept on coming
As if we flew slowly, their formations
Lifting us toward some dazzle of blessing

One wrong thought might darken. As if the fallen
World and salmon were over. As if these
Were the imperishable fish

That had let the world pass away –

There, in a mauve light of drifted lupins,   20
They hung in the cupped hands of mountains

Made of tingling atoms. It had happened.
Then for a sign that we were where we were
Two gold bears came down and swam like men

Beside us. And dived like children.
And stood in deep water as on a throne
Eating pierced salmon off their talons.

So we found the end of our journey.

So we stood, alive in the river of light
Among the creatures of light, creatures of light.

30

The River

Fallen from heaven, lies across
The lap of his mother, broken by world.

But water will go on
Issuing from heaven

In dumbness uttering spirit brightness
Through its broken mouth.

Scattered in a million pieces and buried
Its dry tombs will split, at a sign in the sky,

At a rending of veils.
It will rise, in a time after times,

After swallowing death and the pit
It will return stainless

For the delivery of this world.
So the river is a god

Knee-deep among reeds, watching men,
Or hung by the heels down the door of a dam

It is a god, and inviolable.
Immortal. And will wash itself of all deaths.

Last Night

The river seemed evil.
                    On the high fields, a full moon
Kept the world familiar. Moon-hazed
Hill over hill, the summer night
Turned on its pillow.
                    But down in the tree-cavern river,
The waded river, the river level with my knees,
The river under hangings of hemlock and nettle, and alder and oak,
Lay dark and grew darker. An evil mood
Darkened in it. Evil came up
Out of its stillest holes, and uncoiled
In the sick river, the drought river of slimes –
Like a sick man lying in the dark with his death.
Its darkness under roots, under old flood-battered boles
Was dark as blood,
Rusty peaty blood-dark, old-blood dark.
Something evil about the sunken river
In its sick-bed darkness. I stood in a grave
And felt the evil of fish. The strange evil
Of unknown fish-minds. Deep fish listening to me
In the dying river.

The Gulkana

Jumbled iceberg hills, away to the North –
And a long wreath of fire-haze.

The Gulkana, where it meets the Copper,
Swung, jade, out of the black spruce forest,
And disappeared into it.

Strange word, Gulkana. What does it mean?
A pre-Columbian glyph.
A pale blue thread – scrawled with a child's hand
Across our map. A Lazarus of water
Returning from seventy below.   10
                    We stumbled,
Not properly awake
In a weird light – a bombardment
Of purplish emptiness –

Among phrases that lumped out backwards. Among rocks
That kept startling me – too rock-like,
Hypnagogic rocks –
                    A scrapyard of boxy shacks
And supermarket refuse, dogs, wrecked pick-ups,
The Indian village where we bought our pass
Was comatose – on the stagnation toxins
20   Of a cultural vasectomy. They were relapsing
To Cloud-like-a-boulder, Mica, Bear, Magpie.

We hobbled along a tightrope shore of pebbles
Under a trickling bluff
That bounced the odd pebble onto us, eerily.
(The whole land was in perpetual, seismic tremor.)
Gulkana –
Biblical, a deranging cry
From the wilderness – burst past us.
A stone voice that dragged at us.
30   I found myself clinging
To the lifted skyline fringe of rag spruce
And the subsidence under my bootsoles
With balancing glances – nearly a fear,
Something I kept trying to deny

With deliberate steps. But it came with me
As if it swayed on my pack –
A nape-of-the-neck unease. We'd sploshed far enough
Through the spongy sinks of the permafrost
For this river's
40   Miraculous fossils – creatures that each midsummer
Resurrected through it, in a blood-rich flesh.
Pilgrims for a fish!
Prospectors for the lode in a fish's eye!

In that mercury light, that ultra-violet,
My illusion developed. I felt hunted.
I tested my fear. It seemed to live in my neck –
A craven, bird-headed alertness.
And in my eye
That felt blind somehow to what I stared at
50   As if it stared at me. And in my ear –
So wary for the air-stir in the spruce-tips
My ear-drum almost ached. I explained it

To my quietly arguing, lucid panic
As my fear of one inside me,
A bodiless twin, some doppelgänger
Disinherited other, unliving,
Ever-living, a larva from prehistory,
Whose journey this was, who now exulted
Recognising his home,
And whose gaze I could feel as he watched me   60
Fiddling with my gear – the interloper,
The fool he had always hated. We pitched our tent

And for three days
Our tackle scratched the windows of the express torrent.

We seemed underpowered. Whatever we hooked
Bent in air, a small porpoise,
Then went straight downriver under the weight
And joined the glacial landslide of the Copper
Which was the colour of cement.

Even when we got one ashore   70
It was too big to eat.

But there was the eye!
                    I peered into that lens
Seeking what I had come for. (What had I come for?
The camera-flash? The burned-out, ogling bulb?)
What I saw was small, crazed, snake-like.
It made me think of a dwarf, shrunken sun
And of the black, refrigerating pressures
Under the Bering Sea.

We relaunched their mulberry-dark torsos,
Those gulping, sooted mouths, the glassy visors –   80

Arks of an undelivered covenant,
Egg-sacs of their own Eden,
Seraphs of heavy ore

They surged away, magnetised,
Into the furnace boom of the Gulkana.

Bliss had fixed their eyes
Like an anaesthetic. They were possessed
By that voice in the river
And its accompaniment –

90   The flutes, the drumming. And they rose and sank
         Like voices, themselves like singers
         In its volume. We watched them, deepening away.
         They looked like what they were, somnambulists,
         Drugged, ritual victims, melting away
         Towards a sacrament –
                             a consummation
         That could only be death.
         Which it would be, within some numbered days,
         On some stony platform of water,
         In a spillway, where a man could hardly stand –
100   Aboriginal Americans,
         High among rains, in an opening of the hills,
         They will begin to circle,
         Shedding their ornaments,
         In shufflings and shudders, male by female,
         Begin to dance their deaths –
         The current hosing over their brows and shoulders,
         Bellies riven open and shaken empty
         Into a gutter of pebbles
         In the orgy of eggs and sperm,
110   The dance orgy of being reborn
         From which masks and regalia drift empty,
         Torn off – at last their very bodies,
         In the numbed, languorous frenzy, as obstacles,
         Ripped away –
                             ecstasy dissolving
         In the mercy of water, at the star of the source,
         Devoured by revelation,
         Every molecule drained, and counted, and healed
         Into the amethyst of emptiness –

         I came back to myself. A spectre of fragments
120   Lifted my quivering coffee, in the aircraft,
         And sipped at it.
         I imagined the whole 747
         As if a small boy held it
         Making its noise. A spectre,
         Escaping the film's flicker, peered from the porthole
         Under the sun's cobalt core-darkness
         Down at Greenland's corpse
         Tight-sheeted with snow-glare.

The voice of the river moved in me.
It was like lovesickness.   130
A numbness, a secret bleeding.
Waking in my body.
                          Telling of the King
Salmon's eye.
                  Of the blood-mote mosquito.

And the stilt-legged, subarctic, one-rose rose
With its mock-aperture
Tilting towards us
In our tent-doorway, its needle tremor.

And the old Indian Headman, in his tatty jeans and socks,
     who smiled
Adjusting to our incomprehension – his face
A whole bat, that glistened and stirred.   140

In the Dark Violin of the Valley

All night a music
Like a needle sewing body
And soul together, and sewing soul
And sky together and sky and earth
Together and sewing the river to the sea.

In the dark skull of the valley
A lancing, fathoming music
Searching the bones, engraving
On the glassy limits of ghost
In an entanglement of stars.   10

In the dark belly of the valley
A coming and going music
Cutting the bedrock deeper

To earth-nerve, a scalpel of music

The valley dark rapt
Hunched over its river, the night attentive
Bowed over its valley, the river

Crying a violin in a grave
All the dead singing in the river

The river throbbing, the river the aorta

And the hills unconscious with listening.

Low Water

This evening
The river is a beautiful idle woman.

The day's August burn-out has distilled
A heady sundowner.
She lies back, bored and tipsy.

She lolls on her deep couch. And a long thigh
Lifts from the flash of her silks.

Adoring trees, kneeling, ogreish eunuchs
Comb out her spread hair, massage her fingers.

She stretches – and an ecstasy tightens
Over her skin, and deep in her gold body

Thrills spasm and dissolve. She drowses.

Her half-dreams lift out of her, light-minded
Love-pact suicides. Copulation and death.

She stirs her love-potion – ooze of balsam
Thickened with fish-mucus and algae.

You stand under leaves, your feet in shallows.
She eyes you steadily from the beginning of the world.

A Rival

The cormorant, commissar of the hard sea,
Has not adjusted to the soft river.

He lifts his pterodactyl head in the drought pool
(Sound-proof cellar of final solutions).

The dinosaur massacre-machine
Hums on in his skull, programme unaltered.

That fossil eye-chip could reduce
All the blood in the world, yet still taste nothing.

At dawn he's at it, under the sick face –
Cancer in the lymph, uncontrollable.

Level your eye's aim and he's off
Knocking things over, out through the window –

An abortion-doctor
Black bag packed with vital organs

Dripping unspeakably.
                              Then away, heavy, high
Over the sea's iron curtain –

The pool lies there mutilated,
                              face averted,
Dumb and ruined.

August Evening

Blue space burned out. Earth's bronzes cooling.
September
Edges this evening. Skyline trees hang charred.
The thistles
Survive a biological blaze – burnt splinters,
Skeletal carbons, crowned with ashes. The fuel
Nearly all gone.
                    And the river
Cools early, star-touched. New moon,
Not new leaf-curl tender, but crisp.
                                        Mist
Breathes on the sliding glass. The river
Still beer-tinted from the barley disaster
Is becoming wintry.
                        The sea-tribes are here,
They've come up for their weddings, their Michaelmas fair,
The carnival on the gravels.
                                Wet fog midnight,
A sheathing sea-freeze, hardens round my head,
Stiffens my fingers. Oaks and alders

Fume to black blots opposite.
The river lifts to a ghostly trail of smoke.

Too serious to stir, the longships
Of the sea-trout
Secretive under the land's levels,
Holds crammed with religious purpose,
Cobble the long pod of winter.
They will not play tonight.

Their procession kneels, in God-hush.
Robed in the stilled flow of their Creator
They inhale unending. I share it a little.

Slowly their white pathway sinks from the world.

The river becomes terrible.

Climbing out, I make a silent third
With two owls reassuring each other.

Performance

Just before the curtain falls in the river
The Damselfly, with offstage, inaudible shriek
Reappears, weightless.

Hover-poised, in her snake-skin leotards,
Her violet-dark elegance.

Eyelash-delicate, a dracula beauty,
In her acetylene jewels.

Her mascara smudged, her veils shimmer-fresh –

Late August. Some sycamore leaves
Already in their museum, eaten to lace.
Robin song bronze-touching the stillness
Over posthumous nettles. The swifts, as one,
Whipcracked, gone. Blackberries.
                            And now, lightly,
Adder-shock of this dainty assassin
Still in mid-passion –
                            still in her miracle play:
Masked, archaic, mute, insect mystery

Out of the sun's crypt.
                         Everything is forgiven
Such a metamorphosis in love!
Phaedra Titania
Dragon of crazed enamels!   20
Tragedienne of the ultra-violet,
So sulphurous and so frail,

Stepping so magnetically to her doom!

Lifted out of the river with tweezers
Dripping the sun's incandescence –
                              suddenly she
Switches her scene elsewhere.

        (Find him later, halfway up a nettle,
        A touch-crumple petal of web and dew –

        Midget puppet-clown, tranced on his strings,
        In the nightfall pall of balsam.)   30

September Salmon

Famously home from sea,
Nobly preoccupied with his marriage licence,
He ignores the weir's wrangle. Ignores
The parochial down-drag
Of the pool's long diphthong. Ignores
Festivals of insect fluorescence.

He serves his descendants. And his homage
Is to be patient, performing, slowly, the palsy
Of concerted autumn
In the upside-down cage of a tree.

Does he envy the perennial eels and the mongrel minnows?
He is becoming a god,
A tree of sexual death, sacred with lichens.

Sometimes, for days, lost to himself.
                              Mid-morning,
At the right angle of sun
You can see the floor of his chapel.
There he sways at the altar –

A soul
Hovering in the incantation and the incense.

Over his sky the skeeters traffic, godlike and double-jointed.
He lifts
To the molten palate of the mercurial light
And adds his daub.

Eighty, and Still Fishing for Salmon

He holds
The loom of many rivers.
An old rowan now, arthritic, mossed,
Indifferent to man, roots for grave.

He's watching the Blackwater
Through hotel glass. Estuary nets
Empty. The river fishless. He's a trophy
Of the Great Days – his wrinkles, his tweeds,

And that armchair. And the Tussaud stillness.
Probably he's being tossed
Across a loch on Harris.
Both worlds have been lost

By the ritual mask
That hangs on its nail.
Soon he'll be out there, walking the sliding scree
Of the river – and over and over

His fly will come round on the vacant swirl.

An old Noh dancer, alone in the wind with his dance.
An air-fed, mountain prayer-wheel
Loyal to inbuilt bearings, touch of weather,
Though the heavens fail.

September

There's another river. In this river
Whose grandmotherly, earth-gnarled, sweetened hands
Welcome me with tremblings, give me the old feel
Of reality's reassurance –

There's a fishy nostalgia. The Balsam flower
Dangling loosely beside the gaze and pout,
Electric fingers parting a door curtain
Where smoky music shakes out.

An Eel

I

The strange part is his head. Her head. The strangely ripened
Domes over the brain, swollen nacelles
For some large containment. Lobed glands
Of some large awareness. Eerie the eel's head.
This full, plum-sleeked fruit of evolution.
Beneath it, her snout's a squashed slipper-face,
The mouth grin-long and perfunctory,
Undershot predatory. And the iris, dirty gold
Distilled only enough to be different
From the olive lode of her body,
The grained and woven blacks. And ringed larger
With a vaguer vision, an earlier eye
Behind her eye, paler, blinder,
Inward. Her buffalo hump
Begins the amazement of her progress.
Her mid-shoulder pectoral fin – concession
To fish-life – secretes itself
Flush with her concealing suit: under it
The skin's a pale exposure of deepest eel
As her belly is, a dulled pearl.
Strangest, the thumb-print skin, the rubberised weave
Of her insulation. Her whole body
Damascened with identity. This is she
Suspends the Sargasso
In her inmost hope. Her life is a cell
Sealed from event, her patience
Global and furthered with love
By the bending stars as if she
Were earth's sole initiate. Alone
In her millions, the moon's pilgrim,
The nun of water.

Where does the river come from?
And the eel, the night-mind of water –
The river within the river and opposite –
The night-nerve of water?

Not from the earth's remembering mire
Not from the air's whim
Not from the brimming sun. Where from?

From the bottom of the nothing pool
Sargasso of God
Out of the empty spiral of stars

A glimmering person

Fairy Flood

A brown musically moving beauty, the earth's fullness
Slides towards the sea. An escape
Of earth-serpent, with all its hoards, casting the land, like an
   old skin,
Pulling its body from under the eye.
                                        Escaping daughter
Her whole glass castle melting about her
In full magic –

Some mask of crumpling woe disfigures
Her deep liberation, which is actually jubilant,
As she brings down earth and sky blamelessly
In this headlong elopement without finery,
Weeps past – a freed out-heaping
Of accusative love and abandon.

The fatherly landscape upbraids and harangues,
Claws weakly at her swollen decision
With gaping beard and disarrayed robe,
Undoes his stained bandages,
Exposes his bone-open wounds –

The river cries out once, tosses her hair, hides her eyes,
Bleeding him empty remorselessly.

Riverwatcher

How easy the moist flash, the long eye-slit,
The river's polished key-hole
Opens to ghost – a holy fool
In the bauble mosque of the skull!

O birdwatcher, sit brambly still
Till wrens alight on you, O twilit angler
Tucked in your blood-knot, lift off deftly
As a sedge-fly, keep your head clear

Of the river-fetch –
                        (the epileptic's strobe,
The yell of the Muezzin
Or the 'Bismillah!'
That spins the dancer in

Her whole body liquefied
Where a body loves to be
Rapt in the river of its own music) –

With dry difficulty

Cling to the gnat, the dead leaf
In the riding whorls
That loosen and melt
Into the bellies of pools.

October Salmon

He's lying in poor water, a yard or so depth of poor safety,
Maybe only two feet under the no-protection of an outleaning
    small oak,
Half under a tangle of brambles.

After his two thousand miles, he rests,
Breathing in that lap of easy current
In his graveyard pool.

About six pounds weight,
Four years old at most, and hardly a winter at sea –
But already a veteran,
Already a death-patched hero. So quickly it's over!

10

So briefly he roamed the gallery of marvels!
Such sweet months, so richly embroidered into earth's beauty-dress,
Her life-robe –
Now worn out with her tirelessness, her insatiable quest,
Hangs in the flow, a frayed scarf –

An autumnal pod of his flower,
The mere hull of his prime, shrunk at shoulder and flank,

With the sea-going Aurora Borealis
Of his April power –
20   The primrose and violet of that first upfling in the estuary –
Ripened to muddy dregs,
The river reclaiming his sea-metals.

In the October light
He hangs there, patched with leper-cloths.

Death has already dressed him
In her clownish regimentals, her badges and decorations,
Mapping the completion of his service,
His face a ghoul-mask, a dinosaur of senility, and his whole body
A fungoid anemone of canker –

30   Can the caress of water ease him?
The flow will not let up for a minute.

What a change! from that covenant of polar light
To this shroud in a gutter!
What a death-in-life – to be his own spectre!
His living body become death's puppet,
Dolled by death in her crude paints and drapes
He haunts his own staring vigil
And suffers the subjection, and the dumbness,
And the humiliation of the role!

40   And that is how it is,
That is what is going on there, under the scrubby oak tree, hour
    after hour,
That is what the splendour of the sea has come down to,
And the eye of ravenous joy – king of infinite liberty
In the flashing expanse, the bloom of sea-life,

On the surge-ride of energy, weightless,
Body simply the armature of energy
In that earliest sea-freedom, the savage amazement of life,

The salt mouthful of actual existence
With strength like light –

Yet this was always with him. This was inscribed in his egg.   50
This chamber of horrors is also home.
He was probably hatched in this very pool.

And this was the only mother he ever had, this uneasy channel
    of minnows
Under the mill-wall, with bicycle wheels, car-tyres, bottles
And sunk sheets of corrugated iron.
People walking their dogs trail their evening shadows across him.
If boys see him they will try to kill him.

All this, too, is stitched into the torn richness,
The epic poise
That holds him so steady in his wounds, so loyal to his doom,   60
    so patient
In the machinery of heaven.

Torridge

Which ones
Of the eager faces, garlic or iris
Come back for the new herons?

Once the floods have wiped away their pollen
Have undressed them
And folded them into winter?

Venus and Jupiter, year in and year out
Contend for the crown
Of morning star and of evening star.

And the fish worship the source, bowed and fervent,
But their hearts are water.

The river walks in the valley singing
Letting her veils blow –

A novelty from the red side of Adam.

April in the lift of her arm
December in the turn of her shoulder

As if her sauntering were a long stillness.

She who has not once tasted death.

Salmon Eggs

The salmon were just down there –
Shivering together, touching at each other,
Shedding themselves for each other –

Now beneath flood-murmur
They peel away deathwards.

                              January haze,
With a veined yolk of sun. In bone-damp cold
I lean and watch the water, listening to water
Till my eyes forget me

And the piled flow supplants me, the mud-blooms

10   All this ponderous light of everlasting
Collapsing away under its own weight

Mastodon ephemera

Mud-curdling, bull-dozing, hem-twinkling
Caesarean of Heaven and Earth, unfelt

With exhumations and delirious advents –

                                        Catkins
Wriggle at their mother's abundance. The spider clings to his craft.

Something else is going on in the river

More vital than death – death here seems a superficiality
20   Of small scaly limbs, parasitical. More grave than life
Whose reflex jaws and famished crystals
Seem incidental
To this telling – these tidings of plasm –
The melt of mouthing silence, the charge of light
Dumb with immensity.

                         The river goes on
Sliding through its place, undergoing itself
In its wheel.

I make out the sunk foundations
Of dislocated crypts, a bedrock
Time-hewn, time-riven altar. And this is the liturgy
Of Earth's advent – harrowing, crowned – a travail   30
Of raptures and rendings. Perpetual mass
Of the waters
Wells from the cleft.
                              This is the swollen vent

Of the nameless
Teeming inside atoms – and inside the haze
And inside the sun and inside the earth.

It is the font, brimming with touch and whisper,
Swaddling the egg.
                              Only birth matters
Say the river's whorls.
                              And the river
Silences everything in a leaf-mouldering hush   40
Where sun rolls bare, and earth rolls,

And mind condenses on old haws.

UNCOLLECTED (1983–86)

The Mayfly

The Mayfly is a frail accompaniment
The way Aurora Borealis is frail.

What is it doing on earth? And under the river?

Its shadow
Is the nightmare of the sunk pebble
That feels the claws grip lightly.

The demon has unearthly ideas.

When the Mayfly
Hauls its green, dragonish torso
Out of its sleeping bag, and shimmers into air,
Evolution hides.

Who dances above the trees, rising and falling?
Titania and Oberon
In The Midsummer Night's Dream
Of the lungfish.

Poetic atoms
With their vision of the sun's skirts,
Mad for the Holy Grail,
Dress themselves in Mayfly, a lace of blackish crystals,

Leave hollow earthliness clinging under the leaves.

This religion is fierce. It crucifies them
Through a sacrament of copulation
Onto the face of water,
                              where Heaven shudders.

The Pigeon's Wings

                    Gouge height.
A minnow shoal of light plays under the drinking brambles.
The tom-tit concentrated, intent, doubtful.
The heron launches its marquee, unknotting and affronted.

The ploughed and disparate fields will never meet.
Light rays through grids of sky, we walk in stencil.

A moth eddies its directions of adjustment.
The weir flashes, the river's elaborate buckle.

The Live-Bait

The live-bait, numb with shock,
Rolls down, arms spread, past crying.

A Mighty Intelligence
Has brought the hook-point out at his navel.

Space-vacuums loom up
Taste him and spit him out and vanish
With quakings of cosmos.

Shoal under shoal of flame-tails flee past him,
Preoccupied eyes and chitterings.

He sinks, writhing slowly.

A coil is rearing from under the floor of everything –
Eyes of intent, a conger of glimmers.

Its vortex closes on him, and drinks him in.
The Mighty Intelligence hauls

Setting the hook. And the coil shudders –

Gapings cannot disgorge the barbed bait.

Alerted galaxies wheel in
To tear lumps from the convulsion.
Stars pour from the wounds, staining space.

Wild red suns, black suns
Scoop down and shear off, with streaming mouthfuls.

The spine's armature is ripped to tatters.
Death-orgasm supernovae

Flood from the bitten-away gills.
The star-pouring gullet swallows into emptiness.

Crushed inside the maw
The live-bait grips the hook-steel through his belly

Among clouding asteroids and meteors.
And the Mighty Intelligence, saddened,

Drags his catch to light –
All that remains of it:

The jaws, the flayed skull and savaged neck-stump
Of an undreamed mathematical system.

And finds the bait still alive, though pulpy.
He unhooks him, grateful, to save him –

Lays him carefully on a rock
With navel bleeding and face clenched.

Waste

Neither prohibition of the word *Pain*
Nor sixty years thrown into a small suitcase
Nor foreign eyes among your own children

Nor mass epidemic of the raving muzzle
Nor green bones among what was Sunday dress
Nor the re-arming of Asia

Make history

Unarguable to the blue-eyed sand-flea
Who argues so quietly
Through the Geiger Counter.

The Hare

I

That Elf
Riding his awkward pair of haunchy legs

That weird long-eared Elf
Wobbling down the highway

Don't overtake him, don't try to drive past him,
He's scatty, he's all over the road,
He can't keep his steering, in his ramshackle go-cart,
His big loose wheels, buckled and rusty,
Nearly wobbling off

And all the screws in his head wobbling and loose

And his eyes wobbling

II

The Hare is a very fragile thing.
The life in the hare is a glassy goblet, and her yellow-fringed
  frost-flake belly says: Fragile.

The hare's bones are light glass. And the hare's face –

Who lifted her face to the Lord?
Her new-budded nostrils and lips,
For the daintiest pencillings, the last eyelash touches

Delicate as the down of a moth,
And the breath of awe
Which fixed the mad beauty-light
In her look
As if her retina
Were a moon perpetually at full.

Who is it, at midnight on the A30,
The Druid soul,
The night-streaker, the sudden lumpy goblin
That thumps your car under the belly
Then cries with human pain
And becomes a human baby on the road
That you dare hardly pick up?

Or leaps, like a long bat with little headlights,
Straight out of darkness
Into the driver's nerves
With a jangle of cries
As if the car had crashed into a flying harp

So that the driver's nerves flail and cry
Like a burst harp.

III

Uneasy she nears
As if she were being lured, but fearful,
Nearer.
Like a large egg toppling itself – mysterious!

Then she'll stretch, tall, on her hind feet,
And lean on the air,
Taut – like a stilled yacht waiting on the air –

And what does the hunter see? A fairy woman?
A dream beast?
A kangaroo of the March corn?

The loveliest face listening,
Her black-tipped ears hearing the bud of the blackthorn
Opening its lips,
Her black-tipped hairs hearing tomorrow's weather
Combing the mare's tails,
Her snow-fluff belly feeling for the first breath,
Her orange nape, foxy with its dreams of the fox –

Witch-maiden
Heavy with trembling blood – astounding
How much blood there is in her body!
She is a moony pond of quaking blood

Twitched with spells, her gold-ringed eye spellbound –

Carrying herself so gently, balancing
Herself with the gentlest touches
As if her eyes brimmed –

IV

I've seen her,
A lank, lean hare, with her long thin feet
And her long, hollow thighs,
And her ears like ribbons
Careering by moonlight
In her Flamenco, her heels flinging the dust
On the drum of the hill.

And I've seen him, hobbling stiffly
God of Leapers
Surprised by dawn, earth-bound, and stained
With drying mud,
Painfully rocking over the furrows

With his Leaping-Legs, his Power-Thighs
Much too powerful for ordinary walking,
So powerful

They seem almost a burden, almost a problem,
Nearly an aching difficulty for him
When he tries to loiter or pause,
Nearly a heaving pain to lift and move
Like turning a cold car-engine with a bent crank handle –

Till a shock, a terror, with a bang
Grabs at her ears. An oven door
Bangs open, both barrels, and a barking
Bursts out of onions –
                              and she leaps
And her heels
Hard as angle-iron kick salt and pepper
Into the lurcher's eyes –
                              and kick and kick
The spinning, turnip world
Into the lurcher's gullet –
                              as she slips
Between thin hawthorn and thinner bramble
Into tomorrow.

Waterlicked

Bluster-shower August – exploded thunderlight
Tumbling in a crystal.

Eastward an hour, defectors, fishing like truants.

August Bank-Holiday millions roaming in disquiet.

A thought of pike, thoroughly ravenous,
In Bridgewater canal. Woe on the hope!

Flow-combed pond-weed folded the dull water
In a sunk hammock, where our plug-baits garishly popped.

All afternoon, with between-cloud glare, and the long hurt
Of the bent narrows. A weariness wore us.

A thin madness of windy-glitter water and its empty fractures.

All afternoon, Esox inert subombra
Like a fixed eternal number, ferocious and lucid.
Absent as baby's dreams.
                              In a migraine of dazzle and gloom

We flitted away Westward, among spark emeralds,
To the blue twilit lintel.

Familiar

Eighty-four years dead, younger than I am,
Your hair still full red, you sip your medicine.
The Methodist Minister brings you flowers, the Catholic
Priest a bottle of whisky. A lifted glass –

So the fungal root and pale petal
Of tuberculosis
Raised a last bloom. I imagine your breathed
'Rocked in the Cradle of the Deep' –

My Dad just four. The Dyer's vat pickled to ninety
Or killed quickly (even the Sage, Cragg Jack).   10
Near eighty, your daughter stirred my tea,
Dug up and turned over this and that

Flotsam, heirloom bits of ghost
Under your Grace Darling heaving at the oars
Among mountainous, tenebrous foam.
Now I stand right there. And large as life

You step out of Stubbing Wharfe pub.
(Like my father?) I can't see your face.
I see you pause. (Like me?) I see you squint
Down at your fob. It slips from your hand. And you boot it   20

Along the canal bank – all the way home.
Time scramble. Now you're getting numb,
Chin-deep in the canal, clinging to grass.
Granny (she's already trotted past you)

Told at the Pub you've gone, finds you, strips you,
Rubs you dry, wraps you in a blanket, sets you
By the fire. In the blink of an eye you're away –
Back in the Stubbing Wharfe – shrouded – singing –

Fading
Into such an empty negative   30
Even your grave's lost. You were a seed
Of the Great Hunger, fallen among stones.

Embryo, re-absorbed in the acid-sodden
Grit of the Calder crevasse. But you escaped
Granny's Andalusian blacks, the Sabbath
Toll of the valley prison.
                              And I'm proof
You've come through alive.
                              You reach a hand
As I touch at your elegy. Sweep
Me and my words aside.
                              Drink, deeper,
At this mirror meniscus of paper.

Disarmament

Somewhere – preserved – fire-signed – Hitler's
Head-bone. Tap it.
Imagine stroking the wasp-nest lightness. Listen
At the caves of chalk
For the sea.

Napoleon's exists – within touch.
Ethnic. A dried gourd.
A nesting box
For the wren of the mind.

The skull of Stalin! Imagine
That stained helm
Loosely wrapped, inside its public appearance.
The goblet of dry dregs.
Deforestation of souls! Pipelines of blood!

What unworldliness – (what space-flier!) –
Crowns itself
With such eggshell grails?

Each one lies
Precisely where it lies – slightly smaller
Than a tissue-paper party hat
From a party cracker –

But actually just let fall.
Simply forgotten, by something that lifted off

The brain-casque of a shrew
(I keep it in a cup
Drained, now too fragile to feel)

The skull of a tiger, my room-mate,
Executed 1905
By Lord Curzon (Viceroy Of India).
The whole thing is jaw,
Twice the weight of a famine baby.
The same shape, size and colour
As our Christmas turkey dangling
Out there at this moment for bluetits.

The Lord's eye dwelt there
For the crucial moment. My tongue tip
Hunted and dug
The husk of a wheat-grain
From between gum and cheek-flesh, to be spat out
(After the chain-gang, dust-gagged, marathon
Ache of threshing, all day up on the stacks
Knee-deep among sheaves, ear-drums battered
An eternal day in the inferno
Between bouncing rats and the levering forks
Of the Herrenvolk P.O.W.s
Who sweated grime, who chewed grains)

The shuck of a diatom – imagine it –
Let fall
Through dark miles
Empty
To the sea-floor

From a touch of sun –
                              a passing

Thirst of light
For a taste of earth.

Aspiring Head

Fingers of gimlet fire jerked him awake.
Flashes – a jag-winged indictment.
Faces of fire-turmoil and sunspot.

Now he kneels, in the rust-red chamber.
The prepared blade is a jet of atoms
Perpetually honing its glare.

Be he knows his kneeling is flying
And this room is liberation
And the blade
That judges him, that shears through him and through him

As if mere spectrum in water motes

Is severing the bonds

Halfway Head

He wanted to be here.
Toes guaranteed it. Fingers
Were ready for just this.

And ears. And eyes
Machined to the millionth,

Foretested at the limits.
A clone of triumphs.

So why does he stare as if blinded

Like a new ghost – blinded
By the sudden sun of afterlife?

Body, and its tongue, after all
Cannot move an atom.

Time ruffles its wings, and preens.
Space looks clean through him.

He half stands, half hangs
Mirrored over the river of life

A cenotaph, hacked in clay,
Worn with rains of unbeing.

Landmark Head

If you doubt this face, this is my face
You demanded hands, this is what I have

I found what I could of me, I brought it
I give it you refuse it I give it

I fitted it together I set it up
On the stone near water my tent

Air its song world its instrument
I called on it to live to be lived in

But a cowardliness of membrane
A lethargy of mineral in blood-colour

And spirit
Cried and would not come near it

Cries and flees from it sees a fear
Stands over it in sun-space and mourns it

This is my world-hope my courtship
My emptiness my knowledge.

What's the First Thing You Think Of?

'My brother bent at his airplane, in his attic.
I crept out. I'd left a tell-tale blood-splash
On the shavings. I'd been hewing the brass
Off a cartridge case picked up in a grouse-butt.
My knife had a deer's foot. I found our cat
And hid, nursing it, under my parents' bed.
In the end, they tracked me down by the blood.'

Or: 'The Heights Road. My brother launching a glider
Below where an airplane crashed above the golf-links

(Before the war, before the R.A.F.).
And the first hawk I ever saw and knew
Flew past with a small bird in its claw.
Another small bird bounced after it, crying,
Towed through the air on an invisible string.'

Or: 'A beeswax helm, a viking prow,
Delicate, polished, silent beside some sea
Wilder than any on earth –
        – and for all his baby-bird distress at the food
        I'd tried to spoon into him, and for all the gaping
wound of his look, his stricken, unrecognisable look,
        that could no longer recognise me –
I had to re-launch it. I re-launched it, somehow.
I imagine – out from Flamborough. Impossibly.
(So I still cannot get it afloat or light it.)'

Conscripts

That first night in our billet, I woke hours early.
Got up, dressed. Folded my blankets. In the dark.
Not a soul stirred. I sat on my bed-springs, knees up,
Waiting for reveille. And watched

Their profiles float into dawn.
All still strangers. And me – new to myself.
All helpless, mummy-like, foetal –
They seemed to drift becalmed in spermaceti.

Childhood, mother's touch, glittered in their hair.
Precarious – they were like seedlings
Their first night in the field. Each one damaged
By the clumsy exposure to uniform.

Was it dawn or moonlight?
It was a phosphor crypt – where saints lay
In their humble wax. It was dawn
Raw as in the maternity ward –

Lifting us, brightening moment by moment,
Toward a windowsill
Where the world whitened.
Roofs darkened.

The Best Worker in Europe

The best worker in Europe
  Is only six inch long.
You thought he'd be a bigger chap?
  Wait till you hear my song, my dears,
  Wait till you hear my song.
    No Union cries his Yea or Nay.
    He works for all, both night and day,
    With neither subsidy nor pay.

He comes out of a heap of stones
  Like some old-fashioned elf.
And all he asks is plain water,
  Such as you drink yourself, my dears,
  Such as you drink yourself.
    Two years toiling secretly
    He fits his craft, without a sigh
    To rest his head or close his eye.

And then one day he's off to sea.
  And only six inch long
Into the Black Hole, under the Ocean,
  Rows himself along, my dears,
  He rows himself along.
    To Hell with Russian, Viking, Hun!
    This great-hearted simpleton
    Takes the whole Atlantic on.

He hauls his trawl from Scilly Isles
  To the Subarctic shore.
No overheads, no crew to pay
  Whose wives will cry for more, my dears,
  Wives always cry for more.
    Through storm and freeze, with cheerful grin,
    Candelfish and Capelin,
    He crams the Ocean's goodness in.

A catch that all but splits his seam!
  Although, like a magician,
He's magnified his mass by ninety
  (He too's gone a-fishin', my dears,
  He too's gone a-fishin').
    Such a God-like magic, one's

Suddenly summed in millions
And understated metric tonnes.

Then in from Ocean's curve he brings
His National Gross Achievement.
Even the miracle of two fishes
Cries: "'Tis past believement, my dears,
'Tis simply past believement!'
Nobody's had to lift a hand!
No prayer, no contract, no command,
And he could feed the entire land!

Nobody has to lift a finger
Or to wet a shoe!
This is the worker for the job that
God alone could do, my dears,
That God alone could do.
What a production line, where he
Processes the open sea
To solid feast, and delivers it free.

The best worker in Europe
Is only six inch long –
Suddenly all his labours fail.
But still he sings: 'What's wrong, my dears?
I'll tell you just what's wrong.
My respiration, my circulation,
Compulsory-purchased by the Nation,
Are now Sewers of your Civilisation.

God help the slave', sings the Salmon Smolt,
'Who is owned by everyone.
The Donkey used, flogged, owned by all
Is protected by none, my dears,
He is protected by none –
And the wolf takes him easily.
O every wave upon the sea
Carries a wolf that lives on me.'

Grouse-Butts

A grouse-butt's good for grouse.
A nest of guns, you thought,
The bird-murderer's house –
No, it's the last earth-fort

Where an ancient bird hangs on,
An Aboriginal Brit,
Against an opinion
That would exterminate

The hunters who husband their prey,
The harvesters of a seed
Saved from yesterday,
Who nurse and worship the breed

And protect its sanctuary lands
From what I was, in the past,
When a boy crawled, down on his hands,
And would have slaughtered the last

And emptied these horizons
Of the grouse's laughter and cheer,
In wanton ignorance,
As they are emptied of deer.

Too easy to eat or sell.
Butts gone, the last wild grouse
Blown clean out of its shell
In the egg-collector's house

But millions crying in a shed –
For the gourmet millions.
Better a freedom defended
By the Keeper's numbered guns

And a nest right under the guns,
To inherit the moor. And, after,
Bequeath to daughters and sons
Grouse-life and grouse-laughter

And eyes that watch the dawn
Rise on the place they were born.

Edith

Sitting under the soot and brick, in Mexborough,

She dreamed about freedom. Herself on horseback,
A horizon silhouette, a storm fragment
Tossing over the moor, in romantic black –
Belated, errant, furious Brontë figment.

Her girlish, hungry passion,
Roaming the moors, had caught it.
Now she nursed it. Till she climbed again,
Her cheek bared so the wind and rain could hurt it,

Close to seventy, walking and walking the moor,
Herself the uncontainable weather,
Hurling her delight anywhere –
All she needed was a twist of heather –

Riding and riding and riding the wind
Away over the last edge – and beyond –
Into great breakers of light
Where earth itself reared up and cried out.

Rights

As I lay under Bridestones, on that lovely bit of grass
Which I supposed must have been the bed
Of many an old world newlywed lad and lass

(It sanctified their couplings, I fancied.
They had that lumpen, warty rock for God,
Heather-honey for stamina, Moon for Goddess) –

Anyway, there I lay, more or less brand-new,
Reading *Coriolanus*. I felt uplifted
Like champagne in a thin, bright glass

Into the sizzling blue, among mares' tails,
By that acclamation of hills
Between tremendous acts. Stupefied

In the vibrant black stone's ionisation,
Worked on by its etheric whispers
And drained into my book, I lay helpless

Letting whatever wanted take possession.
A sudden, officious dog barked at my face.
Three or four guns were walking up the heather.

Next thing I was stood around. And stared at.
'What the bloody hell are you doing here?
Don't you know – this is a private shoot?'

'This rock is a public monument. I've come here
For some public privacy. So I stay.'
'Look, you're scaring our grouse. Bugger off.'

'Who rented you this shoot? Who are you?'
'We're the Halifax – Bloody Hell! Cocky Bugger!
Look, bugger off. Bloody Hell!'

'I represent the public so I stay.'
'Bloody Hell!'
'You're wasting your time and your money, anyway,

This bit of moor's been cleaned out – by the public.'
Some things have changed, some haven't.
None of us were quite sure which. So they trooped off.

And I went on lying there, in a turmoil.
Reading *Coriolanus*.

The Pike

In the reservoir, behind the mirror

The pike, a stone
Under the flame-flutter
Complexion of water.

The pike, a sunk stone
Tip-tilted on stones
Under the crawling nape of light.

The pike
Non-participant
Under the lake's slow lungs.

The pike that will only be heavier
Stonier

When all this dammed water,
Like an ouined wife, has frittered away
In housework.

The pike that has somehow, unmoving
Sailed out of the sun

Into this measured hole.
A cold
Finger of the silence of space.

A smile
Of the deafness of earth

Making the skull creak.

Mayday

It's a hard-labour factory-asylum
Of committed birdsong. The world is being made over
By voices which are tools.

Each bird is a tree, air-stirred,
Of its noises.
What is amazing all the day long

Is the almost-madness
Of the eye, the near-frenzy
Wiping the beak on the twig –

The blur to the next job.
No effort – this labour comes easy,
Rooted, that is, as the tree's

Unsleeping slog
At the millionfold uplift
Of perfected hands,

Its pumping tonnage, its heart-column.
Country life
Wears me out, as I fit my brains into it –

My auxiliary cog of nylon
Melted after a few hours
In this all-out production of eggs and nuts.

Sketching a Thatcher

Bird-bones is on the roof. Seventy-eight
And still a ladder squirrel,
Three or four nitches at a time, up forty rungs,
Then crabbing out across the traverse,
Cock-crows of insulting banter, liberated
Into his old age, like a royal fool
But still tortured with energy. Thatching
Must be the sinless job. Weathered
Like a weathercock, face bright as a ploughshare,
Skinny forearms of steely cable, batting   10
The reeds flush, crawling, cliff-hanging,
Lizard-silk of his lizard-skinny hands,
Hands never still, twist of body never still –
Bounds in for a cup of tea, 'Caught you all asleep!'
Markets all the gossip – cynical old goblin
Cackling with wicked joy. Bounds out –
Trips and goes full length, bounces back upright,
'Haven't got the weight to get hurt with!' Cheers
Every departure – 'Off for a drink?' and 'Off
To see his fancy woman again!' – leans from the sky,   20
Sun-burned-out pale eyes, eyes bleached
As old thatch, in the worn tool of his face,
In his haggard pants and his tired-out shirt –
They can't keep up with him. He just can't
Stop working. 'I don't want the money!' He'd
Prefer a few years. 'Have to sell the house to pay me!'
Alertness built into the bird-stare,
The hook of his nose, bill-hook of his face.
Suns have worn him, like an old sun-tool
Of the day-making, an old shoe-tongue   30
Of the travelling weathers, the hand-palm, ageless,
Of all winds on all roofs. He lams the roof
And the house quakes. Was everybody
Once like him? He's squirmed through
Some tight cranny of natural selection.
The nut-stick yealm-twist's got into his soul,
He didn't break. He's proof
As his crusty roofs. He ladder-dances
His blood light as spirit. His muscles
Must be clean as horn.   40

And the whole house
Is more pleased with itself, him on it,
Cresting it, and grooming it, and slapping it
Than if an eagle rested there. Sitting
Drinking his tea, he looks like a tatty old eagle,
And his yelping laugh of derision
Is just like a tatty old eagle's.

Lamenting Head

A head uprooting itself from earth
Shaking its grass and working its pools
Came for me

A brain pain-detector spider-spirit
A snuffer of oozing joys a mesh for after-pangs
Came for me

Hands machinery of soft hunger with chewed nails
Crustacea of discernment
Came for me

A heart shepherd of blood came for me

Belly came for me the worm of man

I hid I hid O I hid
But though I hid in the sun's centre the winking candle found me

And the weak talons caught me
The wet worm of the mouth held me
The gentle drum numbed me
The skin downed like a leaf lifted me

And nailed this face to me

Reckless Head

When it comes down to it
Hair is afraid. Words from within are afraid.

They sheer off, like a garment,
Cool, treacherous, no part of you.

Hands the same, feet, and all blood
Till nothing is left. Nothing stays

But what your gaze can carry.
And maybe you vomit even that, like a too-much poison.

Then it is
That the brave hunger of your skull

Supplants you. It stands where you stood
And shouts, with a voice you can't hear,

For what you can't take.

Sacrificed Head

Because the Black One in Earth
Hungers for the Sun, you were chosen.

Dressed with a corona – you are a sun.

Blackened with vinegar blood
A temporary preservative in air

Black, but still a sun,
Like the Sun's negative.

So you are hung up – a black sun
Where the Black One can find you

And gnaw at you. There you hang, immortal –

Eaten by the Black One
But restored by the Sun, perpetually.

Where the Black One can go on eating you.

This is the satisfaction of Earth.
And it is the sleight

By which the Sun gets clear.

from FLOWERS AND INSECTS (1986)

Narcissi

The Narcissi shiver their stars
In the green-gold wind of evening sunglare.
Their happiness is weightless.
Their merriment is ghostly.

Tonight, too, will be precarious stars
On the Moon's hill
And an April frost.

The Narcissi are untouchable
In a rustling, silent film
Of speeded-up dancing
And laughing children
From the 1918 Armistice.

Their tiny faces are pinched
Under big, loose bows of pale ribbon.

But this is happiness now
To be grown up –
                    skinny, modish girls,
Hair blown back, thin lips parted, pressing
Into a cold sunglare, cheekbones flared
And delicate as lit ice.

They will never be hurt.

(Even among the mourners,
Harrowed with solemnity, and chilled,
They will be safe –

Bulbs in earth
Under the shock of the wreath.)

                    Starry wreath.

Ghost-lights in the orchard.

A Violet at Lough Aughresberg

The tide-swell grinds crystal, under cliffs.

Against the opened furnace of the West –
A branch of apple-blossom.

A bullock of sooted bronze
Cools on an emerald
That is crumbling to granite embers.

Milk and blood are frail
In the shivering wind off the sea.

 Only a purple flower – this amulet
 (Once Prospero's) – holds it all, a moment,
 In a rinsed globe of light.

Brambles

The whole air, the whole day
Swirls with the calls of jackdaws. The baby jackdaw
Generation is being initiated
Into jackdawdom – that complicated
Court-world of etiquette

And precedence, jingoism and law.
Nearly a prison world – with bars
Of cries and signals. The jailors
Are all the other jackdaws. Tearing a track
Through the intertangled briars

I thought again: do they feel this?
Briars are such a success, their defences
So craftsmanlike,
Their reachings so deliberate, are they awake?
Surely some nimbus of pain and pleasure

Sits on their naked coronet,
Their sexual offer. Surely they aren't just numb,
A blind groping. Yet why not?
Aren't my blood-cells the same?
What do even brain-cells fear or feel

Of the scalpel, or the accident?
They too crown a plant
Of peculiar numbness. And the jackdaws
Work darkly to be jackdaws
As if they were seeds in the earth.

The whole claque is a benighted religion
Around the godlike syntax and vocabulary
Of a mute cell, that does not know who we are
Or even that we are here,
Unforthcoming as any bramble-flower.

Daffodils

I'd bought a patch of wild ground.
In March it surprised me. Suddenly I saw what I owned.
A cauldron of daffodils, boiling gently.

A gilding of the Deeds – treasure trove!
Daffodils just came. And kept coming –

'Blown foam,' I wrote, 'Vessels of light!'
They raced under every gust
On the earth-surge. 'Their six-bladed screws
Churning the greeny-yellows
Out of the hard, over-wintered Chlorophyl.'   10

I was still a nomad.
My life was still a raid. The earth was booty.
I knew I'd live forever. I had not learned
What a fleeting glance of the everlasting
Daffodils are. Did not recognise
The nuptial flight of the rarest ephemera –
My own days!
Hardly more body than a hallucination!
A dream of gifts – opening their rustlings for me!

I thought they were a windfall. I picked them. I sold them.   20

Behind the rainy curtains of that dark April
I became intimate
With the soft shrieks
Of their jostled stems –
The wet shocks shaken
Of their girlish dance-frocks –
Fresh-opened Dragonflies, wet and flimsy.

To each scared, bright glance
I brought a defter cruelty. So many times
Slid my fingers down her slenderness,   30

Felt for the source, her chilly fount,
The watery flicker she peered from,
And nipped her off close to the bulb.

I piled their frailty lights on a carpenter's bench,
Distributed leaves among the dozens
(Buckling blade-leaves, limber, groping for air, zinc-silvered)
Propped their raw butts in bucket water
(Their oval, meaty butts)
And sold them, sevenpence a bunch. The whole lot went.

40   Yet they stayed. That night, on my pillow,
My brain was a chandelier of daffodils!

Wings pouring light, faces bowed,
Dressed for Heaven,
The souls of all those daffodils, as I killed them,
Had gone to ground inside me – there they were packed.

I could see right into their flame-stillness
Like seeing right into the eye-pupil
Of a person fast asleep, as if I'd lifted the eyelid –

I could study
50   That scarf of papery crinkle, fawn and perfunctory, at their throats,
And the tissue of their lips. I learned
That what had looked like a taffeta knot, undone
And re-tied looser, crumpled,
Was actually membrane of solid light.

And that their metals were odourless,
More a deep grave stoniness, a cleanness of stone,
As if ice had a breath –

They began to alarm me. Were these
My free girls, my Saturnalian nunnery
60   With their bloomers of scrambled egg-yolk, their flounces,
Their core so alive and kicking, their bare shoulders in frills,
That set the cold stars shaking
Loose and wetly
Inside walking, darkly-coated people?

I tried to picture them out there – in the garden –

These rigid, gold archangels somehow
Drank up my attempt.

They became awful,
Like the idea of atoms. Or like the idea
Of white-frosted galaxies, floating apart.   70

As I sank deeper, each towered heavier,
Cathedral interior lit,
Empty or all-seeing angel stare
Leaning through me –

                    It was Resurrection!
The trumpet!
The earth-weight of nightmare!
                              I wrenched free.
I flitted
With my world, my garden, my unlikely
Baby-cries leached from the thaw –
                              my shiverers
In the draughty wings of the year –   80

Two Tortoiseshell Butterflies

Mid-May – after May frosts that killed the Camellias,
After May snow. After a winter
Worst in human memory, a freeze
Killing the hundred-year-old Bay Tree,
And the ten-year-old Bay Tree – suddenly
A warm limpness. A blue heaven just veiled
With the sweatings of earth
And with the sweatings-out of winter
Feverish under the piled
Maywear of the lawn.   10
                    Now two
Tortoiseshell butterflies, finding themselves alive,
She drunk with the earth-sweat, and he
Drunk with her, float in eddies
Over the Daisies' quilt. She prefers Dandelions,
Settling to nod her long spring tongue down
Into the nestling pleats, into the flower's
Thick-folded throat, her wings high-folded.
He settling behind her, among plain glistenings
Of the new grass, edging and twitching
To nearly touch – pulsing and convulsing   20

Wings wide open to tight-closed to flat open
Quivering to keep her so near, almost reaching
To stroke her abdomen with his antennae –
Then she's up and away, and he startlingly
Swallowlike overtaking, crowding her, heading her
Off any escape. She turns that
To her purpose, and veers down
Onto another Dandelion, attaching
Her weightless yacht to its crest.
30   Wobbles to stronger hold, to deeper, sweeter
Penetration, her wings tight shut above her,
A sealed book, absorbed in itself.
She ignores him
Where he edges to left and to right, flitting
His wings open, titillating her fur
With his perfumed draughts, spasming his patterns,
His tropical, pheasant appeals of folk-art,
Venturing closer, grass-blade by grass-blade,
Trembling with inhibition, nearly touching –
40   And again she's away, dithering blackly. He swoops
On an elastic to settle accurately
Under her tail again as she clamps to
This time a Daisy. She's been chosen,
Courtship has claimed her. And he's been conscripted
To what's required
Of the splitting bud, of the talented robin
That performs piercings
Out of the still-bare ash,
The whole air just like him, just breathing
50   Over the still-turned-inward earth, the first
Caresses of the wedding coming, the earth
Opening its petals, the whole sky
Opening a flower
Of unfathomably-patterned pollen.

Cyclamens in a Bowl

A pink one. A white one. Each
A butterfly – caught by an uptwisting
Slender snake and held. Without hurt.
Without fear.

Now, it seems, a serpent of plants
Rearing and angling, gently writhing
Has opened a butterfly face.

The five petals elated –
A still of tensile flight!

The great, wide-awake ears
Of the most lady-like of gazelles
A gerenuk, in mid-leap,
Over the ambush of clumsy body-leaves.

The flower escapes

The leaves and stems toil in sturdy pursuit,
Debating their manoeuvres with each other,
Arranging their groupings in a workaday world.

The flower floats off into trance
Unattached
At the open window –

Deepening, with skirts up over its head,
Into the breathless
Brightenings that embrace it –

(The lambent, electric shock-waves
Of our simply, quietly gazing at it)

Cool flame-tongue, spectre flower of the lungs!
Wing-beat that nests in the pelvis!
Soul-bird of the bowels!
The heart's very throb
As a winged Hallelujah!

Uplifted, upheld
Letting the God-light glow through –

While the solid leaves, physiques of substance,
Forest-dark, patched pale with experience,
Burdened with passionate, lush, vulnerable veins,
Open their palms to the air, simple and good,

Under those rearing, plunging fillies of spirit!

Saint's Island
for Barrie Cooke

This is a day for small marvels.
The Mayflies are leaving their Mother.

Seven horse-power, our bows batter
The ridgy Lough.
Weird womb. Beneath us
It gestates a monster –

Monstrous, but tiny. When it appears
We'll call it The Green Drake.
At the moment, down there in the mud,
It's something else –
The dream of an alchemist,

The nightmare
Of the sunk pebble
That feels the claws grip lightly.

But today – it wants to be born.
It's had enough of the mud. At a brainwave,
Overpowered by it does not know what
(What is it doing on earth, anyway?)
It kicks off from its burrow.
                              It rises
Fuelled by the manias of space
And inspiration
That coil round the sun's mask.

It rises, as if it fell,
Towards that magnet core, where blindness glances,
The sun's water-image
Shivered by our shock-wave, as we bounce past.

The Mayflies are leaving their Mother.

I glimpse one labouring – a close-up
In the brow of a wave.

I glimpse the midget sneeze –
A dream bursts its bubble.
As much machinery
As the upsurge of a big oak.
(One time I found one had failed.

It wallowed in the oil of light.
I saw through my lens a tiny leech
Corkscrewed into its head.)
Luckier, in millions,
A catkin-green, dragonish torso
Hauls from its sleeping bag –
A yacht has a blown, stubborn moment –
Falters, lifts from the Lough's melt –

The Mayflies are leaving their Mother.

And there they go. The Lough's words to the world.
This is what it thinks.
This is what it aspires to, finally.
This is the closest it comes
To consciousness, and the flight into light –

Into life?

All morning, leaving their Mother, the Mayflies
Spinning on their weak centres,
Poetic electrons
With their vision of the sun's skirts
(An idea faceted like a fly's eye,
A rose-window in blood-cells,
A Holy Grail of neurons)
Blow and dither downwind

Toward the Island,
Toward the grey crumble of Monastery.

They crowd in under the boughs,
Keels under every leaf,
Dangle on claws, cluster their ripenings,
Letting the sun touch them through Chlorophyl,

Spooky fruit

Spooky because this isn't their world
Their world is over.
Their feastings are complete. Their jaws are tied up.
This is their underworld,
Their beach-head in death, because they are already souls –

So many
They gauze and web the Maybush bloom and leaf

As they digest their shock,
The vision.
It nourishes them,
It consumes them.
It peels off the last drudgery
Of the Lough

And they are creeping out of their lives.
None resist or defer it,
Or settle for terms, or evade it.
Already
They have dressed themselves in Mayfly, a lace of blackish crystals

(As if our lives were lichenous rock
Or a sleep of roots. Or a tin of sardines,
An apple, a watch, a thermos.)

Everywhere under the leaves
You see their mummy moulds,
The refuse of their earthliness, clinging empty,
The blood-chart in their wings still perfect,
Still waiting (already seeming dusty),

But they've gone up into sunlight, a wet shimmer

In their smudgy veils,
Sooty fairies.

We watch them through binocs. On and off
All day till evening
They are dancing above the trees, rising and falling
To woodwind airs, clouded or sunny,
To bowings
Of thermometer and barometer,
Over and over, a reel unending and Irish –

What time will they come out? Will they come out?

No hurry,
The long-bellied females, pith-naked,
Tender two inch snippets of live, nerve-cord
Tipped with the three black fork hairs even longer,
And the males darker, smaller –
They are rediscovering each other.
Familiars of the ten billion years

They jig in a spin, in a column. They are tossed and are tossed –

Their happiness is to prolong this. To prolong it
Till the moment opens – and it happens –
And an escaping climax of the music
Lifts them over the top –

And they are coming out!

But now like Dervishes, truly they are like those,
Touched by God,
Drunk with God, they hurl themselves into God –

They have caught the moment,
Their dancing has found that fault in time
To break through – to break out –
Into beyond –
They are casting themselves away,
They abandon themselves, they soar out of themselves,
They fall through themselves –

Where can they go?

Space can't hold them. The blue air is snowing.

All round us
Trickling giddily down, they try to pirouette.

The wind carries them out.

Under the outer waves of the Lough
The big trout wait.
Under the Island lee, anchored in the mirror,
Between light and dark, on the skin of shivers,
We wait.
        (What are we doing on earth?)

All round us
Fanatics faint and wreck shuddering, gently,
Onto the face of evening.

Where I Sit Writing My Letter

Suddenly hooligan baby starlings
Rain all round me squealing,
Shouting how it's tremendous and everybody
Has to join in and they're off this minute!

Probably the weird aniseed corpse-odour
Of the hawthorn flower's disturbed them,
As it disturbs me. Now they all rise
Flutter-floating, oddly eddying,

Squalling their dry gargles. Then, mad, they
Hurl off, on a new wrench of excitement,
Leaving me out.
                I pluck apple-blossom,
Cool, blood-lipped, wet open.

And I'm just quieting thoughts towards my letter
When they all come storming back,
Giddy with hoarse hissings and snarls
And clot the top of an ash sapling –

Sizzling bodies, snaky black necks craning
For a fresh thrill – Where next? Where now? Where? – they're off
All rushing after it
Leaving me fevered, and addled.

They can't believe their wings.

Snow-bright clouds boil up.

Tern
for Norman Nicholson

The breaker humps its green glass.
You see the sunrise through it, the wrack dark in it,
And over it – the bird of sickles
Swimming in the wind, with oiled spasm.

That is the tern. A blood-tipped harpoon
Hollow-ground in the roller-dazzle,
Honed in the wind-flash, polished
By his own expertise –

Now finished and in use.
The wings – remote-controlled
By the eyes
In his submarine swift shadow

Feint and tilt in their steel.
Suddenly a triggered magnet
Connects him downward, through a thin shatter,
To a sand-eel. He hoists out, with a twinkling,

Through some other wave-window.
His eye is a gimlet.
Deep in the churned grain of the roller
His brain is a gimlet. He hangs,

A blown tatter, a precarious word
In the mouth of ocean pronouncements.
His meaning has no margin. He shudders
To the tips of his tail-tines.

Momentarily, his lit scrap is a shriek.

Sketch of a Goddess

We have one Iris. A Halberd
Of floral complications. Two blooms are full,
Floppily opened, or undone rather.
                              Royal
Seraglio twin sisters, contending
For the Sultan's eye. Even here
One is superior.
Rivalry has devastated
Everything about them except
The womb's temptation and offer.

That one's past it. But this one's in her prime.
She utters herself
Utterly into appeal. A surrender
Of torn mucous membranes, veined and purpled,
A translucence of internal organs
In a frisson,
Torn open,
The core debauched,

All loosely dangling helplessness
And enfolding claspers –

Delicately holding herself
As if every edge were cringing round a nerve.

Actually
She's lolling her tongue right out,
Her uvula arched,
Her uterus everted –

An overpowered bee buries its face
In the very beard of her ovaries.

It deafens itself
In a dreadful belly-cry – just out of human hearing.

The Honey Bee

The Honey Bee
Brilliant as Einstein's idea
Can't be taught a thing.
Like the sun, she's on course forever.

As if nothing else at all existed
Except her flowers.
No mountains, no cows, no beaches, no shops.
Only the rainbow waves of her flowers

A tremor in emptiness

A flying carpet of flowers

            – a pattern
Coming and going – very loosely woven –
Out of which she works her solutions.

Furry goblin midgets
(The beekeeper's thoughts) clamber stickily
Over the sun's face – gloves of shadow.

But the Honey Bee
Cannot imagine him, in her brilliance,

Though he's a stowaway on her carpet of colour-waves
And drinks her sums.

In the Likeness of a Grasshopper

A trap
Waits on the field path.

A wicker contraption, with working parts,
Its spring tensed and set.

So flimsily made, out of grass
(Out of the stems, the joints, the raspy-dry flags).

Baited with a fur-soft caterpillar,
A belly of amorous life, pulsing signals.

Along comes a love-sick, perfume-footed
Music of the wild earth.   10

The trap, touched by a breath,
Jars into action, its parts blur –

And music cries out.

A sinewy violin
Has caught its violinist.

Cloud-fingered summer, the beautiful trapper,
Picks up the singing cage

And takes out the Song, adds it to the Songs
With which she robes herself, which are her wealth,

Sets her trap again, a yard further on.   20

Sunstruck Foxglove

As you bend to touch
The gypsy girl
Who waits for you in the hedge
Her loose dress falls open.

Midsummer ditch-sickness!

Flushed, freckled with earth-fever,
Swollen lips parted, her eyes closing,
A lolling armful, and so young! Hot

Among the insane spiders.
You glimpse the reptile under-speckle
Of her sunburned breasts
And your head swims. You close your eyes.

Can the foxes talk? Your head throbs.
Remember the bird's tolling echo,
The dripping fern-roots, and the butterfly touches
That woke you.

Remember your mother's
Long, dark dugs.

Her silky body a soft oven
For loaves of pollen.

Big Poppy

Hot-eyed Mafia Queen!
At the trim garden's edge

She sways towards August.
A Bumble Bee
Clambers into her drunken, fractured goblet –

Up the royal carpet of a down-hung,
Shrivel-edged, unhinged petal, her first-about-to-fall.
He's in there as she sways. He utters thin

Sizzling bleats of difficult enjoyment.
Her carnival paper skirts, luminous near-orange,
Embrace him helplessly.

Already her dark pod is cooking its drug.
Every breath imperils her. Her crucible
Is falling apart with its own fierceness.

A fly, cool, rests on the flame-fringe.

Soon she'll throw off her skirts
Withering into vestal afterlife,

Bleeding inwardly
Her maternal nectars into her own
Coffin – (cradle of her offspring).

Then we shall say:
'She wore herself in her hair, in her day,
And we could see nothing but her huge flop of petal,

Her big, lewd, bold eye, in its sooty lashes,

And that stripped, athletic leg, hairy,
In a fling of abandon—'

Nightjar

The tree creeps on its knees.
The dead branch aims, in the last light.
The cat-bird is telescopic.

The sun's escape
Shudders, shot
By wings of ashes.

The moon falls, with all its moths,
Into a bird's face.

Stars spark
From the rasp of its cry.

Till the moon-eater, cooling,
Yawns dawn
And sleeps bark.

UNCOLLECTED (1987–89)

Devon Riviera

Under the silk nightie of the August evening
The prepared resort, a glowing liner,
Leans towards happiness, unmoving.
The whole vessel throbs with dewy longing.

Grey, dazed heads, promenading their pots,
Their holiday shirts, their shrunk, freckled forearms,
With hobbling wives who look more like their mothers,
Smell rejuvenation in the ebb.

And lard-thickened ex-footballers, with their high-tension scowls,
Trailing headache wives and swollen kids
Towards another compulsory steak and chips
Sniff the beery skirts of liberation.

Mauve-dusted, balanced pairs of spinsters,
Walking to interest an appetite,
Venture their compass-delicate stomachs
Among guffaws and squeals and gaping perfumes.

Decent couples, rigid with loneliness,
Expose themselves
Intermittently, with buttoned faces,
To the furnace interiors of fun-halls.

And easy girls from the North, their half-closed eyes
Fixed on the wine-dark sea-haze towards Jersey,
Loll back in cliff alcoves, above the town out-fall,
While waiters from Pisa gnaw their necks.

They see gulls dangling stainless cries
And colliding for tossed-up fish-guts
Above my chugging boat
That nudges happily home, through the purple,

Hauling the rich robe of sewage.

First Things First

(An Election Duet, performed in the Womb by foetal Twins,
4 June 1987)

FIRST TWIN:

If the cost of a mountain of butter is
    poisoned water in your tap and Cot-Death

If the cost of a mountain of grain is
    poisoned bread on your plate and for the farmer's child
    (and yours) Leukaemia

If the cost of the Gross National Product is
    for trees no leaves
    and waters no fish
    and for you cortical plaques, neurofibrillary tangles
10   Presenile Dementia

And if the cost of Annual Expansion of the World Chemical
    Industry taken as a whole over the last two decades is a
    40% drop in the sperm count of all human males (nor can
    God alone help the ozone layer or the ovum)

Then let what can't be sold to your brother and sister be
    released on the 3rd World and let it return by air and sea
    to drip down the back of your own throat at night

Because

BOTH TWINS (singing):

Man's brain is such a toxin
20   (O hear our foetal shout)
Nothing surer than man's brain
    Will wipe the menace out.

SECOND TWIN:

Man's riddle is: 'Why aren't I right?'
    So to correct his error
He can only double it
    In exponential terror.

Snap your fingers at Death's frown.
    Eat, drink and be jolly.

The only folly of our fun
    Is to bewail our folly.

Who wants to last forever?
    Then take another sup
For everything pitched in the ditch
    Comes back into the cup.

    BOTH TWINS (singing):

Then off to bed, for every head's
    In labour with the pains
Until the Monkey Mutant
    Can bear a brain with brains.

A Full House

1 QUEEN OF HEARTS

Venereal, uterine heat.
Smothering breast-fruit.
The poor boy gasped to be out.

Hell-mouth he could hear.
The many mouthed hound in there
Started his heart a hare.

Daddy jumped, the god of war,
From under her skirts, as a scythe-tusked boar.
Mortal frailty tore.

Willy's blood a shower
Of fertiliser for,
Where he fell, a flower.

2 QUEEN OF SPADES

The Serpent of Old Nile
Coiled in a fig-tree
Queen Cleopatra's
Affable, familiar
Hypodermic smile.

Fruit of the tree he seized
And was darkly kissed.

And melted into air
Twenty years had gone
Dreaming of passion on
That bed in the East.

3 QUEEN OF CLUBS

Three Corbies in a tree
Sang to Macbeth
Maid, Wife, Mother
We are tragedy
Queen of Birth and Death
And there is no other.

Your Fate's a double coil.
For Will to grab the crown
Mother, Maid, Wife
You must kill your Soul
(We'll help you get it done)
And still hang on to your life.

Such soulful, wilful acts
The shadows of your limbs
Wife, Mother, Maid
Shall be history's facts ...
The crown plucked in these dreams
Paid for by Cromwell's head.

4 QUEEN OF DIAMONDS

My son told such a tale ...
His father killed by an Owl!

Dressed for the funeral
He started to play the Fool.

Dreaming he'd married me
He cried: 'It cannot be!'

His sanity took the veil
In Avon's darkest pool.

Succession in a pall
Crazed him to murder us all ...

Pausing for no farewell
I fled into this pearl.

5 KING OF HEARTS

My Will shall be
What I have planned:
My treasure, my land
Split into three.

One third I pay
To help Anne's age
Put her youth's rage
And hate away.

To Judith one
For who will marry
Memento Mori
Of my son?

And for Sue
The final part
Includes my heart
That is pierced through

By my own Lance
In young Edmund's
Bastard Edmund's
Lineal hands.

Envoi

And to God, Her
   Of triple power
Locked with the hoodlum
   Of this hour.

6 KING OF SPADES

Tarquin the King's
Besieging eye
Sacked Lucrece's
Chastity.

Which, it seems,
Wore such a crown

Kingship itself
Was tumbled down.

The bubble of State
We see from this
Balloons from lips
That were made to kiss.

7 KING OF CLUBS

A cripple soon
Can find a fault.
Speak of my lameness
I straight will halt.

I carry a sack
Of limbless pain.
Body deposed
The mind will reign.

The nimble fools
Of human pride
Shall be the toys
Of what I hide.

8 KING OF DIAMONDS

The Cabalist is old.
Crucibles thrice thirteen
Alchemised air to gold,

His soul's incarnate stain,
The tigerish, upstart crow,
To a self of diamond stone.

Sword and Cup can go;
All trumpery that held
The invisible in awe.

Familiar, daemon child,
A howling banshee, rides
A rainbow from the world.

And as the pageant fades,
Warming his master's grave
The calloused Golem hides

Clutching the broken staff
Three fathoms under the prayer
And terminal, wild laugh

Of his great lord who prays
The sea-monster ashore
And feeds it with his plays.

9 KNAVE OF HEARTS

Hal moistens his lips.
   After many a try
At last he slips
   Through the needle's eye

To sew the tap-
   -estry of a new England.
But he's only the tip
   Of the glory-hole tangle

Old Adam packed in
   To the quaking sack
Of the fat Knight's skin ...
   Will the thread break?

10 KNAVE OF SPADES

The Sulphur, Charcoal, Nitrate of his gunnery
Proportioned Othello.
Who fell for this fellow?
A blonde pure as a taper in a nunnery.

A light, light lass, a dark, heavy chap,
And a touch of evil laughter ...
Boom, the whole lot goes up
Unhappily ever after.

11 KNAVE OF CLUBS

Nature's child
Looks at men's graves
As the sun
Watches the waves.

And as the wind
Does what it likes

Finds no bar
To his thoughts and looks.

Wherefore should he
Be other than
Death itself
To play at man?

For all it needs
To rule alone
Taking all
Is to love none.

12 KNAVE OF DIAMONDS

As Mary bore
The Son so mourned
Tortured, murdered
And returned

Timon gives all.
Hands close and take.
Open to render
Hatred back.

In X-ray blink
Baboons revealed
The skulls for which
Their lips had smiled.

He hurls the bomb
From his mother's womb
That blows the species
To kingdom come.

13 JOKER

On all my stages
Not to be heard
On all my pages
Never a word

Where there is nobody
A soothing
Suffering all
Suffers nothing

Birthday Greetings
for Charles Causley

I meant to rhyme your dream:
All Cornwall
A willawaw sea
Of Moors and Mounts
Bursting to granite foam,
A tide-rip cemetery –
One erupting tomb
Of oracular Menhir bones
Which called each other by name
To limber up their tons
Dancing in circles
Backs to the centre backwards
To undo time

    But you were polishing a find.
       You were rehearsing
          The perfect pitch
             Of a granny's retort
                To the postman's laugh
                    That morning in Launceston.

I had meant to paint
With Turneresque tints
Your spectacles' reflection
Of a storm-haven –
Boscastle to Penzance –
And anchored there
In the gold roads of evening,
Above those bleak, wet chapels,
On cabbage-leaf and quernstone
Cornwall's fleet of saints

    But you were bent
      At Altarnun
         To a gravestone relief
            Cut with a nail –
              And the heart-broken sculptor,
                His fame abandoned,
                  Curled in straw.

I had found an image:
You lie in the Irish Sea.
Like any son
Fallen from heaven
Across his mother's knee.
The Moon keeps the tides
Working the mines
That centuries of tinners
Deepened in your sides –
And whispering up your veins
Every one of the waves
Is a rough old Cornishman
Telling of his lives

But you were at thirty thousand feet
   Entering Canadian air-space or were just
      Touching down on the tarmac home
         From home in Sydney.

No matter where. Cornwall
   Is in you the same
As in Camel River
   That stone with the name

Of the King who fell there
   Under the overhang,
Is the freed water's
   Threshold and tongue.

Congratulations, Charles.
God give us half the wit
To recognise our own
And to stick with it.

Chinese History of Colden Water

A fallen immortal found this valley –
Leafy conch of whispers
On the shore of heaven. He brought to his ear
The mad singing in the hills,
The prophetic mouth of the rain –

These hushings lulled him. So he missed
The goblins toiling up the brook.
The clink of fairy hammers forged his slumber
To a migraine of head-scarves and clatter
Of clog-irons and looms, and gutter water   10
And clog-irons and biblical texts.

Till he woke in a terror, tore free, lay panting.
The dream streamed from him. He blinked away
The bloody matter of the Cross
And the death's head after-image of 'Poor'.

Chapels, chimneys, roofs in the mist – scattered.

Hills with raised wings were standing on hills.
They rode the waves of light
That rocked the conch of whispers

And washed and washed at his eye.   20
                              Washed from his ear
All but the laughter of foxes.

Kore

What ghosts gather
Over the moonlit grave mounds
Of your breasts?

The common infantry – whose job it is
To cease in approximate numbers
Within the overall event.

What bat-webbed things flitter
About the holy cave
Between your thighs?

The warriors – the selfless ones
Who simply failed to reassemble
From the all-out scrimmage.

Now the shadowy terrace of your lip,
The silent arches of your eyelids
Are their Valhalla.

Are the heroes happy in heaven?

He who wakes
Beside your sleeping face
In the dawn,
And touches you, to make you even more real.
And watches you breathe

He hears the sighs and the sobbings.

Glimpse

When I peered down
Onto Greenland's appalling features
Sheeted with snow-glare
Under a hole of blaze in the violet

(I had slid open the shutter
Of the jet's port-hole –
I wanted to escape
The film about a daughter's rebellion)

I mourned a little
For my father. I thought of the pierced seal
Down there under the ice
Far from its breathing hole

Straining as he finally strained
With last breaths
Against the steely bond
Held by those aliens –

His bones, his family.

If

If the sky is infected
The river has to drink it

If earth has a disease which could be fatal
The river has to drink it

If you have infected the sky and the earth
Caught its disease off you – you are the virus

If the sea drinks the river
And the earth drinks the sea

It is one quenching and one termination

If your blood is trying to clean itself
In the filter of your corrupted flesh
And the sores run – that is the rivers

The five rivers of Paradise

Where will you get a pure drink now?

Already – the drop has returned to the cup

Already you are your ditch, and there you drink

Mayday

Away, Cuckoo!
Your first cry in April tapped at the blood
Like a finger-tip at a barometer.
Away, Cuckoo!

Sudden popping up of a lolling Priapus –
Hooha! Hooha!
(The orchard flushed, and the hairy copse grew faint
With bluebells.)

Cuckoo jinked in – sleight of a conjurer –
Dowsed with a hawk-fright crucifix
Over the brambly well of the nest-bird's eye
And left its shadow in the egg.

Then came ducking under gates, pursued by a husband.
Or hid – letting the cry flee *in flagrante*,
Hunted by inwit, hill to hollow,
Dodging the echo double that dogged it.

Elsewhere – clockwork woe. O tick-tock fact,
With heartless blow on blow, all afternoon –
Opening hairfine fractures through the heirloom
Porcelain of hearts in rose cottages.

Seven weeks. Eight.
                    Then you and your witchy moll

Cavorting on pylons, chuckling, plotting,
Syncopating that lewd loopy shout
Into your ghoulish, double-act, hiccuping
Gag about baby-murder.

                              Away, Cuckoo!

Lines about Elias
for Thom Gunn

Did music help him? Indeed it helped him.
His crude music, instruments
Imitated uncannily but weirdly
Restored the order of music
Within the terror of the Camp.
They could have been baboons
In some demented phase of tribal breakdown
During a famine, or under the effects
Of a poisonous dust from space.
Yet his music, for its few moments
Ushered them into a formation
Where the Camp did not exist
Where their sorrowful bodies did not exist.

So the scabies on his belly the sores and
Inflammations which made Elias
That ferocious clown crow
And ridiculed him, ripping down his trousers
Fighting with him in the mud
They did not touch his music
Did not adhere to any note of it
Or disturb his performance
Through which his fellow-prisoners escaped
Their rags, their last few horrible hours, their next few
Frightful possibly fatal days, sooner
Or later nearly certainly fatal days
Standing aside from them, stepping a little
Out of the time corridor, standing in a group
Just outside it, where the air was still,

In the solidarity of souls, where music uttered
The dumbness of naked bodies
As if it were the inside of the earth

And everything else –
The hours where their soft surfaces
Tore against the hard –
Were merely rags
It happened to wear, and could ignore.

Music poured out of nowhere
Strange food
And made them for those moments unaware
Of their starvation and indifferent
To their humanity
While the guards too, shedding and
Escaping their humanity
Lowered themselves into the sound
As into a communal bath
Where all were anonymous new-born
Innocent all equally
Innocent equally defenceless

The guards indeed more defenceless
More terribly naked needing
The music more

from WOLFWATCHING (1989)

A Sparrow Hawk

Slips from your eye-corner – overtaking
Your first thought.

Through your mulling gaze over haphazard earth
The sun's cooled carbon wing
Whets the eyebeam.

Those eyes in their helmet
Still wired direct
To the nuclear core – they alone

Laser the lark-shaped hole
In the lark's song.

You find the fallen spurs, among soft ashes.

And maybe you find him

Materialised by twilight and dew
Still as a listener –

The warrior

Blue shoulder-cloak wrapped about him
Leaning, hunched,
Among the oaks of the harp.

Astrological Conundrums

I THE FOOL'S EVIL DREAM

I was just walking about.
Trees here, trees there, ferny accompaniment.
Rocks sticking through their moss jerseys.
A twilight like smoked spectacles, depressive.

I saw a glowing beast – a tigress.
Only different with flower-smells, wet-root smells,
Fish-still-alive-from-their-weed-river smells
And eyes that hurt me with beauty.

She wanted to play so we gambolled.
She promised to show me her cave   10

Which was the escape route from death
And which came out into a timeless land.

To find this cave, she said, we lie down
And you hold me, so, and we fly.
So it was I came to be folded
In the fur of a tiger. And as we travelled

She told me of a very holy man
Who fed himself to a tigress
Because hunger had dried up her milk
And as he filled her belly he became

The never-dying god who gives everything
Which he had always wanted to be.
As I heard her story I dissolved
In the internal powers of tiger

And passed through a dim land
Swinging under her backbone. Till I heard
A sudden cry of fear, an infant's cry –
Close, as if my own ear had cried it.

I sat up
Wet and alone
Among starry rocks.

A bright spirit went away weeping.

II NEARLY AWAKE

The bulls swing their headweights,
Eyes bulging storms and moon-terrors.
Their cleft roots creak all round you
Where you lie, face-bedded, vegetable.

A frozen stone – the stone of your headbone.
The Universe flies dark.
The bulls bulk darker, as their starred nostrils
Blow and ponder your spine.

You lie, helpless as grass. Your prayer,
Petrified into the earth's globe,
Supports you, a crest of fear
On its unstirring.

The wild bulls of your mother have found you.
Huge nudgings of blood, sperm, saliva
Rasp you alive, towel you awake with tongues.
Now they start gnawing the small of your back.

The cry you dare not cry in these moments
Will last you a lifetime.

III TELL

This was my dream. Suddenly my old steel bow
Sprang into my hand and my whole body
Leaned into the bend a harp frame
So perfectly strung it seemed weightless.

I saw the Raven sitting alone
On the crest of the globe. I could see
The Raven's eye agleam in the sky river
Like an emblem on a flowing banner.

I saw the Raven's eye watching me
Through the slitted fabric of the skyflow.   10
I bent the bow's full weight against the star
In that eye until I could see nothing

But that star. Then as I sank my aim
Deeper into the star that had grown
To fill the Universe I heard a whisper:
'Be careful. I'm here. Don't forget me.'

With all my might – I hesitated.

Slump Sundays

Humped around me, mourners ate cold mutton,
Or maybe tripe, ham, piccalilli,
Sliced onions in vinegar, pickled beetroots,
Bread, jam, cheese, cakes, tea –

Something stirred in the half-light.
The tea stirred it. The valley god
Was pulling itself together
In the smokers' haze. Then a mushroomy whiff

Soured off the wet mills.
Souls were mouldering
Inside those great barns – the seed-corn
Lugged back from the Somme.

It served for a mother-tongue. Oracular spore-breath
Of a kind of fungus:
The homegrown hallucinogen
Of a visionary defeat.

Inhaling it, I came to
Under a rainy ridge, in a goblin clump
Of agaric.
Girlish birches waved at the window.

And a scraggy sheep at the moor-edge
Like a boulder tipped from the quarry
Took on the wild look of a hope
Returning from no man's land.

Climbing into Heptonstall

The Tourist Guide, with his Group, in the ring of horizons,
Looked down on to Hebden. 'You will notice
How the walls are black.'
                              'Wash the black walls!'
Came the madman's yell. Bird-like. Wordless.

It meant: 'Wash the blood
Wash the Calder
Of all that still weeps down
Out of the walls

The weaver's baffled, half-deaf shout
Congealed in the walls

The birth–death confinement
A candle over the psalms
The breathed-in and breathed-out
Sour odour of mould
In the survival cells

Soots of the cold
And substitute
Flame lit by Wesley.

So spring-clean the skull. Sweep from the soul's attic
Spinners, weavers, tacklers, dyers, and their infants.   20
All agitators of wool and cotton
Caught in the warp and the woof. In a nook of the hills,
In the web of the streets (the Mill's own web) –

All the jackets that hung there, the prayers that twitched!
And in the web of the Chapel (the graveyard web) –
The shiver of empty names! So scrub

The stomach lining, rid it
Of the arthritic and vinegar cud
Of their swallowed heart-burn. "Penny-hunger",
That anaesthetic herb, choked this valley.   30
Spirit-flower of a stone-deep deprivation.
Rampant – perennial – their one plenty. So
Burn the record break the monument.
Time broke their machine. Let forgetting
Ease down the old gut of the glacier.
Let the seas recycle their atoms.

What survived
Nothing's left
Barely a temper
Less than a nothing   40
                     a hymn, a hymn
Of going
Without
Without
Without – '
                    And he kicked up his legs,
A clowning dance, and let out a tuneless yodel:

'This is what made the wild harebell
So beautifully witless.
The trout under the stone so light-hearted!'

Then his voice hardened – to a wail

And he lurched off, bird-faced, stiff-kneed, downhill.   50
   The Guide

Half-smiled, recovering his flock. And,
With an opening sweep of his arm:
                              'Before us –
Stands yesterday.'

Macaw

Sorcerer! How you hate it all!
Trampling it under slowly – kneading it all
To an ectoplasmic pulp.

Your trampling is your dance. With your eye –
Your head-writhing
Evil eye – fixing the enemy,

You writhe you weave you entangle
All the cords of his soul
And so drag him towards you, and trample him under.

10   Gomorrah! Sodom! Your eye squirms on its pin
In its socket of ashes. In the sulphurous hand-axe
You have to use for a face. That cowl,

That visor of black flint
Is also your third foot. And your flint cup
Serves you for under-jaw, crudely chipped to fit.

Such a pale eye will never forgive!
The egg-daub daffodil shirt
Is no consolation. And that puppet

Prussian blue hauberk of feathers
20   Is a mockery.
                    Nothing will help, you know,
When you come, finally, to grips

With the dancing stars
Who devised this
Trembling degradation and prison and this

Torture instrument of brittle plastic
Jammed askew
Athwart your gullet.

Dust As We Are

My post-war father was so silent
He seemed to be listening. I eavesdropped
On the hot line. His lonely sittings
Mangled me, in secret – like T.V.
Watched too long, my nerves lasered.
Then, an after image of the incessant
Mowing passage of machine-gun effects,
What it filled a trench with. And his laugh
(How had that survived – so nearly intact?)
Twitched the curtain never quite deftly enough   10
Over the hospital wards
Crowded with his (photographed) shock-eyed pals.

I had to use up a lot of spirit
Getting over it. I was helping him.
I was his supplementary convalescent.
He took up his pre-war *joie de vivre*.
But his displays of muscular definition
Were a bleached montage – lit landscapes:
Swampquakes of the slime of puddled soldiers
Where bones and bits of equipment   20
Showered from every shell-burst.
                                   Naked men
Slithered staring where their mothers and sisters
Would never have to meet their eyes, or see
Exactly how they sprawled and were trodden.

So he had been salvaged and washed.
His muscles very white – marble white.
He had been heavily killed. But we had revived him.
Now he taught us a silence like prayer.
There he sat, killed but alive – so long
As we were very careful. I divined,   30
With a comb,
Under his wavy, golden hair, as I combed it,
The fragility of skull. And I filled
With his knowledge.
                          After mother's milk
This was the soul's food. A soap-smell spectre
Of the massacre of innocents. So the soul grew.

A strange thing, with rickets – a hyena.
No singing – that kind of laughter.

Wolfwatching

Woolly-bear white, the old wolf
Is listening to London. His eyes, withered in
Under the white wool, black peepers,
While he makes nudging, sniffing offers
At the horizon of noise, the blue-cold April
Invitation of airs. The lump of meat
Is his confinement. He has probably had all his life
Behind wires, fraying his eye-efforts
On the criss-cross embargo. He yawns

10   Peevishly like an old man and the yawn goes
Right back into Kensington and there stops
Floored with glaze. Eyes
Have worn him away. Children's gazings
Have tattered him to a lumpish
Comfort of woolly play-wolf. He's weary.
He curls on the cooling stone
That gets heavier. Then again the burden
Of a new curiosity, a new testing
Of new noises, new people with new colours

20   Are coming in at the gate. He lifts
The useless weight and lets it sink back,
Stirring and settling in a ball of unease.
All his power is a tangle of old ends,
A jumble of leftover scraps and bits of energy
And bitten-off impulses and dismantled intuitions.
He can't settle. He's ruffling
And re-organizing his position all day
Like a sleepless half-sleep of growing agonies
In a freezing car. The day won't pass.

30   The night will be worse. He's waiting
For the anaesthetic to work
That has already taken his strength, his beauty
And his life.

He levers his stiffness erect
And angles a few tottering steps

Into his habits. He goes down to water
And drinks. Age is thirsty. Water
Just might help and ease. What else
Is there to do? He tries to find again
That warm position he had. He cowers   40
His hind legs to curl under him. Subsides
In a trembling of wolf-pelt he no longer
Knows how to live up to.
                    And here
Is a young wolf, still intact.
He knows how to lie, with his head,
The Asiatic eyes, the gunsights
Aligned effortless in the beam of his power.
He closes his pale eyes and is easy,
Bored easy. His big limbs
Are full of easy time. He's waiting   50
For the chance to live, then he'll be off.
Meanwhile the fence, and the shadow-flutter
Of moving people, and the roller-coaster
Roar of London surrounding, are temporary,
And cost him nothing, and he can afford
To prick his ears to all that and find nothing
As to forest. He still has the starlings
To amuse him. The scorched ancestries,
Grizzled into his back, are his royalty.
The rufous ears and neck are always ready.   60
He flops his heavy running paws, resplays them
On pebbles, and rests the huge engine
Of his purring head. A wolf
Dropped perfect on pebbles. For eyes
To put on a pedestal. A product
Without a market.
                    But all the time
The awful thing is happening: the iron inheritance,
The incredibly rich will, torn up
In neurotic boredom and eaten,
Now indigestible. All that restlessness   70
And lifting of ears, and aiming, and re-aiming
Of nose, is like a trembling
Of nervous breakdown, afflicted by voices.
Is he hearing the deer? Is he listening
To gossip of non-existent forest? Pestered

By the hour-glass panic of lemmings
Dwindling out of reach? He's run a long way
Now to find nothing and be patient.
Patience is suffocating in all those folds
80   Of deep fur. The fairy tales
Grow stale all around him
And go back into pebbles. His eyes
Keep telling him all this is real
And that he's a wolf – of all things
To be in the middle of London, of all
Futile, hopeless things. Do Arctics
Whisper on their wave-lengths – fantasy-draughts
Of escape and freedom? His feet,
The power-tools, lie in front of him –
90   He doesn't know how to use them. Sudden
Dramatic lift and re-alignment
Of his purposeful body –

                                    the Keeper
Has come to freshen the water.

And the prodigious journeys
Are thrown down again in his
Loose heaps of rope.
The future's snapped and coiled back
Into a tangled lump, a whacking blow
That's damaged his brain. Quiet,
100   Amiable in his dogginess,
Disillusioned – all that preparation
Souring in his skin. His every yawn
Is another dose of poison. His every frolic
Releases a whole flood
Of new hopelessness which he then
Has to burn up in sleep. A million miles
Knotted in his paws. Ten million years
Broken between his teeth. A world
Stinking on the bone, pecked by sparrows.

110   He's hanging
Upside down on the wire
Of non-participation.
He's a tarot-card, and he knows it.
He can howl all night
And dawn will pick up the same card

And see him painted on it, with eyes
Like doorframes in a desert
Between nothing and nothing.

Telegraph Wires

Take telegraph wires, a lonely moor,
And fit them together. The thing comes alive in your ear.

Towns whisper to towns over the heather.
But the wires cannot hide from the weather.

So oddly, so daintily made
It is picked up and played.

Such unearthly airs
The ear hears, and withers!

In the revolving ballroom of space,
Bowed over the moor, a bright face

Draws out of telegraph wires the tones
That empty human bones.

Source

Where did all those tears come from?
Were they the natural spring?
He'd returned, happiness,
He'd won the war. End of the table
Every evening, so bursting with presence
He alarmed his children. What were your tears
Looking for? Something you'd lost? Something
Still hurting? Or
You'd got into a habit,
Maybe during the war, of connecting yourself
To something beyond life, a mourning
That repaired you
And was necessary. You were so happy
Your sisters-in-law lived embittered
With envy of you. Hadn't your tears heard?
The sparrows on the chimney

Cared nothing for God,
Did without the grief-bump,
Tear-ducts, they simply went plop
When your eldest shot them, and dropped backwards
Into the soot-hole. Your sorrowing
Was its own blindness. Or was it
Blinded with tears of the future? Your future,
Fulfilling your most secret prayers, laid wrinkles
Over your face as honours. Your tears didn't care.
They'd come looking for you
Wherever you sat alone. They would find you
(Just as I did
On those thundery, stilled afternoons
Before my schooldays). You would be bowed
In your workroom, over your sewing machine.
They would snuggle against you. You would
Stop the needle and without a word
Begin to weep quietly. Like a singing.
With no other care, only to weep
Wholly, deeply, as if at last
You had arrived, as if now at last
You could rest, could relax utterly
Into a luxury of pure weeping –
Could dissolve yourself, me, everything
Into this relief of your strange music.

Sacrifice

Born at the bottom of the heap. And as he grew upwards
The welts of his brow deepened, fold upon fold.
Like the Tragic Mask.
Cary Grant was his living double.

They said: When he was little he'd drop
And kick and writhe, and kick and cry:
'I'll break my leg! I'll break my leg!'
Till he'd ground his occiput bald.

While the brothers built cords, moleskins, khakis
Into dynastic, sweated ziggurats,
His fateful forehead sank
Away among Westerns, the ruts of the Oregon Trail.

Screwdriver, drill, chisel, saw, hammer
Were less than no use.
A glass-fronted cabinet was his showpiece.
His wife had locked him in there with the china.

His laugh jars at my ear. That laugh
Was an elastic vault into freedom.
Sound as a golfball.
He'd belt it into the blue.   20

He never drank in a bar. When he stood
Before he'd stepped she'd plumped the cushions beneath him.
So perfectly kept.
Sundays they drove here and there in the car.

An armchair Samson. Baffled and shorn,
His dream bulged into forearms
That performed their puppet-play of muscles
To make a nephew stare. He and I

Lammed our holly billets across Banksfields –
A five-inch propeller climbing the skylines   30
For two, three seconds – to the drop. And the paced-out length
Of his leash! The limit of human strength!

Suddenly he up and challenged
His brothers for a third of the partnership.
The duumvirate of wives turned down their thumbs.
Brotherly concern – Rain from Rochdale!

Snow from Halifax! Stars over valley walls!
His fireside escape
Simple as leaping astride a bare-back pinto
Was a kick at the ceiling, and that laugh.   40

He toiled in his attic after midnight
Mass-producing toy ducks
On wooden wheels, that went with clicks.
Flight! Flight!

The brothers closed their eyes. They quivered their jowls:
British Columbia's the place for a chap like thee!
The lands of the future! Look at Australia –
Crying out for timber buildings! Get out there!

On the canal bridge bend, at Hawkscluffe,
50   A barrel bounced off a lorry.
His motorbike hit the wall.
'I just flew straight up – and when I dropped

I missed the canal! I actually missed the canal!
I nearly broke the bank! For once
I landed smack on my feet!
My shoelaces burst from top to bottom!'

His laugh thumped my body.
When he tripped
The chair from beneath him, in his attic,
60   Midsummer dusk, his sister, forty miles off,

Cried out at the hammer blow on her nape.
And his daughter
Who'd climbed up to singsong: 'Supper, Daddy'
Fell back down the stairs to the bottom.

For the Duration

I felt a strange fear when the war-talk,
Like a creeping barrage, approached you.
Jig and jag I'd fitted much of it together.
Our treasure, your D.C.M. – again and again
Carrying in the wounded
Collapsing with exhaustion. And as you collapsed
A shell-burst
Just in front of you lifting you upright
For the last somnambulist yards
10   Before you fell under your load into the trench.
The shell, some other time, that buried itself
Between your feet as you walked
And thoughtfully failed to go off.
The shrapnel hole, over your heart – how it spun you.
The blue scar of the bullet at your ankle
From a traversing machine-gun that tripped you
As you cleared the parapet. Meanwhile
The horrors were doled out, everybody
Had his appalling tale.
20   But what alarmed me most

Was your silence. Your refusal to tell.
I had to hear from others
What you survived and what you did.

Maybe you didn't want to frighten me.
Now it's too late.
Now I'd ask you shamelessly.
But then I felt ashamed.
What was my shame? Why couldn't I have borne
To hear you telling what you underwent?
Why was your war so much more unbearable   30
Than anybody else's? As if nobody else
Knew how to remember. After some uncle's
Virtuoso tale of survival
That made me marvel and laugh –
I looked at your face, your cigarette
Like a dial-finger. And my mind
Stopped with numbness.

Your day-silence was the coma
Out of which your night-dreams rose shouting.
I could hear you from my bedroom –   40
The whole hopelessness still going on,
No man's land still crying and burning
Inside our house, and you climbing again
Out of the trench, and wading back into the glare

As if you might still not manage to reach us
And carry us to safety.

Anthem for Doomed Youth

> *He gave us the morning star,*
> *The medicine bag.*
> *Swagged with forests and rivers, and the game*
> *Quaking the earth like a drum.*

8th, 9th, 10th, 11th of August,
The rifle elated,
The Ford in third, the climb out
Over the top towards Oxenhope.

And again, over the top towards Burnley,
10   Days heather plumped to the macadam.
All adolescence there, still tucked intact
Into the magazine of the rifle.

Who owned the moors? O we did!
The Mighty Gitchimanitou, in our tent,
Had handed us the charter –
Blowing Lord Savile's feather off it.

Heads cocked for the Law
We crawled
Through the war's drizzling afterdawn
20   In the utility makeshift early fifties.

You there, manly from Africa,
Steadying the dodgy globe of your future
As you lined up, quiet-eyed,
Backsight and foresight.

But who's that in the backseat?
Blondy curls, blue lamps –
Your soul, a warm egg,
In her beringed fist.

And who's that other beside her?
30   And what does she hold?
Mother! Mother!
It was a bumper year for the portly birds.

Our switching glances, shadow-low,
Hawked across the purple,
And the tame, fuddled coveys
Trickled up their ginnels, to outlooks –

Lighthouses swivelling their simple minds,
Surprised by darkness,
Dropped to numbers,
40   Fluffing together in the boot.

Crack! And the echo: Crack! Dumb and deaf
The Winchester 69's
Dialogue with history. It woke us –
Conscripts of a dream!

The dream broke there.
Only the dodo birds
Trooped up and fell open –
Suddenly big, dark-hearted poppies.

The Black Rhino

I

This is the Black Rhino, the elastic boulder, coming at a gallop.
The boulder with a molten core, the animal missile,
Enlarging towards you. This is him in his fame –

Whose past is Behemoth, sixty million years printing the strata
Whose present is the brain-blink behind a recoiling gunsight
Whose future is a cheap watch shaken in your ear

Listen – bedrock accompanies him, a drumbeat
But his shadow over the crisp tangle of grass-tips hesitates,
    passes, hesitates, passes lightly
As a moth at noon

For this is the Black Rhino, who vanishes as he approaches   10
Every second there is less and less of him
By the time he reaches you nothing will remain, maybe, but the
    horn – an ornament for a lady's lap

Quick, now, the light is perfect for colour – catch the wet, mud caul,
    compact of extinct forms, that protects his blood from the rays
Video the busy thirst of his hair-fringed ears drinking safety
    from the burnt air
Get a shot of his cocked tail carrying its own little torch of
    courageous whiskers

Zoom in on the lava peephole where prehistory peers from the
    roots of his horn
(Every moment more and more interested)
Get a close-up of his horn

Which is an electric shock to your bootsoles (you bowed over
    your camera), as if a buried thing burst from beneath you, as
    if he resurrected beneath you,
Erupting from dust and thorns,   20
At a horn-down gallop, the hieroglyph of amazement –

Quickly, quick, or even as you stare
He will have dissolved
Into a gagging stench, in the shimmer.

Bones will come out on the negative.

II

This vision came
To a man asleep
Over a book
Beside his candle.
A beast came up
Into the flame
As into the dock.
The sleeper spoke:

'I have to laugh.
10   You stand accused
And convicted
Of being born
The Unicorn,
God's other Child
Whose nature heals
With earthlier stuff,
But just the same
To be sacrificed –
That opiate beast
20   Worshipped by
The humbly addicted
Bodily ills
And misery
Of the whole East:
Your every grain
Both anodyne
And Eucharist.

No wonder man
Craving his drug
30   Divides you small
Strips every scrap
And bloody rag
Off your wraith,
Hooked on his faith

Or senile hope
Your relics will heal
And restore all.

And carves your horn
To adorn
The dagger that stands   40
His touchy pride's
Totem pole –
The sentinel
Over the hole
Of his navel
And what it hides.

You are to blame.
With your horn's length
You have nailed your strength
To Eden's coffin   50
Tree, the tree
Of sophistry,
Too solidly
To tug yourself free.
So now you die.'

Already dead
The Rhino cried
From a puddle of blood
Almost dried
In the African dust: 60
'What can you know
Of wrong or right
Of evil or good?
You are the crime.
I accept
I no more exist
Outside your dream
And lethal whim
Of what I am
Than the Beetle can –   70
Though on many a plaque
Where the dead go
Beneath Egypt
The rising sun

And horn of light –
Be other than black.'

Then the man sighed
And sniffed the waft
Of a candle snuffed
80 And lay back in the crypt
Of his time-warped skull
Under a wall
Where long ago
The Rhino had left
Its lowly name
As a silhouette
Writ in soot.

III

The Black Rhino is vanishing.
Horribly sick, without knowing,

She is vanishing. She is infected
With the delusions of man. She has become a delusion.

Every cell of her body is ruptured with human delusion.
She is vanishing

Into a hallucination. She has blundered somehow into man's
   phantasmagoria, and cannot get out.
Even the Ox-pecker cries in fear and the White Egret snatches
   away his shadow.

The Black Rhino wheels and is baffled. Who can help her?
10 Feints of delirium flush under her crusty wraps of sunned clay
   where the flies dig for a way in

The first fatal tokens prickle awake
A torn wisp of stars – a free-fall glimpse of the constellated
   night-bazaars of Japan and Indo-China – blinding migraine

Waves of nausea ripples of mirage
A sensation about the mouth of oiled euphoria, while fifty
   thousand North Yemenite warrior youths come of age in the
   camera (the same number as next year)

The symptoms far-fetched but exact
Each gripping a dagger by the hilt of rhino horn at eight or nine
thousand dollars a handful

The Black Rhino snatched at by terrors
Stares into the black hole in her head, is it hunger in the
electron anti-matter basic void

A bat's eye view of Dubai, counting the dhows in the bay,
flitting from bedroom to bedroom, counting the notes in the
wallets and the purses
And taking a turn between the sheets   20

Feels the undertow of abyss a spinning
Is vanishing

Sways blurs in her outline tries to hear
Tries to hold on to the cool wallow of her earthenware self, the
mouthful of thorns, the superb, mauling brawls of courtship,
the monumental couplings

Hypnagogic shouts jabber taunts of the youngest wife a craving
in the roots of the eye-teeth
Makes a last effort a few steps

Snoring frowns of African bigshots, in the strobe glare and
rumble of airports, uttering grunts of hard currency
Ballistic data in the inter-tribal Swahili of the Kálashnikov

The flies boom
Twenty-five pounds sterling feeds a family for ten weeks   30

The Black Rhino stands stock still is giddy

The thorny scrub has nothing to say. The waterholes are silent.
The horizon mountain-folds are silent.

The Black Rhino
Is vanishing

Into a soft
Human laugh

Leaf Mould

In Hardcastle Crags, that echoey museum,
Where she dug leaf mould for her handfuls of garden
And taught you to walk, others are making poems.

Between finger and thumb roll a pine-needle
Feel the chamfer, feel how they threaded
The sewing machines.
                              And
Billy Holt invented a new shuttle
As like an ant's egg, with its folded worker,
As every other.
You might see an ant carrying one.
                              And
The cordite conscripts tramped away. But the cenotaphs
Of all the shells that got their heads blown off
And their insides blown out
Are these beech-bole stalwarts.
                              And oak, birch,
Holly, sycamore, pine.
                              The lightest air-stir
Released their love-whispers when she walked
The needles weeping, singing, dedicating
Your spectre-double, still in her womb,
To this temple of her *Missa Solemnis*.

White-faced, brain-washed by her nostalgias,
You were her step-up transformer.
She grieved for her girlhood and the fallen.
You mourned for Paradise and its fable.

Giving you the kiss of life
She hung round your neck her whole valley
Like David's harp.
Now, whenever you touch it, God listens
Only for her voice.

Leaf mould. Blood-warm. Fibres crumbled alive
Between thumb and finger.
Feel again
The clogs twanging your footsoles, on the street's steepness,
As you escaped.

Manchester Skytrain

Remember that nightmare straight into the camera –
Dice among dice, jounced in a jouncing cup.
Never any nearer, bouncing in a huddle, on the spot.
Struggling all together glued in a clot.

The first dead cert I ever backed was Word
From The Owner's Mouth. Week before
There was my jockey – 'a day in the life of' –
Starred in *Picture Post*. Who? Somewhere

In the nineteen forty-seven
Strata of the British Museum.   10
He's gone. He went
Even as I watched. And the horse's name?

Gone with my money. It cartwheeled
Smack in front of me, over the first fence.
Left its jockey flat – killed – and galloped on
Long after the finish, in a drugged trance –

(Doncaster). One can't bear to be groomed:
Arcs into shudders, chewing at a scream.
One rolls on the ground and whirls hammers
Refusing to cross a stream,   20

Ending up shot. The stables – asylums
Of these blue-blooded insane –
Prefer the introverts. Here's one. A razor-faced
Big-eyed schizophrene.

Every known musical instrument,
The whole ensemble, packed
Into a top-heavy, twangling half ton
On the stilts of an insect.

They're all dangerous to touch. It nearly takes off –
Just stays. Like a flying saucer's   30
Anti-gravity coil magnet, still space-radioactive,
Eased hot from the wreck. It scares

Even itself. We stand, nervous. Metaphors
Fail the field of force.
Jokey disparagements
The torque of vertigo. A dark horse.

Walt

Going up for the assault that morning
They passed the enclosure of prisoners.
'A big German stood at the wire,' he said,
'A big German, and he caught my eye.
And he cursed me. I felt his eye curse me.'

Halfway up the field, the bullet
Hit him in the groin. He rolled
Into a shell-hole. The sun rose and burned.
A sniper clipped his forehead. He wormed
Deeper down. Bullet after bullet
Dug at the crater rim, searching for him.
Another clipped him. Then the sniper stopped.

All that day he lay. He went walks
Along the Heights Road, from Peckett to Midgley,
Down to Mytholmroyd (past Ewood
Of his ancestors, past the high-perched factory
Of his future life). Up the canal bank,
Up Redacre, along and down into Hebden,
Then up into Crimsworth Dene, to their old campground
In the happy valley,
And up over Shackleton Hill, to Widdop,
Back past Greenwood Lea, above Hardcastles,
To Heptonstall – all day
He walked about that valley, as he lay
Under High Wood in the shell-hole.

I knew the knot of scar on his temple.

We stood in the young March corn
Of a perfect field. His fortune made.
His life's hope over. Me beside him
Just the age he'd been when that German
Took aim with his eye and hit him so hard
It brought him and his wife down together,
With all his children one after the other.

A misty rain prickled and hazed.
'Here,' he hazarded. 'Somewhere just about here.
This is where he stopped me. I got this far.'

He frowned uphill towards the skyline tree-fringe
As through binoculars
Towards all that was left.

II THE ATLANTIC

Night after night he'd sat there,
Eighty-four, still telling the tale.
With his huge thirst for anaesthetics.
'Time I were dead,' I'd heard. 'I want to die.'

That's altered.
                      We lean to a cliff rail
Founded in tremblings.
Beneath us, two thousand five hundred
Miles of swung worldweight
Hit England's western wall
With a meaningless bump.   10

'Aye!' he sighs. Over and over. 'Aye!'
And massages his temples.

Can he grasp what's happened? His frown
Won't connect. Familiar eagle frown –
Dark imperial eye. The ground flinches.
Mountains of dissolution
Boil cold geysers, bespatter us.
                              Tranquillisers,
Steroids, and a whole crateful
Of escapist Madeira, collided
Three evenings ago –   20

They swamped and drowned
The synapses, the breath-born spinnaker shells
Of consonants and vowels.
                              I found him
Trying to get up out of a chair,
Fish-eyed, and choking, clawing at air,
Dumbness like a bone stuck in his throat
He's survived with a word – one last word.
A last mouthful. I listen.
And I almost hear a new baby's
Eyeless howl of outrage – sobered to 'Aye!'   30
Sighed slow. Like blessed breath. He breathes it.

I dare hardly look at him. I watch.
He'd crept into my care.
A cursed hulk of marriage, a full-rigged fortune
Cast his body, crusted like Job's,
Onto my threshold. Strange Dead Sea creature.
He crawled in his ruins, like Timon.
The Times Index was his morning torture.
Fairy gold of a family of dead leaves.
40   'Why?' he'd cried, 'Why can't I just die?'
His memory was so sharp – a potsherd.
He raked at his skin, whispering 'God! God!'
Nightly, a nurse eased his scales with ointment.

I've brought him out for air. And the cliffs. And there
The sea towards America – wide open.
Untrodden, glorious America!
Look, a Peregrine Falcon – they're rare!

Nothing will connect.
He peers down past his shoes
50   Into a tangle of horizons –

Black, tilted bedrock struggling up,
Mouthing disintegration.

Every weedy breath of the sea
Is another swell of overwhelming.
Meaningless. And a sigh. Meaningless.

Now he's closed his eyes. He caresses
His own skull, over and over, comforting.
The Millmaster, the Caesar whose frown
Tossed my boyhood the baffling coin 'guilty'.
60   His fingers are my mother's. They seem astray
In quaverings and loss
As he strokes and strokes at his dome.
The sea thuds and sighs. Bowed at the rail
He seems to be touching at a wound he dare not touch.
He seems almost to find the exact spot.
His eyelids quiver, in the certainty of touch –

And 'Aye!' he breathes. 'Aye!'

We turn away. Then as he steadies himself,
Still gripping the rail, his reaching stare

Meets mine watching him. I can't escape it
Or hold it. Walt! Walt!
                    I bury it
Hugger-mugger anyhow
Inside my shirt.

Take What You Want But Pay For It

I

Weary of the cries
God spoke to the Soul of Adam
Saying: 'Give me your body.' And He
Took Adam's body and nailed it
To a stake, saying: 'This great beast
Shall destroy your peace no more.'

Then God fortified with buttresses
His house's walls, and so devised a prison
For the contorted body
Of the beast. Outside, the Soul, in a shroud,
Glorified the Majesty
Of the defensive structure, towards which
It fled from the enclosing
And unappeasable cry
Of the surrounding bush. Once inside
The locked sanctuary and seeing
Its own body nailed down
To silence, harmless, and
No longer thirsting, it wept
Astounded at the finished and cold
Beauty of its own torment
And the stony peace
Cupped it like hands, and breathed into it
Grace. No longer life,
Simply Grace, whispering: 'This is Grace.'

II

Then the Soul of Adam
Gasped as if in airlessness and there came
In from his hands and feet up through

His bowels and in
Through his shoulders and down
From all the sutures of his skull a single
Cry braiding together all the uncried

Cries his body could no longer cry
A single flagellant thong
10   With which he drove his ghostly being shuddering
Back into the body and
In that sudden inrush of renewal
The nailed feet and the hands
Tore free of the nails and he fell
From the emptied gibbet to earth

And tried to rise and raised
His blood-anointed head and tried to cry
But could not move. Only raised
The blood-mask and its effort
20   In his broken attempt to get up.
Then God withdrew, horrified
Almost afraid, as He saw

Exhaling from the black pits
Of each nail hole and from each gouged
Inscription of blood an ectoplasm
Bluish, and from the blackest pit of all
That issued the despair and its noise
A misty enfoldment which materialised
As a musing woman, who lifted the body
30   As a child's, effortless, and walked
Out of the prison with it, singing gently

Us He Devours

The long Shrine of hunger. Window spectra
Bleak on the retina. It is the hunger
Humbles the eye-beam.

The slime's Great Orme. Stranded, immense Mollusk!
A carapace of stone, cruciform,
Sculpted, as are all God's creatures, by hunger.

Gill-arches high and dry –
It filters
The breath off the water's face, the salt airs.

Casualty of a peculiar cry:
Eloi Eloi
Which is the only sound it ever utters.

That near-fatal cry alone sustains it.

Calling to the eye of the mind
A lost orphan Lamb
For whom the mouth is a wound.

The spiral nebulae that have turned
Into howlings and gnashings.
And the tiny bird of January

Who flees tap-tapping at every bud in the orchard
With such anguish, such foregone despair
It finds nothing, or barely enough

To keep it alive to its pang and that echoing
Immanence of famine.
The four-inch triangle

Of imperishable artefact that furnished
The gape of *Megalodon*
Carcharadon in the first seas.

The insupportable sun. A gargoyle
(Empty gullet, condemned in stone,
Gulping at the elixirs of damnation)

To which lichens of Gothic adhere lightly.

Little Whale Song
for Charles Causley

What do they think of themselves
With their global brains –
The tide-power voltage illumination
Of those brains? Their X-ray all-dimension

Grasp of this world's structures, their brains budded
Clone replicas of the electron world

Lit and re-imagining the world,
Perfectly tuned receivers and perceivers,

Each one a whole tremulous world
10   Feeling through the world? What
Do they make of each other?

'We are beautiful. We stir

Our self-colour in the pot of colours
Which is the world. At each
Tail-stroke we deepen
Our being into the world's lit substance,

And our joy into the world's
Spinning bliss, and our peace
Into the world's floating, plumed peace.'

20   Their body-tons, echo-chambered,

Amplify the whisper
Of currents and airs, of sea-peoples
And planetary manoeuvres,
Of seasons, of shores, and of their own

Moon-lifted incantation, as they dance
Through the original Earth-drama
In which they perform, as from the beginning,
The Royal House.
                    The loftiest, spermiest

Passions, the most exquisite pleasures,
30   The noblest characters, the most god-like
Oceanic presence and poise –

The most terrible fall.

On the Reservations
for Jack Brown

I SITTING BULL ON CHRISTMAS MORNING

Who put this pit-head wheel,
Smashed but carefully folded
In some sooty fields, into his stocking?
And this lifetime nightshift – a snarl

Of sprung celluloid? Here's his tin flattened,
His helmet. And the actual sun closed
Into what looks like a bible of coal
That falls to bits as he lifts it. Very strange.
Packed in mossy woods, mostly ashes,
Here's a doll's cot. And a tiny coffin.

And here are Orca Tiger Eagle tattered
In his second birthday's ragbook
From before memory began.
All the props crushed, the ceilings collapsed
In his stocking. Torremolinos, Cleethorpes –
The brochures screwed up in a tantrum
As her hair shrivelled to a cinder
In his stocking. Pit boots. And, strange,
A London, burst, spewing tea-leaves,
With a creased postcard of the Acropolis.

Chapels pews broken television.
(Who dumped these, into his stocking,
Under coal-slag in a flooded cellar?)
Pink Uns and a million whippet collars –
Did he ask for these? A jumbo jet
Parcelled in starred, split, patched Christmas wrappings
Of a concrete yard and a brick wall
Black with scribble
In his stocking. No tobacco. A few
Rabbits and foxes broken leaking feathers.

Nevertheless, he feels like a new man –

Though tribally scarred (stitch-tattoos of coal-dust),
Though pale (soiled, the ivory bulb of a snowdrop
Dug up and tossed aside),
Though one of the lads (the horde, the spores of nowhere
Cultured under lamps and multiplied
In the laboratories
Between Mersey and Humber),
He stands, lungs easy, freed hands –
Bombarded by pollens from the supernovae,
Two eyepits awash in the millennia –

With his foot in his stocking.

'My young men shall never work. Men who work cannot dream,
and wisdom comes in dreams.' Smohalla, Nez Percé Indians

She dreams she sleepwalks crying the Don River
relieves its nine
circles through her kitchen her kids
mops and brooms herself a squeegee and not
soaking in but
bulging pulsing out of their pores the
ordure *déjà vu* in Tesco's makes her
giddy

She dreams she sleepwalks crying her Dad alive
dug up is being
pushed into a wood-burning stove
by pensioners who chorus in croaks
While Shepherds
Watched Their television gives her
palpitations

She dreams she sleepwalks crying all the dead
huddle
in the slag-heaps wrong
land wrong
time tepees a final
resting for the epidemic
solution every
pit-shaft a
mass-grave herself
in a silly bottle shawled
in the canal's
fluorescence the message
of the survivors a surplus people
the words
washed off her wrists
and hands she complains keep feeling
helpless

She dreams she sleepwalks mainstreet nightly crying
Stalin
keeps her as an ant
in a formicary in a

garbage-can which is his private office
urinal she thinks her aerials
must be bent

Remembering how a flare of pure torrent
sluiced the pit muck
off his shoulder-slopes while her hands
soapy with milk blossom anointed
him and in their hearth
fingers of the original sun opened
the black
bright book of the stone
he'd brought from beneath dreams
or did she dream it

III THE GHOST DANCER

'We are not singing sportive songs. It is as if we were weeping,
asking for life – ' Owl, Fox Indians

A sulky boy. And he stuns your ear with song.
Swastika limbs, his whole physique – a dance.
The fool of prophecy, nightlong, daylong
Out of a waste lot brings deliverance.

Just some kid, with a demonic roar
Spinning *in vacuo*, inches clear of the floor.

Half-anguish half-joy, half-shriek half-moan:
He is the gorgon against his own fear.
Through his septum a dog's penile bone.
A chime of Chubb keys dangling at each ear.

Temenos Jaguar mask – a vogue mandala:
Half a Loa, half a drugged Oglala.

With woad cobras coiling their arm-clasp
Out of his each arm-pit, their ganch his grasp.

Bracelets, anklets; girlish, a bacchus chained.
An escapologist's pavement, padlock dance.
A mannequin elf, topped with a sugarfloss mane
Or neon rhino power-cone on a shorn sconce,

Or crest of a Cock of the Rock, or Cockatoo shock,
Or the sequinned crown of a Peacock.

779

And snake-spined, all pentecostal shivers,
This megawatt, berserker medium
With his strobe-drenched battle-cry delivers
The nineteenth century from his mother's womb:

The work-house dread that brooded, through her term,
Over the despair of salvaged sperm.

Mau-Mau Messiah's showbiz lightning stroke
Puffs the stump of Empire up in smoke.

Brain-box back to front, heart inside out,
Aura for body, and for so-called soul
Under the moment's touch a reed that utters
Out of the solar cobalt core a howl

Bomblit, rainbowed, aboriginal:
'Start afresh, this time unconquerable.'

CAPRICCIO (1990)

Capriccios

Friday created Adam. Cast out Adam.
Buried Adam. Friday. Today. Friday

The thirteenth: drunken laughter of the festive gods
So lightly reversed by Loki's gift:
Spermy mistletoe and a ship of tinder.

Friday the thirteenth. With a fable
Of the bloodied halo, the sponge and the nail.
Friday the thirteenth unveiled perfumed
America. (Lifting the eyelid
Of Columbus
With the chains from his coffin.)

Friday the 13th
Prestidigitateur
May find odds and ends, even for you.

Maybe Frigga's
Two-faced gift. Imagine the bride's mirror
In the form of a cauldron. Call it a cauldron
Of the soul's rebirth.
                        Under the cold
Epicanthic fold lifted in the bride's
Mirror, a cauldron.
                        Where this one
Forgot death. Where that one
Forgot life. Where this other
Sank without a cry.
                        You will be laughed at
For your superstition.
                        (Even so,
Remembering it: will make your palms sweat,
The skin lift blistering, both your lifelines bleed.)

The Locket

Sleeping and waking in the Song of Songs
You were half-blissful. But on occasion
Casually as a yawn, you'd open
Your death and contemplate it.

Your death
Was so utterly within your power
It was as if you had trapped it. Maybe by somehow
Giving it some part of you, for its food.
Now it was your curio pet,
Your familiar. But who else would have nursed it
In a locket between her breasts!

Smiling, you'd hold it up.
You'd swing it on its chain, to tease life.
It lent you uncanny power. A secret, blueish,
Demonic flash
When you smiled and gently bit the locket.

I have read how a fiery cross
Can grow and brighten in the dreams of a spinster.
But a crooked key turned in your locket.
It had sealed your door in Berlin
With the brand of the burnt. You knew exactly
How your death looked. It was a long-cold oven
Locked with a swastika.

The locket kept splitting open.
I would close it. You would smile.
Its lips kept coming apart – just a slit.
The clasp seemed to be faulty.
Who could have guessed what it was trying to say?
Your beauty, a folktale wager,
Was a quarter century posthumous.

While I juggled our futures, it kept up its whisper
To my deafened ear: *fait accompli*.

The Mythographers

When God had created Man and Woman
He gave them to the Mythographers
For testing. Said the Mythographers:
'Let there be a Lilith. Let this Lilith
Owlish from her hole in the willow
Flap into bedrooms laughing or with a screech
(The abortion of a laugh). Her abortions
(Freeing Woman for Man as Man for Woman)

Decompose to single-cell demons
(Their DNA Lilith), riding the wafts of the garden
Or blueing the exhaust. The hairs on her legs shall detect
Under his finger-ring the Mayday signal.
His fever shall be her, hallucinated,
A dancer with her drummer inside her,
Flogging herself with her hair, phosphorescent,
Riding him upside down through the bed-head.
Lilith', said the Mythographers, 'Shall be immortal.

Next, let there be Nehama. Let Nehama
Take the simpleton
Who has quit his wife because television
Revealed all that her veil
Had hidden from him. Let Nehama's kiss
Convince him he's found it.
Her saliva: instant amnesia.
The cries of his children: pangs
In a torn-off third arm
Which was his deformity. Her fingers,
Her knees, her armpits, flying
Buttresses of Dover Cliffs
Numb him as he falls, euphoric,

To where his bride Nehama possessing
Some woman's divorced and desperate body,
Under her wig bald as a blown egg-shell,
Starts weeping that she's pregnant,
Takes to her bed. Will not get up to drag
Her shadow across another day's carpet
Towards her own corpse
Which she can smell, here, in the room
With her. Let her wig stroke itself
On the tailor's dummy. Let it watch her

In the Irish mirror. A skull grins down
Through her bridegroom's wretched expression
Which understands nothing. And the up-ogling skull
That suckles her breast brings her screaming
From the bedroom. She tries to kill
This baby-skull properly dead and goes through
Death's oven door with it to make sure
It stays dead. She manages. Her last

Backward glance
Seals a star between his eyes.
                              'Let this',
Said the Mythographers, 'Be Nehama's fame.'

Systole Diastole

Heart was the difficulty the mother
The child
The god-head of the body

A lioness of noon sucked his heart
With a cub's lockjaw grip and drank
Blood as deep as a heart could pump it

Was that his heart kicking to be free
Wrenching to be free bruising his ribs
Making his back ache a panic heart

Blood could not glut or appease
The suckling grip she had blood was not enough
She drank blood but thirsted for spirit

In every gulp of his life-blood she tasted
A tear drop of clear spirit he weakened
Pleas of air could never lever apart

Jaws of the soul's iron no bodily force
Could prise open
Jaws of spirit ravenous for spirit

So he ripped it free he hid his heart
He implanted it in the belly
Of a flower, where pollen might repair it

It was desperate magic he tried it
Soaked his deranged heart the torn god
In the nectar of an orchid a lily

A tiger lily almost a lotus
But the crying lioness found it
Though she had died of thirst her ghost found it

And tore up the flower, with ghost fangs
And carried his heart back to her lair, in his chest
Where her ghost could gnaw at it, lick at it, guard it

Descent

You had to strip off Germany
The crisp shirt with its crossed lightnings
And go underground.
You were forced to strip off Israel
The bodice woven of the hairs of the cactus
To be bullet-proof, and go deeper.
You had to strip off Russia
With those ear-rings worn in honour
Of Eugene Onegin. And go deeper.
You had to strip off British Columbia   10
And the fish-skin mock-up waterproof
From the cannery, with its erotic motif
Of porcupine quills, that pierced you
And came with you, working deeper
As you moved deeper.
Finally you had to strip off England
With your wedding rings
And go deeper.
              Then suddenly you were abandoned
By the gem-stones, rubies, emeralds, all you had hoarded
In a fold of paper   20
At the back of a drawer – you had thought
These would protect you in the end,
Urim and Thummim. Cowardly
They scattered in the splinters of weeping
As your own hands, stronger than your choked outcry,
Took your daughter from you. She was stripped from you,
The last raiment
Clinging round your neck, the sole remnant
Between you and the bed
In the underworld   30
              Where Inanna
Has to lie naked, between strata
That can never be opened, except as a book.

Folktale

He did not know she had risen out of cinders.
She knew he had nothing.
So they ransacked each other. What he wanted
Was the gold, black-lettered pelt
Of the leopard of Ein-Gedi.
She wanted only the runaway slave.
What he wanted was Turgenev's antimacassar.
She wanted escape without a passport.
What he wanted was Bach's aerobatic
Gutturals in Arabic.
She wanted the enemy without his gun.
He wanted the seven treasures of Asia –
Skin, eyes, lips, blood, hair knotted roughly
In seven different flags.
She wanted the silent heraldry
Of the purple beech by the noble wall.
He wanted Cabala the ghetto demon
With its polythene bag full of ashes.
She wanted only shade from the noon's
Broken-armed Catherine Wheel
Under an island leaf. She wanted
A love-knot Eden-cool as two lob-worms
And a child of acorn.
He wanted a mother of halva.
She wanted the hill-stream's tabula rasa.
He wanted the thread-end of himself.
So they ransacked each other for everything
That could not be found. And their fingers met
And were wrestling, like flames
In the crackling thorns
Of everything they lacked –
                              as midnight struck.

Fanaticism

You had lifted off your future and laid it lightly
Before the door of Aphrodite's temple
As the drowned leave their clothes folded.

Exchanged your face for the mask of Aphrodite
Marriage for the manic depression
Of the ovaries, for the ocean's heave and spill.

Exchanged the plain security of your life-line
For those holy years: the blood-clepsydra
Limit of Aphrodite's epiphany.

'After forty I'll end it,' you laughed
(You were serious) as you folded your future
Into your empty clothes. Which Oxfam took.

Snow

Snow falling. Snowflakes clung and melted
In the sparkly black fox fur of your hat.
Soft chandeliers, ghostly wreckage
Of the Moscow Opera. Flakes perching and
Losing their hold on the heather tips. An unending
Walk down the cobbled hill into the oven
Of empty fire. Among the falling
Heavens. A short walk
That could never end was
Never ending. Down, on down   10
Under the thick, loose flocculence
Of a life
Burning out in the air. Between char-black buildings
Converted to closed cafés and Brontë gift-shops.
Beyond them, the constellations falling
Through the Judaean thorns, into the fleeces
Of the Pennine sheep. Deepening
Over the faces of your school-friends,
Beside their snowed-under tanks, locked into the Steppe
Where the mud had frozen again   20
While they drank their coffee. You escaped
Deeper into the falling flakes. They were clinging
To the charcoal crimped black ponyskin
Coat you wore. Words seemed warm. They
Melted in our mouths
Whatever was trying to cling.
                        Leaning snow

Folded you under its cloak and ushered you away
Down the hill. Back to where you came from.

I watched you. Feeling the snow's touch.

30   Already, it was burying your footprints,
Drawing its white sheet over everything,
Closing the air behind you.

The Other

She had too much so with a smile you took some.
Of everything she had you had
Absolutely nothing, so you took some.
At first, just a little.

Still she had so much she made you feel
Your vacuum, which nature abhorred,
So you took your fill, for nature's sake.
Because her great luck made you feel unlucky
You had redressed the balance, which meant
Now you had some too, for yourself.
As seemed only fair. Still her ambition
Claimed the natural right to screw you up
Like a crossed-out page, tossed into a basket.
Somebody, on behalf of the gods,
Had to correct that hubris.
A little touch of hatred steadied the nerves.

Everything she had won, the happiness of it,
You collected
As your compensation
For having lost. Which left her absolutely
Nothing. Even her life was
Trapped in the heap you took. She had nothing.
Too late you saw what had happened.
It made no difference that she was dead.
Now that you had all she had ever had
You had much too much.
                              Only you
Saw her smile, as she took some.
At first, just a little.

Possession

Maybe it was possible. Your dresses
The door-curtains and incense
Of a seance that could only be suffered,
Never credited. Possession
By ancestors become demons.
A kind of poltergeist. Maybe
That's what set the Alsatians
Snarling through the mouths and eyes
Of your schoolfriends' mothers. African
Exorcists take it for granted. Estelle Roberts
Dealt, face to face, with some hard cases.
Yours were all female. Where from? Who?
Their provenance was the bed
Of the subterranean river system
In the palm of your hand. Priestess of Thammuz
In the temple on Zion rock (in that cave?)
Josiah's anathema. The Babylonian
Mystery who ground between her thighs
The crown of thorns. Your oiled smile
Folded all that in its offer. A hysteric,
Brainwashed by Aurora Borealis,
Spinning in the dust and the smoke
Beside a smoulder of ass-dung,
Shaking from her, with quivering eyelids,
The cries of Mongolian birds
Before the arrival of the voice
Which split the threshold granite
And the future. I saw plain
Her flailing limbs. Tabubu
Mesmerist Priestess of Bastet
Who stripped the son of the Pharaoh
To the last swollen shame and wet fever
Of his infatuation: and let him awake
Copulating with the dust of the highway
Stared at by his own children
All still alive, as if resurrected
(Days before, for her, he had thrown them
To the dogs):

The Coat

No help that it was only dyed marmot
And not natural tiger. No help
That being draped idly over chairs in bars
To soak up the nicotine, it was not
Gripping him by the broken small of the back
And forcing him through brambles. It made no difference.
No good that it left his limbs
Watermarked not with the lickings
Of what had fed but with the perfume-dating
Of that summer, like the imprinting shock
Noon-stench of a discovered corpse. Nobody
Can deter what saunters
Up the ferny path between
The cool, well-ironed sheets, or what spoor
Smudges the signature of the contract.

No help that it was only the lining
The grass-shadow
Of eye-lashes and a hunger heedless as time
That ate faces. It was the bed horror
Of the Passover night. It lifted away
Screams that split bodies. It left
Roofs falling in, the morning empty.
The sun itself silenced. The face
Of after-shock that only dusty stones
Know how to wear.

Smell of Burning

Blackly the Black Forest began dancing.
And you were a tree in the Black Forest.
You wore the sign of lightning to ward off lightning.
You were storm-dancing in other words marching.

A small girl a Black Forest Giant.
And everybody was happy so you were happy
Singing the lightning could not hit you
Marching among the totems idols.

Then came Thunder. After that, the burning.
Blinded by smoke your father stumbled with you
Into a stone land a bare hearth
Incombustible a land of cinders.

But still you could smell the fire in your fingers.
Claws of charcoal almost Hebrew letters
Dropped onto your page from the smouldering
Conifer inside you.

Then smoke spiralled out of your cigarette.
And the Negev Desert had failed
As a firebreak. Stretched out naked, on your bed,
You watched your fear making the moon brown.

Your mother burst from her room homesick weeping
With the smart of smothered embers. Your father murmured:
'None of it matters. We are ghosts in a mask-shop
Where the masks are shapes of smoke.'

But the smoke burned your lungs and you glimpsed in it
The occasional flicker of real flame
As the native resins in your body
Gulped at the oxygen. Coughing for oxygen

Were you a German burning tree trying
To flee from burning Germany or
From the burning German tree the victim
Condemned to hang on it?

The Pit and the Stones

You thought of him as one for your collection.
The brimming power of your gaze
Was mainly the accumulated protein
Of trophies digested.
He was a tethered goat. He thought
He was bleating. Actually he was screaming
Like those African goats, that scream
As if a slashed throat could scream,
Though a goat merely calls for a goat.
Your amusement was like the movement
Of the most magnificent tigress.

But under the goat was the pit.
And in the pit the spikes.
                              He made nothing
Of the hands that had held him,
Had led him, tethered him, left him.
What prompted those hands? Or those mouths
With voices like empty cans tumbled? Darkness
Was the only sense of the darkness. He saw
Absolutely no sense in his tether
But his own weakness.
                              So you took him
With you into the pit
Beneath him, where you were impaled

By the eyes in the faces, incomprehensible
To you as to him. They crowded
The hatch of dawning sky, their jubilation
Like tin cans wildly shaken:
Each with a stone in it.

Shibboleth

Your German
Found its royal licence in the English
Your mother had bought (peering into the future)
By mail order, from Fortnum and Mason. Your Hebrew
Survived on bats and spiders
In the guerrilla priest-hole
Under your tongue. Nevertheless,
At the long-weekend Berkshire county table,
In a dizzy silence, your cheekbones
(From the Black Sea, where the roses bloom thrice)
Flushed sootier:
Stared at by English hounds
Whose tails had stopped wagging. When the lips lifted,
The trade-routes of the Altai
Tangled in your panic, tripped you. It was
The frontier glare of customs.
The gun-barrels
Of the imperious noses

Pointed at something pinioned. Then a drawl:
'Lick of the tar-brush?'

There you saw it,
Your lonely Tartar death,
Surrounded and 'dumb like the bound
Wolf on Tolstoy's horse'.

The Roof

The roof. Any roof. After the roof
The silk-lined curtain-folds, the Bach fugues,
The bursting wardrobe. The small fob-watch on the chain.
How could a roof be stolen from twenty million,
Each of whom died once, with a cry or no cry?
Each as horribly as possible, which is to say murdered.

Though they were all out there, under the great rains,
Your roof belonged to them.
Or maybe to their murderers.
You weren't sure. Either could evict you.

Either way, your rent was accepted
Only so long as you lived incognito.

Either way you lived
Waiting for the knock on the door.

The Error

When her grave opened its ugly mouth
Why didn't you just fly,
Wrap yourself in your hair and make yourself scarce,
Why did you kneel down at the grave's edge
To be identified
Accused and convicted
By all who held in their hands
Pieces of the gravestone grey granite
Proof of their innocence?

You must have misheard a sentence.   10
You were always mishearing

795

Into Hebrew or German
What was muttered in English.
Her grave mouthed its riddle right enough.
But maybe you heard in the air somewhere
An answer to one of your own
Unspoken enigmas. Misheard,
Mistook, and kneeled meekly.

Maybe they wouldn't stone you
20   If you became a nun
And selflessly incinerated yourself
In the shrine of her death.
Because that is what you did. From that moment
Shops, jobs, baby daughter, the German au pair
Had to become mere shapes
In the offered-up flames, a kind of writhing
That enfolded you and devoured
Your whole life.
I watched you feeding the flames.
30   Why didn't you wrap yourself in a carpet
Get to a hospital
Drop the whole mistake – simply call it
An error in translation?

Instead you fed those flames
Six full calendar years –
Every tarred and brimstone
Day torn carefully off,
One at a time, not one wasted, patient
As if you were feeding a child.
40   You were not feeding a child.
All you were doing was being strong,
Waiting for your ashes
To be complete and to cool.

Finally they made a small cairn.

Opus 131

Opus 131 in C Sharp Minor
Opened the great door
In the air, and through it

Flooded horror. The door in the hotel room
And the curtain at the window and even
The plain homely daylight blocking the window
Were in the wrong dimension
To shut it out. The counterpoint pinned back
The flaps of the body. Naked, faceless,
The heart panted there, like a foetus.
Where was the lifeline music? What had happened
To consolation, prayer, transcendence –
To the selective disconnecting
Of the pain centre? Dark insects
Fought with their instruments
Scampering through your open body
As if you had already left it. Beethoven
Had broken down. You strained listening
Maybe for divorce to be resolved
In the arithmetic of vibration
To pure zero, for the wave-particles
To pronounce on the unimportance
Of the menopause. Beethoven
Was trying to repair
The huge constellations of his silence
That flickered and glinted in the wind.
But the notes, with their sharp faces,
Were already carrying you off,
Each with a different bit, into the corners
Of the Universe.

Familiar

Of all creatures a horse!
Why a horse? A mare.
It was a chalk-white shire.
A great moon-boulder mare

Walking out through a woman's dark face
A blanched mare with big bones
The bones got up off a windy plain
Where starlight had sucked them empty

Got up from some atrocity's ground-shadow
History's unquestioning slave

Work-horse of massacre and pogrom
Warriorless an oceanless waif

Lay on your bed gazed out at Highbury Common
Wherever you were you were aware
The silent mare was there the coincidence
That preferred you to non-existence

You were its field
It did nothing wanted nothing
Merely warmed itself at your body
Into a continuing nearness

You neither liked it nor disliked it
'Am I it or is it me
Or do we simply happen to have connected
As a bird lands on a ship a tired migrant?

Which of us is the tired migrant?'

Flame

For oxygen mask
You had Green Farm, near Hexham.
The dusty chemistry
Of the bared, bedroom floorboards
Gave you enough, in a few breaths.
You brought it away. The salmon
Under the stained current of the North Tyne
Added a suspect ingredient:
The one, crucial grain of too-much.
10   But the rent was next to nothing, measured out
In exact proportion. And though the oracular book
Had to fall open at:
'Be absolute for death: either death or life ...'
As if the Master himself had undersigned
A different contract, the Dower House at Park End
Was your back-up fail-safe:
The rent a guarantee and the only snag
A gardener for the paradaisal gardens.
Manchester provided, as extras,
20   Bed coverlet and blankets, to muffle your ears
From any bang and limit any damage.

But climbing into the train at Manchester Central
With all that First Aid kit
And all those protective devices
You did not know how history had already
Cast you to repeat itself.
You had no idea
What signed bit of paper had found you at last
After so many years, what detonator
Waited in your flat   30
To include even your wildest hopes
As so much dirty cobalt
In the nuclear reaction:
Synchrony so precisely attuned
You barely had time to open the envelope
And grab for the telephone
Before it was all over.

Chlorophyl

She sent him a blade of grass, but no word.
Inside it
The witchy doll, soaked in Dior.
Inside it
The gravestone. Inside it
A sample of her own ashes. Inside it
Her only daughter's
Otherwise non-existent smile.
Inside it, the keys
Of a sycamore.
Inside those, falling
The keys
Of a sycamore. Inside those,
Falling and turning in air the
Keys
Of a sycamore.

RAIN-CHARM FOR THE DUCHY

and other Laureate poems (1992)

SOLOMON'S DREAM

A Soul is a wheel.
A Nation's a Soul
With a Crown at the hub
To keep it whole

Rain-Charm for the Duchy
A Blessed, Devout Drench for the Christening
of His Royal Highness Prince Harry
21 December 1984

After the five-month drought
My windscreen was frosted with dust.
Sight itself had grown a harsh membrane
Against glare and particles.

Now the first blobby tears broke painfully.

Big, sudden thunderdrops. I felt them sploshing like vapoury petrol
Among the ants
In Cranmere's cracked heath-tinder. And into the ulcer craters
Of what had been river pools.

Then, like taking a great breath, we were under it.
Thunder gripped and picked up the city.
Rain didn't so much fall as collapse.
The pavements danced, like cinders in a riddle.

Flash in the pan, I thought, as people scampered.
Soon it was falling vertical, precious, pearled.
Thunder was a brass-band accompaniment
To some festive, civic event. Squeals and hurry. With tourist bunting.

The precinct saplings lifted their arms and faces. And the
    heaped-up sky
Moved in mayoral pomp, behind buildings,
With flash and thump. It had almost gone by
And I almost expected the brightening. Instead, something like
    a shutter

Jerked and rattled – and the whole county darkened.
Then rain really came down. You scrambled into the car
Scattering oxygen like a drenched bush.
What a weight of warm Atlantic water!

The car-top hammered. The Cathedral jumped in and out
Of a heaven that had obviously caught fire
And couldn't be contained.
A girl in high heels, her handbag above her head,

Risked it across the square's lit metals.
We saw surf cuffed over her and the car jounced.

Grates, gutters, clawed in the backwash.
She kept going. Flak and shrapnel

Of thundercracks
Hit the walls and roofs. Still a swimmer
She bobbed off, into sea-smoke,
Where headlights groped. Already

Thunder was breaking up the moors.
It dragged tors over the city –
Uprooted chunks of map. Smeltings of ore, pink and violet,
Spattered and wriggled down

Into the boiling sea
Where Exeter huddled –
A small trawler, nets out.
'Think of the barley!' you said.

You remembered earlier harvests.
But I was thinking
Of joyful sobbings –
The throb

In the rock-face mosses of the Chains,
And of the exultant larvae in the Barle's shrunk trench, their
    filaments ablur like propellors, under the churned ceiling of light,
And of the Lyn's twin gorges, clearing their throats, deepening
    their voices, beginning to hear each other
Rehearse forgotten riffles,

And the Mole, a ditch's choked whisper
Rousing the stagnant camps of the Little Silver, the Crooked
    Oak and the Yeo
To a commotion of shouts, muddied oxen
A rumbling of wagons,

And the red seepage, the smoke of life
Lowering its ringlets into the Taw,

And the Torridge, rising to the kiss,
Plunging under sprays, new-born,
A washed cherub, clasping the breasts of light,

And the Okement, nudging her detergent bottles, tugging at her
    nylon stockings, starting to trundle her Pepsi-Cola cans,

And the Tamar, roused and blinking under the fifty-mile drumming,
Declaiming her legend – her rusty knights tumbling out of their
  clay vaults, her cantrevs assembling from shillets,
With a cheering of aged stones along the Lyd and the Lew, the
  Wolf and the Thrushel,

And the Tavy, jarred from her quartzy rock-heap, feeling the
  moor shift
Rinsing her stale mouth, tasting tin, copper, ozone,

And the baby Erme, under the cyclone's top-heavy, toppling
  sea-fight, setting afloat odd bits of dead stick,

And the Dart, her shaggy horde coming down
Astride bareback ponies, with a cry,
Loosening sheepskin banners, bumping the granite,
Flattening rowans and frightening oaks,

And the Teign, startled in its den
By the rain-dance of bracken
Hearing Heaven reverberate under Gidleigh,

And the highest pool of the Exe, its coil recoiling under the sky-shock
Where a drinking stag flings his head up
From a spilled sheet of lightning –

My windscreen wipers swam as we moved.
                                    I imagined the two moors
The two stone-age hands
Cupped and brimming, lifted, an offering –
And I thought of those other, different lightnings, the patient,
  thirsting ones

Under Crow Island, inside Bideford Bar,
And between the Hamoaze anchor chains,
And beneath the thousand, shivering, fibreglass hulls
Inside One Gun Point, and aligned

Under the Ness, and inside Great Bull Hill:

The salmon, deep in the thunder, lit
And again lit, with glimpses of quenchings,
Twisting their glints in the suspense,
Biting at the stir, beginning to move.

Two Poems for
Her Majesty Queen Elizabeth the Queen Mother
on Her Eighty-fifth Birthday
  4 August 1985

THE DREAM OF THE LION

It was an ancient Land. The Land of the Lion.
  New to earth, each creature woke,
  Licked awake to speak, and spoke
The mother-tongue, the rough tongue of the Lion.

Where was this Land? The Land belonged to the Lion.
  Not to the Mare, the chalk-hill's flower.
  Not to the Raven in the Tower.
The eye that opened the mind was the eye of the Lion.

Wild Dog, Hyena, Wolf, maned as a Lion,
  Rolled on her back, and motherly smiled,
  Suckling the Lion's human child
Under the lifted, golden eye of the Lion.

It could not fade, the vision of the Land of the Lion.
  Each clear creature, crystal-bright,
  Honey-lit with Lion-light,
Dreamed that single dream: the dream of the Lion.

Surprised by being, and listening only for the Lion,
  And as fragments of the Sun,
  Globed like it, around it run,
Each, in the heart's mirror, gazed at a Lion.

What was this Lion, the Lion of the Land of the Lion?
  The dream of childhood lasted yet,
  Pondered Mother's face, and met
Watching through her gaze the eyes of the Lion.

Growing into an afterglow of Lion,
  Stranger, strangely humanized,
  Sleepwalker, half hypnotized,
Saw the Lion a Queen in the Land of the Lion.

And on standard and icon a Lion. And Lion
  The name our long-ship Island bore
  Through the night-seas of the war
Till dawn came as a Lion awakening a Lion.

In the relief of light, the Dream of the Lion
    Dropping from air as manna dew,
    Cleansing all, condensed on you:
And the climbing sun revealed you, the Lion.

LITTLE SALMON HYMN

Between the sea's hollows and inland hills,
Naked as at birth
The salmon slips, a simple shuttle
Clothing the earth.

Say the constellations are flocks. And the sea-dawns,
Collecting colour, give it,
The sea-spray the spectrum. Salmon find
The fibre and weave it.

Salmon fishers in Eden bow down,
Lift heavy from the loom
A banner with a salmon woven on it –
As the babe from the womb

Wrapped in the electric fleece
Of constellations,
Robed in the rainbow nakedness
Of oceans.

A Birthday Masque
For Her Majesty Queen Elizabeth II's Sixtieth Birthday
  21 April 1986

I THE FIRST GIFT

Flying from the zenith
An Angel of Water.
All the kingdom's hurt rivers flicker
In its veins.
Wells marked with a cross, blocked wells, lost wells
For pores.
For purity
The light and silence of all eyes –
The re-offering of light
Washed from the refuse of gutters.

It flies through the hair on the head
And through the manna of March hail.
It flies under the dream-flutter of eyelids
And through the crucifixion
Of streetlight and star in a tear.
Its wingbeat
Shatters from the taps.

The Angel is flying with cupped hands.
In its dripping hands a perfect mirror.
In its blazing hands
Sixty million rays drink a sun,
In the mirror a face
Bends to drink the wholeness of that water.

2 AN ALMOST THORNLESS CROWN

Let the first be a Snowdrop, neck bowed
Over her modesty –
Her spermy, fattening gland
Cold under the ground.
                              She links an arm
With a Foxglove, raggily dressed,
Long-bodied, a rough blood-braid
Of dark nipples.
                              Who links now
With a Daffodil –
Scrubbed face and naked throat so pale,
So true and so pure, she is penitential,
The hail on her nape, her bare feet in mire.

Let her twine her arm around one a Rose
Who just now woke
And wakes wider, seems
To stretch awake, to peel back
Bedclothes, to fling off nightdress – to step
Into the shower, almost to sing
Flush with morning light – yet cannot
Wake below the neck, or let sunbeams
Through to the sleeping earth (who makes this
Effort in its dream, stirring a little).

Let her be linked
With somebody slender – tall, September Balsam,

The full pitcher trembling, at evening –
Humid, soul-drinking insect,
Like a child bride from Nepal
Dressed by temple harlots
In her pinkish-purple sari (slightly too big for her).

Weave in among
More Daffodils – more nervy daughters,   30
Sober sisters, bonnets bowed stiffly
Watching gravestones,
Equinox
Flint-raw in their glances,
Touching at themselves with cold fingers
Thinking upright thoughts.
(Or they wake in a scare
Laughing, hearing the mad can-can music,
And it comes over them
To dash off, giddier every minute,   40
Bare-legged in their tatters, away
Alongside scruffy, rough rivers –

But they recover, they shiver their faces, bow,
Become the silent bells of the gust
That frightens the big tree.)
                         Here and there
A Pansy, little pug-face,
Baby panda –
A masterly Chinese brush
Dabbed her signature.
                    Now twine over
And under hot and tipsy Honeysuckles,   50
Their gawky grace, their dark, burgundy flushes
Already silked a little
As each one dips her neck through our exclamations,
And opens a drugged hydra
To sip human dreams,
Lips parted, a filament of salmon
Between the tongue and the teeth, a child's eye in a woman's body,
This little rhubarb dragon,
This viper in the leaves
Bites a numbness, in an anaesthetic perfume,   60
Her damage done so gently

Her clutch of heart-shock, splitting trumpets
Doubles as a scrollwork of eyelashes.
And now an Arum Lily, anorexic,
Her cheekbones flared,
Recites in silence from *Imitatio Christi*
With a demented grin.
Hunches her fleshless scapulae.
Her sweat congeals to pearl
70   In a nunnery of the profane.
Fallen stars her sole nutriment.
Link her with a last Rose
Whose dumb utterance cannot be decoded.
Not a lyrical cry, like the anguished Lily
But a muffled thunder of perturbation.
Wide open, but her secret averted,
Mountain beyond mountain, dawn beyond dawn.

Now a Cyclamen – stilled in her mid-air dance
Ballerina soaring
80   Over her astounded audience.

Then a tumbling peal of Rhododendron,
Knickerbocker lobes, an excess crumple of lips
Cored with bloodier darkness,
A cry from deep in the plant, hurting the throat and the mouth
    helpless open,
A rejoicing, announcing burden of cry,
An offering cry, and the mouth hanging open –
Like the body offering of a beast, that bewilders the eyes of the beast,
Love-offering of eyes, that bewilders the eyelids –
A faint prickle of dark freckles flushing the fine tissues.

90   Link all into a circle
With more Snowdrops – these half under snow
Waiting to be freed,
Like nineteenth-century vicarage maidens
At a tea-party,
Erect, bare-shouldered, bowed, waiting for grace,
Faces elvish, childish.
A congregation of bells
Tiny domes
Of serious worship –

Flying in from the dark perimeter
A care-worn Angel. An old midwife crone
With the touch of Earth.
Earth's past under one arm
As a roll of *TV Times*
For bandages.
Earth's future under the other
Her first aid kit
An anaesthetic telly.

This Angel is flying
Through skin, bones, bricks and dusty mortar.
A hag with bat's wings
That are silky soft as caul tissue.
An Angel with the Earth's healing touch
Flying with cupped hands
Through the worm, into the germ of wheat
A speck into the ovum.

A rusty old bread-knife for scalpel
Or stone-age shard of a bottle.

Not frankincense, not myrrh, not spermacetti,
Not the four gemstones.
In her mountainous hands
She has scooped up something brighter than blinding snow.

She calls it the goodness of earth
As from every corner of the islands
As for creating an Adam.

4 THE RING

Here the horn-scarred hunter and the tall stag
Have exchanged places. Each is dancing
Inside the other. Now the salmon
So many, so sudden, so hard full-throttle
Through the ford's thoroughfare
Knock them off their feet.

And here the wanderer who dared to be born
Out of the Mediterranean's
Clangorous womb.

Crept up the Tamar.
In the orchard of the blest
Planted granite.

And here the knowle of the Raven King
To Tower Hill from Harlech
Singing and telling
Tales to kill sorrow.
And Lir who hid words
In the skin of a heron.

And here, on Cordelia's lip, a down-feather
Of the bronze eagle.
The tongue branded
By Caesar's coinage.
And in the ear's crypt
The bones of Mithras.

And here, twin wolf-heads, the mercenary brothers,
As if appalled –
Such a land, peopled
By puling slaves –
From rabbity girls
Bred howling berserkers.

And here the shoulders that warped the dragons
Over Humber mud.
And the broad-vowelled women
Of the Dales, as if they sang
Nursing the North
Sea's hard-hacked edges.

And here the Conqueror's bull's-eye bolt:
His prize: England
Yoked in the furrow,
And the bride-bed of English –
(Her vengeance: her bastard's
Upstart scutcheon).

And here the poltergeist Luther who married
Mary to Beelzebub,
And their babe, Cromwell –
Macbeth reborn
To step from the cauldron
Into the bloodstream.

And here the harp-strings that opened Eildon
To Thomas the Rymer:
The Queen of the Gael
So spaced her chords –
Supplanting the bars
In the tongue's dungeon.

And here in the boil the peacock oils
From Siva's thumb.
The Hoopoe's cry
From the tower. The seed-flame
From the eye-pupil's
African violet.

Here, for the mould, a melt of strange metals.
To be folded and hammered,
Re-folded, re-hammered,
Till millionfold
It is formed, is the living
Crown of a kingdom

The ring of the people.

5 THE THIRD GIFT

Flying from the depth as from the mouth
Of a furnace –
An Angel of Blood.

A lucky vision. Only
The darkest hour
Finds this star.

Only the emptiest eye lights upon it
Between the faintest stars, the slightest smudge
Of mission will miss it.

Wingbeat behind the eye
As your heartbeat's aurora
Over the roof of your mouth.

Unheard, a drum
In your fingertips
Before dawn, on the coverlet, waiting for you.

Unfelt
As the shared circulation through the warm dark inside the
    warm darkness
Of unborn child inside mother.

And single
As the garment of blood that sews stranger to stranger
Behind the sequin separateness of faces,
The garment patched from the rags of placenta.

Single
As the crimson, tangled, twisted yarn
Of lineage and language.

Single as the sun after midnight –
It flies towards us from under the soles of the feet.

6 CANDLES FOR THE CAKE

(*Thirty Birds, Looking for God, Find the Crown*)

Crow who willed his children all
His worldly goods
And inherited Sun and Moon

Comes with two candles. He calls
Cuckoo and her echo
(All is forgiven!) –
            Four candles.

The Lark who swinging sings
Over the drop, dropping
Samphire and Edelweiss
Drops to earth –
            Six candles.

Sparrow who squats on the pavement
His own rag doll, a cockney street-cry
Penny for the Guy, Penny for the Guy –
            Eight candles.

Deep-chested Nightingale convulsed
In the soul-catcher's
Star-tangle –
            Ten candles.

Thrush and Blackbird, ringing alarms
For worms who lie too late in the dew, while dawn
Snorts and tramples in the dark stable –
              Fourteen candles.

Bowed head, jockey shoulders,
Snipe, hurling upwards
As if flung downwards,
Over the Bens, a flying drum –
              Sixteen candles.

What shall Heron do? Dance
The Alphabet she cannot utter?
Laugh, and be silent –
              Eighteen candles.

Tawny Owl who fills the aisles
With a question, and the White Owl
Who waits at the altar
Turn dark eyes –
              Twenty-two candles.

Wren, tail barred like a falcon's.
Lonely keeper of the gold
In the tumbled cleave.
A bird out of Merlin's ear.
Silent watcher. Suddenly
Singing, like a martyr on fire,
Glossolalia –

Robin Redbreast, with his kitchen-garden
Dungfork folk-tune
Turning the human darkness
Bares a lost ringstone with clasped hands –

And Peregrine, who dangles off Hartland
His tilting geometry
Of the rock-dove's
Passionate outburst –

And Buzzard, as Tarzan
Pendulum on his liana
(The snatch frightens the eye!)
Rescues the partridge
Poult from the coming guns –

And Gull flips over, a scream and a scarf in the sea-cliff's
Wheel of wind. Or down there under the wind
Wing-waltzes her shadow
Over the green hollows –

And Wagtail between moorland boulders, tiddly
With sipping
The quick winks of quick water –

And Swift whose nightlong, daylong, yearlong, lifelong
Flight will be seven times
To the Moon and back –
          Forty candles.

Beery Grouse who grittily
Tells the Curlew
To stop whingeing and drooping –
          Forty-four candles.

Peewit, out of control,
Always saved at the last moment
From a nose-dive crash, letting his voice
Cut in as automatic pilot –
(Can't stop
But manages a wild wave in the fly-past) –
          Forty-six candles.

Magpie who
In his whites, his innocence of colour,
In his spectrum blacks, infra and ultra,
Acts Hamlet
Struts across the tragic rainbow
Between caterpillar and diamond –
          Forty-eight candles.

And Swallow, weaned on midges in a mud-hovel,
Now the sun's own navigator –
Compass-tremor tail-needles
Flickering on the dial –
          Fifty candles.

And Yaffle, who laughs
To count his gains
Red quiff on end

Scared out of his wits
By his golfball brains –

And Arctic Tern who shrieks so sharp, over Orkney,
Like a knife-opened sardine-can, on Skaill,
Where the winds crack brine-soaked whips –

And Pheasant who roosts high, who rests
His inlaid head in the East
And cools in the day's embers
On the finger of Lord Buddha –

And Swan, snowdrop lyrical daughter, possessed
By the coil
Of a black and scowling serpent –

And Raven, with wings clipped, who can topple upwards
Can somersault in a cloud above Meldon
As he walks the Bloody Tower for the realm's freedom.

Lift their wings

Thirty birds
Searching for God
Have found a Queen.
Sixty wings
Alight as a halo
Making Holy
A family of Islands.
Sixty wings
Making a crown.
Petals of a flower
From the other world
That hushes this one –

Sixty candles.

The Song of the Honey Bee

For the Marriage of His Royal Highness
Prince Andrew and Miss Sarah Ferguson
  23 July 1986

When all the birds of Roxburghshire
  Danced on the lawns, and all
The Salmon of the Tweed cavorted
  Over the Garden Wall
                    Gold as the Honey Bee

A helicopter snatched you up.
  The pilot, it was me.
The props, like a roulette wheel,
  Stopped at felicity
                    Soft as the Thistle's Crown

But now the abbey columns
  Stand like your ancestors
And your 'I do' has struck a root
  Down through the abbey floors
                    Gold as the Honey Bee

Now like a North Pole and a South
  You bear the magnet globe
And axis of our spinning land
  Where chaos plays its strobe
                    Soft as the Thistle's Crown

But as the day's commandment
  Which can no longer wait
Yokes Unicorn and Lion both
  To haul the coach of state
                    Gold as the Honey Bee

While royal ghosts in silence
  Bend at the register
And gaze into the letters
  That you have written there
                    Soft as the Thistle's Crown

Like splitting amplification
  Of thunder come the cheers

And set my meaning humming in
   Your honeymooning ears
                        Gold as the Honey Bee

Dance as dancing Eve and Adam
   Kicked their worries off
In Paradise, before they heard
   God politely cough
                        Soft as the Thistle's Crown

Dance on like a tuning fork
   That wakes unearthly stars
In human hearts, and makes them throb
   Like noble, old guitars
                        Gold as the Honey Bee

And dance and dance like Sirius
   Inseparably two
Who twirls in heaven, to show the earth
   What harmony can do
                        Soft as the Thistle's Crown

For from this day, that gives you each
   To each as man and wife
That's the dance that makes the honey
   Happiness of life
                        Gold, gold as the Honey Bee
                        Soft as the Thistle's Crown.

Two Songs

1 For Her Royal Highness Princess Beatrice of York
Born 8.18, 8/8/88

Time sieved every
Hour and date
For Leo's every
Lucky Eight –
Linked and locked them
Into a necklace
For so fortunate
A Fate,

Let bankrupt sense
Rule that the name
Of such a birth
's coincidence.
Who's won the game
If a dicey shake
Of Heaven and Earth
Shook you awake?

What sceptics call
The abyss could bless
Your days with all
This amulet
Now promises –
As easy as
It did create you
A Princess.

2 For the Christening of Her Royal Highness
Princess Beatrice of York

To every Leo born on Earth
    Descends a number Eight.
This Angel strives to make her child
    Blessed and fortunate.
Six Angels came, six bright Blessings
    Hover above your Fate.

The first one bears a Baby Doll –
    The tear inside it kept
Will cure the sick and poisoned seas
    The moment it is wept.

The second bears an Alphabet –
    Within it waits a word
Will cleanse the airs that choke the globe
    The moment it is heard.

The third one bears a Christening Cup
    That brims a cry of fear
Will scour the poison from the wells
    When it shall find an ear.

The fourth one bears a Silver Spoon
  Which being filled shall feed
The famine of this poisoned glut
  That withers womb and seed.

The fifth one bears a Book of Prayer –
  The groan inside it hung
Will break the heart that spoils the earth
  When it shall find a tongue.

The sixth one bears a Day of Fright
  For all whose heady mirth
Totting up your Birthday Blessings
  Questions what they're worth.
Blest are you, born when such Angels
  Poise above the Earth.

A Masque for Three Voices
For the Ninetieth Birthday of
Her Majesty Queen Elizabeth the Queen Mother
  4 August 1990

I

A royalty mints the sovereign soul
  Of wise man and of clown.
What substitute's debased those souls
  Whose country lacks a crown
Because it lies in some Swiss bank
  Or has been melted down.

Tragic drama gives its greatest
  Roles to royalty.
The groundling sees his crowned soul stalk
  The stage of history –
'I know,' he mutters, 'But not how,
  That majesty is me.'

  While, elsewhere,
  Three ravens, wise
  As Magi, drop
  From heaven and stop
  Their play to watch

A painter bent
Patient to paint
A crumbling tower
Where history tries
To shore up
Yesterday's woes –
Yet cannot touch
One holy creature's
Milky gaze.

Being British is the mystery. Can you see
That it is you or you or you or me?
I do not understand how this can be.

When Britain wins, I feel that I have won.
Whatever Britain does, I feel I have done.
I know my life comes somehow from the sun.

I hardly understand what I can mean
When I say Britain's Queens and Kings are mine.
How am I all these millions, yet alone?

II

This century dawned at your first smile
    Lit with another wonder:
The Boer War brimmed such lightnings
    They spilled the Kaiser's thunder:
'Britain's flag has gone too far.
    It must be trampled under.'

While the Hapsburg Empire
    Dreamed on about some war
Where every bombshell seemed a Serb
    In a runaway motor car.
And Queen Victoria laid aside
    Sunset and evening star.

But here, a drama
None has revised
Since it rehearsed
The first scene first:
A mother of heather,
Her gravelly burns,
Her ballad of weather,

Her cradle where turns
A salmon beneath
A breathing shawl
Of bubbles, and somewhere
The baby waul
Of a lamb, or a grouse,
In her lofty, draughty,
Everlasting,
Roofless house.

Briton by a mere accident of birth,
I thought my family was all the earth:
One mother made us all of equal worth.

Came Irish, English, Welsh, Moor, Spaniard, Scot
As missionaries to my humble pot:
One way I am what made me, one way not.

III

Einstein bent the Universe
　　To make war obsolete.
Ford swore his wished-for wheels would rush
　　The century off its feet.
The Soviet Butcher Bird announced
　　The new age with a tweet.

As Bleriot flew to Dover Cliff
　　Through a solid wall of sea
Woman unlocked her freedom.
　　An atom none could see
Opened its revolving doors
　　Into infinity.

Pictures, amazed at motion, talked.
　　Crete's labyrinth unfurled
The pain centre to Aspirin.
　　Whatever howls were hurled
Stravinsky and Picasso
　　Undid the old world.

To balance the euphoria
　　That Mephistophelist
Faust played Kaiser Wilhelm's part
　　Whose conjuring whisper hissed

Warship after warship out
      Into the North Sea mist.

Then from the Kaiser's fontanelle
      Sprouted a magic wand,
A spike of steel, a tuning fork
      For which all Europe donned
Pierrot costume and went waltzing
      Into the beyond.

      My stage, a white stone
      In the North Esk north
      Of Glamis, and beneath
      Swift water gone
      Before you can say
      I am here, now,
      This day, this moment,
      Watching that fish,
      Stilled, as at anchor,
      Tired from the ocean –

      A weightlessness
      Nudging the future
      That presses and freshens,
      Resting,
      With a shiver,
      There, where, wordless,
      The eyes of the bear
      Watched that same sleeked
      Silhouette stroked
      By the flow, on the same
      White stone where,
      A moment ago,
      It slid into place
      A sliver of ocean,
      Barbed, fletched, notched –

      So strange, so near,
      So like love's touch,
      Almost a fear –

      Now, while you watch it,
      This moment, and this,
      It rests there.

Kitchener's aim, cold as an enemy's,
Singled a self I met without surprise:
'British' his finger wrote between my eyes.

I died those million deaths. Yet each one bled
Back into me, who live on in their stead,
A dusty blossom of the British dead.

Still spellbound by that oath at Agincourt,
That palace jewel – the bullet Nelson bore.
But Passchendaele and Somme disturb me more.

Being British may be fact, faith, neither or both.
I only know what ghosts breathe in my breath –
The shiver of their battles my Shibboleth.

IV

Kaiser and Czar pupated.
  The fierce air of Versailles
Matured the first, who burst with Hitler's
  Tarantula cry
And Deutschland danced the goosestep for
  What it was bitten by.

But one voice: 'Hold That Tiger!' took
  Possession of the air.
Allcock and Brown brought Mickey Mouse
  Who brought his Teddy Bear.
And Tutankhamun's tomb disclosed
  What the war-weary wear.

The Czar of Asia's bearskin split –
  Marx lurched on to the stage.
Lenin devoured him with a smile
  And opened Stalin's cage
Whose Cheka and Red Army took
  Whole peoples for a wage.

  I lift my curtains
  From dark Bens
  Tasselled with rains –
  Their wraiths aslant
  Through orange light
  Where a girl walks

To see the lit Lochs
Far below
Creep and fret
In corroded holes.
She lifts her hand
Closer to an eagle
That hangs watching
The strangest sight –
The German Fleet
In Scapa Flow
Melting at anchor
To empty flickerings
Of ocean light.

While the heather, just purpling,
Each bell tipped
With a wet crystal
Listens to the garbled
Intercom
From Jupiter
Through interference
Of earth-warmed air –
Dixieland
And Tiger Rag
Riding the updraught
That lifts the eagle
Another orbit
And the girl's hair.

Dancebands banished the pangs of victory.
But when I slept, as far as I could see
Boots marched in slow motion soundlessly.

No matter though I danced until I dropped,
My pants so baggy and my hair so cropped,
The heart of money failed until it stopped.

The swastika's reversal of the sun,
Hammers and sickles by the billion ton,
Had countersigned the future of the fun.

Peace in our time, calm of the gathering storm.
Being British felt once more like uniform,
Once more King and Queen the only norm.

V

When Adolf and Benito signed
    In blood the Pact of Steel,
Their every step a kind of kick
    Which any child could feel,
And dreams of tripping Franco woke
    Under Stalin's heel

Then turning the omens upside down
    Jazz played a fever chart.
Recycled gunfire sounded
    Like Louis Armstrong's heart.
The radio told the telephone
    The future now could start.

But tyranny's forgings alchemised
    Its antidote, the true.
A Coronation honoured
    The Koh-i-noor anew
And centred on a million suns
    The atom's angels flew.

    At first light
    Where the hardworking burn
    Boils its dark liquor
    Like black coffee
    By second sight
    I watch a hind
    Lightly climb
    Crowned with the peaks
    Of her own home

    And easily spot
    Near the quick water
    Through the squint
    Of my sea-drilled flint
    That her new-dropped fawn
    Tucked among ferns
    Is a Queen's daughter.

At last the actors understood the play.
Somme and Versailles had seemed to go away,
But Mephistopheles had come to stay.

The audience that had seemed not to suspect
Somme and Versailles a first enormous act
Found being British the simple tragic fact.

No soccer final our side had to win.
When losing meant the Wehrmacht marching in
King and Queen made the whole country kin.

A sanctuary Church, a garrison.
Mother and Father of fifty million –
Their surname British and their future one.

VI

War took off, like a black sun,
        And everything went black.
And a bang on the door and a shout meant
        My window leaked a crack,
And my soul was an Anderson shelter
        Somewhere out the back.

Rome, Berlin and Tokyo
        Chopped the globe in three
And the Empire of a thousand years
        Re-styled humanity
A slave-camp of convenience
        For the gods of Destiny.

When Dunkirk's gunless columns trudged
        Up Main Street in their sleep,
And the cinder mote of a Hurricane
        Could make a county weep,
Old wounds of their watching fathers
        Re-opened twice as deep.

For the riddle of the machine-gun
        That stumped the First World War
Was nothing to the stupor
        That saw the Death-heads pour
Out over earth, cloned by the Satan
        Murder-gear they wore.

Then London fell on Britain's head
        In a single flame.
Yet through that glare, which scorched the hair,

Two untouched figures came,
Like Mother and like Father
For all who knew their name –

And it was there
That the Gulf Stream weather
Cooled in the Cairngorms
It was there
That the snowmelt speechless water spilling
Off the island's
Highest, holiest hill – the hidden hill
Unveiled only at the last moment,
Flowed through a Queen's arms,
Poured from the palms of her hands
Into the powdered shape on the stretcher,
Into the burnt thirst, the bomb-wounds.
So she healed each.
And each felt it. When each
Shape was the whole island's.

Deafened ears and seared eyes found how war
Sanctifies King and Queen until they are
One sacred certainty that all can share.

Eyes in the round glow of the burning earth
Saw what mattered, and how much it was worth,
That King and Queen must bear, like a new birth.

Being British was no mystery when man's future
Depended on one nation's soul – a creature
No zoologist ever glimpsed in nature.

VII

A new and other Britain
Was born that year of grace.
Her midwife was a U-boat pack
Like eyes from outer space.
Her christening was the morning dew
Of shrapnel in the grass.

On film, on page, the record lies
To be interpreted.
But records miss the infant soul
That for its Bible read

The toll of missing, and upon
    A National Anthem fed.

Hitler and Mussolini rose
    Into the conflagration
That they had puffed from their own sparks
    But over that elation
Bloomed the Hiroshima cloud
    As if the whole Creation

Had struck a match to find God's face –
    Then bending fearfully
Lit candles for the forty-fifth
    Anniversary
Of a British Queen and her
    Surviving century.

The British dreamed they thought they saw,
    As if a statue stirred,
She nursed the nation's infant soul
    That watched without a word
Through their own eyes, though all deny
    This miracle occurred

When the burns
That washed
The torn breasts of glens, the hill shoulders,
Mourning in veils
Not the passing of Arthur,
And the holy wells
In meadows, by roads,
That burst into cries
For the King's shadow

Wet the lips
And cleansed the blood
Of such a child
As hardly knew
How to live,
What to do,
But to go wild
Under its chatter
Of left and of right,
Its naming of names,

Nor how to utter
Life, love
For her who nursed it,
As in her arms,
So from flames.

Much like the heart that carries us about,
The fearless hope beneath the fearful doubt,
You have worn the Nazi and Soviet Empires out.

Much like our heartbeat, like our verb 'to be',
You thread the events of such a century
Some ask whether the earth herself can bear it.

The wheel of the Zodiac is the earth's jewellery.
Out of our decades of calamity
You made a great necklace, and radiantly you wear it.

Your birthday shares this present with the world.
Simply yourself, like the first smile you smiled,
A small blue figure, bending to a child.

The Unicorn
The Fortieth Anniversary of the Accession
of Her Majesty Queen Elizabeth II
6 February 1992

I X-RAY

Forty years

Invisibly
The spine of a people.
Pillar
Of the scales

Where Left and Right
In alternation
Tremble.
The fulcrum

Behind her eyes.
Forty years
Weighing
The people.

These equably British
In two minds or
Suspended
Hover

Bound by neither
So free
Upright
Level –

Envied.

2 FALSTAFF

Born Court Jesters tout their parts,
Hire out their tongues, cash in their hearts
To the tabloid howl that tops the charts.

Falstaff's our only true-bred Fool,
His belly-laugh the only school
Where liberty guarantees the rule.

Let Licensed Clowns grab ears and eyes.
Britain, Falstaff in disguise,
Laughs with the Queen and keeps her wise.

3 THE UNICORN

Forty years
The Unicorn
Has kept watch.
Her Lion sleeps

In the people.
While the Hyena
Laughing cries:
I feed all

Yet fare ill.
Her Lion dreams.
His colour runs
Into her corgis

To be near.
They are his imps.

But he will wake
Only for War.

She leaves her horn to guard her crown.
She sends her horse to gallop the down.
She walks as a woman into the town.

Democracies and Tyrannies
Are up in the air or on their knees –
The globe's a trampoline to these.

The Ape's brow bursts to reinvent
What govern and bewilder meant –
Madness comes where most thought went.

Those oceanic tears are dry.
Thermodynamic anarchy
Boils the dream in every eye.

Earth's solar fate is non-elective:
This geopolitical corrective
Puts power-junkies in perspective.

Only in Albion a magic hand,
A Unicorn's horn or Queen Mab's wand,
Or Prospero's word, holds all spellbound.

The Island's Ariel reappears,
Tiptoes the tightrope of our fears
And franks our freedom forty years.

Under the course's jumpy skin
Yin gobbles Yang, Yang gobbles Yin.
But her Favourite's cool, as if still to begin.

Villains, disasters in the sun –
How could such odds trouble one
Who has done what she has done?

The Unicorn can only win
The race that she was born to run.
If hearts are gold, the money's on.

5 ENVOI

Just come of age
I met her eyes
Wide in surprise
To have been
Just made a Queen
On a front page.

Forty years later
Looking at her
All see the Crown.
Some, their mother.
One, his wife.
Some, their life.

UNCOLLECTED (1992–97)

Lobby from Under the Carpet

In 1987 *The Times*
  Invited me to write
Vatic stanzas for the victors
  Of Election Night.

My Muse reared up with doleful cry:
  'Give each incumbent Member
While they fiddle their power bases
  One thing to remember.

'To drumbeats Britain's brides repeat:
  Hubby's eager sperms
Since the Sixties are down forty
  Per cent in real terms.

'I dreamed a Waste-Disposal man
  Hires each sperm as a tanker
To lug his poisons off somewhere –
  While he winks at the Banker.

'Or in plain terms at the top of my voice:
                    the cost of the World
Chemical Industry taken as a whole over the last
two decades
is
a 40% drop
in the sperm count of all Western Males
nor can God alone help the ozone layer or the ovum'

The Shareholders, they gagged my Muse,
  'No commas? No full-stops?
This illiterate free-verse rubbish!
  Give me top of the pops!'

My Muse had read
'The Poisoned Womb'.
  I thought her heart would break.
I sent a copy to Maggie: 'O Maggie,
  Read Elkington, and awake!'

Five years reversed the problem.
  Britain became the pit

Of Europe's and the whole world's waste
    For us to scavenge it.

But now Professor Skakkebaek
    Blows his angelic trump,
Revealing, like Christ's cradle,
    The Ministerial dump . . .

And that virility packet
    You take home to your wife
Is down not forty but fifty per cent
    i.e. half its life.

'The population problem solved!'
    Ticks the tittering tock.
But she feels lacking, somehow,
    And he goes off half-cock.

Our only hope's the Premier!
    The sperm will have to stand,
And the ovum, ravaged by toxins,
    Poor dumb pair, hand in hand.

Outside the door of Number Ten,
    While the whole building's a-quake,
With every bankrupt Industry
    Bawling: 'Awake! Awake!'

Three Poems for J.R.

WAIF

You were a waif in our human mystery.
Your large eyes, so pleading and intense,
Looked from the Southern Cross
Like a dog's eyes
From its kennel – at home, and lost.

You moved with your muse
Inside what clothes you had put on
Like a howl inside a fugue.
Never enough Pacific Surf
Between the dry soles of your shoes.

Defending your family from your own wildness
As if Joan of Arc, in the flames,
Had begged God
To remember the innocent stake
And the poor sticks, no less.

You made even friendship seem like your first.
Your smile, like bomb-smoke, your Cheshire Cat grin,
Hovered afterwards. Or returned, pinned on the skull
Of a stone-age, Polynesian love-goddess – dug up
With a ten thousand year thirst.

LOVESICK

You barely touched the earth. You lived for love.
How many loves did you have?
Was there even one?

Or you just loved love.
Love, they say, meaning Dante's God,
Which has a sense in heaven – on earth, none.

Or Love, meaning biology: gene tactics
Of the reproductive system:
Faceless, mindless, almost the fire in the sun.

The Sun
Is its own Aztec victim, tearing for food
Its own heart out, eating only its own.

What was your love? Eyes, words, hands, rooms,
Children, marriages, tears, letters
Were merely the anaesthetics – the lulling flutes
As you fed your heart to its god.

No matter what happened or did not happen

You burned out. You reserved nothing.
You gave and you gave
And that included yourself and that
Was how you burned out
A lonely kind of death.

What you loved most
Apparently was the desert.
And the desert's brother – the sea.
The sea's eldest son – the stone.
And the Gulf – the old hoary father of all.

It was aboriginal incest
Of your firestick-naked, billabong spirit
That came bounding
Over the gibber flats
While your mother's dream lay moon open.

Or her immigrant pallor, in the downunder drought glare,
Drank the dark moisture and its shadow
From the black man's eye. Or her yawn
Had been violated, through the open window,
By snake-genes, blowing in the dust.

Maybe. You were feminist aggressive
With the best. But all the time
Your betrothed, the desert,
Was decorating you, night after night,
With his dead shells, and the inland sea

Slithered away off you
Every dawn, and the stone, shrinking again,
Left inside you the cold germ
Of the fossil fish.
Till the Gulf

Provoked by your reckless, hungry glances,
Your incantatory whisperings, your prayers to be carried off
By boundless Tao –
Came in the dream you just managed to tell,
Skull-eyed, big-winged, and took you.

Two Photographs of Top Withens

The house is ruinous enough, in my snapshot.
But most of the roofslabs are in place.
You sit holding your smile, in one of the sycamores.

We'd climbed from Stanbury.
And through all the leaves of the fierce book
To touch Wuthering Heights – a fouled nest.

My Uncle wrinkles his nose
At something distasteful.
Emily's dream has flown.

But you smile in the branches – still in your twenties,   10
Ear cocked for the great cries.
'We could buy this place and renovate it!'

Except, of course, except,
On second thoughts, maybe, except
For the empty horror of the moor –

Mad heather and grass tugged by the mad
And empty wind
That has petrified or got rid of

Everything but the stones.
The stones are safe, being stone.   20
Even the spirit of the place, like Emily's,

Hidden beneath stone.
Nothing's left for sightseers – only a book.
It was a blue day, with larks, when I aimed my camera.

We had all the time in the world.
Walt would live as long as you had lived.
Then the timeless eye blinked.
                              And weatherproofed,
Squared with Water Authority concrete, a roofless
Pissoir for sheep and tourists marks the site
Of my Uncle's disgust.   30
                  But the tree –
That's still there, unchanged beside its partner,
Where my camera held (for that moment) a ghost.

1984 on 'The Tarka Trail'

I

The river is suddenly green – dense bottle green.
Hard in the sun, dark as spinach.

Drought pools bleach their craters.
The river's floor is a fleece –
Tresses of some vile stuff
That disintegrates to a slime as you touch it
Leaving your fingers fouled with a stink of diesel.

The river's glutted – a boom of plenty for algae.
A festering olla podrida, poured slowly.
Surfactants, ammonia, phosphates – the whole banquet
Flushed in by sporadic thunderbursts
But never a flood enough to scour a sewer,
Never enough to resurrect a river.

A bottleful is like sap, a rich urine,
With minuscule flying saucers whizzing in it.
Down near the estuary – this goes into the mains.
But nothing can help the patient. In the August afternoon
The golden picnic sunrays, leaning dustily
Through the conifers, gaze down
At a ditch-carcase, a puddled horror –
Bile draining from rags, the hulk of ribs.

Charlie found a stranded mussel. He brought it
Up the fishing ladder.
The lips gaped. We peered in, and pried wider,
Parted her pearly gates to get a peek
At her curtained uvula: Queen of the River
Still in her silken chamber, or was it – ?
A yawn of putrid phlegm.

Then the stench hit us. He yelled
And flailed it from his fingers as if it had burnt him
Into a blaze of willow-herb
'God! The river's dead! Oh God!
Even the mussels are finished!'

The tale of a dying river
Does not end where you stand with the visitors
At a sickbed, feeling the usual
Nothing more than mangled helplessness.
You cannot leave this hospital because
Peter, the good corn farmer, with his three plus
Tons of quality grain to the acre (behind him
The Min. of Ag. and Fish.'s hard guarantee

Which is the hired assurance of hired science)
Heaps the poisons into you too.

His upriver neighbour – just as overwhelmed –
Wades through slurry and silage. Where his dad
Milked a herd of twenty, he milks ninety –
Oozing effluent 'equal to the untreated
Sewage of a city the size of Gloucester'.

But Peter, our clean corn farmer, nature protector,
Striding between lush hedgebanks he lets go bush
To gladden the spider, past his carefully nursed
Neglected nettles (a crèche for the butterflies),
The birdwatcher, binoculars thumping his sternum,
Has measured his medicines towards that maximum yield
Into your dish for years. Yes, and smiled
Up towards the colluding sun. And returned
Over his corn (which now, near ripe, seems burned
Oak-dark with some fungus) thirteen times
Between the drill and the reaper.

Three hundredweight of 20–10–10 to the acre,
A hundredweight and a half straight Nitram.
Pesticides, herbicides, fungicides, the grand slam –
Each time twenty gallons to the acre
Into your dish, with top-ups. And slug-pellets
A bonus, with the rest, into your cup
(Via the lifeless ditch – meaning your tap).
Now you are as loaded with the data
That cultivate his hopes, in this brief gamble
As this river is –
                              as he is too,
He can't escape either, nor can his lively young wife,
Who laughs if you ask them why they do what they do
(Her voice ventriloqual, her shoulders jerking on their strings)
'But the children have to be educated.'

II NYMET

No map or Latin ever
Netted one deity from this river.
Taw meant simply *water*.
What was her true name

When with yellow smoky nettle pollen
And the first thorn's confetti
She crushed the May bridegroom's
Head into her flood?

Afterwards she bore him, unfailing,
All summer the splendour
Of eel-wreaths, the glut of white peal,
The glow-cold, sea-new salmon.

Deepening together
Her coombe and her name.
Where is she now?
A fairy

Drowned in the radioactive Irish Sea.
Blood-donor
To the South West Water Authority.
Her womb's been requisitioned

For the cloacal flux, the accountancy curse
Of the Express Dairy Cheese Factory –
'Biggest In Europe'.
A miasma

Mourns on the town bridge, at odd hours,
Over her old home, now her grave.
That's her.
She rots

But still stirs – a nightly, dewy spectre,
Nameless revenant
In her grave-shroud, resurrected
By her maternal despair

For her doomed parr. She wipes their lips
Of the stuff that weeps
From her curdled dug since it became
The fistula of a thousand farms. That's her –

Now she truly can be called: Sewer.
(More truly: The Washer at the Ford.
As in the old story.
The death-rags that she washes and washes are ours.)

Be a Dry-Fly Purist

Barely prick the meniscus. Lightly caress
The last gleam on the river. Lift off deftly
As a sedge-fly. Keep your head clear
Keep your body keep your soul clear

Of the river-fetch –
                                 (the epileptic's strobe,
The yell of the Muezzin
Or the 'Bismillah!'
That spins the dancer in

Her whole body liquefied
Where a body loves to be
Rapt in the river of its own music) –

Or be lost.
                    (*And she said:*
                                 '*When I hooked*
My first salmon, that salmon
In the Ferry Pool, it was I never
Expected nobody ever told I had never
Known anything not
Riding over jumps all I could think it
Was like having my first baby – ')

The Bear
   For Alan Hancox

The day darkened in rain. In the bottom of the gorge
The big tarp awning we sat approximately under
Bucked in its ropes. Pans took off.
Nothing we could do
Could alter anything. River rising by the minute.
The rapids churning fog. Ron came in:
'The rain's warm! Feel the warmth of that wind!'

The mountains stood above us in their saunas.
Our flood-indicators were the cataracts
Dangling down their chests and faces   10
From under their hoods of snow.

When would the rain end?
Maybe it wouldn't, maybe this was The Rains –
The winter coming early. Maybe the river
Never would surrender Ehor's wine-cache
Already four feet under the sliding concrete
Till maybe next June. So why were we happy?
How could we get out? We couldn't.
What else could we be doing? Nothing.
20   Hands tight hidden, hats down over our ears.
Patience welled up like a comfort.
And Life, said Jay, is simple – just a clock
Of good cooking and even better coffee.
And of calculating, shouted Ehor,
By those heavenly egg-timers above us
Occasionally to be glimpsed through the cloud-rags,
And by the deepening bow-wave of that log-jam
What a fantastic upriver flood of Steelhead
This will leave us to deal with!
30   This gloomy wash-out, my friends, is our bonanza!
And the streamy danglers
That decorate the mountains' Indian faces
Mean the rain is getting excited for us
And wanting the mountains to dance. It has dressed the mountains
For a dance – the dance of the Steelhead,
The rain-storm dance, the snow-melt. Those ribbons
Are our dance regalia –

We could have appreciated it all,
We could have let the spirits, clamped in our weatherproofs,
40   Magnify themselves and dance with the mountains
And the whirling wind in robes
Of rain and elemental nostalgia –
But what those busy tickertapes were telling
Was bigger water, river out of control,
The Steelhead hugging deeper
As if they were under an avalanche
Their more and more unthinkable finger-holds,
While our fishing days and our flown-in dreams
Rumbled away over them tossing driftwood,
50   Bleeding us downstream. Our dance was to sit tight,
Freshly sawn-off stumps, hugging our roots,
Stumps of abandoned sawn-off totem poles

At a glum remove from our enterprise
Suspended in the clouds literally,
Clouds that were dragging up and down the gorge
Simultaneously in opposite directions,
A dance that mimed the hope of hopelessness
To squalls that slapped gunshots out of the tent,
Our gossip out of our mouths, and scattered our coffee.
While rain ripped at the tarp. And taps were spluttering   60
At every corner – every edge tasselled or bucketing
As the tarp jumped. And dangledrops were descending
Along every cord, or snapped off.
We could only watch it all and know
Everything was worsening.
                    But we sat there
And enjoyed it. And the Steelhead down there
They were enjoying it too, this was what they were made of,
And made by, and made for, this was their moment.
The thousand-mile humping of mountains
That looked immovable, was in a frenzy,   70
Metabolism of stars, melt of snows –
Was shivering to its ecstasy in the Steelhead.
This actually was the love-act that had brought them
Out of everywhere, squirming and leaping,
And that had brought us too – besotted voyeurs –
Trying to hook ourselves into it.
And all the giddy orgasm of the river
Quaking under our feet –

                    'What's that? It's a bear!'
A black snag reeled past on the blue-white swirls – a tree root?
'It's a goddamned bear!' It was a bear.   80
The night before's mystery upstream gunshot
Materialized, saluted us, and vanished
As a black sea-going bear, a scapegoat, an offering.

The Mayfly is Frail

The way the shivering Northern Lights are frail.

Erupting floods, flood-lava drag across farms,
Oak-roots cartwheeling –
The inspiration was seismic.

Some mad sculptor
In frenzy remaking the river's rooms
Through days and nights of bulging shoulders
And dull bellowing – cooled with cloudbursts –
Needed all his temperament.

Now he sprawls – flat in the sun –
Apparently burned out.

And now comes the still small voice.

Out of his glowing exhaustion
Heals a giddy mote,
A purity in a mould

And the mould splits at a touch of the air.

A shimmering beast
Dawns from the river's opened side.

High Water

In the cragged pool
The river-smithy
Goes on labouring all night.

River-goblins
Toil the bellows, in the underglow.

Sledge-hammers of big water, rock anvils
Pound in the den of glooms.

With fling of glare metals and shadow-struggle.

Under the corrugated roof
Bulging and flashing mares
Slam down their heels, and are held.

Electrical stallions
Surge and, with oaths, are quieted.

A string of the sea's Arctic horses
Came up yesterday, with the salmon,
To be doctored, to be groomed, to be shod.

Two days, and the pool will be idle again.

Everything is on its Way to the River

A near-sonnet, to assure Gavin Ewart that he isn't getting any older

The bull – planting a tree – on its hind legs,
The dandelion clock – salvoes of dryness,
The elephants of granite – herds of slowness,
And the moonlighting hare with fleas in its lugs

Are on their way to the river.

With the stink-horn fungus' satyriasis,
The girl's blush that spills down over her breasts,
The hive's drunk legs – its bellyful of dark beasts,
The shivering favourite – lightning in its face.

The Lord's rainbow processions, in pomp, to the river.
Tombstone letters are wriggling lights on the river.
Continents are the hourglass grains of the river.
All things draw to the river.
                              Under them all
The river, itself and unalterable.

Why the '21st Child' Could Not Be Lifted

The arms
Of newspapers and air-waves were strong
But the twenty-first child was too heavy.

Behind one living eye
The mass grave
Of fourteen thousand dead children.
And behind the other
The mass grave, with its huge spoil heap,
Of every child
Still to be killed in that war.

Maybe all that could have been lifted
With more air-waves
And more sheets of newspaper.
But the twenty-first child also held
In one hand locked with hysteria
Every weapon used by that war.

And in the other
Tibet.

The Last of the 1st/5th Lancashire Fusiliers
A Souvenir of the Gallipoli Landings

The father capers across the yard cobbles
Look, like a bird, a water-bird, an ibis going over pebbles
We laughed like warships fluttering bunting.

Heavy-duty design, deep-seated in ocean-water
The warships flutter bunting.
A fiesta day for the warships
Where war is only an idea, as drowning is only an idea
In the folding of a wave, in the mourning
Funeral procession, the broadening wake
10   That follows a ship under power.

War is an idea in the muzzled calibre of the big guns.
In the grey, wolvish outline.
War is a kind of careless health, like the heartbeat
In the easy bodies of sailors, feeling the big engines
Idling between emergencies.

It is what has left the father
Who has become a bird.
Once he held war in his strong pint mugful of tea
And drank at it, heavily sugared.
20   It was all for him
Under the parapet, under the periscope, the look-out
Under Achi Baba and the fifty billion flies.

Now he has become a long-billed, spider-kneed bird
Bow-backed, finding his footing, over the frosty cobbles
A wader, picking curiosities from the shallows.

His sons don't know why they laughed, watching him through
    the window
Remembering it, remembering their laughter
They only want to weep

As after the huge wars

Huge senseless weeping.

Snapshot

Sheep with their short minds
Bullocks bound in leather
Farmer, his skull stuffed with small print
Like a mouse's nest

Are stuck among wild, stumpy daffodils
Watching meaningless water
Pour away the sands of their hourglass –
One gravity drain gulping down

Time's toxins and all that abattoir blood.

O salmon, arc up, shatter the goggling lens –
Fall back into the cradle of beginning
And ending, the round of unending water.

Playing with an Archetype

While they gambled for their clothes
It was amusing.
Soon he lost every last stitch.

When they gambled for body privileges
It was exciting
Even when she won his last hair, to do as she liked with.

Seeing the possible gains
And thinking: Nothing more to lose –
He gambled on.

He hadn't reckoned
Earth, Sun, Moon and Stars were still to be lost –
They went in one throw.
She put them into her bag.

The Past and the Future – one throw.

All attendant and invisible worlds –
One throw.

She put them into her bag.

So he hung there, echoless, in nothing,
The simple cry of his loss
Nailed where the moment he occupied
Crossed the single place he occupied.

And now, with a finalising smile
She won his cry

Louder and louder he unravelled it for her
And worse and tearing worse, and on and on

Endlessly into her bag.

Epigraph [*from* Earth Dances]
for Reg

The suffering of stony high horizons,
Under the stir of air, sharpens.
And the water-torture of gorges, hoarse wounds
That cannot cease to be, deepens.

Listening to moorland is a headfull of ether.
The bones of the eye-socket
Go inane. The bones of the ear
Hallucinate a ghost.

The soul clings to its skull
Like a tremor
To a tuft of bog-cotton.
Or leaps onto a lark's back

With an idiot song, lost in air.

Old Oats

'Mad Laughter', your sister – her grey perm
Rayed out in electrified frazzles.
But you were the backfiring
Heart of your double-humped,

Sooty, two hundred acres.
Alex cracked. Strabismic, pitiable,
Gawky, adopted Alex!
That morning on the stack – and you
In a Führer frenzy,
Your coalface vocabulary
Going up in one flame!
Alex never came back.
Where did you end up?
Chimpanzee, dangle-pawed,
Shambling, midget ogre. Jehovah
Of my fallen Eden.
Undershot, bristly jowl –
Chimpanzee. That dazzled scowl –
Chimpanzee. Shoulder wing-stumps
In the waistcoat bossed
And polished to metal –
Chimpanzee. Cap an oil-rag,
Chewing your twist,
Raw disintegrating boots –
Your free knuckles lay quaking
At ease on the mudguard
Or pointed out to me
The bright, startling, pretty
Shrapnel in the stubble.
Your spittle curse, bitten off
Among the unshaven silver,
You'd give me the damned farm!
Nothing too stubborn,
Ferguson brains, running on pink paraffin,
Up in the dark, head in the cow's crutch
Under the throb of Dorniers,
Staring into the warm foam,
Hobbling with a bucket and a lantern
Under the sky-burn of Sheffield,
Breaking your labourers with voice –
A royal succession of Georges!
What was it all for?
Collapsing between the stooks,
Up again, jump-starting your old engine
With your hip-flask,
Hoisting the top-heavy stackyard

Summer after summer. How many horses
Worn to chaffy dust? How many tractors
Battered to scrap? What's become of you? Nobody
Could have kept it up. Only
One thing's certain. Somewhere
You rest.

Anniversary

My mother in her feathers of flame
Grows taller. Every May Thirteenth
I see her with her sister Miriam. I lift
The torn-off diary page where my brother jotted
'Ma died today' – and there they are.
She is now as tall as Miriam.
In the perpetual Sunday morning
Of everlasting, they are strolling together
Listening to the larks
Ringing in their orbits. The work of the cosmos,
Creation and destruction of matter
And of anti-matter
Pulses and flares, shudders and fades
Like the Northern Lights in their feathers.

My mother is telling Miriam
About her life, which was mine. Her voice comes, piping,
Down a deep gorge of woodland echoes:
'This is the water-line, dark on my dress, look,
Where I dragged him from the reservoir.
And that is the horse on which I galloped
Through the brick wall
And out over the heather simply
To bring him a new pen. This is the pen
I laid on the altar. And these
Are the mass marriages of him and his brother
Where I was not once a guest.' Then suddenly
She is scattering the red coals with her fingers
To find where I had fallen
For the third time. She laughs
Helplessly till she weeps. Miriam
Who died at eighteen

Is Madonna-like with pure wonder
To hear of all she missed. Now my mother
Shows her the rosary prayers of unending worry,
Like pairs of shoes, or one dress after another,
'This is the sort of thing,' she is saying,
'I liked to wear best.' And: 'Much of it,
You know, was simply sitting at the window
Watching the horizon. Truly
Wonderful it was, day after day,
Knowing they were somewhere. It still is.
Look.'

And they pause, on the brink
Of the starry dew. They are looking at me.
My mother, darker with her life,
Her Red Indian hair, her skin
So strangely olive and other-worldly,
Miriam now sheer flame beside her.
Their feathers throb softly, iridescent.
My mother's face is glistening
As if she held it into the skyline wind
Looking towards me. I do this for her.

She is using me to tune finer
Her weeping love for my brother, through mine,
As if I were the shadow cast by his approach.

As when I came a mile over fields and walls
Towards her, and found her weeping for him –
Able for all that distance to think me him.

The Oak Tree

Your tap-root, deep in starry heaven,
   Brought your life to you.
Your eyes opened and Creation
   Looked calmly through.

Deep into Scotland's battlefields
   Your second root sank.
Richer than all the tartans
   Was the blend you drank.

Through the British trenches
   Your third root struck.
Your leaves bronzed on the lost mystery
   That it brought back.

Then under the throne of England
   Your fourth root went down.
Your leaves and acorns glittered as
   The jewels of the crown.

Your fifth root wrapped so light around
   This island's bedrock.
When pyromanic Swastikas
   Sent Europe up in smoke
Our stone raft rode the open sea
   In the hold of an oak.

Survivors, who knew what it meant
   To be fumes in a shell-hole
Or scattered like shrapnel, were eager
   To let your sixth root steal
Through all their veins, your leaves their faces
   You their one oak bole.

The survivors and their children –
   Dazed in the after-shock –
No longer knew the oak from the island
   Or themselves from the oak.

Their century became a tree
   Of fifty million lives,
And the tree-spirit you, your smile
   The glance among the leaves.

Now the roar of saws in the boughs
   Is the song of our island race.
The crown of oak-leaves amplifies
   A global market-place.

Yet under it all, each year your oak
   Deepens its deep roots,
Renewing itself from the hidden core
   With bare, pure leaf-shoots.

The rings of age in the heartwood
  As the years in your face
Carry the strength of the oak tree
  And the strength's grace.

Your oak's years are not fallen.
  Each year, like a relief,
This tree lifts our only future
  Leaf – after leaf.

A Trout?

for Norman MacCaig

Up here, everything leans, easy,
On everything else.

But the stealthiest peering-in
Is a bull, closing its eyes
To the water-face's Veronica.

Guess ghosts down, gloved with pressure.
Senses dazzled or shut.
Mind fingering after.

Might this be him?
                    Steel of patience.

Hair-trigger
Bomb of suddenness. Shadow-shuttle.
Otherworldling.

Is he still here?

                    Maybe
You can believe him into being.
Maybe he'll pretend.

                    Faint migraine
Gropes the strange, watery underbelly

Of what has no weight
With what is all doubt.

Black Hair

I remember her hair as black
Though I know it was brown.
Dark brown. I first saw it as black.
She was combing it. Probably it was wet.
She was combing it out after washing it.
Black, straight, shining hair down over her breasts.
That's the memory. I must have been sitting
On the kitchen table, looking down
Where she sat on the chest, at the fireside.
Bowing her head slightly towards me
She combed a centre parting. And I thought
She's Red Indian
And that's why her nose is Red Indian.
And that's why her skin seems so dark.
My eyes are blue-green, but hers are dark.

So a big thought in my third or fourth year
Photographed her
Combing black, North American hair
That has outlasted her,
And that I would learn, as I began to learn better,
Was brown. Was grey.
Was fine as baby silk – every hair
Half the thickness in the micrometer
Of the next finest hair we measured
At school in metalwork.
So fine, I could hardly feel it
As I stroked it through those days she lay
Vanishing under my fingers.

Platform One

Holiday squeals, as if all were scrambling for their lives,
Panting aboard the 'Cornish Riviera'.
Then overflow of relief and luggage and children,
Then ducking to smile out as the station moves.

Out there on the platform, under the rain,
Under his rain-cape, helmet and full pack,

Somebody, head bowed reading something,
Doesn't know he's missing his train.

He's completely buried in that book.
He's forgotten utterly where he is.   10
He's forgotten Paddington, forgotten
Timetables, forgotten the long, rocking

Cradle of a journey into the golden West,
The coach's soft wingbeat – as light
And straight as a dove's flight.
Like a graveyard statue sentry cast

In blackened old bronze. Is he reading poems?
A letter? The burial service? The raindrops
Beaded along his helmet rim are bronze.
The words on his page are bronze. Their meanings bronze.   20

Sunk in his bronze world he stands, enchanted.
His bronze mind is deep among the dead.
Sunk so deep among the dead that, much
As he would like to remember us all, he cannot.

Comics

My brother was born blue with his head jammed
Hard against the stony dead-end
Of the industrial tunnel. The birth-cord
Tight around his neck. His escape tool
Was Comics, Westerns. Freedom
Opened away North of the Great Divide
Inside the head. His talisman, his compass,
The rifle
Fallen into his hands from the Paleolithic,
Invisibly engraved
With Bison and Cave Bear. But the Comic Mags
Collected anyhow
Were the drug that took him
Up through the smoke-hole, out through the attic skylight.
Mother feared their visions.
The Wesleyan prudery of her girlhood –
Or what? – again and again she crammed them
Into the ash-bin. Again and again he retrieved them –

Stock to trade for others. She feared
The stars in the eyes, the bear path
Leading out of the valley
Into the den of a strange woman. The snare
Of a temple harlot.
The wrong gods: 'If you do this, that or that –
You'll kill me. Those Magazines
Are my dreams being torn into tiny pieces
By godless men who dream of bad women –
This valley and all its works, all we've slaved for,
Dumped in the ash-bin. Chapels and godliness,
Next to cleanliness, torn up and dumped in an ash-bin.'
That is what she meant, dumping his comics –
As if they were true maps
Locating Gold Fields sown with spent bullets
And upturned toes. Or Paradise East of the Sun.
Or the folly-stone of the Alchemists
In a nest of hocus-pocus.
She didn't know what she was doing
That was so clairvoyant –
As when she clawed in the blazing coals
For a screwed up ten shilling note she'd idly tossed there –
Only knowing that she was desperate
And that it was all too late.

Mother-Tongue

I hear her talking.
She is trying out a flute.
Not the flute but the flute's notes.
Not the flute's notes but the ceilings
And the floors
Of the flute's palace.
And all the winding stairs, a dancing
To the searching voice in the flute.

Now she sways over a cello.
The hairs of the bow
Are the hairs of my body miraculously lengthened.
She regards them as hers.

She uses them with abandon, flings her arm
And the hand holding the bow.

The strings of the cello are the fibres
Of the umbilicus
We shared long ago. So long ago
My memory of our sharing it, in the cave mouth,
Is lost, far beyond the event horizon,
In the black hole
Out of which her music still pours.

6 September 1997

Mankind is many rivers
That only want to run.
Holy Tragedy and Loss
Make the many One.
Mankind is a crowned, Holy
Mother and her Son.
For worship, for mourning:
God is here, is gone.
Love is broken on the Cross.
The Flower on the Gun.

TALES FROM OVID

Twenty-four Passages from the *Metamorphoses*
(1997)

Creation; Four Ages; Flood; Lycaon

Now I am ready to tell how bodies are changed
Into different bodies.

I summon the supernatural beings
Who first contrived
The transmogrifications
In the stuff of life.
You did it for your own amusement.
Descend again, be pleased to reanimate
This revival of those marvels.
Reveal, now, exactly   10
How they were performed
From the beginning
Up to this moment.

Before sea or land, before even sky
Which contains all,
Nature wore only one mask –
Since called Chaos.
A huge agglomeration of upset.
A bolus of everything – but
As if aborted.   20
And the total arsenal of entropy
Already at war within it.

No sun showed one thing to another,
No moon
Played her phases in heaven,
No earth
Spun in empty air on her own magnet,
No ocean
Basked or roamed on the long beaches.

Land, sea, air, were all there   30
But not to be trodden, or swum in.
Air was simply darkness.
Everything fluid or vapour, form formless.
Each thing hostile
To every other thing: at every point
Hot fought cold, moist dry, soft hard, and the weightless
Resisted weight.

God, or some such artist as resourceful,
Began to sort it out.
40 Land here, sky there,
And sea there.
Up there, the heavenly stratosphere.
Down here, the cloudy, the windy.
He gave to each its place,
Independent, gazing about freshly.
Also resonating –
Each one a harmonic of the others,
Just like the strings
That would resound, one day, in the dome of the tortoise.

50 The fiery aspiration that makes heaven
Took it to the top.
The air, happy to be idle,
Lay between that and the earth
Which rested at the bottom
Engorged with heavy metals,
Embraced by delicate waters.

When the ingenious one
Had gained control of the mass
And decided the cosmic divisions
60 He rolled earth into a ball.
Then he commanded the water to spread out flat,
To lift itself into waves
According to the whim of the wind,
And to hurl itself at the land's edges.
He conjured springs to rise and be manifest,
Deep and gloomy ponds,
Flashing delicious lakes.
He educated
Headstrong electrifying rivers
70 To observe their banks – and to pour
Part of their delight into earth's dark
And to donate the remainder to ocean
Swelling the uproar on shores.

Then he instructed the plains
How to roll sweetly to the horizon.
He directed the valleys
To go deep.

And the mountains to rear up
Humping their backs.

Everywhere he taught   80
The tree its leaf.

Having made a pattern in heaven –
Two zones to the left, two to the right
And a fifth zone, fierier, between –
So did the Wisdom
Divide the earth's orb with the same:
A middle zone uninhabitable
Under the fire,
The outermost two zones beneath deep snow,
And between them, two temperate zones   90
Alternating cold and heat.

Air hung over the earth
By just so much heavier than fire
As water is lighter than earth.
There the Creator deployed cloud,
Thunder to awe the hearts of men,
And winds
To polish the bolt and the lightning.

Yet he forbade the winds
To use the air as they pleased.   100
Even now, as they are, within their wards,
These madhouse brothers, fighting each other,
All but shake the globe to pieces.

The East is given to Eurus –
Arabia, Persia, all that the morning star
Sees from the Himalayas.
Zephyr lives in the sunset.
Far to the North, beyond Scythia,
Beneath the Great Bear, Boreas
Bristles and turns.   110
Opposite, in the South,
Auster's home
Is hidden in dripping fog.

Over them all
Weightless, liquid, ether floats, pure,
Purged of every earthly taint.

Hardly had he, the wise one, ordered all this
Than the stars
Clogged before in the dark huddle of Chaos
120   Alit glittering in their positions.

And now to bring quick life
Into every corner
He gave the bright ground of heaven
To the gods, the stars and the planets.
To the fish he gave the waters.
To beasts the earth, to birds the air.

Nothing was any closer to the gods
Than these humble beings,
None with ampler mind,
130   None with a will masterful and able
To rule all the others.

Till man came.
Either the Maker
Conceiving a holier revision
Of what he had already created
Sculpted man from his own ectoplasm,
Or earth
Being such a new precipitate
Of the etheric heaven
140   Cradled in its dust unearthly crystals.

Then Prometheus
Gathered that fiery dust and slaked it
With the pure spring water,
And rolled it under his hands,
Pounded it, thumbed it, moulded it
Into a body shaped like that of a god.

Though all the beasts
Hang their heads from horizontal backbones
And study the earth
150   Beneath their feet, Prometheus
Upended man into the vertical –
So to comprehend balance.
Then tipped up his chin
So to widen his outlook on heaven.

In this way the heap of all disorder
Earth
Was altered.
It was adorned with the godlike novelty
Of man.

And the first age was Gold.   160
Without laws, without law's enforcers,
This age understood and obeyed
What had created it.
Listening deeply, man kept faith with the source.

None dreaded judgement.
For no table of crimes measured out
The degrees of torture allotted
Between dismissal and death.
No plaintiff
Prayed in panic to the tyrant's puppet.   170
Undefended all felt safe and were happy.

Then the great conifers
Ruffled at home on the high hills.
They had no premonition of the axe
Hurtling towards them on its parabola.
Or of the shipyards. Or of what other lands
They would glimpse from the lift of the ocean swell.
No man had crossed salt water.

Cities had not dug themselves in
Behind deep moats, guarded by towers.   180
No sword had bitten its own
Reflection in the shield. No trumpets
Magnified the battle-cries
Of lions and bulls
Out through the mouth-holes in helmets.

Men needed no weapons.
Nations loved one another.
And the earth, unbroken by plough or by hoe,
Piled the table high. Mankind
Was content to gather the abundance   190
Of whatever ripened.
Blackberry or strawberry, mushroom or truffle,
Every kind of nut, figs, apples, cherries,

Apricots and pears, and, ankle deep,
Acorns under the tree of the Thunderer.
Spring weather, the airs of spring,
All year long brought blossom.
The unworked earth
Whitened beneath the bowed wealth of the corn.
200   Rivers of milk mingled with rivers of nectar.
And out of the black oak oozed amber honey.

After Jove had castrated Saturn,
Under the new reign the Age of Silver –
(Lower than the Gold, but better
Than the coming Age of Brass) –
Fell into four seasons.

Now, as never before,
All colour burnt out of it, the air
Wavered into flame. Or icicles
210   Strummed in the wind that made them.
Not in a cave, not in a half-snug thicket,
Not behind a windbreak of wattles,
For the first time
Man crouched under a roof, at a fire.
Now every single grain
Had to be planted
By hand, in a furrow
That had been opened in earth by groaning oxen.

After this, third in order,
220   The Age of Brass
Brought a brazen people,
Souls fashioned on the same anvil
As the blades their hands snatched up
Before they cooled. But still
Mankind listened deeply
To the harmony of the whole creation,
And aligned
Every action to the greater order
And not to the moment's blind
230   Apparent opportunity.

Last comes the Age of Iron.
And the day of Evil dawns.
Modesty,

Loyalty,
Truth,
Go up like a mist – a morning sigh off a graveyard.

Snares, tricks, plots come hurrying
Out of their dens in the atom.
Violence is an extrapolation
Of the cutting edge   240
Into the orbit of the smile.
Now comes the love of gain – a new god
Made out of the shadow
Of all the others. A god who peers
Grinning from the roots of the eye-teeth.

Now sails bulged and the cordage cracked
In winds that still bewildered the pilots.
And the long trunks of trees
That had never shifted in their lives
From some mountain fastness   250
Leapt in their coffins
From wavetop to wavetop,
Then out over the rim of the unknown.

Meanwhile the ground, formerly free to all
As the air or sunlight,
Was portioned by surveyors into patches,
Between boundary markers, fences, ditches.
Earth's natural plenty no longer sufficed.
Man tore open the earth, and rummaged in her bowels.
Precious ores the Creator had concealed   260
As close to hell as possible
Were dug up – a new drug
For the criminal. So now iron comes
With its cruel ideas. And gold
With crueller. Combined, they bring war –
War, insatiable for the one,
With bloody hands employing the other.
Now man lives only by plunder. The guest
Is booty for the host. The bride's father,
Her heirloom, is a windfall piggybank   270
For the groom to shatter. Brothers
Who ought to love each other
Prefer to loathe. The husband longs

To bury his wife and she him.
Stepmothers, for the sake of their stepsons,
Study poisons. And sons grieve
Over their father's obdurate good health.
The inward ear, attuned to the Creator,
Is underfoot like a dog's turd. Astraea,
280   The Virgin
Of Justice – the incorruptible
Last of the immortals –
Abandons the blood-fouled earth.

But not even heaven was safe.
Now came the turn of the giants.
Excited by this human novelty – freedom
From the long sight and hard knowledge
Of divine wisdom – they coveted
The very throne of Jove. They piled to the stars
290   A ramp of mountains, then climbed it.

Almighty Jove
Mobilised his thunderbolts. That salvo
Blew the top off Olympus,
Toppled the shattered
Pelion off Ossa
And dumped it
Over the giants.
They were squashed like ripe grapes.

Mother Earth, soaked with their blood,
300   Puddled her own clay in it and created
Out of the sludgy mortar new offspring
Formed like men.

These hybrids were deaf
To the intelligence of heaven. They were revolted
By the very idea
Of a god and sought only
How to kill each other.
The paternal bent for murder alone bred true.

Observing all this from his height
310   Jove groaned. It reminded him
Of what Lycaon had done at a banquet.
As he thought of that such a fury

Took hold of the Father of Heaven
It amazed even himself.

Then the gods jump to obey
His heaven-shaking summons to council.
The lesser gods come hurrying
From all over the Universe.
They stream along the Milky Way, their highway,
To the Thunderer's throne   320
Between wide-open halls, ablaze with lights,
Where the chief gods
Are housed in the precincts of Jove's palace
At the very summit of heaven
As in their own shrines.

When the gods had taken their seats
Jove loomed over them,
Leaning on his ivory sceptre.
He swung back his mane
With a movement that jolted   330
The sea, the continents and heaven itself.
His lips curled from the flame of his anger
As he spoke: 'When the giants
Whose arms came in hundreds,
Each of them a separate sea-monster,
Reached for heaven, I was less angered.
Those creatures were dreadful
But they were few – a single family.
Many venomous branches, a single root.
They could be plucked out with a single gesture.   340
But now, to the ocean's furthest shore,
I have to root out, family by family,
Mankind's teeming millions.
Yet I swear
By the rivers than run through the underworld
This is what I shall do.
You think heaven is safe?
We have a population of demi-gods,
Satyrs, nymphs, fauns, the playful
Spirits of wild places,   350
Astral entities who loiter about.
When we denied these the freedom of heaven

We compensated them
With their grottoes and crags, their woods and their well-springs,
Their dells and knolls. In all these sanctuaries
We should protect them.
Imagine their fears
Since the uncontrollable Lycaon
Plotted against me, and attempted
360   To do away with me – Jove, King of Heaven,
Whose right hand
Rests among thunderheads and whose left
Sways the assemblies of heaven?'

The gods roared their outrage.
They shouted
For instant correction
Of this madman.
Just as when those gangsters
Tried to wash out Rome's name
370   With Caesar's blood,
Mankind recoiled stunned
As at the world's ending and
The very air hallucinated horrors.

O Augustus, just as you see now
The solicitude of all your people
So did the Father of Heaven
Survey that of the gods.

Just so, too, the majesty of Jove
Quieted heaven with a gesture.
380   'This crime,' he told them,
'Has been fully punished. What it was
And how I dealt with it, now let me tell you.
The corruption of mankind
Rose to my nostrils, here in heaven,
As a stench of putrid flesh.
Seeking better news of the species
I left Olympus, and in the shape of a man
Walked the earth.
If I were to recount, in every detail,
390   How man has distorted himself
With his greed, his lies, his indifference,
The end of time, I think,

Would overtake the reckoning.
Alerted as I was
I was still unprepared for what I found.
I had crossed Maenalus –
The asylum of lions and bears.
I had passed Cyllene
And the shaggy heights and gorges
Of freezing Lycaeus.   400
At nightfall
I came to the unwelcoming hearth
Of the Arcadian King.
I revealed, with a sign,
The presence of a god.
But when the whole court
Fell to the ground and worshipped,
King Lycaon laughed.
He called them credulous fools.
"The simplest of experiments," he snarled,   410
"Will show us whether this guest of ours
Is the mighty god he wants us to think him
Or some common rascal. Then the truth
Will stare us all in the face."

'Lycaon's demonstration
Was to be the shortest of cuts.
He planned to come to my bed, where I slept that night,
And kill me.
But he could not resist embellishing
His little test   420
With one introductory refinement.

'Among his prisoners, as a hostage,
Was a Molossian. Lycaon picked this man,
Cut his throat, bled him, butchered him
And while the joints still twitched
Put some to bob in a stew, the rest to roast.

'The moment
He set this mess in front of me on the table
I acted.
With a single thunderbolt   430
I collapsed his palazzo.
One bang, and the whole pile came down

Onto the household idols and jujus
That this monster favoured.
The lightning had gone clean through Lycaon.
His hair was in spikes.
Somehow he staggered
Half-lifted by the whumping blast
Out of the explosion.
440 Then out across open ground
Trying to scream. As he tried
To force out screams
He retched howls.
His screams
Were vomited howls.
Trying to shout to his people
He heard only his own howls.
Froth lathered his lips.
Then the blood-thirst, natural to him,
450 Went insane.
From that moment
The Lord of Arcadia
Runs after sheep. He rejoices
As a wolf starved near death
In a frenzy of slaughter.
His royal garments, formerly half his wealth,
Are a pelt of jagged hair.
His arms are lean legs.
He has become a wolf.

460 'But still his humanity clings to him
And suffers in him.
The same grizzly mane,
The same black-ringed, yellow,
Pinpoint-pupilled eyes, the same
Demented grimace. His every movement possessed
By the same rabid self.

'So one house is destroyed.
But one only. Through the whole earth
Every roof
470 Is the den of a Lycaon.
In this universal new religion
All are fanatics – suckled
Not by the sweet wisdom of heaven

But by a wolf. All adore, all worship
Greed, cruelty, the Lycaon
In themselves. All are guilty.
Therefore all must be punished. I have spoken.'

As he ended, one half the gods
Added their boom of approval
To his rage. The other deepened it   480
With solid and silent assent.
All were quietly appalled
To imagine mankind annihilated.
What would heaven do
With a globeful of empty temples?
Altars attended
Only by spiders? Was earth's beauty
Henceforth to be judged
Solely by the single-minded
Palates of wild beasts   490
And returned to the worm
Because man had failed?

God comforted the gods.
If everything were left to him, he promised,
He could produce a new humanity –
Different from the first model and far
More prudently fashioned.

So now Jove set his mind to the deletion
Of these living generations. He pondered
Mass electrocution by lightning.   500
But what if the atoms ignited,
What if a single ladder of flame
Rushing up through the elements
Reduced heaven to an afterglow? Moreover,
God as he was, he knew
That earth's and heaven's lease for survival
Is nothing more than a lease.
That both must fall together –
The globe and its brightness combined
Like a tear   510
Or a single bead of sweat –
Into the bottomless fires of the first, last forge.

Afraid that he might just touch off that future
With such weapons, forged in that same smithy,
He reversed his ideas.
He dipped his anger in the thought of water.
Rain, downpour, deluge, flood – these
Could drown the human race, and be harmless.

In a moment he had withdrawn the blast
520   That fixes the Northern ice.
He tethered the parching winds
Off mountains and out of deserts
That bare the flaring blue and crack lips.
He gave the whole earth to the South Wind.
Darkening into the East, and into the West,
Two vast wings of water opened. One
Thunderhead filled heaven,
Feathered with darkness, bringing darkness
From below the Equator.
530   The face of this South Wind, as he came,
Boiled with squalling tempest.
Beard and hair were a whorl of hurricanes.
He dragged whole oceans up, like a peacock shawl.
And as he drubbed and wrung the clouds
Between skyfuls of fist, quaking the earth,
Shocks of thunder dumped the floods.
Juno's messenger, the rainbow,
Swept from earth to heaven, topping up the darkness.
Every crop was flattened. The farmer's year
540   Of labour dissolved as he wept.

But still there was not water enough in heaven
To satisfy Jove's fury.
So Neptune, his brother, god of the seas,
Brought up tidal waves,
And assembled every river
There in the bottom of the ocean
And ordered them to open their aquifers
Ignoring all confines.
The rivers raced back to their sources
550   And erupted.
Neptune himself harpooned the earth with his trident.
Convulsed, it quaked open

Crevasse beneath crevasse
Disgorging the subterranean waters.

Now flood heaps over flood.
Orchards, crops, herds, farms are scooped up
And sucked down
Into the overland maelstrom.
Temples and their statues liquefy
Kneeling into the swirls. 560
Whatever roof or spire or turret
Resists the rip of currents
Goes under the climbing levels.
Till earth and sea seem one – a single sea
Without a shore.
A few crowds are squeezed on diminishing islets
Of hill-tops.
Men are rowing in circles aimlessly, crazed,
Where they ploughed straight furrows or steered wagons.
One pitches a sail over corn. 570
Another steers his keel
Over his own chimney.
One catches a fish in the top of an elm.
Anchors drag over grazing
Or get a grip under vine roots.
Where lean goats craned for brown tufts
Fat seals gambol over and under each other.

The nereids roam astounded
Through submerged gardens,
Swim in silent wonder into kitchens, 580
Touch the eyes of marble busts that gaze
Down long halls, under the wavering light.

Dolphins churn through copses.
Hunting their prey into oak trees, they shake out acorns
That sink slowly.
Wolves manage awhile,
Resting their heads on drowned and floating sheep.
Lions ride exhausted horses. Tigers
Try to mount foundering bullocks.
The strong stag's fine long legs, 590
Growing weedier, tangle in undercurrents.
The wild boar, the poor swimmer, soon goes under.

Even his faithful heavy defenders,
The thunderbolt and lightning-flash of his tusks,
Have joined the weight against him.
Birds grow tired of the air.
The ocean, with nowhere else to go,
Makes its bed in the hills,
Pulling its coverlet over bare summits.

600   While starvation picks off the survivors.

Drowned mankind, imploring limbs outspread,
Floats like a plague of dead frogs.

Phaethon

When Phaethon bragged about his father, Phoebus
The sun-god,
His friends mocked him. 'Your mother must be crazy
Or you're crazy to believe her.
How could the sun be anybody's father?'

In a rage of humiliation
Phaethon came to his mother, Clymene.
'They're all laughing at me,
And I can't answer. What can I say? It's horrible.
I have to stand like a dumb fool and be laughed at.

'If it's true, Mother,' he cried, 'if the sun,
The high god Phoebus, if he is my father,
Give me proof.
Give me evidence that I belong to heaven.'
Then he embraced her. 'I beg you,

'On my life, on your husband Merops' life,
And on the marriage hopes of my sisters,
Only give me proof that the sun is my father.'
Either moved by her child's distress,
Or piqued to defend her honour against the old rumour,

Clymene responded. She stretched her arms to the sun:
'By the dazzling ball itself
Who is watching us now, and is listening
To everything I say, I swear
You are his child. You are the son

'Of that great star which lights up the whole world.
If I lie, then I pray
To go blind, this moment,
And never again to see the light of day.
But if you want so much to meet your father

'It is not impossible.
He rises from that land beyond our borders.
If you must have the truth about yourself
Go and ask him for it.'
Phaethon

Rushed out, his head ablaze
With the idea of heaven.
He crossed his own land, Ethiopia,
Then India, that trembled in the sun's nearness,
And came to his father's dawn palace.

Fittingly magnificent
Columns underpropped a mass
Of gold strata so bright
The eyes flinched from it.
The whole roof a reflector
Of polished ivory.
The silver doors like sheet flame –
And worked into that flame
Vulcan, the god of fire,
Had set, in relief, a portrait of the creation.
There were the seas. Triton
Cruising in foam, through the swell,
Making his lonely music.
And Proteus, amoebic,
Flitting from form to form,
A submarine, shape-shifting shadow.
And Aegeon, half-reclining,
His arms across two whales.
Dorcas was there with her daughters –
Swimming, riding fishes,
Or sitting on rocks and combing their hair.
Each one quite different
Yet all looking like sisters.
And there, on earth, were the cities, the people,
The woods, the beasts, the rivers, the nymphs

And the spirits of wild places.
Surrounding the whole thing, the Zodiac –
On the right door six signs, and six on the left.

Phaethon climbed the steep approach
And entered the house of his father
Who had brought him so much shame.
He went straight in to the royal presence –
But had to stand back: the huge light was so fierce
He could not go near it.
For there was the god – Phoebus, the sun,
Robed in purple
And sitting on a throne of emeralds
That blazed,
Splitting and refracting his flames.
To right and left of him
His annual retinue stood arrayed –
The seasons, the generations, and the hours.
Spring, crowned with a flower garland. Summer,
Naked but for a coronet of ripe corn.
Autumn, purple from treading the wine-press.
And Winter, shivering in rags,
His white hair and his beard
Jagged with icicles.

The boy stared dumbfounded,
Dazed by the marvel of it all.
Then the great god
Turned on him the gaze that misses nothing
And spoke: 'Phaethon, my son!

'Yes, I call you my child – or rather, a man
A father might be proud of. Why are you here?
You must have come with a purpose. What is it?'
Phaethon replied: 'O God, Light of Creation!
O Phoebus, my father – if I may call you father! –

'If Clymene is not protecting herself
From some shame by claiming your name for me
Give me the solid proof.
Let it be known to the whole world
That I am your son. Remove all doubt.'

His father doffed his crown of blinding light
And beckoning Phaethon closer, embraced him.
'Do not fear to call me father.
Your mother told you the truth.
To free yourself from doubt – ask me for something.

'Anything, I promise you shall have it.
And though I have never seen the lake in hell
By which we gods in heaven make our oaths
Inviolable, I call on that lake now
To witness this oath of mine.'

Phoebus had barely finished before Phaethon
Asked for the chariot of the sun
And one whole day driving the winged horses.
His father recoiled. He almost
Cursed his own oath. His head shook

As if it were trying to break its promise.
'Your foolish words,' he said,
'Show me the tragic folly of mine.
If promises could be broken
I would break this. I would deny you nothing

'Except this. Be persuaded
The danger of what you ask is infinite –
To yourself, to the whole creation.
The forces, the materials, the laws
Of all Creation are balanced

'On the course of that chariot and those horses.
A boy could not hope to control them.
You are my son, but mortal. No mortal
Could hope to manage those reins.
Not even the gods are allowed to touch them.

'Only see how foolish you are.
The most conceited of the gods
Knows better
Than to dream he could survive
One day riding the burning axle-tree.

'Yes, even Jupiter
High god of all heaven, whose hand
Cradles the thunderbolt –

He keeps his fingers off those reins.
And who competes with him?

'Our first stretch is almost vertical.
Fresh as they are, first thing,
It is all the horses can do to get up it.
Then on to mid-heaven. Terrifying
To look down through nothing

'At earth and sea, so tiny.
My heart nearly struggles out of my body
As the chariot sways.
Then the plunge towards evening –
There you need strength on the reins. Tethys,

'Who waits to receive me
Into her waters, is always afraid
I shall topple –
And come tumbling
Head over heels in a tangled mass.

'Remember, too,
That the whole sky is revolving
With its constellations, its planets.
I have to force my course against that –
Not to be swept backwards as all else is.

'What will you do,
Your feet braced in the chariot, the reins in your hands,
When you have to counter the pull
Of the whirling Poles? When the momentum
Of the whole reeling cosmos hauls you off sideways?

'Maybe you expect
To come across delectable cities of the gods,
Groves and temples beautifully appointed,
Much as on earth. It is not like that.
Instead, benighted gulches, with monsters.

'Even if you were able to stick to the route
You have to pass
The horns of the Great Bull, the nasty arrows
Of the Haemonian Archer, the gaping jaw
Of the infuriated Lion,

'And the Scorpion's lifted spike, its pincers
That grab for you from one side while the Crab
Rushes at you with its double crushers
From the other.
And how could you cope with the horses?

'Even for me
It is not easy, once they are fired up
With the terrible burners
That they stoke in their deep chests
And that belch flames from their mouths and nostrils.

'Once their blood is up
They will hardly obey me, and they know me.
Think again. Do not ask me
For what will destroy you.
You ask me for solid proof that you are my son:

'My fears for your life are proof, solid enough.
Look at me. If only your eyes
Could see through to my heart and see it
Sick with a father's distress.
Choose anything else in Creation – it is yours.

'But this one thing you have chosen –
I dare not grant it. Choose again, Phaethon.
You have asked me not for an honour, as you suppose,
But for a punishment. O my son,
This is no honour, this is a punishment.

'You throw your arms around my neck and persist.
You have no notion of what you are asking for.
But I have sworn by Styx and you shall have
Whatever you desire. Only, my son,
Ask again, for something different, wiser.'

Phaethon seemed not to have heard.
He wanted nothing but to drive
The chariot and horses of the sun.
His father could find no other means to delay him.
He led him out to the chariot.

Vulcan had made it. The axle-tree was gold,
And the chariot-pole gold. The wheel-rims were gold.
The wheel-spokes silver. The harness, collar and traces,

Crusted with chrysolites and other jewels
Blazed in the beams of the sun-god.

And as Phaethon stood there, light-headed with confidence,
Giddy with admiration
Of the miraculous workmanship and detail,
Dawn opened her purple doors behind him,
Letting the roses spill from her chambers.

The stars decamped – their vanishing detachments
Supervised by the morning star
Who followed them last.
When the sun-god saw that, and the reddening sky
And the waning moon seeming to thaw

He called the Hours to yoke the horses.
The light-footed goddesses brought them
Swinging in steam from the high stables,
Blowing soft flames, fat with ambrosia.
Yoked to the chariot, they champed at the jangling bits.

But now as Phoebus anointed Phaethon
With a medicinal blocker
To protect him from the burning
And fixed the crown of rays on the boy's head
He saw the tragedy to come

And sighed: 'At least, if you can,
Stick to these instructions, my son.
First: use the whip not at all, or lightly.
But rein the team hard. It is not easy.
Their whole inclination is to be gone.

'Second: avoid careering
Over the whole five zones of heaven.
Keep to the broad highway that curves
Within the three zones, temperate and tropic.
Avoid the Poles, and their killing blizzards.

'Keep to that highway, follow the wheel ruts.
Share your heat fairly
Between heaven and earth, not too low
And not crashing in among the stars. Too high
You will set heaven aflame – and, too low, earth.

'The middle way is best, and safest.
And do not veer too far to the right
Where your wheels might crush the Serpent, nor to the left
Where they might be shattered against the Altar.
Take a bearing between them.

'Now Fortune go with you. And I pray
She will take care of you better
Than you have taken care of yourself.
We have talked too long. Night has gone down
Behind the world westward. No more delays.

'Our great light is looked for.

'Grasp the reins. Or better, with a changed mind,
While your feet are still on the earth,
Before you have hurled your idiot emulation
Among the terrors of space,
Grasp my advice.

'Leave my chariot to me.
Let me give the world the light it expects,
A light for you to smile at in safety.'
But Phaethon, too drunk with his youth to listen,
Ignored the grieving god

And leapt aboard, and catching the reins
From his father's hands, joyfully thanked him.
Pyrois, Eous, Aethon, Phlegon –
The four winged horses stormed to be off.
Their whinnyings quaked the air-waves,

A writhing crackle of interference
Throughout heaven. And their pawing hooves
Racketed at the barred gate.
Then Tethys (who knew nothing
Of the part about to be played by her grandson)
Lifted the bars – and all space
Lay open to the racers.

They burst upwards, they hurled themselves
Ahead of themselves,
Winged hooves churning cloud.
They outstripped those dawn winds from the East –
But from the first moment

They felt something wrong with the chariot.
The load was too light.
More like a light pinnace
Without ballast or cargo,
Without the deep-keeled weight to hold a course,
Bucking and flipping
At every wave,
Sliding away sidelong at every gust.
The chariot
Bounced and was whisked about as if it were empty.

When the horses felt this
They panicked.
They swerved off the highway
And plunged into trackless heaven.
Their driver, rigid with fear,
Gripped the chariot rail. It was true,
He had neither the strength nor the skill
To manage those reins.
And even if he could have controlled
The wild heads of the horses
He did not know the route.

For the first time
The stars of the Plough smoked.
And though the Arctic Ocean
Was forbidden to them they strained
To quench themselves in it.

And the Serpent
That hibernated close to the Pole Star
Harmless, and inert in the cold, woke
Scorched, lashing, furious to cool itself.

Even slow Bootes puffed and scrambled
To get away from the heat,
Dragging his plough like an anchor.

And now Phaethon looked down
From the zenith –
And saw the earth
So far below, so terrifyingly tiny,
His whole body
Seemed suddenly bloodless.

His knees wobbled, his eyes
Dazzled and darkened.
He wished he had never seen his father's horses.
He wished he had never learned
Who his father was. He wished his father
Had broken his promise.
He wanted only to be known
As the son of Merops.

Meanwhile the chariot bounded along
Like a ship under a gale
When seas have smashed the rudder
And the ropes have gone
And the helmsman
Crouches and clings in the scuppers,
And prays,
Hiding his eyes with his arm.

What could he do?
Much of the sky was behind him,
But always more ahead.
He looked East, trying to measure
What he had covered.
He looked West – where his Fate lay waiting.
Either way, nothing could help him.

His wrists were looped in the reins he no longer
Had the strength to cling to.
Even the horses' names had gone out of his head.

And now he saw the monsters
Littered among the constellations.
The Scorpion loomed,
Suspending his tail
Over the wide embrace of his claws,
Sprawling across two signs of the Zodiac.
When Phaethon saw that, when he saw
The ponderous talon of the sting, bulbed with poison,
He dropped the reins.
They fell in a tangle over the horses.
Then the horses took off, blindly.
Uncontrolled, they let their madness
Fling them this way and that
All over the sky.

They dashed in among the stars
Switching the chariot along
Like a whip-tail.
They swept low – till the clouds boiled in their wake
And the moon was astonished
To see her brother's chariot below her.

Earth began to burn, the summits first.
Baked, the cracks gaped. All fields, all thickets,
All crops were instant fuel –
The land blazed briefly.
In the one flare noble cities
Were rendered
To black stumps of burnt stone.
Whole nations, in all their variety,
Were clouds of hot ashes, blowing in the wind.
Forest-covered mountains were bonfires.
Athos burned.
Cilician Taurus and Tmolus,
Oeta and Ida, formerly blessed for its springs,
Helicon, home of the Muses, all burned.
And Haemus, that Orpheus would make famous.
The twin peaks of Parnassus, and Cynthus and Eryx,
Were pillars of fire. Etna convulsed
In multiple eruptions.
The snows of Rhodope
Boiled off, and the ridges glowed.
Othrys, Mimas, Dindyma, Mycale
And Cithaeron, dancing place of the Bassarids,
Were ablaze.
Scythia's freezing winds could not protect it.
Ossa, Pindus, Olympus bigger than either,
The Alps that look across Europe
And the Apennines, their clouds gone,
Burned like fleeces.

Now Phaethon saw the whole world
Mapped with fire. He looked through flames
And he breathed flames.
Flame in and flame out, like a fire-eater.
As the chariot sparked white-hot
He cowered from the showering cinders.
His eyes streamed in the fire-smoke.

And in the boiling darkness
He no longer knew where he was
Or where he was going.
He hung on as he could and left everything
To the horses.

That day, they say,
The Ethiopians were burnt black.
That day,
Lybia, in a flash of steam,
Became a shimmering desert,
Where the nymphs of the springs and lakes
Wandered like wraiths, wailing for lost water.
Boeotia wept for the fountain of Dirce,
Argos for Amymone, Ephyre for Pyrene.
Strong rivers fared no better.
The shallows of Tanais fried. Old Peneus,
Mysian Caecus and the headlong Ismenus –
Their shallows and riffles bubbled as if over pebbles
That were red-hot.
And Trojan Xanthus, who would be burned again.
Yellow Lycormas poured a reeking soup.
Looped Meander steamed like a scalded serpent.
Melas in Thrace, Eurotas in Sparta,
Euphrates in Babylon,
Orontes, Thermodon, Ganges, Phasis and Hister
Seemed to smoulder in their beds.
Alpheus dived through fire. Sperchius
Crept between banks that broke into flame.
The gold in Tagus melted.
The singing swans of Cayster
Cried in dismay as the river boiled,
Scalding and stripping their plumage.
The terrified Nile
Escaped into Africa, and hid his head
Among smouldering mountains, leaving the seven
Delta channels
To blow into dunes.
Ismarus' bed was a gully of burning dust.
The Rhine, the Rhône, the Po and the Tiber
Which had been promised an Empire
Were bubbling pits of quag in scabby trenches.

The earth cracked open. And the unnatural light
Beamed down into hell
Scaring the king and queen of that kingdom
With their own terrific shadows.
The seas shrank, baring deserts.
Submarine mountains emerged as islands,
Multiplying the Cyclades.
Fish hugged the bottom of their deepest holes.
Seals bobbed belly up, lifeless.
And the dolphins stayed far down.
Three times
Neptune reared his angry head and shoulders
Above the bubbling surface
And each time plunged again
To escape the searing flames of the air.

Then the Goddess of Earth
Alarmed by the waters crowding into her bowels
Pushed up through the embers
And lifted her head and neck into the furnace.

She spread her hand
To shield her face from the sun.
The terror
That shook her body shook the whole earth.
She crouched lower and cried
With her holy voice:
'You God of the gods,
If my annihilation
Has been decided, why drag it out?
Where are your thunderbolts
To finish the whole thing quickly?
If I am to end in fire
Let it be your fire, O God,
That would redeem it a little.
I can hardly speak.'
She choked in a squall of ashes.
'See my hair singed to the roots,
My eyes cauterised by your glare.
Are these my reward
For my fertility, my limitless bounty,
My tireless production?
Is this my compensation

For undergoing the ploughshare,
The pick and the mattock,
My flesh gouged and attacked and ground to a tilth
Year in year out? Is this how you pay me
For foddering fat beasts,
For plumping the milky grain that suckles man,
For concocting the essences and rich herbs
That smoke on your altars?
Even if I have somehow deserved all this
How are the seas guilty, or your brother?
Why should the oceans, that are his portion,
Cringe and shrink from the sky?
But if you are deaf to us
What about your own heaven? Look at it.
Both Poles are glowing. Once they go
Your whole realm flies off its axle,
Your palace is rubbish in space.
And look at Atlas. He is in trouble.
His shoulders are fabulous, but who can carry
The incineration of a Universe?'

Then heat overcame her. Little by little
She drew in her smoking head,
Like a tortoise, and sank into herself –
Into the caves, close to the land of ghosts.

The Almighty, aroused,
Called on the gods,
Including Phoebus who had lent the chariot –
He asked them to witness
That heaven and earth could be saved only
By what he now must do.
He soared to the top of heaven,
Into the cockpit of thunder.
From here he would pour the clouds
And roll the thunders and hurl bolts.
But now he was cloudless –
There was not a drop of rain in all heaven.

With a splitting crack of thunder he lifted a bolt,
Poised it by his ear,
Then drove the barbed flash point-blank into Phaethon.
The explosion

Snuffed the ball of flame
As it blew the chariot to fragments. Phaethon
Went spinning out of his life.

The crazed horses scattered.
They tore free, with scraps of the yoke,
Trailing their broken reins.
The wreckage fell through space,
Shattered wheels gyrating far apart,
Shards of the car, the stripped axle,
Bits of harness – all in slow motion
Sprinkled through emptiness.

Phaethon, hair ablaze,
A fiery speck, lengthening a vapour trail,
Plunged towards the earth
Like a star
Falling and burning out on a clear night.

In a remote land
Far from his home
The hot current
Of the broad Eridanus
Quenched his ember –
And washed him ashore.
The Italian nymphs
Buried his remains, that were glowing again
And flickering little flames
Of the three-forked fire from God.
Over his grave, on a rock they wrote this:
  Here lies Phoebus' boy who died
  In the sun's chariot.
  His strength too human, and too hot
  His courage and his pride.

His father mourned, hidden,
Eclipsed with sorrow.
They say no sun showed on that day.
But the fires of the burning earth
Were so far useful, to give some light.
And now Clymene's outcry
Equalled the catastrophe.
Mad with grief, she searched the whole earth
To find the boy's limbs, or his bones.

She came to the grave. With her breasts naked
She embraced the engraved rock.

The daughters of the sun grieved as keenly,
Beating their breasts,
Throwing themselves down on their brother's tomb,
Calling incessantly
For the one who would never hear them.
Days, weeks, months, they mourned.
Their lamentations were obsessive,
As if they could never exhaust them
They wore out four full moons with their wailings
Until at last Phaethusa –
As she flung herself to the ground –
Cried out that her feet were fixed of a sudden.
And Lampetie, as she stepped to help her,
Found her own feet rooted, immovable.

A third, tearing her hair,
Brought away handfuls of leaves.
One screamed that a tree bole
Had imprisoned her calves and thighs.
Another was whimpering with horror
To find her arms crooking into stiff branches.
And as they all struggled in vain
To escape or understand, tree bark,
Rough and furrowed, crept on upwards
Over their bodies, throats, faces –
Till it left only their lips, human enough
To call for their mother.

And what could she do
But stagger to and fro
In growing terror –
Torn this way and that,
Kissing the mouths she could still find?
And when she tried to free her daughters
Ripping at the bark, and snapping the branches –
A liquid, like blood,
Came welling out of the wounds,

And the mouths screamed:
'O Mother, do not hurt us.
Though we are trees

We are your daughters –
Oh now we must leave you.'

So their last words were silenced
By the sealing bark.
But then, through that bark,
There oozed lymph like tears, that in the sun's light
Solidified as amber.
These dropped from the boughs
Into the hurrying river
Which carried them off
To adorn, some day far in the future,
Roman brides.

Callisto and Arcas

After Phaethon's disaster
Jove was repairing the earth,
Clothing the burnt lands again with life –

But even such a labour of love,
So urgent, has to yield
To one even more urgent.

And there she was – the Arcadian beauty, Callisto.
He stared. Lust bristled up his thighs
And poured into the roots of his teeth.

She wasn't the sort
That sat at home, her eyes in a daze
On the whirl of a spinning wheel, or a mirror.

She loped along with the huntress Diana,
Her tunic pinned with a bold brooch,
Her ponytail in a white ribbon

And in her hand a bow or a javelin.
Of all Maenalus' nymphs she was Diana's
Favourite. But favourites have to fall.

The sun was well past noon when this girl
Came in under the massive cooling columns
Of a virgin forest. She slackened her bow

And setting her quiver as a pillow
Flung herself down among the anemones
On the sun-littered floor of the woodland.

And that is where Jupiter spotted her.
Defenceless, drowsing, languid. 'A wonder!'
He breathed, 'that my wife need never disturb,

Or if she happens to, the price will be worth it.'
Callisto woke to a voice. Above her
Diana's perfect double, gazing down,

Was speaking to her: 'Best-loved of all my virgins
Where did you hunt today? On which ridges,
Down which valleys?' The girl sat up, astonished –

'O Goddess, O my divine mistress –
Greater than Jupiter –
And I don't care if he hears me – ' Jove smiled

Secretly behind his disguise
Delighted to receive more adulation
Than himself. He stretched beside her and kissed her,

A kiss more than maidenly, that roughened –
A kiss that, as she tried to answer him,
Gagged her voice, while his arms tightened round her,

Straitjacketing her body, and his action
Revealed
The god – irresistible and shameless.

Callisto's piety had limits.
She fought. If Juno had seen how she fought
Her final cruelty might have been modified.

But it was no good. Desperately as she denied him
The God of gods went off home contented
As if from heavenly bliss to heavenly bliss.

The girl wept. Suddenly, she hated the forest,
The flowers, that had watched while it happened.
She was in such a hurry to get away

She almost abandoned her bow and her quiver.
Diana, coming along the ridge of Maenalus
With her virgin troop, after hard hunting,

Saw her darling, and called her. Callisto's
Jumpy terror of Diana's likeness
Grabbed with electric hands, and she bolted –

But then recognised her friends, the virgins
Who ran with the goddess,
And knew this could not be Jove. So she joined them.

But changed now. How hard it is
To keep guilt out of the face!
She no longer led the troop –

Was no longer the boisterous nearest
To the goddess. She hung back, eyes to the ground,
As if slinking along from hiding to hiding.

If any spoke to her she blushed, then paled.
Without her divinity Diana
Could not have missed the thousand human tokens

That were no puzzle to the nymphs.
Nine months passed. Finally came the day,
Heated with hunting under the hot sun

Diana led her company into a grove
With a cool stream over smooth pebbles.
'Here is a place,' she called,

'Where we can strip and bathe and be unseen.'
The Arcadian girl was in a panic.
The rest were naked in no time – she delayed,

She made excuses. Then all the others
Stripped her by force – and with shrill voices
Exclaimed at her giveaway belly

That she tried pitifully to hide
With her hands. The goddess, outraged,
Cried: 'Do not defile this water or us.

'Get away from us now and for ever.'
Meanwhile, Juno had seen everything.
She was merely waiting for an occasion

To exact the exemplary punishment.
The moment Jove's bastard was born –
A boy, Arcas! – her fury exploded.

She stared in wild hatred at the new infant.
'So,' she screamed at Callisto, 'the world can see
You have perfected your insult – and my shame.

'Now see me perfect my revenge
On this beauty of yours
That so unbalanced my husband.'

She grabbed the girl by the hair
Above her forehead, and jerked her down flat on her face.
As Callisto lay there, pleading for mercy

With outstretched arms – those arms the god had caressed
Suddenly bushed thick with black hair,
Her hands curved into scoops of long talons –

They had become feet. And her mouth
That Jupiter had kissed in his rapture
Was fanged jaws, like a torn open wound.

Then to empty her cries of their appeal
The goddess nipped off her speech. Instead of words
A shattering snarl burst from her throat, a threat –

Callisto was a bear.
Yet her mind was unaltered. Her lament
Was the roar of a bear – but her grief was human.

And though they were a bear's forepaws
That she raked at heaven's face with,
Her despair over Jove's ingratitude,

Though she could not speak it, was a girl's.
Afraid of sleeping in the woods, she crept into the gardens
Of what had been her home.

Often she galloped for her life
Hearing the hounds. Often she laboured, gasping,
Hunted across the hillsides where she had hunted.

Sometimes she forgot what she was
And hid from the other creatures. As before –
Above all, what this bear feared were the bears.

She also feared the wolves,
Though her own father
Was out there among them, one of them.

Meanwhile, Arcas grew to his fifteenth year.
He knew nothing at all
About his mother. Hunting was his passion.

One day, after choosing the ground carefully,
Reckoning with the wind
And with the lie of the land

Arcas had pitched his nets
Among the scrubby coverts of Erymanthis.
As he started the drive, of a sudden

Out of the long grass his mother
Reared upright to face him,
Standing tall to see him better, fearless,

As if she recognised him. She recognised him.
Arcas backed slowly, mouth dry,
Terror, three parts wisdom, staring

Fixedly at the eyes that stared at him.
But when she dropped on all fours
And he saw her shaggy shoulders

Humping through undergrowth towards him
He could not think what this great beast intended
If not to kill him. He braced himself

Behind his spear
To meet her momentum
And drive that long, keen-ground blade as deeply

Into her body as he could. Jupiter
Saw it all. He stooped down from heaven
And blocked the bronze point with his fingertip.

Then spun mother and son up in a whirlwind.
So these two, about to be reunited
In that bloody crime and tragic error,

Found themselves far out in space, transformed
To constellations, the Great Bear and the Small,
Dancing around the Pole Star together.

The Rape of Proserpina

Ceres was the first
To split open the grassland with a ploughshare.
The first
To plant corn and nurse harvests.
She was the first to give man laws.

Everything man has he owes to Ceres.
So now I sing of her
And so I pray my song may be worthy
Of this great goddess,
For surely she is worthy of the song.

The giant Typhon, that upstart who had dared
To hope for a home in heaven,
Felt his strength returning. He stirred,
Squashed
Under the massive slab of Sicily.

His right hand, reaching towards Rome,
Was crushed under Pelorus,
His left hand under Pachynnus,
His legs under Lilybaeum
And his enormous head under Etna.

Flat on his back, he vomited ashes,
Flame, lava, sulphur. His convulsions
Shrugged off cities,
Quaked mountains to rubble.
The whole of Sicily trembled.

The Lord of Hell was aghast to see bedrock
Heaving in waves, like ocean. He looked upwards
For earth's crust to come caving in
Letting the sunglare into hell's glooms,
Dazzling the spectres. Anxious

In a black chariot, behind black horses,
The King of Terrors
Thundered up
To reconnoitre the roof of his kingdom.
He scrutinised the island's foundations,

Double-checked every crevasse, crack, fault,
For sign of a shift.
Probed every weak spot with his sceptre
Tapping rocks and analysing echoes.
Everything seemed to be sound

And he began to feel better. It was then
Aphrodite, sitting on her mountain,
Noticed him.
She woke her winged boy, embraced him, kissed him.
'My child,' she whispered, 'you who are all my power,

'You who are my arms, my hands, my magic,
Bend your bow, my darling,
And sink your shaft, which never missed a challenge,
Into the heart of that god
Who rules hell.

'The deities of the upper world are yours
Whenever you please. Even great Jupiter –
Like a helpless figment of your fancy –
Whatever folly you plot, he will perform it.
The gods of the sea, no less,

'Dance to your prompting arrows, your spurs,
Your goads, your tickling barbs.
That great earth-shaker, Neptune,
Is no more than your trophy.
Over all these your rule is hardly questioned.

'It is time to expand our empire, my child,
Into that third realm – the underworld.
A third of Creation – there for the taking.
Heaven mocks our forbearance, and exploits it.
Your power is less than it was, and mine too.

'I have lost Pallas
And the great huntress Diana – both gone.
And now Ceres' daughter, Proserpina,
Wants to stay a virgin. Do we permit it?
Now is your opportunity.

'If you have any pride in our dominion
Fasten that goddess and her grim uncle
Together with one bolt.'

Even as he listened to his mother
Cupid's fingers found the very arrow

For the job – one in a thousand –
True as a ray of the sun tipped with a photon.
He set the soles of his feet to the belly of the bow
And hauling the fletched notch to his chin dimple
Buried it in the dark heart of Pluto.

Near Enna's walls is a deep lake
Known as Pergusa.
The swans on that surface make a music
Magical as the songs
On the swift currents of Cayster.
Trees encircling it
Knit their boughs to protect it
From the sun's flame.
Their leaves nurse a glade of cool shade
Where it is always spring, with spring's flowers.

Proserpina was playing in that glade
With her companions.
Brilliant as butterflies
They flitted hither and thither excitedly
Among lilies and violets. She was heaping
The fold of her dress with the flowers,
Hurrying to pick more, to gather most,
Piling more than any of her friends into baskets.
There the Lord of Hell suddenly saw her.
In the sweep of a single glance
He fell in love
And snatched her away –
Love pauses for nothing.

Terrified, she screamed for her mother,
And screamed to her friends. But louder
And again and again to her mother.
She ripped her frock from her throat downwards –
So all her cherished flowers scattered in a shower.
Then in her childishness
She screamed for her flowers as they fell,
While her ravisher leaped with her
Into his chariot, shouting to the horses
Each one by name,

Whipping their necks with the reins, like the start of a race,
And they were off. They were gone –
Leaving the ripped turf and the shocked faces.

Over deep lakes they went,
And over the fumaroles of the Palici
Where reeking pools boil sulphur.
Past the walled stronghold
Of the Bacchiae, who came from Corinth
And built their city
Between a large and a small harbour.

Near Cyane and Pisaean Arethusa
Jagged headlands clasp a narrow cove
Named after Cyane, who lives there –
Among all Sicily's nymphs the most famous.
Cyane
Reared from the water to her waist
And recognised Proserpina.
'You have gone too far, Pluto,' she cried.
'You cannot be son-in-law to Ceres
If she does not want you.
You should not have kidnapped this child
But asked for her hand according to custom.
The comparison is remote
But I was loved by Anapis.
He did not carry me off in a violent passion.
He never alarmed me. He was gentle.
And after a courtship of prayers
I was willingly won.'

Cyane stretched her arms as she spoke,
To block the path of the horses.
Then the son of Saturn, in a fury,
Plunged his royal sceptre
Down through the bed of her pool
And called to his savage horses.
The bottom of the pool split wide open,
And they dived –
Horses, chariot, Pluto and his prize –
Straight into hell.

Cyane bewailed the rape of the goddess
And the violation of her fountain.

She wept over these wrongs
In secret, as if her heart
Were weeping its blood.
Nothing could comfort her.
Gradually, her sorrow
Melted her into the very waters
Of which she had been the goddess.
Her limbs thinned, her bones became pliant,
Her nails softened. Swiftly she vanished
Into flowing water – first
Her slighter parts, her hair, fingers,
Feet, legs, then her shoulders,
Her back, her breasts, her sides, and at last
No longer blood but clear simple water
Flowed through her veins, and her whole body
Became clear simple water. Nothing remained
To hold or kiss but a twisting current of water.

In despair
Ceres ransacked the earth.
No dawn sodden with dew
Ever found her resting. The evening star
Never found her weary.

She had torn up two pine trees,
Kindled both in Etna,
And holding them high
Through the long nights
Lit her path of glittering frost.

When the sun rose to console her,
Melting the stars, she strode on –
From rising to setting seeking her daughter.
But fatigue and, worse than fatigue, thirst,
Finally overtook her.

Looking for a stream, she found a cottage.
She knocked and asked for water.
An old woman brought her a drink
Of crushed herbs and barley.
While Ceres drank, a boy stared at her –

A cocky brat, who jeered
And called her a greedy guzzling old witch.

His mouth was still wide, his eyes laughing,
When the whole jugful of broth hit him in the face.
The goddess went on glaring at him

As the speckles of the herbs and barley
Stained into his skin, and his arms
Shrank to legs but skinnier,
His whole bodyful of mischief
Shrank to a shape smaller than a lizard

With a long tail.
The old woman let out a cry
And reached for him, but was frightened to touch him
As he scrambled for cover –
He had become a newt.

The lands and the seas
Across which Ceres roamed
Make too long a list.
Searching the whole earth she found herself
Right back where she had started – Sicily.

And so she came to the fount of Cyane,
Who would have told her everything
But her mouth and tongue were dumb water.
Yet they could convey something.
Proserpina's girdle had fallen

Into the pool. Now Cyane's currents
Rolled this to the surface, floating it
Past the startled eyes of the mother.
It was as if only now
Ceres first heard of her loss.

She ripped her hair out in knots.
She hammered her breasts with her clenched fists.
Yet still she knew nothing
Of where her daughter might be.
She accused every country on earth,

Reproached them all for their ingratitude,
Called them unworthy of their harvests.
Above the rest, she cursed Sicily
That had kept this token of her daughter.
Then she slew man and beast in the furrow

With an instant epidemic, throughout the island.
She broke up the ploughs with her bare hands,
Forbade the fields to bear a crop
Of any kind. She made all seed sterile.
This island, that had boasted its plenty

Throughout the world, lay barren.
As soon as the blade showed green – the grain died.
Floods, heatwaves, and tempests
Sluiced away or dried and blew off the tilth.
The bared seeds were collected by birds.

Whatever managed to grow
Grew clogged and matted
With what nobody wanted –
Briars, thistles, thick, fat, creeping weeds
That defied the farmer.

Then Arethusa, the nymph that Alpheus loved,
Lifted her head from her pool,
Swept back her streaming hair, and called to Ceres:
'Great Mother of earth's harvests,
You who have searched through the whole world

'For your vanished daughter,
You have laboured enough, but have raged too much
Against the earth, which was always loyal to you.
The earth is innocent. If she opened herself
To the ravisher, who struck her so cruelly,

'She was far from willing. I am not defending
My own land. I am from Elis,
Born in Pisa. Though I arrived here
A stranger to Sicily, now I love it
Above all other places.

'This is now the home of Arethusa.
I shall live here for ever. And I beg you,
Goddess, to protect it.
Some day, when you are happier,
There will be time for me to tell you

'Why I left my home, and crossed the seas
To come to Ortygia.
Enough that I roamed through the earth, under the earth.

The earth's deepest caves opened a pathway,
Till I came up here – and raising my head

'Recognised the stars I had almost forgotten.
But while I was under the earth
As I slid through the Stygian pool
In the underworld, I felt myself
Reflecting a face that looked down at me.

'It was your Proserpina.
She was not happy. Her face was pinched with fear.
Nevertheless, she was a great queen –
The greatest in that kingdom of spectres.
She is the reigning consort of hell's tyrant.'

Ceres seemed to be turning to stone
As she listened.
For a long time she was like stone.
Then her stupor was shattered by a scream of fury
As she leaped into her chariot.

Jupiter was astonished
When she materialised in front of him,
Her hair one wild snarl of disarray,
Her face inflamed and swollen with sobbing,
And her voice hacking at him, attacking:

'She is your daughter –
Not only mine, but yours too –
You have to do something.
If her mother's pleas are powerless
Maybe her father's heart will stir for her.

'Don't love her any the less
For my part in her.
After my long search, our daughter is found.
If you can call it finding to have unearthed her
Where she is lost for ever.

'Only let me have her back now
And I would forgive whoever took her,
Even though not a hair of her were mine.
A bandit, a ruffian, is no husband
For a daughter of Jove.'

The high god answered calmly:
'I love our daughter no less than you do.
I am bound to her by blood no less than you are.
But see things as they stand. Let your words
Fit the facts. Is this a theft

'Or an act of love? Once you accept him,
This is a son-in-law to be proud of.
Even if he were worthless
He is still the brother of Jupiter.
As it is, in everything

'He is my equal, only not so lucky
In the lottery
That gave heaven to me and hell to him.
Still, if you are determined to take her from him
You can have her – but on one condition.

'The sole condition –
Fixed by the Fates –
Is this:
She can return to heaven
On condition, hear me, on condition

'That she never tasted hell's food.'
Jupiter finished. And Ceres was away
To collect her daughter.
But the Fates stopped her.
Proserpina had eaten something.

Absently straying through Pluto's
Overloaded orchard, she had plucked
A pomegranate. Picked its hard rind open
And sucked the glassy flesh from seven seeds.
Almost nothing, but more than enough.

And she had been observed, as she nibbled,
By Ascalaphus. Orphne,
A nymph well known
In the sunless forest of Avernus,
Impregnated by Acheron, her husband,

Had produced this tell-tale,
Who now blabbed
What he had spied through the leaves,

So closing hell's gates on Proserpina.
The Queen of the Underworld groaned,

Scooped a handful of water
From the infernal river Phlegethon
And throwing it in the face of that babbler
Transformed it to an owl's –
A face all beak and huge eyes.

Ascalaphus fainted.
He came to
Between big brown wings,
His human shape gone.
Now nearly all head,

The rest of him – long feathery legs,
With feet that were nothing
But bunches of long hooks,
And wings that seemed almost too heavy to lift.
He had become an owl,

A sleepy owl, hated by men,
The bird with a screech you'd think a corpse
Might make if a corpse
Could float up from the underworld
With bad news for you and yours.

And maybe that spy got his deserts
For his mischief.
But what did the daughters of Achelous do wrong?
They too were turned into birds
In everything but their faces.

Was it bad luck by association
To have been Proserpina's playmates
At the flower-picking –
And did their singing, their miraculous chorus,
Fail to redeem them?

No, they too had gone searching for her
All over the world. In the end
They prayed for wings to cross the seas
And tell the ocean depths of their trouble.
The gods consented, and the amazed girls

Saw their bodies equipped with golden plumage,
And the wings and feet of birds. But their singing,
So loved by the gods, escaped this mutation.
Their tongues, their throats, their voices remained unaltered –
Live shrines of unearthly human voices.

Now Jupiter intervened
Between his brother and his grieving sister.
He parted the year's round into two halves.
From this day, Proserpina,
The goddess who shares both kingdoms, divides her year

Between her husband in hell, among spectres,
And her mother on earth, among flowers.
Her nature, too, is divided. One moment
Gloomy as hell's king, but the next
Bright as the sun's mass, bursting from clouds.

Arethusa

Ceres, happy again to have her daughter,
Returned to Arethusa, curious
To learn why she ran from home, and just how
She became a sacred fountain.

The pool grew calm as the goddess
Rose out of the depth.
She gathered up her green hair and from it
Wringing the heavy water began
The old story of how she was loved by a river.

'I was a nymph of Achaia.
None loved the woods,
And setting their hunting nets, as keenly as I did.
I was all action and energy,
And never thought of my looks.
Even so, my looks, yes, my beauty
Made others think of me.
The fame of my appearance burdened me.
The attractions
That all the other girls were sick to have
Sickened me, that I had them.
Because they attracted men, I thought them evil.

'There came a day
I had exhausted myself
In the Stymphalian Forest. The heat was frightening.
And my efforts, harrying the game,
Had doubled its effect on me.
I found a stream, deep but not too deep,
Quiet and clear – so clear,
Every grain of sand seemed magnified.
And so quiet, the broad clarity
Hardly dimpled.
The poplars and willows that drank at it
Were doubled in a flawless mirror.
I waded in – footsoles, ankles, knees.
Then stripped,
Hung my clothes on a willow
And plunged.
As I played there, churning the surface,
To and fro, diving to the bottom,
Swimming on my back, my side, my belly,
I felt a strange stir bulge in the current –
It scared me so badly
I scrambled up on to the bank.
A voice came after me:
"Why leave in such a hurry, Arethusa?"
It was Alpheus, in the swirl of his waters.
"Why leave in such a hurry?" he cried again.
I saw my clothes on the willow across the river.
I had come out on the wrong bank.
Naked as I was, I just ran –
That brought him after me
All the more eagerly – my nakedness
Though it was no invitation
Gave his assault no option.
I was like the dove in a panic
Dodging through trees when the hawk
Rides its slipstream
Tight as a magnet.

'The peak of Orchomenus went past,
And Psophis –
They were stepping stones
That my feet barely touched. Then Cyllene

And the knapped, flinty ridges
Of Maenalus, Erymanthus, and Elis –
The map rolled under me
As in a flight in a dream. He could not
Overtake me
But he could outlast me.
Over savannahs, mountains black with forest,
Pathless crags and gorges. But soon
The sun pressed on my back and I saw
That I ran in a long and leaping shadow –
The very shape of my terror –
And I heard the stones flying
From his striding feet, and his panting breath
That seemed to tug at my hair.

'In an agony of effort
I called to Diana:
"Help, or it's all over with me.
Remember how I carried your bow,
Your quiverful of arrows. Help me,
Help me, Oh help me."

'The goddess heard and was stirred.
She brought up a dense mist
And hid me.
I smothered my gasping lungs. I tried
To muffle my heartbeat. And I froze.
I could hear the river-god, Alpheus,
Blindly casting about –
Twice he almost trod on me
Where I crouched under deep weeds.
"Arethusa!" he kept shouting, "Arethusa!"
As if I would answer!
You can imagine what I was feeling –
What the lamb feels when the wolf's jaws
Are ripping the edge of the shed door.
Or what the hare feels
Peering through the wall of grass blades
When the circling hounds lift their noses.
But Alpheus persisted.
Circling the clump of mist, he could see clearly
My track that had gone in had not come out.
When I understood this

A sudden sweat chilled my whole body.
It streamed from me.
It welled from my hair. It puddled under my feet.
In the time it takes to tell you this
I had become a spring, a brisk stream,
A river, flowing away down the hillside.
But the river-god recognised me.
And he too dissolved his human shape,
Poured himself into his true nature
And mingled his current with my current.

'But Diana helped me again. She split earth open.
I dived into the gorge
And underground I came to Ortygia –
This land,
Which bears the name of my own beloved goddess,
Brought me back to light. That is my story.'

Tiresias

One time, Jupiter, happy to be idle,
Swept the cosmic mystery aside
And draining another goblet of ambrosia
Teased Juno, who drowsed in bliss beside him:
'This love of male and female's a strange business.
Fifty-fifty investment in the madness,
Yet she ends up with nine-tenths of the pleasure.'

Juno's answer was: 'A man might think so.
It needs more than a mushroom in your cup
To wake a wisdom that can fathom which
Enjoys the deeper pleasure, man or woman.
It needs the solid knowledge of a soul
Who having lived and loved in woman's body
Has also lived and loved in the body of a man.'

Jupiter laughed aloud: 'We have the answer.
There is a fellow called Tiresias.
Strolling to watch the birds and hear the bees
He came across two serpents copulating.
He took the opportunity to kill

Both with a single blow, but merely hurt them –
And found himself transformed into a woman.

'After the seventh year of womanhood,
Strolling to ponder on what women ponder
She saw in that same place the same two serpents
Knotted as before in copulation.
"If your pain can still change your attacker
Just as you once changed me, then change me back."
She hit the couple with a handy stick,

'And there he stood as male as any man.'
'He'll explain,' cried Juno, 'why you are
Slave to your irresistible addiction
While the poor nymphs you force to share it with you
Do all they can to shun it.' Jupiter
Asked Tiresias: 'In their act of love
Who takes the greater pleasure, man or woman?'

'Woman,' replied Tiresias, 'takes nine-tenths.'
Juno was so angry – angrier
Than is easily understandable –
She struck Tiresias and blinded him.
'You've seen your last pretty snake, for ever.'
But Jove consoled him: 'That same blow,' he said,
'Has opened your inner eye, like a nightscope. See:

'The secrets of the future – they are yours.'

Echo and Narcissus

When the prophetic vision awoke
Behind the blind eyes of Tiresias
And stared into the future,

The first to test how deeply he saw
And how lucidly
Was Liriope, a swarthy nymph of the fountain.

She was swept off her feet by the river Cephisus
Who rolled her into the bed of a dark pool,
Then cast her up on the shingle pregnant.

The boy she bore, even in his cradle,
Had a beauty that broke hearts.
She named this child Narcissus. Gossips

Came to Tiresias: 'Can her boy live long
With such perfect beauty?' The seer replied:
'Yes, unless he learns to know himself.'

All regarded these words as a riddle –
Till time solved them with a strange madness.
A stranger death completed the explanation.

In his sixteenth year Narcissus,
Still a slender boy but already a man,
Infatuated many. His beauty had flowered,

But something glassy about it, a pride,
Kept all his admirers at a distance.
None dared be familiar, let alone touch him.

A day came, out on the mountain
Narcissus was driving and netting and killing the deer
When Echo saw him.

Echo who cannot be silent
When another speaks. Echo who cannot
Speak at all
Unless another has spoken.
Echo, who always answers back.

In those days, this nymph was more than a voice.
She had a pretty body.
But her prattle was the same –
Never anything more
Than the last word or two, the tail end
Of what she heard uttered by others,
Which she repeated over and over.

Juno had stricken her
With this odd affliction.
When Juno, following a tip-off,
Would be stalking Jupiter, to catch him
In some dell, with a nymph,
Echo made it her duty
To engage the goddess in an unending
Rigmarole of chatter. Till the nymph

Had pleased the god enough
To be let go.
Echo did this so often,
And so artfully, Juno
In a rage turned on her: 'Your tongue
Has led me in such circles,
Henceforth
It will have to trail
Helplessly after others, uttering
Only the last words, helplessly,
Of what you last heard.'

The moment Echo saw Narcissus
She was in love. She followed him
Like a starving wolf
Following a stag too strong to be tackled.
And like a cat in winter at a fire
She could not edge close enough
To what singed her, and would burn her.
She almost burst
With longing to call out to him and somehow
Let him know what she felt.
But she had to wait
For some other to speak
So she could snatch their last words
With whatever sense they might lend her.

It so happened, Narcissus
Had strayed apart
From his companions.
He hallooed them: 'Where are you?
I'm here.' And Echo
Caught at the syllables as if they were precious:
'I'm here,' she cried, 'I'm here' and 'I'm here' and 'I'm here.'

Narcissus looked around wildly.
'I'll stay here,' he shouted.
'You come to me.' And 'Come to me,'
Shouted Echo. 'Come to me,
To me, to me, to me.'
Narcissus stood baffled,
Whether to stay or go. He began to run,
Calling as he ran: 'Stay there.' But Echo

Cried back, weeping to utter it, 'Stay there,
Stay there, stay there, stay there.'
Narcissus stopped and listened. Then, more quietly,
'Let's meet halfway. Come.' And Echo
Eagerly repeated it: 'Come.'

But when she emerged from the undergrowth
Her expression pleading,
Her arms raised to embrace him,
Narcissus turned and ran.
'No,' he cried 'no, I would sooner be dead
Than let you touch me.' Echo collapsed in sobs,
As her voice lurched among the mountains:
'Touch me, touch me, touch me, touch me.'

Echo moped under the leaves.
Humiliated, she hid
In the deep woods. From that day
Like a hurt lynx, for her
Any cave was a good home.
But love was fixed in her body
Like a barbed arrow. There it festered
With his rejection. Sleeplessly
She brooded over the pain,
Wasting away as she suffered,
The petal of her beauty
Fading and shrivelling, falling from her –
Leaving her voice and bones.
Her bones, they say, turned
Into stone, sinking into the humus.
Her voice roamed off by itself,
Unseen in the forest, unseen
On the empty mountainside –
Though all could hear it
Living the only life left to Echo.

Narcissus had rebuffed her adoration
As he had the passionate attentions
Of many another nymph of the wilderness
And many another man.
One of these, mocked and rejected,
Lifted his hands to heaven:
'Let Narcissus love and suffer

As he has made us suffer.
Let him, like us, love and know it is hopeless.
And let him, like Echo, perish of anguish.'
Nemesis, the corrector,
Heard this prayer and granted it.

There was a pool of perfect water.
No shepherd had ever driven sheep
To trample the margins. No cattle
Had slobbered their muzzles in it
And befouled it. No wild beast
Had ever dashed through it.
No bird had ever paddled there preening and bathing.
Only surrounding grasses drank its moisture
And though the arching trees kept it cool
No twigs rotted in it, and no leaves.

Weary with hunting and the hot sun
Narcissus found this pool.
Gratefully he stretched out full length,
To cup his hands in the clear cold
And to drink. But as he drank
A strange new thirst, a craving, unfamiliar,
Entered his body with the water,
And entered his eyes
With the reflection in the limpid mirror.
He could not believe the beauty
Of those eyes that gazed into his own.
As the taste of water flooded him
So did love. So he lay, mistaking
That picture of himself on the meniscus
For the stranger who could make him happy.

He lay, like a fallen garden statue,
Gaze fixed on his image in the water,
Comparing it to Bacchus or Apollo,
Falling deeper and deeper in love
With what so many had loved so hopelessly.
Not recognising himself
He wanted only himself. He had chosen
From all the faces he had ever seen
Only his own. He was himself
The torturer who now began his torture.

He plunged his arms deep to embrace
One who vanished in agitated water.
Again and again he kissed
The lips that seemed to be rising to kiss his
But dissolved, as he touched them,
Into a soft splash and a shiver of ripples.
How could he clasp and caress his own reflection?
And still he could not comprehend
What the deception was, what the delusion.
He simply became more excited by it.
Poor misguided boy! Why clutch so vainly
At such a brittle figment? What you hope
To lay hold of has no existence.
Look away and what you love is nowhere.
This is your own shadow.
It comes with you. While you stay it stays.
So it will go
When you go – if ever you can go.

He could not go.
He wanted neither to eat nor to sleep.
Only to lie there – eyes insatiably
Gazing into the eyes that were no eyes.
This is how his own eyes destroyed him.

He sat up, and lifting his arms
Called to the forest: 'You trees,
Was there ever a love
As cruel as mine is to me?
You aged voyeurs, you eavesdroppers,
Among all the lovers who have hidden
Under your listening leaves
Was there ever a love
As futureless as mine?
What I love is untouchable.
We are kept apart
Neither by seas nor mountains
Nor the locked-up gates of cities.
Nothing at all comes between us –
Only the skin of water.
He wants my love as I want his.
As I lean to kiss him
He lifts up his face to kiss me –

Why can't I reach him? Why can't he reach me?
In that very touch of the kiss
We vanish from each other – he vanishes
Into the skin of water.

'Who are you? Come out. Come up
Onto the land. I never saw beauty
To compare with yours. Oh why do you always
Dodge away at the last moment
And leave me with my arms full of nothing
But water and the memory of an image.
It cannot be my ugliness
Or my age that repels you,
If all the nymphs are so crazy about me.
Your face is full of love
As your eyes look into my eyes
I see it, and my hope shakes me.
I stretch my arms to you, you stretch yours
As eagerly to me. You laugh when I laugh.
I have watched your tears through my tears.
When I tell you my love I see your lips
Seeming to tell me yours – though I cannot hear it.

'You are me. Now I see that.
I see through my own reflection.
But it is too late.
I am in love with myself.
I torture myself. What am I doing –
Loving or being loved?
What can my courtship gain?
What I want, I am.
But being all that I long for –
That is my destitution.
Why can't I get apart from my body?
This is a new kind of lover's prayer.
To wish himself apart from the one he loves.

'This impotent grief
Is taking my strength
And my life.
My beauty is in full bloom –
But I am a cut flower.
Let death come quickly –

Carry me off
Where this pain
Can never follow.
The one I loved should be let live –
He should live on after me, blameless.
But when I go – both of us go.'

Then Narcissus wept into the pool.
His tears shattered the still shrine
And his image blurred.
He cried after it: 'Don't leave me.
If I cannot touch you at least let me see you.
Let me nourish my starving, luckless love –
If only by looking.'
Then he ripped off his shirt,
And beat his bare chest with white fists.

The skin flushed under the blows.
When Narcissus saw this
In the image returned to perfection
Where the pool had calmed –
It was too much for him.
Like wax near the flame,
Or like hoar-frost
Where the first ray of the morning sun
Creeps across it,
He melted – consumed
By his love.
Like Echo's the petal of his beauty
Faded, shrivelled, fell –
He disappeared from his own eyes.
Till nothing remained of the body
That had driven Echo to distraction.

Echo was watching all this misery.
Remembering how it happened before
To her, when he ran from her,
Her anger blazed
But her pity smothered it.
And when he moaned, 'Alas,' she wept,
And groaned. 'Alas.' His last words,
As he gazed into the dark pool,
'Farewell, you incomparable boy,

I have loved you in vain'
Returned from her lips with sorrow doubled:
'I have loved you in vain.'
And after his last 'Farewell'
Came her last 'Farewell.'
He pillowed his head on the grass.
So finally death
Closed the eyes that had loved themselves too much.

When he entered the Land of the Dead
Narcissus could not resist it –
He ran straight to the banks of the Styx
And gazed down at the smear of his shadow
Trembling on the fearful current.
His sisters, the nymphs of the fountains,
Cropped their hair and mourned him
In a lamenting song – and far off,
Wandering heartbroken among the hills
Echo sang the refrain.

When men came with timber
To build a pyre, and with crackling torches
For the solemnity
That would reduce Narcissus
To a handful of dust in an urn –
No corpse could be found.
But there, in the pressed grass where he had perished,
A tall flower stood unbroken –
Bowed, a ruff of white petals
Round a dainty bugle centre
Yellow as egg yolk.

Yes, it was this quiet woodland flower
Trumpeted the fame of Tiresias
Throughout Achaia.

Erisychthon

Some are transformed just once
And live their whole lives after in that shape.
Others have a facility
For changing themselves as they please.

Proteus, who haunts the shadowy seas
That scarf this earth, is glimpsed as a young man
Who becomes of a sudden a lion
That becomes a wild boar ripping the ground,

Yet flows forward, hidden, through grass, without sound
As a serpent, that emerges
As a towering bull under down-bent horns,
Or hides, among stones, a simple stone.

Or stands as a tree alone.
Or liquefies, and collapses, shapeless,
Into water, a pouring river. Sometimes
He is the river's opposite – fire.

Another with a similar power
Was Erisychthon's daughter,
The wife of Autolycus. Her father
Gave to the gods nothing but mockery.

Without a qualm he cut down every tree
In the sacred grove of Ceres –
An ancient wood that had never, before that day,
Jumped to the axe's stroke.

Among those trees
One prodigious oak was all to itself
A tangled forest. Its boughs were bedecked with wreaths
And votive tributes – each for a prayer

Ceres had some time granted. Dryads there
Danced a holy circle around its bole
Or joined hands to embrace it –
A circumference of twenty paces.

Erisychthon ignores all this as
He assesses the volume of its timber,
Then orders his men to fell it.
Seeing their reluctance, he roars:

'If this tree were your deity, that every clown adores,
And not merely a tree you think she favours,
Nevertheless, those twigs away there at the top
Would have to come down now, as the rest falls.'

He snatches an axe – and hauls
The weight of the broad head up and back.
But in that moment, as the blade hangs
Poised for the first downstroke, shudderings

Swarm through the whole tree, to its outermost twigs
And a groan bursts out of the deep grain.
At the same time
Every bough goes grey – every leaf

Whitens, and every acorn whitens.
Then the blade bites and the blood leaps
As from the neck of a great bull when it drops
Under the axe at the altar.

Everybody stares paralysed.
Only one man protests. The Thessalian
Erisychthon turns with eyes stretched
Incredulous. 'Your pious cares,' he bellows,

'Are misplaced.' And he follows
That first swing at the oak with another
At the protester's neck, whose head
Spins through the air and bounces.

Then the oak, as he turns back to it, pronounces,
In a clear voice, these words:
'I live in this tree. I am a nymph,
Beloved by Ceres, the goddess.

'With my last breath, I curse you. As this oak
Falls on the earth, your punishment
Will come down on you with all its weight.
That is my consolation. And your fate.'

Erisychthon ignored her. He just kept going,
Undercutting the huge trunk, till ropes
Brought the whole mass down, jolting the earth,
Devastating the underbrush around it.

All the nymphs of the sacred grove mourned it.
Dressed in black, they came to Ceres,
Crying for the criminal to be punished,
Bewailing the desecration. The goddess listened.

Then the summer farms, the orchards, the vineyards,
The whole flushed, ripening harvest, shivered
As she pondered how to make his death
A parable of her anger.

If his cruelty, greed, arrogance
Had left him a single drop of human feeling
What the goddess did now
Would have drained mankind of its pity.

She condemned him
To Hunger –
But infinite, insatiable Hunger,
The agony of Hunger as a frenzy.

Destiny has separated Hunger
So far from the goddess of abundance
They can never meet, therefore Ceres
Commissioned a mountain spirit, an oread:

'Hear what I say and do not be afraid.
Far away to the north of Scythia
Lies a barren country, leafless, dreadful:
Ice permanent as iron, air that aches.

'A howling land of rocks, gales and snow.
There mad Hunger staggers. Go. Bid Hunger
Take possession of Erisychthon's belly.
Tell her she has power over all my powers

'To nourish Erisychthon. Let all I pour
Or push down this fool's gullet only deepen
His emptiness. Go. My dragon-drawn chariot
Will make the terrific journey seem slight.'

The nymph climbed away and her first halt
Was the top of Caucasus.
She soon found Hunger raking with her nails
To bare the root of a tiny rock-wort

Till her teeth could catch and tear it.
In shape and colour her face was a skull, blueish.
Her lips a stretched hole of frayed leather
Over bleeding teeth. Her skin

So glossy and so thin
You could see the internal organs through it.
Her pelvic bone was like a bare bone.
The stump wings of her hip bones splayed open.

As she bowed, her rib-cage swung from her backbone
In a varnish of tissue. Her ankle joints
And her knee joints were huge bulbs, ponderous, grotesque,
On her spindly shanks. The oread

Knew danger when she saw it. She proclaimed
The command of the goddess from a safe distance,
The whole speech only took a minute or so –
Yet a swoon of hunger left her trembling.

She got away fast.
All the way back to Thessaly
She gave the dragons their head.
Now hear me.

Though Hunger lives only in opposition
To Ceres, yet she obeys her. She soars through darkness
Across the earth, to the house of Erisychthon
And bends above the pillow where his face

Snores with open mouth.
Her skeletal embrace goes around him.
Her shrunk mouth clamps over his mouth
And she breathes

Into every channel of his body
A hurricane of starvation.
The job done, she vanishes,
She hurtles away, out of the lands of plenty,

As if sucked back
Into the vacuum –
Deprivation's hollow territories
That belong to her, and that she belongs to.

Erisychthon snores on –
But in spite of the god of sleep's efforts
To comfort him, he dreams he sits at a banquet
Where the food tastes of nothing. A nightmare.

He grinds his molars on air, with a dry creaking,
Dreaming that he grinds between his molars
A feast of nothing, food that is like air.
At last he writhes awake in twisting, knotted

Cramps of hunger. His jaws
Seem to have their own life, snapping at air
With uncontrollable eagerness to be biting
Into food and swallowing – like a cat

Staring at a bird out of reach.
His stomach feels like a fist
Gripping and wringing out
The mere idea of food.

He calls for food. Everything edible
Out of the sea and earth. When it comes
Dearth is all he sees where tables bend
Under the spilling plenty. Emptying

Bowls of heaped food, all he craves for
Is bigger bowls heaped higher. Food
For a whole city cannot sate him. Food
For a whole nation leaves him faint with hunger.

As every river on earth
Pours its wealth towards ocean
That is always sweeping for more,
Draining the continents,

And as fire grows hungrier
The more fuel it finds
So, famished by food,
The gullet of Erisychthon, gulping down

Whatever its diameter can manage
Through every waking moment,
Spares a mouthful
Only to shout for more.

This voracity, this bottomless belly,
As if his throat opened
Into the void of stars,
Engulfed his entire wealth.

His every possession was converted
To what he could devour
Till nothing remained except a daughter.
This only child deserved a better father.

His last chattel, he cashed her in for food.
He sold her, at the market.
But she was far too spirited
To stay as a bought slave.

Stretching her arms towards the sea, she cried:
'You who ravished my maidenhead, save me.'
Neptune knew the voice of his pretty victim
And granted the prayer. Her new owner,

Who minutes ago was admiring the girl he had bought,
Now saw only Neptune's art – featured
And clothed like a fisherman. Perplexed,
He spoke to this stranger directly.

'You with your fishing tackle, hiding your barbs
In tiny gobbets of bait – may you have good weather
And plenty of silly fish that never notice
The hook till it's caught them! – Can you tell me

'Where is the girl who was here a moment ago?
Her hair loose, and dressed in the cheapest things,
She was standing right here where her footprints –
Look – stop, and go no further. Where is she?'

The girl guessed what the god had done for her.
She smiled to hear herself asked where she might be.
Then to the man parted from his money:
'I'm sorry, my attention has been fixed

'On the fish in this hole. But I promise you,
By all the help I pray for from Neptune,
Nobody has come along this beach
For quite a while – and certainly no woman.'

The buyer had to believe her. He went off, baffled.
The girl took one step and was back
In her own shape. Next thing,
She was telling her father. And he,

Elated, saw business. After that
On every market he sold her in some new shape.
A trader bought a horse,
Paid for it and found the halter empty

Where a girl sat selling mushrooms.
A costly parrot escaped its purchaser
Into an orchard – where a girl picked figs.
One bought an ox that vanished from its pasture

Where a girl gathered cowslips.
So Erisychthon's daughter plied her talent
For taking any shape to cheat a buyer –
Straight and crooked alike.

All to feed the famine in her father.
But none of it was enough. Whatever he ate
Maddened and tormented that hunger
To angrier, uglier life. The life

Of a monster no longer a man. And so,
At last, the inevitable.
He began to savage his own limbs.
And there, at a final feast, devoured himself.

Semele

Juno was incensed when she learned it:
Jove had impregnated Semele.
Curses
Came bursting out of her throat, but she swallowed them
Hissing: 'Anger is lost on Jupiter. Only

'Let me get my hands on that woman.
As sure as I am Juno, the Queen of Heaven,
As sure as I grasp the sceptre
And am Jove's wife and sister,
As sure as I am at very least his sister,

'I shall destroy that whore.
Let others excuse her. They say she takes nothing
If this taste of his love is all she takes.

They say she's no more trespassed on my marriage
Than a cloud-shadow crossing a mountain.

'They should know the fact.
His brat is in her womb.
And that is a kind of marriage –
Durable as the life of that creature.
Jupiter's own child – out of her womb!

'More than I ever gave him.
A splendid-looking woman –
And so pleased with herself, to be so splendid.
Her pleasure is a delusion.
Her beauty comes at a cost, she will find.

'I am not the daughter of Saturn
If she does not stumble very soon
Headlong into hell's horrible river,
Pushed there and shoved under
By the loving caresses of none other

'Than her darling, the high god Jupiter.'
Juno rose from her throne
Like a puff of smoke from a volcano.
In a globe of whirling light
She arrived at the home of Semele.

Semele
Looked up at a shadow. There,
Standing on her threshold, a gummy old woman –
White wisps,
A sack of shrivelled skin propped on a stick,

Bent as if broken-backed,
Tottering at each step to stay upright,
And her voice
Quavering like a dying pulse. This figure
Was the very double of Beroe –

Semele's old nurse from Epidaurus.
Semele recognised and welcomed
Her old nurse. She never doubted a moment.
Their gossiping began to circle,
Touching at Semele's swollen belly.

Juno sighed. Her lizard throat trembled.
'Ah, I pray you are right.
I pray that Jupiter is the sire, as you say.
But who can be sure?
Something about it smells fishy to me.

'You wouldn't be the first simple virgin
To hear an unscrupulous seducer
Reveal his greatest secret – that he is a god.
Even if he spoke the truth and you are right –
Even if the babe in your womb is Jove's –

'Supposition will not satisfy
The questions
That will surely occur to the coming child.
That child
Is going to demand real proof.

'Jupiter should give you real proof
That he is himself. Ask him to face you
Naked as for Juno in heaven,
In all his omnipotence and glory,
The great god of the triple-headed sceptre.'

Listening to the twisty words of Juno
Semele heard
Only the purest wisdom.
She asked her divine lover for a love-gift –
A gift she would name only if it were granted.

Jupiter smiled: 'Whatever you want – name it,
You shall have it. I swear
On the terror who holds all heaven in awe,
The god of hell's river, you shall have it.'
Semele's laugh was as triumphant

As she was ignorant
Of the game she was playing.
She laughed
To have won the simple trick
That would wipe her out of existence

So easily. 'I want to see you,' she said,
'Exactly as Juno sees you when she opens
Her arms and body to you. As if I were Juno,

Come to me naked – in your divine form.'
Too late

Jove guessed what she was asking.
He tried to gag her
With his hand but her tongue
And her lips had hurried it all out
And he had heard it. He groaned.

His oath could no more be retracted
Than her words could be unuttered.
Yes, God wept a little
Gathering the foggy clouds around him
As he withdrew into heaven.

Now he piled above him the purple
Topheavy thunderheads
Churning with tornadoes
And inescapable bolts of lightning.
Yet he did what he could to insulate

And filter
The nuclear blast
Of his naked impact –
Such as had demolished Typhoeus
And scattered his hundred hands.

He chose
A slighter manifestation
Fashioned, like the great bolts, by the Cyclops
But more versatile – known in heaven
As the general deterrent.

Arrayed in this fashion
Jove came to the house of Cadmus' daughter.
He entered her bedchamber,
But as he bent over her sleeping face
To kiss her

Her eyes opened wide, saw him
And burst into flame.
Then her whole body lit up
With the glare
That explodes the lamp –

In that splinter of a second,
Before her blazing shape
Became a silhouette of sooty ashes
The foetus was snatched from her womb.
If this is a true story

That babe was then inserted surgically
Into a makeshift uterus, in Jove's thigh,
To be born, at full term, not from his mother
But from his father – reborn. Son of the Father.
And this was the twice-born god – the god Bacchus.

Peleus and Thetis

Proteus, old as the ocean,
Said to Thetis: 'Goddess
Of all the salt waters,
When you bear a son the boy will be
The wonder of the world.
He will make a man of himself
So far superior to his father
His father's fame will be – to have been his father.
Jupiter heard the prophecy just in time
To deflect his lust
From the maidenhead of Thetis.
He switched it
To the next on his list. But as a precaution,
Too well aware of his own frailty,
He sent a substitute to neutralise
The prize of the prediction and its sequel:
Peleus, his grandson, son of Aeacus.
'Go,' he commanded. 'No matter what it takes
To bring it about, impregnate that virgin.'

Tucked into Hamonia's coast is a bay
Between promontories, deep incurved,
Like a sickle.
A perfect harbour if only the water were deeper.
But the sea sweeps in
Barely covering a plain of pale sand.
The beach is perfect,
No seaweed, and the sand

Powdery light, yet firm to the foot.
The hanging bulge of the land is plumped with myrtles.
Beneath those leaves a cave climbs from the sea.
It looks like the work of man. But a deity used it.
This was the secret bedchamber of Thetis.
Naked, she surfed in on a dolphin
To sleep there. And there Peleus found her.

He woke her with a kiss.
First she was astonished, then furious.
He applied all his cunning to seduce her.
He exhausted his resources. None of it worked.
His every soft word hardened her colder.
If they had been two cats, he was thinking,
She would have been flattened to the wall,
Her mask fixed in a snarl, spitting at him.
He took his cue from that. Where argument
Fails, violence follows. His strength
Could have trussed her up like a chicken
If she had stayed the woman he woke with a kiss.
But before he knew
He was grappling with an enormous sea-bird,
Its body powerful as a seal, and its beak
Spiking his skull like a claw-hammer.
A bird that was suddenly a wren
Escaping towards the tangle of myrtles,
Bolting past his cheek like a shuttlecock
That he caught with a snatch of pure luck,
And found himself
Gripping a tigress by the shag of her throat
As her paw hit him with the impact
Of a fifty-kilo lump of snaggy bronze
Dropped from a battlement.
He rolled from the cave and landed flat on his back
In cushioning shallow water.

Then he slaughtered sheep,
Burned their entrails, heaped incense
Onto the fatty blaze, poured wine
Into the salt wash and called on the sea-gods,
Till a shade, from the depth-gloom beyond,
Darkened into the bay's lit shallows,
And a voice hissed from the tongues of suds

That shot up the sand: 'Son of Aeacus,
This woman can be yours if you can catch her
Sleeping as before in her cavern.
But this time, bind her, bind her tight with thongs,
Before she wakes. Then hang on to her body
No matter what it becomes, no matter what monster.
Do not let her scare you –
However she transforms herself, it is her,
Dodging from shape to shape, through a hundred shapes.
Hang on
Till her counterfeit selves are all used up,
And she reappears as Thetis.'
This was the voice of Proteus. It ceased
And the long shape faded from the shallows.

Peleus hid in the myrtles. Towards sundown
The goddess came up from the deep water,
Rode into the bay, climbed into her cave
And stretched out on her couch.

She was hardly asleep
When the noosed thongs jerked tight.
Her ankles and her wrists made one bunch.
Her feet and hands were a single squirming cluster,
As if she were to be carried, slung from a pole,
Like an animal.

Peleus clinched his knot, then bundled her up
In his arms, and embraced her with all his might
As her shapes began to fight for her.
He shut his eyes and hung on, ignoring
Her frenzy of transformations
Till they shuddered to stillness. She knew she was beaten
By that relentless grip. 'Heaven has helped you,'
She panted. 'Only heaven
Could have given me to you, and made me yours.'

Then he undid her bonds. As he massaged
The circulation into her hands and feet
His caresses included her whole body.
She was content to let them take possession
Of her skin, her heart, and, at last, of her womb
Where now he planted Achilles.

Actaeon

Destiny, not guilt, was enough
For Actaeon. It is no crime
To lose your way in a dark wood.

It happened on a mountain where hunters
Had slaughtered so many animals
The slopes were patched red with the butchering places.

When shadows were shortest and the sun's heat hardest
Young Actaeon called a halt:
'We have killed more than enough for the day.

'Our nets are stiff with blood,
Our spears are caked, and our knives
Are clogged in their sheaths with the blood of a glorious hunt.

'Let's be up again in the grey dawn –
Back to the game afresh. This noon heat
Has baked the stones too hot for a human foot.'

All concurred. And the hunt was over for the day.
A deep cleft at the bottom of the mountain
Dark with matted pine and spiky cypress

Was known as Gargaphie, sacred to Diana,
Goddess of the hunt.
In the depths of this goyle was the mouth of a cavern

That might have been carved out with deliberate art
From the soft volcanic rock.
It half-hid a broad pool, perpetually shaken

By a waterfall inside the mountain,
Noisy but hidden. Often to that grotto,
Aching and burning from her hunting,

Diana came
To cool the naked beauty she hid from the world.
All her nymphs would attend her.

One held her javelin,
Her quiverful of arrows and her unstrung bow.
Another folded her cape.

Two others took off her sandals, while Crocale
The daughter of Ismenus
Whose hands were the most artful, combing out

The goddess' long hair, that the hunt had tangled,
Bunched it into a thick knot,
Though her own hair stayed as the hunt had scattered it.

Five others, Nephele, Hyale, Phiale
Psecas and Rhanis, filled great jars with water
And sluiced it over Diana's head and shoulders.

The goddess was there, in her secret pool,
Naked and bowed
Under those cascades from the mouths of jars

In the fastness of Gargaphie, when Actaeon,
Making a beeline home from the hunt
Stumbled on this gorge. Surprised to find it,

He pushed into it, apprehensive, but
Steered by a pitiless fate – whose nudgings he felt
Only as surges of curiosity.

So he came to the clearing. And saw ripples
Flocking across the pool out of the cavern.
He edged into the cavern, under ferns

That dripped with spray. He peered
Into the gloom to see the waterfall –
But what he saw were nymphs, their wild faces

Screaming at him in a commotion of water.
And as his eyes adjusted, he saw they were naked,
Beating their breasts as they screamed at him.

And he saw they were crowding together
To hide something from him. He stared harder.
Those nymphs could not conceal Diana's whiteness,

The tallest barely reached her navel. Actaeon
Stared at the goddess, who stared at him.
She twisted her breasts away, showing him her back.

Glaring at him over her shoulder
She blushed like a dawn cloud
In that twilit grotto of winking reflections,

And raged for a weapon – for her arrows
To drive through his body.
No weapon was to hand – only water.

So she scooped up a handful and dashed it
Into his astonished eyes, as she shouted:
'Now, if you can, tell how you saw me naked.'

That was all she said, but as she said it
Out of his forehead burst a rack of antlers.
His neck lengthened, narrowed, and his ears

Folded to whiskery points, his hands were hooves,
His arms long slender legs. His hunter's tunic
Slid from his dappled hide. With all this

The goddess
Poured a shocking stream of panic terror
Through his heart like blood. Actaeon

Bounded out across the cave's pool
In plunging leaps, amazed at his own lightness.
And there

Clear in the bulging mirror of his bow-wave
He glimpsed his antlered head,
And cried: 'What has happened to me?'

No words came. No sound came but a groan.
His only voice was a groan.
Human tears shone on his stag's face

From the grief of a mind that was still human.
He veered first this way, then that.
Should he run away home to the royal palace?

Or hide in the forest? The thought of the first
Dizzied him with shame. The thought of the second
Flurried him with terrors.

But then, as he circled, his own hounds found him.
The first to give tongue were Melampus
And the deep-thinking Ichnobates.

Melampus a Spartan, Ichnobates a Cretan.
The whole pack piled in after.
It was like a squall crossing a forest.

Dorceus, Pamphagus and Oribasus –
Pure Arcadians. Nebrophonus,
Strong as a wild boar, Theras, as fierce.

And Laelaps never far from them. Pterelas
Swiftest in the pack, and Agre
The keenest nose. And Hylaeus

Still lame from the rip of a boar's tusk.
Nape whose mother was a wolf, and Poemenis –
Pure sheep-dog. Harpyia with her grown pups,

Who still would never leave her.
The lanky hound Ladon, from Sicyon,
With Tigris, Dromas, Canace, Sticte and Alce,

And Asbolus, all black, and all-white Leuca.
Lacon was there, with shoulders like a lion.
Aello, who could outrun wolves, and Thous,

Lycise, at her best in a tight corner,
Her brother Cyprius, and black Harpalus
With a white star on his forehead.

Lachne, like a shaggy bear-cub. Melaneus
And the Spartan-Cretan crossbreeds
Lebros and Agriodus. Hylactor,

With the high, cracked voice, and a host of others,
Too many to name. The strung-out pack,
Locked onto their quarry,

Flowed across the landscape, over crags,
Over cliffs where no man could have followed,
Through places that seemed impossible.

Where Actaeon had so often strained
Every hound to catch and kill the quarry,
Now he strained to shake the same hounds off –

His own hounds. He tried to cry out:
'I am Actaeon – remember your master,'
But his tongue lolled wordless, while the air

Belaboured his ears with hounds' voices.
Suddenly three hounds appeared, ahead,
Raving towards him. They had been last in the pack.

But they had thought it out
And made a short cut over a mountain.
As Actaeon turned, Melanchaetes

The ringleader of this breakaway trio
Grabbed a rear ankle
In the trap of his jaws. Then the others,

Theridamus and Oristrophus, left and right,
Caught a foreleg each, and he fell.
These three pinned their master, as the pack

Poured onto him like an avalanche.
Every hound filled its jaws
Till there was hardly a mouth not gagged and crammed

With hair and muscle. Then began the tugging and the ripping.
Actaeon's groan was neither human
Nor the natural sound of a stag.

Now the hills he had played on so happily
Toyed with the echoes of his death-noises.
His head and antlers reared from the heaving pile.

And swayed – like the signalling arm
Of somebody drowning in surf.
But his friends, who had followed the pack

To this unexpected kill,
Urged them to finish the work. Meanwhile they shouted
For Actaeon – over and over for Actaeon

To hurry and witness this last kill of the day –
And such a magnificent beast –
As if he were absent. He heard his name

And wished he were as far off as they thought him.
He wished he was among them
Not suffering this death but observing

The terrible method
Of his murderers, as they knotted
Muscles and ferocity to dismember

Their own master.
Only when Actaeon's life
Had been torn from his bones, to the last mouthful,

Only then
Did the remorseless anger of Diana,
Goddess of the arrow, find peace.

Myrrha

Cinyras, the son of Paphos,
Might well have been known as Fortune's darling
If only he'd stayed childless.

The story I am now going to tell you
Is so horrible
That fathers with daughters, wherever you are,
Had better not listen to it –
I beg you to stay clear.
Or if you find my song irresistible
Let your ear
Now become incredulous.
May you convince yourselves this never happened.

Or if you find yourselves
Believing this crime and horrified by it –
You must, above all, believe
In the punishment, the awesome punishment,
The gods allotted to it.

If nature can let any person fall
Into crimes as vile as this
I congratulate our corner of the world –
So lucky to lie so far
From the soil
That nursed this enormity.

Let Panchaia be praised for its balsam,
Zedoary, cinnamon, and for the teeming
Variety of its herbs, and for its abundance
Of trees bearing incense –
But while myrrh grows there it cannot be envied.

The cost of that bush was too great.
Whatever arrow pierced the heart of Myrrha
Cupid absolutely disowns it.

Whatever torches kindled the flames in her body
He denies they were his.

One of hell's three horrible sisters
Brought a firebrand from the flickering tarpit
And an armful of serpents
Anointed with their own venom
And took possession of her.

Hatred for one's father is a crime.
Myrrha's love for her father
Was a crime infinitely worse.

The court of King Cinyras hummed with suitors.
From every degree of the compass they had come,
The princes of the East –
Haughty rivals for the King's daughter
Who wanted nothing to do with any of them.
Choose, Myrrha, before the story twists,
Choose from all these men in your father's palace –
Excluding only one.

Myrrha felt the stirring secret
Serpent of her craving and the horror
That came with it.
'What is happening to me?' she whispered.
'What am I planning?'
She prayed to the gods: 'You watchers in heaven,
Help me to strangle this.
I pray
By the sacred bond between child and parent
Let me be spared this.
Do not permit this criminal desire
To carry me off – if it is criminal.
Is it criminal?
Is it unnatural?
For all the creatures it is natural –
When the bull mounts the heifer, his daughter,
Neither feels shame.
A stallion fights to breed from his own daughter.
A billy goat will impregnate his daughter
As soon as any other little nanny.
And the birds – the birds –
No delicate distinctions deter them.

All mate where they can.
How lucky they are, those innocents,
Living within such liberties.
Man has distorted that licence –
Man has made new laws from his jealousy
To deprive nature of its nature,
Yet I have heard that nations exist
Who make a virtue of just this – fathers
Marry their daughters, mothers marry their sons –
To keep the blood in the family,
And give to both daughters and sons
Possession of their deepest happiness –
The bliss of their infancy as a wedding present.

'But I was born here, not there.
Born into the prison of this palace,
A prisoner of these laws. What am I doing?
Thoughts are running away with me.
I must not let such hopes roam so freely.
And yet, by every contract and custom,
Cinyras owns my love.
It would be a crime indeed to withhold it.
And if it were not for one small accident –
That he begat me –
I could give him my love, as his bride.

'But – because I am his – he can never be mine.
How if I were a stranger?
I should get away,
Get out of this land – but could I ever
Get out of my guilt? Out of my love?
My evil obsession keeps me here
Where I can be near him,
Look at him, speak to him, touch him, kiss him,
Though that is the limit of it.
Wretch, what more can you hope for?
Do you want to lie netted
In a mesh of family conundrums –
Sister to your son,
Co-wife to your mother, your brother's mother?
Remember the Furies,
The snake-haired, dreadful sisters
Who climb from the hell of conscience

Whirling their torches.
Be careful. While you are still guiltless,
Before you have set a foot wrong,
Do not so much as think of taking
The first step. Mighty Nature
Set this prohibition
Between a human father and his daughter.
Fear it.
I know what you want. It is because
You are who you are that you cannot have it.
Cinyras is noble. He lives by law.
And yet what if he fell
Into just such agonies of love – '

Meanwhile
Cinyras was wholly preoccupied
By the superfluity of suitors.
He saw only one solution.
He cited their names and lands and possessions
To his daughter –
Then simply asked her to choose.

Long minutes
Myrrha stood staring at her father.
For her, nothing else existed.
Her brain stormed – but to no purpose,
While her eyes brimmed as if they melted.
Cinyras pitied his child.
What he saw was modesty tormented.
He dried her face and kissed her.
He told her not to cry – while she clung
To his neck, half swooning at his kisses.
And when he asked her just what kind of husband
She wanted, she whispered: 'One like you.'
Cinyras understood nothing. He laughed:
'My darling, never let anything change your devotion
To me.' When she heard that word 'devotion'
Her heart broke up in her body. She stood there
Like a beast at the altar, head hanging.

Midnight. Mankind sprawled
In sleep without a care.
But Myrrha writhed in her sheets.

To cool the fiery gnawings throughout her body
She drew deep gasping breaths.
They made the flames worse.
Half of her prayed wildly —
In despair under the crushing
Impossibility — and half of her coolly
Plotted how to put it to the test.
She was both aghast at her own passion
And reckless to satisfy it.

Like a great tree that sways,
All but cut through by the axe,
Uncertain which way to fall,
Waiting for the axe's deciding blow,
Myrrha,
Bewildered by the opposite onslaughts
Of her lust and her conscience,
Swayed, and waited to fall.
Either way, she saw only death.
Her lust, consummated, had to be death;
Denied, had to be death.

With a huge effort
She got up out of bed,
Tied her girdle to a door lintel
And made a noose.
'Cinyras,' she sobbed. 'O my darling,
When you see this, please understand it.'
She pushed her numb, drained face
Through the noose. But as she drew the knot
Tight to the nape of her neck
She fainted. The lintel jerked at her weight.

Her old nurse, who lay in the next room,
Slept lightly as a sparrow.
She found herself listening
To the girl's despairing soliloquy.
Instantly she was up and through the door.
She shrieked at the suicide.
She tugged the knot loose.
She tore her own garments, and beat at her breasts,
She laid the limp girl on the floor —

Then she wept –
Embraced the girl and wept
And asked her why she should want to do such a thing.
Myrrha had recovered. She lay silent.
She simply lay there
Letting her worst moment do its worst.
Too slow to end it all
And then being caught in the act
Seemed to leave her now with less than nothing.

But the old nurse was persistent.
She clawed down her white hairs,
She bared the shrivelled skins of her breasts
And begged the girl, by this ruin
Of the cradle of her first years,
To tell her the secret.

Myrrha moaned and twisted from the questions.

The nurse came in closer, determined
To get at the truth. And she promised
Not only to keep her secret:
'I may be old,' she said,
'But that may make it easier for me to help you.
If some lunatic fit has fallen on you
From some power in the air,
From something you have eaten, some place you have sat in,
I know who can cure it.
If somebody has bewitched you, I know
The rituals to unwind the spell and bind it
Round the witch's neck.
Or if you have unsettled the gods
I know which offerings can appease them.
What else can it be?
Your home and future are secure.
Your father and mother are happy, they reign in their prime.'

As if she had heard nothing else
That single word 'father' went through Myrrha
Like a hot iron, and she sighed in misery.
The nurse missed that clue. But she guessed
Love was at the bottom of it.
So she dug away stubbornly
Embracing and straining the girl's ripeness

To her own withered rack.
'I know,' she whispered at last, 'I know your sickness.
You are in love.
And I am the very one who can best help you.
Not a breath of this shall come to your father.'

Again at the word 'father'
Myrrha choked a cry.
'Go away,' she wailed. She wrenched herself
From the nurse's clasp
And pitched onto her bed,
Burying her face in pillows.
'Leave me alone,' she sobbed.
'Don't take the last rag of my self-respect.'

And when the nurse persisted: 'Stop. Don't ask.
What you are wanting to know is pure evil.'
The old woman recoiled.
And now it was fear, not age, that made her tremble.

But more determined than ever
She clutched Myrrha's feet in her old fingers
Threatening to tell her father everything
About that noose
Unless she shared her secret. At the same time
She promised perfect loyalty
If she would confide it –
Yes, and her help. She promised her help.

Myrrha looked up and flung her arms
Around her old nurse. Her tears
Splashed down the scraggy breasts.
Now she tried to confess. But every effort
Was stifled as she hid her face again
And gagged herself with her robe.
At last she managed: 'My mother is so lucky
To have such a man for her husband – '
Then her voice was overwhelmed
By the flood of sobs that came with it.

But the nurse had heard enough.
Now she knew she had the truth
As her white hair bushed out
In a halo of horror

And she felt her body go cold.
Her slow words of caution, of wisdom,
Dragging up
From some rarely used depth,
Began to admonish Myrrha.
As if mere words could have a hope
Of altering such a passion.
Myrrha shook them off
As she shook the tears from her eyes.

She knew
The nurse's words were all true.
But her passion was deaf
As well as blind.
And if it could not satisfy itself
No matter what it destroyed in the act
It was happy to die that very moment.

'This is great folly,' the nurse said then.
'Death is never an option, only an error.
Myrrha, you shall have – ' Here she paused.
Her tongue shied from the words 'your father'.
'You shall have – I promise it, I call
Heaven to witness, you shall have your will.'

Now came the festival of Ceres.
Married women, robed in laundered whiteness,
Brought the goddess the first-fruits
Of the harvest. For these women
Through nine days and nights
Love or the slightest contact with a man
Was forbidden.

Cenchreis, the wife of Cinyras,
The mother Myrrha so painfully envied,
Was one of the celebrants
Wrapped in the white gown of the mysteries.
Nine days and nine nights
The King's bed was to be empty.

That first evening Cinyras drowsily
Sipping a last glass, found himself
Listening to the nurse's strange news –
About an incredibly beautiful girl

Madly in love with him.
Idly, he asked the girl's age,
And the nurse said, 'Same as Myrrha.'
'Bring her tonight,' said the King, with hardly a thought.

The nurse returned to Myrrha, jubilant –
'Success,' she hissed. 'Success.'
It was then, as that sharp word success
Went past her ear
That Myrrha felt a premonitory shiver,
The quick touch of a shadow of terror.
Then she let her joy lift her off her feet.

The moon had gone down,
Clouds covered the stars,
When Myrrha, like a wide-eyed sleepwalker,
Hypnotised by a dream of wild lust
Stepped from her chamber –
The heavens above gave her no light.
Icarus had covered his face
And Erigone, lifted to heaven by pure love of her father,
Hid her eyes.

Three times
Myrrha stumbled
As if her very feet rebuked her.
Three times
A screech owl, death's *doppelgänger*,
The bird with the sewn-up face,
Saluted her evil fate
With its rasping laugh.
But she ignored all omens,
Finding refuge from her shame
In the pitch darkness, that hid her almost from herself.

Her left hand
Clung to the hand of her old nurse.
Her right hand
Groped for invisible obstacles
As if she were blind.
The old woman went swiftly.
She knew the map of the palace with her eyes closed.

And here
Was the door of the King's bedroom.
The door swung wide.
Suddenly Myrrha was standing
In the dark chamber
Where the King breathed.

Her legs almost went from beneath her.
The blood drained from her face and head –
Unrecognised, she knew
She still had time to get out.

But more and more horrified by herself
More and more sick with guilt,
She let the old nurse
Lead her toward the bed where the King waited.

'She is yours,'
Was all the old woman whispered.
Gently she pushed Myrrha forward
Till she felt that reluctant, trembling body
Lifted weightless from her
Into the dark tent of the bed.

Then she crabbed away in the dark
Fleeing the disaster she had created
And that had already forgotten her.

The father
Welcomed his own flesh and blood
Into the luxury
Of the royal bed.
He comforted her,
Mistaking her whimpering struggle of lust and conscience
For girlish panic.

It could be
To soothe her he called her 'my child'
Or even 'my daughter'
And maybe when she called him 'father'
He supposed that made her first yielding
Somehow easier for her –
So the real crime, that the King thought no crime,
Let nothing of its wickedness be omitted.

After her father had crammed her with his seed
Myrrha left him
Finding her way now without difficulty –
Her womb satisfied
With its prize:
A child conceived in evil.

The next night father and daughter did it again
In the pitch darkness.
The same, night after night. On the ninth night
Cinyras made a mistake.
He let curiosity take over.
He prepared a lamp. That he lit
And held high, as she lay there,
Revealing the form and the face
Of his bedmate –
His daughter.

Now all the guilt was his.
Too huge and elemental
For words
His anguish
Was a roar throughout the palace.

He snatched his sword from its scabbard.
But Myrrha dived from his chamber
Into the night, dodging like a bat,
And escaped him.

She went on,
Crossed her father's kingdom,
Forsook Panchaia,
Left Arabia's palms far behind her.

Till a nine-month meandering journey
Brought her to Sabaea.
There she rested the kicking freight
That she could carry no further,
Utterly disgusted with her life
But afraid of dying.
She had no idea what to pray for,
So prayed without thinking:

'O you gods,
If there are any gods with patience enough

To listen to me
Who deserve
The most pitiless judgement
Which I would welcome –
I only fear that by dying
I would pollute the dead.
Just as my life contaminates the living.
Give me some third way, neither wholly dead
Nor painfully alive. Remove me
From life and from death
Into some nerveless limbo.'

Venus and Adonis (and Atalanta)

A power in the air hears the last prayer
Of the desperate. Myrrha's prayer to be no part
Of either her life or her death was heard and was answered.

The earth gripped both her ankles as she prayed.
Roots forced from beneath her toenails, they burrowed
Among deep stones to the bedrock. She swayed,

Living statuary on a tree's foundations.
In that moment, her bones became grained wood,
Their marrow pith,

Her blood sap, her arms boughs, her fingers twigs,   10
Her skin rough bark. And already
The gnarling crust has coffined her swollen womb.

It swarms over her breasts. It warps upwards
Reaching for her eyes as she bows
Eagerly into it, hurrying the burial

Of her face and her hair under thick-webbed bark.
Now all her feeling has gone into wood, with her body.
Yet she weeps,

The warm drops ooze from her rind.
These tears are still treasured.   20
To this day they are known by her name – Myrrh.

Meanwhile the meaty fruit her father implanted
Has ripened in the bole. Past its term,
It heaves to rive a way out of its mother.

But Myrrha's cramps are clamped in the heart-wood's vice.
Her gagged convulsions cannot leak a murmur.
She cannot cry to heaven for Lucina.

Nevertheless a mother's agony
Strained in the creaking tree and her tears drench it.
For pity, heaven's midwife, Lucina,

Lays her hands on the boughs in their torment
As she recites the necessary magic.
The trunk erupts, the bark splits, and there tumbles

Out into the world with a shattering yell
The baby Adonis. Nymphs of the flowing waters
Cradle him in grasses. They wash him

With his mother's tears. Bittermost envy
Could only glorify such a creature.
A painter's naked Cupid to perfection –

The god's portrait without his arrow quiver
Or his bow. Here, subtlest of things,
Too swift for the human eye, time slips past.

And this miraculous baby of his sister,
Sired by his grandpa, just now born of a bush,
Barely a boy, in the blink of an eye is a man

Suddenly more beautiful than ever –
So beautiful the great Venus herself,
Hovering over the wonder, feels awe.

Then the boy's mother, pent by Venus
In that shrub of shame, finds her revenge.
The goddess falls helplessly for Adonis.

Venus plucking kisses from her Cupid
Snagged her nipple on an unnoticed arrow
Sticking from his quiver. She pushed him away –

But was wounded far worse than she feared.
Pierced by the mortal beauty of Adonis
She has forgotten Cythera's flowery island,

Forgotten the bright beaches of Paphos,
Forgotten Cnidos, delicate as its fish,
Amathus, veined with costly metals. Neglected 60

Even Olympus. She abstains from heaven
Besotted by the body of Adonis.
Wherever he goes, clinging to him she goes.

She who had loved equally the shade
And her indolence in it, who had laboured
Only as a lily of the valley,

Now goes bounding over the stark ridges,
Skirts tucked high like the huntress, or she plunges
Down through brambly goyles, bawling at hounds,

Hunting the harmless; the hare who sees best backwards, 70
Hinds with painful eyes like ballerinas,
Tall stags on their dignity. She has nothing

To do with fatal boars. She shuns wolves,
Their back teeth always aching to crack big bones.
Bears with a swipe like a dungfork. Lions,

Lank bellies everlastingly empty,
That lob over high bomas, as if weightless,
With bullocks in their jaws. 'These,' she cried,

'O my beloved, are your malefic planets.
Never hesitate to crush a coward 80
But, challenged by the brave, conceal your courage.

'Leave being bold, my love, to the uglier beasts.
Else you stake my heart in a fool's gamble.
Let Nature's heavier criminals doze on

'Or you may win your glory at my cost.
The beauty, the youth, the charms that humbled Venus,
Feel silly and go blank when suddenly a lion

'Looks their way. They have no influence
On whatever lifts a boar's bristles,
Or on the interests or on the affections 90

'Of any of that gang. The tusk of the boar
Is the lightning jag that delivers the bolt.
The ignorant impact of solidified

'Hunger in the arrival of a lion
Turns everything to dust. I abhor them!'

'But why should you abhor them?'
    'There is a lesson

'These coarse brutes can teach us. But first,
This hunters's toil is more than my limbs are used to.
Look, that kindly poplar has made cool

'A bed of shade in the grass, just for us.'
So Venus pillowed her head on the chest of Adonis.
Then, to her soft accompaniment of kisses:

    'Once the greatest runner was a woman – so swift
    She outran every man.
    It is true. She could and she did.
    But none could say which was more wonderful –
    The swiftness of her feet or her beauty.

    'When this woman questioned the oracle
    About her future husband
    The god said: "Atalanta,
    Stay clear of a husband.
    Marriage is not for you. Nevertheless

    ' "You are fated to marry.
    And therefore fated, sooner or later, to live
    Yourself but other." The poor girl,
    Pondering this riddle, alarmed,
    Alerted, alone in a thick wood,

    'Stayed unmarried.
    The suitors who kept at her stubbornly
    She met
    With a fearful deterrent:
    "You can win me," she told them,

    ' "Only if you can outrun me.
    That is to say, if you will race against me.
    Whoever wins that race – he is my husband.
    Whoever loses it – has lost his life.
    This is the rule for all who dare court me."

    'Truly she had no pity.
    But the very ferocity

Of this grim condition of hers
Only lent her beauty headier power –
Only made her suitors giddier.

'Hippomenes watched the race.
"What fool," he laughed, "would wager life itself
Simply to win a woman –
With a foregone conclusion against him?
This is a scheme to rid the world of idiots."

'But even as he spoke he saw the face
Of Atalanta. Then as her dress opened   140
And fell to her feet
He saw her dazzling body suddenly bared.
A beauty, O Adonis, resembling mine

'Or as yours would be if you were a woman.
Hippomenes' brain seemed to turn over. His arms,
As if grabbing to save himself as he slipped,
Were reaching towards her, fingers hooked,
And he heard his own voice
Coming like somebody else's: "What am I saying?

' "I did not know, I never guessed   150
What a trophy
You run for – "
And there, as he stammered and stared,
His own heart was lost.

'Suddenly he was terrified of a winner.
He prayed that all would fail and be executed.
"But why," he muttered, "am I not out among them
Taking my chance?
Heaven helps those who give it something to help."

'These words were still whirling in his head   160
As her legs blurred past him.
Though her velocity was an arrow
As from a Turkish bow of horn and sinew
The shock-wave was her beauty.

'Her running redoubled her beauty.
The ribbon-ties at her ankles
Were the wing-tips of swallows.

The ribbon-ties at her knees
Were the wing-tips of swifts.

170   'Her hair blazed above her oiled shoulders.
And the flush on her slender body
Was ivory tinted
By rays that glow
Through a crimson curtain.

'And while this hero gazed with drying mouth
It was over.
Atalanta stood adjusting her victor's chaplet
And her defeated suitors, under the knife,
Sprawled as they coughed up her bloody winnings.

180   'Hippomenes ignored the draining corpses.
He stepped forward – his eyes gripping hers.
"Why do you scry for fame, Atalanta,
In the entrails
Of such pathetic weaklings?

' "Why not run against me?
If I win
You will not be shamed – only surpassed
By the son of Megareus, who was sired by Onchestius,
190   Who was sired by Neptune, god of the sea.

' "I am Hippomenes –
A great-grandson of the god of the oceans.
I have not disappointed expectations.
If my luck fails, by the fame of Hippomenes
Your fame shall be that much more resplendent."

'Atalanta was astonished as she felt
Her heart falter. Her legs began to tremble.
Her wild rage to conquer seemed to have kneeled
In a prayer to be conquered.
200   She murmured:

' "Which god, jealous of beautiful youth,
Plots now to slay this one?
Putting it into his head to fling away life.
As I am the judge:
Atalanta is not worth it.

' "It is not his beauty that makes me afraid
Though it well might.
It is his innocence, his boyishness
Touches me, and hurts me.
He is hardly a boy. He is a child.   210

' "Yet with perfect courage,
Contemptuous of death.
Also fourth in descent, as he claims, from the sea-god.
Also he loves me
And is ready to die if he cannot have me.

' "Listen, stranger,
Get as far away from me as you can
By the shortest route.
Marriage with me is death.
Go while you can move.   220

' "My bridal bed, my virgin bed, is a sump
Under the executioner's block.
Go and go quickly.
No other woman will refuse you.
The wisest will do all she can to win you.

' "Yet why should I bother myself?
After so gladly killing so many
Why should I care now? Die if you must.
If these poor corpses here cannot deter you,
If you are so sick of your life – then die.   230

' "They will say: because he dared to love her
She killed him. I shall have to hear:
Her thanks for his fearless love was a shameful death.
This will bring me fame – but ill-fame.
Yet none of it is my fault.

' "You cannot win, Hippomenes,
Forget me.
If only your insanity could shrink
Into your feet as a superhuman swiftness!
Look at him. His face is like a girl's.   240

' "In me there sleeps evil for both of us.
Do not wake it up. Go quietly away.
You belong to life. But believe me,

If Fate had not made my favour lethal
You alone would be my choice."

'Atalanta knew nothing about love
So she failed
To recognise love's inebriation
As it borrowed her tongue to pronounce these words.
250   She was hardly aware of what they meant.

'But her father, and the crowd, demanded the race.
And Hippomenes was already praying: "O Venus,
You gave me this great love – now let me keep it."
A quirk of air brought his prayer to my hearing.
Moved, I moved quickly.

'The most precious acre in Cyprus
Is my temple's orchard. A tree grows there
Of solid gold. With leaves of green gold
On boughs of white gold. Among those leaves
260   Hang apples of red gold. I picked three.

'Visible only to Hippomenes
I taught him the use of these apples.
Then at a blast from the trumpets
Both shot from their marks.
Their feet flickered away and the dust hung.

'They could have been half-flying over water
Just marring the shine.
Or over the silky nape of a field of barley.
Hippomenes felt the crowd's roar lifting him on:
270   "Hippomenes! You can win! Hippomenes!"

'And maybe Atalanta
Was happier than he was to hear that shout
As she leaned back on her hips, reining back
The terrible bolt of speed in her dainty body,
And clung to him with her glance even as she left him

'Tottering as if to a halt, labouring for air
That scorched his mouth and torched his lungs,
With most of the course to go. This was the moment
For flinging one of my apples out past her –
280   He bounced it in front of her feet and away to the left.

'Startled to see such a gorgeous trinket
Simply tossed aside, she could not resist it.
While she veered to snatch it up
Hippomenes was ahead, breasting the crest
Of the crowd's roar.

'But Atalanta came back in with a vengeance.
She passed him so lightly he felt to be stumbling.
Out went the second apple.
As if this were as easy she swirled and caught it
Out of a cloud of dust and again came past him.   290

'Now he could see the flutter of the crowd at the finish.
"O Venus," he sobbed, "let me have the whole of your gift!"
Then with all his might he hurled
The last apple
Past and beyond her – into a gulley

'Choked with tumbled rock and thorn. She glimpsed it
Vanishing into a waste
Of obstacles and lost seconds.
With two gold apples heavier at each stride
And the finish so near, she tried to ignore it.   300

'But I forced her to follow. And the moment she found it
That third apple I made even heavier.
Lugging her three gold prizes far behind
Her race was lost. Atalanta belonged to the winner.
So their story begins.

'But tell me, Adonis, should he have given me thanks
And burned costly perfumes in my honour?
Neither thanks nor perfumes arrived. He forgot my help.

'Anger overtook me. I was hurt.   310
I swore I would never again be slighted so.
My revenge would scare mankind for ever.

'Now hear the end of the story. This fine pair
Worn out with their wanderings, in a deep wood
Found a temple
Built long since for Cybele, Mother of the Gods,
Whose face is a black meteorite.

'Both thought they were tired enough that night
To sleep on the stone paving. Till I kissed

The ear of Hippomenes
320   With a whisper. As my lips touched him he shivered
Into a fit of lust like epilepsy.

'Under the temple was a cave shrine
Hollowed in solid bedrock and far older
Than the human race. An unlit crypt.
It was walled
With wooden images of the ancient gods.

'This was the sanctum doomed Hippomenes
Now defiled,
Sating himself on the body of Atalanta.
330   The desecrated wooden images
Averted their carved faces in horror.

'And the tower-crowned Mother of All, Cybele,
Considered plunging both
As they copulated
Into Styx, the tarpit of bubbling hell.
But that seemed insufficient to her.

'Instead she dropped maned hides
Over their sweating backs. Hardened and hooked
Their clutching fingers into talons. Let
340   Their panting chest-keels deepen. Let them sweep
The dust with long tails. Gargoyle-faced,

'And now with speech to match, these godless lovers
Rumble snarls, or cough, or grunt, or roar.
They have the thorny scrub for a nuptial chamber
And are lions – their loathsome fangs obedient
Only to the bridle-bits of Cybele.

'O dear love,
These and the others like them, that disdain
To give your hounds a run but come out looking for the hunter,
350   For my sake, O dear boy, let them lie.
Do not ruin our love with your recklessness.'

Her lesson done, the goddess climbed with her swans
Towards lit clouds. Meanwhile, as Adonis
Pondered her parable to find a meaning,

His hounds woke a wild boar in a wallow.
When this thug burst out his boar-spear's point
Glanced off the bone into the hump of muscle.

The boar deftly hooked the futile weapon
Out of the wound and turned on the hunter,
Overtook the boy's panic scramble,   360

Bedded its dagger tusks in under his crotch
Then ploughed him with all its strength as if unearthing
A tough tree's roots, till it hurled him aside, mangled.

Venus, afloat on swansdown in the high blue,
Still far short of Paphos, felt the shock-wave
Of the death-agony of Adonis.

She banked and diving steeply down through cirrus
Sighted her darling boy where he sprawled
Wallowing in a mire of gluey scarlet.

She leapt to the earth, ripping her garment open.   370
She clawed her hair and gouged her breasts with her nails,
Pressing her wounds to his wounds as she clasped him

And screaming at the Fates: 'You hags shall not
Have it all your way. O Adonis,
Your monument shall stand as long as the sun.

'The circling year itself shall be your mourner.
Your blood shall bloom immortal in a flower.
Persephone preserved a girl's life

'And fragrance in pale mint. I shall not do less.'
Into the broken Adonis she now dripped nectar.   380
His blood began to seethe – as bubbles thickly

Bulge out of hot mud. Within the hour
Where he had lain a flower stood – bright-blooded
As those beads packed in the hard rind

Of a pomegranate. This flower's life is brief.
Its petals cling so weakly, so ready to fall
Under the first light wind that kisses it,

We call it 'windflower'.

Pygmalion

If you could ask the region of Amathis
Where the mines are so rich
Whether it had wanted those women
The Propoetides,
You would be laughed at, as if you had asked
Whether it had wanted those men
Whose horned heads earned them the name Cerastae.

An altar to Zeus,
God of hospitality, stood at the doors
Of the Cerastae, soaked –
A stranger would assume – with the blood
Of the humbly sacrificed
Suckling calves and new lambs of Amathis.
Wrong. They butchered their guests.

Venus was so revolted to see offered
Such desecrated fare
She vowed to desert Ophiusa
And her favoured cities.
But she paused: 'The cities,' she reasoned,
'And the places I love –
What crime have these innocents committed?

'Why should I punish all
For a few? Let me pick out the guilty
And banish or kill them –
Or sentence them to some fate not quite either
But a dire part of both.
The fate for such, I think, is to become
Some vile thing not themselves.'

The horns of the Cerastae suggested
One quick solution for all –
Those men became bullocks. As for the others,
The Propoetides –
Fools who denied Venus divinity –
She stripped off their good names
And their undergarments, and made them whores.

As those women hardened,
Dulled by shame, delighting to make oaths

Before the gods in heaven
Of their every lie, their features hardened
Like their hearts. Soon they shrank
To the split-off, heartless, treacherous hardness
Of sharp shards of flint.

The spectacle of these cursed women sent
Pygmalion the sculptor slightly mad.
He adored woman, but he saw
The wickedness of these particular women
Transform, as by some occult connection,
Every woman's uterus to a spider.
Her face, voice, gestures, hair became its web.
Her perfume was a floating horror. Her glance
Left a spider-bite. He couldn't control it.

So he lived
In the solitary confinement
Of a phobia,
Shunning living women, wifeless.
Yet he still dreamed of woman.
He dreamed
Unbrokenly awake as asleep
The perfect body of a perfect woman –
Though this dream
Was not so much the dream of a perfect woman
As a spectre, sick of unbeing,
That had taken possession of his body
To find herself a life.

She moved into his hands,
She took possession of his fingers
And began to sculpt a perfect woman.
So he watched his hands shaping a woman
As if he were still asleep. Until
Life-size, ivory, as if alive
Her perfect figure lay in his studio.

So he had made a woman
Lovelier than any living woman.
And when he gazed at her
As if coming awake he fell in love.

His own art amazed him, she was so real.
She might have moved, he thought,
Only her modesty
Her sole garment – invisible,
Woven from the fabric of his dream –
Held her as if slightly ashamed
Of stepping into life.

Then his love
For this woman so palpably a woman
Became his life.

Incessantly now
He caressed her,
Searching for the warmth of living flesh,
His finger-tip whorls filtering out
Every feel of mere ivory.

He kissed her, closing his eyes
To divine an answering kiss of life
In her perfect lips.
And he would not believe
They were after all only ivory.

He spoke to her, he stroked her
Lightly to feel her living aura
Soft as down over her whiteness.
His fingers gripped her hard
To feel flesh yield under the pressure
That half wanted to bruise her
Into a proof of life, and half did not
Want to hurt or mar or least of all
Find her the solid ivory he had made her.

He flattered her.
He brought her love-gifts, knick-knacks,
Speckled shells, gem pebbles,
Little rainbow birds in pretty cages,
Flowers, pendants, drops of amber.
He dressed her
In the fashion of the moment,
Set costly rings on her cold fingers,
Hung pearls in her ears, coiled ropes of pearl
To drape her ivory breasts.

Did any of all this add to her beauty?
Gazing at her adorned, his head ached.
But then he stripped everything off her
And his brain swam, his eyes
Dazzled to contemplate
The greater beauty of her naked beauty.

He laid her on his couch,
Bedded her in pillows
And soft sumptuous weaves of Tyrian purple
As if she might delight in the luxury.
Then, lying beside her, he embraced her
And whispered in her ear every endearment.

The day came
For the festival of Venus – an uproar
Of processions through all Cyprus.
Snowy heifers, horns gilded, kneeled
Under the axe, at the altars.

Pygmalion had completed his offerings.
And now he prayed, watching the smoke
Of the incense hump shapelessly upwards.
He hardly dared to think
What he truly wanted
As he formed the words: 'O Venus,
You gods have power
To give whatever you please. O Venus
Send me a wife. And let her resemble – '
He was afraid
To ask for his ivory woman's very self –
'Let her resemble
The woman I have carved in ivory.'

Venus was listening
To a million murmurs over the whole island.
She swirled in the uplift of incense
Like a great fish suddenly bulging
Into a tide-freshened pool.
She heard every word
Pygmalion had not dared to pronounce.

She came near. She poised above him –
And the altar fires drank her assent

Like a richer fuel.
They flared up, three times,
Tossing horns of flame.

Pygmalion hurried away home
To his ivory obsession. He burst in,
Fevered with deprivation,
Fell on her, embraced her, and kissed her
Like one collapsing in a desert
To drink at a dribble from a rock.

But his hand sprang off her breast
As if stung.
He lowered it again, incredulous
At the softness, the warmth
Under his fingers. Warm
And soft as warm soft wax –
But alive
With the elastic of life.

He knew
Giddy as he was with longing and prayers
This must be hallucination.
He jerked himself back to his senses
And prodded the ivory. He squeezed it.
But it was no longer ivory.
Her pulse throbbed under his thumb.
Then Pygmalion's legs gave beneath him.
On his knees
He sobbed his thanks to Venus. And there
Pressed his lips
On lips that were alive.
She woke to his kisses and blushed
To find herself kissing
One who kissed her,
And opened her eyes for the first time
To the light and her lover together.

Venus blessed the wedding
That she had so artfully arranged.
And after nine moons Pygmalion's bride
Bore the child, Paphos,
Who gave his name to the whole island.

Hercules and Dejanira

Hercules, the son of Jupiter,
Was bringing his new bride home
When he came to the river Evenus.

Burst banks, booming torrent
Where there had been a ford. Hercules
Had no fear for himself, only for his wife.

A centaur galloped up. This was Nessus
Familiar with the bed of that river.
Broad haunch, deep shoulder, powerful vehicle
For forcing a way through strong water.

'Let me take her over,' he offered.
'Big as you are, Hercules,
You will be swept off your feet, but you can swim.'

Thinking only of getting across
This earth-shaking menace
That stunned the air with mist,
The Boeotian hero hoisted his darling
Onto the centaur's back.

Dejanira clung there, white with fear –
Paralysed
Between her dread of the river
And her dread of the goat-eyed centaur.
Who now plunged straight into
The high-riding boils of brown water.

Hercules wasted no time either.
He hurled his club and his heavy bow
Right across to the far bank, and muttered:
'No river resists me.'
Then, without pausing
To seek some broader, quieter reach of water,
Leapt in as he was, at the narrowest place,
Dragging the drogue of his arrow quiver
And the ponderous pelt of the lion,
Breasting the race right there, where it tightened
In a blaze of brown foam through the narrows.

He came out hard-skinned and glistening
On the other side
And had just picked up his bow
When a human scream tossed clear
Of the river's rumbling stampede
And he saw Nessus
Galloping away with Dejanira.

'You fool,' roared Hercules,
'Do you think your horse hooves are equal
To your mad idea?
Do you think you can plant your family tree
Between me and mine?
Nessus, the cure for you is on its way.
Neither respect for me
Nor your father's howls in hell
Chained on his wheel of fire
Can deflect you from the forbidden woman.
But I shall overtake you,
Not on my feet, but flying
On the feather of a weapon.'

As these words left the mouth of Hercules
His arrow arrived,
And Nessus was looking down
At the barbed head, raw with blood,
Jutting from his breastbone
Before he felt it splinter his vertebrae.

He wrenched the arrow clean through him
And the blood burst free,
Thudding jets, at front and back –
Blood already blackened
By the arrow's medication –
The lethal juices of the Lernaean Hydra.

This blood brought a last brain-wave to Nessus.
He saw its use. 'Let me,' he groaned,
'Leave an avenger behind me.'
Then stripping off his shirt
And soaking it in the hot fountain
Pumping from his chest
Gave it to Dejanira.
'With my dying words,' he whispered,

'I give you this love-charm, to win man's love.
No man who wears it can resist it.'

The years went by. The triumphs of Hercules
Grew familiar to the whole world
As did Juno's hatred of him.

*

His conquest of Oechalia,
That looked like just another, was his last.
Returning from this victory, intending
To offer up thanks to Jupiter
At Cenaeum, on flaming altars,
Hercules himself was overtaken
By a whisper,
By rumour –
Rumour who loves to spice big bowls of the false
With a pinch of the true,
And who, gulping her own confections,
Grows from nearly nothing to fill the whole world.
Rumour reached his wife well before him
And offered her something irresistible,
Telling her that her husband, the tower of man,
Had fallen for Iole. What you fear
Overtakes you. Dejanira
Had always dreaded this moment.
Her screams had waited too long
For exactly this. After the screams
She fell to the ground sobbing.
But straightaway pulled herself together:
'Why wail – except to amuse my rival?
She'll be at the door any minute.
A plan! Cunning!
The brain – before it's too late!
Before he marries her.
Scold? Or be silent?
Go home to Calydon, and hide there
Under your father's throne?
Or sit it out here?
Disappear, and mystify both –
Or stay and poison their pleasures
With my noise and nuisance

If nothing else?
Or remind myself I am the sister
Of Meleager
And frighten the life out of everybody
With the way I kill her –
Illustrating my agony on her body,
Demonstrating, incidentally,
What it means to be jilted?'

As she revolved her options
She recalled the dying gaze of the centaur –
And his last breath – making sacred
The promise in the strawberry shirt of blood.
She saw her perfect solution.
Unknowing as she was
Of any hidden meaning in the garment
This unfortunate woman handed the shirt
That would complete her misery
To Hercules' factotum – one Lichas.

She called it a welcoming,
A homecoming gift, for her husband.

Unknowing as she sent it, the hero received it –
Put off his lion pelt
And pulled over his shoulders the bile
That made his arrows fatal –
Bile crushed from the gall
Of the Hydra so famously defeated.

He had lit the first altar flames
For the high god.
Now he sprinkled incense into the flames
Chanting his prayers of gratitude, and pouring
Wine from goblets over the altar marble.

But already the venom in the weave of his shirt,
Softened and activated
By the heat of the altar,
Was soaking into his skin.
It reached and touched his blood. Then of a sudden
Struck through his whole body.

Amazed at the flush of pain
But refusing to acknowledge it

Or that anything of the sort could be happening
To him
Hercules for a while
Did not even gasp.
He thought he had shrugged off worse.
Then came a bigger pang –
A prong of pure terror
That jabbed his very centre
And opened
A whole new order of agony.
At last he understood.
His roar shook the woods of Oeta.
His frantic hands knew they were too late
As he scattered the altarstones and tore
At the folds of the horrible garment.
Wherever the weave came away
It lifted sheets of steaming skin with it.
Either it clung,
Stronger than he was, or tore free
Only where the muscles tore free,
Writhing rags and rope-ends of muscle,
Baring the blue shine of thick bones.

The blood in all his veins had become venom.
His body was one blaze,
As if steam exploded
Where a mass of white-hot iron
Plunged into ice.

All being was agony, bottomless.
His heart pounded flame.
His shape melted in bloody plasm.
His sinews cracked and shrank.
His bones began to char.

Clawing at the stars, he cried:
'O Juno, daughter of Saturn,
Are you gloating?
Lean out of heaven and smile
At what is happening to me.
Glut your depraved heart on this banquet.
Or if I am so pathetic
That even my destroyer, yes, even you

Have to pity me
Then let me be rid of my life.
You are my stepmother, give me a gift,
A fitting gift from you,
Give me this death quickly,
Remove this soul you hate so much
And torture so tirelessly,
This soul that has survived, in relentless toil,
For this finale.
Did I rid the earth of Busiris,
The king who draped his temples
With the blood of travellers?
Did I pluck Antaeus
From the nurse of his infinite strength –
The breasts of his mother Earth –
Denying him any refreshment there,
Till he perished?
Is this why I never hesitated
To embrace those three-bodied horrors,
The Spanish herdsman, and Cerberus,
The dog at the gate of hell?
Are these the hands
That twisted the head of the giant bull down
And pinned his horn in the earth?
The hands that helped Elis
And the waters of Stymphalus
And the woods of Parthenius –
The hands that brought me
The prize of the Amazons,
A sword-belt of worked gold –
The hands that picked the apples of Hesperus
From the coils of the unsleeping serpent?
I barely paused for the Arcadian boar.
The centaurs were helpless against me.
The multiplication of the Hydra's heads
Were profitless to the monster.
And the man-eating horses of Diomed,
Gorged on human flesh,
Grown homicidal on their diet –
Drinking human blood, stalled and bedded
On the rags of human corpses –
I saw them, I slaughtered them,

And threw their master's carcase on top of the heap.
The Nemean lion went limp
In the grip of these fingers.
I took revolving heaven on these shoulders.
I never wearied of the labours
You, Juno, forced me to undertake.
You ran out of commands
Before I grew tired of obeying them.
But this is one labour too many.
Fire is turning me into itself.
Courage and weapons are futile.
I have become a leaf in a burning forest.
While King Eurystheus, my enemy,
Eats and laughs and feels invigorated
Among all the others who trust in gods.'

This was the speech
That burst from the bloody wreckage
Of the great warrior
As he careered over the hills of Oeta –
Like a wild bull
Dragging the barbed spear
That the hunter fixed in his vitals
Before he fled.

Some saw him
Tugging at the shirt's last tatters,
Now inextricably
The fibres of his own body,
Uprooting trees, belabouring the faces of cliffs,
Reaching for his father in heaven.

In the blur of this frenzy, Hercules
Saw the feet of Lichas
Sticking from a crevice.
He had crammed his head and body in there
With such desperate fear
He thought he was all hidden.
But Hercules' pain had become madness.
He screamed: 'Lichas – you
Threw this net over me. You trapped me
In this instrument of torture.
You were great Juno's catspaw

To strip my skeleton.'
And Lichas was jerking in air
Like a rabbit
Dragged out by the hind legs.
He babbled excuses and scrabbled
For Hercules' knees to embrace them –

Too late, Hercules' arm
Was already whirling like a sling,
And like a slingstone Lichas
Shot into the sky, a dwindling speck
Out over the Euboean Sea.
As he went he hardened to stone.
As rain, they say, in the freezing winds
Hardens to snow, and the spinning snow
Is packed into hard hailstones.
Terror, we're told, boiled off his body liquids,
Baking him to stone. So, petrified,
He began to fall.
A rock, he splashed
Into the sea, far out.
He is still there, a crag in the swell,
A man-shaped clinker of fear,
Feared by sailors, who shun it
As if it might be alive. They call it Lichas.

Now Hercules, most famous
Son of the high god,
Felled thick trees on the top of Oeta,
And built a pyre.
He summoned Philoctetes, son of Poeas,
And gave him his bow, his quiver
And the arrows
Destined to return to the city of Troy.

With the help of Philoctetes
He kindled the squared stack of tree trunks.
And draping over it
His robe – the skin of the Nemean lion –
He stretched himself full length on top of that,
Head pillowed on his club,
And as the flames took hold, and the smoke boiled up,
Gazed into space like a guest

Lolling among the wine-cups,
Head wreathed with festive garlands.

Now flames savaged the whole pile
With elemental power
Like a pride of squabbling lions,
Worrying at limbs that ignored them,
Engulfing a hero who smiled in contempt.

The gods watched, distraught
To see the champion of the earth
Disintegrating in a blue shimmer,
Till Jupiter consoled them.

'You are anxious for my son. That is good.
I am happy to rule
Over gods who feel gratitude
Towards one who helped them.
His exploits have earned your admiration.
Your admiration for him warms me too.
His honour is my honour.
But do not be perturbed by these flames
Where Oeta seems to erupt.
The fire can take pleasure in Hercules
Only through what he had from his mother.
What he had from me
Is incombustible, indestructible,
Eternal –
Immune to flame, intangible to death.
That part has completed its earthspan.
So now – I shall lift it into heaven
Knowing you will rejoice to welcome it.

'If there is one among you
Who resents
This deification of my son
They will have to swallow all ill-feeling
And agree
Hercules has earned his reward.'

The gods approved. Even Juno
Heard her husband out with a calm gaze.
Only the slightest frown flicked her eyebrow
At the touch of that last sentence.

While Jupiter was speaking, the fire
Removed every trace of Hercules
That fire could get a grip on.
His mother's boy had vanished.
In his place glowed the huge cast
Of the child of Jove.
The snake sloughs its age and dullness
In a scurf of opaque tatters,
Emerging, new-made, in molten brilliance –
So the Tirynthian hero emerged
More glorious, greater, like a descended god.

Then his omnipotent father hoisted him
Through clouds, in a four-horse chariot,
And fixed him among the constellations, massive.
Atlas grunted under the new weight.

The Birth of Hercules

Old Alcmene of Argolis,
Hercules' mother, had Iole
To hear her incessant grieving remembrance

Of her son's triumphs – that the world had watched
In amazement. To her, his anxious mother,
Each new task had come as a fresh disaster.

At the end, Hercules had asked Hyllus
To take Iole in, to his hearth and heart.
Iole carried the hero's unborn child.

'O Iole,' cried Alcmene, 'when your time comes
And you call on Lucina to help you,
I pray you may find favour, as I did not.

'Lucina, she who eases the way for women
When they perform their miracle of labour,
For me did the opposite. Having to listen

'To Juno's command, not to my prayers,
She made my time almost fatal to me.
The sun had gone through nine signs, entering the tenth,

'And Hercules, created for travail,
Was so enormous in me, it was plain
Only Jove could have sired him.

'My cramps were soon beyond what can be borne.
Now as I think of it a deathly sweat
Chills me. The old terror snatches at me.

'Seven days and nights I lay screaming.
I clawed at the sky, begging Lucina
To help me with her attendants – the gods of birth.

'She came, but she came from Juno –
Already bribed by Juno, and happy,
To toss my life to Juno's malevolence.

'She listened to me as if I were her music,
Sitting alone by the altar, at the front door,
Her right leg over and twisted around her left.

'And her hands knitted together with locked fingers
Blocking my baby's birth.
As my pushing began, she muttered her magic,

'Trapping the babe in the tunnel.
I writhed, I was out of my mind with pain.
I cursed Jupiter for his unconcern.

'None of it was any good.
My cries would have softened flint.
I begged to be let die.

'The women of Thebes, who were with me,
Amplified my cries, my prayers, my pleading,
Trying to comfort me. It was all useless.

'But I had a servant there, a quick-witted girl,
Galanthis – the most beautiful hair, red gold –
Low-born, but dear to me for her loyalty.

'She recognised Juno's mischief.
And running in and out with cloths and water,
Noticed Lucina, sitting contorted at the altar,

'And in mid-stride cried: "Good news.
Whoever you are, now is your lucky chance
To congratulate a fortunate woman.

' "Alcmene of Argolis is thanking the gods!
At last – her beautiful child is beautifully born."
Lucina leaped to her feet in dismay

'Freeing her tangled limbs and braided fingers
And as Lucina's body undid its knot
My child slid out, effortless, into the world.

'They say Galanthis laughed at Lucina –
Openly, to have fooled her so completely.
But as she laughed the angered goddess caught her

'By that hair, and dragged her to the ground full length,
And held her there, however she fought to get up,
And there transformed her forearms into short legs,

'And changed her whole body, and, letting her hair
Keep its colour and cover her, released her
A bounding and spitting weasel. A weasel!

'And since a lie issuing between her lips
Had helped a woman deliver her baby,
The weasel delivers her offspring through her mouth.

'But she is brisk and tireless as ever
And as before is here, there, everywhere,
All over my house.'

The Death of Cygnus

Under Troy's wall, in mid-battle,
Cygnus, the son of Neptune,
Had gone through the Greeks twice
And sent a freshly butchered thousand
Tumbling into the underworld. Opposite –
The chariot of Achilles, through the Trojans,
A tornado through a dense forest,
Had left a swathe of shattered trunks,
Vital roots in the air, a tangle of limbs.
Achilles was looking for Hector.
But Hector's humiliation
Had been deferred a decade into the future.
Meanwhile, here stood Cygnus,
With arrogant scowl and blood-washed weapons,

The champion of the moment. Achilles
Fixed his attention on him.
'Think yourself lucky,' he shouted,
'As you leave your pretty armour to me,
That it was Achilles who killed you.'
Then he drove his team straight at him,
And sent a spear between their white necks
To drop Cygnus under their hooves.
The aim was perfect,
But the blade, that should have split the sternum,
And the heavy shaft,
That should have carried clean through the body,
Bounced off, like a reed thrown by a boy.
Achilles, astounded, skidded his team to a halt.
Cygnus was laughing.
'I know which goddess was your mother.
The Queen of the Nereids.
But why be surprised if you cannot kill me?
Do you think I wear this helmet
Crested with the tails of horses
For protection? Or that I present this shield
To save my skin? Or tuck myself in a breastplate
Because I am nervous?
I carry these for ornament only,
Just as Mars himself does. Naked,
My skin would still be proof
Against the whole Greek arsenal,
Including yours. This is what it means
To be the son not of a sea-nymph
But of Neptune, lord of the whole ocean
And all its petty deities.'
His spear followed his words –
Achilles, with a gesture, caught it
On the boss of his shield.
The bronze could not stop it.
Nine hardened ox-hides behind the bronze
Could not stop it. The tenth ox-hide stopped it.
Achilles shook it off,
And sent a second spear –
Its shaft vibrating in air –
That bounced off Cygnus, as if off the wall of Troy.
A third as heavy, as fast, and as accurate,

Did no better. Cygnus stood open-armed.
Laughing to welcome these guests
That knocked on his chest. By now Achilles
Was groaning with anger
Like the bull that pivots in the arena
Among the scarlet cloaks, his tormentors,
Who cannot be pinned down, but flutter away
From every swipe of his points.

Achilles retrieved his failed spears –
And could hardly believe what he found:
The great blades
Sharp and intact as ever.
'What's happened to my strength?' he muttered.
'Is there something about this fellow that has spellbound
The power of my arm –
The same arm
That pulled down the wall of Lyrnessus
When I smashed Thebes
Like a pitcher
Full of the blood of the entire populace?
When I dug such trenches with my weapon
The river Caicus drained
Whole nations of their crimson?
Here, too, this arm has slaughtered so many
Their heaped corpses make monuments – pyramids
All along the shore, to remind me
What strength is in it.'

As he pondered this, he noticed
Menoetes, one of the Lycians.
Exasperated, to reassure himself,
He hurled a spear, like a yelled oath.
It went through the breastplate of Menoetes
As if through a letter
He happened to be reading.
It drove on,
And clattered the stones beyond as if it had missed –
But splashing them with blood.
As Menoetes –
Like a crocodile straining to get upright –
Beat his brow on the earth towards which he crumpled,
Achilles recovered the spear. 'This corpse, this spear

And this arm, I have proved, are perfect Achilles.
Now with the help of heaven,' he cried, 'let Cygnus
Join us in a similar combination.'
And he flung the spear – and it travelled
As if along a beam
That passed through the left nipple of the target.
But at a clang the shaft bowed
And sprang off sideways. Nevertheless
At that point of impact a splat of blood
Brought a cry from Achilles –
A cry of joy, ignorant
That what he saw was the blood of Menoetes.
He leapt onto Cygnus like a tiger,
Hacking at him from every direction
With his aerobatic sword.
The flaring helmet flew off in shards
Like the shell of a boiled egg.
And the shield
Seemed to be making many wild efforts
To escape in jagged fragments.
But Achilles' blade
Bit no deeper. With a pang of despair
He saw its edge turning, like soft lead,
As he hewed
At the impenetrable neck sinews
Of this supernatural hero.

With a bellow of fury
He lifted his shield
And slammed the boss full in the face of Cygnus,
Spreading the nose like a crushed pear
And denting the skull-front concave
In a shower of teeth. At the same time
He pounded the top of his skull with the sword pommel,
Left, right, left, right, boss and pommel.
Cygnus staggered backwards,
His head on its anvil, under two giant hammers,
His neck-bones splintering, his jawbone lolling to his
   chest.
Terror and bewilderment had already
Removed the world from Cygnus.
A big rock blocked his retreat, he fell over

Splayed backwards across it,
Like a victim on an altar.
And now Achilles hoisted him
By his helpless legs, and whirled his head
On the diameter of his noble height
Like an axe. Through the vertical arc
Slam down onto the edged stones.
Then dropped on him, knee staving the rib-cage.
He gripped and twisted the thong –
All that remained of the fled helmet –
Under his chin, a tourniquet that tightened
With the full berserk might of Achilles
Till the head almost came off,
And Cygnus was dead.

Achilles' eyes cleared, as he kneeled there
Panting and cooling.
But now, as he undid the buckles
That linked the corpse's gorgeous armour,
He found his plunder empty.

In those moments
Neptune's word had breathed in off the ocean
And carried away Cygnus
On white wings, their each wingstroke
Yelping strangely – a bird with a long
Undulating neck and a bruised beak
Aimed at a land far beyond the horizon.

Arachne

Minerva, goddess of weavers,
Had heard too much of Arachne.
She had heard
That the weaving of Arachne
Equalled her own, or surpassed it.

Arachne was humbly born. Her father
Laboured as a dyer
Of Phocaean purple. Her mother
Had been humbly born. But Arachne
Was a prodigy. All Lydia marvelled at her.

The nymphs came down from the vines on Tmolus
As butterflies to a garden, to flock stunned
Around what flowered out of the warp and the weft
Under her fingers.
Likewise the naiads of Pactolus

Left sands of washed gold
To dazzle their wonder afresh
On her latest. They swooned at all she did.
Not only as it lay done, but as each inch crept
From under her touches.

A grace like Minerva's, unearthly,
Moved her hands whether she bundled the fleeces
Or teased out the wool, like cirrus,
Or spun the yarn, or finally
Conjured her images into their places.

Surely, only Minerva could have taught her!
Arachne
Laughed at the suggestion.
Her sole instructor, she claimed, was her inborn skill.
'Listen,' she cried, 'I challenge Minerva

'To weave better than I weave,
And if she wins
Let her do whatever she wants with me,
I shan't care.'
Minerva came to Arachne

As an old woman
Panting and leaning on a stick.
'Some things that age brings,' she began,
'Are to be welcomed. Old experience teaches
The thread of consequence cannot be broken.

'Listen to my warning. Give to mortals
The tapestries that make you
Famous and foremost among mortal weavers,
But give to the goddess
Your gratitude for the gift.

'Leave it to her to boast of you, if she wants to,
And ask her to forgive you
For your reckless remarks

Against her.
She will hear and she will be merciful.'

Arachne turned from her loom.
She reared like a cobra, scowling,
And came near to striking the old woman,
Her eyes hard with fury.
As she spat at her: 'Your brain totters

'Like your decrepit body.
You have lived too long.
If you possess daughters or granddaughters
Waste your babble on them.
I am not such a fool

'To be frightened by an owl-face and a few screeches.
I make up my own mind,
And I think as I always did.
If the goddess dare practise what she preaches
Why doesn't she take up my challenge?

'Why doesn't she come for a contest?'
As Arachne spoke, the old woman
Seemed to flare up
To twice her height, crying: 'She has come.'
All the nymphs fell prostrate.

The women of Mygdonia bowed and hid
Their faces in terror.
Only Arachne brazenly
Defied the goddess, with a glare. She flushed deep red
In the rush of her anger, then paled –

As the dawn crimsons then pales.
But she stuck to her challenge. Too eager
For the greater glory now to be won,
She plunged with all her giddy vanity
Into destruction.

Minerva bent to the contest
Without another word. She rigged up her loom.
The shuttles began to fly.
Both rolled their upper garments down
Under their breasts to give their arms freedom

For every inspiration.
So concentrated on the outcome
Neither was aware how hard she was working,
Feeding the cloth with colours
That glowed every gradation

Of tints in the rainbow
Where the sun shines through a shower
And each hue dissolves
Into its neighbour too subtly
For human eye to detect it.

Minerva portrayed the divine
History of her city, Athens,
And how it came to be named.
There were the twelve high gods surrounding Jove.
She characterised each one:

Jove in his majesty and thunders,
Neptune splitting a crag
With his trident, and the ocean
Gushing from the crevasse –
By which he claimed the city.

And herself, with a shield and a long spear,
The high-ridged helmet on her head
And over her breasts the aegis.
And, where she speared the earth, silvery olives
Springing up, with berries.

The gods gazed astonished. A winged
Victory perfected the assembly.
Then the goddess
Filled each corner with an illustration
Of the kind of punishment

Arachne could now expect for her impudence.
In one corner, two snowy summits,
Rhodope and Haemon, had been human
Before they assumed for themselves
The names of the greatest gods.

In another corner the Queen of the Pygmies
Who had challenged Juno and lost
Had become a crane

Warring against her own people.
In the third corner Antigone,

Who had challenged Juno, cried in vain
To her father Laomedon and to the city of Troy
As the goddess turned her into a stork.
She tries to cheer herself with the white flash
Of her broad wings and her beak's clatter.

In the fourth corner Cinyras
Embraced the temple steps – all that remained
Of his daughter, his tears
Splashing the stones.
Finally

With an embroidered border of tangled olives –
Pallas framed her design
And completed the work
With her own tree, like a flourish,
The tree of peace, an olive.

Arachne's tapestry followed a different theme.
It showed Europa crying from out at sea
Astride the bull that had deceived her.
The high god Jupiter, in his bull form,
Carrying her off –

And glistening with effort.
You could see her feet recoiling
From the swipe of the waves through which he heaved.
And Asteria was there
Fighting to keep her clothes on

Under the storming eagle.
And Leda, bared
Under the blizzard of the swan.
Across the growing pattern Jupiter
Varied and multiplied

His amorous transformations:
A satyr
Planted Antiope with her divine twins.
The lady of Tyris yielded her body
Only to one she thought Amphitryon.

The lap of Danae opened
Only to a shower of gold. Here
The god has gone into the eye of a candle
To comfort Asopus' daughter.
There he's a shepherd, knowing Mnemosyne

Adores that flute.
And there as a freckled serpent
He has overcome Demeter's daughter.
In each of these Arachne
Gave Jove rich new life.

Then moved on to Neptune –
Who had become a great bull, too, to cope
With the daughter of Aeolus.
And as the god of a river
Sweeps Aloeus' wife away in a grasp

That casts her up imprinted with twin sons.
Here a ram
Surprises Bisaltis. There a masterful horse
Circumvents the modesty of Demeter.
A dolphin dives with Melantho. And the curse

Of Medusa's grisly beauty
Softens for a bird.
Arachne captures them all as if she had copied
Each as it happened.
Then she brings on Phoebus –

As a peasant, a falcon, a lion, last as a shepherd
Seducing Isse, Macareus' daughter.
Then Bacchus, with a bunch of grapes
That are no grapes, deceiving Erigone.
And there in the glowing weave,

Saturn a stallion
Begetting Chiron – half man and half pony.
Arachne bordered her picture, to close it,
With a sparkling wreath of cunningly knotted
Flowers and ivy. So it was finished.

And neither the goddess
Nor jealousy herself
Could find a stitch in the entire work

That was not perfection. Arachne's triumph
Was unbearable.

Minerva tore from the loom
That gallery of divine indiscretions
And ripped it to rags.
Then, all her power gone
Into exasperation, struck Arachne

With her boxwood shuttle
One blow between the eyes, then another,
Then a third, and a fourth. Arachne
Staggered away groaning with indignation.
She refused to live

With the injustice. Making a noose
And fitting it round her neck
She jumped into air, jerked at the rope's end,
And dangled, and spun.
Pity touched Minerva.

She caught the swinging girl: 'You have been wicked
Enough to dangle there for ever
And so you shall. But alive,
And your whole tribe the same through all time
Populating the earth.'

The goddess
Squeezed onto the dangling Arachne
Venom from Hecate's deadliest leaf.
Under that styptic drop
The poor girl's head shrank to a poppy seed

And her hair fell out.
Her eyes, her ears, her nostrils
Diminished beyond being. Her body
Became a tiny ball.
And now she is all belly

With a dot of head. She retains
Only her slender skilful fingers
For legs. And so for ever
She hangs from the thread that she spins
Out of her belly.

Or ceaselessly weaves it
Into patterned webs
On a loom of leaves and grasses –
Her touches
Deft and swift and light as when they were human.

Bacchus and Pentheus

So the fame of the blind
Seer Tiresias
Flared up in all the Greek cities.
Only Pentheus, King of Thebes,
Laughed at the old man's prophecies.
'In-fill for empty skulls,'
He jeered at this dreamer.
'Dreams,' he explained,
'Which this methane-mouth
Tells us are the dark manifesto   10
Of the corrector,
In fact are corpse-lights, the ignes fatui,
Miasma from the long-drop
And fermenting pit
Of what we don't want, don't need,
And have dumped.
They rise from the lower bowel. And lower.'
The laughter of Pentheus
Clanged through his malodorous prisons and echoed
Into the underworld and into heaven.   20

Tiresias replied with his usual riddle:
'How lucky for you, Pentheus,
If only you, like me, had managed
To get rid of your two eyes
That so sharply
Supervise everything and see nothing.
Then you would not have to watch
What Bacchus will do to you.
These dreams, that you miscall ridiculous,
And that attract your derision,   30
Just as your own dear face
Will be unrecognisable

Because of a glittering mask of blowflies –
These dreams
Have shown me this new god, son of Semele,
And they have shown me a preview, in full colour,
Of a banquet
Bacchus will hold for you, Pentheus,
At which you will be not only guest of honour
40   But the food and drink. Think of it.
Your expensive coiffure
With your face wrapped in it
Wrenched off like a cork, at the neck,
Your blood
Poured out over your mother and sisters,
Your pedigree carcase
Ripped by unthinking fingers
Into portions, and your blue entrails,
Tangled in thorns and draped over dusty rocks,
50   Tugged at by foxes.
All this, Pentheus, as clear as if
It had already happened. I saw it
In a silly dream
Which this new god, outlawed by you,
Gave to me on a street corner.
Gave to me – for me to give to you.
What can it mean?'

Pentheus with a roar
Kicked the old blind man
60   Like a stray befouling dog
From his palazzo. A lifetime too late
To alter himself or his fate.

The god has come. The claustrophobic landscape
Bumps like a drum
With the stamping dance of the revellers.
The city pours
Its entire population into the frenzy.
Children and their teachers, labourers, bankers,
Mothers and grandmothers, merchants, agents,
70   Prostitutes, politicians, police,
Scavengers and accountants, lawyers and burglars,
Builders, layabouts, tradesmen, con-men,

Scoundrels, tax-collectors, academicians,
Physicians, morticians, musicians, magicians,
The idle rich and the laughing mob,
Stretched mouths in glazed faces,
All as if naked, anonymous, freed
Into the ecstasy,
The dementia and the delirium
Of the new god.   80

Pentheus rushes about, his voice cracks.
He screams like an elephant:
'This is a disease –
Toads have got into the wells,
The granaries have all gone to fungus,
A new flea is injecting bufotenin.
You forget, you Thebans,
You are the seed of the god Mars.
Remember your ancestry
Under the tongue of the great serpent   90
Inaccessible to folly.
You veterans, what has happened to your hearing –
It was cured and seasoned
By the crash of weaponry and the war-cries
And the dying cries of the enemy.
How can you go capering
After a monkey stuffed with mushrooms?
How can you let yourselves be bitten
By this hopping tarantula
And by these glass-eyed slavering hydrophobes?   100
You pioneers, you first settlers, heroes,
You who raised our city, stone by stone,
Out of the slime of the salt marsh,
And hacked its quiet, with your sword's edge,
Out of the very solar system
To shield a night light for your babes and toddlers,
How can you
Go rolling your eyes and waggling your fingers
After that claque of poltroons?
Remember   110
How often you dragged yourselves, by your teeth and nails,
Out of the mass graves
And the fields of massacre,

Clutching your wives and new-born,
Fighting off the hyenas –
Can a fed-back, millionfold
Amplified heartbeat
And some drunken woman's naked heel tossed over your heads
Bounce you out of your wits –
120   Like bobbing unborn babies?
Iron warriors, menhirs of ancient manhood,
Tootling flutes
Wet as spaghetti?
And you philosophers,
Metaphysicians, where are your systems?
What happened to the great god Reason?
And to the stone table of Law
That you fitted back together
Out of the Absolute's shattering anger
130   Against backsliders?
You have become sots,
You have dunked it all, like a doughnut,
Into a mugful of junk music –
Which is actually the belly-laugh
Of this androgynous, half-titted witch.
You are forgetting the other.
You forget the hard face of the future
With its hungry mouth and its cry
Which is the battle cry
140   That waits behind the time of plenty
Hungry for all you have,
And that massacres for amusement, for thrills,
And to liberate your homes and your land
From your possession.
You forget the strangers who are not friendly.
They are coming over the earth's bulge
Out of the wombs of different mothers.
As sure as the moon's tide,
They will lift off your roofs and remove your walls like driftwood
150   And take all you have.
With ground steel they will separate you from it,
Leaving you hugging the burnt earth.
If Thebes has to fall
That would be better.
We could succumb to such a fate with honour.

Then our despair would resemble a noble trophy,
Our tears would be monumental.
But you have surrendered the city
Not to war's elemental chaos
And heroes harder and readier than yourselves   160
But to a painted boy, a butterfly face,
Swathed in glitter.
A baboon
Got up as an earring
In the ear of a jigging whore.

'As for this lewd, blasphemous joke
About his birth –
Begotten by God himself, a divine by-blow,
Then snatched by his father's scorched fingers
Out of the incineration of his mother –   170
Sodden, squirming, no bigger than a newt,
Then gestated full term, an implant,
In the thigh of Almighty God.
By which he implies – like a papoose
In God's scrotum.
Do you hear this fairy tale?
How can you swallow it? Bring the juggler to me.
Let me get my thumbs on that Adam's apple,
I'll pop this lie out of him, with squeals,
Like the pip of yellow   180
Out of a boil. Like a pulp of maggot,
A warble-fly chrysalis
From under the hide of a bull.
Bring him.'

With the dry foam framing his lips
Pentheus sent his praetorian guard
To arrest this creature, this Bacchus,
Acclaimed as a new god.

His grandfather, blear-eyed but long-sighted,
Tried to restrain him.   190
The wise elders, too tottery and arthritic
To go dancing, tried to restrain him.
Their warnings fell like holy water sprinkled
Onto a pan of boiling pig-fat.
Their head-shakings, white-haired, white-bearded,

Like a log-jam in a big river
Only broke his momentum into bellowings,
Frothings, and the plunge
Of a cataract.

200   The guards come back bruised and dishevelled.
They bring to Pentheus not the Bacchus he wanted
But a different prisoner. They call him
'A priest of the new rites.'
Hands bound, a jackal-faced Etruscan.
Pentheus' glare, a white-hot branding iron,
Bears down on the face of this prisoner.
With difficulty he calms
His homicidal hands, as he speaks:
'Your death approaches
210   Very fast, simply because
Your friends need the warning. So: quickly:
What is your homeland, your family, and your name?
And how does it come about
That you end up here, the manikin doll
Of this ventriloquial, mesmeric,
Itinerant common fraud?'

The voice that answers him is quite fearless.
'I am Acoetes, out of Maeonia.
My parents were poor.
220   My father possessed neither stock
Nor ground for it to stand on.
His wealth
Was a barbed hook and the art
Of finding fish with it.
These, and the wilderness of waters,
Were his bequest to me.
But I grew weary of wading among herons.
I took to open water.
I pushed a prow out through breakers.
230   I stretched my cunning
Between the tiller, the sail
And the constellations.
As I learned the moods
Of the menagerie of heaven –
Of squally Capricornus, the saturnine goat,
Of the Hyades, the little piglets

Showering summer stars,
Of the two bears revolving in their clock –
All the winds of ocean
Became familiar, and their safe havens.   240

'One time,
My destination Delos, I was blown
Onto the coast of Chios.
Skill with the oars got us ashore safely.
That night we camped there. At dawn
I sent Opheltes, the bosun, with men
To find fresh water,
While I climbed a headland
To study the wind, the sky-signs, the horizons.
Everything looked promising. I returned   250
To the ship, recalling my crew.
"Look what we've found," shouted Opheltes.
He shoved ahead of him a strange boy,
A little boy, beautiful as a girl.
They'd picked him up on the hillside.
Straight away they'd recognised plunder.
The child staggered,
Mouth half open, eyelids heavy.
He was ready to collapse
With wine, or sleep, or both.   260
But I saw, I knew, by everything
About him, this boy was more than mortal.
His face, his every movement,
Told me he was a god.
I said to the crew: "I do not know
Which god you have found but I am certain
This child is divine."
Then I spoke to the boy: "Whoever you are,
Preserve our lives in the sea, bless our voyage,
And forgive these fellows   270
Their rough words and their rough hands."

' "None of that rubbish," cried Dictys. "This boy's ours."
His anger was quick – like his body,
Quickest of all, like a gibbon,
To hurtle here and there in the ship's rigging.
Lybis roared agreement. He was a dullard.
Always feeling he was being robbed

Or outwitted, always wanting a fight.
Melanthus joined them – he was sharper, our look-out,
280   But bored with too much emptiness
In front of and behind his blond eyelashes.
Alcemidon likewise. He thought only
Of what he could get away with.
And black Epopus, whose voice was a maul,
Literally, one huge muscle
All to itself, the timekeeper
And metronome of the oarsmen,
Always craving for exercise. And the rest,
They bent their voices to his
290   Just as out on the sea they bent their bodies.
The girlish boy
Was a landfall, a whole port
For these testy sailors. But I blocked
The top of the gangplank.
"Bestial sacrilege," I told them,
"Shall not defile this vessel
While I am master of it."

'The worst man among them pretended to retch.
Lycabus. He was so reckless
300   He seemed to be searching everywhere
With a kind of desperation
For his own violent death.
Tuscany had thrown him out
For murdering a neighbour.
He grabbed at my throat with his rower's fingers
And would have pitched me overboard
But I caught hold of a rope, and between my knee
And his pelvic bone
Gave his testicles the fright of their lives.
310   The whole crew bellowed, with one voice,
For him to get up
And finish what he had started.
The uproar
Seemed to rouse the boy.
The great god Bacchus awoke.
"My friends," he cried,
"What was that awful noise? It sounded awful!
Where am I? How did I get here?

Are you planning to take me somewhere?
Tell me where."   320
Proreus found a soft voice.
"Nothing to be afraid of. You seemed lost.
We thought you'd like a lift.
Where do you want to go?
Wherever you say – and we'll drop you off."
Then the god said:
"Naxos is my home. Take me there
And many friends for life
Will give you a welcome to remember."

'Those criminals   330
With sudden hilarity
Swore by the sea and all its gods to take him.
And they urged me to get under way –
To do the boy this easy favour.
I took them at their word
Since Lycabus still sprawled
Groaning and vomiting in the scuppers.
I set the painted prow
Towards Naxos.

'Then Opheltes, in a hissing whisper,   340
Asked me if I was crazy.
And the rest of the crew, their faces,
Their mouthings, their gestures, made it plain –
They wanted me to take the boy where they pleased,
Very far from Naxos.
I could not believe
They could suppose a god could be tricked by men.
I told them:
"This is not only wicked – it is stupid.
I'll have no part in it."   350
Then one of them, Aethalion,
Shouldered me from the helm.
"In that case," he said, "leave our fortunes to us."

'As the ship heeled, the god of actors
Went reeling off balance. He clutched the gunwale,
Stared at the churned swerve in the wake
And pretended to weep.
"This is not the way home," he wailed.

"The sun should be on that side. We were
360   Right before. What have I done wrong?
What is the world going to say
If the whole crew of you
Kidnap one small boy?"
Those bandits laughed at his tears
And they laughed at me too, for mine.
But I swear
By the god himself
(And there is no god closer to hear me)
That the incredible
370   Truly now did happen.

'First, the ship stops dead in the sea
As if rammed into a dry dock.
The oarsmen are amazed. They grimace
And force the blood from under their fingernails
To budge the hull or shear the rowlocks.
The sails are helpless,
Flogging in their ropes. Then suddenly ivy
Comes swarming up the oars, it cumbers the oar-strokes
And tumbles in over the deck,
380   Coiling up the masts, boiling over
To spill great bundles, swinging in the wind,
Draping the sails. And the god
Is standing there, mid-ship, crowned
With clusters of fat grapes.
He brandishes a javelin
Twined with stems and leaves of the vine.
And around him are heaped, as if real,
The great shapes of big cats, yawning, blinking,
The striped and the spotted, leopards, lynxes,
390   Tigers and jungle cats.

'Then either in panic terror or godsent madness
Every man leaps up, as if for his life,
And overboard into the sea.
Medon was the first to go black.
His spine arched into a half-wheel, mid-air.
Lycabus gibbered at him. "Look he's changing
Into a sea-monster – "
As his own gape widened
Backwards beneath his ears, in the long smile

Of a dolphin, and his nose flattened,   400
His body slicked smooth, his skin toughened.
And Libys – his hands slipped from the oar
Because they were already shrinking.
Before he hit the wave he knew they were fins.
Another was reaching up
To free the ropes from the ivy
And found he had no arms. With a howl
He somersaulted over the stern
In a high arc
Flailing the black half-moon of a dolphin tail   410
That was suddenly his.
These creatures crash round the ship.
They fling sheets of spray over the ivy
As they plunge under. Or they burst upwards
Like a troupe of acrobatic dancers –
Blasting out in a fume, through their blowholes,
The sea they gulp as they frolic.
I was the survivor of twenty,
Shuddering with fear, barely sane.
But the god was kind.   420
"Now steer towards Dia," he told me.
And I did so. And there I was rewarded.
I entered the priesthood of this mighty god.'

Now Pentheus spoke:
'You have dreamed us a long dream,
With a deal of ocean bluster,
But my anger has neither slept nor cooled.'
He called for slaves.
'Break this man on the rack elaborately.
Send him down to hell grateful   430
For the respite.'

So Acoetes was dragged off, and slammed
Into a strongroom.
But it is told:
While the executioner's implements
Of fire, pincers, choppers, and incidentals,
Were being readied
To gratify Pentheus, of a sudden
Bolts shot out of their sockets and went skittering
Over the floors. Locks exploded   440

In a scatter of components curiously fractured.
Doors flew open untouched.
And untouched the shackles
Fell off Acoetes.

Pentheus heard of this. But from it
Learned nothing. Instead, his brain temperature
Rose a degree. Something insane
Behind his eyes
Tore off its straitjacket.
450 He thought no more of bodyguards
Than of jailers, warders, doctors, nurses.
Alone he climbed Cithaeron,
The mountain consecrated to Bacchus,
Where the air
Pounded his eardrums like mad fists
And seemed to pound in his heart,
And the screaming songs of the possessed
Were like the screams of a horse, reverberating
Inside the horse's own skull.
460 Pentheus was like that horse
On a battlefield, when the unfought fury
Shimmers in mid-air before the attack,
And the blast of the trumpets
Goes like lightning
Through every supercharged nerve,
And he whinnies, rolls his eyeballs,
Champs foam and paws at the far sky
To be first at the enemy –
Pentheus was like that
470 When he heard the unbearable howls
And ululations
Of the Bacchantes, and the clash of their cymbals.
And when he stumbled in his fury
And fell on all fours,
When he clutched the sod and felt their stamping
Shaking the mountain beneath his fingers,
When Pentheus
Saw the frightened worms
Twisting up out of their burrows
480 Then the red veil came over his vision.

Halfway up the slope is a level clearing.
Pentheus bounded into the open
And halted –
Utterly unprepared
For what he had surprised.
He stared, in a stupor,
Into the naked mysteries.

The first to see him,
The first to come for him
Like a bear defending her cubs,   490
The first to drive her javelin into him
Was his own mother –
Screeching as she came:
'It's the boar that ploughed up our gardens!
I've hit it! Quickly, sisters, now we can kill it!
I've hit it.' Pentheus falls
And the whole horde of women
Pile on top of him
Like a pack of wild dogs,
Like a squabbling heap of vultures.   500
Every one claws to get hold of something
And pull it away.

A changed man, Pentheus,
Emptied with terror,
Tries to crawl.
His mouth bites at new words,
Strange words, words that curse himself,
That renounce himself, that curse Pentheus.
He convicts himself,
Begs for forgiveness   510
With blood coming out of his mouth.
He heaves upright,
Shouting to his aunt: 'Autone,
Remember your darling Actaeon
Torn to rags by the hounds that loved him.
Pity me.' The name Actaeon
Sounds to her like the scream of a pig
As she wrenches his right arm
Out of its socket and clean off.
While Ino, with the strength of the god,   520
Twists the other likewise clean off.

Armless, he lurches towards his mother.
'Mother,' he sobs, 'Mother, look at me,
Recognise me, Mother!'
Agave stares, she blinks, her mouth wide.
She takes her son's head between her hands
And rips it from his shoulders.
She lifts it, like a newborn baby,
Her red fingers hooked into the hair
530   Letting the blood splash over her face and breasts –
'Victory!' she shrieks. 'I've done it! I did it!'

Swiftly, like a light breeze at dawn,
After the first hard night-frost of the year
Has left a tree's leaves
Numbed and precariously clinging,
So swiftly
The hands of those women
Separated the King's bones and stripped them.

The lesson
540   Was not lost on Thebes, the city of letters.
Women made sure, thereafter,
That this sleepy child
Was acknowledged, was honoured
And made happy by all who played with him
In his ritual play,
Blessing all who blessed him.

Midas

Peasants crowded to gawp at Silenus –
The end-product of a life
They could not imagine.
They chained him with flowers and dragged him,
In a harness of flowers, to their king, Midas,
As if he were some
Harmless, helpless, half-tapir or other
Charming monster.
When Midas recognised him,
And honoured him, fat and old and drunk as he was,
As the companion of Bacchus,
And restored him to the god,

Bacchus was so grateful
He offered to grant Midas any wish —
Whatever the King wanted, it would be granted.
Midas was overjoyed
To hear this first approach, so promising,
Of his peculiar horrible doom.
He did not have to rack his brains.
A certain fantasy
Hovered in his head perpetually,
Wistfully fondled all his thoughts by day,
Manipulated all his dreams by night.
Now it saw its chance and seized his tongue.
It shoved aside
The billion — infinite — opportunities
For Midas
To secure a happiness, guaranteed,
Within the human range
Of what is possible to a god.
It grasped, with a king's inane greed,
The fate I shall describe.

Midas said: 'Here is my wish.
Let whatever I touch become gold.
Yes, gold, the finest, the purest, the brightest.'
Bacchus gazed at the King and sighed gently.
He felt pity —
Yet his curiosity was intrigued
To see how such stupidity would be punished.
So he granted the wish, then stood back to watch.

The Phrygian King returned through the garden
Eager to test the power — yet apprehensive
That he had merely dreamed and now was awake,
Where alchemy never works. He broke a twig
From a low branch of oak. The leaves
Turned to heavy gold as he stared at them
And his mouth went dry.
He felt his brain move strangely, like a muscle.
He picked up a stone and weighed it in his hand
As it doubled its weight, then doubled it again,
And became bright yellow.
He brushed his hand over a clump of grass,
The blades stayed bent — soft ribbons

Of gold foil. A ripe ear of corn
Was crisp and dry and light as he plucked it
But a heavy slug of gold, intricately braided
As he rolled it between his palms.
It was then that a cold thought seemed to whisper.
He had wanted to chew the milky grains –
But none broke chaffily free from their pockets.
The ear was gold – its grain inedible,
Inaccessibly solid with the core.
He frowned. With the frown on his face
He reached for a hanging apple.
With a slight twist he took the sudden weight
No longer so happily. This was a fruit
He made no attempt to bite, as he pondered its colour.

Almost inadvertently he stroked
The door pillars, as he entered the palace,
Pausing to watch the brilliant yellow
Suffuse the dark stone.
He washed his hands under flowing water, at a fountain.
Already a hope
Told him that the gift might wash away,
As waking up will wash out a nightmare.
But the water that touched him
Coiled into the pool below as plumes
Of golden smoke, settling heavily
In a silt of gold atoms.

Suddenly his vision
Of transmuting his whole kingdom to gold
Made him sweat –
It chilled him as he sat
At the table
And reached for a roasted bird. The carcase
Toppled from his horrified fingers
Into his dish with a clunk,
As if he had picked up a table ornament.
He reached for bread
But could not break
The plaque of gold that resembled a solid puddle
Smelted from ore.
Almost in terror now
He reached for the goblet of wine –

Taking his time, he poured in water,
Swirled the mix in what had been translucent
Rhinoceros horn
But was already common and commoner metal.
He set his lips to the cold rim
And others, dumbfounded
By what they had already seen, were aghast
When they saw the wet gold shine on his lips,
And as he lowered the cup
Saw him mouthing gold, spitting gold mush –
That had solidified, like gold cinders.
He got up, reeling
From his golden chair, as if poisoned.

He fell on his bed, face down, eyes closed
From the golden heavy fold of his pillow.
He prayed
To the god who had given him the gift
To take it back. 'I have been a fool.
Forgive me, Bacchus. Forgive the greed
That made me so stupid.
Forgive me for a dream
That had not touched the world
Where gold is truly gold and nothing but.
Save me from my own shallowness,
Where I shall drown in gold
And be buried in gold.
Nothing can live, I see, in a world of gold.'

Bacchus, too, had had enough.
His kindliness came uppermost easily.
'I return you,' said the god,
'To your happier human limitations.
But now you must wash away
The last stain of the curse
You begged for and preferred to every blessing.
A river goes by Sardis. Follow it upstream.
Find the source
Which gushes from a cliff and plunges
Into a rocky pool. Plunge with it.
Go completely under. Let that river
Carry your folly away and leave you clean.'

Midas obeyed and the river's innocent water
Took whatever was left of the granted wish.
Even today the soil of its flood plain
Can be combed into a sparse glitter.
And big popcorns of gold, in its gravels,
Fever the fossicker.

Midas never got over the shock.
The sight of gold was like the thought of a bee
To one just badly stung –
It made his hair prickle, his nerves tingle.
He retired to the mountain woods
And a life of deliberate poverty. There
He worshipped Pan, who lives in the mountain caves.
King Midas was chastened
But not really changed. He was no wiser.
His stupidity
Was merely lying low. Waiting, as usual,
For another chance to ruin his life.

                *

The cliff-face of Tmolus watches
Half the Mediterranean. It falls away
To Sardis on one side, and on the other
To the village of Hypaepa.
Pan lives in a high cave on that cliff.
He was amusing himself,
Showing off to the nymphs
Thrilling them out of their airy bodies
With the wild airs
He breathed through the reeds of his flute.
Their ecstasies flattered him,
Their words, their exclamations, flattered him.
But the flattered
Become fools. And when he assured them
That Apollo, no less,
Stole his tunes and rearranged his rhythms
It was a shock
For Pan
To find himself staring at the great god
Hanging there in the air off the cave mouth,
Half eclipsed with black rage,

Half beaming with a friendly challenge.
'Tmolus, the mountain,' suggested the god, 'can judge us.'

Tmolus shook out his hair,
Freed his ears of bushes, trees, birds, insects,
Then took his place at the seat of judgement,
Binding his wig with a whole oak tree –
The acorns clustering over his eyebrows,
And announced to Pan: 'Your music first.'

It so happened
Midas was within hearing
Collecting nuts and berries. Suddenly he heard
Music that froze him immobile
As long as it lasted. He did not know
What happened to him as Pan's piping
Carried him off –
Filled him with precipices,
Lifted him on weathered summits,
Poured blue icy rivers through him,
Hung him from the stars,
Replaced him
With the fluorescent earth
Spinning and dancing on the jet of a fountain.

It stopped, and Tmolus smiled,
As if coming awake –
Back, he thought, hugely refreshed
From a journey through himself.
But now he turned
To Apollo, the great, bright god.
As he turned, all his forests
Dragged like a robe.

Apollo was serious.
His illustrious hair burst
From under a wreath of laurel picked
Only moments ago on Parnassus.
The fringe of his cloak of Tyrian purple
Was all that touched the earth.
In his left hand the lyre
Was a model, in magical code,
Of the earth and the heavens –
Ivory of narwhal and elephant,

Diamonds from the interiors of stars.
In his right hand he held
The plectrum that could touch
Every wavelength in the Universe
Singly or simultaneously.
Even his posture
Was like a tone – like a tuning fork,
Vibrant, alerting the whole earth,
Bringing heaven down to listen.

Then the plectrum moved and Tmolus,
After the first chords,
Seemed to be about to decompose
Among the harmonics.
He pulled himself together – but it was no use,
He was helpless
As the music dissolved him and poured him
Through the snakes and ladders
Of the creation and the decreation
Of the elements,
And finally, bringing the sea-horizon
To an edge clean as a knife,
Restored him to his shaggy, crumpled self.

Pan was humbled. Yes, he agreed –
Apollo was the master. Tmolus was correct.
The nymphs gazed at Apollo. They agreed.
But then a petulant voice,
A hard-angled, indignant, differing voice
Came from behind a rock.

Midas stood up. 'The judgement,' he cried,
'Is ignorant, stupid, and merely favours power.
Apollo's efforts
Are nothing but interior decoration
By artificial light, for the chic, the effete.
Pan is the real thing – the true voice
Of the subatomic.'

Apollo's face seemed to writhe
Momentarily
As he converted this clown's darkness to light,
Then pointed his plectrum at the ears
That had misheard so grievously.

Abruptly those ears lolled long and animal,
On either side of Midas' impertinent face.
Revolving at the root, grey-whiskered, bristly,
The familiar ears of a big ass.
The King,
Feeling the change, grabbed to hang on to his ears.
Then he had some seconds of pure terror
Waiting for the rest of his body to follow.
But the ears used up the power of the plectrum.
This was the god's decision. The King
Lived on, human, wagging the ears of a donkey.

Midas crept away.
Every few paces he felt at his ears and groaned.
He slunk back to his palace. He needed
Comfort. He was bitterly disillusioned
With the spirit of the wilderness.
He hid those ears – in a turban superb
As compensation could be.

But a king needs a barber.
Sworn to secrecy or impalement
The barber, wetting his lips,
Clipped around the gristly roots
Of the great angling ears as if the hair there
Might be live nerve-ends.
What he was staring at,
And having to believe, was worse
For him than for their owner,
Almost. He had to hide this news
As if it were red-hot
Under his tongue, and keep it there.
The ultimate shame secret
Of the ruler of the land.
It struggled to blurt
Itself out, whenever
He opened his mouth.
It made him sweat and often
Gasp aloud, or strangle
A groan to a sigh. Or wake up
In the middle of the silent night
Certain he had just
Yelled it out, at the top of his voice,

To the whole city.
He knew, this poor barber,
He had to spit it out somehow.

In the lawn of a park he lifted a turf
After midnight. He kneeled there
And whispered into the raw hole
'Ass's ears! Midas has ass's ears!'
Then fitted the turf back, trod flat the grave
Of that insuppressible gossip,
And went off, singing
Under his breath.

But in no time,
As if the barber had grafted it there
From some far-off reed-bed,
A clump of reeds bunched out, from that very sod.
It looked strange, on the park lawn,
But sounded stranger.
Every gust brought an articulate whisper
Out of the bending stalks. At every puff
They betrayed the barber's confidence,
Broadcasting the buried secret.
Hissing to all who happened to be passing:
'Ass's ears! Midas has ass's ears!'

Niobe

Niobe had known Arachne.
She, too, scorned the gods –
For a different reason. Arachne's fate
Taught Niobe nothing.
Niobe was proud. She was proud

Of the magical powers of her husband –
Amphion, the King. And she was proud
Of the purity of the noble blood
They both shared. And proud
Of their kingdom's envied might and splendour.

But above all these, her greatest pride
Was her family – her fourteen children.
And it is true, Niobe, of all mothers

Would have been the most blest
If only she had not boasted

That she, of all mothers, was the most blest.

The daughter of Tiresias, Manto,
Whose prophetic frenzy
Opened the three worlds to her,
Came raving into the streets, possessed by vision.
She screamed at the women of Thebes:

'The goddess is speaking through my mouth.
She commands you all:
Twist laurels round your heads, gather at the temple,
Burn incense – give prayers and offerings
To Leto and the children of Leto.'

The Theban women asked no questions.
If that was what the goddess wanted
That is what they would give her.
They filled the temple, their worshipping cries went up
To Leto and the children of Leto.

But suddenly, in a swirl of attendants,
Niobe was among them.
She looked magnificent –
Like a great flame, in her robes of golden tissue.
She reared her spectacular head,

Her hair coiled and piled like a serpent
Asleep on a heap of jewels.
Anger made her beauty awesome.
From her full height she raked the worshippers
With a glare of contempt.

'Isn't this insane?
Aren't you all out of your minds
To offer tributes to these gods in the sky
Who exist only by hearsay?
How can you do this

'And at the same time ignore
Real divinity such as your eyes can see?
You worship Leto
Who lives only in a story
At altars built specially for her.

'But who has built an altar to acknowledge
What is divine in me?
My father was Tantalus –
Among all mortals only he
Sat at the feasts of the gods.

'Only he clinked glasses with them. My mother
Is a sister of the Pleiades.
And that great god among the greatest, Atlas,
Who bears the globe of heaven on his back –
He is my grandfather. And who forgets

'That my grandfather on the other side
Is Jupiter himself?
And it is no boast
When I remind you that great Jupiter
Is also my father-in-law.

'All Phrygia kneels and pays homage
To me. I rule over this city
That rose into place, stone by stone,
As if weightless, obedient
To my husband's magical music.

'I am the Queen of the Royal Palace of Cadmus.
Wherever my eyes rest in my house
They rest on fabulous wealth.
Nor can it be denied – my own beauty
Is not equalled on any face in heaven.

'No – I have been blessed above all women.
Who can deny it? Who can doubt
That my great fortune will continue to grow?
It is too great – far, far too great
For Fate to reverse.

'Ill-fortune
Cannot lay a finger on me.
Let her take whatever she will –
Whatever she can take, still she leaves me
Far more than she takes.

'Tell me,
How can I fear ill-fortune?
Even if it came to the worst –

If I lost some of my children –
I could never be left with only two.

'Only two!
Two is all that Leto ever had.
Two children! You might as well have none.
Get rid of these laurels. Back to your homes.
Finish with this nonsense. Finish, I say.'

Cowed, the women of Thebes obeyed her.
They dropped the laurel wreaths, broke off their worship,
Left the altars –
But their prayers to Leto, like
Subterranean rivers, could not

Be stopped or diverted.
They flowed on, unspoken, heard only by Leto.
And Leto was enraged.
She climbed to the top of Cynthus
And cried out to her children – the twins:

None other than Apollo and Diana,
So lightly dismissed by the Phrygian Queen.
'Your mother is calling you,' she cried.
'Your mother, who is so proud of being your mother.
In heaven I take second place to none

'Except Juno herself. Hear me, my children.
Your mother's divinity is being denied.
Women loyal to me from the beginning
Are forbidden to worship at my altar.
Niobe has forbidden it. Oh help me.

'The daughter of Tantalus has inherited
All her father's blasphemous folly.
Not only has she emptied my temples,
She drives me mad
With insults, derision,

'And tells the whole world her fourteen children
Are a thousand times superior
To my two. Compared to her I am childless.
O my children, double her mockery – back
Into her own mouth, let her swallow its meaning.'

Leto would have gone on
But her great son Apollo spoke: 'Mother,
Your words merely prolong Niobe's delusion.'
He exchanged a signal with his sister.
Together they sailed through the sky

Like an eclipse in a cloud
Till they hung over the city of Cadmus.
Outside the city
A broad plain smoked like a burning ground,
Pounded bare and hard
By charioteers and horsemen, to and fro
Exercising their horses.
Niobe's sons were out there
Astride gaudy saddle-cloths,
Their gold-studded reins bunched in their fingers,
Managing muscular horses.

Ismenus, Niobe's eldest,
Was reining his horse hard,
Bringing it round in a tight circle
When his spine snapped
And a bellow forced his mouth open
As a broad-headed bright-red arrow
Came clean through him.
The reins fell loose. For a moment
He embraced the horse's neck, limply,
Then slid from its right shoulder.

Sipylus looked wildly upward.
He heard a quiver rattle high in the air
And urged his horse to a full gallop –
As the ship's pilot
Seeing the overtaking squall behind him
Puts out every inch of canvas
To catch every breath and escape it –
But it was no good.
The god's arrow was already there,
The feathers squatting in the nape of his neck,
The long shaft sticking from his Adam's apple.
He bowed
Over the horse's mane and simply
Rolled on forward and down

Under the hooves
That churned his limbs briefly, scattering the blood.

Phaedimus was no luckier.
With his brother –
Who had inherited the ominous name
Of his grandfather, Tantalus –
He had left the horses. These two
Were doing what they loved best –
Wrestling together, with oiled bodies,
And were locked chest to chest,
Each straining to fold the other backwards
When the arrow
From the unerring bow of Apollo
Slammed through both, and nailed them together.
Each thought his backbone broken by the other.
With a single groan they collapsed,
Crumpling sideways
A monster with eight limbs, clawing for life,
Dying a single death from the one wound.

Alphenor could not understand
What was happening.
He hammered his chest with his fists and tore at it
With his fingers. He tried
To lift his two brothers back on their feet –
But as he struggled there, with all his strength
Braced under their dead weights,
A forked barb of Apollo
Touched him beneath his left shoulder-blade.
It came out under his ribs, on the right,
With a rag of his liver.
He felt his heart kicking against the shaft
As he dropped into darkness
Beneath his brothers.

Long-haired Damasichthon was not so lucky
To escape so smoothly.
The arrow that brought him down
Had gone in behind the knee.
He flung back his head,
Showing heaven a mask of agony
As he made one huge effort to wrench

The barbs from their anchorage
Behind his tendons.
The second arrow found him in that posture.
It went in
At the base of his throat, in the fork
Of his clavicle –
And drove straight down through the aorta.
A column of blood
Ejected it and he fell
Like a broken fountain –
The blood jetting in twisting and showering arcs
From his flailing body.

Ilioneus was last.
He dropped to his knees and lifted his arms –
'You gods,' he cried, 'all of you, hear me,
Spare me, protect me.'
But ignorant of his mother's folly
He was ignorant
Which gods to appeal to.

Apollo the Archer, touched with pity,
Regretted the arrow
That his eye was following.
But the wound was instantly fatal,
Surgical, precise, minimal –
It stopped his heart before he felt the impact.

Now the news came looking for Niobe.
Rumour like an electrical storm-wind
Whisking the dust at street corners –
People huddling together, then scattering
In an uproar of wails. Till at last
Her own family burst in on her, shrieking.

She heard it unable to believe –
Knowing it all true,
As the severed limb cannot feel.
Astounded that the gods could do so much
So swiftly,
Aghast that they had the power to do it,
Enraged that they had dared.

The final blow fell on her
As if she were already senseless.
Amphion, her husband, hearing the news
Had stabbed himself, ending his grief with his life.

This was no longer Niobe the Queen
Who had driven her people, as with a whip,
From Leto's altars,
Who had stalked through her own city
Like a conqueror
Viewing a conquest –
When her beauty, her pride, her arrogance
Sickened the people with envy and hatred.

Now even those who hated her most
Pitied her. She bowed
Over the cooling bodies of her sons.
She kissed them, as if she could give them
A lifetime of kisses in these moments.
She lifted her bruised arms:
'Leto,' she cried, 'feast yourself
On your triumph, which is my misery.
I have died seven deaths – at your hands.
In each of these seven corpses I died
In agony and lie dead.
Gloat. And exult. And yet
Your victory is petty.
Though you have crushed me I am still far, far
More fortunate than you are.
I still have seven children.'
Demented with her losses,
Niobe no longer knew
How to be frightened or prudent.

And even as she spoke
Terror struck
With an invisible arrow
All who heard
A bowstring thud in the air.

The seven sisters of the dead brothers
Stooped by the seven biers,
Loose hair over their shoulders, mourning.
One of them, as she eased

The arrow from the heart of her brother,
Fell on him,
An arrow through her own,
Already dead, her mouth on his mouth.

Another, consoling her mother,
Stopped mid-sentence, bent
Over her sudden wound and collapsed,
Mouth closed and eyes vacant.
Another, running, seemed to stumble –
But her sprawl was lifeless.
Another tripping over her body
Was dead in the air as she fell.
One of them
Squeezed her head and shoulders
Under a dead brother, another
Stood in the open sobbing,
Paralysed with fear.

When six of them lay dead
Niobe grabbed the seventh and covered her
With her limbs and body,
And tried to protect her
In swathes of her robes, crying:
'Leave me my youngest.
Leave me one. Leave me the smallest.
Of all my children let me keep this one.'
But a slender arrow
Had already located
The child
She tried to hide and pray for.

Niobe gazed at the corpses.
All her children were dead.
Her husband was dead.
Her face hardened
And whitened, as the blood left it.
Her very hair hardened
Like hair carved by a chisel.
Her open eyes became stones.
Her whole body
A stone.

Life drained from every part of it.
Her tongue
Solidified in her stone mouth.
Her feet could not move, her hands
Could not move: they were stone,
Her veins were stone veins.
Her bowels, her womb, all stone
Packed in stone.
And yet
This stone woman wept.

A hurricane caught her up
And carried her
Into Phrygia, her homeland,
And set her down on top of a mountain.
And there, a monument to herself,
Niobe still weeps.
As the weather wears at her
Her stone shape weeps.

Salmacis and Hermaphroditus

Among those demi-gods, those perfect girls
Who sport about the bright source and live in it,
The beauty of Salmacis, the water-nymph,
Was perfect,
As among damselflies a damselfly's,
As among vipers the elegance
Of a viper, or a swan's grace among swans.
She was bending to gather lilies for a garland
When she spied Hermaphroditus.
At that first glimpse she knew she had to have him.   10
She felt she trod on prickles until she could touch him.
She held back only a moment,
Checked her girdle, the swing of her hem, her cleavage,
Let her lust flood hot and startled
Into her cheek, eyes, lips – made her whole face
Open as a flower that offers itself,
Wet with nectar. Then she spoke:
'Do you mind if I say – you are beautiful?
Seen from where I stand, you could be a god.

20   Are you a god? If you are human,
      What a lucky sister! As for the mother
      Who held you, and pushed her nipple between your lips,
      I am already sick with envy of her.
      I dare not think of a naked wife in your bed.
      If she exists, I dare not think of her bliss.
      Let me beg a taste, one little sip
      Of her huge happiness. A secret between us.
      But if you are unmarried – here I am.
      Let us lie down and make our own
30   Bridal bed, where we can love each other
      To sleep. And awaken each other.'

      The boy blushed – he had no idea
      What she was talking about.
      Her heart lurched again when she saw
      How his blush bewildered his beauty.
      Like the red side of an apple against a sunset,
      Or the ominous dusky flush
      That goes over the cold moon
      When the eclipse grips its edge
40   And begins to swallow it inch by inch
      In spite of all the drums and pans and gongs
      Beaten on earth beneath to protect it.

      Then the nymph slid her arms
      Around his neck, and asked for a kiss,
      One kiss, one brotherly kiss –
      'Get away,' he cried. 'Let me go,
      Or I'm off. And you can sit here
      On your basket of tricks all by yourself!'
      That scared Salmacis, she thought he really might go.
50   'Oh no, forgive me!' she sobbed. 'Forgive me!
      I couldn't help it. I'm going. Oh, I'm spoiling
      This lovely place for you. I'm going. I'm going.'

      So, lingering her glances, she goes,
      And truly she seems to have gone.
      In fact, she has ducked behind a bush.
      There she kneels, motionless, head lifted –
      Her eye fixed, like the eye of a leopard.

      He plays, careless as a child,
      Roams about happily

Thinking he's utterly alone. 60
He paddles into the pool's edge, goes deeper.
The cool pulse of the spring, warping the clarity,
Massages his knees, delicious.
He peels off his tunic and the air
Makes free with all that had been hidden,
Freshens his nudity. Under the leaves
Salmacis groaned softly
And began to tremble.
As the sun
Catches a twisting mirror surface 70
With a splinter of glare
Her own gaze flamed and hurt her. She was already
Up and leaping towards him,
She had grabbed him with all her strength –
Yet still she crouched where she was
Shaking all over, letting this go through her
Like a dreadful cramp. She watched him
Slap his pale shoulders, hugging himself,
And slap his belly to prepare it
For the plunge – then plunge forward. 80
And suddenly he was swimming, a head bobbing,
Chin surging through the build of a bow-wave,
Shoulders liquefied,
Legs as if at home in the frog's grotto,
Within a heave of lustre limpid as air
Like a man of ivory glossed in glass
Or a lily in a bulb of crystal.

'I've won!' shrieked Salmacis. 'He's mine!'
She could not help herself.
'He's mine!' she laughed, and with a couple of bounds 90
Hit the pool stark naked
In a rocking crash and thump of water –
The slips of her raiment settling wherever
They happened to fall. Then out of the upheaval
Her arms reach and wind round him,
And slippery as the roots of big lilies
But far stronger, her legs below wind round him.
He flounders and goes under. All his strength
Fighting to get back up through a cloud of bubbles
Leaving him helpless to her burrowing kisses. 100

Burning for air, he can do nothing
As her hands hunt over him, and as her body
Knots itself every way around him
Like a sinewy otter
Hunting some kind of fish
That flees hither and thither inside him,
And as she flings and locks her coils
Around him like a snake
Around the neck and legs and wings of an eagle
110   That is trying to fly off with it,
And like ivy which first binds the branches
In its meshes, then pulls the whole tree down,
And as the octopus –
A tangle of constrictors, nippled with suckers,
That drag towards a maw –
Embraces its prey.

But still Hermaphroditus kicks to be free
And will not surrender
Or yield her the least kindness
120   Of the pleasure she longs for,
And rages for, and pleads for
As she crushes her breasts and face against him
And clings to him as with every inch of her surface.
'It's no good struggling,' she hisses.
'You can strain, wrestle, squirm, but cannot
Ever get away from me now.
The gods are listening to me.
The gods have agreed we never, never
Shall be separated, you and me.'

130   The gods heard her frenzy – and smiled.

And there in the giddy boil the two bodies
Melted into a single body
Seamless as the water.

Tereus

Pandion, the King of Athens, saw
King Tereus was as rich
And powerful as himself.

He was also descended from the god Mars.
So Pandion gave his daughter to Tereus,
And thought himself happy.

Hymen and Juno and the Graces,
Those deities who bless brides, shunned this marriage.
Instead the bridal bed was prepared by the Furies
Who lit the married pair to it with torches
Stolen from a funeral procession.
Then an owl

Flew up from its dark hole to sit on the roof
Directly above their bed. All that night
It interrupted their joy –
Alternating little mewing cries
With prophetic screams of catastrophe.
And this was the accompaniment of omens

When Tereus, the great King of Thrace,
Married Procne, and begot Itys.
But all Thrace rejoiced. Thereafter,
The day of their wedding and the Prince's birthday
Were annual jubilees for the whole nation.
So ignorant are men.

Five years passed. Then Procne spoke to her husband,
Stroking his face. 'If you love me
Give me the perfect gift: a sight of my sister.
Let me visit her. Or, better still,
Let her visit us. Go – promise my father
Her stay here can be just as brief as he pleases.'

At a command from Tereus, oar and sail
Brought him to Athens. There King Pandion
Greeted his son-in-law. Tereus
Began to explain his unexpected arrival –
How Procne longed for one glimpse of her sister.
But just as he was promising

The immediate return of Philomela
Once the two had met, there, mid-sentence,
Philomela herself – arrayed
In the wealth of a kingdom – entered:
Still unaware that her own beauty
Was the most astounding of her jewels.

She looked like one of those elfin queens
You hear about
Flitting through the depths of forests.
Tereus felt his blood alter thickly.
Suddenly he himself was like a forest
When a drought wind explodes it into a firestorm.

She was to blame – her beauty. But more
The King's uncontrollable body.
Thracians are sexually insatiable.
The lust that took hold of him now
Combined the elemental forces
Of his national character and his own.

His first thought was: buy her attendants
And her nurses with bribes.
Then turn the girl's own head
With priceless gifts –
Cash in your whole kingdom for her.
His next thought was

Simply to grab her
And carry her off –
Then fight to keep her. He was the puppet
Of instant obsession. No insane plan
Gave him pause if it promised to make her his.
All of a sudden, wildly impatient

He pressed Pandion again with Procne's request –
The glove of his own greed. Passion
Made him persuasive. When he went too far
He swore Procne
Sickened to see her sister.
He even wept as he spoke,

As if he had brought her tears with him
As well as her pleading words.
God in heaven, how blind men are!
Everybody who witnessed it marvelled
At what this man would do for his wife's sake,
The lengths he would go to! And yet

The acting was irresistible!
Philomela was overwhelmed. She wept too,
Hugging her father, pleading through her tears.

As he loved her and lived for her happiness
She begged him to grant her this chance –
The worst that any woman ever suffered.

Tereus stared at the Princess,
Imagining her body in his arms.
His lust
Was like an iron furnace – first black,
Then crimson, then white
As he watched her kiss and caress her father.

He wished himself her father –
In which case
His intent would have been no less wicked.
King Pandion surrendered at last
To the doubled passion of his daughters.
Ecstatic, Philomela

Wept and thanked him for his permission
As if he had bestowed
Some enormous prize on her and her sister,
Rather than condemned them, as he had,
To the fate
That would destroy them both.

The sun went down.
A royal banquet glittered and steamed.
The guests, replete, slept.
Only the Thracian King, Tereus, tossed,
Remembering Philomela's every gesture,
Remembering her lips,

Her voice, her hair, her hands, her glances,
And seeming to see
Every part her garments concealed
Just as he wanted it.
So he fed his lust and stared at the darkness.
Dawn lit the wharf at last

For their departure. Now King Pandion
Implored his son-in-law to guard his charge:
'I lend her to you
Because you and she and her sister were persuasive.
By your honour, by the gods, by the bond between us,
Protect her like a father.

'Send her home soon,
This darling of my old age.
Time will seem to have stopped till I see her again.
Philomela, come back soon, if you love me.
Your sister's absence alone is more than enough.'
The King embraced his daughter and wept.

Then asked both – Tereus and the girl –
To give him their hands, as seals of their promise.
He joined their hands together –
Beseeching them to carry his blessing
To his far-off daughter and his grandson.
There the father choked

On his goodbye.
His voice collapsed into sobs,
Overwhelmed of a sudden
By fear –
Inexplicable, icy,
A gooseflesh of foreboding.

The oars bent and the wake broadened
Behind the painted ship.
Philomela watched the land sinking
But Tereus laughed softly:
'I've won. My prayers are granted. She is mine.'
He was in a fever for the delights

That he deferred only with difficulty.
And the nape of her neck was aware
Of his eyes
As he gloated on her – like an eagle
That has hoisted a hare in its gripe
To its inescapable tower.

The moment the ship touched his own shore
Tereus lifted Philomela
Onto a horse, and hurried her
To a fort, behind high walls,
Hidden in deep forest.
And there he imprisoned her.

Bewildered and defenceless,
Failing to understand anything
And in a growing fear of everything,

She begged him to bring her to her sister.
His answer was to rape her, ignoring her screams
To her father, to her sister, to the gods.

Afterwards, she crouched in a heap, shuddering –
Like a lamb still clinging to life
After the wolf has savaged it
And for some reason dropped it.
Or like a dove, a bloody rag, still alive
Under the talons that stand on it.

Then like a woman in mourning
She gouged her arms with her nails,
She clawed her hair, and pounded her breasts with her fists,
Shrieking at him: 'You disgusting savage!
You sadistic monster!
The oaths my father bound you to –
Were they meaningless?
Do you remember his tears – you are inhuman,
You couldn't understand them.
What about my sister waiting for me?
What about me?
What about my life?
What about your marriage?
You have dragged us all
Into your bestial pit!
How can my sister think of me now?
Your crime is only half done –
Kill me and complete it.
Why didn't you kill me first
Before you destroyed me that other way?
Then my ghost at least
Would have been innocent.
But the gods are watching –
If they bother to notice what has happened –
If they are more than the puffs of air
That go with their names –
Then you will answer for this.
I may be lost,
You have taken whatever life
I might have had, and thrown it in the sewer,
But I have my voice.
And shame will not stop me.

I shall tell everything
To your own people, yes, to all Thrace.
Even if you keep me here
Every leaf in this forest
Will become a tongue to tell my story.
The dumb rocks will witness.
All heaven will be my jury.
Every god in heaven will judge you.'

Tereus was astonished
To be defied and raged at and insulted
By a human being. And startled
By the sudden clutch of fear
As her words went home. Speechless, mindless,
In a confusion of fear and fury

He hauled her up by the hair,
Twisted her arms behind her back and bound them,
Then drew his sword.
She saw that
As if she were eager, and bent her head backwards,
And closed her eyes, offering her throat to the blade –

Still calling to her father
And to the gods
And still trying to curse him
As he caught her tongue with bronze pincers,
Dragged it out to its full length and cut it
Off at the root.

The stump recoiled, silenced,
Into the back of her throat.
But the tongue squirmed in the dust, babbling on –
Shaping words that were now soundless.
It writhed like a snake's tail freshly cut off,
Striving to reach her feet in its death-struggle.

After this, again and again –
Though I can hardly bear to think about it,
Let alone believe it – the obsessed King
Like an automaton
Returned to the body he had mutilated
For his gruesome pleasure.

Then, stuffing the whole hideous business
Deep among his secrets,
He came home, smooth-faced, to his wife.
When she asked for her sister, he gave her
The tale he had prepared: she was dead.
His grief, as he wept, convinced everybody.

Procne stripped off her royal garments
And wrapped herself in black. She built a tomb
Without a body, for her sister,
And there she made offerings to a ghost
That did not exist, mourning the fate of a sister
Who endured a fate utterly different.

A year went by. Philomela,
Staring at the massive stone walls
And stared at by her guards, was still helpless,
Locked up in her dumbness and her prison.
But frustration, prolonged, begets invention,
And a vengeful anger nurses it.

She set up a Thracian loom
And wove on a white fabric scarlet symbols
That told in detail what had happened to her.
A servant, who understood her gestures
But knew nothing of what she carried,
Took this gift to Procne, the Queen.

The tyrant's wife
Unrolled the tapestry and saw
The only interpretation
Was the ruin of her life.
She sat there, silent and unmoving,
As if she thought of something else entirely.

In those moments, her restraint
Was superhuman. But grief so sudden, so huge,
Made mere words seem paltry.
None could lift to her lips
One drop of its bitterness.
And tears were pushed aside

By the devouring single idea
Of revenge. Revenge
Had swallowed her whole being. She had plunged

Into a labyrinth of plotting
Where good and evil, right and wrong,
Forgot their differences.

Now came the festival of Bacchus
Celebrated every third year
By the young women of Thrace.
The rites were performed at night –
All night long the din of cymbals
Deafened the city.

Dressed as a worshipper
Procne joined the uproar. With a light spear,
Vine leaves round her head, and a deer pelt
Slung over her left shoulder, she became
A Bacchante, among her attendants. Berserk
She hurled herself through the darkness, terrifying,

As if possessed by the god's frenzy.
In fact, she was crazy with grief.
So she found the hidden fort in the forest.
With howls to the god, her troop tore down the gate,
And Procne freed her sister, disguised her
As a Bacchante, and brought her home to the palace.

Philomela felt she might die
Of sheer fear, when she realised
She was in the house of her ravisher.
But Procne,
Shut in the safety of her own chamber,
Bared her sister's face and embraced her.

Philomela twisted away.
Shame tortured her.
She would not look at her sister –
As if she herself were to blame
For the King's depravity.
She fixed her eyes on the ground like a madwoman.

While her gestures flailed
Uselessly to tell the gods all
That Tereus had done to her
Doubling his cruelty on her body,
Despoiling her name for ever.
Procne took her shoulders and shook her.

She was out of her mind with anger:
'Tears can't help us,
Only the sword
Or if it exists
Something more pitiless
Even than the sword.

'O my sister, nothing now
Can soften
The death Tereus is going to die.
Let me see this palace one flame
And Tereus a blazing insect in it,
Making it brighter.

'Let me break his jaw. Hang him up
By his tongue and saw it through with a broken knife.
Then dig his eyes from their holes.
Give me the strength, you gods,
To twist his hips and shoulders from their sockets
And butcher the limbs off his trunk

'Till his soul for very terror scatter
Away through a thousand exits.
Let me kill him – Oh! However we kill him
Our revenge has to be something
That will appal heaven and hell
And stupefy the earth.'

While Procne raved Itys came in –
Her demented idea
Caught hold of his image.
'The double of his father,' she whispered.
Silent, her heart ice,
She saw what had to be done.

Nevertheless as he ran to her
Calling to her, his five-year-old arms
Pulling at her, to be kissed
And to kiss her, and chattering lovingly
Through his loving laughter
Her heart shrank.

Her fury seemed to be holding its breath
For that moment
As tears burned her eyes. She felt

Her love for this child
Softening her ferocious will – and she turned
To harden it, staring at her sister's face.

Then looked back at Itys
And again at her sister, crying:
'He tells me all his love – but she
Has no tongue to utter a word of hers.
He can call me mother, but she
Cannot call me sister.

'This is the man you have married!
O daughter of Pandion!
You are your father's shame and his despair.
To love this monster Tereus, or pity him,
You must be a monster.
It is monstrous!'

Catching Itys by the arm she gave herself
No more time to weaken.
Like a tiger on the banks of the Ganges
Taking a new-dropped fawn
She dragged him into a far cellar
Of the palace.

He saw what was coming. He tried
To clasp her neck screaming: 'Mama, Mama!'
But staring into his face
Procne pushed a sword through his chest –
Then, though that wound was fatal enough,
Slashed his throat.

Now the two sisters
Ripped the hot little body
Into pulsating gobbets.
The room was awash with blood
As they cooked his remains – some of it
Gasping in bronze pots, some weeping on spits.

A feast followed. Procne invited
One guest only, her husband.
She called it a ritual
Peculiar to her native land
And special for this day, when the wife
Served her lord, without attendant or servant.

Tereus, ignorant and happy,
Lolled on the throne of his ancestors
And swallowed, with smiles,
All his posterity
As Procne served it up. He was so happy
He called for his son to join him:

'Where is Itys? Bring him.'
Procne
Could not restrain herself any longer.
This was her moment
To see him fall helpless onto the spike
In the pit she had dug for him.

'Your son,' she said, 'is here, already.
He is here, inside,
He could not be closer to you.'
Tereus was mystified –
He suspected some joke, perhaps Itys
Was hiding under his throne.

'Itys,' he called again. 'Come out,
Show yourself.' The doors banged wide open,
Philomela burst into the throne-room,
Her hair and gown bloody. She rushed forward,
And her dismembering hands, red to the elbows,
Jammed into the face of Tereus

A crimson, dripping ball,
The head of Itys.
For moments, his brain
Refused to make sense of any of it.
But the joy she could not speak
Philomela released in a scream.

Then it was his turn.
His roar tore itself
Out of every fibre in his body.
He heaved the table aside –
Shouting for the Furies
To come up out of hell with their snake-heads.

He tugged at his rib-cage,
As if he might rive himself open
To empty out what he had eaten.

He staggered about, sobbing
That he was the tomb of his boy.
Then gripped his sword-hilt and steadied himself

As he saw the sisters running.
Now his bellow
Was as homicidal
As it was anguished.
He came after them and they
Who had been running seemed to be flying.

And suddenly they were flying. One swerved
On wings into the forest,
The other, with the blood still on her breast,
Flew up under the eaves of the palace.
And Tereus, charging blind
In his delirium of grief and vengeance,

No longer caring what happened –
He too was suddenly flying.
On his head and shoulders a crest of feathers,
Instead of a sword a long curved beak –
Like a warrior transfigured
With battle-frenzy dashing into battle.

He had become a hoopoe.
Philomela
Mourned in the forest, a nightingale.
Procne
Lamented round and round the palace,
A swallow.

Pyramus and Thisbe

Throughout the East men spoke in awe of Thisbe –
A girl who had suddenly bloomed
In Babylon, the mud-brick city.

The house she had grown up in adjoined
The house where Pyramus, so many years a boy,
Brooded bewildered by the moods of manhood.

These two, playmates from the beginning,
Fell in love.
For angry reasons, no part of the story,

The parents of each forbade their child
To marry the other. That was that.
But prohibition feeds love,

Though theirs needed no feeding. Through signs
Their addiction to each other
Was absolute, helpless, terminal.

And the worse for being hidden.
The more smothered their glances, the more
Agonised the look that leapt the gap.

In the shared wall that divided their houses,
Earth-tremors had opened a fissure.
For years, neither household had noticed.

But these lovers noticed.
Love is not blind. And where love cannot peer
Pure clairvoyance whispers in its ear.

This crack, this dusty crawl-space for a spider,
Became the highway of their love-murmurs.
Brows to the plaster, lips to the leak of air

And cooking smells from the other interior,
The lovers kneeled, confessing their passion,
Sealing their two fates with a fracture.

Sometimes they slapped the wall, in frustration:
'How can a wall be so jealous!
So deaf to us, so grudging with permission!

'If you can open this far for our voices
Why not fall wide open, let us kiss,
Let us join bodies as well as voices.

'No, that would be too much. That would mean
The wall repaired to part us utterly.
O wall, we are grateful. Nowhere in the world

'But in this tiny crack may our great loves,
Invisibly to us, meet and mingle.'
Then each would kiss the crack in the cold plaster,

Their own side of the wall, with a parting kiss.
This could not go on for long.
One day at their confessional, they decided

To obey love and risk everything.
They made their plan: that night they would somehow
Escape from their guarded houses,

Leave the city, and tryst in the open country –
Their rendezvous the mulberry tree
Over the tomb of Ninus, a famous landmark.

At this time of the year the tree was loaded
With its milk-white fruit, that a cool spring
Made especially plump and succulent.

Their plan enthralled them – with the joy it promised.
A promise that seemed so sure
No possible snag or snarl, no shadow of an error,

No shiver of apprehension troubled it.
Their sole anxiety was the unrelenting
Glare of the sun in the day, that seemed to have stopped.

But suddenly it was dark.
Thisbe had oiled the hinges. Now they helped her
Slip from the house like the shadow of a night-bird

Leaving the house-eaves. The moonlight
That lit her path from the city
Found the sparks of her eyes, but not her pallor –

Her veil hid all but her eyes from night watchers.
So she came to the tomb. Sitting in the shadow
Of the tree dense with fruit

That reflected the moon, like new snow,
She stared out into the brilliant jumble
Of moonlight and shadows. She strained

To catch the first stirring of a shadow
That would grow into Pyramus. It was then,
As she peered and listened,

And felt the huge silence, the hanging weight
Of the moonlit cliff above her,
And, above the cliff, the prickling stars,

That the first fear touched her.
She froze, her breath shrank, slight as a lizard's.
Only her eyes moved.

She had seen, in her eye-corner, a shadow
That seemed to have shifted.
Now she could hear her heart. Her head swivelled.

Somebody was walking towards her.
She stood, she leaned to the tree, her legs trembling.
She realised she was panting.

And almost cried out: 'Pyramus!'
But at that moment
The shadow coughed a strange cough – hoarse, cavernous,

And was much nearer, moving too swiftly.
A strangely hobbling dwarf, bent under something.
Then her brain seemed to turn over.

Plain in the moonlight she saw
That what had looked like a dwarf
Was nothing of the kind. A lioness

Was slouching directly towards her
Under its rippling shoulders, coming
To wash its bloody jaws,

And quench its hanging belly, its blood-salt surfeit,
In the spring beside her.
Without another thought, Thisbe was running –

She left her veil floating
To settle near the water. She ran, ducking
Behind the tomb of Ninus, too frightened to scream,

And squeezing her eyes shut, squeezed herself
Into a crevice under the cliff.
The lioness drank, then found the veil,

The perfumed veil perfumed again
By a woman's excitement, and her fear.
The beast began to play with the veil –

Forepaws tore downwards, jaw ripped upwards.
And the veil towelled the blood
From the sodden muzzle, and from the fangs.

Soon the beast lost interest
In this empty skin, so savourless,
And the beautiful weave was abandoned.

The lioness went off. She was absorbed
Among the moonlit rocks
As if she had never happened. Only the veil

Waited for Pyramus
Who now emerged running, his shadow vaulting beside him.
Both stopped at the spring.

The lion's footprints, alien, deep, unwelcome,
Printed the spring's margin.
Pyramus picked up the veil, too familiar

Blackened by blood though it was –
Blood so fresh and glistening. He groaned,
Not unlike the lioness

But groaning words: 'Did our planning
Foresee this double death as a fitting
Finale to our love which was forbidden?

'But Thisbe should have escaped the lion and lived.
I am to blame – for appointing this wild place
But failing to be here before her.'

Then he roared aloud: 'Are there any more lions
Living in the cliff there?
Come out and punish a criminal.'

He groaned again, to himself:
'Cowards call for death – but courage
Does something about it.'

He swayed, weeping into the sticky remnant:
'Let our blood mingle
As never in love, in this veil torn by a lion.'

He set his sword point to his chest
And ran at the tree, burying the blade to the hilt,
Then with his last effort pulled it from the wound.

When a lead conduit splits, the compressed water
Jets like a fountain.
His blood shot out in bursts, each burst a heartbeat,

Showering the fruit of the tree –
Till the white fruits, now dyed hectic purple,
Dripped his own blood back onto his body

That spilled the rest of its life, in heavy brimmings,
To the tree roots that drank it
And took it up to the fruits, that fattened darker.

Thisbe's fear for Pyramus and the lion,
And, almost worse, the thought that he might have arrived
And be at the tomb without her

Brought her running. But when she saw
The tree that had been snow-white with its fruit
Now purple-dark, blackish in the moonlight,

Her new fear was that she had lost her bearings
And come to the wrong place. Then she heard
A grunting cough in the tree's shadow

And saw the body sprawl, as if in sleep,
Into the moonlight.
Now she screamed. Unafraid of the lion

Again and again she screamed.
She embraced his corpse, fierce as any lion,
More passionately than she had ever dreamed

Of embracing it in life. She screamed to him
To wake up and speak to her.
His eyes opened a moment, but death

Was closing their light as they gazed at her.
Thisbe looked down at her hand, it was clutching
The soggy rag of her veil.

She saw his scabbard empty. 'It was your love
That persuaded your own hand to kill you.
My love is as great, my hand as ready.

'Once I am with you
My story can be told: the cause of your death,
But your consolation for ever.

'Death has divided us, so it is right
That death should bring us together
In an unbreakable wedlock. Parents,

'As you find our bodies,
Limbs entwined, stiffened in a single knot,
Do not separate us. Burn us as we lived

'In the one flame.
And you who live on, with your boughs laden,
Over two stripped of their blossom, their seed and their life,

'Remember how we died. Remember us
By the colour of our blood in your fruit.
So when men gather your fruit, and crush its ripeness,

'Let them think of our deaths.'
She spoke, then set the point of the warm sword
Beneath her breast and fell on it.

With her last strength she wound him with her arms and legs.

The gods were listening and were touched.
And the gods touched their parents. Ever after
Mulberries, as they ripen, darken purple.

And the two lovers in their love-knot,
One pile of inseparable ashes,
Were closed in a single urn.

BIRTHDAY LETTERS (1998)

Fulbright Scholars

Where was it, in the Strand? A display
Of news items, in photographs.
For some reason I noticed it.
A picture of that year's intake
Of Fulbright Scholars. Just arriving –
Or arrived. Or some of them.
Were you among them? I studied it,
Not too minutely, wondering
Which of them I might meet.
I remember that thought. Not
Your face. No doubt I scanned particularly
The girls. Maybe I noticed you.
Maybe I weighed you up, feeling unlikely.
Noted your long hair, loose waves –
Your Veronica Lake bang. Not what it hid.
It would appear blond. And your grin.
Your exaggerated American
Grin for the cameras, the judges, the strangers, the frighteners.
Then I forgot. Yet I remember
The picture: the Fulbright Scholars.
With their luggage? It seems unlikely.
Could they have come as a team? I was walking
Sore-footed, under hot sun, hot pavements.
Was it then I bought a peach? That's as I remember.
From a stall near Charing Cross Station.
It was the first fresh peach I had ever tasted.
I could hardly believe how delicious.
At twenty-five I was dumbfounded afresh
By my ignorance of the simplest things.

Caryatids (1)

What were those caryatids bearing?
It was the first poem of yours I had seen.
It was the only poem you ever wrote
That I disliked through the eyes of a stranger.
It seemed thin and brittle, the lines cold.
Like the theorem of a trap, a deadfall – set.
I saw that. And the trap unsprung, empty.

I felt no interest. No stirring
Of omen. In those days I coerced
Oracular assurance
In my favour out of every sign.
So missed everything
In the white, blindfolded, rigid faces
Of those women. I felt their frailty, yes:
Friable, burnt aluminium.
Fragile, like the mantle of a gas-lamp.
But made nothing
Of that massive, starless, mid-fall, falling
Heaven of granite
                    stopped, as if in a snapshot,
By their hair.

Caryatids (2)

Stupid with confidence, in the playclothes
Of still growing, still reclining
In the cushioned palanquin,
The nursery care of nature's leisurely lift
Towards her fullness, we were careless
Of grave life, three of us, four, five, six –
Playing at friendship. Time in plenty
To test every role – for laughs,
For the experiment, lending our hours
To perversities of impulse, charade-like
Improvisations of the inane,
Like prisoners, our real life
Perforce deferred, with the real
World and self. So, playing at students, we filled
And drunkenly drained, filled and again drained
A boredom, a cornucopia
Of airy emptiness, of the brown
And the yellow ale, of makings and unmakings –
Godlike, as frivolous as faithless,
A dramaturgy of whim.
That was our education. The world
Crossed the wet courts, on Sunday, politely,
In tourists' tentative shoes.
All roads lay too open, opened too deeply

Every degree of the compass.
Here at the centre of the web, at the crossroads,
You published your poem
About Caryatids. We had heard
Of the dance of your blond veils, your flaring gestures,
Your misfit self-display. More to reach you
Than to reproach you, more to spark
A contact through the see-saw bustling
Atmospherics of higher learning
And lower socialising, than to correct you
With our archaic principles, we concocted
An attack, a dismemberment, laughing.
We had our own broadsheet to publish it.
Our Welshman composed it – still deaf
To the white noise of the elegy
That would fill his mouth and his ear
Worlds later, on Cader Idris,
In the wind and snow of your final climb.

Visit

Lucas, my friend, one
Among those three or four who stay unchanged
Like a separate self,
A stone in the bed of the river
Under every change, became your friend.
I heard of it, alerted. I was sitting
Youth away in an office near Slough,
Morning and evening between Slough and Holborn,
Hoarding wage to fund a leap to freedom
And the other side of the earth – a free-fall
To strip my chrysalis off me in the slipstream.
Weekends I recidived
Into Alma Mater. Girl-friend
Shared a supervisor and weekly session
With your American rival and you.
She detested you. She fed snapshots
Of you and she did not know what
Inflammable celluloid into my silent
Insatiable future, my blind-man's-buff
Internal torch of search. With my friend,

After midnight, I stood in a garden
Lobbing soil-clods up at a dark window.

Drunk, he was certain it was yours.
Half as drunk, I did not know he was wrong.
Nor did I know I was being auditioned
For the male lead in your drama,
Miming through the first easy movements
As if with eyes closed, feeling for the role.
As if a puppet were being tried on its strings,
Or a dead frog's legs touched by electrodes.
I jigged through those gestures – watched and judged
Only by starry darkness and a shadow.
Unknown to you and not knowing you.
Aiming to find you, and missing, and again missing.
Flinging earth at a glass that could not protect you
Because you were not there.

Ten years after your death
I meet on a page of your journal, as never before,
The shock of your joy
When you heard of that. Then the shock
Of your prayers. And under those prayers your panic
That prayers might not create the miracle,
Then, under the panic, the nightmare
That came rolling to crush you:
Your alternative – the unthinkable
Old despair and the new agony
Melting into one familiar hell.

Suddenly I read all this –
Your actual words, as they floated
Out through your throat and tongue and onto your page –
Just as when your daughter, years ago now,
Drifting in, gazing up into my face,
Mystified,
Where I worked alone
In the silent house, asked, suddenly:
'Daddy, where's Mummy?' The freezing soil
Of the garden, as I clawed it.
All round me that midnight's
Giant clock of frost. And somewhere
Inside it, wanting to feel nothing,

A pulse of fever. Somewhere
Inside that numbness of the earth
Our future trying to happen.
I look up – as if to meet your voice
With all its urgent future
That has burst in on me. Then look back
At the book of the printed words.
You are ten years dead. It is only a story.
Your story. My story.

Sam

It was all of a piece to you
That your horse, the white calm stallion, Sam,
Decided he'd had enough
And started home at a gallop. I can live
Your incredulity, your certainty
That this was it. You lost your stirrups. He galloped
Straight down the white line of the Barton Road.
You lost your reins, you lost your seat –
It was grab his neck and adore him
Or free-fall. You slewed under his neck,
An upside-down jockey with nothing
Between you and the cataract of macadam,
That horribly hard, swift river,
But the propeller terrors of his front legs
And the clangour of the iron shoes, so far beneath you.

Luck was already there. Did you have a helmet?
How did you cling on? Baby monkey
Using your arms and legs for clinging steel.
What saved you? Maybe your poems
Saved themselves, slung under that plunging neck,
Hammocked in your body over the switchback road.

You saw only blur. And a cyclist's shock-mask,
Fallen, dragging his bicycle over him, protective.
I can feel your bounced and dangling anguish,
Hugging what was left of your steerage.
How did you hang on? You couldn't have done it.
Something in you not you did it for itself.
You clung on, probably nearly unconscious,

Till he walked into his stable. That gallop
Was practice, but not enough, and quite useless.

When I jumped a fence you strangled me
One giddy moment, then fell off,
Flung yourself off and under my feet to trip me
And tripped me and lay dead. Over in a flash.

The Tender Place

Your temples, where the hair crowded in,
Were the tender place. Once to check
I dropped a file across the electrodes
Of a twelve-volt battery – it exploded
Like a grenade. Somebody wired you up.
Somebody pushed the lever. They crashed
The thunderbolt into your skull.
In their bleached coats, with blenched faces,
They hovered again
To see how you were, in your straps.
Whether your teeth were still whole.
The hand on the calibrated lever
Again feeling nothing
Except feeling nothing pushed to feel
Some squirm of sensation. Terror
Was the cloud of you
Waiting for these lightnings. I saw
An oak limb sheared at a bang.
You your Daddy's leg. How many seizures
Did you suffer this god to grab you
By the roots of the hair? The reports
Escaped back into clouds. What went up
Vaporised? Where lightning rods wept copper
And the nerve threw off its skin
Like a burning child
Scampering out of the bomb-flash. They dropped you
A rigid bent bit of wire
Across the Boston City grid. The lights
In the Senate House dipped
As your voice dived inwards
Right through the bolt-hole basement.

Came up, years later,
Over-exposed, like an X-ray –
Brain-map still dark-patched
With the scorched-earth scars
Of your retreat. And your words,
Faces reversed from the light,
Holding in their entrails.

St Botolph's

Our magazine was merely an overture
To the night and the party. I had predicted
Disastrous expense: a planetary
Certainty, according to Prospero's book.
Jupiter and the full moon conjunct
Opposed Venus. Disastrous expense
According to that book. Especially for me.
The conjunction combust my natal Sun.
Venus pinned exact on my mid-heaven.
For a wait-and-see astrologer – so what?
Touch of a bat's wing easily exorcised.
Our Chaucer would have stayed at home with his Dante.
Locating the planets more precisely,
He would have pondered it deeper. What else? I left it
For serious astrologers to worry
That conjunction, conjunct my Sun, conjunct
With your natal ruling Mars. And Chaucer
Would have pointed to that day's Sun in the Fish
Conjunct your Ascendant exactly
Opposite my Neptune and fixed
In my tenth House of good and evil fame.
Our Chaucer, I think, would have sighed.
He would have assured us, shaking his sorrowful head,
That day the solar system married us
Whether we knew it or not.
                              Falcon Yard:
Girl-friend like a loaded crossbow. The sound-waves
Jammed and torn by Joe Lyde's Jazz. The hall
Like the tilting deck of the *Titanic*:
A silent film, with that blare over it. Suddenly –
Lucas engineered it – suddenly you.

First sight. First snapshot isolated
Unalterable, stilled in the camera's glare.
Taller
Than ever you were again. Swaying so slender
It seemed your long, perfect, American legs
Simply went on up. That flaring hand,
Those long, balletic, monkey-elegant fingers.
And the face – a tight ball of joy.
I see you there, clearer, more real
Than in any of the years in its shadow –
As if I saw you that once, then never again.
The loose fall of hair – that floppy curtain
Over your face, over your scar. And your face
A rubbery ball of joy
Round the African-lipped, laughing, thickly
Crimson-painted mouth. And your eyes
Squeezed in your face, a crush of diamonds,
Incredibly bright, bright as a crush of tears
That might have been tears of joy, a squeeze of joy.
You meant to knock me out
With your vivacity. I remember
Little from the rest of that evening.
I slid away with my girl-friend. Nothing
Except her hissing rage in a doorway
And my stupefied interrogation
Of your blue headscarf from my pocket
And the swelling ring-moat of tooth-marks
That was to brand my face for the next month.
The me beneath it for good.

The Shot

Your worship needed a god.
Where it lacked one, it found one.
Ordinary jocks became gods –
Deified by your infatuation
That seemed to have been designed at birth for a god.
It was a god-seeker. A god-finder.
Your Daddy had been aiming you at God
When his death touched the trigger.

                                    In that flash

You saw your whole life. You ricocheted
The length of your Alpha career
With the fury
Of a high-velocity bullet
That cannot shed one foot-pound
Of kinetic energy. The elect
More or less died on impact –
They were too mortal to take it. They were mind-stuff,
Provisional, speculative, mere auras.
Sound-barrier events along your flightpath.
But inside your sob-sodden Kleenex
And your Saturday night panics,
Under your hair done this way and done that way,
Behind what looked like rebounds
And the cascade of cries diminuendo,
You were undeflected.
You were gold-jacketed, solid silver,
Nickel-tipped. Trajectory perfect
As through ether. Even the cheek-scar,
Where you seemed to have side-swiped concrete,
Served as a rifling groove
To keep you true.
                    Till your real target
Hid behind me. Your Daddy,
The god with the smoking gun. For a long time
Vague as mist, I did not even know
I had been hit,
Or that you had gone clean through me –
To bury yourself at last in the heart of the god.

In my position, the right witchdoctor
Might have caught you in flight with his bare hands,
Tossed you, cooling, one hand to the other,
Godless, happy, quieted.
                    I managed
A wisp of your hair, your ring, your watch, your nightgown.

Trophies

The panther? It had already dragged you
As if in its jaws, across Europe.
As if trailing between its legs,
Your mouth crying open, or not even crying any more,
Just letting yourself be dragged. Its real prey
Had skipped and escaped. So the fangs,
Blind in frustration,
Crushed your trachea, strangled the sounds. The Rorschach
Splashing of those outpourings stained
Your journal pages. Your effort to cry words
Came apart in aired blood
Enriched by the adrenalins
Of despair, terror, sheer fury –
After forty years
The whiff of that beast, off the dry pages,
Lifts the hair on the back of my hands.
The thrill of it. The sudden
Look that locked on me
Through your amber jewels
And as I caught you lolling locked
Its jaws into my face. The tenacity
Of the big cat's claim
On the one marked down and once disabled
Is a chemical process – a combustion
Of the stuff of judgement.

So it sprang over you. Its jungle prints
Hit your page. Plainly the blood
Was your own. With a laugh I
Took its full weight. Little did I know
The shock attack of a big predator
According to survivors numbs the target
Into drunken euphoria. Still smiling
As it carried me off I detached
The hairband carefully from between its teeth
And a ring from its ear, for my trophies.

18 Rugby Street

So there in Number Eighteen Rugby Street's
Victorian torpor and squalor I waited for you.
I think of that house as a stage-set –
Four floors exposed to the auditorium.
On all four floors, in, out, the love-struggle
In all its acts and scenes, a snakes and ladders
Of intertangling and of disentangling
Limbs and loves and lives. Nobody was old.
An unmysterious laboratory of amours.
Perpetual performance – names of the actors altered,
But never the parts. They told me: 'You
Should write a book about this house. It's possessed!
Whoever comes into it never gets properly out!
Whoever enters it enters a labyrinth –
A Knossos of coincidence! And now you're in it.'
The legends were amazing. I listened, amazed.

I lived there alone. Sat alone
At the hacked, archaic, joiner's bench
That did for desk and table,
And waited for you and Lucas.
Whatever I was thinking I was not thinking
Of that Belgian girl in the ground-floor flat,
Plump as a mushroom, hair black as boot polish:
The caged bird and extra-marital cuddle
Of the second-hand-car dealer who kept
The catacomb basement heaped with exhaust mufflers,
Assorted jagged shards of cars, shin-rippers
On the way to the unlit and unlovely
Lavatory beneath the street's pavement.
That girl had nothing to do with the rest of the house
But play her part in the drama. Her house-jailer
Who kept her in solitary was a demon
High-explosive, black, insane Alsatian
That challenged through the chained crack of the door
Every entrance and exit. He guarded her,
For the car dealer, from all, too well finally.
Not, seven years in the future, from her gas-oven.
She was nothing to do with me. Nor was Susan
Who still had to be caught in the labyrinth,

And who would meet the Minotaur there,
And would be holding me from my telephone
Those nights you would most need me. On this evening
Nothing could make me think I would ever be needed
By anybody. Ten years had to darken,
Three of them in your grave, before Susan
Could pace that floor above night after night
(Where you and I, the new rings big on our fingers,
Had warmed our wedding night in the single bed)
Crying alone and dying of leukaemia.

Lucas was bringing you. You were pausing
A night in London on your escape to Paris.
April 13th, your father's birthday. A Friday.
I guessed you were off to whirl through some euphoric
American Europe. Years after your death
I learned the desperation of that search
Through those following days, scattering your tears
Around the cobbles of Paris. I deferred for a night
Your panics, your fevers, your worst fear –
The toad-stone in the head of your desolation.
The dream you hunted for, the life you begged
To be given again, you would never recover, ever.
Your journal told me the story of your torture.

I guess how you visited each of your sacred shrines
In raging faith you'd catch him there, somehow,
By clairvoyance, by coincidence –
Normally child's play to a serious passion.
This was not the last time it would fail you.
Meanwhile there was me, for a few hours –
A few pence on the fare, for insurance.
Happy to be martyred for folly
I invoked you, bribing Fate to produce you.
Were you conjuring me? I had no idea
How I was becoming necessary,
Or what emergency surgery Fate would make
Of my casual self-service. I can hear you
Climbing the bare stairs, alive and close,
Babbling to be overheard, breathless.
That was your artillery, to confuse me:
Before coming over the top in your panoply
You wanted me to hear you panting. Then –

Blank. How did you enter? What came next?
How did Lucas delete himself, for instance?
Did we even sit? A great bird, you
Surged in the plumage of your excitement,
Raving exhilaration. A blueish voltage –
Fluorescent cobalt, a flare of aura
That I later learned was yours uniquely.
And your eyes' peculiar brightness, their oddness,
Two little brown people, hooded, Prussian,
But elvish, and girlish, and sparking
With the pressure of your effervescence.
Were they family heirlooms, as in your son?
For me yours were the novel originals.
And now at last I got a good look at you.
Your roundy face, that your friends, being objective,
Called 'rubbery' and you, crueller, 'boneless':
A device for elastic extremes,
A spirit mask transfigured every moment
In its own séance, its own ether.
And I became aware of the mystery
Of your lips, like nothing before in my life,
Their aboriginal thickness. And of your nose,
Broad and Apache, nearly a boxer's nose,
Scorpio's obverse to the Semitic eagle
That made every camera your enemy,
The jailer of your vanity, the traitor
In your Sexual Dreams Incorporated,
Nose from Attila's horde: a prototype face
That could have looked up at me through the smoke
Of a Navajo campfire. And your small temples
Into which your hair-roots crowded, upstaged
By that glamorous, fashionable bang.
And your little chin, your Pisces chin.
It was never a face in itself. Never the same.
It was like the sea's face – a stage
For weathers and currents, the sun's play and the moon's.
Never a face until that final morning
When it became the face of a child – its scar
Like a Maker's flaw. But now you declaimed
A long poem about a black panther
While I held you and kissed you and tried to keep you

From flying about the room. For all that,
You would not stay.

We walked south across London to Fetter Lane
And your hotel. Opposite the entrance
On a bombsite becoming a building site
We clutched each other giddily
For safety and went in a barrel together
Over some Niagara. Falling
In the roar of soul your scar told me –
Like its secret name or its password –
How you had tried to kill yourself. And I heard
Without ceasing for a moment to kiss you
As if a sober star had whispered it
Above the revolving, rumbling city: stay clear.

A poltroon of a star. I cannot remember
How I smuggled myself, wrapped in you,
Into the hotel. There we were.
You were slim and lithe and smooth as a fish.
You were a new world. My new world.
So this is America, I marvelled.
Beautiful, beautiful America!

The Machine

The dark ate at you. And the fear
Of being crushed. 'A huge dark machine',
'The grinding indifferent
Millstone of circumstance'. After
Watching the orange sunset, these were the words
You put on a page. They had come to you
When I did not. When you tried
To will me up the stair, this terror
Arrived instead. While I
Most likely was just sitting,
Maybe with Lucas, no more purpose in me
Than in my own dog
That I did not have. A real dog
Might have stared at nothing
Hair on end
While the grotesque mask of your Mummy-Daddy

Half-quarry, half-hospital, whole
Juggernaut, stuffed with your unwritten poems,
Ground invisibly without a ripple
Towards me through the unstirred willows,
Through the wall of The Anchor,
Drained my Guinness at a gulp,
Blackly yawned me
Into its otherworld interior
Where I would find my home. My children. And my life
Forever trying to climb the steps now stone
Towards the door now red
Which you, in your own likeness, would open
With still time to talk.

God Help the Wolf after Whom the Dogs Do Not Bark

There you met it – the mystery of hatred.
After your billions of years in anonymous matter
That was where you were found – and promptly hated.
You tried your utmost to reach and touch those people
With gifts of yourself –
Just like your first words as a toddler
When you rushed at every visitor to the house
Clasping their legs and crying: 'I love you! I love you!'
Just as you had danced for your father
In the home of anger – gifts of your life
To sweeten his slow death and mix yourself in it
Where he lay propped on the couch,
To sugar the bitterness of his raging death.

You searched for yourself to go on giving it
As if after the nightfall of his going
You danced on in the dark house,
Eight years old, in your tinsel.

Searching for yourself, in the dark, as you danced,
Floundering a little, crying softly,
Like somebody searching for somebody drowning
In dark water,
Listening for them – in panic at losing
Those listening seconds from your searching –
Then dancing wilder in the silence.

The Colleges lifted their heads. It did seem
You disturbed something just perfected
That they were holding carefully, all of a piece,
Till the glue dried. And as if
Reporting some felony to the police
They let you know that you were not John Donne.
You no longer care. Did you save their names?
But then they let you know, day by day,
Their contempt for everything you attempted,
Took pains to inject their bile, as for your health,
Into your morning coffee. Even signed
Their homeopathic letters,
Envelopes full of carefully broken glass
To lodge behind your eyes so you would see

Nobody wanted your dance,
Nobody wanted your strange glitter – your floundering
Drowning life and your effort to save yourself,
Treading water, dancing the dark turmoil,
Looking for something to give –
                                        Whatever you found
They bombarded with splinters,
Derision, mud – the mystery of that hatred.

Fidelity

It was somewhere to live. I was
Just hanging around, courting you,
Afloat on the morning tide and tipsy feelings
Of my twenty-fifth year. Gutted, restyled
À la mode, the Alexandra House
Became a soup-kitchen. Those were the days
Before the avant-garde of coffee bars.
The canteen clatter of the British Restaurant,
One of the war's utility leftovers,
Was still the place to repair the nights with breakfasts.
But Alexandra House was the place to be seen in.
The girls that helped to run it lived above it
With a retinue of loose-lifers, day-sleepers
Exhausted with night-owling. Somehow
I got a mattress up there, in a top room,

Overlooking Petty Cury. A bare
Mattress, on bare boards, in a bare room.
All I had, my notebook and that mattress.
Under the opening, bud-sticky chestnuts,
On into June, my job chucked, I laboured
Only at you, squandering all I'd saved.
Free of University I dangled
In its liberties. Every night
I slept on that mattress, under one blanket,
With a lovely girl, escaped freshly
From her husband to the frontier exposure
Of work in the soup-kitchen. What
Knighthood possessed me there? I think of it
As a kind of time that cannot pass,
That I never used, so still possess.
She and I slept in each other's arms,
Naked and easy as lovers, a month of nights,
Yet never once made love. A holy law
Had invented itself, somehow, for me.
But she too served it, like a priestess,
Tender, kind and stark naked beside me.
She traced out the fresh rips you had inscribed
Across my back, seeming to join me
In my obsession, in my concentration,
To keep my preoccupation intact.
She never once invited, never tempted.
And I never stirred a finger beyond
Sisterly comforting. I was like her sister.
It never seemed unnatural. I was focused,
So locked onto you, so brilliantly,
Everything that was not you was blind-spot.
I still puzzle over it – doubtful, now,
Whether to envy myself, or pity. Her friend,
Who had a bigger room, was wilder.
We moved in with her. That lofty room
Became a dormitory and H.Q.
Alternative to St Botolph's. Plump and pretty,
With a shameless gap-tooth laugh, her friend
Did all she could to get me inside her.
And you will never know what a battle
I fought to keep the meaning of my words
Solid with the world we were making.

I was afraid, if I lost that fight
Something might abandon us. Lifting
Each of those naked girls, as they smiled at me
In their early twenties, I laid them
Under the threshold of our unlikely future
As those who wanted protection for a new home
Used to bury, under the new threshold,
A sinless child.

Fate Playing

Because the message somehow met a goblin,
Because precedents tripped your expectations,
Because your London was still a kaleidoscope
Of names and places any jolt could scramble,
You waited mistaken. The bus from the North
Came in and emptied and I was not on it.
No matter how much you insisted
And begged the driver, probably with tears,
To produce me or to remember seeing me
Just miss getting on. I was not on it.
Eight in the evening and I was lost and at large
Somewhere in England. You restrained
Your confident inspiration
And did not dash out into the traffic
Milling around Victoria, utterly certain
Of bumping into me where I would have to be walking.
I was not walking anywhere. I was sitting
Unperturbed, in my seat on the train
Rocking towards King's Cross. Somebody,
Calmer than you, had a suggestion. So,
When I got off the train, expecting to find you
Somewhere down at the root of the platform,
I saw that surge and agitation, a figure
Breasting the flow of released passengers,
Then your molten face, your molten eyes
And your exclamations, your flinging arms
Your scattering tears
As if I had come back from the dead
Against every possibility, against
Every negative but your own prayer

To your own gods. There I knew what it was
To be a miracle. And behind you
Your jolly taxi-driver, laughing, like a small god,
To see an American girl being so American,
And to see your frenzied chariot-ride –
Sobbing and goading him, and pleading with him
To make happen what you needed to happen –
Succeed so completely, thanks to him.
Well, it was a wonder
That my train was not earlier, even much earlier,
That it pulled in, late, the very moment
You irrupted onto the platform. It was
Natural and miraculous and an omen
Confirming everything
You wanted confirmed. So your huge despair,
Your cross-London panic dash
And now your triumph, splashed over me,
Like love forty-nine times magnified,
Like the first thunder cloudburst engulfing
The drought in August
When the whole cracked earth seems to quake
And every leaf trembles
And everything holds up its arms weeping.

The Owl

I saw my world again through your eyes
As I would see it again through your children's eyes.
Through your eyes it was foreign.
Plain hedge hawthorns were peculiar aliens,
A mystery of peculiar lore and doings.
Anything wild, on legs, in your eyes
Emerged at a point of exclamation
As if it had appeared to dinner guests
In the middle of the table. Common mallards
Were artefacts of some unearthliness,
Their wooings were a hypnagogic film
Unreeled by the river. Impossible
To comprehend the comfort of their feet
In the freezing water. You were a camera
Recording reflections you could not fathom.

I made my world perform its utmost for you.
You took it all in with an incredulous joy
Like a mother handed her new baby
By the midwife. Your frenzy made me giddy.
It woke up my dumb, ecstatic boyhood
Of fifteen years before. My masterpiece
Came that black night on the Grantchester road.
I sucked the throaty thin woe of a rabbit
Out of my wetted knuckle, by a copse
Where a tawny owl was enquiring.
Suddenly it swooped up, splaying its pinions
Into my face, taking me for a post.

A Pink Wool Knitted Dress

In your pink wool knitted dress
Before anything had smudged anything
You stood at the altar. Bloomsday.

Rain – so that a just-bought umbrella
Was the only furnishing about me
Newer than three years inured.
My tie – sole, drab, veteran R.A.F. black –
Was the used-up symbol of a tie.
My cord jacket – thrice-dyed black, exhausted,
Just hanging on to itself.

I was a post-war, utility son-in-law!
Not quite the Frog-Prince. Maybe the Swineherd
Stealing this daughter's pedigree dreams
From under her watchtowered searchlit future.

No ceremony could conscript me
Out of my uniform. I wore my whole wardrobe –
Except for the odd, spare, identical item.
My wedding, like Nature, wanted to hide.
However – if we were going to be married
It had better be Westminster Abbey. Why not?
The Dean told us why not. That is how
I learned that I had a Parish Church.
St George of the Chimney Sweeps.
So we squeezed into marriage finally.

Your mother, brave even in this
U.S. Foreign Affairs gamble,
Acted all bridesmaids and all guests,
Even – magnanimity – represented
My family
Who had heard nothing about it.
I had invited only their ancestors.
I had not even confided my theft of you
To a closest friend. For Best Man – my squire
To hold the meanwhile rings –
We requisitioned the sexton. Twist of the outrage:
He was packing children into a bus,
Taking them to the Zoo – in that downpour!
All the prison animals had to be patient
While we married.
                          You were transfigured.
So slender and new and naked,
A nodding spray of wet lilac.
You shook, you sobbed with joy, you were ocean depth
Brimming with God.
You said you saw the heavens open
And show riches, ready to drop upon us.
Levitated beside you, I stood subjected
To a strange tense: the spellbound future.

In that echo-gaunt, weekday chancel
I see you
Wrestling to contain your flames
In your pink wool knitted dress
And in your eye-pupils – great cut jewels
Jostling their tear-flames, truly like big jewels
Shaken in a dice-cup and held up to me.

Your Paris

Your Paris, I thought, was American.
I wanted to humour you.
When you stepped, in a shatter of exclamations,
Out of the Hôtel des Deux Continents
Through frame after frame,
Street after street, of Impressionist paintings,

Under the chestnut shades of Hemingway,
Fitzgerald, Henry Miller, Gertrude Stein,
I kept my Paris from you. My Paris
Was only just not German. The capital
Of the Occupation and old nightmare.
I read each bullet scar in the Quai stonework
With an eerie familiar feeling,
And stared at the stricken, sunny exposure of pavement
Beneath it. I had rehearsed
Carefully, over and over, just those moments –
Most of my life, it seemed. While you
Called me Aristide Bruant and wanted
To draw *les toits*, and your ecstasies ricocheted
Off the walls patched and scabbed with posters –
I heard the contrabasso counterpoint
In my dog-nosed pondering analysis
Of café chairs where the S.S. mannequins
Had performed their *tableaux vivants*
So recently the coffee was still bitter
As acorns, and the waiters' eyes
Clogged with dregs of betrayal, reprisal, hatred.
I was not much ravished by the view of the roofs.
My Paris was a post-war utility survivor,
The stink of fear still hanging in the wardrobes,
Collaborateurs barely out of their twenties,
Every other face closed by the Camps
Or the Maquis. I was a ghostwatcher.
My perspectives were veiled by what rose
Like methane from the reopened
Mass grave of Verdun. For you all that
Was the anecdotal aesthetic touch
On Picasso's portrait
Of Apollinaire, with its proleptic
Marker for the bullet. And wherever
Your eye lit, your immaculate palette,
The thesaurus of your cries,
Touched in its tints and textures. Your lingo
Always like an emergency burn-off
To protect you from spontaneous combustion
Protected you
And your Paris. It was diesel aflame
To the dog in me. It scorched up

Every scent and sensor. And it sealed
The underground, your hide-out,
That chamber, where you still hung waiting
For your torturer
To remember his amusement. Those walls,
Raggy with posters, were your own flayed skin –
Stretched on your stone god.
What walked beside me was flayed,
One walking wound that the air
Coming against kept in a fever, wincing
To agonies. Your practised lips
Translated the spasms to what you excused
As your gushy burblings – which I decoded
Into a language, utterly new to me
With conjectural, hopelessly wrong meanings –
You gave me no hint how, at every corner,
My fingers linked in yours, you expected
The final face-to-face revelation
To grab your whole body. Your Paris
Was a desk in a *pension*
Where your letters
Waited for him unopened. Was a labyrinth
Where you still hurtled, scattering tears.
Was a dream where you could not
Wake or find the exit or
The Minotaur to put a blessed end
To the torment. What searching miles
Did you drag your pain
That were for me plain paving, albeit
Pecked by the odd, stray, historic bullet.
The mere dog in me, happy to protect you
From your agitation and your stone hours,
Like a guide dog, loyal to correct your stumblings,
Yawned and dozed and watched you calm yourself
With your anaesthetic – your drawing, as by touch,
Roofs, a traffic bollard, a bottle, me.

You Hated Spain

                            Spain frightened you. Spain
Where I felt at home. The blood-raw light,
The oiled anchovy faces, the African
Black edges to everything, frightened you.
Your schooling had somehow neglected Spain.
The wrought-iron grille, death and the Arab drum.
You did not know the language, your soul was empty
Of the signs, and the welding light
Made your blood shrivel. Bosch
Held out a spidery hand and you took it
Timidly, a bobby-sox American.
You saw right down to the Goya funeral grin
And recognised it, and recoiled
As your poems winced into chill, as your panic
Clutched back towards college America.
So we sat as tourists at the bullfight
Watching bewildered bulls awkwardly butchered,
Seeing the grey-faced matador, at the barrier
Just below us, straightening his bent sword
And vomiting with fear. And the horn
That hid itself inside the blowfly belly
Of the toppled picador punctured
What was waiting for you. Spain
Was the land of your dreams: the dust-red cadaver
You dared not wake with, the puckering amputations
No literature course had glamorised.
The juju land behind your African lips.
Spain was what you tried to wake up from
And could not. I see you, in moonlight,
Walking the empty wharf at Alicante
Like a soul waiting for the ferry,
A new soul, still not understanding,
Thinking it is still your honeymoon
In the happy world, with your whole life waiting,
Happy, and all your poems still to be found.

Moonwalk

A glare chunk of moon.
The hill no colour
Under the polarised light.
Like a day pushed inside out. Everything
In negative. Your mask
Bleak as cut iron, a shell-half –
Shucked off the moon. Alarming
And angering moon-devil – here somewhere.
The Ancient Mariner's Death-in-Life woman
Straight off the sea's fevered incandescence
Throwing black-and-white dice.
A sea saracen and cruel-looking.
And your words
Like bits of beetles and spiders
Retched out by owls. Fluorescent,
Blue-black, splintered. Bat-skulls. One day, I thought,
I shall understand this tomb-Egyptian,
This talking in tongues to a moon-mushroom.
Never wake a sleepwalker. Let the blame
Hit the olive-trees.
The black blood of their shadows
Might cry out like Abel's.
Who's here? That's the question: Who's here?
The doctor who humours, and watches
As the patient dies in his care.
Something else shares the skin of the day.
The mimicry of possession, the set of the mouth,
Would be awful in a dream. Awake
It's a question of patience. Like a phantom
Womb-tumour. The full moon of radium
Had stripped herself for the operation –
Stripped herself of everything
But moon. What is moon? The raw lump
Of ore, not yet smelted and shaped
Into your managed talent. Or it flings
Onto the X-ray plate the shape of the ape
Being led by the virgin, both helpless
In her hell. The moon
Takes things like that seriously –
As it stares at the kitchen implements.

I was the gnat in the ear of the wounded
Elephant of my own
Incomprehension. Curator
Of the tar-pit. Around us
On the moon-brown hills, the stars rested
Their possible anaesthesia,
All the mythologies, all inaccessible.
The sardine-boats – off with Cassiopeia.
Every stone a rosetta
Of moon-marks. I could no more join you
Than on the sacrificial slab
That you were looking for. I could not
Even imagine the priest. I walked beside you
As if seeing you for the first time –
The moon-shadow of a strange dog,
The silent shadow of a dog
That had befriended you. Your eyes
Were in their element
But uncomprehending and
Terrified by it. Like the surfaced Kraken
You took in the round
Of moon and starred sea, littered heaven and
Moon-blanched, moon-trenched sea-town
And its hook of promontory halving
The two wings of beach. A great bird
Fallen beside the Mediterranean.
A sea of lapis lazuli painted
Glitteringly afresh, just for you,
By de Chirico.
You carried it all, like shards and moults on a tray,
To be reassembled
In the poem to be written so prettily,
And to be worn like a fiesta mask
By the daemon that gazed through it
As through empty sockets – that still gazes
Through it at me.

Drawing

Drawing calmed you. Your poker infernal pen
Was like a branding iron. Objects
Suffered into their new presence, tortured
Into final position. As you drew
I felt released, calm. Time opened
When you drew the market at Benidorm.
I sat near you, scribbling something.
Hours burned away. The stall-keepers
Kept coming to see you had them properly.
We sat on those steps, in our rope-soles,
And were happy. Our tourist novelty
Had worn off, we knew our own ways
Through the town's runs. We were familiar
Foreign objects. When he'd sold his bananas
The banana seller gave us a solo
Violin performance on his banana stalk.
Everybody crowded to praise your drawing.
You drew doggedly on, arresting details,
Till you had the whole scene imprisoned.
Here it is. You rescued for ever
Our otherwise lost morning. Your patience,
Your lip-gnawing scowl, got the portrait
Of a market-place that still slept
In the Middle Ages. Just before
It woke and disappeared
Under the screams of a million summer migrants
And the cliff of dazzling hotels. As your hand
Went under Heptonstall to be held
By endless darkness. While my pen travels on
Only two hundred miles from your hand,
Holding this memory of your red, white-spotted bandanna,
Your shorts, your short-sleeved jumper –
One of the thirty I lugged around Europe –
And your long brown legs, propping your pad,
And the contemplative calm
I drank from your concentrated quiet,
In this contemplative calm
Now I drink from your stillness that neither
Of us can disturb or escape.

Fever

You had a fever. You had a real ailment.
You had eaten a baddie.
You lay helpless and a little bit crazy
With the fever. You cried for America
And its medicine cupboard. You tossed
On the immovable Spanish galleon of a bed
In the shuttered Spanish house
That the sunstruck outside glare peered into
As into a tomb. 'Help me,' you whispered, 'help me.'

You rambled. You dreamed you were clambering
Into the well-hatch and, waking, you wanted
To clamber into the well-hatch – the all-clear
Short cut to the cool of the water,
The cool of the dark shaft, the best place
To find oblivion from your burning tangle
And the foreign bug. You cried for certain
You were going to die.
                                    I bustled about.
I was nursemaid. I fancied myself at that.
I liked the crisis of the vital role.
I felt things had become real. Suddenly mother,
As a familiar voice, woke in me.
She arrived with the certain knowledge. I made a huge soup.
Carrots, tomatoes, peppers and onions,
A rainbow stir of steaming elixir. You
Had to become a sluice, a conduit
Of pure vitamin C. I promised you,
This had saved Voltaire from the plague.
I had to saturate you and flush you
With this simmer of essences.
                                    I spooned it
Into your helpless, baby-bird gape, gently,
Masterfully, patiently, hour by hour.
I wiped your tear-ruined face, your exhausted face,
All loose with woe and abandon.
I spooned more and you gulped it like life,
Sobbing 'I'm going to die.'
                                    As I paused
Between your mouthfuls, I stared at the readings

On your dials. Your cry jammed so hard
Over into the red of catastrophe
Left no space for worse. And I thought
How sick is she? Is she exaggerating?
And I recoiled, just a little,
Just for balance, just for symmetry,
Into sceptical patience, a little.
If it can be borne, why make so much of it?
'Come on, now,' I soothed. 'Don't be so scared.
It's only a bug, don't let it run away with you.'

What I was really saying was: 'Stop crying wolf.'
Other thoughts, chilly, familiar thoughts,
Came across the tightrope: 'Stop crying wolf,
Or else I shall not know, I shall not hear
When things get really bad.'
                                        It seemed easy
Watching such thoughts come up in such good time.
Plenty of time to think: 'She is crying
As if the most impossible of all
Horrible things had happened –
Had already happened, was going on
Still happening, with the whole world
Too late to help.' Then the blank thought
Of the anaesthesia that helps creatures
Under the polar ice, and the callous
That eases overwhelmed doctors. A twisting thought
Of the overload of dilemma, the white-out,
That brings baffled planarian worms to a standstill
Where they curl up and die.

You were overloaded. I said nothing.
I said nothing. The stone man made soup.
The burning woman drank it.

55 Eltisley

Our first home has forgotten us.
I saw when I drove past it
How slight our lives had been
To have left not a trace. When we first moved in there
I looked for omens.

Vacated by a widow gathered to her family
All it told me was: 'Her life is over.'
She had left the last blood of her husband
Staining a pillow. Their whole story
Hung – a miasma – round that stain.
Senility's sour odour. It had condensed
Like a grease on the cutlery. It confirmed
Your idea of England: part
Nursing home, part morgue
For something partly dying, partly dead.
Just so the grease-grimed shelves, the tacky, dark walls
Of the hutch of a kitchen revolted you
Into a fury of scouring. I studied the blood.
Was it mouth-blood, or ear-blood,
Or the blood of a head-wound, after some fall?
I took possession before
Anything of ours had reconditioned
That crypt of old griefs and its stale gas
Of a dead husband. I claimed our first home
Alone and slept in it alone,
Only trying not to inhale the ghost
That clung on in the breath of the bed.
His death and her bereavement
Were the sole guests at our house-warming.
We splurged ten pounds on a sumptuous Chesterfield
Of Prussian blue velvet. Our emergency
Kit of kitchen gadgets adapted
That rented, abandoned, used-up grubbiness
To the shipyard and ritual launching
Of our expedition. One mirage
Of the world as it is and has to be
Seemed no worse than another. Already
We were beyond the Albatross.
You yourself were a whole Antarctic sea
Between me and your girl-friends. You were pack-ice
Between me and any possible mention
Of my might-have-beens. I had accepted
The meteorological phenomena
That kept your compass steady.
Like polar apparitions only Wendy
And Dorothea, by being visionary
Fairy godmothers, were forgiven their faces.

I pitied your delirium of suspicion.
Through the rainbow darkness I plodded,
Following a clue of Patanjali.
Hand in hand we plodded. For me, that home
Was our first camp, our first winter,
Where I was happy to stare at a candle.
For you, it was igloo comfort.
Your Bell Jar centrally heated
By a stupefying paraffin heater.
But you were happy too, warming your hands
At the crystal ball
Of your heirloom paperweight. Inside it,
There, in miniature, was your New England Christmas,
A Mummy and a Daddy, still together
Under the whirling snow, and our future.

Chaucer

'Whan that Aprille with his shoures soote
The droghte of March hath perced to the roote . . .'
At the top of your voice, where you swayed on the top of a stile,
Your arms raised – somewhat for balance, somewhat
To hold the reins of the straining attention
Of your imagined audience – you declaimed Chaucer
To a field of cows. And the Spring sky had done it
With its flying laundry, and the new emerald
Of the thorns, the hawthorn, the blackthorn,
And one of those bumpers of champagne
You snatched unpredictably from pure spirit.
Your voice went over the fields towards Grantchester.
It must have sounded lost. But the cows
Watched, then approached: they appreciated Chaucer.
You went on and on. Here were reasons
To recite Chaucer. Then came the Wyf of Bath,
Your favourite character in all literature.
You were rapt. And the cows were enthralled.
They shoved and jostled shoulders, making a ring,
To gaze into your face, with occasional snorts
Of exclamation, renewed their astounded attention,
Ears angling to catch every inflection,
Keeping their awed six feet of reverence

Away from you. You just could not believe it.
And you could not stop. What would happen
If you were to stop? Would they attack you,
Scared by the shock of silence, or wanting more – ?
So you had to go on. You went on –
And twenty cows stayed with you hypnotised.
How did you stop? I can't remember
You stopping. I imagine they reeled away –
Rolling eyes, as if driven from their fodder.
I imagine I shooed them away. But
Your sostenuto rendering of Chaucer
Was already perpetual. What followed
Found my attention too full
And had to go back into oblivion.

Ouija

Always bad news from the Ouija board.
We spelt out the alphabet, fringed the arena
Of your coffee table with the letters.
Two goals: 'Yes' at one end, 'No' at the other.
Then leaned, our middle fingers lolling
On the bottom of the upturned glass. Frivolity
Darkening to solemn apprehension.
Respectfully, we summoned a spirit.
It was easy as fishing for eels
In the warm summer darkness. Hardly a minute
Before the glass began to nose at the letters,
Then to circle thoughtfully. Finally, 'Yes'.
Something was there. A spirit offered to be named.
She nudged out her name. And she was
Despairing, depressed, pathetic. She concocted
Macabre, gloomy answers. Every answer
Was 'rottenness' or 'worms' or simply 'bones'.
She left a peculiar guilt – a befouled
Feeling of jeopardy, a sense that days
Would be needed now to cleanse us
Of the pollution. Some occult pickpocket
Had slit the soul's silk and fingered us.
But we explained it easily: some rejected
Dream's drop-out had found its way to the glass

Where the power had gone to its head.
                                        Far better
We fish up discredited clairvoyance,
Assume we hummed on all creation's wavelengths,
Attune Ouija to the frequencies
Of omniscience, of prophecy.
A case of locating the right spirit.
Once again we leaned
Over the brink of letters and called down
Into the well of Ouija. This time
We announced the requirements in firm tones,
And as the glass began to prowl repeated
Clearly the qualifications for the job.
Suddenly the glass, with a whizzing flourish,
Was wrenched almost from under our fingers to 'Yes'.
As if we'd hooked a fish right there at the surface.
This one promised only truth. To prove it
He offered to fill in that week's football coupon
And make our fortune in the next five minutes.
He picked thirteen draws. 'That's not many.'
'Just enough,' he replied. He was right –
But spaced all down the column of matches
His accurately picked-off thirteen draws,
The whole clutch, were adrift by a single match
Ahead of the day's results. 'Too eager?' 'Yes.'
He apologised. He swore to correct himself.
Five days then of tiptoe internal hush.
Finally the stalk, the taking aim –
And there again he got the total number,
Eighteen, precisely. But his cluster, spot on
If it had not been split
And adrift in two groups in opposite directions –
Two before, three behind – fell
Through the safety nets I'd spread for his errors.
'Gambling fever's beginning to give him the shakes.
He's getting too interested in some of the teams.
He's wanting winners and losers, and he's losing
Simple solidarity with the truth.
There's a lesson here,' I thought, as I watched
His week-by-week collapse to the haphazard,
Juggling hopes and fantasy, human and anxious.
He preferred to talk about poetry. He made poems.

He spelled one out:
                    'Nameless he shall be
The myriad of daughters
Tending his image
Washing the mountain slopes with tears
To slake the parched plains'.
                         'Is that a good poem?'
I asked him. 'That poem', he declared,
'Is a great poem.' His favourite poet
Was Shakespeare. His favourite poem *King Lear*.
And his favourite line in *King Lear*? 'Never
Never never never never' – but
He could not remember what followed.
We remembered but he could not remember.
When we pressed him he circled, baffled, then:
'Why shall I ever be perplexed thus?
I'd hack my arm off like a rotten branch
Had it betrayed me as my memory.'
Where did he find that? Or did he invent it?
It was an odd joke. He liked jokes.
More often serious. Once, as we bent there, I asked:
'Shall we be famous?' and you snatched your hand upwards
As if something had grabbed it from under.
Your tears flashed, your face was contorted,
Your voice cracked, it was thunder and flash together:
'And give yourself to the glare? Is that what you want?
Why should you want to be famous?
Don't you see – fame will ruin everything.'
I was stunned. I thought I had joined
Your association of ambition
To please you and your mother,
To fulfil your mother's ambition
That we be ambitious. Otherwise
I'd be fishing off a rock
In Western Australia. So it seemed suddenly. You wept.
You wouldn't go on with Ouija. Nothing
I could think of could explain
Your shock and crying. Only
Maybe you'd picked up a whisper I could not hear,
Before our glass could stir, some still small voice:
'Fame will come. Fame especially for you.
Fame cannot be avoided. And when it comes

You will have paid for it with your happiness,
Your husband and your life.'

The Earthenware Head

Who modelled your head of terracotta?
Some American student friend.
Life-size, the lips half-pursed, raw-edged
With crusty tooling – a naturalistic attempt
At a likeness that just failed. You did not like it.
I did not like it. Unease magnetised it
For a perverse rite. What possessed us
To take it with us, in your red bucket bag?
November fen-damp haze, the river unfurling
Dark whorls, ferrying slender willow yellows.   10
The pollard willows wore comfortless antlers,
Switch-horns, leafless. Just past where the field
Broadens and the path strays up to the right
To lose the river and puzzle for Grantchester,
A chosen willow leaned towards the water.
Above head height, the socket of a healed bole-wound,
A twiggy crotch, nearly an owl's porch,
Made a mythic shrine for your double.
I fitted it upright, firm. And a willow tree
Was a Herm, with your head, watching East   20
Through those tool-stabbed pupils. We left it
To live the world's life and weather for ever.

You ransacked thesaurus in your poem about it,
Veiling its mirror, rhyming yourself into safety
From its orphaned fate.
But it would not leave you. Weeks later
We could not seem to hit on the tree. We did not
Look too hard – just in passing. Already
You did not want to fear, if it had gone,
What witchcraft might ponder it. You never   30
Said much more about it.
                              What happened?
Maybe nothing happened. Perhaps
It is still there, representing you
To the sunrise, and happy

In its cold pastoral, lips pursed slightly
As if my touch had only just left it.
Or did boys find it – and shatter it? Or
Did the tree too kneel finally?

Surely the river got it. Surely
40 The river is its chapel. And keeps it. Surely
Your deathless head, fired in a furnace,
Face to face at last, kisses the Father
Mudded at the bottom of the Cam,
Beyond recognition or rescue,
All our fears washed from it, and perfect,
Under the stained mournful flow, saluted
Only in summer briefly by the slender
Punt-loads of shadows flitting towards their honey
And the stopped clock.
                                        Evil.
50 That was what you called the head. Evil.

Wuthering Heights

Walter was guide. His mother's cousin
Inherited some Brontë soup dishes.
He felt sorry for them. Writers
Were pathetic people. Hiding from it
And making it up. But your transatlantic elation
Elated him. He effervesced
Like his rhubarb wine kept a bit too long:
A vintage of legends and gossip
About those poor lasses. Then,
After the Rectory, after the chaise longue
Where Emily died, and the midget hand-made books,
The elvish lacework, the dwarfish fairy-work shoes,
It was the track from Stanbury. That climb
A mile beyond expectation, into
Emily's private Eden. The moor
Lifted and opened its dark flower
For you too. That was satisfactory.
Wilder, maybe, than ever Emily knew it.
With wet feet and nothing on her head
She trudged that climbing side towards friends –

Probably. Dark redoubt
On the skyline above. It was all
Novel and exhilarating to you.
The book becoming a map. *Wuthering Heights*
Withering into perspective. We got there
And it was all gaze. The open moor,
Gamma rays and decomposing starlight
Had repossessed it
With a kind of blackening smoulder. The centuries
Of door-bolted comfort finally amounted
To a forsaken quarry. The roofs'
Deadfall slabs were flaking, but mostly in place,
Beams and purlins softening. So hard
To imagine the life that had lit
Such a sodden, raw-stone cramp of refuge.
The floors were a rubble of stone and sheep droppings.
Doorframes, windowframes –
Gone to make picnickers' fires or evaporated.
Only the stonework – black. The sky – blue.
And the moor-wind flickering.

                            The incomings,
The outgoings – how would you take up now
The clench of that struggle? The leakage
Of earnings off a few sickly bullocks
And a scatter of crazed sheep. Being cornered
Kept folk here. Was that crumble of wall
Remembering a try at a garden? Two trees
Planted for company, for a child to play under,
And to have something to stare at. Sycamores –
The girth and spread of valley twenty-year-olds,
They were probably ninety.

                          You breathed it all in
With jealous, emulous sniffings. Weren't you
Twice as ambitious as Emily? Odd
To watch you, such a brisk pendant
Of your globe-circling aspirations,
Among those burned-out, worn-out remains
Of failed efforts, failed hopes –
Iron beliefs, iron necessities,
Iron bondage, already
Crumbling back to the wild stone.

                           You perched

In one of the two trees
Just where the snapshot shows you.
Doing as Emily never did. You
Had all the liberties, having life.
The future had invested in you –
As you might say of a jewel
So brilliantly faceted, refracting
Every tint, where Emily had stared
Like a dying prisoner.
And a poem unfurled from you
Like a loose frond of hair from your nape
To be clipped and kept in a book. What would stern
Dour Emily have made of your frisky glances
And your huge hope? Your huge
Mortgage of hope. The moor-wind
Came with its empty eyes to look at you,
And the clouds gazed sidelong, going elsewhere,
The heath-grass, fidgeting in its fever,
Took idiot notice of you. And the stone,
Reaching to touch your hand, found you real
And warm, and lucent, like that earlier one.
And maybe a ghost, trying to hear your words,
Peered from the broken mullions
And was stilled. Or was suddenly aflame
With the scorch of doubled envy. Only
Gradually quenched in understanding.

The Chipmunk

A rippling, bobbing wood-elf, the chipmunk came
Under the Cape Cod conifers, over roots,
A first scout of the continent's wild game,
Midget aboriginal American. Flowing
On electrical accurate feet
Through its circuitry. That was the first real native –
Dodging from flashlit listening still
To staring flashlit still. It studied me
Sitting at a book – a strange prisoner,
Pacing my priceless years away, eyes lowered,
To and fro, to and fro,
Across my page. It snapped a tail-gesture at me –

Roused me, peremptory, to this friendship
It would be sharing with me
Only a few more seconds.
                              Its eyes
Popping with inky joy,
Globed me in a new vision, woke me,
And I recognised it.
                          You stayed
Alien to me as a window model,
American, airport-hopping superproduct,
Through all our intimate weeks up to the moment,
In a flash-still, retorting to my something,
You made a chipmunk face. I thought
An eight-year-old child was suddenly a chipmunk.
Pursed mouth, puffed cheeks. And suddenly,
Just in that flash – as I laughed
And got my snapshot for life,
And shouted: 'That's my first ever real chipmunk!' –
A ghost, dim, a woodland spirit, swore me
To take his orphan.

Horoscope

You wanted to study
Your stars – the guards
Of your prison yard, their zodiac. The planets
Muttered their Babylonish power-sprach –
Like a witchdoctor's bones. You were right to fear
How loud the bones might roar,
How clear an ear might hear
What the bones whispered
Even embedded as they were in the hot body.

Only you had no need to calculate
Degrees for your ascendant disruptor
In Aries. It meant nothing certain – no more
According to the Babylonian book
Than a scarred face. How much deeper
Under the skin could any magician peep?

You only had to look
Into the nearest face of a metaphor

Picked out of your wardrobe or off your plate
Or out of the sun or the moon or the yew tree
To see your father, your mother, or me
Bringing you your whole Fate.

Flounders

Was that a happy day? From Chatham
Down at the South end of the Cape, our map
Somebody's optimistic assurance,
We set out to row. We got ourselves
Into mid-channel. The tide was flowing. We hung
Anchored. Northward-pulling, our baited leads
Bounced and bounced the bottom. For three hours –
Two or three sea-robins. Cruisers
Folded us under their bow-waves, we bobbed up,
Happy enough. But the wind
Smartened against us, and the tide turned, roughening,
Dragged seaward. We rowed. We rowed. We
Saw we weren't going to make it. We turned,
Cutting downwind for the sand-bar, beached
And wondered what next. It was there
I found a horse-shoe crab's carapace, perfect,
No bigger than a bee, in honey-pale cellophane.
No way back. But big, good America found us.
A power-boat and a pilot of no problems.
He roped our boat to his stern and with all his family
Slammed back across the channel into the wind,
The spray scything upwards, our boat behind
Twisting across the wake-boil – a hectic
Four or five minutes and he cast us off
In the lee of the land, but a mile or more
From our dock. We toiled along inshore. We came
To a back-channel, under beach-house gardens – marsh grass,
Wild, original greenery of America,
Mud-slicks and fiddler-crab warrens, as we groped
Towards the harbour. Gloom-rich water. Something
Suggested easy plenty. We lowered baits,
And out of about six feet of water
Six or seven feet from land, we pulled up flounders
Big as big plates, till all our bait had gone.

After our wind-burned, head-glitter day of emptiness,
And the slogging row for our lives, and the rescue,
Suddenly out of water easy as oil
The sea piled our boat with its surplus. And the day
Curled out of brilliant, arduous morning,
Through wind-hammered perilous afternoon,
Salt-scoured, to a storm-gold evening, a luxury
Of rowing among the dream-yachts of the rich
Lolling at anchor off the play-world pier.

How tiny an adventure
To stay so monumental in our marriage,
A slight ordeal of all that might be,
And a small thrill-breath of what many live by,
And a small prize, a toy miniature
Of the life that might have bonded us
Into a single animal, a single soul –

It was a visit from the goddess, the beauty
Who was poetry's sister – she had come
To tell poetry she was spoiling us.
Poetry listened, maybe, but we heard nothing
And poetry did not tell us. And we
Only did what poetry told us to do.

The Blue Flannel Suit

I had let it all grow. I had supposed
It was all O.K. Your life
Was a liner I voyaged in.
Costly education had fitted you out.
Financiers and committees and consultants
Effaced themselves in the gleam of your finish.
You trembled with the new life of those engines.

That first morning,
Before your first class at College, you sat there
Sipping coffee. Now I know, as I did not,
What eyes waited at the back of the class
To check your first professional performance
Against their expectations. What assessors
Waited to see you justify the cost

And redeem their gamble. What a furnace
Of eyes waited to prove your metal. I watched
The strange dummy stiffness, the misery,
Of your blue flannel suit, its straitjacket, ugly
Half-approximation to your idea
Of the proprieties you hoped to ease into,
And your horror in it. And the tanned
Almost green undertinge of your face
Shrunk to its wick, your scar lumpish, your plaited
Head pathetically tiny.
                                    You waited,
Knowing yourself helpless in the tweezers
Of the life that judged you, and I saw
The flayed nerve, the unhealable face-wound
Which was all you had for courage.
I saw that what gripped you, as you sipped,
Were terrors that had killed you once already.
Now, I see, I saw, sitting, the lonely
Girl who was going to die.
                                    That blue suit,
A mad, execution uniform,
Survived your sentence. But then I sat, stilled,
Unable to fathom what stilled you
As I looked at you, as I am stilled
Permanently now, permanently
Bending so briefly at your open coffin.

Child's Park

What did they mean to you, the azalea flowers?
Those girls were so happy, rending the branches,
Embracing their daring bouquets, their sumptuous trousseaux,
The wet, hot-petalled blossoms. Seizing their day,
Having a good time. Your homicidal
Hooded stare met them head on.
As if they were stealing the brands
Of your own burning. I hurried you off. Bullfrogs
Took you down through lily tangle. Your fury
Had to be quenched. Heavy water,
Deeper, deeper, cooling and controlling
Your plutonium secret. You breathed water.

Freed, steadied, resurfaced, your eyes
Alit afresh on colour, so delicate,
Splitting the prism,
As the dragonflies on the solid lilies.
The pileated woodpecker went writhing
Among the catalpas. It clung
To undersides and swooped
Like a pterodactyl. The devilry
Of the uncoiling head, the spooky wings,
And the livid cry
Flung the garden open.
                              You were never
More than a step from Paradise.
You had instant access, your analyst told you,
To the core of your Inferno –
The pit of the hairy flower.
                              At a sunny angle
The fountain threw off its seven veils
As the air swayed it. Here was your stair –
Alchemy's seven colours.
I watched you as you climbed it all on your own
Into the mouth of the azalea.

You imagined a veil-rending defloration
And a rebirth out of the sun – mixed up together
And somehow the same. You were fearless
To meet your Father,
His Word fulfilled, there, in the nuclear core.

What happens in the heart simply happens.

I stepped back. That glare
Flinging your old selves off like underthings
Left your whole Eden radioactive.

9 Willow Street

Willow Street, poetical address.
Number nine, even better. It confirmed
We had to have it. We got it.
A tower of the Muses. Freed from school
For the first time in your life, this was the cage

Your freedom flew to – a view of the Charles River
And Cambridge beyond it. Over my table
I covered the windows with brown paper,
Pushed ear-plugs in on my inflamed nerves
And sank. In the other room,
Perched up in the glare, on the cliff-edge,
You hammered your new Hermes,
Your Panic Bird chipping at the old egg,
While I rolled in my sack, with my lumber,
Along the bottom of the Charles. We huddled. Me
In my black sack striking sulphur matches
To find the eyes of Jung's nigredo. You
In a paralysis of terror-flutters
I hardly understood. I folded
Black wings round you, wings of the blackness
That enclosed me, rocking me, infantile,
And enclosed you with me. And your heart
Jumped at your ribs, you gasped for air.
You grabbed for the world,
For straws, for your morning coffee – anything
To get airborne. My bubbles
Wobbled upwards and burst emptily
In the reverberations of the turbines
Home and College had assembled in you,
That thundered the parquet
And shook you to tremblings. Your day
Was twenty-four rungs of a fire-escape
Hanging in ghastly swirls, over nothing,
Reaching up towards nothing.
What an airy Hell!
                        Boston clanged
All its atoms below, through all its circles
Between Harvard and Scollay Square. Alone
Either of us might have met with a life.
Siamese-twinned, each of us festering
A unique soul-sepsis for the other,
Each of us was the stake
Impaling the other. We struggled
Quietly through the streets, affirming each other,
Dream-maimed and dream-blind.
                        Your typewriter,
Your alarm clock, your new sentence

Tortured you, a cruelty computer
Of agony niceties, daily afresh –
Every letter a needle, as in Kafka.
While I, like a poltergeist fog,
Hung on you, fed on you – heavy, drugged
With your nightmares and terrors. Inside your Bell Jar
I was like a mannikin in your eyeball.
What happened casually remains –
Strobes of a hallucinating fever
In some heaving dimension of chemical horror.
Our only escape was into arms
That reached upwards or reached downwards
And rolled us all night eastward with each other
Over the bottom, in the muddy current.
What a waste!
What did our spectre-blinded searching reach
Or wake to, that was worth it?
                          Happiness
Appeared – momentary,
Peered in at your window
Like a wild migrant, an oriole,
A tanager, a humming-bird – pure American,
Blown scraps of the continent's freedom –
But off course and gone
Before we could identify it.

It took me a dizzy moment to make out
Something under the chestnuts, struggling
On a path of the Common, down near the Swan-boats.
What looked like a slug, black, soft, wrinkled,
Was wrestling, somehow, with the fallen
Brown, crumpled lobe of a chestnut leaf.
Suddenly, plainly, it was a bat.
A bat fallen out of its tree
Mid-afternoon. A sick bat? I stooped
Thinking I'd lift it again to tree-bark safety.
It reared up on its elbows and snarled at me,
A raving hyena, the size of a sparrow,
Its whole face peeled in a snarl, fangs tiny.
I tried to snatch it up by the shoulders
But it spun, like a fighter, behind its snarl.

A crowd collected, entertained to watch me
Fight a bat on Boston Common. Finally
I had to give it my finger.
Let the bite lock. Then, cradling it,
Gently lifted it and offered it up
To the wall of chestnut bark. It released me
And scuttled upwards backwards, face downwards,
A rearguard snarl, triumphant, contorted,
Vanishing upwards into where it had come from.

At home I looked at the blood, and remembered:
American bats have rabies. How could Fate
Stage a scenario so symbolic
Without having secreted the tragedy ending
And the ironic death? It confirmed
The myth we had sleepwalked into: death.
This was the bat-light we were living in: death.

The Literary Life

We climbed Marianne Moore's narrow stair
To her bower-bird bric-à-brac nest, in Brooklyn.
Daintiest curio relic of Americana.
Her talk, a needle
Unresting – darning incessantly
Chain-mail with crewel-work flowers,
Birds and fish of the reef
In phosphor-bronze wire.
Her face, tiny American treen bobbin
On a spindle,
Her voice the flickering hum of the old wheel.
Then the coin, compulsory,
For the subway
Back to our quotidian scramble.
Why shouldn't we cherish her?

You sent her carbon copies of some of your poems.
Everything about them –
The ghost gloom, the constriction,
The bell-jar air-conditioning – made her gasp
For oxygen and cheer. She sent them back.
(Whoever has her letter has her exact words.)

'Since these seem to be valuable carbon copies
(Somewhat smudged) I shall not engross them.'
I took the point of that 'engross'
Precisely, like a bristle of glass
Snapped off deep in my thumb.
You wept
And hurled yourself down a floor or two
Further from the Empyrean.
I carried you back up.
And she, Marianne, tight, brisk,
Neat and hard as an ant,
Slid into the second or third circle
Of my Inferno.

A decade later, on her last visit to England,
Holding court at a party, she was sitting
Bowed over her knees, her face,
Under her great hat-brim's floppy petal,
Dainty and bright as a piece of confetti –
She wanted me to know, she insisted
(It was all she wanted to say)
With that Missouri needle, drawing each stitch
Tight in my ear,
That your little near-posthumous memoir
'OCEAN 1212'
Was 'so wonderful, so lit, so wonderful' –

She bowed so low I had to kneel. I kneeled and
Bowed my face close to her upturned face
That seemed tinier than ever,
And studied, as through a grille,
Her lips that put me in mind of a child's purse
Made of the skin of a dormouse,
Her cheek, as if she had powdered the crumpled silk
Of a bat's wing.
And I listened, heavy as a graveyard
While she searched for the grave
Where she could lay down her little wreath.

The Bird

Under its glass dome, behind its eyes,
Your Panic Bird was not stuffed. It was looking
For you did not know what. I could feel
For the glass – not there and yet there –
A zoo gecko glued against nothing
With all its life throbbing in its throat,
As if it stood on ether. The Princess
Let her hair right down to the ground
From her solitary high window. Remember,
Circling Boston Common together,
The defective jailbird walk we perfected,
Feet swinging from the knees. A Tyrolean
Clockwork, revolving under glass,
To a tinkling. You told me
Everything but the fairy tale. Step for step
I walked in the sleep
You tried to wake from.
                                    You widened your pupils
For thunderclap dawn – at the wharf,
And in came that ice-caked ship,
Fretworked chandelier of lacy crystals,
A whole wedding vessel lifted from under
The ocean salt – flash-frozen. Then you turned,
Your eyelashes clogged, and stretched your eyes
At the charred-out caves of apartment block
That had burned all night, a flame-race upwards
Under the hoses, behind the Senate. You howled
With your sound turned off and your screen dark
For tragedy to go on – to hell with the curtain.
You willed it to get going all over again,
Spit one spark of woe through the frozen suds
That draped the gutted building
Like a solid Niagara.

What glowed into focus was blood suddenly
Weltering dumb and alive
Up through the tattooed blazon of an eagle.
Your homeland's double totem. Germany's eagle
Bleeding up through your American eagle
In a cloud of Dettol. It jabbed

Its talons at the glass. It wanted
To be born, pecking at the glass. Tears were no good.
Though you could smash a mahogany heirloom table
With a high stool for an axe,
Tears were rain on a window.

We stood married, in a packed room, drinking sherry,
In some Cambridge College. My eyes
Had locked on a chunky tumbler
Solid with coins (donations to pay for the booze),
Isolated on a polished table.
I was staring at it when it vanished
Like a spinning grenade, with a bang.
The coins collapsed in a slither. But the table
Was suddenly white with a shatter of tiny crystals.
A cake of frozen snow
Could have crashed in from space. Every crumb
Of smithereen that I peered into
Was flawed into crystals infinitely tiny

Like crumbs of the old, slabbed snow
That all but barricaded London
The day your bird broke free and the glass dome
Vanished – with a ringing sound
I thought was a telephone.
I knew the glass had gone and the bird had gone.
Like lifting an eyelid I peered for the glass –
But I knew it had gone. Because of the huge
Loose emptiness of light
Wheeling through everything.
                              As if a gecko
Fell into empty light.

Astringency

I always think of the Charles River
Frozen. The word 'Astringency'
Was the cant for years.
Slackly I strolled there. A big event:
A million dead worms
Littering the lawny grass along the walkway.
Modern times had caught them up

And overtaken. String ends
Too short to be saved. The cindery air,
A waft of roasted iron, blew from Cambridge.
'Lit Crit,' my friend said, 'and Agrochemicals
Are Siamese twins.' What? Were you with me
When I saw an amazing thing,
Right there at the edge of the Charles?
A fisherman, hoping for God knows what,
Had just caught a goldfish.
Out of that brown mass, from under
The hundred miles and the thousand false faces
Of the Charles River
That I had assumed 100 per cent proof toxic.
A goldfish! Thick, deep and very frisky.
Nine inches long – obviously thriving.
Somebody's apartment darling – flushed?
But caught again! Brainstorm of the odds!
He let it go. It swam off.
It dissolved in the murk. That same spot
We – you and me – watched small, ranked waves
Washing over a nipple of rock at the edge there.
You and me, standing on America,
Together, silent, thinking of nothing, watching
The sliding ring of ripple
That each small, tired wave threw over the rock
'Like a lariat,' you said.

The sole metaphor that ever escaped you
In easy speech, in my company –
Past the censor? Past the night hands?
Past the snare
Set in your throat by whom? Who caught all
That teeming population, every one,
To hang their tortured eyes and tongues up
In your poems? To what end? The constrictor
Not to be tugged out, or snapped.

The Badlands

Right across America
We went looking for you. Lightning
Had ripped your clothes off
And signed your cheekbone. It came
Out of the sun's explosion
Over Hiroshima, Nagasaki,
As along the ridge of a mountain
Under the earth, and somehow
Through death-row and the Rosenbergs.
They took the brunt of it.
You weren't too logical about it.
You only knew it had come and had gripped you
By the roots of the hair
And held you down on the bed
And stretched across your retina
The global map of nerves in blue flames,
Then left you signed and empty. But already
You had got clear –
Jumped right out of your crackling cast
Through that hole over your cheekbone
And gone to ground, gone underground, into moonland
Somewhere in America.
                    We came to a stone
Beside a lake flung open before dawn
By the laugh of a loon. The signs good,
I turned the stone over. The timeless one,
Head perfect, eyes waiting – there he lay.
Banded black,
White, black, white, coiled. I said:
'Just like the coils on the great New Grange lintel.'
One thing to find a guide,
Another to follow him.
                    In North Dakota
We met smoke of the underground burning –
A fistula of smouldering bitumen.
Hellish. Or lit by lightning. Or
Dante's, to coach us. Ignited
By the moon's collision. I saw it in a dream
Coming bigger and closer till almost
The size of the earth it crashed

Into the Atlantic —
I watched it from the point of Manhattan.
The earth took it with a tremendous jolt —
Impact and penetration. Next thing
The moon was inside the earth,
Cramming its phosphor flames
Under the scabby humped pelt of the prairies.
And above me the towers of Manhattan
Swayed like curtains of ash.
                              In the Badlands
We got deeper. A landscape
Staked out in the sun and left to die.
The Theodore Roosevelt National Park.
Long ago dead of the sun. Loose teeth, bone
Coming through crust, bristles.
Or a smashed industrial complex
For production
Of perpetual sacrifice, of canyons
Long ago disembowelled.
When Aztec and Inca went on South
They left the sun waiting,
Starved for worship, raging for attention,
Now gone sullenly mad.
As it sank it stared at our car.
Middle distance, yellow, the Missouri
Crawled, stagnated, crawled.

The silence, at least,
Like a cooling incinerator
Was an afterlife. As it cooled
Every clinker inched its shadow wider
And darker
Like a little door. There we camped.
The most inimical place I ever was in.
Too late to go on. I remember

A lone tree near the campsite.
I kept looking towards it —
For comfort? It gave none.
As we pitched our tent
You were uneasy. You kept being overwhelmed
By the misery of the place, like a nausea.
You kept having to stand up and look round.

We were tired.
Easy prey. We went for a walk.
Everything watched us. We stood, not chilled yet,
Watching the sun go –
A half, a quarter, as if it were being drained.
Then all gone.
                At that moment something
Heaved out of the land and was there.
Empty, horrible, archaic – America.
Planetary – before the eye touched it.
A land with maybe one idea – snake.

But then, suddenly, near us
Something hectic in a rickety thorn-bush.
It was a tiny terror, a maniac midget
Hurtling in top-gear uncontrol –
Like a ball on a pin-table, clash and ricochet,
Terror bounce and back, clash and back,
Through the maze of the thorn-bush. I thought
A panicky bird, fluttering maybe tethered
By a slim snake like a bootlace
Couldn't break out of the thorns. I thought
Some electrical predator hunted
Electrical tiny prey. Or two
Tiny birds of desert ferocity
Fought in there. It was a solitary mouse.

Somewhere in that iron-hearth, ashen landscape
He had found dewdrops enough for his eyes
And was protecting them – with an energy
More like torturing poison
Than what could be found in food. Where was his food?
And what was he doing here
In this solar furnace
Of oxides and firedust?
And what was he up to in his gymnasium,
All on his own, burning up calories,
Blazing off nervous tension, having a breakdown –
Overloaded with emergency fury
Or some uncontainable surplus of joy?
He skittered about his flimsy
Castle of spines, dodging maybe
The deadly radiation of our attention

As we peered in from the sky – and
He'd vanished. His scatter of intricate racket
Went on some seconds after him.

The canyons cooled. Indigo darkened,
Oozing out of the earth like ectoplasm,
A huge snake heaping out. 'This is evil,'
You said. 'This is real evil.'
Whatever it was, the whole landscape wore it
Like a plated mask. 'What is it?'
I kept saying. 'What is it?'
As if that might force the whatever
To materialise, maybe standing by our car,
Maybe some old Indian.
                              'Maybe it's the earth,'
You said. 'Or maybe it's ourselves.
This emptiness is sucking something out of us.
Here where there's only death, maybe our life
Is terrifying. Maybe it's the life
In us
Frightening the earth, and frightening us.'

Fishing Bridge

Nearly happy. Brilliantly lit –
That threshold of the great lake
Spilling its river. Naive pioneers,
We had no idea what we were seeing
When we watched the cut-throat beneath our boat,
Marching, massed, over the sunken threshold
Of the Yellowstone.
                              Petty precautions
To keep our skulls clear of the whizzing leads
Catapulted from the lashing rods
Of the holiday anglers – a cram of colour
Along the bank and the bridge – took all our forethought.
We did not see what infinite endowment
Leaned over that threshold, beckoning us
With that glitter of distance as it gathered
The trout into its bounty.
                              Little finesse,

With bumping leads and earthworms. No problem
Catching our limit dozen
Of those weary migrants, pushing and pushed
Towards their spawning gravels. What I remember
Is the sun's dazzle – and your delight
Wandering off along the lake's fringe
Towards the shag-headed wilderness
In your bikini. There you nearly
Stepped into America. You turned back,
And we turned away. That lake-mouth
Was only one of too many thresholds –

Every one of them a glittering offer.
We half-closed our eyes. Or held them wide
Like sleepwalkers while a voice on a tape,
Promising, directed us into a doorway
Difficult and dark. The voice urged on
Into an unlit maze of crying and loss.
What voice? 'Find your souls,' said the voice.
'Find your true selves. This way. Search, search.'
The voice had never heard of the shining lake.
'Find the core of the labyrinth.' Why? What opens
At the heart of the maze? Is it the doorway
Into the perfected vision? Masterfully
The voice pushed us, hypnotised, bowing our heads
Into its dead-ends, its reversals,
Dreamy gropings, baffled ponderings,
Its monomaniac half-search, half-struggle,
Not for the future – not for any future –

Till it stopped. Was that the maze's centre?
Where everything stopped? What lay there?
The voice held me there, by the scruff of the neck,
And bowed my head
Over the thing we had found. Your dead face.
Your dead lips, dry, pale. And your eyes
(As brown-bright, when I lifted the lids,
As when you gazed across that incandescence)
Unmoving and dead.

The 59th Bear

We counted bears – as if all we wanted
Were more bears. Yellowstone
Folded us into its robe, its tepees
Of mountain and conifer.
Mislaid Red Indian Mickey Mouse America
Pointered us from campground to campground –
We were two of many. And it was as novel-astonishing
To you as to me. Paradise, we saw,
Was where wild bears ate from the hands of children.
Were these real wild bears? We saw Daddies
Supporting their babies piggyback on dark bears
In a dancing ring of guffaws and cameras.
The bears were in on the all-American family,
Originals of those board cut-out bears,
Uncle Bruins in Disneyland overalls,
Who warned against forest fires. Bears waited –
Welcoming committees – at every parking,
Lifting their teddybear ears and quizzing buttons
At the car windows. Twenty, we counted.
Thirty. Forty. Fifty. Once
As I opened the car door at a café
A bear that just happened to be passing
Shouldered it shut.
Everywhere people were entertaining
Bears and bears were entertaining people.

We roamed, soon at home in the marvellous abundance.
Eagles were laid on too. We leaned at a rail
And looked down onto floating black flecks
That turned out to be eagles – we were swept
Into the general exclamatory joy
By somebody's binoculars. I stared
Down through the spread fingers of an eagle
Into a drop that still scares me to remember.
But it all refused to be translated.
The Camp Ranger notices seemed perfunctory,
Make-believe. Through coy nicknames magma
Bubbled its colours, belched its labouring sighs –
Prehistory was still at boiling point,
Smoking round us.

Each evening
Bears raided the campgrounds. Camera stars,
They performed at the sunken trash-bins. Delight –
Every few days a whole new class of campers
Squealing for fearless close-ups before
The warnings sank in.
                    Somehow that night
The warnings had sunk in. You were nervous.
It had been a day of worsening nerves.
We had driven just too far. The gas
Had got too low and the evening too late.

Your spirits as usual had gone right down with
The fuel-gauge to the bottom, and bobbed there –
You saw us in a vision, a headline,
Devoured in the night-woods. One curve in the road
Became dreadful – nearly impassable.
A giant elk detached itself abruptly
From the conifer black, wheeled its rigging
Right above the bonnet and vanished, like a sign
From some place of omens. We reached our tent
In the dusk of campfires.
                    Three cold fried trout
Were surplus from breakfast. But
It was too late to sit up under the stars
Sipping and eating – 'The bears!' The bears were coming!
With a racket of clatter-pans, and a yelling
From the far end of the campground – 'Bears! Bears!' –
You panicked into the tent and pleaded.
I saw a big brown bear and a smaller, darker,
Romping like big rubber toys,
Bouncing along, like jolly inflatables
Among the tents and tables. Awesome, fluid,
Unpredictable, dodging swiftness! And cries.
The whole campground was jumpy – a cacophony
Of bangings and shouts urging the bears
On and away elsewhere – anywhere away
Pestering somebody else. I locked everything
Into the car. Each thing carefully checked.
One thing I missed.
                    Did we sleep?
The campground slept. The bears had been scared off,

To other campgrounds. How safe we felt
In our green breathing walls! Hidden breathers,
Safe and chrysalis in our sleeping bags,
Trusting each moment to elide into another
As quiet as itself. Vast, bristling darkness
Of America. Under my pillow –
Drastic resource for a drastic emergency –
I kept the hatchet, purposefully sharpened.

What time was it? A rending crash – too close –
Had me head up and alert, listening,
As if I watched what made it. Then more rendings
Of real awful damage going on,
Still being done – and you were awake too,
Listening beside me. I got up
And peered through the tent's window mesh into moonlight.
Everything clear, black-shadowed. The car
Five paces away, looked natural enough.
Then more rippings inside it, and it shook,
And I saw the dark blockage, a black mass
Filling the far rear window. 'Those damned bears!
One's getting into the car.'
                                    A few shock-shouts,
I thought, a close-up assault of human abuse,
And the bear would be off. I'd take my hatchet
Just in case. I got out my hatchet,
Pitifully unimaginative.
I was remembering those amiable bears.
That's how it happens. Your terrors
Were more intelligent, with their vision –
And I was not so sure. Then for an hour
He was unpacking the car, unpuzzling our bags,
Raking and thumping. I imagined
Every scrap of fabric ripped from the springs.
It sounded like a demolition. We lay
Decoding every variety of sound
As he battered and squelched, crunched and scraped
With still intervals of meditation.
I got up again. In first faint light
I made him out wrestling our steel freezer
Between his paws. 'It's the big brown one.' We'd heard
He was the nasty one. Again we lay quiet,

Letting him do what he wanted.
                                    And at last
A new sound – the caress, ushering closer,
The lullaby reveille of a cruising engine:
The Camp Ranger's car, doing the dawn rounds.
The bear heard it. And we had the joy –
Awful incredulity like joy –
Of hearing his claw-bunches hurry-scuffle
To the secret side of our tent. He was actually there,
Hiding beside our tent! His breathing,
Heavy after the night's gourmandising,
Rasped close to the canvas – only inches
From your face that, big-eyed, stared at me
Staring at you.
                    The car cruised easily away
Into the forest and lake silence. The bear
Faded from his place, as the tent walls paled.
Loons on the glassed lake shook off their nightmares.
The day came.
                    A ghoul had left us,
Leaving our freezer buckled open, our fish
Vanished from their stains, every orange
Sucked flat, our pancake mix
Dabbled over yards of dust, everything
Edible gone, in a scatter of wrappers
And burst cartons. And the off rear window of the car
Wrenched out – a star of shatter splayed
From a single talon's leverage hold,
A single claw forced into the hair-breadth odour
Had ripped the whole sheet out. He'd leaned in
And on claw hooks lifted out our larder.
He'd left matted hairs. I glued them in my Shakespeare.

I felt slightly dazed – a strange pride
To have been so chosen and ego-raked
By the deliberations of that beast.

But you came back from the wash-house
With your last-night's panic double-boosted
For instant flight.
                    Some doppelgänger,
That very night, at the next campground,
Had come out of his tent to shoo off a bear

With a torch and a few shouts. He'd learned –
Briefly, in what flash of reckoning
He'd been allowed – what I had hardly guessed:
A bear's talons, which by human flesh
Can be considered steel, braced on tendons
Of steel hawser, are on the end of an arm
That can weigh sixty, seventy, eighty pounds
Moving at 90 m.p.h.
Your terror had the mathematics perfect.
You had met a woman in the wash-house
Who'd driven terrified from that other campground.
And you just knew, it was that very same bear.
Having murdered a man, he'd romped through the woods
To rob us.
That was our fifty-ninth bear. I saw, well enough,
The peril that see-saws opposite
A curious impulse – what slight flicker
In a beast's brain electrifies tonnage
And turns life to paper. I did not see
What flicker in yours, what need later
Transformed our dud scenario into a fiction –
Or what self-salvation
Squeezed the possible blood out of it
Through your typewriter ribbon.
                              At that time
I had not understood
How the death hurtling to and fro
Inside your head, had to alight somewhere
And again somewhere, and had to be kept moving,
And had to be rested
Temporarily somewhere.

Grand Canyon

Not a brimming glass of orange juice –
But you were suddenly more than careful
Not to spill a drop. There on the rim,
Watching the mules tilt down
Was almost nausea.
Miles off, opposite, the miles-high rampart cliff.
Miles below, the unshaved, two-day bristle

Was an eighty-foot ponderosa.
So they said. And the heat down there was hellish.

Too vast to be visible in,
A quarry from which the sculpture
Of something
Had been hacked, then left there
Too big to move.
America's big red mamma!
Now letting the sun, with changing colours,
Caress her, as she lay open.
We drifted our gaze through – like a feather
Lost in the afterglow of her sensations.

Six weeks pregnant and you were scared of the mules.
Yet here was the oracle.
This was America's Delphi. You wanted a sign.
We settled for the cougar-hunter. Scrawny,
Cantankerous old-timer. Stagey tales of the early canyon.
He showed slides without a joke.
Made his bag of five hundred lions
Sound as likely as finished.
You took against him
Even as his words played at your eardrums
And rippled their faint, canyon thunder
And lightning over her foetus.

We'd brought our water-cooler bag through the cinders of
    the Mojave.
Slung under the front bumper, au fait.
We seemed to be saving it. We still hadn't broached it.
We were stoned
With the heaped-up coils of highway crammed in our heads,
The mountains, the forests, the cities, the boysenberry pies
Jammed in our body-sacks. We were numbed by the shock-waves
Coming off the sky-vistas at us –
The thunder-beings that swept against us and through us
Out of the road's jackrabbits and the beer-can constellations
We drove into after dark.

We had sweated the labour, the pilgrimage.
Now we wanted the blessing.
Some word – from before this translation
Of the canyon lion to the dollar eagle.

We had big hope the Navajo dancers
Up there on their platform would deliver it.

PAUM! It came
The first thud of that drum
Before a single dancer popped up.

PAUM! The gorge spoke
Through that membrane,
The first summons
Out of its vertigo and nausea.
And every hair on my body
Jumped as if it were old dust on a drumskin.

PAUM!
Swallowed the whole memory,
The dancers, the crowd, the cameras, everything there on the
    canyon rim
Swallowed by a solitary thud.
You, me, and her – suspended
In her quaking echo-chamber – swallowed
As a bad accident
Wipes the memory just before and after –
The whole scene gone
Into *PAUM!*

I made a note so I know
We sleepwalked back to the car and found our water-bag stolen.

Nothing is left. I never went back and you are dead.
But at odd moments it comes,
As if for the first time, like a hand grabbing
And shaking me from light sleep,
Through all these years, and after thirty years,
Close, itself, ours as the voice of your daughter –

PAUM!

Karlsbad Caverns

We had seen the bats in the Karlsbad caves,
Thick as shaggy soot in chimneys
Bigger than cathedrals. We'd made ourselves dots

On the horizon of their complete world
And their exclusive lives.
Presumably the whole lot were happy —

So happy they didn't know they were happy,
They were so busy with it, so full of it,
Clinging upside down in their stone heavens.

Then we checked our watches. The vanguard bats,
To the minute, started to flicker and whirl
In the giant mouth of the cavern

That was our amphitheatre, where they were the drama.
A flickering few thickened to a million
Till critical boiling mass tore free of the magnet

Under the earth. The bats began to hurl out —
Spill out, smoke out, billow out,
For half an hour was it, an upward torrent

Of various millions of bats. A smoky dragon
Out of a key-hole in earth,
A great sky-snake writhing away southwards

Towards the Rio Grande
Where every night they caught their tons of insects —
Five tons, somebody said.

And that was how it should be.
As every night for how many million years?
A clockwork, perfected like their radar.

We weren't sure whether to stay that night or go.
We were where we had never been in our lives.
Visitors — visiting even ourselves.

The bats were part of the sun's machinery,
Connected to the machinery of the flowers
By the machinery of insects. The bats' meaning

Oiled the unfailing logic of the earth.
Cosmic requirement — on the wings of a goblin.
A rebuke to our flutter of half-participation.

Thoughts like that were stirring, when somebody yelled.
The sky-dragon of bats was making a knot.

'They're coming back!'
                              We stared and we saw,

Through the bats, a mushrooming range
Of top-heavy thunderheads, their shutters flashing
Over the Rio Grande. The bats had a problem.

Wings above their heads like folding umbrellas
They dived out of the height
Straight back into the cave – the whole cloud,

The vast ragged body of the genie
Pouring back into the phial. All over the South
The storm flashed and crawled like a war.

Those bats had their eyes open. Unlike us,
They knew how, and when, to detach themselves
From the love that moves the sun and the other stars.

Black Coat

I remember going out there,
The tide far out, the North Shore ice-wind
Cutting me back
To the quick of the blood – that outer-edge nostalgia,
The good feeling. My sole memory
Of my black overcoat. Padding the wet sandspit.
I was staring at the sea, I suppose.
Trying to feel thoroughly alone,
Simply myself, with sharp edges –
Me and the sea one big tabula rasa,
As if my returning footprints
Out of that scrim of gleam, that horizon-wide wipe,
Might be a whole new start.

My shoe-sole shapes
My only sign.
My minimal but satisfying discussion
With the sea.
Putting my remarks down, for the thin tongue
Of the sea to interpret. Inaudibly.
A therapy,
Instructions too complicated for me

At the moment, but stowed in my black box for later.
Like feeding a wild deer
With potato crisps
As you do in that snapshot where you exclaim
Back towards me and my camera.

So I had no idea I had stepped
Into the telescopic sights
Of the paparazzo sniper
Nested in your brown iris.
Perhaps you had no idea either,
So far off, half a mile maybe,
Looking towards me. Watching me
Pin the sea's edge down.
No idea
How that double image,
Your eye's inbuilt double exposure
Which was the projection
Of your two-way heart's diplopic error,
The body of the ghost and me the blurred see-through
Came into single focus,
Sharp-edged, stark as a target,
Set up like a decoy
Against that freezing sea
From which your dead father had just crawled.

I did not feel
How, as your lenses tightened,
He slid into me.

Portraits

What happened to Howard's portrait of you?
I wanted that painting.
Spirits helped Howard. 'Sometimes
When I'm painting, I hear a voice, a woman's,
Calling *Howard, Howard* – faint, far-off,
Fading.'
          He got carried away
When he started feeding his colours
Into your image. He glowed
At his crucible, on its tripod.

10 How many sessions?
Yaddo fall. Woodstoves. Rain,
Rain, rain in the conifers. Tribal conflict
Of crows and their echoes. You deepened,
Molten, luminous, looking at us
From that window of Howard's vision of you.
Yourself lifted out of yourself
In a flaming of oils, your lips exact.

Suddenly – 'What's that? Who's that?'
Out of the gloomy neglected chamber behind you
20 Somebody had emerged, hunched, gloating at you,
Just behind your shoulder – a cowled
Humanoid of raggy shadows. Who?
Howard was surprised. He smiled at it.
'If I see it there, I paint it. I like it
When things like that happen. He just came.'

Came from where? Mystery smudge extra,
Stalking the glaze wetness
Of your new-fired idol brilliance.
I saw it with horrible premonition.
30 You were alone there, pregnant, unprotected
In some inaccessible dimension
Where that creature had you, now, to himself.
As if Howard's brush-strokes tethered you there
In a dark emptiness, a bait, an offering,
To bring up – not a man-eater, not a monster,
Not a demon – what? Who?
                              We watched
A small snake swim out, questing
Over the greenhouse dust – a bronze prong
Glistening life, tentative and vital
40 As a snail's horn, lifting its flow
Magnetically towards – 'Beautiful!'
That's what I cried. 'Look, Howard, beautiful!
So intense it's hypnotic!' Howard laughed.
Snakes are snakes. 'You like it,' he said,
'Because it's evil. It's evil, so it thrills you.'

You made no comment. Hardly a week before –
Entranced, gnawing your lips, your fingers counting
The touches of your thumb, delicately

Untangling on your fingers a music
That only you could hear, you had sat there,   50
Bowed as over a baby,
Conjuring into its shrine, onto your page,
This thing's dead immortal doppelgänger.

Stubbing Wharfe

Between the canal and the river
We sat in the gummy dark bar.
Winter night rain. The black humped bridge and its cobbles
Sweating black, under lamps of drizzling yellow.
And the hillsides going straight up, the high woods,
Massed with tangled wintry wet, and the moorland
Almost closing above us. The shut-in
Sodden dreariness of the whole valley,
The hopeless old stone trap of it. Where shall we live?
That was the question, in the yellow-lit tap-room
Which was cold and empty. You having leapt
Like a thrown dice, flinging off
The sparkle of America, pioneer
In the wrong direction, sat weeping,
Homesick, exhausted, disappointed, pregnant.
Where could we start living? Italy? Spain?
The world was all before us. And around us
This gloomy memorial of a valley,
The fallen-in grave of its history,
A gorge of ruined mills and abandoned chapels,
The fouled nest of the Industrial Revolution
That had flown. The windows glittered black.
If this was the glamour of an English pub, it was horrible.
Like a bubble in the sunk *Titanic*.
Our flashing inter-continental sleeper
Had slammed into a gruesome, dead-end tunnel.
Where could we camp? The ideal home
Was trying to crawl
Up out of my Guinness. Where we sat,
Forty years before I was born
My drunken grandad, dragged out of the canal,
Had sat in a sheet singing. A house of our own
Answering all your problems was the answer

To all my problems. All we needed
Was to get a home – anywhere,
Then all our goblins would turn out to be elves,
Our vampires guides, our demons angels
In that garden. Yes, the garden. The garden
Swelled under all our words – like the presence
Of what swelled in you.
                              Everything
Was there in my Guinness. Where, exactly?
That was the question – that dark
Peculiar aftertaste, bitter liquorice
Of the secret ingredient. At that black moment
Prophecy, like a local owl,
Down from the deep-cut valley opposite
Made a circuit through its territory –
Your future and mine. 'These side-valleys,' I whispered,
'Are full of the most fantastic houses,
Elizabethan, marvellous, little kingdoms,
Going for next to nothing. For instance
Up there opposite – up that valley – '
My certainty of the place was visionary,
Waiting there, on its walled terrace – an eyrie
Over the crevasse of trees and water.
You had no idea what I was talking about.
Your eyes were elsewhere –
The sun-shot Atlantic lift, the thunderous beaches,
The ice-cream summits, the whisper of avalanches,
Valleys brimming gentians – the Lawrentian globe
Lit the crystal globe you stared into
For your future – while a silent
Wing of your grave went over you. Up that valley
A future home waited for both of us –
Two different homes. Where I saw so clearly
My vision house, you saw only blackness,
Black nothing, the face of nothingness,
Like that rainy window.
                              Then five bowlers
Burst in like a troupe of clowns, laughing.
They thumped down their bowls and ordered. Their star turn
Had a raging ulcer, agony.
Or the ulcer was the star. It kept
The five of them doubled up – tossing helpless

On fresh blasts of laughter. It stoked them
Like souls tossing in a hell, on a grill
Of helpless laughter, agony, tears
Streaming down their faces
Like sweat as they struggled, throats gulping,
To empty their glasses, refilling and emptying.
I had to smile. You had to smile. The future
Seemed to ease open a fraction.

Remission

A fragile cutting, tamped into earth,
You took root, you flourished only
In becoming fruitful – in getting pregnant,
In the oceanic submissions
Of giving birth. That was the you
You loved and wanted to live with.
The kernel of the shells – each prettily painted –
Of the doll from the Polish corridor,
The inmost, smiling, solid one, the joy-being,
Venus of Willendorf or the Wyf of Bath.

That was the you you shared with the wild earth.
It was your membership
Of a sorority of petals and creatures
Whose masonic signs are beauty and nectar
In the love-land, the Paradise
Your suicide had tried to drag you from.

And it was the you that escaped death
In the little woven vessel
On the most earthly river
Of that Paradise. Your Indian midwife
(Of all your fairy godmothers the timeliest,
For you she was a deity from the Ganges,
Black with alluvial wisdom) stroked your hair
And made you weep with relief, and stowed you aboard,
Folded you from yourself, lulled the passage
Of yourself from your bleeding self
With the face-mask of nitrous oxide that was empty,
With yoga breath,
With monkey-fine dark fingers delivered you

In a free-floating crib, an image that sneezed
And opened a gummed mouth and started to cry.
I was there, I saw it. As I helped you

Escape incognito
The death who had already donned your features,
The mask of his disguise.

Isis

The morning we set out to drive around America
She started with us. She was our lightest
Bit of luggage. And you had dealt with Death.
You had come to an agreement finally:
He could keep your Daddy and you could have a child.

Macabre debate. Yet it had cost you
Two years, three years, desperate days and weepings.
Finally you had stripped the death-dress off,
Burned it on Daddy's grave.
Did it so resolutely, made
Such successful magic of it, Life
Was attracted and swerved down –
Unlikely, like a wild dove, to land on your head.
Day of America's Independence
You set out. And I, not Death,
Drove the car.
                    Was Death, too, part of our luggage?
Unemployed for a while, fellow traveller?
Did he ride on the car top, on the bonnet?
Did he meet us now and again on the road,
Smiling in a café, at a gas station?
Stowaway in our ice-box?
Did he run in the wheel's shadow?

Or did he sulk in your papers, back in your bedroom,
Waiting for your habits
To come back and remember him? You had hidden him
From yourself and deceived even Life.
But your blossom had fruited and in England
It ripened. There your midwife,
The orchardist, was a miniature Indian lady

Black and archaic, half-Gond,
With her singing manner and her lucky charm voice,
A priestess of fruits.
Our Black Isis had stepped off the wall
Shaking her sistrum –
Polymorphus Daemon,
Magnae Deorum Matris – with the moon
Between her hip-bones and crowned with ears of corn.

The great goddess in person
Had put on your body, waxing full,
Using your strainings
Like a surgical glove, to create with,
Like a soft mask to triumph and be grotesque in
On the bed of birth.

It was not Death
Weeping in you then, when you lay among bloody cloths
Holding what had come out of you to cry.

It was not poetic death
Lifted you from the blood and set you
Straightaway lurching – exultant –
To the phone, to announce to the world
What Life had made of you,
Your whole body borrowed
By immortality and its promise,
Your arms filled
With what had never died, never known Death.

Epiphany

London. The grimy lilac softness
Of an April evening. Me
Walking over Chalk Farm Bridge
On my way to the tube station.
A new father – slightly light-headed
With the lack of sleep and the novelty.
Next, this young fellow coming towards me.

I glanced at him for the first time as I passed him
Because I noticed (I couldn't believe it)
What I'd been ignoring.

Not the bulge of a small animal
Buttoned into the top of his jacket
The way colliers used to wear their whippets –
But its actual face. Eyes reaching out
Trying to catch my eyes – so familiar!
The huge ears, the pinched, urchin expression –
The wild confronting stare, pushed through fear,
Between the jacket lapels.
                                        'It's a fox-cub!'
I heard my own surprise as I stopped.
He stopped. 'Where did you get it? What
Are you going to do with it?'
                                        A fox-cub
On the hump of Chalk Farm Bridge!

'You can have him for a pound.' 'But
Where did you find it? What will you do with it?'
'Oh, somebody'll buy him. Cheap enough
At a pound.' And a grin.
                                        What I was thinking
Was – what would you think? How would we fit it
Into our crate of space? With the baby?
What would you make of its old smell
And its mannerless energy?
And as it grew up and began to enjoy itself
What would we do with an unpredictable,
Powerful, bounding fox?
The long-mouthed, flashing temperament?
That necessary nightly twenty miles
And that vast hunger for everything beyond us?
How would we cope with its cosmic derangements
Whenever we moved?

The little fox peered past me at other folks,
At this one and at that one, then at me.
Good luck was all it needed.
Already past the kittenish
But the eyes still small,
Round, orphaned-looking, woebegone
As if with weeping. Bereft
Of the blue milk, the toys of feather and fur,
The den life's happy dark. And the huge whisper
Of the constellations

Out of which Mother had always returned.
My thoughts felt like big, ignorant hounds
Circling and sniffing around him.
                              Then I walked on
As if out of my own life.
I let that fox-cub go. I tossed it back
Into the future
Of a fox-cub in London and I hurried
Straight on and dived as if escaping
Into the Underground. If I had paid,
If I had paid that pound and turned back
To you, with that armful of fox –

If I had grasped that whatever comes with a fox
Is what tests a marriage and proves it a marriage –
I would not have failed the test. Would you have failed it?
But I failed. Our marriage had failed.

The Gypsy

The Cathedral was there,
Impotent, for show, for others, for other
Ages. The spectacular up-spearing
Of its tonnage pierced us
With the shadow-gloom and weight of the sacred.
Not the first time I'd seen Rheims. The last.
I shall never go near it again.
The lightning stroke of what happened
Burnt up the silkiest, secretive, tentative
Map of France I was weaving
Ahead of us – as a spider weaves its walkway,
For our future, maybe. Our first
Exploration beyond Paris together,
Reconnoitring, note-making, enthralled
By everything. We sat in the square
Dunking our buttered croissants in hot chocolate.
You were writing postcards, concentrated.
In your mac. Midmorning, the air fresh.

The dark stub gypsy woman
Was suddenly there. Busy, business-like
As a weasel testing every crevice,

Or the blade of a waiter splitting oysters,
Flinging without a pause
The bad one into the bin, the top shell
Into the bin, then at the next, attentive,
Finding the key-hole. She was holding out
A religious pendant – a Nicholas, a Mary –
Palm upwards. Expert, without a side-glance,
Almost before she spoke you had refused her,
A practised reflex, sprung like a trap, hard
Your vehemence met her vehemence.
Her racing routine demand stopped at your 'Non.'
And she did stop, stung, stunned, as sudden
As if you had slapped her. Like a pistol her finger
Came up to your face, all her momentum
Icicled into a pointer: 'Vous
Crèverez bientôt.' Her dark face
A knot of oiled leather, a quipu,
Like Geronimo's. Bitter eyes
Of grappa-dreg revenge, old Gallic malice,
Raisins of bile. And as abruptly
She had gone on, hither, thither,
Among the tables and vanished, leaving her words
Heavier than the Cathedral,
Bigger, darker, founded far deeper –
My whole body taking their weight
Like a newer or much older religion
In me alone, to be carried
Everywhere with me – deeper catacombs,
And with a stronger God.
                                    But you
Went on writing postcards. For days I rhymed
Talismans of power, in cynghanedd,
To neutralise her venom. I imagined
Returning to Rheims, how I would find her
And give her a coin – bribe her to call home
Her projectile. But you
Never mentioned it. Never recorded it
In your diary. And I hung in a hope
You hadn't even heard it. Deafened, maybe,
By closer explosions. Closed, maybe,
In a solider crypt.

A Dream

Your worst dream
Came true: that ring on the door-bell –
Not a simple chance in a billion
But a meteorite, straight down our chimney,
With our name on it.

Not dreams, I had said, but fixed stars
Govern a life. A thirst of the whole being,
Inexorable, like a sleeper drawing
Air into the lungs. You had to lift
The coffin lid an inch.
In your dream or mine? Strange letter box.
You took out the envelope. It was
A letter from your Daddy. 'I'm home.
Can I stay with you?' I said nothing.
For me, a request was a command.

Then came the Cathedral.
Chartres. Somehow we had got to Chartres.
Not the first time for you.
I remember little
But a Breton jug. You filled it
With everything we had. Every last franc.
You said it was for your mother.
You emptied our oxygen
Into that jug. Chartres
(I salvaged this)
Hung about your face, a mantilla,
Blackened, a tracery of char –
As after a firestorm. Nun-like
You nursed what was left of your Daddy.
Pouring our lives out of that jug
Into his morning coffee. Then you smashed it
Into shards, crude stars,
And gave them to your mother.

'And for you,' you said to me, 'permission
To remember this dream. And think about it.'

The Minotaur

The mahogany table-top you smashed
Had been the broad plank top
Of my mother's heirloom sideboard –
Mapped with the scars of my whole life.

That came under the hammer.
The high stool you swung that day
Demented by my being
Twenty minutes late for baby-minding.

'Marvellous!' I shouted, 'Go on,
Smash it into kindling.
That's the stuff you're keeping out of your poems!'
And later, considered and calmer,

'Get that shoulder under your stanzas
And we'll be away.' Deep in the cave of your ear
The goblin snapped his fingers.
So what had I given him?

The bloody end of the skein
That unravelled your marriage,
Left your children echoing
Like tunnels in a labyrinth,

Left your mother a dead-end,
Brought you to the horned, bellowing
Grave of your risen father –
And your own corpse in it.

The Pan

When he stopped at last in the long main street
Of the small town, after that hundred
And ninety miles, the five-o'clock, September,
Brassy, low, wet Westcountry sun
Above the street's far end, and when
He had extricated his stiffness
From the car crammed with books, carrier bags
Of crockery, cutlery and baby things,
And crossed the tilting street in that strange town

To buy a pan to heat milk and babyfood
The moment they arrived
Hours ahead of their furniture
Into their stripped new house, in their strange new life,
He did not notice that the ironmonger's
Where he bought the pan had been closed
And empty for two years. And returning
With the little pan he did not notice
A man on the pavement staring at him,
His arm round a young woman who wore
A next-to-nothing long evening dress
Slashed to the hip, and a white, silk, open-work shawl
Round her naked shoulders, and leopard-claw earrings,
He did not recognise, nor did his wife
As he squeezed back weary beside her
Behind the wheel of the Morris Traveller,
That this man, barely two yards from them,
Staring at them both so fixedly,
The man so infinitely more alive
Than either of them there in the happy car
Was himself – knowing their whole future
And helpless to warn them.

Error

I brought you to Devon. I brought you into my dreamland.
I sleepwalked you
Into my land of totems. Never-never land:
The orchard in the West.
                          I wrestled
With the blankets, the caul and the cord,
And you stayed with me
Gallant and desperate and hopeful,
Listening for different gods, stripping off
Your American royalty, garment by garment –
Till you stepped out soul-naked and stricken
Into this cobbled, pictureless corridor
Aimed at a graveyard.
                          What had happened
To the Italian sun?
Had it escaped our snatch

Like a butterfly off a nettle? The flashing trajectory,
The trans-continental dream-express
Of your adolescence – had it
Slammed to a dead-end, crushing halt, fatal,
In this red-soil tunnel? Was this why
We could not wake – our fingers tearing numbly
At the mesh of nettle-roots?
                              What wrong fork
Had we taken? In a gloom orchard
Under drumming thatch, we lay listening
To our vicarage rotting like a coffin,
Foundering under its weeds. What did you make of it
When you sat at your elm table alone
Staring at the blank sheet of white paper,
Silent at your typewriter, listening
To the leaking thatch drip, the murmur of rain,
And staring at that sunken church, and the black
Slate roofs in the mist of rain, low tide,
Gleaming awash.
                    This was Lyonnesse.
Inaccessible clouds, submarine trees.
The labyrinth
Of brambly burrow lanes. Bundled women –
Stump-warts, you called them –
Sniffing at your strangeness in wet shops.
Their eyes followed you everywhere, loamy badgers,
Dug you out of your sleep and pawed at your dreams,
Jabbered hedge-bank judgements, a dark-age dialect,
Peered from every burrow-mouth.
                                  The world
Came to an end at bullocks
Huddled behind gates, knee-deep in quag,
Under the huddled, rainy hills. A bellow
Shaking the soaked oak-woods tested the limits.
And, beside the boots, the throbbing gutter –
A thin squandering of blood-water –
Searched for the river and the sea.

And this was what we had chosen finally.
Remembering it, I see it all in a bubble:
Strange people, in a closed brilliance,
Laughing and crying soundlessly,

Gazing out of the transparency
At a desolation. A rainy wedding picture
On a foreign grave, among lilies –
And just beneath it, unseen, the real bones
Still undergoing everything.

The Lodger

Potatoes were growing in the yard corner
That September. They were the welcome wagon!
First fruits of our own ground. And their flavour
Was the first legend. Pioneer
In our own life, those mornings –
I bought the spades, the forks, the overalls, the boots.
And the books. The books! I was a student
Gluttonous to swallow all horticulture,
The whole cornucopia. I began to dig.
I had to start right – I double-dug
The entire garden. And my heart,
And whatever hid in my heart, dug with me.
I assumed I was doomed – a matter of time
Before the heart jumped out of my body
Or simply collapsed. After a few hours digging
Suddenly something gave, the sweat burst out,
I was shaking. Heart. By now I was accustomed.
It could only be heart. The pangs. The poundings.
At night on my pillow the syncopated stagger
Of the pulse in my ear. Russian roulette:
Every heartbeat a fresh throw of the dice –
A click of Russian roulette. Strange
To be lying on my bed
Contemplating my heart as it knocked me to pieces,
As if I were attending the ache of a tooth.
And yet my heart was me. I was my heart.
My heart, that had always sung me through
My frenzies of exertion. How could it fail me?
I carried it everywhere with me, a dying child,
Weighing at my chest. A sudden spike
Under my left shoulder-blade.
Or a sword – horrible image of the thin blade
Pushed down vertically beside my neck

Inside the clavicle. Or a gnawing
At my ribs, from the inside. Worst
The unpredictable faintness – instant gear-slip
From infinite energy to ghostly nothing,
The drive jolted into neutral, and my motor
Racing uselessly. How many times a day?
Hypochondria walked, holding my arm
Like a nurse, her fingers over my pulse.
Well, I was going to die.
I started a diary – observations
Of my heart's errata.
My waking with strengthless hands. My going to bed
With fingers that throbbed so hard
They jerked the book I clung to and stared at.
The timing of the double-fisted blow
That came down between my shoulder-blades
'Soft but stunning like the kick of a camel'.
The sudden lapping at my throat of loose blood
Like a bird escaped, broken-winged,
From a cat briefly. Efforts to make my whole
Body a conduit of Beethoven,
To reconduct that music through my aorta
So he could run me clean and unconstrained
And release me. I could not reach the music.
All the music told me
Was that I was a reject, belonged no longer
In the intact, creating, resounding realm
Where music poured. I was already a discard,
My momentum merely the inertias
Of what I had been, while I disintegrated.
I was already posthumous.
Whatever I looked at, any cat or dog,
Saw me already dead, merely
Lurching on a few paces, perfunctory vision
Still on my retina.
                              My new study
Was all the ways a heart can kill its owner
And how mine had killed me. Of all this one,
Two, three years I told you nothing.
                                        Meanwhile
Who was using my heart,
Who positioned our bee-hive and planted,

With my unwitting hands, to amuse himself,
Nine bean rows? Who was this alien joker
Who had come to evict us,
Sharing my skin, just as he shared yours,
Watching my digging, so calmly? And gazing
Over your shoulder, into the poems you polished
As into this or that or the other mirror
That tried to ignore him?

Daffodils

Remember how we picked the daffodils?
Nobody else remembers, but I remember.
Your daughter came with her armfuls, eager and happy,
Helping the harvest. She has forgotten.
She cannot even remember you. And we sold them.
It sounds like sacrilege, but we sold them.
Were we so poor? Old Stoneman, the grocer,
Boss-eyed, his blood-pressure purpling to beetroot
(It was his last chance,
He would die in the same great freeze as you),
He persuaded us. Every Spring
He always bought them, sevenpence a dozen,
'A custom of the house'.

Besides, we still weren't sure we wanted to own
Anything. Mainly we were hungry
To convert everything to profit.
Still nomads – still strangers
To our whole possession. The daffodils
Were incidental gilding of the deeds,
Treasure trove. They simply came,
And they kept on coming.
As if not from the sod but falling from heaven.
Our lives were still a raid on our own good luck.
We knew we'd live for ever. We had not learned
What a fleeting glance of the everlasting
Daffodils are. Never identified
The nuptial flight of the rarest ephemera –
Our own days!

We thought they were a windfall.
Never guessed they were a last blessing.

So we sold them. We worked at selling them
As if employed on somebody else's
Flower-farm. You bent at it
In the rain of that April – your last April.
We bent there together, among the soft shrieks
Of their jostled stems, the wet shocks shaken
Of their girlish dance-frocks –
Fresh-opened dragonflies, wet and flimsy,
Opened too early.

We piled their frailty lights on a carpenter's bench,
Distributed leaves among the dozens –
Buckling blade-leaves, limber, groping for air, zinc-silvered –
Propped their raw butts in bucket water,
Their oval, meaty butts,
And sold them, sevenpence a bunch –

Wind-wounds, spasms from the dark earth,
With their odourless metals,
A flamy purification of the deep grave's stony cold
As if ice had a breath –

We sold them, to wither.
The crop thickened faster than we could thin it.
Finally, we were overwhelmed
And we lost our wedding-present scissors.

Every March since they have lifted again
Out of the same bulbs, the same
Baby-cries from the thaw,
Ballerinas too early for music, shiverers
In the draughty wings of the year.
On that same groundswell of memory, fluttering
They return to forget you stooping there
Behind the rainy curtains of a dark April,
Snipping their stems.

But somewhere your scissors remember. Wherever they are.
Here somewhere, blades wide open,
April by April
Sinking deeper
Through the sod – an anchor, a cross of rust.

The Afterbirth

Huddled on the floor, the afterbirth
Was already offal.
There was the lotus-eater's whole island
Dragged out by its roots, into the light,
And flopped onto blood-soaked newsprint – a tangled
Puddle of dawn reds and evening purples,
To be rubbished. You were laughing and weeping
Into the glare. A tear-splitting dazzle
Like the noon sun finally stared at
Had burst into the bedroom when the Gorgon
Arrived and ripped her face off
And threw it to the floor. Such a shocking
Beauty born. I saw it flash up
That sunburned German with all his strength
Slamming the sea-tripes of the octopus
Hard down onto our honeymoon quay –
In the blue-blackish glare
Of my sunstroke.
                        You were weeping
Your biggest, purest joy. The placenta
Already meaningless, asphyxiated.
Your eyes dazzling tears as I thought
No other brown eyes could, ever,
As you lifted the dazzler. I eased
The heavy, fallen Eden into a bowl
Of ovenproof glass. A bowl with a meaning
All to itself – a hare crouching
In its claret – the curled-up, chopped-up corpse
That weeks before I had jugged in it. I felt
Like somebody's shadow on a cave wall.
A figure with a dog's head
On a tomb wall in Egypt. You watched me
From your bed, through the window,
As I buried the bowlful of afterbirth
In a motherly hump of ancient Britain,
Under the elms. You would eat no more hare
Jugged in the wine of its own blood
Out of that bowl. The hare nesting in it
Had opened its eyes. As if some night,
Maybe with a thick snow falling softly,

It might come hobbling down from under the elms
Into our yard, crying: 'Mother! Mother!
They are going to eat me.'
                              Or bob up,
Dodging ahead, a witchy familiar, sent
To lock error beyond repair when it
Died silent, a black jolt,
Under my offside rear wheel
On the dawn A30. You heard nothing.
But it bled out of my pen. And re-formed
On my page. The hieroglyph of the hare.
You picked it up, curious.
And it screamed in your ear like a telephone –
The moon-eyed, ripped-up flower of it screamed.
Disembowelled, a stunned mask,
Unstoppably, like a burst artery,
The hare in the bowl screamed –

Setebos

Who could play Miranda?
Only you. Ferdinand – only me.
And it was like that, yes, it was like that.
I never questioned. Your mother
Played Prospero, flying her magic in
To stage the Masque, and bless the marriage,
Eavesdropping on the undervoices
Of the honeymooners in Paris
And smiling on the stair at her reflection
In the dark wall. My wreckage
Was all of a sudden a new wardrobe, unworn,
Even gold in my teeth. Ariel
Entertained us night and day.
The voices and sounds and sweet airs
Were our aura. Ariel was our aura.
Both of us alternated
Caliban our secret, who showed us
The sweetest, the freshest, the wildest
And loved us as we loved. Sycorax,
The rind of our garden's emptied quince,
Bobbed in the hazy surf at the horizon

Offshore, in the wings
Of the heavens, like a director
Studying the scenes to come.

Then the script overtook us. Caliban
Reverted to type. I heard
The bellow in your voice
That made my nape-hair prickle when you sang
How you were freed from the Elm. I lay
In the labyrinth of a cowslip
Without a clue. I heard the Minotaur
Coming down its tunnel-groove
Of old faults deep and bitter. King Minos,
Alias Otto – his bellow
Winding into murderous music. Which play
Were we in? Too late to find you
And get to my ship. The moon, off her moorings,
Tossed in tempest. Your bellowing song
Was a scream inside a bronze
Bull being roasted. The laughter
Of Sycorax was thunder and lightning
And black downpour. She hurled
Prospero's head at me,
A bounding thunderbolt, a jumping cracker.
The moon's horns
Plunged and tossed. I heard your cries
Bugling through the hot bronze:
'Who has dismembered us?' I crawled
Under a gabardine, hugging tight
All I could of me, hearing the cry
Now of hounds.

A Short Film

It was not meant to hurt.
It had been made for happy remembering
By people who were still too young
To have learned about memory.

Now it is a dangerous weapon, a time-bomb,
Which is a kind of body-bomb, long-term, too.

Only film, a few frames of you skipping, a few seconds,
You aged about ten there, skipping and still skipping.

Not very clear grey, made out of mist and smudge,
This thing has a fine fuse, less a fuse
Than a wavelength attuned, an electronic detonator
To what lies in your grave inside us.

And how that explosion would hurt
Is not just an idea of horror but a flash of fine sweat
Over the skin-surface, a bracing of nerves
For something that has already happened.

The Rag Rug

Somebody had made one. You admired it.
So you began to make your rag rug.
You needed to do it. Played on by lightnings
You needed an earth. Maybe. Or needed
To pull something out of yourself –
Some tapeworm of the psyche. I was simply
Happy to watch your scissors being fearless
As you sliced your old wool dresses,
Your cast-offs, once so costly,
Into bandages. Dark venous blood,
Daffodil yellow. You plaited them
Into a rope. You massaged them
Into the new life of a motley viper
That writhed out of the grave
Of your wardrobe. Like the buried wrapping
Of old mummy non-selves. You bowed
Like a potter
Over the turning hub of your rich rag rug
That widened its wheel,
Searching out the perimeter of a music –
The tongues of the loose ends flickering in air,
Issuing like a fugue out of the whorls
Of your fingertips. It calmed you,
Creating the serpent that coiled
Into a carpet. And the carpet
Lifted us, as it turned and returned,
Out of that crimson room of our cardiac days.

It freed me. It freed you
To do something that seemed almost nothing.
Whenever you worked at your carpet I felt happy. 30
Then I could read Conrad's novels to you.
I could cradle your freed mind in my voice,
Chapter by chapter, sentence by sentence,
Word by word: *The Heart of Darkness*,
The Secret Sharer. The same, I could feel
Your fingers caressing my reading, hour after hour,
Fitting together the serpent's jumbled rainbow.
I was like the snake-charmer – my voice
Swaying you over your heaped coils. While you
Unearthed something deeper than our verses. 40
A knowledge like the halves of a broken magnet.

I remember
Those long, crimson-shadowed evenings of ours
More like the breath-held camera moments
Of reaching to touch a falcon that does not fly off.
As if I held your hand to stroke a falcon
With your hand.
                    Later (not much later)
Your diary confided to whoever
What furies you bled into that rug.
As if you had dragged it, like your own entrails, 50
Out through your navel.

Was I the child or the mother? Did you braid it,
That umbilicus between us,
To free yourself from my contraction or was it
Pushing me out and away? Did you coil it,
Your emergency magic operation,
To draw off the tangle of numb distance
Secreting itself between us? Or was it
A drooled curse
From some old bitter woman's rusty mouth 60
That stays awake when she sleeps – her malediction
Spellbinding tiered labyrinths of confusion
Into the breadth of a hearth-rug? The coils,
Impassable, became a mamba, fatal.
Its gentle tap, when you trod on it for finality,
Would alter your blood. When I stepped over it
Would alter my nerves and brain.

I dreamed of our house

Before we ever found it. A great snake
Lifted its head from a well in the middle of the house
70   Exactly where the well is, beneath its slab,
In the middle of the house.
A golden serpent, thick as a child's body,
Eased from the opened well. And poured out
Through the back door, a length that seemed unending –
Till its tail tapered over the threshold,
The deep-worn, cracked threshold, soon to be ours.
That was after the whole house, in my dream,
Had capsized. And a perfect replica
Double of the house – the well-world's own
80   Upside-down reflection duplicate –
Had swung uppermost, and locked upright
Under its different stars, with an earthquake jolt,
Shaking the snake awake.

The rag rug

That had heaped out onto your lap
Slid to the floor. There it lay, coiled
Between us. However it came,
And wherever it found its tongue, its fang, its meaning,
It survived our Eden.

The Table

I wanted to make you a solid writing-table
That would last a lifetime.
I bought a broad elm plank two inches thick,
The wild bark surfing along one edge of it,
Rough-cut for coffin timber. Coffin elm
Finds a new life, with its corpse,
Drowned in the waters of earth. It gives the dead
Protection for a slightly longer voyage
Than beech or ash or pine might. With a plane
I revealed a perfect landing pad
For your inspiration. I did not
Know I had made and fitted a door
Opening downwards into your Daddy's grave.

You bent over it, euphoric
With your Nescafé every morning.
Like an animal, smelling the wild air,
Listening into its own ailment,
Then finding the exact herb.
It did not take you long
To divine in the elm, following your pen,
The words that would open it. Incredulous
I saw rise through it, in broad daylight,
Your Daddy resurrected,
Blue-eyed, that German cuckoo
Still calling the hour,
Impersonating your whole memory.
He limped up through it
Into our house. While I slept he snuggled
Shivering between us. Turning to touch me
You recognised him. 'Wait!' I said. 'Wait!
What's this?' My incomprehension
Deafened by his language – a German
Outside my wavelengths. I woke wildly
Into a deeper sleep. And I sleepwalked
Like an actor with his script
Blindfold through the looking glass. I embraced
Lady Death, your rival,
As if the role were written on my eyelids
In letters of phosphorus. With your arms locked
Round him, in joy, he took you
Down through the elm door.
He had got what he wanted.
I woke up on the empty stage with the props,
The paltry painted masks. And the script
Ripped up and scattered, its code scrambled,
Like the blades and slivers
Of a shattered mirror.

And now your peanut-crunchers can stare
At the ink-stains, the sigils
Where you engraved your letters to him
Cursing and imploring. No longer a desk.
No longer a door. Once more simply a board.
The roof of a coffin
Detached in the violence

From your upward gaze.
It bobbed back to the surface –
It washed up, far side of the Atlantic,
A curio,
Scoured of the sweat I soaked into
Finding your father for you and then
Leaving you to him.

Apprehensions

Your writing was also your fear,
At times it was your terror, that all
Your wedding presents, your dreams, your husband
Would be taken from you
By the terror's goblins. Your typewriter
Would be taken. Your sewing-machine. Your children.
All would be taken.
This fear was the colour of your desk-top,
You almost knew its features.
That grain was like its skin, you could stroke it.
You could taste it in your milky coffee.
It made a noise like your typewriter.
It hid in its own jujus –
Your mantelpiece mermaid of terracotta.
Your coppery fondue pan. Your linen. Your curtains.
You stared at these. You knew it was there.
It hid in your Schaeffer pen –

That was its favourite place. Whenever you wrote
You would stop, mid-word,
To look at it more closely, black, fat,
Between your fingers –
The swelling terror that would any moment
Suddenly burst out and take from you
Your husband, your children, your body, your life.
You could see it, there, in your pen.

Somebody took that too.

Dream Life

As if you descended in each night's sleep
Into your father's grave
You seemed afraid to look, or to remember next morning
What you had seen. When you did remember
Your dreams were of a sea clogged with corpses,
Death-camp atrocities, mass amputations.

Your sleep was a bloody shrine, it seemed.
And the sacred relic of it
Your father's gangrenous, cut-off leg.
No wonder you feared sleep.
No wonder you woke, saying: 'No dreams.'

What was the liturgy
Of that nightly service, that cult
Where you were the priestess?
Were those poems your salvaged fragments of it?

Your day-waking was a harrowed safety
You tried to cling to – not knowing
What had frightened you
Or where your poetry followed you from
With its blood-sticky feet. Each night
I hypnotised calm into you,
Courage, understanding and calm.
Did it help? Each night you descended again
Into the temple-crypt,
That private, primal cave
Under the public dome of father-worship.
All night you lolled unconscious
Over the crevasse
Inhaling the oracle
That spoke only conclusions.

Hackings-off of real limbs,
Smoke of the hospital incinerator,
Carnival beggars on stumps,
The gas-chamber and the oven
Of the camera's war – all this
Was the anatomy of your God of Sleep,

His blue eyes – the sleepless electrodes
In your temples

Preparing his Feast of Atonement.

Perfect Light

There you are, in all your innocence,
Sitting among your daffodils, as in a picture
Posed as for the title: 'Innocence'.
Perfect light in your face lights it up
Like a daffodil. Like any one of those daffodils
It was to be your only April on earth
Among your daffodils. In your arms,
Like a teddy bear, your new son,
Only a few weeks into his innocence.
Mother and infant, as in the Holy portrait.
And beside you, laughing up at you,
Your daughter, barely two. Like a daffodil
You turn your face down to her, saying something.
Your words were lost in the camera.
                              And the knowledge
Inside the hill on which you are sitting,
A moated fort hill, bigger than your house,
Failed to reach the picture. While your next moment,
Coming towards you like an infantryman
Returning slowly out of no-man's-land,
Bowed under something, never reached you –
Simply melted into the perfect light.

The Rabbit Catcher

It was May. How had it started? What
Had bared our edges? What quirky twist
Of the moon's blade had set us, so early in the day,
Bleeding each other? What had I done? I had
Somehow misunderstood. Inaccessible
In your dybbuk fury, babies
Hurled into the car, you drove. We surely
Had been intending a day's outing,

Somewhere on the coast, an exploration –
So you started driving.
                    What I remember
Is thinking: She'll do something crazy. And I ripped
The door open and jumped in beside you.
So we drove West. West. Cornish lanes
I remember, a simmering truce
As you stared, with iron in your face,
Into some remote thunderscape
Of some unworldly war. I simply
Trod accompaniment, carried babies,
Waited for you to come back to nature.
We tried to find the coast. You
Raged against our English private greed
Of fencing off all coastal approaches,
Hiding the sea from roads, from all inland.
You despised England's grubby edges when you got there.
That day belonged to the furies. I searched the map
To penetrate the farms and private kingdoms.
Finally a gateway. It was a fresh day,
Full May. Somewhere I'd bought food.
We crossed a field and came to the open
Blue push of sea-wind. A gorse cliff,
Brambly, oak-packed combes. We found
An eyrie hollow, just under the cliff-top.
It seemed perfect to me. Feeding babies,
Your Germanic scowl, edged like a helmet,
Would not translate itself. I sat baffled.
I was a fly outside on the window-pane
Of my own domestic drama. You refused to lie there
Being indolent, you hated it.
That flat, draughty plate was not an ocean.
You had to be away and you went. And I
Trailed after like a dog, along the cliff-top field-edge,
Over a wind-matted oak-wood –
And I found a snare.
Copper-wire gleam, brown cord, human contrivance,
Sitting new-set. Without a word
You tore it up and threw it into the trees.

I was aghast. Faithful
To my country gods – I saw

The sanctity of a trapline desecrated.
You saw blunt fingers, blood in the cuticles,
Clamped round a blue mug. I saw
Country poverty raising a penny,
Filling a Sunday stewpot. You saw baby-eyed
Strangled innocents, I saw sacred
Ancient custom. You saw snare after snare
And went ahead, riving them from their roots
And flinging them down the wood. I saw you
Ripping up precarious, precious saplings
Of my heritage, hard-won concessions
From the hangings and the transportations
To live off the land. You cried: 'Murderers!'
You were weeping with a rage
That cared nothing for rabbits. You were locked
Into some chamber gasping for oxygen
Where I could not find you, or really hear you,
Let alone understand you.
                                    In those snares
You'd caught something.
Had you caught something in me,
Nocturnal and unknown to me? Or was it
Your doomed self, your tortured, crying,
Suffocating self? Whichever,
Those terrible, hypersensitive
Fingers of your verse closed round it and
Felt it alive. The poems, like smoking entrails,
Came soft into your hands.

Suttee

In the myth of your first death our deity
Was yourself resurrected.
Yourself reborn. The holy one.
Day in day out that was our worship –
Tending the white birth-bed of your rebirth,
The unforthcoming delivery, the all-but-born,
The ought-by-now-to-be-born.

We were patient.
The gruelling prolongueur of your labour-pangs

Gave our dedication altitude.
What would you be – begotten
By that savage act of yours committed
On your body, battering your face to the concrete,
Leaving yourself for dead
(And hoping you were dead) for three days?

We feared
Our new birth might be damaged,
Injured in that death-struggle conception.
Our hope was also dread. The dolorous
Agony you performed was also happy:
The part of your own mother. I was midwife.
And the daily busyness of life
Was no more than more towels, kettles
Of hot water, then the rubber mask
Of anaesthetic that had no gas in it,
The placebo you kept grabbing for,
Gulping it like cocaine.

Your labour frightened you.
What was trying to come frightened you.
You had no idea what it might be –
Yet it was the only thing you wanted.
Night after night, weeks, months, years
I bowed there, as if over a page,
Coaxing it to happen,
Laying my ear to our unborn and its heartbeat,
Assuaging your fears. Massaging
Your cramps into sleep with hypnosis
And whispering to the star
That would soon fall into our straw –
Till suddenly the waters
Broke and I was dissolved.
Much as I protested and resisted
I was engulfed
In a flood, a dam-burst thunder
Of new myth.
In the warp of pouring glair,
Me bowled under it, I glimpsed
Your labour cries refracted, modulating –
Just as in a film – not to the cries
Of the newborn in her creams and perfumes,

Not to the wauling of joy,
But to the screams
Of the mourner
Just after death far-off in prehistory.
After death and outside our time.
The now of it
A scream stuck in a groove – unstoppable.
And you had been delivered of yourself
In flames. Our newborn
Was your own self in flames.
And the tongues of those flames were your tongues.
I had delivered an explosion
Of screams that were flames.
'What are these flames?' was all I managed to say,
Running with my midwife's hands
Not to wash them, only to extinguish
The screeching flames that fed on them and dripped from them.
I could not escape the torching gusher.
You were a child-bride
On a pyre.
Your flames fed on rage, on love
And on your cries for help.
Tears were a raw fuel.
And I was your husband
Performing the part of your father
In our new myth –
Both of us drenched in a petroleum
Of ancient American sunlight,
Both of us consumed
By the old child in the new birth –
Not the new babe of light but the old
Babe of dark flames and screams
That sucked the oxygen out of both of us.

The Bee God

When you wanted bees I never dreamed
It meant your Daddy had come up out of the well.

I scoured the old hive, you painted it,
White, with crimson hearts and flowers, and bluebirds.

So you became the Abbess
In the nunnery of the bees.

But when you put on your white regalia,
Your veil, your gloves, I never guessed a wedding.

That Maytime, in the orchard, that summer,
The hot, shivering chestnuts leaned towards us,

Their great gloved hands again making their offer
I never know how to accept.

But you bowed over your bees
As you bowed over your Daddy.

Your page a dark swarm
Clinging under the lit blossom.

You and your Daddy there in the heart of it,
Weighing your slender neck.

I saw I had given you something
That had carried you off in a cloud of gutturals –

The thunderhead of your new selves
Tending your golden mane.

You did not want me to go but your bees
Had their own ideas.

You wanted the honey, you wanted those big blossoms
Clotted like first milk, and the fruit like babies.

But the bees' orders were geometric –
Your Daddy's plans were Prussian.

When the first bee touched my hair
You were peering into the cave of thunder.

That outrider tangled, struggled, stung –
Marking the target.

And I was flung like a headshot jackrabbit
Through sunlit whizzing tracers

As bees planted their volts, their thudding electrodes,
In on their target.

Your face wanted to save me
From what had been decided.

You rushed to me, your dream-time veil off,
Your ghost-proof gloves off,

But as I stood there, where I thought I was safe,
Clawing out of my hair

Sticky, disembowelled bees,
A lone bee, like a blind arrow,

Soared over the housetop and down
And locked onto my brow, calling for helpers

Who came –
Fanatics for their God, the God of the Bees,

Deaf to your pleas as the fixed stars
At the bottom of the well.

Being Christlike

You did not want to be Christlike. Though your father
Was your God and there was no other, you did not
Want to be Christlike. Though you walked
In the love of your father. Though you stared
At the stranger your mother.
What had she to do with you
But tempt you from your father?
When her great hooded eyes lowered
Their moon so close
Promising the earth you saw
Your fate and you cried
Get thee behind me. You did not
Want to be Christlike. You wanted
To be with your father
In wherever he was. And your body
Barred your passage. And your family
Who were your flesh and blood
Burdened it. And a god
That was not your father
Was a false god. But you did not
Want to be Christlike.

The Beach

You lashed for release, like a migrant eel in November.
You needed the sea. I knew not much more
About Westcountry beaches than you did.
We are surrounded, I said, by magnificent beaches.
You'd seen the cliffs – a slashed and tilted gorge
Near Hartland, where we'd picked blackberries
That first somnambulist week of your ecstasy
With your brother. But now you needed a beach
Like your drug. Your undertow withdrawal
Blinded and choked you. It darkened a darkness darker.
England was so filthy! Only the sea
Could scour it. Your ocean salts would scour you.
You wanted to be washed, scoured, sunned.
That 'jewel in the head' – your flashing thunderclap miles
Of Nauset surf. The slew of horse-shoe crabs
And sand-dollars. You craved like oxygen
American earlier summers, yourself burnt dark –
Some prophecy mislaid, somehow. England
Was so poor! Was black paint cheaper? Why
Were English cars all black – to hide the filth?
Or to stay respectable, like bowlers
And umbrellas? Every vehicle a hearse.
The traffic procession a hushing leftover
Of Victoria's perpetual funeral Sunday –
The funeral of colour and light and life!
London a morgue of dinge – English dinge.
Our sole indigenous art-form – depressionist!
And why were everybody's
Garments so deliberately begrimed?
Grubby-looking, like a camouflage? 'Alas!
We have never recovered,' I said, 'from our fox-holes,
Our trenches, our fatigues and our bomb-shelters.'

But I remembered my shock of first sighting
The revolving edge of Manhattan
From the deck of the *Queen Elizabeth* –
That merry-go-round palette of American cars.
Everywhere the big flower of freedom!
The humming-bird of light at the retina!
Then the weird shameful pain of uncrumpling

From wartime hibernation, cramped, unshucking
My utility habit – deprivation
Worn with the stupid pride of a demob outfit,
A convalescence not quite back into the world.

Now I wanted to show you such a beach
Would set inside your head another jewel,
And lift you like the gentlest electric shock
Into an altogether other England –
An Avalon for which I had the wavelength,
Deep inside my head a little crystal.

For some reason I'd fixed on Woolacombe Sands.
I had seen that mile of surf in its haze
But only across the bay from Baggy headland
Where the peregrine went over and the shark under,
And the seal came in, and the sea-flash
Was gathered and crimped, tucked and crewelled
Into needlework by the cliff-top flora –
A brilliant original for Hilliard's miniatures.

Your crisis came late in the day. It was dusk when we got there
After a steamed-up hour of November downpour
And black cars sploshing through pot-hole puddles.
The rain had stopped. Three or four other cars
Waited for walkers – distant and wrapped in their dowds.
A car-park streetlamp made the whole scene hopeless.
The sea moved near, stunned after the rain,
Unperforming. Above it
The blue-black heap of the West collapsed slowly,
Comfortless as a cold iron stove
Standing among dead cinders
In some roofless ruin. You refused to get out.
You sat behind your mask, inaccessible –
Staring towards the ocean that had failed you.
I walked to the water's edge. A dull wave
Managed to lift and flop. Then a weak hiss
Rolled black oil-balls and pushed at obscure spewage.

So this was the reverse of dazzling Nauset.
The flip of a coin – the flip of an ocean fallen
Dream-face down. And here, at my feet, in the suds,
The other face, the real, staring upwards.

Dreamers

We didn't find her – she found us.
She sniffed us out. The Fate she carried
Sniffed us out
And assembled us, inert ingredients
For its experiment. The Fable she carried
Requisitioned you and me and her,
Puppets for its performance.

She fascinated you. Her eyes caressed you,
Melted a weeping glitter at you.
Her German the dark undercurrent
In her Kensington jeweller's elocution
Was your ancestral Black Forest whisper –
Edged with a greasy, death-camp, soot-softness.
When she suddenly rounded her eyeballs,
Popped them, strangled, she shocked you.
It was her mock surprise.
But you saw hanged women choke, dumb, through her,
And when she listened, watching you, through smoke,
Her black-ringed grey iris, slightly unnatural,
Was Black Forest wolf, a witch's daughter
Out of Grimm.

Warily you cultivated her,
Her Jewishness, her many-blooded beauty,
As if your dream of your dream-self stood there,
A glittering blackness, Europe's mystical jewel.
A creature from beyond the fringe of your desk-lamp.
Who was this Lilith of abortions
Touching the hair of your children
With tiger-painted nails?
Her speech Harrod's, Hitler's mutilations
Kept you company, weeding the onions.
An ex-Nazi Youth Sabra. Her father
Doctor to the Bolshoi Ballet.

She was helpless too.
None of us could wake up.
Nightmare looked out at the poppies.
She sat there, in her soot-wet mascara,
In flame-orange silks, in gold bracelets,

Slightly filthy with erotic mystery –
A German
Russian Israeli with the gaze of a demon
Between curtains of black Mongolian hair.

After a single night under our roof
She told her dream. A giant fish, a pike
Had a globed, golden eye, and in that eye
A throbbing human foetus –
You were astonished, maybe envious.

I refused to interpret. I saw
The dreamer in her
Had fallen in love with me and she did not know it.
That moment the dreamer in me
Fell in love with her, and I knew it.

Fairy Tale

Forty-nine was your magic number.
Forty-nine this.
Forty-nine that. Forty-eight
Doors in your high palace could be opened.
Once you were gone off every night
I had forty-eight chambers to choose from.
But the forty-ninth – you kept the key.
We would open that, some day, together.

You went off, a flare of hair and a plunge
Into the abyss.
Every night. Your Ogre lover
Who recuperated all day
Inside death, waited in the chasm
Under the tingling stars.
And I had forty-eight keys, doors, chambers,
To play with. Your Ogre
Was the sum, crammed in one voodoo carcase,
Of all your earlier lovers –
You never told even your secret journal
How many, who, where, when.
Only one glowed like a volcano
Off in the night.

But I never looked, I never saw
His effigy there, burning in your tears
Like a thing of tar.
Like a sleeping child's night-light,
It consoled your cosmos.
Meanwhile, that Ogre was more than enough,
As if you died each night to be with him,
As if you flew off into death.

So your nights. Your days
With your smile you listened to me
Recounting the surprises of one or other
Of the forty-eight chambers.
Your happiness made the bed soft.
A fairy tale? Yes.

Till the day you cried out in your sleep
(No, it was not me, as you thought.
It was you.) You cried out
Your love-sickness for that Ogre,
Your groaning appeal.

Icy-haired, I heard it echoing
Through all the corridors of our palace –
High there among eagles. Till I heard it
Beating on the forty-ninth door
Like my own heart on my own ribs.
A terrifying sound.
It beat on that door like my own heart
Trying to get out of my body.

The first next night – after your plunge
To find again those arms
Arching towards you out of death –
I found that door. My heart hurting my ribs
I unlocked the forty-ninth door
With a blade of grass. You never knew
What a skeleton key I had found
In a single blade of grass. And I entered.

The forty-ninth chamber convulsed
With the Ogre's roar
As he burst through the wall and plunged
Into his abyss. I glimpsed him

As I tripped
Over your corpse and fell with him
Into his abyss.

The Blackbird

You were the jailer of your murderer –
    Which imprisoned you.
And since I was your nurse and your protector
    Your sentence was mine too.

You played at feeling safe. As I fed you
    You ate and drank and swallowed
Sliding me sleepy looks, like a suckling babe,
    From under your eyelids.

You fed your prisoner's rage, in the dungeon,
    Through the key-hole –
Then, in a single, stung bound, came back up
    The coiled, unlit stairwell.

Giant poppy faces flamed and charred
    At the window. 'Look!'
You pointed and a blackbird was lugging
    A worm from its bottleneck.

The lawn lay like the pristine waiting page
    Of a prison report.
Who would write what upon it
    I never gave a thought.

A dumb creature, looping at the furnace door
    On its demon's prong,
Was a pen already writing
    Wrong is right, right wrong.

Totem

To ward it off (whatever it was) or attract it
You painted little hearts on everything.
You had no other logo.
This was your sacred object.

Sometimes you painted around it the wreath
Of an eight-year-old's flowers, green leaves, yellow petals.
Sometimes, off to the side, an eight-year-old's bluebird.
But mostly hearts. Or one red simple heart.

The frame of the big mirror you painted black –
Then, on the black, hearts.
And on your old black Singer sewing-machine –
Hearts.
The crimson on the black, like little lamps.

And on the cradle I made for a doll you painted,
Hearts.
And on the threshold, over which your son entered,
A heart –
Crimson on the black, like a blood-splash.

This heart was your talisman, your magic.
As Christians have their Cross you had your heart.
Constantine had his Cross – you, your heart.
Your Genie. Your Guardian Angel. Your Demon Slave.

But when you crept for safety
Into the bosom of your Guardian Angel
It was your Demon Slave. Like a possessive
Fish-mother, too eager to protect you,
She devoured you.

Now all that people find
Is your heart-coloured book – the empty mask
Of your Genie.
The mask
Of one that opening arms as if to enfold you
Devoured you.

The little hearts you painted on everything
Remained, like the track of your panic.
The splashes of a wound.

The spoor
Of the one that caught and devoured you.

Robbing Myself

I came over the snow – the packed snow
The ice-glaze hardened and polished,
Slithering the A 30, two hundred miles,
The road unnatural and familiar,
A road back into myself
After the cosmic disaster –
The worst snow and freeze-up for fifteen years,
Twenty miles an hour, over fallen heaven.

I came to the house
In the blue December twilight.
Just light enough
To fork up my potatoes, to unbed them
From my careful clamp. I shelled off their snowed-over coverlet.
They seemed almost warm in their straw.
They exhaled the sweetness
Of the hopes I'd dug into them. It was a nest
Secret, living, the eggs of my coming year,
Like my own plump litter, my secret family,
Little earthen embryos, little fists
And frowning brows and the old, new sleep-smell of earth.

I picked over my apples,
My Victorias, my pig's noses,
In the dark outhouse, and my fat Bramleys.
My spring prayers still solid,
My summer intact in spite of everything.
I filled for you
A sack of potatoes and a sack of apples.
And I inspected my gladioli bulbs
In the dusty loft, in their dry rags, hibernating
(I did not know they were freezing to death).

Then I crept through the house. You never knew
How I listened to our absence,
A ghostly trespasser, or my strange gloating
In that inlaid corridor, in the snow-blue twilight,
So precise and tender, a dark sapphire.
The front room, our crimson chamber,
With our white-painted bookshelves, our patient books,
The rickety walnut desk I paid six pounds for,

The horse-hair Victorian chair I got for five shillings,
Waited only for us. It was so strange!
And the crimson cataract of our stair Wilton
Led up to caverns of twelfth-century silence
We had hardly disturbed, in our newness.
Listening there, at the bottom of the stair,
Under the snow-loaded house
Was like listening to the sleeping brain-life
Of an unborn baby.

The house made newly precious to me
By your last lonely weeks there, and your crying.
But sweet with cleanliness,
Tight as a plush-lined casket
In a safe
In the December dusk. And, shuttered by wintering boughs,
The stained church-windows glowed
As if the sun had sunk there, inside the church.

I listened, as I sealed it up from myself
(The twelve-hour ice-crawl ahead).
I peered awhile, as through the key-hole,
Into my darkened, hushed, safe casket
From which (I did not know)
I had already lost the treasure.

Blood and Innocence

In the wilderness
Between the locusts and the honey
They demanded it. Oh, no problem.
If that's all you want,
You said, and you gave it.
Your electrocution, with all its zigzags.
A St Anthony at the bad moment
The demons got him.
The flute-like soul sundered into all its needles –
Bamboo dynamited. Electrodes
Sizzling under your blond bang –
Your smile slightly tense. Waving their feelers
They tugged it away down their tunnels.

They came back. They demanded that other –
That one. Oh, no problem,
You said, easier in fact.
Yourself by Frankenstein, stiff-kneed,
Matricidal, mask in swollen plaster
Like Beethoven's. Magnified thumb
Under her Adam's apple, her tongue a foot long –
And herself a doll, your semblable,
Your pendant on a maple by Paradise Pond.
But yourself a babe again, born again
Not of mother's blood nor of Christ's –
Washed and reborn only in your own.

No, these weren't what they wanted. They wanted
That – that other. Oh, no problem,
Why on earth didn't you say.
Daddy unearthed. And the nine-year-old howl
Come of age
Round his good ankle, a cart-rope –
Hauling him into the light.
And a hoof-like thunder on the moor –
The gutturals of Thor
For accompaniment
To the howl.

Thor's voice its very self
Doing a hammer-dance on Daddy's body,
Avenging the twenty-year forsaken
Sobs of Germania –

Grinning squabbling overjoyed they
Dragged it into the thorns. How is that,
Is that O.K.? you asked.
You looked round for some acknowledgement
From the demanding mouths

In a gilded theatre suddenly empty
Of all but the faces
The faces faces faces faces

Of Mummy Daddy Mummy Daddy –
Daddy Daddy Daddy Daddy
Mummy Mummy

Costly Speech

Manhattan's full moon between skyscrapers
Forbade it.
The new moon, her whole family of phases,
Running the gleam of the rails
From rising to falling forbade it.

Even the beaver, way up in Alaska,
Treading water, to watch your son
Doing something strange in a glide of the Deshka,
Forbade it.
Yosemite's oldest root on earth, needle
By needle was adamant,
Onto your daughter's page, with signatures.
Every prairie-dog in Wyoming
Whether or not it ate the grapes you tossed
Forbade it.
Bubbles from Yellowstone's boiling paint-pots
Forbade it. They dubbed their prohibition
Sound-track onto your snapshot portrait fixtures.
Even the sluggish fish in Pontchartrain
Lobbed out right beside you where you swam
To forbid it. Night after night.
Nauset groaned in its sleep
And mumbled and mouthed, to forbid it –
Miles of shuddering lifted and fell back
A thunderclap veto.
And from a distant land your grandma's
Wedding photo hurried to forbid it.

Just as your own words
Irrevocably given to your brother,
Hostage guarantors,
And my own airier words, conscripted, reporting for duty,
Forbade it and forbade it.

They were simple guards and all were yawning,
Ignorant how your left hand wrote in a mirror
Opposite your right,
Half of you mortified, half of you smiling.

And ignorant of the spooky chemistry
Of opportunity, of boom and bust

In the optic nerve of editors.
Ignorant of the tumblers in the lock
Of U.S. Copyright Law
Which your dead fingers so deftly unpicked.

The Inscription

Snow-cakes banked the streets. Frozen grey
Barricades of dirty sugar. Hard
Cold. Cold
His morning flat in bright sun,
Sooted in Soho. Brick light. New light.
Cargo-dumped empty lightness.
Packing-case emptiness, lightness. Ice-breaker
Her bows had butted through, the missing supplies
Warm in her hold. Cracked through the frozen sea
A rigid lightning of icy but open water
Where she moved closer. So here he was.
She had got what she wanted – to see
The islet or reef or rock he'd ended up on.
Her eyes went over the walls and into
Every corner, like a dog in a new home. Like a dog
That had seen a rat vanish, that smelt a rat.
There was his bed, yes. There was his phone.
But she had that number. Most of all
She wanted his assurance, weeping she begged
For assurance he had faith in her. Yes, yes. Tell me
We shall sit together this summer
Under the laburnum. Yes, he said, yes yes yes.
The laburnum draped deathly in the blue dusk.
The laburnum like a dressed corpse in full yellow.
The huge clock of the laburnum stuck at noon,
Striking noon noon noon –
What kind of faith did she mean? Yes, he had faith.
He had promised her everything she asked for,
And she had told him all she wanted
Was for him to get out of the country, to vanish.
I'll do whatever you want. But which do you want?
Go together next week North
Or for me to vanish off the earth?
She wept, pleading for reassurance – that he have

Faith in her, and he reeled when he should have grabbed:
'Do as you like with me. I'm your parcel.
I have only our address on me.
Open me or readdress me.' Then
She saw his Shakespeare. The red Oxford Shakespeare
That she had ripped to rags when happiness
Was invulnerable. Resurrected.
Wondering, with unbelieving fingers,
She opened it. She read the inscription. She closed it
Like the running animal that receives
The fatal bullet without a faltering check
In its stride, she started again
Begging for that reassurance and he gave it
Over and over and over and over he gave
What she did not want or did
Want and could no longer accept or open
Helpless-handed as she hid from him
The wound she had given herself, striking at him
Had given herself, that had emptied
From her hands the strength to hold him against
The shock of her words from nowhere, that had
Fatally gone through her and hit him.

Night-Ride on Ariel

Your moon was full of women.
Your moon-mother there, over your bed,
The Tyrolean moon, the guttural,
Mourning and remaking herself.
It was always Monday in her mind.
Prouty was there, tender and buoyant moon,
Whose wand of beams so dainty
Put the costly sparkle
Into Cinderella. Beutscher
Moon of dismemberment and resurrection
Who found enough parts on the floor of her shop
To fill your old skin and get you walking
Into Tuesday. Mary Ellen Chase,
Silver nimbus lit, egg eyes hooded,
The moon-owl who found you
Even in England, and plucked you out of my nest

And carried you back to college,
Dragging you all the way, your toes trailing
In the Atlantic.   Phases
Of your dismal-headed
Fairy godmother moon. Mother
Making you dance with her magnetic eye
On your Daddy's coffin
(There in the family film). Prouty
Wafting you to the ballroom of broken glass
On bleeding feet. Beutscher
Twanging the puppet strings
That waltzed you in air out of your mythical grave
To jig with your Daddy's bones on a kind of tightrope
Over the gap of your real grave.
Mary Ellen Moon of Massachusetts
Struck you with her chiming claw
And turned you into an hourglass of moonlight
With its menstrual wound
Of shadow sand. She propped you
On her lectern,
Lecture-timer.   White-faced bolts
Of electrocuting moonlight –
Masks of the full or over-full or empty
Moon that tipped your heart
Upside down and drained it. As you flew
They jammed all your wavelengths
With their criss-cross instructions,
Crackling and dragging their blacks
Over your failing flight,
Hauling your head this way and that way
As you clung to the sun – to the last
Shred of the exploded dawn
In your fist –

That Monday.

Telos

Too many Alphas. Too much Alpha. Sunstruck
With Alpha. Eye-sick,
Head-sick, sick sick sick O
Sick of Alpha. You kicked school it
Collapsed in Alphas. You shook
The lightning conductor between your teeth –
All the sky-signs registered Alpha.
You burrowed for a way back out of it all.
Down into a cellar. There in the dark
Your eyes tight shut
You turned your mother inside out
Like ripping a feather-pillow
And came up covered with Alphas.
You stamped and stamped
Like Rumpelstiltskin
On your Daddy's coffin and the whole band
Started up Alpha. The whole stadium
Clapped Alpha, roared Alpha. You sniped at
Ping-pong balls boy-friend after boy-friend
Jogging on pin-jet fountains and bull's-eyed
A straight row of Alphas. Won a huge
Plastic Alpha with blond hanks. You smashed her
With a kitchen stool and out fell
Tick-tock Alpha. Bloodprints
Of your escaping heel
Signed the street-scene snowscape Alpha.
                              Anyhow,
Anywhere to lose
The Furies of Alpha you crawled under
Or hurdled every letter in the Alphabet
And hurling yourself beyond Omega
                              fell
Into a glittering Universe of Alpha.

Brasilia

You returned
In your steel helm. Helpless
We were dragged into court, your arena,

Gagged in the hush.
Titterings of horror
And the bead of sweat in the spine's furrow.
You delivered
The three sentences. Not a whisper
In the hush.
Your great love had spoken.
Only the most horrible crime
Could have brought down
The blade of lightning
That descended then. Dazzled,
All coughed in the ozone.
Even the dogs were stunned. And the same flash
Snatched you up into Heaven.
Some Colosseum flunkeys
Carry out your father's body.
Another carries his head. Your mother
Stands, and to huge amazement
Staggers out, carrying her own head.
Other flunkeys carry me and mine.

Every day since, throughout your Empire,
Like the motherly wraith who nightly
Wailed through the streets of Tenochtitlán
Just before Cortés ended it –
Your effigies cry out on their plinths,
Dry-eyed. Your portraits, tearlessly,
Weep in the books.

The Cast

Daddy had come back to hear
All you had against him. He
Could not believe it. Where
Did you get those words if not
In the tails of his bees? For others
The honey. For him, Cupid's bow
Modified in Peenemünde
Via Brueghel. Helpless
As weightless, voiceless as lifeless,
He had to hear it all

Driven into him up to the feathers,
Had to stand the stake
Not through his heart, but upright
In the town square, him tied to it
Stark naked full of those arrows
In the bronze of immortal poesy.

So your cry of deliverance
Materialised in his
Sacrificed silence. Every arrow
Nailing him there a star
In your constellation. The giant
Chunk of jagged weapon –
His whole distorted statue
Like a shard of shrapnel
Eased out of your old wound. Rejected
By your body. Daddy
No longer to be borne. Your words
Like phagocytes, ridding you with a roar
Of the heavy pain.

Healed you vanished
From the monumental
Immortal form
Of your injury: your Daddy's
Body full of your arrows. Though it was
Your blood that dried on him.

The Ventriloquist

We caught each other by the body
    And fell in a heap.
Your doll in the dark bedroom woke
    With her scream a whip.

With your arms around my neck
    I ran through a thorny wood.
The doll screamed after us, to the world,
    Daddy was no good.

You sobbed against my chest.
    I waded the river's freeze.

The doll had put your Mummy on show –
   The Kraken of the seas.

As you lay on the bed
   I leaned to the locked door.
The doll sat on the roof and screamed
   I was with a whore.

The doll broke in that night
   Killed you and was gone
Screaming at the stars to look
   And see Justice done.

Life after Death

What can I tell you that you do not know
Of the life after death?

Your son's eyes, which had unsettled us
With your Slavic Asiatic
Epicanthic fold, but would become
So perfectly your eyes,
Became wet jewels,
The hardest substance of the purest pain
As I fed him in his high white chair.
Great hands of grief were wringing and wringing
His wet cloth of face. They wrung out his tears.
But his mouth betrayed you – it accepted
The spoon in my disembodied hand
That reached through from the life that had survived you.

Day by day his sister grew
Paler with the wound
She could not see or touch or feel, as I dressed it
Each day with her blue Breton jacket.

By night I lay awake in my body
The Hanged Man
My neck-nerve uprooted and the tendon
Which fastened the base of my skull
To my left shoulder
Torn from its shoulder-root and cramped into knots –
I fancied the pain could be explained

If I were hanging in the spirit
From a hook under my neck-muscle.
Dropped from life
We three made a deep silence
In our separate cots.

We were comforted by wolves.
Under that February moon and the moon of March
The Zoo had come close.
And in spite of the city
Wolves consoled us. Two or three times each night
For minutes on end
They sang. They had found where we lay.
And the dingos, and the Brazilian-maned wolves –
All lifted their voices together
With the grey Northern pack.

The wolves lifted us in their long voices.
They wound us and enmeshed us
In their wailing for you, their mourning for us,
They wove us into their voices. We lay in your death,
In the fallen snow, under falling snow,

As my body sank into the folk-tale
Where the wolves are singing in the forest
For two babes, who have turned, in their sleep,
Into orphans
Beside the corpse of their mother.

The Hands

Two immense hands
Dandled your infancy.
Later the same hands quietly
Positioned you in the crawl space
And fed you the pills,
Gloved so you would not recognise them.

When you woke in the hospital
You got help to recognise
The fingerprints inside what you had done.
You could not believe it. It was hard
For you to believe.

Later, inside your poems
Which they wore like gloves, the same hands
Left big fingerprints. The same
Inside your last-stand letters
Which they wore like gloves.
Inside those words you struck me with
That moved so much faster than your mouth
And that still ring in my ears.

Sometimes I think
Finally you yourself were two gloves
Worn by those two hands.
Sometimes I even think that I too
Was picked up, a numbness of gloves
Worn by those same hands,
Doing what they needed done, because
The fingerprints inside what I did
And inside your poems and your letters
And inside what you did
Are the same.

The fingerprints
Inside empty gloves, these, here,
From which the hands have vanished.

The Prism

The waters off beautiful Nauset
Were the ocean sun, the sea-poured crystal
Behind your efforts. They were your self's cradle.
What happened to it all that winter you went
Into your snowed-on grave, in the Pennines?
It goes with me, your seer's vision-stone.
Like a lucky stone, my unlucky stone.
I can look into it and still see
That salty globe of blue, its gull-sparkle,
Its path of surf-groomed sand
Roaming away north
Like the path of the Israelites
Under the hanging, arrested hollow of thunder
Into promise, and you walking it
Your sloped brown shoulders, your black swim-suit,

Towards that sea-lit sky.
                              Wherever you went
It was your periscope lens,
Between your earthenware earrings,
Behind your eye-brightness, so lucidly balanced,
Such a flawless crystal, so worshipped.

I still have it. I hold it –
'The waters off beautiful Nauset'.
Your intact childhood, your Paradise
With its pre-Adamite horse-shoe crab in the shallows
As a guarantee, God's own trademark.
I turn it, a prism, this way and that.
That way I see the filmy surf-wind flicker
Of your ecstasies, your visions in the crystal.
This way the irreparably-crushed lamp
In my crypt of dream, totally dark,
Under your gravestone.

The God

You were like a religious fanatic
Without a god – unable to pray.
You wanted to be a writer.
Wanted to write? What was it within you
Had to tell its tale?
The story that has to be told
Is the writer's God, who calls
Out of sleep, inaudibly: 'Write.'
Write what?

Your heart, mid-Sahara, raged
In its emptiness.
Your dreams were empty.
You bowed at your desk and you wept
Over the story that refused to exist,
As over a prayer
That could not be prayed
To a non-existent God. A dead God
With a terrible voice.
You were like those desert ascetics
Who fascinated you,

Parching in such a torturing
Vacuum of God
It sucked goblins out of their finger-ends,
Out of the soft motes of the sun-shaft,
Out of the blank rock face.
The gagged prayer of their sterility
Was a God.
So was your panic of emptiness – a God.

You offered him verses. First
Little phials of the emptiness
Into which your panic dropped its tears
That dried and left crystalline spectra.
Crusts of salt from your sleep.
Like the dewy sweat
On some desert stones, after dawn.
Oblations to an absence.
Little sacrifices. Soon

Your silent howl through the night
Had made itself a moon, a fiery idol
Of your God.
Your crying carried its moon
Like a woman a dead child. Like a woman
Nursing a dead child, bending to cool
Its lips with tear-drops on her fingertip,
So I nursed you, who nursed a moon
That was human but dead, withered, and
Burned you like a lump of phosphorus.

Till the child stirred. Its mouth-hole stirred.
Blood oozed at your nipple,
A drip-feed of blood. Our happy moment!

The little god flew up into the Elm Tree.
In your sleep, glassy-eyed,
You heard its instructions. When you woke
Your hands moved. You watched them in dismay
As they made a new sacrifice.
Two handfuls of blood, your own blood,
And in that blood gobbets of me,
Wrapped in a tissue of story that had somehow
Slipped from you. An embryo story.
You could not explain it or who

Ate at your hands.
The little god roared at night in the orchard,
His roar half a laugh.

You fed him by day, under your hair-tent,
Over your desk, in your secret
Spirit-house, you whispered,
You drummed on your thumb with your fingers,
Shook Winthrop shells for their sea-voices,
And gave me an effigy – a Salvia
Pressed in a Lutheran Bible.
You could not explain it. Sleep had opened.
Darkness poured from it, like perfume.
Your dreams had burst their coffin.
Blinded I struck a light

And woke upside down in your spirit-house
Moving limbs that were not my limbs,
And telling, in a voice not my voice,
A story of which I knew nothing,
Giddy
With the smoke of the fire you tended
Flames I had lit unwitting
That whitened in the oxygen jet
Of your incantatory whisper.

You fed the flames with the myrrh of your mother
The frankincense of your father
And your own amber and the tongues
Of fire told their tale. And suddenly
Everybody knew everything.
Your God snuffed up the fatty reek.
His roar was like a basement furnace
In your ears, thunder in the foundations.

Then you wrote in a fury, weeping,
Your joy a trance-dancer
In the smoke in the flames.
'God is speaking through me,' you told me.
'Don't say that,' I cried. 'Don't say that.
That is horribly unlucky!'
As I sat there with blistering eyes
Watching everything go up
In the flames of your sacrifice

That finally caught you too till you
Vanished, exploding
Into the flames
Of the story of your God
Who embraced you
And your Mummy and your Daddy –
Your Aztec, Black Forest
God of the euphemism Grief.

Freedom of Speech

At your sixtieth birthday, in the cake's glow,
Ariel sits on your knuckle.
You feed it grapes, a black one, then a green one,
From between your lips pursed like a kiss.
Why are you so solemn? Everybody laughs

As if grateful, the whole reunion –
Old friends and new friends,
Some famous authors, your court of brilliant minds,
And publishers and doctors and professors,
Their eyes creased in delighted laughter – even

The late poppies laugh, one loses a petal.
The candles tremble their tips
Trying to contain their joy. And your Mummy
Is laughing in her nursing home. Your children
Are laughing from opposite sides of the globe. Your Daddy

Laughs deep in his coffin. And the stars,
Surely the stars, too, shake with laughter.
And Ariel –
What about Ariel?
Ariel is happy to be here.

Only you and I do not smile.

A Picture of Otto

You stand there at the blackboard: Lutheran
Minister manqué. Your idea
Of Heaven and Earth and Hell radically
Modified by the honey-bee's commune.

A big shock for so much of your Prussian backbone
As can be conjured into poetry
To find yourself so tangled with me –
Rising from your coffin, a big shock

To meet me face to face in the dark adit
Where I have come looking for your daughter.
You had assumed this tunnel your family vault.
I never dreamed, however occult our guilt,

Your ghost inseparable from my shadow
As long as your daughter's words can stir a candle.
She could hardly tell us apart in the end.
Your portrait, here, could be my son's portrait.

I understand – you never could have released her.
I was a whole myth too late to replace you.
This underworld, my friend, is her heart's home.
Inseparable, here we must remain,

Everything forgiven and in common –
Not that I see her behind you, where I face you,
But like Owen, after his dark poem,
Under the battle, in the catacomb,

Sleeping with his German as if alone.

Fingers

Who will remember your fingers?
Their winged life? They flew
With the light in your look.
At the piano, stomping out hits from the forties,
They performed an incidental clowning
Routine of their own, deadpan puppets.
You were only concerned to get them to the keys.
But as you talked, as your eyes signalled

The strobes of your elation,
They flared, flicked balletic aerobatics.
I thought of birds in some tropical sexual
Play of display, leaping and somersaulting,
Doing strange things in the air, and dropping to the dust.
Those dancers of your excess!
With such deft, practical touches – so accurate.
Thinking their own thoughts caressed like lightning
The lipstick into your mouth corners.

Trim conductors of your expertise,
Cavorting at your typewriter,
Possessed by infant spirit, puckish,
Who, whatever they did, danced or mimed it
In a weightless largesse of espressivo.

I remember your fingers. And your daughter's
Fingers remember your fingers
In everything they do.
Her fingers obey and honour your fingers,
The Lares and Penates of our house.

The Dogs Are Eating Your Mother

That is not your mother but her body.
She leapt from our window
And fell there. Those are not dogs
That seem to be dogs
Pulling at her. Remember the lean hound
Running up the lane holding high
The dangling raw windpipe and lungs
Of a fox? Now see who
Will drop on all fours at the end of the street
And come romping towards your mother,
Pulling her remains, with their lips
Lifted like dog's lips
Into new positions. Protect her
And they will tear you down
As if you were more her.
They will find you every bit
As succulent as she is. Too late
To salvage what she was.

I buried her where she fell.
You played around the grave. We arranged
Sea-shells and big veined pebbles
Carried from Appledore
As if we were herself. But a kind
Of hyena came aching upwind.
They dug her out. Now they batten
On the cornucopia
Of her body. Even
Bite the face off her gravestone,
Gulp down the grave ornaments,
Swallow the very soil.
                        So leave her.
Let her be their spoils. Go wrap
Your head in the snowy rivers
Of the Brooks Range. Cover
Your eyes with the writhing airs
Off the Nullarbor Plains. Let them
Jerk their tail-stumps, bristle and vomit
Over their symposia.
                        Think her better
Spread with holy care on a high grid
For vultures
To take back into the sun. Imagine
These bone-crushing mouths the mouths
That labour for the beetle
Who will roll her back into the sun.

Red

Red was your colour.
If not red, then white. But red
Was what you wrapped around you.
Blood-red. Was it blood?
Was it red-ochre, for warming the dead?
Haematite to make immortal
The precious heirloom bones, the family bones.

When you had your way finally
Our room was red. A judgement chamber.
Shut casket for gems. The carpet of blood

Patterned with darkenings, congealments.
The curtains – ruby corduroy blood,
Sheer blood-falls from ceiling to floor.
The cushions the same. The same
Raw carmine along the window-seat.
A throbbing cell. Aztec altar – temple.

Only the bookshelves escaped into whiteness.

And outside the window
Poppies thin and wrinkle-frail
As the skin on blood,
Salvias, that your father named you after,
Like blood lobbing from a gash,
And roses, the heart's last gouts,
Catastrophic, arterial, doomed.

Your velvet long full skirt, a swathe of blood,
A lavish burgundy.
Your lips a dipped, deep crimson.
You revelled in red.
I felt it raw – like the crisp gauze edges
Of a stiffening wound. I could touch
The open vein in it, the crusted gleam.

Everything you painted you painted white
Then splashed it with roses, defeated it,
Leaned over it, dripping roses,
Weeping roses, and more roses,
Then sometimes, among them, a little bluebird.

Blue was better for you. Blue was wings.
Kingfisher blue silks from San Francisco
Folded your pregnancy
In crucible caresses.
Blue was your kindly spirit – not a ghoul
But electrified, a guardian, thoughtful.

In the pit of red
You hid from the bone-clinic whiteness.

But the jewel you lost was blue.

HOWLS & WHISPERS (1998)

Paris 1954

I've been watching
That young man, visible through the window, at the table of that café
(I can't read the name at this distance).
But he's sipping the first claret he ever tasted, I know that,
And chewing his first Gruyère. He will spend the rest of his life
Trying to recapture the marvel –
Separately or combined –
Of that wine that cheese and this moment.
So new to his unlived life, so ready for anything,
He could never imagine, and can't hear
The scream that approaches him.

It resembles a white mask with spread fingers
That will grab and drub and wring his heart
Like a bandage impossible to clean.
A scream
Resembling a nuclear melt-down
That will render his whole world untouchable
Or touchable only with a penalty
Of radio-active burn. A scream
That will lock him up in a labyrinth
Made of ordinary streets
As if he were the Minotaur.

                    A scream
Shaped also like a panther
That will find his soul and tear it from him,
And eat it, and take its place
Lying like the gatekeeper of Hell
Between him and the Creator,
Watching him with eyes that never sleep,
Opening its mouth only to scream.

The scream
Already looking for him, as he sits there,
And that will certainly find him, coming closer
Now in the likeness of a girl.
A scream
That has nothing to do with the wine-glass, not even vibrating it,
And is no kind of reflection in it
Is not so much as a faint sweat in the holes of the tough cheese

Not so much as a chance pattern of omen
For some medium to decipher
In the cheese's woven rind,

A scream
Trying to sound like laughter and hope –
Sounding like all happiness, all hope.

I watch him.

Religion

You wanted to eat your mother.
Murder is of a piece
With the mouth,
Roots are torn up, seeds, eggs are plucked out.
Hearts are bitten into.
Your childhood's
Diaries, like a starving child's dreams,
Stuffed with feasts.

A mother was killed but not eaten.
The mouth
Caressed the killing with a healing saliva –
Words of love,
A Holy Writ
Incessantly murmured.

Your father also died
And could not be eaten.
The words of your mouth
Covered his corpse with a healing saliva –
A chrism of love,
A Missa Solemnis
Incessantly murmured.

In that mythos
Projected from the muscles of the jaw,
From the roots of the teeth –
In that Mass
Your father and mother were killed and not eaten.
Your hunger
Went up as a scream of love.

The inexorable murder
Performed, but bloodlessly –
Then washed with Holy Love,
With words
Poured out like warm oil.

So you were your own Church.
Your religion was Love.
Its sacrificial murder –
That killing in heaven –
Was flow of passion here on earth
Where your kiss, your real lips,
And your words
Were the blessing.

The Hidden Orestes

Tragedies of the House of Atreus
Exclude Electra's husband. Gossip has it
He's a befogged buffoon. He can't make out
What's eating his wife. Every woman
Who sits in their home, no matter how friendly,
She hates. Also, he's alarmed
By the uncanny masculine voice
That now and again, before she's aware of it,
Bursts from between her lips
With a demonic snarl
That seems aimless, maybe
While she watches a cricket, at dusk,
Crawling in over the windowsill.

He's not to know that Orestes
Is padding up the long trail
Like a black panther
In inky darkness – the black velvet bagfull
Of family emeralds. So he can't guess
What incognito killer
Pulls on her face, of a sudden,
At a knocking, and leaves their bed
To let in the banshee, the death-shriek
Of her own mother Clytemnestra.
And he will never get clear

How that body, murdered by Electra,
Comes to be her own. As if a tracker
Had swerved onto the wrong spoor
At the last moment. Or how the maternal Furies,
Hunting the guilty one, can be led
By Clytemnestra's ghost, carrying, fiery
And furious as a torch, the corpse of Electra,
And coming for him.

The Laburnum

Tell me
We shall sit together this summer
Under the laburnum. But the laburnum
Has gone. Yes, I said, yes yes yes.
The laburnum draped deathly in the blue dusk.
The laburnum like a dressed corpse in full yellow.
The huge clock of the laburnum stuck at noon
Striking noon noon noon –
Who dug up the laburnum? So far off
From where their words sawed at you, all that week,
Chipped at you. They wanted you to know
Exactly what they thought you should know
About what they had heard. They sharpened
With nail-files
The little teeth, all the cutting edges
To get it over with, as a favour
To you. Their bodies were craving
For the exercise. And their eyes craving
To see the wintry twigs trembling. Hit
Harder, you probably said,
Cut deeper. So they did. Your mother
Typing her letters saw the pods spit out
Poisonous laburnum seeds, sprinkling her pages –
She had to get you from under that tree,
To get that tree from over you. She drove
Her fingers deeper. She had not
Taught the hands to type
All her life for nothing. The laburnum
Strengthened only in my sleep,
Winter barely half over. I need,

You told them, only the truth. They consoled you
With howls from their own divorce, with the revenge
You could not find in yourself, with a future
You could not find in yourself.
With their bare hands they tore up the laburnum
By the roots. Only the truth, you begged it,
Only the truth. They almost laughed
To show you your grave, the raw hole
Of root ends – broken in air. Who else dare
Tell you this truth? We are your true friends.
Then they stepped back to let it happen.

So, in my sleep, without my hearing a whisper
The laburnum fell.

The Difference

When she collapsed to the floor of the kitchen
And threshed there, eyes epileptic,
Screaming her curse at 'Dickie' (not his name),
He knew he was out of his depth,
Not only as a doctor. Shaken
By the exhaustion, the past wrenched open
Like a dress ripped off, by that choking
Revelation as of knotted lovers
Lifted from Pompeii's ashes,
He watched her recovering, sobbing, her hair over her hands,
The blame stunned out of her, as after a car-crash
Skin-of-the-teeth survival.
                        But it was nothing
To seeing the floor actually yawn open
And the screaming one fall through – and beneath her
The stranger, huge-eyed, his arms wide,
Grasp her as she landed on top of him,
And the floor close forever over both.

The Minotaur 2

I saw the plot unfolding and me in it,
Where we touched like cripples. Your first scene.
The surreal mystery of our picnic quarrel
Opened your performance quietly.

And you had opened the vein.
And recognised gold. A cry of bereavement.
You had picked up the skein of blood
That twitched and led you, ignoring me,

Not out of the labyrinth
But to the very centre,
Where the Minotaur, which was waiting to kill you,
Killed you.

Howls & Whispers

What was poured in your ears
While you argued with death?
Your mother wrote: 'Hit him in the purse.'
Reiterated it, like Iago,
'Hit him in the purse.' Her joy
That you were at last ridding yourself
Of this bacterium, whose evil fever
Had aborted your pedigree career –

                                    – and had annulled
The marriage she had prepared you for.
After the event I found her letters.
I felt the gratification of her fury.
'Hit him in the purse,' and 'Be strong
To free yourself: go straight for divorce.'
And from your analyst: 'Keep him out of your bed.
Above all, keep him out of your bed.'

You left me those letters, those war-banners
You had waved in my face.
These were your Intelligence Corps
In our efforts to hear each other.
These were our only Marriage Guidance Council.

Thunderheads of static experience
Unloading into your ear, to waken and jam it.

Then through that last week the go-between
Doing her best, with the tape-recorder
Under her tongue, the confidante
On all sides, that double spy,
The manquée journalist, the professional dopester,
Who had to prove that only she
Knew the facts and the latest – bringing you
In huge dishes of dark eyes
Garblings of what I was said to have said,
Was said to have done. She squatted at your ear.
She was the bug in my bed.
Pretty, innocent-eyed, gleeful Iago.
And her friends, the step-up transformers
Of your supercharged, smoking circuits,
What did they plug into your ears
That had killed you by daylight on Monday?

These were the masks that measured out the voltage
That they wired so tenderly
With placebo anaesthetic
Into your ear, and that killed you
Even as you screamed it at me.

The City

Your poems are a dark city centre.
Your novels, your stories, your journals, are suburbs
Of this big city.
The hotels are lit like office blocks all night
With scholars, priests, pilgrims. It's at night
Sometimes I drive through. I just find
Myself driving through, going slow, simply
Roaming in my own darkness, pondering
What you did. Nearly always
I glimpse you – at some crossing,
Staring upwards, lost, sixty year old.
The crowd piles around you. You stand stock still.
Your face, under the green or orange light,
A desert Indian's, wild, bewildered.

You want to ask something but you can't.
You stare into every face
Trying to recognise somebody.
They ignore you. Then the light goes red
And they all surge past you.
Then you see me in my car, staring at you.
I see you thinking: ought I to know him?
I see you frown. I see you trying
To remember – or suddenly not to remember.

Moon-Dust

Passions had been and gone, in plenty.
You told me about this one.
I read about that one.
I heard about that other, or surmised
Or saw the damage.

And there was your face, like the dandelion
At the edge of the launching pad.

And there was your story, like the cratered moon
Where my story sat
Like a capsule on its tripod,
And where I moved with giant, weightless leaps
Collecting a few rocks, with tongs.

Now you, only your cheek lit,
Sink in the West.
And I study these peculiar rocks,
Like a flower, touching at rocks
As the wind nods it.

The Offers

Only two months dead
And there you were, suddenly back within reach.
I got on the Northern Line at Leicester Square
And sat down and there you were. And there
The dream started that was no dream.
I stared and you ignored me.

Your part in the dream was to ignore me.
Mine was to be invisible – helplessly
Unable to manifest myself.
Simply a blank, bodiless gaze – I rested
The whole weight of my unbelieving stare
On your face, impossibly real and there.
Not much changed, unchanging under my pressure.
You only shuddered slightly as the carriage
Bored through the earth Northward.
You seemed older – death had aged you a little.
Paler, almost yellowish, as you had been
In the morgue, but impassive.
As if the unspooling track and shudder of the journey
Were the film of your life that occupied you.
Your gaze, inward, resisted my gaze.
Your basket on your knee, heavy with packages.
Your handbag on a long strap. Your hands
Folded over the heap. Unshifting
My gaze leaned against you as a gaze
Might lean its cheek on a hand. The impossible
Went on sharing your slight shuddering, your eyelids,
Your lips lightly pursed, your melancholy.
Just as in the dream that insists
On the plainly impossible, and lasts
Second after second after second,
Growing more and more incredible –
As if you slowly turned your face and slowly
Smiled full in my face, daring me
There, among the living, to speak to the dead.
But you seemed not to know the part you were playing.
And just as in the dream, I did not speak.
Only tried to separate the memory
Of your face from this new face you wore.
If you got out at Chalk Farm, I told myself,
I would follow you home. I would speak.
I would make some effort to seize
This offer, this saddened substitute
Returned to me by death, revealed to me
There in the Underground – surely as if
For my examination and approval.

Chalk Farm came. I got up. You stayed.
It was the testing moment.
I lifted your face from you and took it
Outside, onto the platform, in this dream
Which was the whole of London's waking life.
I watched you move away, carried away
Northwards, back into the abyss,
Your real new face unaltered, lit, unwitting,
Still visible for seconds, then gone,
Leaving me my original emptiness
Of where you had been and abruptly were not.

But everything is offered three times.
And suddenly you were sitting in your own home.
Young as before, untouched by death. Like
A hallucination – not to be blinked away.
A migraine image – warping my retina.
You seemed to have no idea you were yourself.
Even borrowing the name of your oldest rival –
As if it had lain handiest. Yet you were
So much yourself my brain's hemispheres
Seemed to have twisted slightly out of phase
To know you you yet realise that you
Were not you. To see you you and yet
So brazenly continuing to be other.
You had even kept your birthdate – exact
As a barb on the impossibility.
And lived only two miles from where we had lived.
Other spirits colluded in a support team
Of new parents for you, a new brother.
You courted me all over again – covertly.
I breathed a bewildering air – the gas
Of the underworld in which you moved so easy
And had your new being. You told me
The dream of your romantic life, that had lasted
Throughout our marriage, there in Paris – as if
You had never returned until now.
Death had repossessed your talent. Or maybe
Had converted it to a quieter thing –
A dumbly savage longing, a submerged
Ferocity of longing in eyes
So weirdly unaltered. I struggled awhile

In my doubled alive and dead existence.
I thought: 'This is coincidence – the mere
Inertia of my life's momentum, trying
To keep things as they were, as if the show
Must at all costs go on, same masks, same parts,
No matter who the actors.' Gasping for air,
At the bottom of the Rhine, barely conscious,
Indolently like somebody drowning
I kicked free.
Your gentle ultimatum relaxed its hold.
True to your ghostly humour, next thing
You sent me a pretty card from Honolulu.
After that, an afterworld memento,
Every year a card from Honolulu.
It seemed you had finessed your return to the living
By leaving me as your bail, a hostage stopped
In the land of the dead.
                            Less and less
Did I think of escape.
Even in my dreams, our house was in ruins.
But suddenly – the third time – you were there.
Younger than I had ever known you. You
As if new made, half a wild roe, half
A flawless thing, priceless, facetted
Like a cobalt jewel. You came behind me
(At my helpless moment, as I lowered
A testing foot into the running bath)
And spoke – peremptory, as a familiar voice
Will startle out of a river's uproar, urgent,
Close: 'This is the last. This one. This time
Don't fail me.'

Superstitions

Friday created Adam. Cast out Adam.
Buried Adam. Friday. Today. Friday

The thirteenth was laughter of the drunken gods
So lightly reversed by Loki's gift:
Spermy mistletoe and a ship of tinder.

Friday the thirteenth, a fable told
Of the bloodied halo, the sponge, and the nail.

And Friday the thirteenth unveiled perfumed
America. (Lifting the eyelid
Of Columbus
With the chains from his coffin.)

Friday the thirteenth
Prestidigitateur
May find odds and ends, even for you.

Maybe Frigga's
Two-faced gift. The cauldron of Valhalla,
Where warriors were reborn.

                              Under the cold
Epicanthic fold lifted in the bride's
Mirror, a cauldron
                  where this one
Forgot death. Where that one
Forgot life. Where this other
Sank without a cry.
                    Let them laugh
At your superstition.

(Remembering it will make your palms sweat,
The skin lift blistering, both your lifelines bleed.)

UNCOLLECTED (1997–98)

from Sir Gawain and the Green Knight

[*The New Year feast at King Arthur's Court is interrupted by the
entry of a Green Knight, on a green horse, who challenges any of
Arthur's knights to chop off his head and agree to submit to the
same blow, from the Green Knight, at the Green Chapel, one year
later. Sir Gawain takes up the challenge. In the following passage
Gawain arrives at the Green Chapel to keep his word.*]

Then he spurred Gringolet, and took up the trail.
Trees overhung him, the steep slope close to his shoulder.
He pushed on down through the rough, to the gorge-bottom.
Wherever he turned his eyes, it looked wilder.
Nothing anywhere near that could be a shelter.
Only cliffy brinks, beetling above him,
Knuckled and broken outcrops, with horned crags.
Clouds dragging low, torn by the scouts.
There he reined in his horse and puzzled awhile.
Turning his doubts over, he searched for the Chapel.
Still he could see nothing. He thought it strange.
Only a little mound, a tump, in a clearing,
Between the slope and the edge of the river, a knoll,
Over the river's edge, at a crossing place,
The burn bubbling under as if it boiled.
The Knight urged his horse and came closer.
He dismounted there, light as a dancer,
And tethered his costly beast to a rough branch.
Then he turned to the tump. He walked all round it,
Debating in himself what it might be.
Shaggy and overgrown with clumps of grass,
It had a hole in the end, and on each side.
Hollow within, nothing but an old cave
Or old gappy rock-heap, it could be either
      Or neither.
   'Ah God!' sighed Gawain,
   'Is the Green Chapel here?
   Here, about midnight,
   Satan could say a prayer.'

'Surely,' he muttered, 'This is desolation.
This oratory is ugly, under its weeds.
The right crypt for that ogre, in his greenery,
To deal with his devotions devil-fashion.

My five wits warn me, this is the evil one,
Who bound me on oath to be here, to destroy me.
The chapel of Mischance – God see it demolished!
It is the worst-cursed Church I ever attended.'
With his helmet on his head, and his lance in his hand,
He clambered up on top of the bushy cell
And heard coming off the hill, from a face of rock,
The far side of the stream, a ferocious din.
What! It screeched in the crag, as if it would split it!
It sounded like a scythe a-shriek on a grind-stone!
What! It grumbled and scoured, like water in a mill!
What! It rushed and it rang, painful to hear!
'By God!' thought Gawain, 'I think that scummer
Is done in your honour, Knight, to welcome you
        As you deserve.
    Let God have his way! Ah well.
    It helps me not one bit.
    What if I lose my life?
    No noise is going to scare me.'

Then the Knight shouted, at the top of his voice:
'Is nobody at home, to collect my debt?
Gawain is here, now, walking about.
If any man is willing, get here quickly.
It is now or never, if he wants payment.'
'Be patient,' came a voice from the crag overhead,
'And I shall satisfy you, as I promised.'
Then he was back at his racket, with fresh fury,
Wanting to finish his whetting, before he came down.
But suddenly he was there, from under a cliff,
Bounding out of a den with a frightful weapon –
A Dane's axe, new fettled to settle the wager.
It had a massive head hooking back to the helve,
Ground bright with a file, and four foot long.
It measured as much by the rich thong that hung from it.
That giant, all got up in green as before,
Both the face and the legs, the hair and the beard,
Came down with plunging strides, in a big hurry,
Planting the axe to the earth and striding beside it.
When he got to the water he would not wade it,
He vaulted across on his axe, and loomed up,
Bursting into the clearing, where he stood

On the snow.
Sir Gawain knew how to greet him –
But not too friendly.
While the other replied: 'I see, Sir Sweetness,
A man can keep his word.'

'Gawain,' said the Green Man, 'God protect you.
Let me welcome you, Knight, to my small holding.
You have timed your coming, as a true man should.
I see you honour the contract sealed between us.
This time twelvemonth back you took a thing from me.
So now, at this New Year, I shall reclaim it.
We have this lonely valley to ourselves.
No Knights are here to part us. We fight as we please.
Get that helmet off, and take your payment.
And give me no more talk than I gave you
When you whipped off my head with a single swipe.'
'Nay,' said Gawain, 'By God that gave me my soul,
I shall not grudge one jot of the damage coming.
Stick to the single stroke and I shall not move
Nor utter a word to warn you from whatever
        You choose.'
    He stretched his neck and bowed
    And bared the white flesh,
    Pretending to fear nothing.
    He would not dare to be fearful.

The Man in Green was eager, and all ready,
Grasping that ugly tool, to hit Gawain.
With all his body's might he hoisted it high,
Aimed it murderously for the utmost hurt.
And if he had brought it down as he had aimed it
The Knight who had never flinched would have been headless.
But Gawain skewed a sidelong glance at the weapon
As it came down to cut him off from the earth,
And shrank his shoulders a little from the sharp iron.
That other checked his stroke. He deflected the blade.
Then he reproached the prince with shaming words:
'You are not Gawain,' he said, 'whose name is so great,
Who never quailed in his life, by hill nor by vale.
Here you are wincing for fear before I touch you.
I never heard such cowardice of that hero.
When you hit me, I never fluttered an eyelid.

I never let out a squeak, in Arthur's hall.
My head rolled over the floor, but I did not flinch.
Before you are touched, your heart jumps out of your body.
It seems to me that I am a warrior far
        Far better.'
    Said Gawain: 'I winced once.
    And that once is the last.
    Though my head rolling on earth
    Can never be replaced.

'But hurry up, warrior, for God's sake come to the point.
Deal me my destiny, and do it quickly.
I shall stand to your stroke with not one stir
Till your axe-head hits me. I give you my word.'
'Then here it comes,' cried the other, and heaved it upwards
With a gargoyle grimace as if he were mad,
And with all his strength hauled down, yet never touched him.
He stopped the blade mid-stroke, before it could harm.
Gawain patiently waited, not a nerve twitched.
He stood there still as a rock or some stiff stump
That grips the stony ground with a hundred roots.
Then the Man in Green spoke pleasantly:
'Now that your heart is whole again, may I ask you,
Let your high rank, that Arthur gave you, preserve you
And recover your neck from my stroke, if it is able.'
Then Gawain ground his teeth and shouted in anger:
'Why, hack away, you savage, you threaten too long.
I think you have frightened yourself with your bragging.'
'What's this?' cried the other, 'Rough words from Sir Gawain?
I will no longer withhold from such an appeal
        Justice.'
    And he braced himself for the stroke –
    Clenching both lip and brow.
    No wonder he did not like it
    Who saw no rescue now.

Lightly he lifted the weapon, then let it down deftly
With the barb of the bit by the bare neck,
And though he swung full strength he hardly hurt him,
But snicked him on that side, so the sheer edge
Sliced through skin and fine white fat to the muscle,
Then over his shoulders the bright blood shot to the earth.
When Gawain saw his blood blink on the snow

He sprang a spear's length forward, in one great stride,
Snatched up his helmet as he went, and crammed it on his head.
A shunt of his shoulders brought his shield to the front
And his sword flashed out as he spoke fiercely:
Since he was first a man born of his mother
Never in this world was he half as happy.
'That's enough, warrior. I take no more.
I have taken the payment blow, without resistance.
If you fetch me another, I shall match it.
I shall repay it promptly, you can trust me,
    And in full.
  I owed a single cut.
  That was our covenant
  Agreed in Arthur's Hall –
  So now, Sir, what about it?'

The Knight in Green stepped back, and leaned on his axe.
Setting the shaft in the snow, he rested on the head
And gazed awhile at the prince who stood before him:
Armed, calm, fearless, undaunted. He had to admire him.
Now as he spoke, his voice was big and cheerful:
'What a brave fellow you are. Do not be angry.
Nobody here has misused you, or done you dishonour.
We kept to the terms agreed in the King's Court.
I promised a blow. You have it. You are well paid.
And I require from you no other quittance.
If I had wanted it, I could have grieved you.
I could have exacted a cut, perhaps, far worse.
But see how I teased you, my worst was a playful feint.
I did not maim you with a gash. I took only justice,
For the contract we agreed on that first night.
You have kept faith with me and the bond between us,
And all that you took you returned – as a good man should.'

Some Pike for Nicholas

Down the black drain, and across the Black Lough
Where whitecaps burned, you came tossing on a saucer
Out of childhood, pulled by lean black pike.
From bridle and bit you freed them, and shook hands.

Lough na Cashel's great Queen granted you your prayer
Which was to take her in your arms, on your mother's birthday,
And give her the kiss of life in the cat's tail shallows.
A loon lauded you and an otter saluted.

The pike's broad grin, ruffed with Lough Gur's ice,
Stoniest, oldest eye of reality,
Welcomed your welcome, where crannogs pondered
My boy, my dream alive without distraction.

Through the November, gale-torn, indigo dusk
You fought Lough Allen. It reared, the size of a man,
Shook blood-lit gills and rode a flying serpent ...
The swipe of that huge tail rocking the memory yet, like a
    hurricane lantern.

Brother Peartree

Yellow and peach pink –
A translucence of late October
Thinner day by day
Reveals what's not there.

I send you fewer letters – fewer and thinner
Year by year. Can I really be thinking
It's just not worth it any more?
What was it I once hoped for?

Paradise. The whole bag of dream
That boyhood was made of
Heavy with rivers and forests. And the game
Quaking the earth like a drum.

Then I made do with a folktale tree
You planted in my orchard.
That's our shared life – that pear-tree.
We're that little in touch.

The year sticks leaves on it – they drop off.
I still stick sentences
On our plans for us –
They drop off.

Pretty yellow and flamey pink.
Till the boughs are an empty crate.
It has never brought me a single pear.
Is it too late?

Or the wrong side of the earth?
Your roots are here, as we say.
Drinking my thoughts. So those branches are roots.
And the real, the flourishing tree

Is on your lawn in Australia. Maybe
The one that ripened for you that gigantic,
Protected, solitary pear
Which you tied with a string to its branch

Just to make double sure –
But you never got it. He did –
Lounging in from your garden, slurping the core,
Your friend's awful kid.

Shakespeare, drafting his will in 1605, plots an autobiographical play for 1606

My Will shall be
As I have planned:
My treasure, my land,
Split into three,

One third I pay
To help Anne's age
Put her youth's rage
And hate away.

To Judith one
Else who would marry
Memento Mori
Of my son?

And for Sue
The final part
Includes my heart
That is pierced through

By my own lance
In young Edmund's
Bastard Edmund's
Lineal hands.

The Prophet
[after Pushkin]

Crazed by my soul's thirst
Through a dark land I staggered.
And a six-winged seraph
Halted me at a crossroads.
With fingers of dream
He touched my eye-pupils.
My eyes, prophetic, recoiled
Like a startled eaglet's.
He touched my ears
And a thunderous clangour filled them,
The shudderings of heaven,
The huge wingbeat of angels,
The submarine migration of sea-reptiles
And the burgeoning of the earth's vine.
He forced my mouth wide,
Plucked out my own cunning
Garrulous evil tongue,
And with bloody fingers
Between my frozen lips
Inserted the fork of a wise serpent.
He split my chest with a blade,
Wrenched my heart from its hiding,
And into the open wound
Pressed a flaming coal.
I lay on stones like a corpse.
There God's voice came to me:
'Stand, Prophet, you are my will.
Be my witness. Go
Through all seas and lands. With the Word
Burn the hearts of the people.'

A Dove

Snaps its twig-tether – mounts –
Dream-yanked up into vacuum
Wings snickering.

Another, in a shatter, hurls dodging away up.

They career through tree-mazes –
Nearly uncontrollable love-weights.

Or now
Temple-dancers, possessed, and steered
By solemn powers
Through insane, stately convulsions.

Porpoises
Of dove-lust and blood splendour
With arcs
And plungings, and spray-slow explosions.

Now violently gone
Riding the snake of the long love-whip
Among flarings of mares and stallions

Now staying
Coiled on a bough
Bubbling molten, wobbling top-heavy
Into one and many.

APPENDICES, NOTES AND INDEXES

In several editions and selections of his poetry, Hughes compiled notes offering brief explanations of the genesis or themes of his various sequences, and, in some cases, commentary upon individual poems. These are reproduced below.

Crow

[*Selected Poems 1957–1981* (1982)]
This is a sequence of poems relating the birth, upbringing and adventures of a protagonist of that name.

Cave Birds

[*Selected Poems 1957–1981* (1982)]
This is a sequence of twenty-nine poems written to accompany drawings – of imaginary birds – by Leonard Baskin. The poems plot the course of a symbolic drama, concerning disintegration and re-integration, with contrapuntal roles played by birds and humans. For the four poems printed here the drawings cannot be reproduced, so it might help to know that the Executioner is a giant raven; the Knight is a decomposing bird of the Crow type; Bride and Groom are human beings with bird attributes, and the Risen is a falcon, the full-fledged emergence of a Horus. Throughout the original sequence the interdependence between drawings and verse is quite close.

[*Three Books* (1993)]
In this sequence, where the dramatis personae are the bird-spirits of people, or people with bird-spirits, each poem is designed as a masque-like tableau, to make an 'alchemical' ritual drama of transformation, with beginning, middle, end, and a good outcome.

Gaudete

[*Gaudete* (1977), prefatory *Argument*]
An Anglican clergyman is abducted by spirits into the other world.
    The spirits create a duplicate of him to take his place in this world, during his absence, and to carry on his work.
    This changeling interprets the role of minister in his own way.
    The narrative recounts the final day of events which lead to his cancellation by the powers of both worlds.
    The original man reappears in this world, but changed.

[*Gaudete* (1979), prefatory *Argument*]
An Anglican Clergyman, the Reverend Nicholas Lumb, is carried away into the other world by elemental spirits. Just as in the Folktale, these spirits want him for some work in their world.

To fill his place in this world, for the time of his absence, the spirits make an exact duplicate of him out of an oak log, and fill it with elemental spirit life. This new Nicholas Lumb is to all appearances exactly the same as the old, has the same knowledge and mannerisms, but he is a log. A changeling.

This changeling proceeds to interpret the job of ministering the Gospel of love in his own log-like way.

He organises the women of his parish into a coven, a love-society. And the purpose of this society, evidently, is the birth of a Messiah to be fathered by Lumb.

While he applies himself to this he begins to feel a nostalgia for independent, ordinary human life, free of his peculiar destiny.

At this point, the spirits who created him decide to cancel him. It may be that the original Lumb has done the work they wanted him to do, and so the changeling's time is up. The result is that all the husbands of the parish become aware of what is happening to their wives.

The narrative recounts the last day of the changeling's life.

At the death of the changeling, the original Nicholas Lumb reappears in this world, in the West of Ireland, where he roams about composing hymns and psalms to a nameless female deity.

Remains of Elmet

[*Remains of Elmet* (1979), prefatory note]
The Calder valley, west of Halifax, was the last ditch of Elmet, the last British Celtic kingdom to fall to the Angles. For centuries it was considered a more or less uninhabitable wilderness, a notorious refuge for criminals, a hide-out for refugees. Then in the early 1800s it became the cradle for the Industrial Revolution in textiles, and the upper Calder became "the hardest-worked river in England". Throughout my lifetime, since 1930, I have watched the mills of the region and their attendant chapels die. Within the last fifteen years the end has come. They are now virtually dead, and the population of the valley and the hillsides, so rooted for so long, is changing rapidly. Fay Godwin set out to capture some impressions of this landscape at this moment, and her photographs moved me to write the accompanying poems. *Remains*.

[*Elmet* (1994), preface]
Elmet is still the name on maps for a part of West Yorkshire that includes the deep valley of the upper Calder and its watershed of Pennine moorland. These poems confine themselves to the upper Calder and the territory roughly encircled by a line drawn through Halifax (on the east), Keighley (on the north east), Colne (on the

north-west), Burnley (on the west), and Littleborough (on the
south-west); an 'island' straddling the Yorks–Lancs border, though
mainly in Yorkshire, and centred, in my mind, on Heptonstall.
Elmet was the last independent Celtic kingdom in England and
originally stretched out over the vale of York. I imagine it shrank
back into the gorge of the upper Calder under historic pressures,
before the Celtic survivors were politically absorbed into England.
But even into the seventeenth century this narrow cleft and its side-
ginnels, under the glaciated moors, were still a 'badlands', a
sanctuary for refugees from the law. Defoe hid in Halifax to escape
his creditors. In those days Halifax was a small country town, and
the main stronghold, further up the valley, was Heptonstall. An old
rhyme takes note of one aspect of the early shift of power:

> Halifax is made of wax,
> Heptonstall of stone.
> Halifax has many pretty girls,
> Heptonstall's got none.

Heptonstall is now a straggly hill-top hamlet.

   Physically inhospitable, cut off to north and south by the
high moorland, the insularity of the valley was in some ways
almost complete, in others anything but. It formed a natural
highway, the pass (just north of the M62) between the Scandinavian
pressures of the North Sea and the Celtic pressures of the Irish Sea,
between Mersey and Humber: this was the top of the tide, from
both seas – where the wrack washed up and stayed. The results –
alternating between pressurized stagnation and fermenting
independence – can be read into the region's history. In the Civil
War, the valley militia formulated their refusal to obey any order
from the King lacking the full consent of Parliament, in a document
that was incorporated into Jefferson's Declaration of Independence
(one of his ancestors, the first Secretary for Virginia, came from the
valley). The region's early prosperity was based on wool, and the
household industry had shaped architectural features in the old
farms and cottages. So, when the time came, the spirit of the place
was ready to take advantage of mass-production, and wherever
water ran mills sprang up. By the end of the nineteenth century, the
Calder was called 'the hardest worked river in England'. The
tributary known as Colden Water (the 'moor-water' in the poem
titled 'Crown Point Pensioners') comes down a small side-valley as
a tiny stream, easy to jump across in many places, yet at one time
even this trickle was the lifeline for no fewer than fourteen mills
(and up near the top of it, in the thirteenth century, the first fulling
mill on record). Following hard on these mills, as Jacob on Esau,
the Chartist Movement came into being here. The main valley, now
shorn of its forest of chimneys (and of most of its mill-buildings),
trying to adapt to tourism, prides itself on the title 'Cradle of the
Industrial Revolution'.

   This confined separateness, with its peculiar conditions and history, had its Darwinian effect on the natives. The most recent and obvious imprint on them was made by Wesley's Methodism, or rather by the local mutation of it. When Wesley first saw the place, and preached here, before the Industrial Revolution, he called it 'the most beautiful valley in England'. But he went on – 'with the most barbarous people'. He was looking at it before that 'barbarous' population became his most fanatic enthusiasts. Which is to say, before they had registered the full impact of Parson Grimshaw, the hell-fire Methodist preacher of Haworth in the latter part of the eighteenth century. In Mrs Gaskell's *Life of Charlotte Brontë* there is a vivid and convincing (familiar) account of the community, the human type, that Grimshaw had to deal with. To judge by the shock-wave, which could still be felt, I think, well into this century, he struck the whole region 'like a planet'. There is a marvellous recreation of his life in Glyn Hughes's novel *Where I Used to Play on the Green*. Grimshaw's unusual force seems to have alarmed even Wesley, a little. To a degree, he changed the very landscape. His heavenly fire, straight out of Blake's *Prophetic Books*, shattered the terrain into biblical landmarks: quarries burst open like craters, and chapels – the bedrock transfigured – materialized standing in them. The crumpled map of horizons became a mirage of the Holy Land. Grimshaw imposed this vision (which was not a little neurotic), then herded the people into it.

The men who built the chapels were the same who were building the mills. They perfected the art of perching their towering, massive, stone, prison-like structures on drop-offs where now you would only just graze sheep. When the local regimes (and combined operation) of Industry and Religion started to collapse in the 1930s, this architecture emerged into spectacular desolation – a grim sort of beauty. Ruin followed swiftly, as the mills began to close, the chapels to empty, and the high farms under the moor-edge, along the spring line, were one by one abandoned. When I came to consciousness there in the 1930s, the process was already far gone, though the communities seemed to be still intact, still entirely absorbed by the life of the factories – or by the slump. But you could not fail to realize that the cataclysms had happened – to the population (in the First World War, where a single bad ten minutes in no man's land would wipe out a street or even a village), to the industry (the shift to the East in textile manufacture), and to the Methodism (the new age). Gradually, it dawned on you that you were living among the survivors, in the remains.

Moortown Diary

[*Moortown Diary* (1989), Preface]
In the early 1970s my wife and I bought a small farm just north of the northern edge of Dartmoor, in what is generally known as North Devon, and farmed it in partnership with her father, Jack Orchard, to whom I have dedicated this book. He was a retired

farmer whose family had farmed in Devon for generations. My own experience of farming had previously been limited to playing and working on farms in West and South Yorkshire when I was a boy, just failing to buy a farm in Australia when I left University, and since then rearing the occasional bullock or two. My mother's mother's family had farmed in West Yorkshire, so I always heard the common saying 'back to the land in three generations' with a cocked ear. However it was, when the opportunity to buy a farm suddenly came, I took it. We had no idea what an interesting moment we had chosen.

Even then, in the early 1970s, the ancient farming community in North Devon was still pretty intact and undisturbed, more so than anywhere else in England. No industrial development or immigrant population had ever disrupted it. A lucky combination of factors kept tourists to the minimum, and those few to the sparse resorts on the rocky fringe. The high rainfall and poor soil deterred the sort of farmer who might try to change things. Cut off by Exmoor to the east, Dartmoor to the south, and that northern coastline of high, wreckers' cliff in which the only harbourage was all but closed by a dangerous bar, North Devon felt like an island. The rest of England had always ignored it. And there was a palpable feeling here that England (along with South Devon and Cornwall) was another country and could be ignored in return. Over the centuries this has bred a curious mentality. Yorkshire farmers are thought to be an independent lot, and those I knew certainly were, but even fifty years ago they were embattled, alert to all the buffeting modern pressures of mass population and industry. The isolated self-sufficiency of the old North Devon farmers was something else altogether, like nothing I had ever encountered.

Buried in their deep valleys, in undateable cob-walled farms hidden not only from the rest of England but even from each other, connected by the inexplicable, Devonshire, high-banked, deep-cut lanes that are more like a defence-maze of burrows, these old Devonians lived in a time of their own. It was common to hear visitors say: 'Everything here's in another century!' But what they really meant, maybe, was that all past centuries were still very present here, wide-open, unchanged, unexorcized, and potent enough to overwhelm any stray infiltrations of modernity. The farmers lived lightly in the day and the year, but heavily in that long backward perspective of their ancient landscape and their homes. The breed was so distinct, so individualized and all of a piece, they seemed to me almost a separate race. I could believe they were still that Celtic tribe the Romans had known as the *Dumnoni*, 'the people of the deep valleys', a confederacy of petty kings, hidden in their strongholds that were only just beginning to emerge out of the old oak forest.

How rapidly that changed within the next decade, how completely that ancient world and its spirit vanished, as the older generation died off and gave way to sons who were plunged into the financial nightmares, the technological revolutions and international market madness that have devastated farmers, farms and farming ever since, intensifying right up to this moment, is no part of what I recorded in the passages of verse collected here. Or it is only a small, indirect part, in so far as my wife and I inevitably belonged, in many respects, to the new wave. Against the strong resistance of her father we did try some of the novelties, lusted after the exotic, foreign breeds of cattle that poured into England during the 1970s, boosted our palpitations on the regular sales blast of *Farmer's Weekly*, with its dazing propaganda for new chemicals, new machinery, more chemicals, new methods, different chemicals, new gimmicks, new short-cuts, every possible new way of wringing that critical extra per cent out of the acreage and the animals. We were dragged, as bewildered as the rest, into that seismic upheaval which has been, probably, one of the biggest extinctions so far in the evolution of English countryside and farming tradition. Few farmers understood what was happening. Within a very short time the last vestige of grandeur in the real work had vanished, the product itself had become a weirdly scandalous, unwanted surplus, the livestock a danger to public health (and nobody knew better than the farmer what he pumped into them), the very soil a kind of poison, the rivers sewers. This deeply satisfying, self-reliant if occasionally gruelling way of life had mutated – into a jittery, demoralized, industrial servitude, in effect farming not stock and land but grants and subsidies, at the mercy of foreign politicians, big business conglomerates, bank managers and accountants. A sharp nose for these things soon enlightened us, and we settled into the old-fashioned routine of running a suckler herd of beef cows, a flock of breeding ewes, and keeping everything going on baler twine.

Even so, whether we liked it or not, we were in the front line of the first campaign of what felt very much like the Third World War conducted by other means – the EEC Agricultural Policy War. At one point, while we were trying to sell some of the animals I mention in these pages, cattle-market prices dropped as low as ever in history. Buying a steak at a butcher's shop you would not have noticed the tremor in the scales, but at that time a farmer sold a calf and with the proceeds managed to buy a Mars Bar; a local farmer leaving Hatherleigh Market found two unfamiliar calves in his trailer – dumped there by the owner who could neither get a price for them nor afford to take them back home and feed them.

The pieces in this collection came about by the way. It occurred to me from time to time that interesting things were happening, and that I ought to make a note of them, a note of the details in particular, partly with the idea of maybe using them at some future time in a piece of writing, and partly to make a fleeting snapshot, for myself, of a precious bit of my life. Over those first years, as the evidence now shows me, that impulse came to me about forty times. And most of the results are here.

I should say something about the form and style in which these pieces are written. I set them down in what appears to be verse for a simple reason. In making a note about anything, if I wish to look closely I find I can move closer, and stay closer, if I phrase my observations about it in rough lines. So these improvised verses are nothing more than this: my own way of getting reasonably close to what is going on, and staying close, and of excluding everything else that might be pressing to interfere with the watching eye. In a sense, the method excludes the poetic process as well.

This sort of thing had to be set down soon after the event. If I missed the moment – which meant letting a night's sleep intervene before I took up a pen – I could always see quite clearly what had been lost. By the next day, the processes of 'memory', the poetic process, had already started. Though all the details were still absolutely fresh, most of them no longer seemed essential to the new pattern taking control. The pieces here which begin to look a little more like 'poems' mark the occasions where I had 'missed the moment' in this way.

I regarded them as casual journal notes, and made no attempt to do anything with them, until one day a magazine editor asked me for a poem. Thinking I might find something to work on, I then looked these pieces over, and picked out 'February 17th'. It didn't take me long to realize that I was in the position of a translator: whatever I might make of this passage, I was going to have to destroy the original. And what was original here was not some stranger's poem but the video and surviving voice-track of one of my own days, a moment of my life that I did not want to lose. I then saw that all the other entries, even the more diffuse, still carried that same souvenir bloom for me. Altering any word felt like retouching an old home movie with new bits of fake-original voice and fake-original actions.

I put them together for my wife, as a memorial to her father. For any other reader who might find something of interest in them I have added a few sentences of introductory context here and there, as I would if I were reading them to an audience.

[*Moortown Diary* (1989), Notes]
'Dehorning' (page 504)
That first year or two, we did all the jobs that required handling of the animals in a small yard. Twenty cows were all it could hold. Most cattle nowadays are dehorned soon after birth, but at that time many of the cows you bought still had horns. Among the unhorned, these soon discovered the point of power. So, in the end, they had to face what I describe here. As it happens, I made another note of the very same occasion, a different kind of observation, which now reminds me what a shattering effect the operation had on me, though I am not squeamish. As if the horns had been repeatedly sawn off me. The 'crush' is an adjustable steel cage for immobilizing a beast.

'Poor birds' (page 505)
This next piece is a scrap of afterbirth from that first description of
our labours in the winter rain. That winter, in particular, was
doubly darkened – by bigger hordes of invading starlings than I had
ever seen. All day long they would be storming down on to the field
beside us, or roaring up, wired to every rumour, in a bewildered
refugee panic, very disturbing, even slightly depressing, and
somehow ominous, since they couldn't be ignored, and wherever
you glanced you saw another tribe of starlings fleeing across the
sky. Yet I was more touched by the redwings, who hurried about in
smaller, quieter detachments, with secretive cries, the lost stragglers
of an army rather than an army. These more diffident foreigners
seemed by contrast much more aware of their plight, much more
exposed to the ultimate fact: that this was all there was.

'Foxhunt' (page 507)
The Reverend Jack Russell, the Victorian inventor of the Jack
Russell terrier, was a fanatical foxhunter, who would and
sometimes did hunt six days a week. When he came as Parson to
Iddesleigh, a small village very close to the setting of this journal,
foxhunting on horseback, to hounds, was unknown in the region,
and he was dismayed to learn that there wasn't a single fox to be
found between Dartmoor, seven miles to the south, and Torrington,
eleven miles to the north, and the same distances to east and west.
Every fox glimpsed in this territory was instantly reported, like a
man-eater, and dug out and killed, by the farmers or by a
commando of villagers. Jack Russell managed to interest two or
three farmers in forming a hunt, and persuaded them to set down
foxes in artificial dens and generally to protect them. More farmers
became interested, and began to half-protect foxes. Pretty soon he
had a thriving hunt going. The country people too, evidently,
adjusted their feelings about foxes. Presumably they found
themselves stirred by the ritual and ceremony of the hunt. Even
after horses had passed out of common use, and that atavistic fear
of what a man becomes when he gets up into the saddle had
revived again, country folk still remained involved in the horse cult.
Maybe because it is such a big part of the lives of girls and women
(a girl or a woman on a horse is a different matter). The whole
business is mysterious, but one consequence has been that the foxes
of North Devon flourish in the most extraordinary way. They
might well disapprove of my hard words against the houndpack.
For all I know, they regard Jack Russell as their patron Saint. At a
recent Meet starting from the Duke Of York in Iddesleigh, when
the first little wood was drawn, just outside the village, foxes ran
out in every direction. An explosion of foxes! The houndpack was
completely bewildered. Observers reckoned 'over twenty foxes'.

'Roe-deer' (page 513)
About two months after this encounter, I met one of these animals

again (one of the same pair, I imagine) in a strange episode that sent me back to re-read my own verses. If those two deer, on that snowy February morning, had gone on downhill, and through the copse visible in the combe (the 'tree dark' from which they had probably started), they would have been stopped, at the bottom of the next field, by the River Taw. In April, I was standing beside that river just after dawn, and looking up the grassy combe, where the first rays of sun rested on the very heavy dew. In other words, I was looking up towards that copse I mention above. I suddenly realized I was being watched – by a figure outlined on the swell of the hill against the copse tucked in behind, a figure I took to be a man. When he started walking towards me I could see that he was unusually small, and somehow unnatural, but in what way unnatural I couldn't at that range quite make out. I kept perfectly still, and he approached me at a walk, so purposefully that I assumed he had seen me and wanted to speak to me. But the closer he came the odder he seemed. I had one of those moments, or rather several long moments, when you wonder whether what you are looking at actually is, at last, a ghost. At that hour in the morning I was ready for anything – certainly for a ghost. With those bright, rather brassy sunbeams full on him he looked absolutely solid and yet – unnatural: I could only think he must be some kind of earthy troll, some little old man living wild, or maybe even a little old woman. It was his confident approach, of course, that blocked the obvious. But my amazement hardly lessened when I realized that it was a roe-deer. It came the whole distance in a dead straight line. Till it stood, within twenty paces, clearly trying to puzzle out what kind of creature I might be, and thinking, perhaps, that I might be a big roe-buck. Then it circled to the left and studied me some more. Finally it turned and loped away up the field, stopping now and again to look back, till it paused, where I'd first seen it, looking back. Then it disappeared behind the hill.

'She has come to pass' (page 521)
By the time we recoiled from the charms of foreign cattle breeds, we had settled our liking on South Devons. This was unorthodoxy. Every North Devon farmer's Bible states quite clearly that South Devon cattle cannot thrive 'north of the A30' which runs, on its way from Penzance to Kensington, about six miles south of the farm. But we knew some of the best of the breed were much further north than that, and anyway we fancied them, even if only as a cross. So we set out to find a South Devon bull.

South Devons are generally reckoned the biggest native breed, but in fact they too are exotic. According to their history, they were introduced by Queen Eleanor, to supply beef and hides for the Fleet at Dartmouth, and came originally from the South of France. The main families still tend to be grouped around Dartmouth. We heard of a sale near Dartmouth where two or three quality bulls were being sold, and decided to go for one of them, a quite young

animal, whose first calves were there to be admired. My wife bid –
past our limit, past double our limit, and finally dropped out close
to a figure three times our set limit. I left it too long before making
a note, and so entirely missed the real point, which was our
infatuation with that animal, and the wild relief at having escaped
paying for him – exactly as if we had just won all that he had now
cost somebody else. Nevertheless, the entry hangs on to something
of the day, so I kept it.

'Birth of Rainbow' (page 521)
What I sharply remember about this piece was how nearly I let it
pass – like many another curious moment. That timing, the cow
dropping the calf just as we set eyes on her (after we had watched
her well into darkness the night before), was almost as peculiar as
the fact that she gave birth under the end of a rainbow; and
thinking about it that night I pushed myself out of bed to make the
note, knowing that by the next day I would for sure have lost the
authentic fingerprints of the day itself. I recall, too, how as I came
to the close, Frost's line 'Something has to be left to God' strayed
into my head, and how I made a quick bow around that, to tie the
piece up. We called the calf Rainbow.

'Orf' (page 522)
Small outbreaks of the ulcerous infection known as Orf or Lewer
are fairly common among sheep and lambs. It generally begins
around the lips and nose, but can spread anywhere (and can even
make the leap on to the shepherd).
    I missed the moment, here, by about two weeks. As I submitted
to what seemed to be the requirements of the writing, I was keenly
aware of all that I was rejecting. Details that were not important to
the writing were still important to me! And still seem important.
The lonely, hunched-up way he stood there, in the cattle pen, on
the lumpy, dry, compacted bedding (which was chicken litter from
a battery farm – probably part of his failure to recover!), and the
way the afternoon sun came on to him from the open opposite end
of the building, and the shockingly-amplified crack of the rifle
under the brittle asbestos roof. That should be there. And maybe
the stony grave in the wood that I dug for him, and the little oak
sapling that I planted on it (an extraordinary sort of funeral for any
livestock casualty).

'Happy calf' (page 523)
I sat close to this calf, where he sat on high ground, outlined
against the bulk of Dartmoor six miles away, and I 'sketched' him
in these words. I remember thinking, as his mother came between
him and the blue shape of those hills, 'What a subject for an old
Chinese painter!' This evoked the idea of a Chinese sage, on his
mountain, in a trance, deep in Tao. The calf was obviously in a
religious daze, the state of steady bliss which must be, one

imagines, the normal mood of relaxing animals, their inborn
defence against natural conditions. Our lost birthright. I kept all
that from intruding with the single word 'meditating'.

'Little red twin' (page 525)
The bulk of these pieces, I'm aware, concern the nursing if not the
emergency hospital side of animal husbandry. All sheep, lambs and
calves are patients: something in them all is making a steady effort
to die. That is the farmer's impression. How many succeed is one
of the things every farmer keeps to himself. On the other hand, the
deepest fascination of stock rearing is this participation in the
precarious birth of these tough and yet over-delicate beasts, and
nursing them against what often seem to be the odds. 'Scour' is a
chronic condition of diarrhoea, very common with young calves,
usually fairly easy to cure, but debilitating while it lasts. Sometimes
it ends in death. This occasion illustrated in an odd way what has
always seemed to me almost a law: if anything can, even by only
the remotest chance, operate as a trap, some animal will end up
trapped in it.

'Teaching a dumb calf' (page 527)
What I call the 'ancient statue' is simply the characteristic position
that a calf takes up when it suckles, facing the opposite way to its
mother, its upcurving back pressed close against the bulge of her
belly, where she can reach round to give him a lick or a sniff. This
makes a compact design, and appears in very early art.

'While she chews sideways' (page 530)
The calf called Struggle, that died in one of the other pieces, was
fathered by this bull, a colossal Charolais, a hired stud. Charolais
bulls can be beautiful, but this one was not. Cows come into season
about every twenty-one days. In a herd of thirty, the bull is always
investigating. For the first month he lives through an ecstatic fugue
of three-day infatuations, enthralled, even enslaved. Then as gaps
begin to appear in the enchantment he becomes progressively more
baffled and unbelieving.

'Sheep I and II' (page 531)
Sometimes we brought an invalid in close to the house, where we
could watch over it constantly. We would set up a small wire pen
on the front lawn. On this occasion, we had brought in a ewe and
her late-born, midget lamb – a lamb that had some quite special
problem in staying alive, as well as being so unnaturally small. The
following day, after he had gone, but before we had shifted his
mother back to the flock, I made the note of Part I.

In Part II, I am being reminded of the first time I ever heard the
uncanny noise that a large flock of sheep makes when the mothers,
separated for the shearing from their still quite young lambs, return
shorn – desperate to find the lambs that are desperate to find their

mothers. There were no sheep on the South Yorkshire farms of my boyhood, and I had never heard a shearing on the moor farms of West Yorkshire either. During my National Service on an isolated RAF radio station I had the use of a powerful receiver, and through the night watches I could amuse myself searching the globe for the kind of music I liked. Late one night, roaming the space waves, I suddenly came into this unearthly lamentation, weaving and crackling through the galactic swells. I had no idea what it could be. I thought it must be, it had to be, the recording of the uproar on a battlefield, just after the attack. I listened for distinct words, or a stray gunshot or explosion. Then I thought it must be an inspired sound-effect for a radio version of Dante's Inferno, maybe an authentic battlefield recording used for a dramatization of Dante's descent, as all Hell opens beneath him. I listened for some explanation, but everything faded into a jabber of foreign commentary. The sound haunted me for two or three years, till I happened to walk in on a sheep-shearing on the moorland near Builth Wells. The flock was very large, and the lambs and their shorn, searching mothers were scattering over a wide valley. And there it was, in that empty landscape: my imagined battlefield, the outcry of the inferno.

On the occasion I record here, all the animals were very close to me, the other side of a high, thick hedge, in a field next to where I was working, so I could see nothing, only hear the sounds.

'A monument' (page 534)
Farmers make especially valuable soldiers, I have read, because they are skilled in so many different ways. Jack Orchard belonged to that tradition of farmers who seem equal to any job, any crisis, using the most primitive means, adapting and improvising with any old bit of metal, and the more massive the physical demand, the more novel the engineering problem, the more intricate the mechanical difficulty, the better; and preferably the whole operation should be submerged under the worst possible weather. The concentration with which he transformed himself into these tasks, and the rapt sort of delight, the inner freedom, they seemed to bring him – all without a word spoken – gave me a new meaning for the phrase 'meditation on matter'. He made me understand how Stonehenge was hauled into place and set up as a matter of course, even if the great bluestones had to come from Limerick.

The episode I noted in 'A monument' brought this home to me because the job itself was such a very slight one – albeit so necessary and in those conditions so laborious – as tensing a strand of barbed wire through a wood. But it could have made no difference to him, except maybe to intensify his satisfaction, if we had been doing it in the dark, or even under bombardment.

'A memory' (page 535)
Throughout whatever he did, he smoked a cigarette. He rarely

seemed to puff at it, just let it smoulder there. He spoke the broadest Devonshire with a very deep African sort of timbre. Unlike the indigenous Devonians who seem to be usually short, and often thick-set, he was very tall, broad and gangly, with immense hands. His line of Orchards came via Hartland, opposite the Isle of Lundy, which at one time was held by Moorish seafarers (hence the Moriscoes), and blood-group factors evidently do reveal pockets of North African genes here and there along the North and South Cornwall and Devon coasts. The Hartland Orchards have a crest: a raven. That could easily be accounted for, I used to tell him, if they had originally been Moorish pirates. We treat it as a joke, but for me it identified his essence.

River

[*Three Books* (1993), Notes]
It is not easy to separate the fascination of rivers from the fascination of fish. Making dams, waterfalls, water-gardens, water-courses, is deeply absorbing play, for most of us, but the results have to be a home for something. When the water is wild, inhabitants are even more important. Streams, rivers, ponds, lakes *without fish* communicate to me one of the ultimate horrors – the poisoning of the wells, death at the source of all that is meant by water. I spent my first eight years beside the West Yorkshire River Calder – in which the only life was a teeming bankside population of brown rats. But the hillside streams and the canal held fish – including, in the canal, big but rare trout. These preoccupied me, as a lifeline might. Later on, in South Yorkshire, the farm which was for years my playground was bounded on one side by the River Don, which drained the industrial belt between Sheffield and Doncaster: a river of such concentrated steaming, foaming poisons that an accidental ducking was said to be fatal. My lifeline there was an old oxbow of the Don, full of fish and waterfowl. One day (early 1940s) I saw all the fish in this lake bobbing their mouths at the surface: the beginning of the end, as it turned out. That same day I noticed a strange ruddy vein in the ditch water that drained from the farm buildings, two or three hundred yards away. And I registered a new smell. I traced the vein to a big stone shed, packed with sodden, dark-stained grass – reeking the new smell. It was the first silage.

'Salmon-taking Times' (page 648)
Atlantic Salmon dig nests, called 'redds', in the river gravel, covering their eggs with more gravel. In the British Isles, spawning begins in November, but might go on into January. After spawning, all the male fish die, as do some of the females – of exhaustion. The baby fish hatch in March, or thereabouts, and stay in the river, feeding on tiny organisms, for two, three, or even four years, depending on the feed and the individuality of the fish. When they

get to five or six inches, one April or May these 'parr', as they are called, decide to go to sea, and begin to change colour. From looking very like brown trout they become silvery 'smolts', and instead of sticking each to its little territory and defending it fiercely, they drop downriver – into the estuary and eventually to sea, travelling in shoals. Where they go then depends on the feed, which depends in turn on changing factors of ocean currents, ocean temperatures. Some reappear after their first winter at sea, by which time they weigh five or six pounds. Others come back after two winters, weighing anything between eight pounds and twice that – or even more. The fish that stay out for three winters begin to be seriously big specimens, if they survive the thousand perils. Here and there, females will be returning to spawn for a second or even a third time.

Nature keeps all options open, so these fish begin to come back as early as February. In the days when nothing disturbed the cycle, smaller or larger shoals went on arriving through the year, entering the rivers and running up at times of high river flow. Each fish is programmed to return to the river, to the tributary, and even to the very pool, perhaps the very gravel patch, of its birth. Some make a mistake, but then might swim long distances to correct it. The moment they enter freshwater, they cease to feed, and so from that moment begin to lose condition, while the eggs or milt, which are small and undeveloped early in the year, begin to grow and ripen, cannibalizing the body-fat and muscle of the parent. In other words, with every day in the river, the salmon grows slightly less tasty. By the time eggs or milt are fully developed, and the moment for spawning arrives, the fish itself is inedible: all goodness has gone into eggs and milt, and the flesh is left whitish, flavourless, even disgusting. Smoked, or otherwise disguised, this is the salmon that country hotel guests often encounter in autumn and winter.

As spawning time approaches, the cock fish in particular go through a physical transformation: their colouring – reds and blacks – can become almost violent, like warpaint. At the same time, their heads and especially their jaws change, the tip of their underjaw hooks up in a 'kipe', sometimes grotesque, like a rhino horn on the chin instead of the nose-end. Meanwhile, if they have been in the river some months, many will have developed patches of fungus – if not the full-blown Ulcerative Dermal Necrosis (that hit rivers in the British Isles at the end of the 1960s, and has all but wiped out some stocks).

Since salmon do not feed in freshwater (though they will catch and crush flies in their mouths, and suck worms), they have to find easy ways of saving energy throughout their wait for November. The favoured solution is to lie as if in coma, inaccessibly preoccupied, immune to any temptation. But for every salmon (at least, this is the faith) there is a time of the day – perhaps only a few minutes – when the fish is alert, active, craving to do something. At this moment they can sometimes be caught. Some experts maintain that the moment coincides with a certain phase in the constantly changing availability of oxygen in the water. It is recognizable externally by an atmospheric feeling, to which birds, insects and animals (and human beings) also seem to respond.

'The Bear' (page 845)
Most of this book was prompted by observations made on rivers in the British Isles. 'The Bear' is a memory of the Dean River, in British Columbia. Steelhead are rainbow trout, born in the river (like salmon), but going to sea and returning (like salmon and the size of salmon) to spawn where they were born. They are an immensely powerful and glamorous fish, with a mystique of their own: the great prize of the Pacific North-West. My three companions, fanatic 'steelheaders', two Canadians and one American, would never dream of killing one of these creatures. 'If we killed them,' they say, 'we'd be like you people in England: we wouldn't have any.'

'That Morning' (page 663)
The river in 'That Morning', like the Gulkana, is in Alaska. King Salmon is the Alaskan name for the Chinook – the biggest of the five species of Pacific salmon. All Pacific salmon die after spawning. The 'drift of Lancasters' is simply a memory of South Yorkshire from a late phase of the Second World War. On many evenings, for the last two hours of daylight (then on into darkness), the whole sky would be full of four-engined bombers, from airfields further north, on their way to the great raids. For those hours everything, the whole landscape, would be gripped by that drumming – a different sensation from sitting in cellars listening to the curious, inside-the-head throbbing of Dorniers, as they crept up the line of the River Don to bomb Sheffield, night after night a few years earlier.

Wolfwatching

[Note to 'The Black Rhino' (page 763)]
This piece was written to help raise funds for the campaign to save the Black Rhinoceros.

By 1980 the formerly vast numbers of African Black Rhino had been reduced to about 17,000. From earliest times, India and all countries eastward of it have regarded the rhino, and especially its horn, as a cornucopia of magical, versatile medicines. Modern marketing has increased the value of the horn at the point of sale, in the East, to three times its weight in gold, and modern weapons have supplied the trade. As much horn again goes to North Yemen, where the outcome of the Civil War combined with the oil crisis to produce a freakish, mass market for the costly rhino-horn-handled *djambia,* the ceremonial curved Yemenite dagger.

In 1986, when the Black Rhino population in Africa was diving towards 4,000, the English writer Martin Booth visited the South Luangwa National Park in Zambia to reconnoitre for a film about the Black Rhino's plight. This park was known at the time to hold one of the densest concentrations of surviving Black Rhino, and the particular region he surveyed held 'upwards of thirty', nearly all identified. Among these he located one large old bull, whom he hoped to make the star of his film. In September 1987, when he went back there with his film crew (and while I was composing this piece), he couldn't find a single Black Rhino. The 'upwards of thirty' of the year before had been reduced to an untraceable 'perhaps three'. He recapitulated the opening section of my poem by finding the skeleton of his old rhino bull.

Rain-Charm for the Duchy

[Notes, 1992]

'Rain-Charm for the Duchy' (page 803)
(First published in the *Observer*, 23 December 1984)
The Duchy is the common name for the royal lands of the Duke of Cornwall, HRH Prince Charles. In this poem I use the term loosely to cover the watersheds of most of Devon's rivers, excluding that part of the Duchy which lies outside Devon, but including some of Devon – everything north of Dartmoor – that lies outside the Duchy. I also exclude that part of Devon which lies east of the River Exe. This means excluding the little River Axe and Coleridge's River Otter.

The map of my poem is therefore the roughly square 'island' bounded on the west by the north–south course of the Tamar, which for most of its length serves as the Devon–Cornwall frontier, entering the sea at Plymouth, and on the east by the parallel north–south course of the Exe, which enters the sea, south of Exeter, at Exmouth. This shape emerged naturally since, in writing my poem, I stuck to those West-country rivers that in some part I know intimately, and as it happens their sources and valleys make a single, symmetrical, interlinked pattern.

The high moors, Dartmoor in the south and Exmoor in the north, lift and cool the prevailing southwesterlies as they come off the Atlantic, giving Devon a high rainfall (on Exmoor one of the highest in England), and a wealth of rivers. Nearly all these rivers rise on one or the other of the moors. Dartmoor's emerge very close together, the distance between their headwaters measured in paces rather than miles. The only two that rise on neither moor are the Torridge and the Tamar, and these first appear away in the north-west corner only a mile or so apart, within half a mile of the sea, just behind the north-coast cliff, near Hartland. The Tamar then flows south right across the peninsula, but on the way picks up its main tributary, the Lyd, from Dartmoor. The Torridge bends in a deep loop southwards then eastwards, turning north to enter the sea through a gap in the north cliff near Bideford (only fifteen miles from its source), but on the way it picks up its main tributary, the Okement, from Dartmoor. In both cases, according to the salmon and sea-trout, these tributaries from Dartmoor bring in the best water. The Taw makes the link between the two moors. Always known as the Torridge's sister river, running parallel and close to it for their last twenty miles, and joining it in the estuary, the Taw rises on Dartmoor but picks up from Exmoor its biggest tributary – the wonderful River Mole, which again according to the salmon and sea-trout brings in the best water. The only two rivers not linked into the Dartmoor (or Duchy) system in this way are the Exe and the two deceptively slender branches of the Lyn (one of which, in 1952, bulldozed away part of Lynmouth), which bring their water from Exmoor.

Salmon spawn in all these rivers. The determination of salmon to get upstream, their leaping at waterfalls, is familiar to all. But this terrific effort is sporadic, or rather opportunist – entirely dependent on the level of water in the river. Though none will spawn before November, the fish start coming in from the Atlantic as early as February or March, and continue to come in through the year, generally in distinct runs, like different tribes. They materialize at the mouth of their home river, and if the river flow is the right height when they arrive they will run straight in, adjusting to freshwater in the estuary mix as they go, then on upriver, leaping the cascades and the weirs. But if the river is low, the usual case, they will accumulate off the river mouth, hanging about, sometimes drifting up the estuary on the flow tide, dropping back on the ebb, waiting for water. When levels remain very low, they are physically unable to get into some of these rivers. Towards the end of summer, as they grow desperate, they will try to run the river on even a slight taste of new water. An eighteenth-century diarist recorded his attempt to ford the Tamar at one of those moments when the assembled salmon (huge numbers in those days) had decided to rush the shrunken river. His horse refused to approach the water, terrified by the massed fish going up over the gravel, through the ford, backs out, tails churning like propellors, moving at their top speed (which is extremely fast). As impressive, in its way, is to see a shoal of baby salmon, each one only two inches long, no more than four months out of the egg, responding to a sudden, fresh rise in river level, leaping at some trickle in the wall of a weir, a constant spray fountain of tiny fish, battering themselves on the stones.

This is how salmon come to be such sensitive glands in the vast, dishevelled body of nature. Their moody behaviour, so unpredictable and mysterious, is attuned, with the urgency of survival, to every slightest hint of the weather – marvellous instruments, recording every moment-by-moment microchange as the moving air and shifting light manipulate the electronics of the water molecules. One of the rewards of having been at some time of your life an obsessive salmon fisher is that salmon remain installed in some depth of your awareness, like a great network of private meteorological stations, one in every pool you know, in every river you ever fished, in that primitive otherworld, inside this one, where memory carries on 'as if real'. You can receive a report from any of these stations at any moment, usually unexpectedly. The motion of a cloud noticed through a window, the sudden stirring of a flower in a mid-city garden border, can be enough.

In the south-west, the drought of 1975 was one of the worst this century. The 1984 drought was as bad, and in some respects worse, because it was the peak of what had become a sequence of summer droughts. At one point, the River Torridge, going over its last weir above the tide – Tarka the Otter's famous Beam Weir – was down to three million gallons a day, which looks about like water being spilled slowly from a tin bath.

Like the 1975 drought, that drought of 1984 broke with a heavy storm. A memorable moment. I recorded it then, in verses, as a fitting splash for the christening of HRH Prince Harry, the Duke of Cornwall's second son.

'Two Poems for Her Majesty Queen Elizabeth the Queen Mother' (page 806)
(First published in the *Observer*, 29 December 1985)
THE DREAM OF THE LION   The basis of this poem is the association of three Lions: the one in Her Majesty Queen Elizabeth the Queen Mother's maiden name, the one in her birth-sign, and the totem animal of Great Britain. The first and the third combined inside my head long ago, during my boyhood obsession with the animal kingdom and my boyhood fanatic patriotism, in a way that was able to stir at the surface again, in these verses, as an experience to some degree widely shared.
LITTLE SALMON HYMN   As Patron of the Salmon And Trout Association, the Queen Mother is also godmother of the salmon itself.

'A Birthday Masque' (page 807)
(First published in *The Times*, 21 April 1986)
In this Masque of images, celebrating Her Majesty the Queen's sixtieth birthday, I set at the centre a Crown and a Nativity. The three gifts greatly needed, in Parts 1, 3 and 5, are brought not by three kings of the Orient, or three Magi – as to the newborn Christ – but by three angels: the Angel of Water, the Angel of Earth and the Angel of Blood. The first brings Water's true nature – purity, the quality of the soul – to the world of polluted waters. The second brings Earth's true nature – what Taoists would call the Way – to the world of external bewilderment and empty distraction. The third brings to the world of conflicting groups Blood's true nature – the lineal unity of mankind, not as an agglomeration of sub-species but as a true family, an orphaned and

bereft family, scattered, like the family in Shakespeare's play *The Comedy of Errors*.

AN ALMOST THORNLESS CROWN   This Crown is slightly thorny (rose-thorny) in that it is the Crown for the Christ of whom the Queen, as head of the English Church, is the earthly representative, exactly as the kings and queens of the earlier world were the earthly representatives of whatever god or goddess represented the spiritual unity of whatever religion then prevailed.

The Crown is slightly thorny, also, in memory of the nettle and weed-flower crown worn by King Lear in Shakespeare's play, at the moment of his rebirth, the point at which he becomes like an idiot-savant, a grey-bearded infant saint in Cordelia's arms, a kind of almost risen Christ in the arms of a kind of Mary. In this way, the Flower Crown associates the Queen with the King who is not only the hero of the crucial work by our national prophet and seer, but is the only King in British legendary history who was originally a god – the Welsh sea-god Llyr, formerly the Irish god Lir, direct heir of a genetic lineage that goes back through Apollo to Ra, the high god of Ancient Egypt, the Sun, in geological time (flower-time) not that long ago.

Again, as in Shakespeare, each flower is also an image of the profane 'sleeping' human being reborn as a sacred 'awakened' one, the bearer of a divinity which is also simply and perfectly natural. 'The divinity in the flower', or 'the god in the flower' is merely one way of naming the 'miraculous' factor in living nature which, in spite of everything, stubbornly insists on being there, peculiar, indescribable and self-evident. The Crown, says this Flower Crown, does not belong to historical time and the tabloid scrimmage of ideologies, but to natural time, where the flower of five million years ago is still absolutely up-to-date, and is even some way in the future, always just ahead of the avant garde of any fashion. The Crown, says this Flower Crown, is the reminder and the presence of this mystery in life – that historical time comes second.

THE RING   This term, 'the ring of the people', occurs in the memoir by the great Sioux Shaman Black Elk, who saw 'the ring' of his people 'broken' in a prophetic vision of the disintegration of the Sioux nation as an independent moral unity. Yet his visionary concept of 'the ring of the people' embraced, finally, all the different peoples of the earth, not only his own tribesmen.
In this poem I combine a 'ring' of some of the past and present invading groups that make up modern Britain with the idea of forging a Crown out of laminated metals, with formal ritual observances, in the manner of forging the blade of a Samurai sword.

CANDLES FOR THE CAKE   This final section is based, not too closely, on the Islamic Sufi masterwork, Attar's *Conference of the Birds*. In Attar's account thirty birds set out, led by the Hoopoe, to find the Simurgh – the God of the Birds. After many ordeals (seven painful valleys of enlightenment) they reach their destination. But each one then finds that the Simurgh is none other than himself or herself, or rather none other than his or her own true self, which is the Divine Self, awakened and revealed by the difficulties of the journey. ('Simurgh' means simply 'thirty birds'.)

In my piece, the birds of the British Isles, thirty of them, not too unlike their Persian brothers and sisters, find their true selves (their spiritual selves) by finding the spiritual unity of the Islands, which is 'the ring of the people', which is also the Crown (of the representative of this 'soul' of the Islands), which is the Queen. As in:

> A Soul is a wheel.
> A Nation's a Soul
> With a Crown at the hub
> To keep it whole

whether the Crown be thorns, feathers, or quivering points in a ring of light on a birthday cake.

'The Song of the Honey Bee' (page 818)
(First published in the *Daily Telegraph*, 23 July 1986)
According to the folklore of the Scottish Borders, HRH Prince Andrew proposed to Miss Sarah Ferguson at a ball in Floors Castle, the magnificent palace of the Duke of Roxburgh, which looks southwards over the River Tweed, just outside Kelso. There is one particular river pool which, because it lies directly under the wall of the old castle gardens, is known as the Garden Wall, and salmon tend to gather down there, in deep water.

For the Royal couple, at the time of their marriage, the College of Heralds devised a composite symbol: a bee hovering over the flower of a thistle. The rich associations of this emblem were a challenge. The Bee has a long ancestry as a manifestation of the Great Goddess. I could see that she was hovering, here, as Venus the Goddess of Love, poised over the flower into which Adonis has just been transformed. Having ended his profane life, he is about to be lifted, reborn, into his new divine life on the breast of the Goddess, as in Shakespeare's favourite tableau. This seemed like rather a lot of fancy dress, for the newlyweds. So I suppressed it, and composed a song made out of glimpses of their more earthly circumstances. This song is being sung by the Bee who, instead of representing the Goddess Venus, is now her son, Cupid, the winged, hovering one, with the arrow and the honey.

'Two Songs' (page 819)
(The first of these first published in the *Daily Telegraph*, 20 December 1988)
According to Astrologers, eight is the lucky number for those born under the sign of Leo. In that case, the perfect birth time, for a Leo looking for maximum good luck, must be eight minutes past eight on the eighth day of the eighth month in the eighty-eighth year of the century. Delaying Princess Beatrice's arrival by exactly ten minutes, the powers that be ensured that she received the full

endowment of eights (maximum six), but also the 'lucky' flaw, the slight, human imperfection that makes the beautiful thing perfect, that intrusive yet minimal 'I', to divert the envy of the gods.

In the First Song, I versify thoughts about the coincidence, pure and simple. In the Second Song, I imagine each of these lucky eights as one of the good fairies, or Angels, who bring the (thought-to-be-impossible) gifts to those who are born into fairy-tales.

'A Masque for Three Voices' (page 821)
(First published in the *Weekend Telegraph,* 4 August 1990)
It would not be so difficult for an epic dramatist to open his drama of the twentieth century, which is also the drama of the modern age, in the year 1900, the year of the birth of Her Majesty Queen Elizabeth the Queen Mother. The two main plots could be shown emerging clearly for the first time from the Boer War and from Russia, though centre-stage is held by the sub-plot, from the Balkans. Major parts begin to appear quietly among the crowd, with Max Planck's quantum theory and Freud's *Interpretation of Dreams* in that first year. The sub-plot and one of the main plots combine to produce the First World War, which gives the other main plot its chance. The two main plots combine where Hitler's tyranny is absorbed by Stalin's. And this drama, as a story with a beginning, middle and end, could be neatly brought to a close in 1990, the year of the Queen Mother's ninetieth birthday, with the collapse of the Soviet system. One self-contained work in the unending cycle.

My poem touches the outlines of this period, seeing it as a drama from the British point of view, with the Queen Mother's role in the foreground. Seeing it, that is, from the point of view of the son of an infantryman of the First World War. This qualification defines the outlook of an offspring of that war, one for whom it was virtually the Creation Story, and such a shattering, all-inclusive, grievous catastrophe that it was felt as a national *defeat,* though victory had somehow been pinned on to it as a consolation medal. At least, it felt so in the tribal lands of the north. In those regions, the impact was naked, with no intellectual anodyne available, no social anaesthetic, certainly not for the very young. Possibly, among the survivors and the children of the survivors of the industrial horde, that sense of a paralysing defeat, the shock of massacre, was sealed by the years of the Great Depression. Yet that numbed mourning for the First World War was ominously enlivened, at a deep level, by a prophetic expectation of the Second. One of my earliest recurrent dreams, long before 1939, was clouds of German parachutists descending on the Calder Valley in West Yorkshire, and my constant fantasy was how this or that part of the valley could be defended, where a sniper might best lie, and who would be traitors. Beneath my rambling daydream was a perpetual unease, that I must prepare myself, become a marksman at least. Everybody felt something similar, in that age of anxiety. Only the style of response varied. No doubt the place of birth, and certainly the timing, which decided the historical horizon, influenced that. My historical horizon, typical for a great many of my generation, was closed by the dead of the First World War and the legend, beyond them, of the slavery of the nineteenth century in the great industrial camps. The inherited mass of general, dumb calamity, unmediated by any theory, meant that the threat of war became, in my head, an assumption of the extreme case – guerrilla escapades against the invader, reprisal executions of our families against the wall of the house – the worst moment. Though the worst moment, in a way, did come, and crushed many homes and lives, obviously it stopped short of occupation by the enemy, but that did not mean we felt free of it, and it had a peculiar effect on our mentality. One who was born of the First World War, who spent his first nine years dreaming of the Second, having lived through the Second went on well into his thirties expecting the nuclear Third and the chaos after. Since these wars were felt to be defensive – against the threats of tyrants and their ideological police-state tyrannies, in which, perhaps, one might not last long – all social theories and even half-political ideas were instinctively screened. Any that smelt of the enemy triggered the response to the threat. The Britons who had fought at the opening of the First World War had fought in the old-fashioned way, innocent professionals, mercenaries, or not knowing why they fought. But they all ended up, transformed by the event, forcibly re-educated, fighting out of a blinded solidarity with their losses, fighting to save somehow the colossal national investment in the dead. They established, for their children, the scale and nature of the investment. Those who fought in the Second World War and waited for the Third not only carried the reckoning of the First World War dead, whom they felt to be their fathers, but had a realistic updated understanding, which emerged from the same arithmetic, of what totalitarian armies of occupation meant, and of the fate of other nations; and the crucial factor in this single-mindedness seems to have been the direct experience, or the innate experience, of the First World War. This would help to explain how the evangelism of ideological dialectics, of alternative, ideal points of view, which were so attractive to a generation born just before the First World War, and became so attractive again, in more sophisticated forms, to a generation born after 1940, sounded to those born between less like the freed intelligence of a new age than like the tyrant's whisper – the double-tongued and ventriloqual tones of one who, when the worst moment came, would suddenly reveal himself as your interrogator, the inquisitor, speaking with the high-minded authority of the torturer and the executioner in the room there just behind him. In the majority, this induced an instinctive, characteristic anti-intellectualism, an immunity, of a certain kind. In a way, it foreclosed our minds against the great European intellectual debate of the next forty years, though an intimately related response produced some compensation in the poetry of that same generation (for whom the worst moment came with a vengeance), in Eastern Europe and Israel. The British outlook that I describe here, I realize, is now almost entirely limited to those born after the First World War but before the late thirties – that slightly different species who took in the blood of the First World War with their mother's milk, and who up to their middle age knew Britain only as a country always at war, or inwardly expecting and preparing for war.

I say this simply to revive a sense of the historical actuality from which I draw these verses and to re-shuffle back into the pack of relative meanings under that word 'nationalism' the British experience of the first half of this century, when both national *and* personal survival were threatened, everything collapsed back to the basic scenario and nothing was listened to but the bulletin from the private crystal set under the breastbone – the sacred tones of 'the ring of the people', on the simplest, human wavelength.

But if this 'last stand' attitude, this biological resilience, is to manifest itself strongly enough to defend itself, it has to be there in the first place – like a dormant genetic resource, ready to be switched on by the 'darkest hour'. Every nation tries to create this secret resource for itself, in some shape or other, as a constitution, or a Holy Book, or a tradition of heroic leaders, or whatever. Some develop it more successfully than others. Those who lack it, or who have lost it, or those artificial conglomerates that have not had the time or occasion to nurture it, soon break into fragments under pressure, and easily collapse. To be effective, it has to be there at the spiritual level as a sacred myth, but in some concrete form, a true palladium, fashioned and purchased at a cost by the nation's real history – only disclosing itself, maybe, in the ultimate trial.

In Britain's case, when the trial came with the Second World War, our sacred myth, the living symbol of a hidden unity, the dormant genetic resource, turned out to be the Crown. As it happened – helped, maybe, by a memory of Elizabeth the First, more surely by a memory of Victoria – the mantle of this palladium settled on the Queen Mother, who was then Queen. A decisive circumstance, it could be, or one that counted heavily, was the accidental fact that for those who fought in and survived the First World War, and entertained brief hopes in the twenties, she was the generation of their wives, and for those who fought in the Second and expected the Third, she was the generation of their mothers. And this enhanced the mythic role of King George VI. Passing time has made it clear that she not only wore the symbol of that 'ring of the people', but, being who she was, rose to the occasion in such a way that she became the incarnation of it.

Then the threat receded – letting certain things sink back out of sight. As new generations began to forget these things, meanings shifted. This was strikingly illustrated to me when this poem, which I had taken pains to make as accessible as possible, was first published in the *Weekend Telegraph*, and a reader complained that he found it incomprehensible. In a sense, it is for him that I have given the piece this general note – which readers of my own age will find superfluous – explaining how the Queen Mother comes to be at the centre of Britain's experience of the drama by which the twentieth century will be remembered.

In the poem, I pass the point of view between three voices, distinguished by the verse form, and by the lighter or darker, the more formal or more intimate tone – as the Three Graeae passed the single eye among themselves, from one to the other. Various moments of the Queen Mother's life come into softer or sharper focus against a procession of simple historical tableaux.

'The Unicorn' (page 813)
(First published in the *Daily Telegraph*, 6 February 1992)
X-RAY   The germ of this whole composition was the idea of a magnetized needle, afloat on the meniscus of a cup or puddle, searching out and pointing to North – a cosmic bearing precariously sustained. At the same time, when the public plan to erect a 25-feet-high bronze Unicorn fountain in Parliament Square, as part of the celebrations of the Royal event, was postponed, I thought of filling the gap, provisionally, with a Unicorn in verse.

The Unicorn's horn coalesced with the needle and became a spine – threaded with the electrical nerve that galvanizes all the aligned and stratified vertebrae as a single, responsive backbone. That spine, influenced by the balancing finger of the needle, became the pillar of a pair of scales – the old-fashioned kind, with the pans hanging down like buckets from the yoke of a milkmaid, old-style. My idea was to let this image of a human scales, weighing the Left and Right of a democracy and responsible for its balance (the fulcrum of that balance being located in the pineal gland, the 'third eye', of a real person), develop itself as a dangling structure of reflections, in various ways counterpointing each other, revolving around each other, slender and quite sparse – like a suspended *mobile*.

FALSTAFF   These verses pose a contrast between two sorts of humour: the not so kind, and the kindly – on the one hand, the sort that depends for its living (for its very survival, like a wretched court jester) on some tyrant, being forced to flatter the peculiar sadism of the Tyrant, and on the other hand, the sort that is (like Falstaff's, with which he nurtures Prince Hal, in Shakespeare's *Henry IV Parts I and II*) bound to nobody, free, affectionate, all-accepting, all-forgiving, illuminating, liberating – as the laughter of a Zen master ought to be.

THE UNICORN   The Unicorn and the Lion were first combined, as the supporters (the beasts on either side) of the royal coat of arms, by James I, in 1603. This pairing of a white and a red beast, rampant and facing each other, in fact resurrected a much older British symbol: two Dragons, one white and one red, perpetually battling deep beneath the mid-point of the Island. One of these mythic

Dragons had become the Dra Goch, the Red Dragon of Britain under which, after the end of the four-hundred-year Roman military occupation, Arthur and his father (Pen-Dragon) fought the invading Germanic tribes, who turned into our Anglo-Saxons, and who, as it happens, fought under a White Dragon. This conflict dragged on, with its Scandinavian variations, until the Norman Conquest, which brought the Frankish (French-German) Red Lion into England (and on to the royal seal and standard of Prince John and Richard I). The island factions of the Red and White Dragons were suppressed, with the dispossessed mass of the population, under the new military occupation of the Norman French. In a sense – politically a real sense – the Norman Red Lion had now taken the place of the Anglo-Saxon White Dragon against the British, and likewise the place of the British Red Dragon against the Anglo-Saxons. It enforced a truce of a kind, and a co-existence of bitter enemies, beneath but also within a single new organism: the Red Lion.

Though the Norman high command and royal court went on speaking French for another four hundred years or so, their slow 'Britishification' jumped a phase when the Tudor Henry VII resuscitated the Welsh Red Dragon and brought it into the Royal Coat of Arms as co-supporter with the Red Lion. This shifting of symbols expressed a reality manifest in the Tudors: the old British were emerging through the Anglo-Saxon, Viking, Norman mix into the control of the national co-existence. This same move must have conjured the subliminal presence, so to speak, of the White Dragon (the recessive Anglo-Saxon) more potently into the Norman Red Lion, in so far as it intensified in a real way the old polarization between Celt and Anglo-Saxon by clarifying the affinity and common interest of Anglo-Saxon and Norman. That this did happen is obvious even today; the consequences are a matter of daily comment, where the Anglo-Saxon's greatest pride is to claim Norman blood and the instinctive antagonism between the Celtic fringe and the Norman–Anglo-Saxon axis is a byword, on both sides.

The Unicorn as a mythic icon belonged to the Scottish crown. At his accession to the British throne, James I substituted the Unicorn for the Welsh Red Dragon on the royal coat of arms. This new rampant white beast now faced the Red (or Golden) Lion. Again, this expressed a political reality, as the assimilation of Scotland to Britain's – now Great Britain's – national Union began. That displacement of the Welsh Red Dragon also expressed a reality: in one sense, Wales had lost power as a family member with turbulent, separate identity, in so far as she had become so physically incorporated into England, even into England's ruling group, through the Tudors, who were now displaced by the Stuarts. But in another sense, the Welsh Dragon had been absorbed by the Unicorn, strengthening the Celtic common quarrel with the Norman–Anglo-Saxon dominance, which eventually pulled southern Ireland out of the marriage truce, still keeps Ulster uncontrollable, and yet has produced the energy for some of Britain's greatest personalities, as well as the steady flow of her cultural wealth.

At the Civil War, the Unicorn and the Lion separated. After the execution of Charles I the Unicorn went with James I's grandson, Charles II, and the Lion stayed with the Commonwealth. By now, perhaps, the Lion was confused: how much was it Norman Lion, how much Anglo-Saxon Dragon, how much the Dragon of the British tribes – how much the Raven, the Horse, the Boar of the older Celts, how much the Raven of the Vikings, and how much remained of the Roman Eagle? As for the British themselves, genetically the most mixed-up gallimaufry of mongrels on earth, the one unity they could cling to, in that crisis, was God and the common language. Since Charles II's Restoration of the Unicorn, in 1660, the red beast and the white, the Lion and the Unicorn, have supported the constitutional monarchy as the God-consecrated shrine of democracy, where the Unicorn is the divine aspect of the Democratic Idea, and the Lion the sacred reality.

This ideogram of the marriage blend of our island races is a magnetic field of genuine influence and meaning. It is curious how it continues to shape Britain at the level on which it operates. The modern transfusion (through Queen Victoria's family) from our Germanic sources, and again (through Her Majesty the Queen Mother's family) from our Celtic sources, can be seen as a consistency, an obedience to the archaic pattern, with a real effect on the dreams that supply the blood to our ideas.

A UNICORN CALLED ARIEL   In this piece, I imagine a supernatural being, a kind of Pegasus-Unicorn, arriving on middle-earth, where (as at the beginning of a film about the supernatural) she divides into three parts – three disguises. The first, her magical horn, her supernatural Majesty, takes on the role of Monarch. The second, her horse-like magical vehicle (named Ariel, after Prospero's magical servant in Shakespeare's *The Tempest*), trots off in the earthly likeness of a racehorse. The third becomes a woman, the racehorse's owner, who likes a bet.

She has landed on a globe where the two alternative political forms, Tyranny and Democracy, are equally helpless in the violent hands of history, and where the human primate, striving to gain control over these erratic forces, promotes them, because of his nature.

In verse five, the statements are abrupt but straightforward. Earth's doom, which is to be absorbed by the expanding sun in a Supernova (some five or six billion years hence), is, like an inherited monarchy, beyond debate: i.e. is 'non-elective'. So much for the first line. In the second line: just as the Russian winter, which froze the armies of Napoleon and Hitler, is a geopolitical fact, so I say the earth's position in the solar system, which will decide the earth's fate, is a geopolitical fact. 'Political corrective' also means what it says. As a fashionable term, to be 'politically correct' means that you behave as those who have power can force you to behave. A 'geopolitical corrective', therefore, is one that brings you into line with its 'geopolitical' law, whether you like it or not. And this particular law, imposing 'political correctness' on a 'solar' scale, puts in perspective (the third line) the human primate's addiction to power – the addiction that pumps the violence into the aforementioned hands of history.

The sixth verse is a riddle, but restricts itself to the iconography of the whole poem. Only in Albion (Albion was the world's name for sacred Great Britain three hundred years before Julius Caesar introduced these islands to history) is this power addiction kept within limits – (a) by that magical Unicorn's horn, (b) by the supernatural immunity of the British Democratic Idea, invested as it is in the monarch, and (c) by the word (the *Logos,* the divine Shakespearean word) of Prospero, who is the genius within the English tongue and who, being the master of Ariel, must also be the woman who owns the thoroughbred. In this verse, the 'magic hand' is Wales (as if it were Merlin's), the 'Unicorn's horn' is Scotland, 'Queen Mab' is Ireland (originally a goddess, she was the principle of royalty in Ulster: whoever married her high priestess – her 'Queen Mab' – became King, and held his crown through her. Later, she became the Queen Maeve of Connaught whose intrigues precipitated the Battle of the Bulls, the theme of the great Irish epic of Cuchulain's single-handed defence of Ulster. Ultimately she became a great figure in the mythos of Yeats, having starred meanwhile in Shakespeare as the 'midwife' of all the 'fairies'), and Prospero is England. The whole assemblage is Great Britain 'spellbound' (that is to say, 'enchanted') by a supernaturally sanctioned democracy. So this verse is a form of the royal coat of arms.

The rest of the poem follows logically. Ariel, her magical or 'divine' mount, gallops his circuits as if tightrope-walking – successfully – over the heavings of a world that is actually the skin of Yin and Yang. This Chinese global symbol of alternating extremes (like two Dragons eating each other from the tail upwards, each living the death of the other) is another form of the 'forces of history' that bounce 'tyrannies and democracies' on the trampoline of the earth's skin. Ariel's successful race is Britain's freedom from such somersaults. 'Villains' – in relationship to Ariel – are the Antonios and Sebastians, the would-be self-serving revolutionary tyrants outwitted and disarmed by Ariel, in *The Tempest.* 'Disasters in the sun' were the dreadful portents, the heralds, of the coup in Rome when a tyrant, Caesar, was toppled by a revolutionary assassin, Brutus, as that event was remembered by Hamlet's friend, Horatio, while he waited on the battlements for the ghost of Hamlet's father. The last lines ride Ariel out of that field of associations to a clear finish.

APPENDIX TWO Variant Titles

ALTERNATIVE TITLE	TITLE IN THIS EDITION
Anecdote	Bedtime Anecdote
Acrobats, The	Acrobats
After There Was Nothing There Was a Woman	After There Was Nothing Came a Woman
Ancient Heroes and the Pilot, The	The Ancient Heroes and the Bomber Pilot
And the Owl Floats	And Owl
Auction	Auction at Stanbury
Bar Room T.V.	Public Bar T.V.
Battle, A	Crow's Account of the Battle
Battle of Osfrontis, The	The Battle of Osfrontalis
Beacon, The (I)	The Stone
Beacon, The (II)	T.V. Off
Beware of the Stars	That Star [Four Tales Told by an Idiot, IV]
Bullfinches	Bullfinch
Cautionary Tale	Criminal Ballad
Chiasmadon	Photostomias, I–III
Cockcrow	Cock-Crows
Crow Goes out to Play	In the Little Girl's Angel Gaze
Crow Goes to the Films	Crow Goes to the Movies
Crow Hymn*	Snake Hymn
Crow Rambles	Life is Trying to be Life
Crow Totem	Crow's Elephant Totem Song
Crow Twice Born	Crow and Mama
Crow's Song about Prospero and Sycorax	Prospero and Sycorax
Crow's Table Talk	Tiger-Psalm
Cuckoo's	Cuckoo
Culprit, The	The Scapegoat
Curlews in April [*Remains of Elmet*]	Curlews, II
Curlews Lift [*Remains of Elmet*]	Curlews, I
Curlews Lift [*SP 1982*]	Curlews, I–II
Dark Women	The Green Wolf
Dead Farms, Dead Leaves	Shackleton Hill
Death-Mask	Ludwig's Death-Mask
Encounter	Full Moon and Little Frieda
Festival of Poets	Poets
Fifth Bedtime Story ('Once upon a time...')	A Bedtime Story
Fifth Bedtime Story ('There was this terrific battle')	Crow's Account of the Battle

Root, Stem, Leaf	*see* A Match, On the Slope, To Be a Girl's Diary
Rules of the Game	The Other
Scapegoat Culprit, The	The Scapegoat
Second Bedtime Story	Lovesong
Sentenced, The	The Risen
Six Years Into Her Posthumous Life	The Dark River
Snake Hymn	A Crow Hymn
Soliloquy of a Misanthrope	Soliloquy
Socrates' Cock	The Accused
Solstice Song	Christmas Card
Starlings Have Come	Starlings Come Suddenly
Stealing Trout	Stealing Trout on a May Morning
The Swallow	A Swallow
These Grasses of Light	Stanbury Moor
Three Voices	What's the First Thing You Think Of?
Toll of Air Raids	Toll
Tomcat	Esther's Tomcat
Two***	Tutorial
Two Astrological Conundrums	Astrological Conundrums
Two Views of the Sea, 1	Fanaticism
Vegetarian	A Vegetarian
Violet	A Violet at Lough Aughrisburg
Watersong	How Water Began to Play [Two Eskimo Songs, 1]
West Dart	The West Dart
What the Serpent Said to Adam	If
When Two Men For The First Time In All	Law in the Country of the Cats
Where the Millstone of Sky	Wadsworth Moor
Where the Mothers	Abel Cross, Crimsworth Dean
White Owl, The	Song Against the White Owl
Woman in the Valley, The	Torridge
Wolf	The Iron Wolf
Word River, The	The River
'X'	Each New Moment My Eyes
'X'	Crow Wakes
You Claw the Door	The Beacon**

* a different poem to 'A Crow Hymn' (p. 200)
** a different poem to the similarly titled poem in *NSP* (where 'The Beacon' is a new title drawing together two formerly separate poems from *Earth-numb*: 'The Stone' and 'T.V. Off')
*** a different poem to 'Two', in *Remains of Elmet*

The following lists reproduce the contents of three texts – *Crow*, *Orts*, *Moortown* (1979) – whose appearance in the *Collected Poems* varies from their contents and ordering as originally published. Also listed are the contents of *Remains of Elmet* and *River* as revised for *Three Books* and *Elmet*.

Crow: From the Life and Songs of the Crow
(expanded edition, Faber and Faber, 1972)

Two Legends
Lineage
Examination at the Womb-Door
A Kill
Crow and Mama
The Door
A Childish Prank
Crow's First Lesson
Crow Alights
That Moment
Crow Hears Fate Knock on the Door
Crow Tyrannosaurus
Crow's Account of the Battle
The Black Beast
A Grin
Crow Communes
Crow's Account of St George
A Disaster
The Battle of Osfrontalis
Crow's Theology
Crow's Fall
Crow and the Birds
Criminal Ballad
Crow on the Beach
The Contender
Oedipus Crow
Crow's Vanity
A Horrible Religious Error
Crow Tries the Media
Crow's Nerve Fails
In Laughter
Crow Frowns
Magical Dangers
Robin Song
Conjuring in Heaven

Crow Goes Hunting
Owl's Song
Crow's Undersong
Crow's Elephant Totem Song
Dawn's Rose
Crow's Playmates
Crowego
The Smile
Crow Improvises
Crowcolour
Crow's Battle Fury
Crow Blacker than Ever
Revenge Fable
A Bedtime Story
Crow's Song of Himself
Crow Sickened
Song for a Phallus
Apple Tragedy
Crow Paints Himself into a Chinese Mural
Crow's Last Stand
Crow and the Sea
Truth Kills Everybody
Crow and Stone
Fragment of an Ancient Tablet
Notes for a Little Play
Snake Hymn
Lovesong
Glimpse
King of Carrion
Two Eskimo Songs
   1. Fleeing from Eternity
   2. How Water Began to Play
Littleblood

Orts (*Rainbow Press, 1978*)

1 The fallen oak sleeps under the bog
2 Let that one shrink into place
3 The Queen of Egypt
4 You have come down from the clouds
5 Skin
6 Air
7 At some juncture the adult dies
8 So much going on
9 Huge global trouble all to earn
10 The earth is strong, faithful, true, and
11 Ophelia
12 The express with a bang

62 He sits grinning, he blurts laughter
63 Before dawn twilight, a sky dry as talc

Moortown (*Faber and Faber, 1979*)

MOORTOWN
Rain
Dehorning
Poor birds
Struggle
Feeding out-wintering cattle at twilight
Foxhunt
New Year exhilaration
Snow smoking as the fields boil
Bringing in new couples
Tractor
Roe-deer
Couples under cover
Surprise
Last night
Ravens
February 17th
March morning unlike others
Turning out
She has come to pass
Birth of Rainbow
Orf
Happy calf
Coming down through Somerset
Little red twin
Teaching a dumb calf
Last load
While she chews sideways
Sheep, I–II
A monument
A memory
The day he died
Now you have to push
The formal auctioneer
Hands

PROMETHEUS ON HIS CRAG
 1 His voice felt out the way. 'I am' he said
 2 Prometheus ... Relaxes
 3 Prometheus ... Pestered by birds roosting and defecating
 4 Prometheus ... Spotted the vulture coming out of the sun
 5 Prometheus ... Dreamed he had burst the sun's mass
 6 Prometheus ... Has bitten his prophetic tongue off
 7 Prometheus ... Arrested half-way from heaven

Remains of Elmet (Three Books, Faber and Faber, 1993)

For Billy Holt
Two Trees at Top Withens
Sunstruck
When Men Got to the Summit
Heather
The Sheep Went on Being Dead
Churn-Milk Joan
The Canal's Drowning Black
Alcomden
Cock-Crows
Walls at Alcomden
The Long Tunnel Ceiling
Shackleton Hill
Two
On the Slope
Curlews Lift
Bridestones
Mount Zion
What's the First Thing You Think of?
The Beacon
Tree
The Sluttiest Sheep in England
Wadsworth Moor
Familiar
Heptonstall Old Church
Crown Point Pensioners
West Laithe Cobbles
Widdop
Emily Brontë
Heptonstall Cemetery

Elmet (*Faber and Faber, 1994*)

The Dark River
Abel Cross, Crimsworth Dene
Football at Slack
Two Photographs of Top Withens
Stanbury Moor
Two Trees at Top Withens
First, Mills
Hill-Stone was Content
The Weasels We Smoked out of the Bank
Leaf Mould
Heptonstall
Wild Rock
Moors
Tick Tock Tick Tock
There Come Days to the Hills
Shackleton Hill

Chinese History of Colden Water
Rhododendrons
Auction at Stanbury
Curlews in April
Curlews Lift
On the Slope
For Billy Holt
Sunstruck
When Men Got to the Summit
Churn-Milk Joan
Heather
Alcomden
The Canal's Drowning Black
The Sheep Went on Being Dead
Bridestones
Cock-Crows
Walls at Alcomden
The Long Tunnel Ceiling
Two
Mount Zion
What's the First Thing You Think of?
Tree
Dick Straightup
The Sluttiest Sheep in England
Wadsworth Moor
Familiar
Heptonstall Old Church
Crown Point Pensioners
West Laithe Cobbles
Widdop
Emily Brontë
Walt
The Horses
The Beacon
Wind
Roarers in a Ring
Pennines in April
Six Young Men
Slump Sundays
Climbing into Heptonstall
Heptonstall Cemetery
Heptonstall
Sacrifice
Telegraph Wires
For the Duration
Anthem for Doomed Youth

River *(Three Books, Faber and Faber, 1993)*

Notes

NOTE ON THE TEXT

The following trade editions and limited editions are referred to in the notes (pamphlets and broadsides are referred to *passim*):

The Hawk in the Rain 1957
Lupercal 1960
Selected Poems [with Thom Gunn] 1962
Recklings 1967 (dated 1966)
Wodwo 1967
Crow: From the Life and Songs of the Crow 1970
Poems [with Ruth Fainlight and Alan Sillitoe] 1971
Crow Wakes 1971
Selected Poems 1957–1967 (1972)
Prometheus on His Crag 1973
Season Songs 1976, 1985
Gaudete 1977
Moon-Bells and Other Poems 1978
Cave Birds 1978
Orts 1978
Moortown Elegies 1978
Adam and the Sacred Nine 1979
Remains of Elmet 1979 (Rainbow Press), 1979 (Faber and Faber)
Moortown 1979
A Primer of Birds 1981
Selected Poems 1957–1981 (1982)
River 1983
Flowers and Insects 1986
Wolfwatching 1989
Moortown Diary 1989
Capriccio 1990
Rain-Charm for the Duchy 1992
Three Books 1993
Elmet 1994
Earth Dances 1994
New Selected Poems 1957–1994 (1995)
Collected Animal Poems (4 vols, 1995)
Tales from Ovid 1997
Birthday Letters 1998
Howls & Whispers 1998

The following abbreviations are used:

CAP   *Collected Animal Poems* (4 vols, Faber and Faber, 1995)
LRB   *London Review of Books*
NSP   *New Selected Poems 1957–1994* (1995)
PBS   Poetry Book Society
Sagar/Tabor   (eds.) Keith Sagar and Stephen Tabor, *Ted Hughes: A Bibliography. 2nd Edition. 1946–1995* (1998)
SP 1972   *Selected Poems 1957–1967* (1972)
SP 1982   *Selected Poems 1957–1981* (1982)
TLS   *Times Literary Supplement*

Details of first publication are given for all uncollected poems. For poems collected in volume-form, details of first periodical publication are given only where variants are involved, or when periodical publication was substantially earlier than volume publication. The publication history of individual collections, from *The Hawk in the Rain* onwards, is summarized in the headnotes.

The copy-text is noted for all poems, i.e. the source for the text as it appears in the present edition, usually the latest printed text to contain revisions. Where a poem underwent revision, the notes record variants in wording between the copy-text and earlier printed versions. No manuscript variants have been recorded. Nor do the notes record differences in punctuation, capitalization or spelling, or minor differences of lineation. Variants are listed in the following sequence: line-number, lemma from the copy-text, square bracket, variant and source. Thus:

12 feet] claws *Three Books*

indicates that in line 12 the copy-text reads 'feet' whereas the variant text – published in *Three Books* – reads 'claws'. Where a variant reading extends to the whole line, or to a substantial proportion of the line, or to more than one line, the lemma and bracket are not used and the variant version alone is given (including its punctuation). Where part of a variant line is given, rather than the entire line, it is preceded by [...], and/or followed by '*etc*'. In recording variants, line-breaks are represented by / and stanza-breaks by //. All line-numbers refer to the text of the poem as it appears on the page in *Collected Poems*; all variants record departures from the text of the poem as it appears on the page in *Collected Poems*.

In the relatively limited cases where there are several variant texts for a poem, the collations work backwards in reverse order of publication, from the copy-text to the earliest variant text, in each case recording additional variants without duplicating shared variants. In some cases a poem differs extensively in two versions, or arguably constitutes different poems; in which case both versions are printed in the text (and entered separately, according to dates of publication) and cross-referenced in the notes.

Hughes frequently changed the titles of poems when moving a poem from one context to another. The present edition invariably prints the title of each poem as it appears in the copy-text, and the endnote records the variant title(s). Appendix Two lists all variant titles.

Orts refers in all cases to the collection of poems published under the title *Orts* (1978), rather than to the sequence of poems collected in *Earth-numb* [*Moortown*] under the title 'Orts'.

Elmet refers in all cases to the revised edition of the *Remains of Elmet*, published as *Elmet* in 1994.

In the text, roman numerals are given for poems divided into sections, and Arabic numbers for individual poems within sequences. In the endnotes likewise: 11.1 refers to section two, line one.

EARLY POEMS AND JUVENILIA (1946–57)

Wild West *Don and Dearne, Whitsuntide 1946. Don and Dearne was the school magazine of Mexborough Grammar School, South Yorkshire, which Hughes attended to July 1949*

Too Bad for Hell *Don and Dearne, July 1948*

The Recluse *Don and Dearne, July 1948*

Initiation *Don and Dearne, July 1948*

Here in the Green and Glimmering Gloom *Don and Dearne, July 1948*

Pastoral Symphony No 1 *Don and Dearne, July 1950. 'Hughes had left Mexborough Grammar School the previous summer and was now doing his National Service at Fylingdales' (Sagar/Tabor p.278); cf. also 'Mayday on Holderness', p.60*

The Little Boys and the Seasons [*text*: Accent, Spring 1957] **2** drive] make **11** The] And the *additional line after* **13**: The pond's untidy with her underclothes, **17** Then] And **18** from] with *additional line after* **22**: And was lying in the marketplace and panting. *additional line after* **23**: The yellow-haired harvest fallen asleep in his arms, *Granta, 8 June 1954. 'This, the first poem Hughes published in Cambridge, appeared (under the pseudonym Daniel Hearing) in the month in which he graduated' – Sagar/Tabor p.278*

The Court-Tumbler and Satirist *(ed.) Karl Miller, Poetry from Cambridge 1952–54, May 1955*

Song of the Sorry Lovers *Chequer, 8 June 1954 (under the pseudonym Peter Crew)*

The Woman With Such High Heels She Looked Dangerous *Delta, Spring 1955*

Poem ('In clear Spring's high ice-breaking heaven') *Chequer, June 1955*

Scene Without An Act *Granta, 12 May 1956; the poem is a longer version of 'Parlour-Piece' (p.25); the final line was adapted to become the final line of 'Thrushes' (p.82)*

Bawdry Embraced *[text*: Reckings] *first published in Poetry (Chicago), Aug 1956.'The first of Hughes's poems to be published beyond Cambridge' [Sagar/Tabor p.279], it was included in the original typescript of The Hawk in the Rain. Draft letter from Hughes to Charles Monteith of Faber and Faber, undated, agreeing to a projected paperback edition of The Hawk in the Rain: 'I deleted a poem from that book at Marianne Moore's request, since she was one of the judges in the YMYWHA prize it got, and there was an element in the piece that might have slightly compromised her if she had seemed to approve. However, it was one of the best pieces, very much in the spirit of the book, and one I would not like to lose, though it seems too late to include among anything I'm doing now. Would it be possible to put it in? First, last or wherever is convenient? I'm enclosing a copy.' [Emory University, Hughes archive]. The poem did not appear in the paperback edition (May 1968), nor in subsequent reprints. It was eventually collected in Recklings (1966). The last six stanzas only were incorporated retrospectively into the Hawk in the Rain section of NSP (1995), under the title 'Song from Bawdry Embraced'. 5 No] Nor Poetry (Chicago), Aug 1956*

The Drowned Woman *Poetry (Chicago), Feb 1957*

THE HAWK IN THE RAIN

Published by Faber and Faber, September 1957. *'The Hawk in the Rain* won the First Publication Award in a contest sponsored in early 1956 by the Young Men's and Young Women's Hebrew Association of New York; the 287 entries were judged by W. H. Auden, Marianne Moore and Stephen Spender. Sylvia Plath typed the manuscript and persuaded Hughes to submit it. On 24 February 1957 a telegram notified the Hugheses that it had won; the prize was immediate publication by Harper, with the opportunity to negotiate independently with a British publisher. Faber accepted the manuscript around 10 May, and returned proofs in about a week.' *(Sagar/Tabor,* p.7). The ordering of the poems differs between the U.S. (Harper) and Faber editions.
  Dedication: To Sylvia

The Hawk in the Rain *title*: The Hawk in the Storm **3** ankle] heel **6** His] Whose **8** Gasping small breaths, catching last sounds, as the wind **10** hawk hangs] hawk **11–12** Like a rapt water-walker springs my dream / With its sleeper staring from the eyes **13** Bloodily] Out of this bloodily **14** strain towards] into **17** suffers] sees *Atlantic Monthly, Feb 1957.*

The Jaguar **17** the] a *Poetry (Chicago), Aug 1957.* **11** As] Like **13** As if in a sudden frenzy: slavering jaw hanging, **14** eye] crazed eye **16–20** But what holds them, from corner to corner swinging, // Swivelling the ball of his heel on the polished spot, / Jerking his head up in surprise at the bars, / Has not hesitated in the millions of years, / And like life-prisoners they through bars stare out. *Chequer, Nov 1954. The variant l.17 – 'Swivelling the ball of his heel on the polished spot' – subsequently became l.14 of 'Second Glance at a Jaguar' (p.151)*

The Thought-Fox **1** this] the *(ed.) Donald Hall, New Poets of England and America 2, June 1962. 'The Thought-Fox' is placed as the opening poem in SP 1972, SP 1982, and NSP*

The Horses *reprinted in Elmet in 1994*

Song *wr. 1949, the earliest poem to be included in one of Hughes's collections*

Parlour-Piece *cf. 'Scene Without An Act', p.12*

Secretary *untitled* **7** Safe home] At home *Saint Botolph's Review, Feb 1956; the Review was a poetry magazine launched in Cambridge by Hughes and friends, early in 1956; the first and only issue contained four poems by Hughes, all included in The Hawk in the Rain*

Soliloquy *untitled Saint Botolph's Review, Feb 1956. Title:* Soliloquy of a Misanthrope *The Hawk in the Rain (but titled 'Soliloquy' in SP 1972, SP 1982, NSP)*

The Dove-Breeder **11** or] and *Granta, 18 May 1957*

Incompatibilities **9–10** But desire, outstripping the hands that mere touch fills, / Has dived *etc* **11** Plummets] Plummeting *The Nation, July 1957*

September *title:* Parting *Spectator, 2 Aug 1957*

Fallgrief's Girl-friends **25–6** mannequin/Leads] mannequins/Lead *Saint Botolph's Review, Feb 1956*

Wind *reprinted in Elmet in 1994*

Roarers in a Ring **13** held] hold *The Nation, 22 Dec 1956. Reprinted in Elmet in 1994*

Law in the Country of the Cats *untitled* **21** mistaking] remembering **23** eye] eyes *Saint Botolph's Review, Feb 1956*

The Casualty **26** Widens] Opens wide **31** edge] lip *[a reading specific to this text of the poem] Poetry (Chicago), Aug 1957.* **16** Hear now] Now **18** touches it] touches **25** his] the **30** their] the **31** tender] precious **34** Till they] At last **35** On] At *Chequer, Nov 1954*

Six Young Men 8 ridiculous] hysterical **13** seven] thirty
15 a rumouring] rumouring **28** It is fearful seeing a man's
photograph **33** one place which] sole place that **34** In his Sunday
best, see *etc* **35** onto] and onto **40** or] nor **41** Your hand's less
vivid than their splashing blood: **43** permanent] actual *Delta,
Summer 1957. Reprinted in Elmet in 1994*

Two Wise Generals *James, Lord of Douglas, known as the Black
Douglas, fought for Scottish independence at the side of Robert the
Bruce, on whose death in 1329 he was entrusted to carry his
monarch's heart on a pilgrimage to the Holy Land and bury it
there, but was killed fighting the Moors in Spain en route to
Palestine in 1330.*

The Ancient Heroes and the Bomber Pilot *title*: The Ancient
Heroes and the Pilot *Poetry (Chicago), Aug 1957*

The Martyrdom of Bishop Farrar *Robert Farrar (or Ferrar), Bishop
of St David's, was burnt at the stake during the reign of Queen
Mary; his unflinching Protestantism is described in Foxe's Book of
Martyrs. According to family tradition Hughes's mother was a
descendant of Farrar. Subsequent to its appearance in The Hawk in
the Rain, the poem was published as a pamphlet by Richard
Gilbertson in March 1970*

UNCOLLECTED (1957–59)

Letter *New Statesman, 28 Sept 1957*

Quest *Grapevine, Feb 1958; wr. 1957*

Constancy *London Magazine, Aug 1958*

Shells *New Yorker, 1 Aug 1959*

Gulls Aloft *Christian Science Monitor, 12 Dec 1959*

Snails *Christian Science Monitor, 15 Dec 1959*

LUPERCAL

Published by Faber and Faber, March 1960. The title refers to the
Roman festival of the Lupercalia, held on 15 February, whose
purpose was to secure fertility for the field, the flocks, and the
people. *Dedication*: To Sylvia

Everyman's Odyssey 2 trust was] smiles were *(ed.) Vernon
Watkins, Landmarks and Voyages, PBS, Dec 1957*

Mayday on Holderness 31 Gallipoli: *Hughes's father fought in
Gallipoli campaign of World War 1, and was one of only seventeen
survivors of an entire battalion of Lancashire Fusiliers; cf. also*

'Out', *in Wodwo (p.165), and 'Dust As We Are' in Wolfwatching* (p.753)

February 2 pineforest] pinewoods seen 3 or that long] the long 5 hairless, knuckled] hairless and knuckled 9 Print] Stand on 10 parkland] forests *London Magazine, April 1959*

Crow Hill 1 oozing] stinking *New Statesman, 15 Mar 1958*

A Woman Unconscious [*text*: NSP] 24 head?] head. *Lupercal.* 5 The quick] And the quick *Poetry (Chicago), Aug 1959*

Strawberry Hill *was the name of the house which Horace Walpole bought in 1747 and converted into a nature-taming monument to the Gothic taste of the time*

Dick Straightup 43 bigger and deeper] deeper and bigger 46 when] as 53–8 ['*Obit.*'] omitted *Northern Broadsheet Summer 1959; the 'Obit.' was added after the death of the original of Dick Straightup. Reprinted in Elmet in 1994*

A Dream of Horses *title*: Groom's Dream 7 pockets and straw] pockets, straw 8 Into a darkness ruining and deafening to horses 10 sleep-dazed] sleep-staring 11 horses] enraged horses 14 this plunging] a plunging blackness 16 lantern] lanterns 20 listening] listening to horses *final stanza is headed 'Envoi'* 25 Now let us, tied, be quartered] Let me, tied, be torn to quarters *London Magazine Aug 1958. First published in the Grecourt Review, Nov 1957*

Esther's Tomcat *title*: Tomcat *New Yorker, 9 Jan 1960.* 9–14 *a version of the South Yorkshire legend of the Barnburgh knight, in which the knight and the cat are both found dead, locked together*

Historian *title*: The Historian *Nation, 15 Nov 1958*

Pennines in April *reprinted in Elmet in 1994*

Hawk Roosting *title*: Roosting Hawk *The Grecourt Review, May 1959*

Nicholas Ferrer *In 1625 Ferrar established a community at Little Gidding in Huntingdonshire, based on The Book of Common Prayer and charitable works in the locality; after his death in 1637 the community was broken up by the Puritans, who feared that it promoted the return of Romish practices to England; Ferrar's manuscripts were burned*

Urn Burial *Urn Burial (1658) is the title of a treatise on funerary customs and meditation on mutability, by Sir Thomas Browne*

Of Cats *an earlier printed version of the poem contains many variants, including a different opening quatrain*: That man's subconscious mind is constituted / Entirely of cats, no wise man for an instant disbelieves – Father to daughter, mother to son inherited / (Whereby the least of cats gets fully nine lives). – *and an* *additional final 'Envoi':* A cat on a shop doorstep gazes steadily through the thick / Street-width of legs, wheels, exhaust: deep in his centuries as in cushions. / From a shop doorway a cat returns her look: / Thus, in the clutter of your brain, the eternals make their assignations. *Harper's Magazine, June 1958*

View of a Pig 36 scour] scrub *TLS, 7 Aug 1959*

Wilfred Owen's Photographs *title: cf. Hughes's review of (ed.) Ian Parsons, Men Who March Away: Poems of the First World War (1965):* 'We know that [Owen] intended his poems – as he intended those photographs of the trenches, emergency operations and like, which he wanted to magnify and display in London – to drive the actuality of the front-line sufferings into the faces of those safe in England.' *The poem refers to an episode from the early career of Charles Stewart Parnell, when the 'obstructionist' Home Rule element among Irish MPs in the 1870s espoused the abolition of flogging in the Navy, as part of a wider tactics of espousal designed to obstruct the workings of the House of Commons*

An Otter 11.1 The hunt's] Now the hunt's 11.15 logic; he] logic and he *Encounter, March 1960*

November [*text*: SP 1972] 12 his] its *Lupercal.* 2 Was sodden] Was black, sodden 3–4 In the sunk lane/The ditch] I took the sunk lane/ Where the ditch 14 the ground. A wind] the ground as a wind 15 fresh] new 17 hand] band 18 hardened] chilled 21 farms. In a moment] farms, and in a moment 33 Under a dark sheltering oak leaned *Critical Quarterly, Summer 1959*

The Perfect Forms 3 *cf. William Blake, The Marriage of Heaven and Hell, Plate 8: 'One thought fills immensity.'*

Thrushes 19 Carving] Paring *Encounter, March 1958; wr. 1957*

Bullfrog 10 fantastical] fantastically 15 To see] Now to see 16 all] with all *New Yorker, 8 Aug 1959*

Pike 23 two feet long] two feet *Encounter, March 1960*

Snowdrop 8 heavy as metal] as heavy as metal *SP 1982; the Lupercal reading was restored in NSP*

Lupercalia 11.2 abides] stays 11.11 engross her bed] bring her to bed *Poetry (Chicago), Aug 1959*

UNCOLLECTED (1960–67)

A Fable *TLS, 9 Sept 1960*

The Storm *translation of a passage from Homer, Odyssey Bk v; broadcast on the Third Programme, 10 Nov 1960; no print-publication*

Lines to a Newborn Baby *Texas Quarterly, Winter 1960*

To F.R. at Six Months *Sewanee Review, Jan–Mar 1963. Title*: For Frieda in her First Months *Western Daily Press, 22 Feb 1961. Title*: Lines to Three Months *Evidence, Winter 1961/2*

Dully Gumption's College Courses *London Magazine, March 1961; cf the related poem, 'Dully Gumption's Addendum', in Recklings (p.126). Section III ('Theology') was collected as a separate poem in Wodwo (p.161); section IV ('Humanities') was collected as a separate poem in Recklings (p.140).* 'The idea of "Dully Gumption's College Courses" was to write a kind of pocket college education for each discipline.' ('*Ted Hughes and Crow: An interview with Ekbert Faas', London Magazine, Jan 1971*)

My Uncle's Wound *Poetry at the Mermaid (PBS), 16 July 1961; cf. 'Under High Wood', p.770*

The Road to Easington [*text*: ed. Robert Conquest, New Lines 2, August 1963] **19** in] into **23** *expanded to*: And its depth calling to the road. Here / The sea's sound sluices everywhere – a grubby scrap-iron **27** envelopes] interesting envelopes *Listener, 23 Aug 1962*

Sunday Evening *Atlantic Monthly, May 1963*

Poem to Robert Graves Perhaps *Poetry (Chicago), Dec 1963*

On Westminster Bridge *Poetry (Chicago), Dec 1963. ll.18–20 reappear with alterations in 'Karma' (p.167, ll.28–31), and were subsequently incorporated into the expanded version of 'Stations' (p.158, III.1–4), from SP 1972 onwards. The poem alludes to Wordsworth's sonnet 'Composed upon Westminster Bridge, September 3, 1802'*

After Lorca *Poetry (Chicago), Dec 1963*

Era of Giant Lizards *Poetry (Chicago), Dec 1963; the poem was adapted to become 'Keats', in Recklings (p.128)*

Small Hours *Poetry (Chicago), Dec 1963*

Bad News Good! *Agenda, Dec–Jan 1963/4*

Dice *Critical Quarterly, Summer 1964. Section VI ('Guinness') was collected as a separate poem in Recklings (p.127)*

O White Elite Lotus *Critical Quarterly, Winter 1964*

Carol *Sunday Times, 19 Dec 1965*

Warm Moors *Critical Quarterly, Spring 1966.* **1** pane] faucet **1** to] by **7** score] stone **8** scoring] squaring **9** This is the way] Step by step *Bookdealer, 13 Nov 1986 (publication of an early draft of the poem). The last four lines of 'Warm Moors' reappear as the last four lines of section V of 'Skylarks' in Wodwo (p.173)*

Folk-Lore *Critical Quarterly, Spring 1966*

Gibraltar *New Statesman, 8 Apr 1966, where it appears together with 'A Colonial' (p.134)*

Birdsong *London Magazine, Sept 1966*

Plum Blossom *Transatlantic Review, Autumn 1966; an expanded version of 'Plum-Blossom' in Recklings (stanzas two and three appear as section 1 of the Recklings version, cf. p.132)*

The Last Migration *ed. Diana Spearman, The Animal Anthology, 25 Oct 1966 (written specifically for the anthology); the first half of the poem is the source for 'Irish Elk', p.497*

The Burning of the Brothel *published as a pamphlet, Goliard Press, Oct–Nov 1966*

To W.H. Auden *Sunday Times, 19 Feb 1967; published on the occasion of Auden's sixtieth birthday*

RECKLINGS

Published in a limited edition by Turret Books, January 1967 (dated 1966), 150 copies. There was no Faber edition. *Recklings* draws on poems written between 1956 and 1966, during the same period as the composition of *Wodwo*. Poems which had appeared together in periodicals were divided between the two collections, which were published within months of each other. Two of the *Recklings* poems are entered elsewhere in the present edition: 'Logos' was published in both *Recklings* and *Wodwo*, and is here placed in *Wodwo* (p.155); 'Bawdry Embraced' was first collected in *Recklings* but originally intended for *The Hawk in the Rain*, and is here entered at its date of first periodical publication (p.13).

'A Match', 'On the Slope', and 'To be a Girl's Diary' were included in the Harper & Row (U.S.) edition of *Wodwo* as a sequence entitled 'Root, Stem, Leaf', and were reprinted thus in *SP 1972* and *SP 1982*, though not thereafter.

'Recklings': the smallest and weakest animals in a litter.

On the Slope *[text: Elmet]* 11 By] *On Three Books.* 10 Foxglove and harebell] Foxglove, harebell *SP 1982.* 5 her] *the Poetry Review, Autumn 1966. Title*: A Pause for Breath 11 By the steep slope] By the steep lane 15 dimming] dimmed *New Yorker, 27 Aug 1966. Collected in the Harper (U.S.) edition of Wodwo – and in SP 1972, SP 1982 – as 'Root, Stem, Leaf, 11'; reprinted as a separate poem in Three Books and Elmet*

Water *first published in the Observer, 6 Jan 1963. Collected in Moon-Bells and in NSP*

Fishing at Dawn *first published in the New Statesman, 26 May 1961*

Dully Gumption's Addendum *an earlier periodical version contains an additional line after each stanza, as follows: 1) What other* prodigies? *2)* Is this the birth of Caedmon? *3)* In the merry head of England? *4)* An eleventh plague? O Egypt! *5)* Where's the Moses for it? *6)* He was a tractable booby! *7)* All this done with smiles? *8)* Tell it all, tell it all! *9)* Would God he had been born African! *10)* Like Elijah? *Poetry (Chicago), May 1962. Cf. 'Dully Gumption's College Courses', p.98*

Guinness *first published as section* VI *of 'Dice' (p.107), Critical Quarterly, Summer 1964*

Flanders *title*: Flanders, 1960 1 eyes] eyeballs 4 Still they] They 5 the] their *Observer, 16 April 1961*

Keats *l.1 and ll.4–5 are adapted from 'Era of Giant Lizards' (p.106)*

Beech Tree *dated 1961 in typescript*

Toll *title*: Toll of Air Raids *Observer, 16 April 1961*

Memory *first published TLS, 14 July 1961. Collected in NSP*

Heatwave *first published in Poetry (Chicago), Dec 1963; collected as poem no. 4 of 'Orts', in Earth-numb [Moortown] (1979)*

Thaw 1 Who'll calibrate] Or calibrate 4 pillows grow deeper] a pillow deepens *New Yorker, 18 Mar 1967*

Plum-Blossom, I-III *a different version of the poem appeared in the Transatlantic Review, Autumn 1966 (cf. p.114); section* II *of the present version was published separately under the title 'More Theology', in Moments of Truth: Nineteen Short Poems by Living Poets, Keepsake Press, Oct 1965*

Public Bar T.V. *a different poem to 'Public Bar T.V.' in Wodwo; never reprinted*

Trees 1 I asked the holly, 'What is your life if ...?' 8 I asked the birch, 'How can you...?' *additional line after* 15: Like a ghost I tried to fade. *New Yorker, 17 July 1965. Collected in NSP*

A Match 12 *omitted SP 1982.* 14 not] but *Critical Quarterly, Spring 1966. Collected in the Harper (U.S.) edition of Wodwo – and in SP 1972, SP 1982 – as 'Root, Stem, Leaf, 1'. Collected in NSP as a separate poem*

Small Events 6 They] For they 19 outward nor inward] inward nor outward *New Yorker, 18 Mar 1967. Collected in NSP*

To be a Girl's Diary *collected in the Harper (U.S.) edition of Wodwo – and in SP 1972, SP 1982 – as 'Root, Stem, Leaf,* III'

Stealing Trout on a May Morning [*text*: NSP] 94 trireme] schooner *Three Books (River). additional line after* 23: Fluffed like souls afloat on their heavenly pastures, 33 wrappers] wrapper 80 river] army of river 82 of] from 92 four] three 101 On] From *Recklings. Title*: Stealing Trout 3 5 a.m.] 4 a.m. 6 reeking] smoking 14 are like brides] like brides are 16 orchards are the] orchards, the

20 open] wide 23 two] five 45 sky] river 51 the night-moor] there
57 *expanded to*: Off ploughlands and lanes – wanting the pure peat
whisky / Fed from the breast on Dartmoor. 58 At first] For minutes
64 *expanded to*: Where the bundled hazel rods, hugging each other,
/ Lean over and peer in and cannot / Make up their minds. Here it
is shallow 77 Now I deepen. And here comes the mob 78 coming
towards me] piling down 79 press through] am missing
84 mapless] high mapless 89 sudden, strong] strike and strong
90 real] genuine 95 It forces] Forces 98 mangy] scabby 99 about]
circa *New Yorker, 21 March 1964. Collected in Recklings, Three
Books (where it is first incorporated into River) and NSP*

Humanities *previously published as section IV of 'Dully Gumption's
College Courses' (cf. p.98), London Magazine, March 1961*

Tutorial *Title*: Two 3 What are those tilted tomes? Boards 5 stew
them up to] stew up words to 6 He is fat] He is gone at the
seams 11 wharfe-weed] warf-weed 12 enquiry] his enquiry
Northern Review, Spring 1965. Title: Tutorial 10 straining]
draining *New Statesman, 2 Nov 1962. Collected in NSP*

Poltergeist *first published in the Spectator, 25 Nov 1960*

Last Lines *first published in the Observer, 16 April 1961*

The Lake 16 Yet how] How *New Yorker, 21 Oct 1961. Collected
in NSP*

Unknown Soldier 5 The] A *first published in Critical Quarterly,
Winter 1960*

WODWO

Published by Faber and Faber, May 1967. Many of the poems had
appeared in periodicals from as early as 1960 onwards. The Harper
& Row (U.S.) edition of *Wodwo* included 'Root, Stem, Leaf'
(comprising three poems from *Recklings* – cf. endnotes to
Recklings), and 'Scapegoats and Rabies', neither of which appeared
in the Faber edition; the latter contained 'Logos', omitted from the
U.S. edition, and added sections II and III of 'Gog'. The texts of
several of the *Wodwo* poems were subsequently revised for their
inclusion in *SP 1972*; these revisions have been incorporated, and
are noted below. Copy-text: *Wodwo* except where otherwise stated.

Part II of *Wodwo*, comprising five short stories and a radio play,
is omitted from the present edition. Hughes prefaced *Wodwo* with
an Author's Note: 'The stories and play in this book may be read
as notes, appendix and unversified episodes of the events behind the
poems, or as chapters of a single adventure to which the poems are
commentary and amplification. Either way, the verse and the prose
are intended to be read together, as parts of a single work.' He
later planned to collect *The Hawk in the Rain, Lupercal* and

Wodwo in one volume (along the lines of *Three Books*), omitting Part II of *Wodwo*.

Dedication: To my Mother and Father

Epigraph: 'Sometimes with dragons he wars, and with wolves also, / Sometimes with wild men of the woods who lived among the crags, / Both with bulls and bears, and boars at other times, / And giants that pursued him over the high fell.' [from *Sir Gawain and the Green Knight, ll. 720–23*]

Thistles 3 Or] And *TLS, 9 Sept 1960*

Still Life 2 the] this *London Magazine, Feb 1962*

Her Husband 8 blood-weight] blood-count 12 slams] claps *Spectator, 24 March 1961*

Cadenza [*text*: NSP] 10 collision] collisions 11 a] as a *Wodwo*. 17 dives shut like a burned land back to] dives back like a burned land to *Agenda, April–May 1965.* 4 bared] bare 11 as a] a 13 An emerald] A turquoise 14 The sea lifts] A sea that lifts 17 Till the sky shuts back like a burned land to its spark *New Yorker, 30 May 1964*

Ghost Crabs [*text*: SP 1982] 23 beds] our beds 39 turmoil] moil [*a reading specific to this text of the poem*] *SP 1972.* 24 rooms] our rooms 25 possessions] our possessions *Wodwo. Title*: Nightfall 26 brains] our brains *Listener, 21 July 1966; broadcast 17 October 1965 (Third Programme) as 'Nightfall'*

Boom *in SP 1972 the title 'Boom' brings together three poems from Wodwo ('Boom', 'Public Bar T.V.' and 'Wino'); 'Tutorial' (from Recklings) and 'Kafka' (section II of 'Wings') were added to 'Boom' in SP 1982; the poems were never reprinted as a sequence thereafter*

Ludwig's Death Mask *title*: Death Mask *New Statesman, 17 June 1966*

Second Glance at a Jaguar 11 mouth] teeth *New Yorker, 25 March 1967*

Public Bar T.V. *title*: Bar-Room T.V. *SP 1982. A different poem to 'Public Bar T.V.' in Recklings; first published in the New Statesman, 27 Oct 1961*

Fern *additional stanza after 4*: A dancer, leftover, among crumbs and remains / Of God's drunken supper, / Dancing to start things up again. / And they do start up – to the one note of silence. 9–10 How many went under? Everything up to this point went under. / Now they start up again / Dancing gravely, like the plume *New Yorker, 18 March 1967*

A Wind Flashes the Grass [*text*: SP 1982] 13 They crowd] And crowd *Wodwo*

A Vegetarian *title*: Vegetarian *Observer, 4 Nov 1962*

Sugar Loaf *first published in the Observer, 16 April 1961*

Bowled Over *title*: One **14** bullet!] bullet? *The Northern Review, Spring 1965; recorded 29 Aug 1962 for 'The Poet Speaks'* (Argo Records)

Wino *first published in the Observer, 16 April 1961*

Logos *previously published in Recklings.* **1** blinding] burning **3–4** [...] Then if it comes / So unlikely far, against such odds *etc* **9** But space shudders in nightmare. Awakening **10** tastes] she tastes **11** its] her **12** which] that *Recklings.* **2** a] the **9** But space shudders in nightmare. Awaking **15** ancient] mangled *Critical Quarterly, Summer 1966*

The Rescue **24** Wait. That's all wrong. How queer! I can see it. / The five never moved. *Atlantic Monthly, March 1962*

Stations [*text*: SP 1972] *section* III *is not present in the Wodwo text, but was added to the poem as reprinted in SP 1972, SP 1982 and NSP; the additional lines were drawn from ll.28–38 of 'Karma' (cf. p.167), which was not included in SP 1972, SP 1982 or NSP*

The Green Wolf [*text*: SP 1982] **1** My] Your **10** I] You **16** me] you *Wodwo. Title*: Dark Women **19** smouldering] flaring [*otherwise this early periodical text is identical with SP 1982*] *Observer, 6 Jan 1963*

Theology *previously published as section* III *of 'Dully Gumption's College Courses' (p.98), London Magazine, March 1961*

Gog, I–III [*text*: NSP, *for section* I, *otherwise Wodwo*] *the Harper (U.S.) ed. of Wodwo, SP 1972, SP 1982, NSP all reprint section* I *only* 1.16 trees] stones *Wodwo.* 1.9 lichens] mosses 11–12 *transposed* 1.15 pound] beat 1.22 horizon bears] horizons bear *The Nation, 22 April 1961.* III *title*: The Knight (A Chorus) *printed separately, Critical Quarterly, Spring 1966*

Kreutzer Sonata *first published in the New Statesman, 23 Aug 1963; cf. Tolstoy's story of the same title*

Out, I–III [*section* III *only*] *title*: Remembrance Day **1** the mouth] a mouth **14** So] Then **15** You] Your *Granta, 19 Oct 1963. To be 'Out' is to be away on military service*

New Moon in January **3** warning] warnings *Observer, 6 Jan 1963*

The Warriors of the North *first published in the Observer, 4 Nov 1962*

Karma *title*: Public Speech *Critical Quarterly, Winter 1966. In SP 1972, SP 1982 and NSP, ll.28–38 were incorporated to become section* III *of the revised text of 'Stations' (p.158); 'Karma' was never collected elsewhere after its publication in Wodwo*

Song of a Rat, I–III *part* I *only is collected as a separate poem in SP 1982; parts* I–III *are collected in NSP*

Heptonstall [*text*: SP 1972] 2 Skull of an idiot] The hill's collapsed skull *Wodwo, Elmet (1994) [the SP 1972 reading was restored in NSP]. Title:* Hill Top 2 Head of an idiot 7 Under] Beneath *New Yorker, 27 Feb 1965. Reprinted in Elmet (1994)*

Ballad from a Fairy Tale *rewritten as 'The Angel' in Remains of Elmet (p.492)*

Skylarks [*text*: NSP] *sections* IV *and* VIII *are not present in the Wodwo text, but were added to the poem as reprinted in SP 1972, SP 1982, NSP.* VII.2 a bonfire] the bonfire *Critical Quarterly, Autumn 1966*

Mountains *first published in the Observer, 5 Aug 1962*

Wings, I–III II [*text*: NSP] *title:* Kafka Writes II.4 wall of glare] glare *Wodwo. In SP 1972 and NSP, section* II *is printed as a separate poem entitled 'Kafka' (omitted from the U.S. ed. of SP 1972); in SP 1982, 'Kafka' is printed as section* V *of a sequence entitled 'Boom' (cf. note to 'Boom', p.1249).* II.6 *the name 'Kafka' in Czech means 'jackdaw'.* III.3 is lifting] lifting III.10 manna] bread *London Magazine, Sept 1966 [prints section* III *only]*

Pibroch 6 A pebble] Stone *(eds.) Paul Engle and Joseph Langland: Poet's Choice, Dial Press Oct 1962, where Hughes appends the following note:* '. . . A Pibroch is a piece of music for bagpipes, a series of variations "chiefly martial, but including dirges". No sound hits me so deeply as bagpipes. A familiar spirit is supposed to serve a family for generations, and I look on this poem as an heirloom.' *First published in Critical Quarterly, Winter 1960*

The Howling of Wolves [*text*: SP 1972] 6 viola] violin *Wodwo*

Gnat-Psalm [*text*: SP 1972] *epigraph:* 'The Gnat is of more ancient lineage than man. – Proverb.' 7 swipes] thrusts 25 Singing] Singing/Singing 30 tree] hill *additional lines after* 30: And the towns, camped by their graveyards, / Saddening into an utter darkness 32 And highways and airways 34–5 *expanded to:* The wind's dance, the death dance / Plunging into marshes and undergrowth / And cities like cowdroppings huddling to dust *Wodwo.* 21 sun] suns *London Magazine, Sept 1966*

Full Moon and Little Frieda *title:* Encounter *divided into two sections, of which the second is omitted from Wodwo:* The cows submerge. / The moon has opened you wide and bright like a pond. // The moon lifts you off the grass – / A cat's cradle of spider webs, where the stars are trembling into place. // The brimming moon looks through you and you cannot move. // Any minute / A bat will fly out of a cat's ear. *(ed.) Chad Walsh, Today's Poets, Nov 1964. Title:* Full Moon. *Atlantic Monthly, Dec 1963. [on its first publication – Observer, 27 Jan 1963 – the title* *and text of the poem were identical with the final version as collected in Wodwo]*

Wodwo *first published in the New Statesman, 15 Sept 1961; 'wodwo' ('wild man', 'satyr', 'troll') is a term taken from Sir Gawain and the Green Knight – cf. the epigraph to the present collection*

UNCOLLECTED (1967–70)

Scapegoats and Rabies [*text*: NSP] 1.23 Their] From their III.3–4 Grow crystal balls/Rolling with visions v.6 But though] Though v.6 has] had v.24 And] But *New Statesman, 13 Jan 1967. Subsequent to its periodical publication the poem was published as a pamphlet (Poet & Printer, April 1967); it was included in the U.S. edition of Wodwo, and collected in SP 1972, SP 1982, NSP*

from **Three Legends** *Journal of Creative Behaviour, Poetry Supplement, Summer 1967; the first of the three 'legends' was collected as the opening poem in Crow, where it appears in the present edition (cf. 'Two Legends', p.217); these are among the earliest Crow poems to appear in print*

T.V. On *Listener, 28 Sept 1967*

The Brother's Dream *ed. George MacBeth, Poetry 1900–1965, 27 Nov 1967 (broadcast 22 Nov 1965, Third Programme)*

Dog Days on the Black Sea *Critical Quarterly, Spring/Summer 1968*

'?' *Critical Quarterly, Spring/Summer 1968*

Crowquill *Poetry Gala (Poetry Society), late 1968*

Ballad of Bauble-Head *New American Review, Jan 1970*

Crow's Feast *Halifax Evening Courier, 30 Jan 1970*

A Crow Hymn *published as a pamphlet, the Sceptre Press, March 1970*

Song of Woe *wr. 1967; Critical Quarterly, Summer 1970*

Existential Song *wr. 1967; London Magazine, July/Aug 1970*

A Lucky Folly *wr. 1968; Workshop, Sept 1970*

Fighting for Jerusalem *wr. 1966; published as a poster, MidNAG, Oct 1970, and in the TLS, 9 Oct 1970*

This Game of Chess *privately printed as a broadside, probably Christmas 1970, and based on a photograph of three Elisabeth Frink sculptures of heads*

[CROW]

Crow is both a single work and a loose grouping of texts, published in instalments between 1967 and 1973, ranging from individual periodical poems to broadsides, pamphlets and limited editions. These both preceded and followed the familiar Faber edition (October 1970), whose subtitle – *From the Life and Songs of the Crow* – suggests both a larger context and the continuous, or discontinued, nature of the process. Many Crow poems were never published, and one-third of the published poems were never integrated into the sequence as established by the Faber edition, whose cover announced that it 'contains the passages of verse from about the first two-thirds of what was to have been an epic folk-tale'. When he gave readings from *Crow*, Hughes usually provided a narrative framework for the poems, and he contemplated publishing the latter as a separate prose work.

The present edition includes all uncollected Crow poems, and retains the sequence of Crow collections, thus: *Four Crow Poems* (August 1970), *A Few Crows* (October 1970), the first Faber edition of *Crow* (October 1970), *Crow Wakes* (April 1971), and the Crow group comprised by the Hughes section of *Poems: Ruth Fainlight, Ted Hughes, Alan Sillitoe* (April 1971). Consequently, eleven poems from the Faber edition are here placed within *Four Crow Poems* and *A Few Crows*.

The American edition of *Crow* (Harper & Row, March 1971) included seven poems absent from the first Faber edition: 'Crow Hears Fate Knock on the Door', 'Crow's Fall', 'The Contender', 'Crow Tries the Media', 'Crow's Elephant Totem Song', 'Crow Paints Himself into a Chinese Mural' and 'The Lovepet'. With the exception of 'The Lovepet', all of these poems were incorporated into the expanded Faber edition of *Crow* (December 1972), which is the copy-text for the present edition. (See Appendix Three for a complete contents list of the expanded *Crow*). For Crow poems not included in that edition, the texts are specified below.

Four uncollected Crow poems – 'The Lovepet', 'Life is trying to be life', 'Prospero and Sycorax', and 'Tiger-psalm' – were later collected in *Earth-numb* (1979), which is where they appear in the present edition.

Four Crow Poems
Published as four broadsides, 25 August 1970

King of Carrion 10 Into the darkness and dumbness and blindness of the gulf *Listener 26 Sept 1968*

Crow and the Birds 5 When] While *Poetry Gala (PBS) Winter 1968*

A Few Crows
Published by the Rougemont Press, October 1970. Illustrated by Reiner Burger

A Kill 7 by] with 12 atom] atoms *A Few Crows*

Notes for a Little Play 20 And this] This *A Few Crows*

A Grin 9 that] but that 17 So] And *A Few Crows*

The Battle of Osfrontalis *title*: The Battle of Osfrontis *A Few Crows*

Crow Tyrannosaurus 13–16 *omitted from A Few Crows, but included in all other texts.* 17 Even man he] And man 19 innocents] victims 25 trapsprung] of itself *Observer, 12 Jan 1969*

Carnival *omitted from Crow; never reprinted*

Crow. From the Life and Songs of the Crow
Published by Faber and Faber, October 1970 (expanded 2nd edition, December 1972). Dedication: In Memory of Assia and Shura.

Two Legends *first published in the Journal of Creative Behaviour, Poetry Supplement, Summer 1967, as the first of 'Three Legends' (cf. p.191)*

Lineage *additional line after* 16: Who begat Yes *Ted Hughes: Animal Poems, published by Richard Gilbertson, Aug 1967*

Crow Alights 5 And he] He *Michigan Quarterly Review, Summer 1970.* 5 horror] terror 6 horror] terror 12 embers] ashes 14 this] a white *Halifax Evening Courier, 30 Jan 1970.* 7 rain-sodden] rain-rotten [*otherwise identical to the text as published in Crow*] *Listener, 24 July 1969*

Crow Hears Fate Knock on the Door *added to the 1972 printing of Crow*

Crow's Account of the Battle *title*: Fifth Bedtime Story 5 hold] reach 23 drain-pipe] tap *additional line after* 46: People fell to bits too easily *New American Review, Jan 1970. Title*: A Battle 4 screams higher groans deeper] screams and whistles higher 5 hold] hear 7 to escape the] from blasts of 15 courses] ways 16 stone, earth] earth, stones 19 So mouths were crying 'Mama' 20 traps] vacuums 24 blanks between stars] gaps between the stars 35 proved] good 50 too] were too 63 the sky] sky *Outposts, Autumn 1967*

A Disaster 14 all the people] the people 20 effort] efforts *Scotsman 22 July 1967; one of the first published Crow poems*

Crow's Fall *added to the 1972 printing of Crow*

Criminal Ballad *title*: Cautionary Tale 8 Drained] Bleached 11 That] Which 14 Gazed towards] Frowned toward 29 the] his 31 calling to] beseeching 34 splinters] fragments 38 the] a *Listener, 6 June 1968*

Oedipus Crow 8 water-spirit] water-spirits 11 she] they *Listener, 1 Oct 1970*

Crow Tries the Media *added to the 1972 printing of Crow* **9** throat] throttle **11** While] And **13** While tycoons gambled with his glands *etc* **16** simply] very simply *New Yorker, 18 July 1970*

In Laughter **17** its] the **18** the] its **26** And rolls] Topples **28** *omitted* **29** slowly] finally *TLS, 14 March 1968*

Crow Goes Hunting **9** But if Crow was Crow what was the hare? *New Statesman, 24 July 1970*

Crow's Elephant Totem Song *added to the 1972 printing of Crow.* **46** Blotched] Soaked *London Magazine, July/Aug 1970.* *Title*: Crow Totem **11–12** *transposed* **11** Take] O take **12** of innocence and kindliness] O innocence O kindliness **20** ran under the Elephant's tail] ran in under the Elephant's knees **36** blaze] glow **41** roof] top **44** the] their *Works in Progress 2, Literary Guild of America, Jan 1971*

Crowcolour *added to the 1972 printing of Crow*

Crow's Battle Fury **18** head] skull **21–25** *omitted* **26** He moves forward a step, then a step, then a step – *Listener, 30 July 1970*

A Bedtime Story *title*: Fifth Bedtime Story **23** funny] silly **29** a] the **37–40** *are inserted after* **33** **34** But somehow] Somehow **49–51** *conflated to*: And saw what he could and did what he could **53** were bits of stick] had become just bits of wood *Listener, 18 July 1968*

Crow Sickened **8** challenging] calling *Critical Quarterly, Summer 1970*

Crow Paints Himself into a Chinese Mural *added to the 1972 printing of Crow.* **24** *omitted* *New Yorker, 14 Nov 1970*

Truth Kills Everybody **6** the famous] famous **16** dragging] sinking **20** He held it and held it and *Halifax Evening Courier, 30 Jan 1970.* **20** He held it and held it and held it and *Listener, 24 July 1969. cf.* 'The war ... was his ideal subject, the burning away of all human pretensions in the ray cast by death ... not truth is beauty only, but truth kills everybody.' – *Introduction to (ed.) Ted Hughes, Selected Poems of Keith Douglas (1964)*

Fragment of an Ancient Tablet **3** notable] famous *Observer, 15 Feb 1970*

Snake Hymn *title*: Crow Hymn *Sunday Times, 24 May 1970*

Lovesong *title*: Second Bedtime Story *Critical Quarterly, Spring/ Summer 1968.* **29** Her love-tricks were clashing of jail-keys **31** Like an animal] An animal *Northwest Review, Fall/Winter 1967–8*

Two Eskimo Songs II. *title*: Watersong *New American Review, Jan 1970. Only section II was included, as a separate poem, 'How Water Began to Play', in SP 1982 and NSP*

Crow Wakes

Published by Poet & Printer Press, April 1971, 200 copies. Of the twelve poems, only 'The Contender' was subsequently incorporated into the main Crow sequence. 'Crow's Table Talk' was later incorporated into Earth-numb [Moortown], under the title 'Tiger-psalm', which is where it is placed in the present edition. Three other poems – 'Song against the White Owl', 'Amulet' and 'I See a Bear' – were reprinted in other contexts (noted below), but are here retained within Crow Wakes. Copytext: Crow Wakes, except where specified

Crow Wakes *wr. 1964; first published as 'X', a dialogue from the play Eat Crow, Encounter, July 1965. Collected in NSP, where it is placed before Wodwo*

Bones *collected in NSP*

Amulet *first published as a separate, by A & G (Woodford Green), Christmas 1970; reprinted in Moon-Bells, and Under the North Star*

I See a Bear *reprinted in Moon-Bells, and Under the North Star. Title: The Grizzly Bear Under the North Star*

Bedtime Anecdote [*text*: NSP] *title*: Anecdote **7** no floor] no floors **22** on] in **26** And he did] And did **36** a monsoon] monsoon *Crow Wakes. Title*: Anecdote **4** *omits parentheses* **15** loose rant] rant *additional line after* **21**: Masticating food that was no food **22** *omits parentheses* **24** But] And *additional line after* **25**: And the weight of his head on the neck that was no neck **31** the ice] and the ice **31** the mouths] and the mouths **38** leopard] fever *Northwest Review Fall/Winter 1967–8. The poem was first collected in NSP, where it is retrospectively inserted into the Crow sequence*

Song against the White Owl 7 loaned] loans *London Magazine, July/Aug 1970; reprinted in A Primer of Birds, under the title 'The White Owl'*

The Contender *included in the Harper (U.S.) edition of Crow, and thereafter in the Faber expanded edition (1972)*

Poems. Ruth Fainlight, Ted Hughes, Alan Sillitoe.

Published by the Rainbow Press (April 1971, c.300 copies). 'Between 1971 and 1979 much of Hughes's writing was first collected in limited editions printed for the Rainbow Press, a publishing imprint owned by Hughes and his sister Olwyn' (Sagar/Tabor, p.4). Contains six Crow poems by Hughes, unreprinted elsewhere with the exception of 'Crow Rambles', which was collected in Moortown as 'Life is Trying to be Life', where it is placed in the present edition.

Crow's Courtship *included in the 1973 Faber limited edition of Crow*

UNCOLLECTED (1971–73)

The Space-Egg was Sailing *New Poems 1970-71 (P.E.N.), 19 April 1971. 29–48 incorporate 'Crow's Song of Himself', previously published in Crow (p.247)*

'In the little girl's angel gaze' *published as a broadside designed by Ralph Steadman, the Steam Press, March 1972. The poem was announced ('in the prospectus of a portfolio edition of broadside poems by various authors' – Sagar/Tabor, p.63) under the title: 'Crow Goes out to Play'*

The New World *six poems set to music by Gordon Crosse in 1969, and published for the Three Choirs Festival, Autumn 1972. Poem 4 ('I Said Goodbye to Earth') was first published as a poster, by Turret Books, Jan 1969, and later incorporated into Gaudete, with variants (cf. p.365)*

An Alchemy *(ed.) Graham Fawcett, Poems for Shakespeare 2, 20 May 1973*

PROMETHEUS ON HIS CRAG

In 1971 Hughes accompanied Peter Brook and the International Centre for Theatre Research to Persia for the Fifth Shiraz Festival. There he wrote *Orghast*, the name both of the play performed at Persepolis and of the invented language in which it is written. 'Our drama combined the *Prometheus Bound* of Aeschylus, Calderon's *Life is a Dream* – both of which stories had early roots in Persia – and archaic bits of myth, mainly early Persian, associated with the figure of Prometheus. It revolved around the complementary fates of this semi-divine figure nailed to the mountain summit and the disinherited figure chained in the mountain's heart.' [Notes to *SP* 1972]. Hughes wrote separately a number of short poems about Prometheus, twenty-one of which were collected as *Prometheus On His Crag*, published by the Rainbow Press, November 1973 [*Rainbow*], 160 copies. The sequence was subsequently collected in *Moortown* (1979), omitting three poems and adding three poems. The present edition prints the *Moortown* text and sequence; the three omitted poems [with their original numbers] are printed below:

[5] Prometheus On His Crag // Knew what was coming and his eyes closed / And his scream started. So all that day / The shuddering chestnut tree tore slowly open // With its arms full, / And under it – the woman again / With her brimming jar // Calling to him. But his scream / Crammed his head and all that day / He saw nothing and he heard nothing.

[12] Prometheus On His Crag // Can see Io fleeting across the map, / A rout of tribulation – a cry / Bucking the bee of the Creator. //

And she can see him – a relief / Carved into summit granite, / Quarried by the Creator's offal-eater. // Is she his secret soul – or is he hers? / If she could rest, would his chains drop off him? / If he could burst his chains, could she rest? // It matters.

[17] Prometheus On His Crag // Was himself the fire / Frozen. / His freedom, as for ice, // Could only be a return to his earliest – / A dissolution / To flame. // The fire wants him back. / Every day its burrowing double tongue / Comes to melt his centre, // Every night the cold repairs the damage.

Poems 9, 16 and 20 were collected in SP in 1982, and numbers 2, 3, 9, 10, 14 and 19 were collected in NSP.

3. 'Prometheus ... Pestered by birds' 3 wind-honed] wind-buffed *Rainbow*

4. 'Prometheus ... Spotted the Vulture' 5 As] While 5 breastbone to crotch] crotch to breastbone 6 peruse] read *South Bank Poetry and Music, Oct 1971*

5. 'Prometheus ... Dreamed he had burst' *first published in Moortown*

7. 'Prometheus ... Arrested half-way' *first published in Moortown*

9. 'Now I know I never shall' 6 mountain water] a sea 8 stays] is it *Antaeus, Winter 1973*

15. 'Prometheus ... Had such an advantageous prospect' 10 prophesying] proclaiming *Réalités, Mar 1973*

17. 'No God – only wind on the flower' *first published in Moortown*

20. 'Prometheus ... Pondered the vulture' 35 Image after image after image. And the vulture *Rainbow.* 2 Speculated about the vulture. Was it 5 Or was it his] Or his 18 Life] living 33 crucial] central 35–6 As the vulture/Circled] The vulture/Only circled *Antaeus, Winter 1973*

21. 'His mother covers her eyes' 4–5 Birth-hacked flesh-ripeness. / The cry bulging, a slow mire 7 is uttering] utters 10 With crocus] Crocus 11 The] A 13–15 Cloud-bird / Midwifes the upglare naphtha, / Opening the shell. 16 And] As 17 And sways to stature *Antaeus, Winter 1973*

UNCOLLECTED (1974–75)

Welcombe *Bananas, Jan/Feb 1975*

Exits *Bananas, Jan/Feb 1975*

The Lamentable History of the Human Calf *New Departures, 1975; the poem has its origins in Hughes's play, Difficulties of a Bridegroom (broadcast 21 Jan 1963)*

Season Songs originated as a set of *Five Autumn Songs for Children's Voices* [*FAS*], printed as a pamphlet for the 1968 Harvest Festival, Little Missenden, for performance by school children. The five untitled poems were subsequently incorporated without change as the Autumn section of *Spring Summer Autumn Winter*, published by the Rainbow Press, September 1974, 140 copies [*SSAW*], where they are given titles – 'Leaves', 'The Defenders', 'The Seven Sorrows', 'The Stag', 'There Came a Day'. *SSAW* extended the sequence by including five poems for each of the other seasons, and was in turn enlarged with the addition of ten further poems to become *Season Songs*, published by Faber and Faber, May 1976 [*SS 1976*].

The second edition of *Season Songs* [*SS 1985*] omitted 'The Stag' and 'Two Horses', and added seven poems. The contents and ordering of the present edition follow *SS 1976*; the copy-text is *SS 1985*. The seven additional poems gathered in *SS 1985* were all initially published elsewhere, and in the present edition are entered at their various periodical publication dates.

Two of the original season songs – 'The Defenders' and 'Hunting the Summer' – were omitted from *SS 1976* and were never reprinted; they are here entered immediately prior to *Season Songs* (p.301), as poems from *SSAW*.

When some of the poems first appeared in periodicals they were described as 'from a cycle of poems of the seasons for children' (*Listener*, 4 April 1974). The song-cycle incorporated progressively more complex material, and Hughes is quoted on the cover of *SS 1976* as stating that '*Season Songs* began as children's poems but they grew up'. He remarked elsewhere that he had tried to keep 'within hearing of children' ('Ted Hughes introduces and reads *Season Songs*', BBC Radio 3, September 1977). The U.S. edition (Viking Press, October 1975, with illustrations by Leonard Baskin) carries no reference to *Season Songs* as a children's book.
Dedication: To Carol

from Spring Summer Autumn Winter

Hunting the Summer *published in Spring Summer Autumn Winter, Sept 1974, but omitted from Season Songs*

The Defenders *first published (untitled) in Five Autumn Songs for Children's Voices, Jan 1969; reprinted in Spring Summer Autumn Winter as 'The Defenders'; omitted from Season Songs*

Season Songs (1976)

A March Calf *reprinted from SSAW.* **14** I block] somebody blocks **19** *omitted Listener, 16 Aug 1973*

The River in March *reprinted from SSAW.* **20** it cannot] cannot *Listener, 16 Aug 1973*

March Morning Unlike Others *first published in SS 1976; the poem was incorporated into the Moortown Diary sequence, p.519*

Spring Nature Notes, I–VI *reprinted from SSAW.* II.8 touch] disturb II.9 touched] disturbed III.1 stiff, quivering] stiff and quivering III.4 sentinels] sentries III.12 veteran] a veteran *SSAW*

April Birthday *reprinted from SSAW.* 11 silvered] silvery 27 float] are floating 29 On] Over 30 everywhere] all over *SSAW*

Icecrust and Snowflake 7 velvet-petalled] miraculous *SS 1976*

Deceptions *reprinted from SSAW.* 14 Eluding] Evading *SSAW*

Swifts 51 Then eyelids] Eyelids *Listener, 16 May 1974*

Mackerel Song *reprinted from SSAW*

Hay *first published in SS 1976*

Sheep, I–III *first published in SS 1976, the poem (parts I and III only) reappeared as part of the Moortown Diary sequence, p.531; in NSP – which prints all three sections – it is placed with Season Songs*

Apple Dumps *first collected in SS 1976.* 13 wings] its wings *Bananas, Jan/Feb 1975*

Work and Play *reprinted from SSAW.* 17 creases] moistures 37 crannies] creases *SSAW*

The Harvest Moon *reprinted from SSAW.* 14 Stare up petrified, while the moon swells *SSAW*

The Golden Boy *reprinted from SSAW*

Leaves *originally published in FAS, untitled.* 17 grave] graves 30 says] said 38 says] said *SSAW, FAS*

Autumn Nature Notes, I–VIII V.9 Blackenings, shrivellings] blackenings shrivel *SS 1976.* VI.20 remains] last possessions VII.9 fondling] and fondles *Listener, 26 Sept 1974. Section V published separately, title*: October V.7 A blue tremor of the air. A gold furred flame V.8–9 [...] one by one/As they peel open] as they peel/And flake open V.10 hardens] stiffens *Outposts, Spring 1974. Section VII published separately, title*: November VII.3 a crossing] wraiths of *Outposts, Spring 1974*

The Seven Sorrows *originally published in FAS, untitled*

A Cranefly in September *first published in SS 1976*

There Came a Day *originally published in FAS, untitled*

The Stag [*text*: SS 1976] *originally published in FAS, untitled; entitled 'The Stag' in SSAW; omitted from SS 1985.* 25 And turned] And the stag turned 26 Hearing the hound-pack smash] hearing how the hound-pack smashed 28 which] that 33 loll-tongued

hounds] hounds and their hanging tongues 34 And] While
34 shouted] cried 35 And the] The *SSAW, FAS*

Two Horses, I–V [*text: SS 1976*] *first collected in SS 1976; omitted
from SS 1985* II.13 Shaggy] Bushy III.4 As I stumbled] I
stumbled IV.4 cries] shouts IV.14 And they] They V.6 shag-haired]
shaggy V.8 wire-spring] spring-wire V.11 *omits* In a steam of dung
and sweat *London Magazine, June/July 1976*

The Warrior of Winter *reprinted from SSAW; additional stanza
after 24*: At dawn he woke white / Past moving or speaking. / His
wounds stuck bleak as blades. / Icicles barred his eyes. / A crow
was watching him. / The star had conquered. *SSAW*

Christmas Card *reprinted from SSAW. title*: Solstice Song 1 the
car, yes] the car 26 swamp woodland] swampy forest 32 watch]
you watch *SSAW*

December River 22 leapfrogged] had leapfrogged 56 towards] at
New Yorker, 24 June 1974

New Year Song *reprinted from SSAW.* 26 snow] the snow 28 A
song comes] Now comes a song *SSAW*

Snow and Snow *reprinted from SSAW.* 15 fairytales] fairylands
SSAW

The Warm and the Cold *reprinted from SSAW.* 18 chuckle] giggle
SSAW. 16 soaring] hurtling *Listener, 8 Nov 1973*

UNCOLLECTED (1976–77)

He called *London Magazine, April/May 1976. This is a heavily
revised version of 'In These Fading Moments' (Cave Birds, p.423)
as originally broadcast in June 1975; the Faber edition of Cave
Birds (1979) reverted to the broadcast text*

Eclipse [*text*: Flowers and Insects] *first published as a pamphlet, the
Sceptre Press, 30 July 1976.* 13 by] with 28 appetites] appetite
83 *expanded to*: Holding forelegs. I went three hundred yards / And
brought a magnifying glass / And studied them from two inches. It
was still obscure 89 the] this 97 realised] noticed 114 dot]
blob 118 Wringing] Cleaning 126 rubbish] refuse 130 antiques.]
antiques? 133 sun's] moon's *Sceptre Press. Collected in Flowers and
Insects, and NSP*

Pets [*text*: Season Songs (1985)] 8 That I left out for her twilight
emergence 10 his] its 11 his] its 12 he] I 14 Grows. A tabby Tom.]
A tabby tom. Grows 19 *expanded to*: Since that last appearance /
When he brought in his remains to die or be doctored *(ed.) George
Macbeth, The Book of Cats, Nov 1976; reprinted in Moon-Bells
(1978)*

Green Mother *Boston University Journal, Winter 1976; the poem is an early version of 'A Green Mother' from Cave Birds (p.431)*

[Caprichos] *These poems are from a projected but unpublished sequence (cf. Sagar/Tabor p.397); several of the Seven Dungeon Songs (pp.559–63) also appeared in periodicals under the general title of* Caprichos, *as did 'Song of Longsight' (from Earth-numb, p.552) and 'Landmark Head' (from Mokomaki, p.695).*

'Who lives in my skin with me?' *Mars, 1977 [no date]*

'If the mouth could properly open' *Aspect, 1978 [no date]; the poem is a different version of 'If mouth could open its cliff' (Seven Dungeon Songs, p.562)*

'When dawn lifts the eyelid behind the eyelid' *Aspect, 1978 [no date]*

'Nevertheless rejoice' *[text:* (ed.) David Harsent, Winter Poetry Supplement (PBS), 1983] **3** This is the shriek] A shriek **5** The surgery overture] A surgery sound **6** blades] knives **7–12** After hard snaky swallowings / The whetted adoration / Smoking from the trachea // All grievances redressed in the grave / Of hydrochloric acids **13** a whole sky] a whole pale heaven **14** He stalks – up to the knees in glittering soul **15** equipoise] afterlife *Aspect, 1978 [no date]. In the PBS text the poem is entitled 'Grace'*

GAUDETE

Published by Faber and Faber, May 1977. *Gaudete* was originally written as a film scenario during 1962–64, but was never adapted to film. It was revised in 1971–72, after *Orghast*, and in 1975 Hughes added an Epilogue consisting of a prose text and forty-five short poems. The present edition includes the complete sequence of Epilogue poems, but omits the main narrative, and omits the prose Epilogue which frames the sequence. Hughes's own practice when excerpting *Gaudete* for *SP 1982* and for *NSP* was to offer a selection (identical in each case) from the Epilogue poems, rather than to excerpt from the *sui generis* narrative which precedes them.

In his notes to *SP 1982*, Hughes describes *Gaudete* as 'a long story in verse which outlines the last day of a changeling – a creature substituted for an Anglican clergyman, as an all but perfect duplicate, by powers of the other world, while the real clergyman remains in the other world as their prisoner (like Thomas the Rhymer in the Scots ballad). At the destruction of the changeling, the man of flesh and blood reappears, and the poems here are taken from his notebook – his diary of coming to his senses, or of trying to come to his senses.' In the 'Argument' which prefaces *Gaudete* (both versions of which are included in Appendix One), Hughes had characterised the Epilogue poems thus: 'the original Nicholas Lumb reappears in this world, in the West of Ireland, where he roams about composing hymns and psalms to a nameless female deity'.

Several of the poems appeared in periodicals in 1975 under the title '*from* Lumb's Remains' – an early version of the *Gaudete* epilogue which was given a first dramatised reading at the Ilkley Festival in 1975. Hughes wrote an introductory note to the Festival programme, which concludes: 'The Epilogue, which you are going to hear, records [Lumb's] first meeting with human beings, after his return from the world of spirits.'

A number of the poems were also collected in *Orts* (1978), cf. the headnote and notes to *Orts*, p.1266.

'**Collision with the earth has finally come** – ' *collected in SP 1982 and in NSP*

'**Once I said lightly**' *collected in SP 1982 and in NSP*

'**This is the maneater's skull**' *collected in SP 1982 and in NSP*

'**I see the oak's bride in the oak's grasp**' [*text*: NSP] *additional line after* 17: A perilously frail safety *Gaudete. Collected in SP 1982 and in NSP*

'**A primrose petal's edge**' *title*: *from* Lumb's Remains 9 *omitted* 11 against] on *Boston University Journal, Winter 1975. Collected in SP 1982 and in NSP*

'**Waving goodbye, from your banked hospital bed**' [*text*: NSP] 16 blinding] glaring *Gaudete. Collected in SP 1982 and in NSP*

'**I said goodbye to earth**' *first published as a poster, Turret Books, 1969; reprinted as one of the six poems for music comprising 'The New World', 1972 (p.276).* 1 earth] the earth 8 Upon] On 12 dark] warm 12 bleed] weep *Turret Books*

'**The swallow** – **rebuilding** – ' *collected in SP 1982 and in NSP*

'**The night wind, muscled with rain**' *title*: *from* Lumb's Remains 2 tug] pull 8 scamper] run *Boston University Journal, Winter 1975*

'**The grass-blade is not without**' 6 on] and *Bananas, Autumn/ Winter 1976. Collected in SP 1982 and in NSP*

'**I know well**' *collected in SP 1982 and in NSP*

'**Sometimes it comes, a gloomy flap of lightning**' *collected in SP 1982 and in NSP*

'**Calves harshly parted from their mamas**' *title*: *from* Lumb's Remains *Boston University Journal, Winter 1975. Collected in SP 1982 and in NSP*

'**A bang** – **A burning** – ' *collected in SP 1982 and in NSP*

'**The dead man lies, marching here and there**' *title*: *from* Lumb's Remains *Boston University Journal, Winter 1975*

'Your tree – Your oak' *title*: The Oak 1–7 A guard / At the pure
well of leaf / A glare / Of upward Lightning / Momentary / Under
the crumbling stars. 13 my] your *additional line after* 20: With a
crow in the top. *Bananas, Jan/Feb 1975. Collected in SP 1982 and
in NSP*

UNCOLLECTED (1977–78)

He Gets Up in Dark Dawn [*text*: Season Songs 1985] *first collected
in Moon-Bells (1978); added to Season Songs 1985.* 17 in] at
20 Squibby-damp, echoless] Echoless, squibby-damp 21 blue
garden] garden *The Listener, 16 June 1977*

Unknown Warrior *(ed.) Gavin Ewart, New Poems 1977–78
(P.E.N.), 21 Nov 1977*

After the Grim Diagnosis *(ed.) Colin Falck, Poetry Supplement
(PBS), 1 Dec 1977*

[1952–1977] 'A Nation's a soul' *TLS, 23 June 1978; commissioned
by Faber and Faber for the Queen Square Trust, and incised in
stone, in commemoration of the Silver Jubilee. The quatrain was
revised to become the epigraph to Rain-Charm for the Duchy,
where it is entitled 'Solomon's Dream' (p.802)*

A Solstice [*text*: (ed.) Michael Morpurgo, All Around the Year,
April 1979] *first published as a pamphlet, Sceptre Press, July 1978*
154 at his chest] deliberately at his chest *Sceptre Press. Uncollected,
although the first fifteen lines were reprinted in Earth Dances
(1994), under the title 'Solstice'. The poem addresses Hughes's older
brother, Gerald, who had emigrated to Australia in December 1948
(cf. 'Two, p.480, and also 'Brother Peartree', p.1192)*

New Foal [*text*: NSP] *title*: Foal 4 fondled by small draughts]
wind-fondled 5–6 A star crashed in from outer space – / Blazed
and burned out in one flash 7 smoulder] remains 13 It baffles him,
like a numbness 16 He's resting 17 blank] huge 17 empty] huge
18 questions] huge questions 27 a giant] as if a giant 28 Strokes]
Stroked 36 Soon] and soon 37 He wants] Wanting 39–40 [...] And
unearthly horse/Surges him, weightless, a tossing of flame 42 And
coils his eyeball and his heels 43 like the awe] like the terror
46 *omitted* 47 fling] flings 48 And full moons and dark moons *(ed.)
Michael Morpurgo, All Around the Year, April 1979. Title*: The
Foal Has Landed *Critical Quarterly, Autumn 1978*

Wycoller Hall [*text*: Remains of Elmet (Rainbow Press)] *collected
in the limited edition of Remains of Elmet, but omitted from all the
Faber editions, and never reprinted* 22 vigilance] ageing *Antaeus,
Summer/Autumn 1978. The poem's rhetorical form derives from
John Skelton's late medieval satire, 'Speke Parrott'*

ORTS

Published by the Rainbow Press, August 1978. 200 copies. There was no Faber edition of *Orts*, and (aside from the poems collected in *Moortown*, as noted below) the majority of the poems were not reprinted. 'Orts' means 'leavings'; one typescript of the collection carries the epigraph 'The lady's leavings are the dog's dainties' (*Sagar/Tabor*, p.95). Several of the poems are left over from 'Lumb's Remains', an early version of the *Gaudete* Epilogue, dating from the mid-1970s. The Rainbow Press publicity-flier described *Orts* as 'a first edition of sixty-three poems, many of which were intended for the second part of *Gaudete* (Faber, 1977) but not included therein'.

Fourteen poems (nos. 10, 12, 13, 16, 20, 22, 23, 25, 35, 39, 47, 58, 59, 63) were subsequently included in the *Earth-numb* section of *Moortown*, under the heading 'Orts', which is where they are placed in the present edition. No. 36 ('Hathershelf') was subsequently collected under a different title in *Remains of Elmet*, where it is placed in the present edition; no. 11 ('Ophelia') was subsequently collected in *River*, where it is placed in the present edition.

2. **'Let that one shrink into place'** *title*: '... part of a new sequence called "Lumb's Remains"' *Listener, 20 March 1975*

5. **'Skin'** 5 somehow nervous] nervous 9 just] first 11 rippings] rendings *Granta, April 1976*

6. **'Air'** 10 The air] Still the air 11 Brings everything it finds 13 Humoured] Humours 15 Rages and starves *Granta, April 1976*

34. **'Stilled at his drink'** *title*: '... part of a new sequence called "Lumb's Remains"' *Listener, 20 March 1975*

42. **'The bulging oak is not as old'** *title*: '... part of a new sequence called "Lumb's Remains"' *Listener, 20 March 1975*

45. **'Why do you take such nervy shape to become'** *title*: '... part of a new sequence called "Lumb's Remains"' *Listener, 20 March 1975*

CAVE BIRDS

Cave Birds originated in 1974 when Hughes was shown a sequence of nine bird drawings by Leonard Baskin, and in response wrote a cycle of nine accompanying poems, separately titled, as follows [Baskin / Hughes]:

  A Hercules-in-the-Underworld Bird / The Summoner
  A Desert Bittern / The Advocate
  A Titled Vulturesss / The Interrogator
  An Oven-Ready Pirhana Bird / The Judge
  A Hermaphroditic Ephesian Owl / The Plaintiff

A Raven of Ravens / The Executioner
A Tumbled Socratic Cock / The Accused
A Ghostly Falcon / The Risen
Goblin / Finale

Baskin in turn produced a further ten drawings, for which Hughes wrote a further ten poems. These ten poems and drawings constitute the first edition of *Cave Birds*, a portfolio containing drawings, texts and facsimiles, which was published in a limited edition of 125 copies in May 1975 [*Scolar Press*], comprising:

A Death-Stone Crow of Carrion / The Knight
A Double Osprey / The Gatekeeper
A Flayed Crow / The Hall of Judgement
A Maze Pelican / The Baptist
A Sunrise of Owl / A Loyal Mother
A Monkey-Eating Eagle / Incomparable Marriage
A Stud Cockerel Hunted in the Desert / The Culprit
A Scarecrow Swift / The Guide
A Crow of Prisms / Walking Bare
An Owl Flower / The Good Angel

Hughes separately wrote twelve further poems (to accompany eight of which Baskin subsequently produced drawings):

The Scream
After the First Fright
She Seemed So Considerate
Your Mother's Bones Wanted to Speak
In These Fading Moments I Wanted to Say
First, the Doubtful Charts of Skin
Something Was Happening
Only a Little Sleep, a Little Slumber
As I Came, I Saw a Wood
After There was Nothing There Was a Woman
His Legs Ran About
Bride and Groom Lie Hidden for Three Days

The Scolar Press edition was published to coincide with the first performance of *Cave Birds*, at the Ilkley Literature Festival in May 1975, during which Baskin's drawings were projected onto a screen and all thirty-one poems given a dramatised reading. The reading was produced by George Macbeth, and broadcast shortly thereafter on BBC Radio 3, with a linking commentary by Hughes (23 June 1975).

The thirty-one poems formed the basis of the much-revised and expanded Faber edition of *Cave Birds* (in which the poems only are given titles), published in October 1978 [*Cave Birds (1978)*]. Two of the BBC broadcast poems – 'The Advocate' and 'Your Mother's Bones' – were omitted from the Faber edition, and were never published by Hughes, but are reproduced in (ed.) Keith Sagar, *The Achievement of Ted Hughes* (1983, pp.346, 348).

The text of the Faber 1978 edition was reprinted with further revisions, and without drawings, in *Three Books* (1993). The present edition prints the revised text of *Three Books**, except where otherwise specified.

    Subtitle: An Alchemical Cave Drama *Cave Birds (1978)*, *Three Books*

    Dedication: To Eric Walter White

[*In June 1993 Faber reissued Hughes's three major illustrated adult sequences – *Remains of Elmet*, *Cave Birds* and *River* – in one volume, without illustrations, under the title *Three Books*. Hughes revised the contents, the ordering and the texts of all three sequences, extensively so in the case of *Remains of Elmet* and *River*. The intention of *Three Books* was to liberate the poems from any presumed dependency upon their visual contexts, and to suggest implicit links between the three sequences.]

The Scream 2 my] was my 3 Shared] Which shared 17 where] and 20 Lifted] Raised *Cave Birds (1978)*. 21 He smiled in half-coma, a smiling doll *Stand Magazine, 1976*

The Summoner *subtitle*: A Hercules-In-The-Underworld Bird *New Statesman, 27 Sept 1974*

The Interrogator *first published as a broadside with a drawing by Leonard Baskin, Ilkley Literature Festival, 24 May 1975* 16 Later] After *Cave Birds (1978)*. *Additional opening lines*: On the sun's first dawning / A snail's spermy signature / Was enough / To incense heaven and set the atoms trembling. 1 Small hope now] So small hope 5–7 He scrutinizes / Everything that craves and has transgressed / Into the masks and amnesias of hunger. 14–15 *omitted Ilkley Literature Festival*

She Seemed So Considerate 4 were sweating] sweated 12 potted pet fern] pet fern 12 spirit] creature 13 withered] died 14 I felt life had decided to cancel me 15 more] better 16 winged being] bird-being *Cave Birds (1978)*

The Judge 5 offal-sack] garbage-sack 14 appeal] substance *Cave Birds (1978)*

The Plaintiff 1 This is the bird of light! *Cave Birds (1978)*

In These Fading Moments I Wanted to Say 1 to flame] to a flame 3 unutterable] unspeakable 11 dusty dead] dead 18 while the door was closing] before the door closed *Cave Birds (1978)*. *'He called'* (p.347) *is a heavily revised version of this poem*

The Executioner *subtitle*: A Raven of Ravens *New Statesman, 27 Sept 1974*

The Accused 11 sacred] the sacred *Cave Birds (1978)*. *Title*: Socrates' Cock *London Magazine, April/May 1976*

First, the Doubtful Charts of Skin 16 tombs] graves 17–18 And a leaning menhir, with my name on it. / And an epitaph, which read: *Cave Birds (1978)*

The Knight 3 Unlacing] And unlacing 34 As] While 35 Deepens] Strengthens *Cave Birds (1978)*. 34 As hour by hour] And hour after hour *Scolar Press*

Something was Happening 10 And all the time 11 glancing up] staring 12 began to burn] was burning 15 see] watch 17–20 As she tried to tell / How it went on getting worse and worse / Till she sank back. 21–2 And when I saw new emerald tufting the quince, in April / And cried in dismay: 'Here it comes again!' 27 furthest] far 28 snow-burned eagle-hunter] eagle-hunter *Cave Birds (1978)*

The Gatekeeper 1 A sphynx 5 You choose – but it is a formality 7 redundant] futile 9 Such fear – your weight *etc* 13 the bare] a bare piece of 15 chitter] chatter 17 turned corpse] corpse 18 As everything] Everything 19 Thumps] Nails *Cave Birds (1978)*. *Additional couplet after* 4: Then, an answer. So this is what I am, finally. / Finally horror. 5 choose] seem to choose 18 comes] has come *Scolar Press*

A Flayed Crow in the Hall of Judgement 1 Darkness has all come together, making an egg. 6 curls me up like a shrimpish foetus] has curled me up like a new foetus 8 a nowhere] an air 12 struggles] struggled 22 Great] A great 26 my soul-skin pinned out] the soul-skin laid out *Cave Birds (1978)*. *Additional line after* 4: Infinity has looked into me. 6 shawl] pellicle 26 skinned] is skinned *Scolar Press*

The Baptist 1 Enfolds you, as in arms] Enfolds you 8 Bearing] Carrying 9 So you] You 10 Like a hard-cornered grief, drop by drop 11 An] Or an 13–14 Or a seed in its armour. *Cave Birds (1978)*. *Additional lines after* 8: Any earthly news of you / Must be a recording you made sometime. *Scolar Press*

A Green Mother 21 A city] The city 22 Like] Is like 23 I am your guide 25–6 This earth is the sweetness/Of all the heavens] This earth is heaven's sweetness 27–8 The grave is her breast / And her milk is endless life *Cave Birds (1978)*. *Title*: A Loyal Mother *Scolar Press. For a variant earlier version of the poem, cf. 'Green Mother', p.351*

As I Came, I Saw a Wood 1 craned] stood 5 none] they 17 saw] could see 23 drink] to drink *Cave Birds (1978)*

A Riddle 8 made good progress] chose your direction 13 caught] received 14 counter-attacked] attacked 15 under] beneath 18 When you arrived empty 19 left] forsook 20–1 Now as you face your death / I offer you your life *Cave Birds (1978)*. *'A Riddle' is a rewriting – for Cave Birds 1978 – of 'Incomparable Marriage' from the 1975 Scolar Press edition, the text of which follows*: I meet you / For the audit. Your spellbound hours / Were a summoning. I have come. / Your creditor – even like water from the rock. // It is too late to pray. Too late to cry. // The thought behind your eye, so lightly fleeting, / Wrought a question / In hooked letters of iron /

1269

From which you now hang. I am that shape. // And you are all I have. / Just as I am all you can see. / A forged face of brass perforce ravenous / For its creator. // I am the hungriest of all the daughters. / And now you are my groom / I shall become / Your saviour mother. // My love has cast out the live evil / That gorged only itself. / Now you come into my womb / For the last pain. // Soon, into a changed, helpless world / Of wind and of sun, of rock and water / I shall deliver you / To cry out. *Scolar Press*

The Scapegoat 15 Let out a mandrake shriek 16 sputter] jabber 22 Lolls] Lolled 24 A wine-skin of riddance, a goat of oaths *Cave Birds (1978)*. *Title*: The Culprit *additional lines after* 16: The conjuror's parrot – unholy fool – / Gagged to crack Logos. *Scolar Press*. *Title*: The Scapegoat Culprit *Transatlantic Review, Spring 1977*

After There was Nothing Came a Woman *title*: After There was Nothing There Was a Woman 1 has arrived at] had reached 5 have] had 7 are] were 8 protects] protected 10 Are as they are] Lay as they did 10 cannot] could not 11 They hung as it were in space 13 found] had found 16 And curtained it with a flowered skirt 17 makes] made 18 looks] looked 20 at] around at *Cave Birds (1978)*. *Additional line after* 17: She could see the excited wind flexing on the face of the water. *London Magazine, April/ May 1976*

The Guide *additional couplet after* 4: The chick ruptures its shell, then stops, dazzled. / I have not stopped. *Scolar Press*

His Legs Ran About 1–2 Till they tangled and seemed to trip and lie down / With her legs intending to hold them there forever 3 felt through] groped in *additional couplet after* 5: Mouth talked its way in and out and finally / Found her mouth and settled deeper deeper 6 came against] came up against 11 pressing] pushing 14 Finding] Seeking 16 truth and greatness] greatness and truth *Cave Birds (1978)*

Walking Bare 14 Ampler] And new 16 blood-worn] blood wrapped 23 inhalation] breath *Cave Birds (1978)*

Bride and Groom Lie Hidden for Three Days 11 incredulous] incredulously *Cave Birds (1978)*. *This poem is incorporated into Crow in Hughes's 1997 Faber audio-cassette reading of Crow*

The Owl Flower 3 writhes apart] separates 4 Fiendish] Plaintive 16 grimace] smile *Cave Birds (1978)*. *Title*: The Good Angel 12 in] on 23 cringing] shivering *Scolar Press*. 21 broody] the broody *TLS, 30 May 1975*

The Risen [*text*: NSP, *which follows Cave Birds (1978) rather than Three Books*] 6 carries] brings 24 wrist.] wrist? *Three Books*. *Title*: The Sentenced: A Ghostly Falcon 21 splendour] beauty *New Statesman, 27 Sept 1974*

Finale *cf.* 'We go on writing poems because one poem never gets the whole account right. There is always something missed. At the end of the ritual up comes a goblin.' (*'Ted Hughes and Crow: An interview with Ekbert Faas', London Magazine, Jan 1971*)

ADAM AND THE SACRED NINE

Published by the Rainbow Press, Spring 1979. 160 copies. The sequence was incorporated into *Moortown* (1979), texts unrevised, but omitting five poems, as noted below. The present edition prints the complete [*Rainbow*] sequence. *SP 1982* included the following endnote to its selection from *Adam and the Sacred Nine*: 'These poems form part of a small sequence in which Adam, fallen prostrate, is visited by nine birds who each in turn bring their gift of "how to live", for him to accept or reject.'

Five of the poems were published in periodical form in 1976 as a sequence entitled 'Five Birds in Paradise'. Seven of the poems were collected in *SP 1982*; none of the sequence was collected in *NSP*.

The Song *collected in SP 1982*

Awake! *omitted from Moortown*

All this time his cry *omitted from Moortown*

He had retreated *omitted from Moortown*

And the Falcon came 1 The] With *New Poetry 2, 18 Nov 1976*. *Collected in SP 1982*

The Wild Duck *collected in SP 1982*

The Swift comes the swift *collected in SP 1982*

The Unknown Wren 12 squatted] squatting 23 trembling] tremblings *New Poetry 2, 18 Nov 1976*

And Owl 1 A masked soul] Mummy-masked as a soul 5 very still] still 15 Because of the Shape] The shape 16 Because of the shape] The shape *New Poetry 2, 18 Nov 1976. Collected in SP 1982*

The Dove Came 8 Piling heaven of violet and silver *Rainbow*. *Collected in SP 1982*

And the Phoenix has come 16 Laughs] Crows *SP 1982*

Light *omitted from Moortown; originally published Granta, April 1976*

Bud-tipped twig *omitted from Moortown*

The sequence exists in four versions. Firstly, the limited edition (Rainbow Press, April 1979, 180 copies) with four photographs by Fay Godwin; secondly, the first Faber edition (May 1979) with sixty-three photographs by Fay Godwin; thirdly, the sequence of poems – without photographs – as revised for inclusion in *Three Books* (Faber and Faber, June 1993); fourthly, a further revised sequence of both photographs and poems, entitled *Elmet* (Faber and Faber, October 1994). These are referred to below as, respectively, *Rainbow*, *Remains*, *Three Books* and *Elmet*.

The four sequences differ from each other as to inclusions, ordering, titles and texts. For *Rainbow* and for *Three Books* Hughes ordered the poems himself. For *Remains* and for *Elmet* he chose the opening and closing poems; Hughes and Godwin then decided together on the sequence of photographs, after which they chose which poems would appear next to which photographs (cf. Fay Godwin, 'Ted Hughes and Elmet', in [ed.] Nick Gammage, *The Epic Poise: A Celebration of Ted Hughes*, Faber and Faber, 1999). The present edition follows *Remains* for contents and for ordering, and the copy-text is *Remains* for the twenty poems subsequently omitted from *Three Books*; otherwise *Three Books* is the copy-text for all revised texts and for all titles (thirteen of the untitled or first-line titled poems in *Remains* were given new titles in *Three Books*).

The contents underwent considerable further revision for the 1994 edition, published as *Elmet* (whose focus broadened to include twelve previously collected poems from *The Hawk in the Rain*, *Lupercal*, *Wodwo* and *Wolfwatching*). *Elmet* introduced some further revisions to individual poems, and these have been incorporated into the present text. Variants between all four editions are noted below. One poem – 'Wycoller Hall' was included in the Rainbow limited edition but omitted from all subsequent editions; it is here entered at its date of first periodical publication (p.388).

Subtitle: A Pennine Sequence *Remains (subtitle omitted from the sequence as reprinted in Three Books and Elmet)*

Dedication: Poems in Memory of Edith Farrar. The Photographs are for Ted (*Remains*). In Memory of My Mother and Father (*Three Books*). In Memory of Edith Farrar and William Hughes. The Photographs are for Ted (*Elmet*)

The Dark River [*text*: Elmet] 17 surrounding] encircling *Three Books. In Remains, the poem is untitled, set in italics to form an epigraph to the collection, and placed prior to the contents page. The opening line refers to the poet's mother, now 'six years into her posthumous life'.* 2 He] And 10–12 He renews his prime exercising what happened, / As his body tries to renew its cells – 13 Empty air] Air 15–16 And the smoky valley opens, the womb that bore him, / Chimney above chimney, hill over hill 17 *omitted* **20** So *omitted* **21–23** *contracted to*: Archaeology of the mouth, / Treasures that crumble at the touch of day – *Remains*

Abel Cross, Crimsworth Dene *title*: Where the Mothers *Remains*

Hardcastle Crags *omitted from Three Books. A heavily revised version of the poem was included in Three Books as 'Leaf Mould' – originally published in the TLS under the title 'Hardcastle Crags', and subsequently collected in Wolfwatching, where it is placed in the present edition (p.768)*

Lumb Chimneys *omitted from Three Books.* **6** Brave] High **6** mortgaged walls] pampered forts **7** finally too much] tossed aside **8** Heirloom] Lineal *Rainbow. Mill chimneys were traditionally referred to in Yorkshire as 'Lumbs'*

Two Trees at Top Withens *title*: Open to Huge Light *Remains*

Stanbury Moor *title*: These Grasses of Light *Remains.* **10** gleam] glare *Texas Arts Journal, 1978*

Moors **19** gleams] light *Rainbow*

The Trance of Light *the poem was later revised and collected in Three Books as 'Chinese History of Colden Water' (p.738)*

West Laithe Cobbles *title*: It Is All *Remains.* **9–10** *transposed Texas Arts Journal, 1978*

Long Screams *omitted from Three Books*

Curlews, 1–11 [*text*: NSP] *Remains, Three Books, and Elmet (1994) all print 'Curlews' as two separate poems, entitled respectively 'Curlews Lift' and 'Curlews in April'; in SP 1982 the two poems were combined as one poem in two sections, entitled 'Curlews Lift', and as one poem in NSP under the title 'Curlews'*

Walls at Alcomden *title*: Hill Walls *Remains.* **14** Here] And here **14** rib] bone *Encounter, Sept 1977*

Walls *omitted from Three Books*

First, Mills **6** The fatal] A single, fatal **6–7** And faces whitening / At the windows] And the faces at windows / Whitened **8** *omitted* **10** The hills were commandeered *Remains*

Hill-Stone Was Content **13** And] Till *Earth Dances.* **14** darkening, dwindling] darkening *Remains.* **14** In their long, hopeless, darkening stand. *Texas Arts Journal, 1978*

Mill Ruins *omitted from Three Books*

Wild Rock [*text*: Elmet] **13** worsteds] worsted *Three Books.* **14** bones] flash *Rainbow*

The Big Animal of Rock *omitted from Three Books*

Tree *first published in Three Books, this poem joins two separate* *poems from Remains, entitled respectively 'Tree' (which became ll.1–19 of the revised poem) and 'A Tree' (which became ll.20–32 of the revised poem)* **1** a different] another **3** black stones, blown water] stones and wild water **13** saw] felt **17** Transfigured, bowed – **20** Gasped a cry *'Tree', Remains.* **24** his] its **32** Lets what happens to it happen. *'A Tree', Remains.* **16** Mind had left him. God had left him. *Rainbow*

Alcomden [*text*: Elmet] **13** numbly] dumbly *Three Books. Title*: Rock Has Not Learned *Remains*

Remains of Elmet *omitted from Three Books.* **14** molars] teeth *Rainbow*

Shackleton Hill *title*: Dead Farms, Dead Leaves *Remains*

When Men Got to the Summit **9** their] the *Elmet (NSP restores the original 'their')*

Churn-Milk Joan [*text*: Elmet] **7** labour] effort **10** Maybe *omitted* **21** wrenched. Then] wrenched, and *Three Books.* **14** Relic of The Plague *omitted additional line after* **20**: Her legendary terror was not suffered. *Remains*

Grouse-Butts *omitted from Three Books. The present text restores the final three stanzas inadvertently omitted from Remains.* **12** The front-line emplacements] They are the front-line strategy **14** costly, beautiful] beautiful *New Statesman, 17 Feb 1978. Cf. the revised periodical version of 'Grouse-Butts', p.699*

High Sea-Light *omitted from Three Books*

Bridestones [*text*: Elmet] **15** horizons] the horizons **20** you] your ghost *Three Books.* **1** Holy of holies – a hill-top chapel. **3** heart-bone] heart-stuff **14** the weather] weather **15** horizons] hills **16** constellations] stars **17** Over] Upon **20** Touches you **23** can always lift] stares into **24** From this perch *Remains.* **3** laid] stripped *Antaeus, Summer/Autumn 1978*

Wadsworth Moor *title*: Where the Millstone of Sky *Remains*

Spring-Dusk *omitted from Three Books.* **4** its wounds] wounds *Rainbow*

Sunstruck [*text*: Elmet] *first published as a pamphlet, Sceptre Press, Aug 1977.* **10** that] the **24** Tethered to] Blocked by *Three Books.* **24** Tethered to] Chained to *Remains*

Willow-Herb *omitted from Three Books*

The Canal's Drowning Black [*text*: Elmet] **11** into] through *Three Books.* **1** the pale] bleached **2** secret] secretive **6–7** Over bridge-reflections, I teetered / On the slime-brink *etc.* **11** down into my reflection] below me **15** So when a monkey] A Monkey **17** They] So they **20** Then] And *Remains. l.25 refers to Mount Zion Wesleyan Chapel (cf. 'Mount Zion', p.480)*

The Long Tunnel Ceiling [*text*: Elmet] 31 sandstone] gritstone [*other texts all read 'sandstone'*] *Three Books*. 7 Bradford] Rochdale 7 baled with] baled 8 With worsteds and cottons, over my head met 9 Rochdale] Bradford 9 ground] fought 13 begun] started 14 Bricks were dropping out of the tunnel ceiling 15 starting] going 18 And the] The *Remains*

Under the World's Wide Rims *omitted from Three Books*

Two [*text*: Elmet] 9 an] its 12 feet] claws *Three Books*. 1 out of] from 2 The stolen grouse were glowing like embers. 9 its oracle of unending] oracles of abundance 10 spread a land] poured out 12 Bringing scorched talons of crows 14 huddled] close 16 swayed] stood still *Remains*

Mount Zion [*text*: Elmet] 13 Moriah] the desert *Three Books*. 13 *omitted* 34 could hear] heard 36 With screwdrivers and chisels *Remains*

The Ancient Briton Lay Under His Rock *omitted from Three Books*. 1 polished] glittering 11 Stinging] Hot *Encounter, Dec 1977*

Crown Point Pensioners [*text*: Elmet] 8 shifts] moves *Three Books*. 6 board-game] game 7 Spreads crumpled] Lies open *additional lines after* 9: Mills are missing. Chapels are missing. / But what has escaped the demolisher / Clings inside their masks – / Puppets of the graveyard's dreams. *additional stanza after* 13: Wild melody, wilful improvisations. / Stirred to hear still the authentic tones / The reverberations their fathers / Drew from these hill-liftings and hill-hollows / Furthered in their throats. *Remains*. [*additional stanza after* 13: *for* Wild *read* Ancient *for* Stirred *read* Proud *Listener, 6 July 1978*]

For Billy Holt *Billy Holt was a self-educated weaver from Todmorden, near Hebden Bridge in Yorkshire; a survivor of the 1914–18 war, he travelled on horseback throughout Europe, and achieved fame as a broadcaster during the Second World War*

Heptonstall *a different poem to 'Heptonstall' in Wodwo.* 28 telegraph] the telegraph *Remains*

The Beacon *originally published in Orts (poem no. 36) under the title 'Hathershelf'. Title*: You Claw the Door *Remains*. 7 eternal silence] eternity *Orts*

Emily Brontë 3 But] And 11 under] in *Rainbow*

Haworth Parsonage *omitted from Three Books. Haworth Parsonage, in West Yorkshire, was the home of the Brontë family*

Top Withens *omitted from Three Books*. 1–2 Hope squared the stone / And laid these roof slabs, and wore the way to them / With a pioneer eye. 3 was] must have looked 5 Here climbed the news 6 slow] rich 6 a] the 7 Blooming with cattle, wheat, oil, cities

8 held out] held 9 dogged] stubborn *Poetry London/Apple Magazine, Autumn 1979*

The Sluttiest Sheep in England *additional line after* 18: In his magnetic heaven 19–20 Has sent his angels to stare at you / In the likeness of beggars. *Remains.* 15 iguana] modified Iguana *Rainbow*

Auction at Stanbury *title*: Auction *Remains*

Light Falls Through Itself *omitted from Three Books*

In April *omitted from Three Books.* 12 With eyes] Eyes *Rainbow*

The Word that Space Breathes *omitted from Three Books*

Heptonstall Old Church 6 crystal] star 11 crystal] star *TLS, 24 June 1977. The Church of St Thomas à Becket, erected in Heptonstall (West Yorkshire) in 1260, has been a ruin since its roof collapsed in the mid-nineteenth century .*

Tick Tock Tick Tock *in J. M. Barrie's story, Peter Pan severs Captain Hook's right arm and throws it to a crocodile; shortly afterwards the crocodile swallows a clock*

Cock-Crows 2 was splitting] splitting *Remains. Title*: Cockcrow 1–2 Standing high to see tidal dawn / Split heaven from earth 5–19 *contracted to*: You heard / Out of deep middle-earth, in the valley cauldron / The fire-crests of the cocks / Toss up flaring, sink back again dimming // And toss harder and brighter and higher / Talon-shouts hooking higher / To hang smouldering from the night's fringes 20 The whole valley brimming with cockcrows 21 A] The 23 Crestings and spurs of glow-metal *Antaeus, Winter 1978*

The Angel *omitted from Three Books; the poem is a rewriting of 'Ballad from a Fairy Tale' in Wodwo (p.171)*

UNCOLLECTED (1979)

Irish Elk *Listener, 18 Jan 1979. The poem derives from the first half of 'The Last Migration' (p.115)*

Barley [*text*: Season Songs 1985] 1 gold bullion] gold 2 pours] flows 28 pitiless] the pitiless 48 Barbaric and tireless, a battalion of Amazons. 49 And that's] This is 51 barbed, feathered] barbed and feathered *(ed.) Michael Morpurgo, All Around the Year: New Poems by Ted Hughes, April 1979*

A Lamb in the Storm *Helix, Aug 1979*

The Rose *Helix, Aug 1979*

In the Black Chapel *published as a broadside (with a drawing by Leonard Baskin), 'on the occasion of the exhibition: Illustrations to Ted Hughes Poems', Victoria and Albert Museum, Sept/Oct 1979*

Moortown (Faber and Faber, October 1979), brought together three works previously published in limited editions by the Rainbow Press – *Prometheus On His Crag, Moortown Elegies* and *Adam and the Sacred Nine*. A fourth section, entitled *Earth-numb*, combines poems selected from *Orts* (also Rainbow Press) with miscellaneous short sequences and a loose grouping of hitherto uncollected poems [see below]. *Moortown* in effect resembles an interim Selected Poems.

In the present edition, *Prometheus On His Crag* and *Adam and the Sacred Nine* have been restored to their separate occasions; Hughes later regretted the bundling of these works together with the 'Moortown' sequence proper, which he later republished separately as *Moortown Diary* (1989), and which is here presented as a separate work.

The thirty-four poems comprising *Moortown Diary* were originally published by the Rainbow Press as *Moortown Elegies* (October 1978, 175 copies), described in the publicity flier as 'a sequence of mostly hitherto uncollected poems and passages from a verse journal about the author's experiences farming in Devon'. The poems are described in the title as *Elegies*, and the sequence dedicated to the memory of Jack Orchard, the poet's father-in-law, with whom Hughes and his wife Carol farmed Moortown Farm in north Devon, from 1972 until Jack Orchard's death in 1976.

Moortown Elegies was retitled *Moortown* when it was reprinted as the opening section of the Faber collection of the same name, in October 1979, with slight changes to the ordering of the poems. The first separate trade edition, re-titled *Moortown Diary* (Faber and Faber, September 1989), incorporated further changes to the ordering, together with the addition of dates of composition for each poem, a retrospective prose Preface, and commentary to individual poems (reproduced in Appendix One).

Texts and ordering follow *Moortown Diary*, and the present edition follows *NSP* in titling the sequence *Moortown Diary*.

Dedication: To the Memory of Jack Orchard

Feeding out-wintering cattle at twilight 25 porridge] porage *Moortown*

Foxhunt 8 expostulates] curses back *Listener, 28 April, 1977. First collected in Moon-Bells*

Struggle *additional lines after* **8**: A cow's face can alter, / Pain, misery, bewilderment alter it / But it can never speak. *Moortown Elegies*

Roe-deer 15–16 *omitted South West Review, Mar 1977. First collected in Moon-Bells*

February 17th 4 bobbed] bogged **23** that baby head] that head *Bananas, Summer 1976*

March morning unlike others *previously published in Season Songs (p.309)*

Birth of Rainbow 23 his] its 25 his] its 26 his] its 27 his] its 28 his] its 29 him] it 40 his] its *Moortown Elegies. First collected in Moon-Bells*

Orf *'orf': cattle plague, murrain*

Coming down through Somerset *first collected in Moon-Bells*

Last load 51 across] over *Moortown Elegies*

Sheep, I–II *previously published in Season Songs (and placed in the Season Songs section in NSP); Moortown omits the second of the three parts of the poem as published in Season Songs (cf. p.318)*

Hands 15 oaken-boarding] cedar-boarding 30 that] a *Moortown*. 26 estranged] aloof *Moortown Elegies*

EARTH-NUMB

The third section of *Moortown* (Faber and Faber, 1979) is entitled *Earth-numb*. Never published separately, it consists of a group of poems drawn from *Orts* (1978), together with several short sequences and miscellaneous poems, most of which had been printed in periodicals between 1966 and 1978. The present edition incorporates *Earth-numb* as a sequence – since Hughes largely adhered to its inclusions and arrangement in his later retrospective selections, *SP 1982* and *NSP* – with two exceptions: 'Heatwave' (originally published in periodical form in 1963) is here restored to the chronology of a previous decade in *Recklings*, where it was first collected; and 'Night Arrival of Sea-Trout' is reserved for *River* (1983), in which sequence it was subsequently collected.

Four uncollected 'Crow' poems, previously published in limited editions, were first collected in *Earth-numb* – 'The Lovepet', 'Life is trying to be life', 'Prospero and Sycorax', and 'Tiger-psalm' – which is where they appear in the present edition.

The text of all poems follows *Moortown* (1979) except where otherwise specified.

Earth-numb *later incorporated into Three Books (River);* 20 hole] pit *Three Books (NSP restores hole). Collected in SP 1982 and NSP*

That girl 10 all the flowers] the flowers 12 bacterium] bacteria *New Statesman, 18 Oct 1974*

Here is the Cathedral 13 hurt] live 48 do you have to be told] do we have to tell you *Listener, 5 Oct 1978. The poem's occasion is the excavation of the Roman garrison bath-house and plague burials at Exeter cathedral*

Postcard from Torquay 1 at] on 20 Gazed over] And *New Statesman, 29 Oct 1974*

Old age gets up *(ed.) Colin Falck, Poetry Supplement (PBS), 1 Dec 1977*

Nefertiti 8 breathe a word] say anything *TLS, 24 June 1977.* 8 breathe a word] say a thing *Poetry Australia, Feb 1977*

A Motorbike 14 The foreman, the boss, as bad] The foreman and the boss were as bad 25 six] five *Listener, 30 Nov 1967. Collected in SP 1982 and NSP*

Deaf School *South West Review, Mar 1977. Collected in SP 1982 and NSP*

Photostomias, I–III *first published as a pamphlet, with a relief print by Claire Van Vliet, for Charles Seluzicki, June 1977. Title:* Chiasmadon [*epigraph omitted*] 1.5 charged] arrayed III.6 fury] frenzy III.11 digits] integers III.13 mucuous and phosphorescence] mucuous – phosphorescence *Charles Seluzicki*

The Lovepet *a Crow poem; originally included in the Harper (U.S.) edition of Crow, and eventually incorporated into the selections from Crow published in SP 1982 and in NSP*

Second Birth *previously unpublished*

Song of Longsight *first published (untitled) as one of 'Poems from Caprichos', Aspect, 1978 (cf. p.352)*

Life is trying to be Life *a Crow poem, first published as 'Crow Rambles', in Poems. Fainlight, Hughes, Sillitoe.* 20 (As for a mother it cannot remember). *Poems. Fainlight, Hughes, Sillitoe. Collected in SP 1982 and NSP*

A Citrine Glimpse, I–II 1:2 a glance] like a glance *section* II omitted *ed. Edward Lowbury, Night Ride and Sunrise, 1 May 1978*

Four Tales Told by an Idiot. *First published as a pamphlet, the Sceptre Press, Aug 1979.* III.3 shapes of me leaning] parts of me standing 5 Twitched] Shook 5 a habit of me to squeak out] bits of me to cry out 6 twists of me still tangle] some of me still tangles 7 Swayed] Shook 8 Swept] Shook 8 impress will not] place would not 9 Stirred papers, parts of me stayed trapped in hooked words 10 motes] scraps 11 Stirred river, which carried most of me away 12 shed] dropped *Sceptre Press.* IV *title:* Beware of the Stars *additional line after* 15: We are totally surrounded *New Departures 10/11, 1975. The fourth of the Four Tales was collected in NSP* **Actaeon** *first published in Atlantic Monthly, Sept 1976*

Seven Dungeon Songs *Several of these poems were published in periodicals under the general title 'Caprichos', and nos. 2–7 were referred to in typescript as 'Caprichos' (cf. Sagar/Tabor, p.397; for other poems from this projected sequence, cf. pp.352–4).*

Dead she became space-earth *title*: from *Caprichos*. 3 goodness]
treasures *Boston University Journal, Spring 1977*
I walk *title*: from *Caprichos*. *additional line after* 15: My futile
stridings tangle it worse *Mars, 1977*
If mouth could open its cliff *for an alternate version of this poem,*
cf. 'If the mouth could properly open', p.353

A Knock at the Door 4 Darkness of person, hairiness of a creature
– 19 bits] pieces 24 A mouth wet and red and agile 43 lips]
face 43 scalding can's metal] hot can's edge 59 *omitted* 60 shining]
glistening 62 church] dark church *additional line after* 65:
Nobody's, humped where gravity glues it, *Critical Quarterly,*
Autumn 1979

Orts The title adverts to the fact that most of the poems in this
sequence are drawn from the limited edition of Orts (1978; cf. the
headnote to Orts); however the sequence also contains poems from
other sources, and previously unpublished poems, as noted below.
1. **Each new moment my eyes** *first published in Orts. Title:* 'X'
(ed.) Dannie Abse, PBS Supplement, Dec 1975
2. **Are they children** *first published in Orts.* 1 or senile] or are they
senile 2 A] You *Orts*
3. **For weights of blood** *first published in Orts*
5. **In the M5 restaurant** *first published in Orts.* 11 freedom
evidently] freedom *Orts. Title:* '... *part of a new sequence called*
"Lumb's Remains"' Listener, 20 March 1975. Collected in NSP
6. **Poets** *title*: Festival of Poets 1 They fringe the earth, a corolla,
wings 5 They chorus a dawn 8 And crazy] Crazy 9–12 Or they
absent / Into the grass-blade glint-atom / Fusing the globe / With
the light that fled *Bananas, Jan/Feb 1975. Collected in NSP*
7. ***Grosse Fuge*** *previously unpublished. Collected in NSP*
8. **Lucretia** *first published in Orts;.* 1 her] its 4 she] it 4 her] its
5 her] its *Orts*
9. **The Cathedral** *first published in Orts*
10. **Pan** *first published as a broadside, Morrigu Press, Aug*
1979 10 convulsion] convulsions *Morrigu Press*
11. **Speech out of shadow** *previously unpublished. Collected in SP*
1982 and NSP
12. **Everything is waiting** *previously unpublished*
14. **Flight from Egypt** *previously unpublished*
15. **Beeches, leafless** *first published in Orts, where it is untitled;*
additional opening lines: The earth is strong, faithful, true and /
Beyond all doubt / Beautiful. // Beeches, leafless *etc* 2 earth's] its
4 anchor of itself] anchor itself *Orts*
16. **Look back** *first published in Orts.* 1 See] Look 3 See] Look
additional lines after 13: // and away / Where the old streets, for
some decades / Leading everywhere, have arrived nowhere *(ed.)*
Tom Wharton, 21 Years of Poetry & Audience, May 1976
17. **Buzz in the window** *previously unpublished. Collected in CAP*
18. **Lumb** *first published in Orts, where it is untitled. Collected in*

SP 1982 and in NSP, where it is placed as one of the Gaudete epilogue poems
19. **The express** *first published in Orts*
20. **T.V. off** *first published in Orts, where it is untitled. Collected in SP 1982 and in NSP (together with 'The Stone'), under the title 'The Beacon, II'*
21. **Ophiuchos** *first published in Orts*
22. **Funeral** *previously unpublished*
23. **Children** *first published in Orts. Collected in NSP*
24. **Prospero and Sycorax** *a Crow poem, first published as 'Crow's Song about Prospero and Sycorax', as part of the pamphlet entitled Shakespeare's Poem, Lexham Press, May 1971; reprinted in the limited edition only of Crow (Faber and Faber, Dec 1973). Collected in SP 1982 and NSP*
25. **Before-dawn twilight, a sky dry as talc** *first published in Orts. Title: '... part of a new sequence called "Lumb's Remains"' Listener, 20 March 1975*

Tiger-psalm *[text: NSP] a Crow poem, first collected in Crow Wakes under the title 'Crow's Table Talk'.* 13 God of her own] The god of his own 18 her] his 26 her] his 38 the fall] a fall 46 Sister] Brother *Moortown.* 26 her] its *Listener, 16 Nov 1978. Title:* Crow's Table Talk 32 exalted] possessed *Crow Wakes.* 5 anaesthetic] an anaesthetic 13 God of her own salvation] the tiger / Is the god himself of his own salvation 23 burn] are 24 the illusion] all illusions 26 her] its 32 Kills with the strength of madness, kills possessed 43 Neither the path of life nor the path of death: *Sad Traffic, Dec 1969. Collected in SP 1982 and NSP*

The Stone *first published in the New Statesman, 6 Sept 1974. Collected in NSP (together with 'T.V. Off') as part one of 'The Beacon'*

Stained Glass *The sequence was first published in Moortown*

A God *first published in (ed.) Howard Sergeant, New Poems 1976–77 (PEN), 1 Nov 1976. Collected in SP 1982 and NSP*

UNCOLLECTED (1980–81)

Unfinished Mystery *LRB, 21 Feb 1980*

Do not Pick up the Telephone *[text: NSP] first published in Ploughshares, 1980, and first collected in SP 1982. additional lines after 8:* Panties are hotting up their circle for somebody to burn in / Nipples are evangelising bringing a sword or at least a razor / Cunt is proclaiming heaven on earth i.e. death to the infidel 28 string] cord *Ploughshares. Collected in NSP, where it is placed before Gaudete*

Lily *Ploughshares, 1980*

Sky Furnace *published as a broadside, Caricia Fine Arts, 1980*

Fort *ed. R.L. Cook, A Garland of Poems for Leonard Clark, Aug 1980*

Fishing the Estuary *Graffiti Spring 1981*

[*Publications of the Morrigu Press, 1979–80*]
Between 1979 and 1983, the Morrigu Press (named after the Crow-headed Celtic water-goddess) published some twenty separate broadsides of individual poems by Hughes, printed by his son Nicholas on an Albion hand press given by the poet's sister Olwyn. Several of these poems were subsequently collected for children, with watercolours by Leonard Baskin, in Under the North Star *(Faber and Faber, April 1981)*
Wolf [*text*: Under the North Star] *first published in First Publications of the Morrigu Press, April 1979, as 'The Iron Wolf', and collected in Under the North Star*
Puma *first published in First Publications of the Morrigu Press, April 1979, and collected in Under the North Star*
Brooktrout [*text*: Under the North Star] *first published as a broadside, Morrigu Press, June 1979, and collected in Under the North Star* **4** gorgeous] splendid **7** current's] torrent's **10** goggling] staring *Brooktrout*
Eagle *first published as a broadside, Morrigu Press, July 1980, and collected in Under the North Star*
Mosquito [*text*: CAP] *first published as a broadside, Morrigu Press, Aug 1980, and collected in Under the North Star* **4** her] his **6** her] his **7** squeezed her kneeled] held him swelled black **8** splintering quartz teeth] with splintering teeth **9** her] his *additional line after* **10**: Winter sank to her knees *Morrigu Press*

Three River Poems
A set of broadsides published by the Morrigu Press, May 1981. 'Visitation' was included in River *(1983); all three poems were later incorporated into the revised* River *sequence in* Three Books *(1993); the texts here follow* Three Books
Catadrome **5** remembering mire] mulling heart *Three River Poems*
Caddis **13** house] home **17** affirms] affirm **20** light] pattering *Three River Poems*
Visitation **4** among] in among *River*

A PRIMER OF BIRDS

Published by the Gehenna Press, July 1981 (225 copies), with woodcuts by Leonard Baskin. *A Primer of Birds* was the first book by Hughes to be published by the press, which was owned by Baskin (and which as early as 1959 had published a broadside of

'Pike', from *The Hawk in the Rain*.). Many of the poems are redrafted versions of holograph poems included in the out-of-series ('embellished') copies of the 1975 limited edition of *Cave Birds* (for an account of which, cf. *Sagar/Tabor* pp.78–79). Several poems were subsequently incorporated into Faber sequences and collections, which is where they appear in the present edition. Thus 'Kingfisher', 'Whiteness' and 'A Rival' were collected in *River* (1983); 'Nightjar' and 'Tern' were collected in *Flowers and Insects* (1986); 'Macaw', 'A Sparrow Hawk' and 'A Dove' were collected in *Wolfwatching* (1989). 'White Owl' has on the contrary been restored to its first appearance in *Crow Wakes* (1971), as 'Song against the White Owl'.

For Leonard and Lisa *a dedicatory poem for Leonard and Lisa Baskin. Sagar/Tabor (p.397) point out that this is a version of an unpublished poem from the Caprichos MS sequence*

Cuckoo [*text*: Listener, 13 June 1985, *a revised version of the Primer of Birds text*] *title*: Cuckoo's 1–4 First cry in April / Taps at the blood suspended / In its ponderous jar 5 as] like 6 the diary trembling] the month shaking 7 The orchard] And the orchard 7 Milkymaids] milky maids 15 woodland to woodland] hillside to hillside 17 The] From the 20 moll] mate 22 heirloom] precarious *additional stanza after* 23: But progress through the shire, April hazy, / With some stateliness – like a day comet / Trailing a vista-shimmering shawl of echo 24 Then comes ducking] As you duck 25–6 Covering your tracks, two of you, three, ventriloqual – / Over the hill, in the wood, and in the egg. 27–8 Soon, bare-faced, you and your wife sit cackling / Chuckling hiccoughing and converting 29 That] Your 31–2 Stuttering / Joke about baby-murder. *A Primer of Birds. 'Mayday' (p.741) is an extensively revised version of 'Cuckoo'*

Swans *previously unpublished; included in the embellished copies of Cave Birds (1975)*

Buzzard *previously unpublished; included in the embellished copies of Cave Birds (1975)*

Black-back Gull *previously unpublished*

Snipe *previously unpublished; included in the embellished copies of Cave Birds (1975)*

A Swallow [*text*: Season Songs 1985] *first collected in A Primer of Birds, added to Season Songs (1985). Title*: The Swallow 1 in] of 7 still too dumb] too dumb 8 at mirage heat] trembling hot 10 buffaloes] camels 14 So she exchanged] Exchanging 24 chimney] chymney 26 And now] And 29 bursts] burst 29 to anchor] and anchored 30 frost] the frost *A Primer of Birds. For an alternate version of the poem, cf. p.634*

Sparrow *previously unpublished; included in the embellished copies of Cave Birds (1975)*

The Hen [*text*: NSP] *previously unpublished; included in the embellished copies of Cave Birds (1975).* 9 of hot ovens] hot ovens 25 reveals to her] allows her to see *A Primer of Birds. Collected in NSP, where it is placed among poems from What Is the Truth?*

Mallard [*text*: ed. Eugene England and Peter Makuck, An Open World: Essays on Leslie Norris, Columbia S.C. 1994] *additional lines after* 2: Everything // Suddenly rubbish. Trees / Trying to take off. 5–6 Myself mixed with it / Inextricably. Blown *additional line after* 7: Gusty skeleton. 8 A space-witch] Space-witch. Sky 12 Has unbalanced] Unbalances 13 As a dark horse – sudden] But a dark horse – a sudden 14 bolts for freedom] is escaping 18–19 [...] And is snatched / Twisting away up // The drumming chimney *A Primer of Birds*

Evening Thrush [*text*: NSP] *previously unpublished; included in the embellished copies of Cave Birds (1975); added to Season Songs (1985).* 1 limes and willows] willows and limes *Season Songs (1985).* 7 head-up, flame-naked] flame-naked 38 With] By *Listener,* 2 *June 1983.* 1 limes and willows] willows and elms 7 head-up, flame-naked] flame-naked, head-back *A Primer of Birds. Collected in NSP*

Magpie *previously unpublished*

Shrike *previously unpublished; included in the embellished copies of Cave Birds (1975)*

Starlings Have Come [*text*: Season Songs 1985] *title*: Starlings Come Suddenly 8–10 Now a close-up seething of fleas. / Starlings, / All, as one, out of control, a doom-panic mob, / A fever of infection, they wrap you 11 assembling] suddenly assembling 17 This Elizabethan] The Elizabethan *A Primer of Birds. Added to Season Songs (1985)*

Bullfinch *title*: Bullfinches *Moon-Bells*

Wren *previously unpublished*

Nightingale *previously unpublished*

The Moorhen *reprinted in Three Books (River)* 17 thistledown] this thistledown 18 Scampered] Scootered 19 sprint-strides] hurdle-strides *Moon-Bells (2nd ed., 1986).* 17 thistledown, black, tip-toe] black tip-toe thistledown 19 Lumpier] Heavier *Quarto, Oct 1980*

Pheasant *previously unpublished; included in the embellished copies of Cave Birds (1975)*

Phoenix *previously unpublished*

UNCOLLECTED (1981–83)

Cows *published as a broadside, 'printed by Nicholas Hughes for the benefit of Farms for City Children', 21 Sept 1981*

'Drove Six or so high miles' *(ed.) David Harsent, New Poetry 7, Nov 1981*

River of Dialectics *(ed.) Andrew Motion, Poetry Supplement (PBS), Nov 1981*

Sing the Rat *LRB, 18 Feb 1982*

Giant Dream of Elephants *published as a 'booklet', Morrigu Press, July 1982*

Remembering Teheran [*text*: NSP] **4** a] the **6** Evin Motel] Motel **10** bosom] bosoms **20** wide] large **20** trees] leaves **21** big males] males **24** among] through **25** Between] Among the **29** a] the **33** script] scripts **40** straightened] turned **41** the wrong] some ultimate **43–4** All round me stood the peculiar thistles – / Desert-fanatics – **47** an optimum] a complete **51** cobalt-cored] violet-edged **53** [...] long-shadowed outriders **54** Cast in perfect metal (radiation-proof), **56** drinking] testing **60–3** I found a wriggle of water / That had somehow smuggled itself down **65** It wriggled these last] Spilling and scribbling its last **67** Its naked little current seemed almost dangerous **78** Sipped] Sipping **84–9** At a giddy moment – / To the belly-dancer, the snakiest, loftiest beauty, / (Though she would not dance on my table or kiss me through her veil, / And though she made her request / Only through her demon-mask warrior drummer) **92** saw] watched *LRB, 19 Aug 1982. First collected in NSP*

The Great Irish Pike [*text*: LRB, 2–29 Dec 1982] *first published as a separate, Appledore Press, 1982, with lithographs by Barrie Cooke. 26 copies*

Thomas the Rhymer's Song *recorded by Shusha Guppy, on 'Durable Fire' (Linnet Records), 1982; never printed*

Madly Singing in the Mountains [*text*: Three Books (River)] **14–15** *conflated to*: Time is afraid of them **16–17** Here in their first infancy, / New-born ancients, they sun themselves *additional final line*: (Time dare hardly breathe as it listens.) *(ed.) Thomas Redshaw, Hill Field: Poems and Memoirs for John Montague on His Sixtieth Birthday, June 1989. Dedication omitted* **15** They cannot learn any more **16** wrinkled ancients *omitted* **17** Ancient sages, they sun themselves **19** time can't touch] God first taught them *additional final line*: Waiting for the beginning to come round. *(ed.) Alan Brownjohn, New Year Poetry Supplement (PBS), Dec 1982. Collected in Three Books*

To Be Harry *New Departures, Jan 1983. written i.m. Harry Fainlight. 'A few details are necessary as explanatory notes to the*

1285

poem. *Harry died alone outside his isolated Welsh cottage, and the body was not found for some days. The title of the only publication in his lifetime, a pamphlet of poems, is* Sussicran *(Narcissus spelt backwards). He participated in a "happening" in which his role was to be the body in a coffin carried into the Underground, and spent several hours travelling around the Circle Line with a cortege of excited mourners.'* – Ruth Fainlight, 'To Be Harry', in *(ed.)* Nick Gammage, The Epic Poise: A Celebration of Ted Hughes, *Faber and Faber, 1999 – where the poem is reprinted, with one variant:* 5 burned] buried

Mice Are Funny Little Creatures *published as a 'booklet',* Morrigu Press, Jan 1983

Weasels At Work *published as a 'booklet',* Morrigu Press, Jan 1983

Fly Inspects *published as a 'booklet',* Morrigu Press, Mar 1983

Swallows Listener, *21 April 1983; an alternate version of 'A Swallow' in* A Primer of Birds *(p.604), with two additional sections; published after the* Primer of Birds *text and before the revised* Primer of Birds *text as collected in* Season Songs *(1985)*

RIVER

River exists in two versions: the first Faber edition, published September 1983 with photographs by Peter Keen; secondly the sequence – without photographs – as revised and reordered for inclusion ten years later in *Three Books* (Faber and Faber, 1993). These are referred to below as, respectively, *River* and *Three Books*. Nine poems were omitted and thirteen poems added to the sequence in *Three Books*. The present edition follows *River* (1983) for the contents and ordering of the sequence; the copytext is likewise *River* for those poems which were not reprinted in *Three Books*; otherwise *Three Books* is followed for texts and for titles, with exceptions noted below. The thirteen poems added to the sequence for the first time in *Three Books* are entered at 1993, if previously unpublished, or variously according to their earlier dates of periodical publication. For *Three Books* Hughes supplied an endnote concerning the sequence, which is included in Appendix One.

The U.S. edition (Harper & Row, 1983) was published without photographs.

Title: originally announced by Faber (for publication in June 1983) as *October Salmon. River Poems and Photographs*.

Dedication: For Andrea and for Nicholas (*River*); For Nicholas (*Three Books*)

The Morning Before Christmas *omitted from Three Books*

Japanese River Tales, 1–11 1.12 raggy] tattered *River*

Flesh of Light 2–5 Inside the sun, the smelting / crawls and glitters among heather-topped stones. // The mill of the galaxy, the generator / Making the atoms dance / with its reverberations, brims out lowly / For cattle to wade. They lift muzzles / That unspool the glair, 7–14 The power-line, alive in its rough trench, / Electrifies the anemones / And the bristling wheat. A chrism of birth // Anoints the earth's bones. Ferns, unfolding baby fists, / Nod into upreaching, eyes of egg-film / Wobble for focus, in the throbbing aura // Of the river's magnetic descent 17 rainbow] inscribed *River*

New Year *omitted from Three Books*

Whiteness 10 away] away up 18 the] its *(ed.) Emma Tennant, Saturday Night Reader, Oct 1979.* 6 hidden man's] man's *(ed.) Geoffrey Elborn, Hand and Eye, Tragara Press, Nov 1977. First collected in A Primer of Birds*
Four March Watercolours *omitted from Three Books*

The Merry Mink 13 like a constellation] a constellation *River.* 9 at] on *Quarto, Oct 1980*

Salmon-Taking Times 1 flood-storm] flood rain 2 loud] wild 3 hillsides] the hillsides 5 Possessed sows and boars, frisk-tailed piglets, *River.* 3–6 Flushed out of the hillsides. Stampeding muscle, / Piglets, tusky old boars, lumbering sows / Quarrelling in the narrows. *etc* 19 membranes] filaments *(ed.) Douglas Dunn, PBS Supplement, Dec 1979*

A Cormorant 7 Pleistocene] Palaeolithic 21 incomprehension] befuddlement 25–6 He's thinking: 'Here's one of those monsters. / Dare I risk another dive?' He dives. *(ed.) Alan Brownjohn, New Year Poetry Supplement (PBS), Dec 1982*

Stump Pool in April 11 limp] broad 12 Creased and humped in their folds, convulse 17 and to fasten – in wedlock –] and somehow to tangle *River*

Go Fishing 7 glistenings] the womb *River.* 20 Mangled] Churned *New Statesman, 26 June 1981*

Milesian Encounter on the Sligachan *[text: NSP] the Sligachan: a river on the Isle of Skye, Scotland; 'milesian': a group of legendary early invaders of Ireland, partial to tall tales; 'gruagach': a young maiden (gaelic); 'glaistig': a fairy haunting a stream (gaelic); 'boggart': a spectre haunting a locale (west Yorkshire).*
5 crusty] a crusty 28 sliding] swinging 36 Searching in from space *River.* 47 sunk there] there *Three Books.* 12 scapulae] scapulars 17 glimpse] glance 36 Searing in from space *Enter Rumour, Spring 1983*

Ophelia *first published in Orts*

Creation of Fishes *omitted from Three Books*

The West Dart *title*: West Dart 1 spiked] pronged 6 granite] moorland *River*

Strangers [*text*: River] 20 And] They 21 strafed hogweed] hogweed 22 aiming] strafing 24 blind] unfeeling *Three Books (the NSP text follows River, rather than Three Books)*

After Moonless Midnight *omitted from Three Books*

An August Salmon 27 *omitted River*

The Vintage of River is Unending *omitted from Three Books*

Night Arrival of Sea-Trout *originally published as a broadside, First Publications of the Morrigu Press, May 1979; reprinted in Earth-numb [Moortown] and in Earth Dances (1994).* 1 her] its 2 her open] its opened 5 tossing] comes tossing 8–9 *conflated to*: The stillness snarls, moon-mouthed, and shivers *LRB, 25 Oct 1979*

The Kingfisher 12 beak full of ingots] a shower of prisms *additional line after* 12: A spilling armful of gems, beak full of ingots *River.* 11 sunken] sunken greasy 12 Bursts from the mirror, showering prisms – *additional line after* 12: Brings up an armful of gems, a beakful of ingots 22 And look! He's / – gone again.] And look! He's back – / He's gone – *A Primer of Birds*

That Morning *first collected in SP 1982, where it is placed as the final poem in the volume, as in the Three Books version of River and in the NSP selection from River.* 16 thought] breath *(ed.) Roger Pringle, A Garland for the Laureate: Poems Presented to Sir John Betjeman, Nov 1981*

The River *title*: River *River. Title*: The Word River 3–4 But the river cannot be killed, whatever. / It goes on, flowing from heaven, 7 Scattered] Broken 8 tombs] tomb 16 door] cascades 18 our] all *New Departures 26 Sept 1980*

The Gulkana [*text*: NSP] *After publication in the Faber edition of River (1983), the poem was substantially revised for its appearance in the Harper (U.S.) edition of River (1984), and further revised for inclusion in Three Books and NSP. The Gulkana: a river in southeastern Alaska; its waters meet the Copper River, whose waters flow south into the Gulf of Alaska.* 1–2 *appear as lines* 4–5 4 Away to the north, jumbled iceberg hills 6 Strange] Fine 9-10 A Lazarus [...] below *omitted* 13 purplish emptiness] ultra-violet 25 in perpetual] was in perpetual 26 And this was the Gulkana 29 A stone voice that] And 33 – nearly] Almost 35 Made my steps strange to me. It stayed with me 36 swayed] rode 37 We'd] I'd 44 In the strange violet light, that mercury light 46 my] the 51 for] of 94 away] from us 98 *omitted* 100 Aboriginal] These aboriginal 102 They will] Will 103 *omitted* 108 a] the 117 drained, and counted, and healed] seized, and tasted and drained 118 the]

that 119 A spectre of fragments] A spectre 121 And sipped at it.
Adrift, convalescent 122 the whole 747] our aircraft 124 A spectre]
And a spectre 126 core-darkness] darkness 127 at] on to 130–1 It
was like lovesickness. Like a mourning / Numbness, a secret
bleeding, a deeper *Three Books*.
1 away to] to 3–5 *omitted* 8 thread] line 8 child's] left 9 Across
our map] Through our crumpled map 10 stumbled] moved
26 And the Gulkana 31 skyline] horizon 41 blood-rich] fruit-
sweet 42 Pilgrims] Pilgrim 44 In the mercury light 55–56 some
doppelgänger/Disinherited other] some disinherited being/And
doppelgänger other 68 glacial] Arctic 77 black, refrigerating]
refrigerating 79 their] the 80 Those] The 81 an undelivered
covenant] undelivered promise 90 The flutes, the drumming] Of
drumming and flutes 93 They looked like what they were,
somnambulists] somnambulists 94 melting away] as they melted
away 95 a sacrament] their sacrament 97 Within numbered
days 98 On] There, on 99 *omitted* 102 circle] dance 105 Begin to]
They will 106 The current hosing] The water sluicing 107 shaken]
poured 111 masks] the masks 112 Torn off – their very bodies
114 Ripped away] Torn off *additional line after* 116: A thin wind
off the peak of a mountain 118 Into that amethyst – 127–8 Down
onto Greenland's corpse / Tight-shrouded with snow-glare.
129–135 The burden of the river moved in me / Like lovesickness. /
Woke deeper, a secret bleeding of mourning, In my cave of body.
While I recorded /The King Salmon's eye. / And the blood-mote
mosquito. / And the stilt-legged, one-rose rose / With its mock
aperture, its brave exposure *River (Harper and Row edition, 1984)*.
Title: Gulkana 1–2 *omitted* 4 Swung out of the black spruce forest,
on a pebbly bend *additional line after* 5: Hazed with forest fires
that had burned for weeks. 6 does] did 8 child's] childish
9–16 *contracted to*: Through our crumpled map. It was water /
More than water, rocks that were more than rocks. // A scrapyard
of boxy shacks 48–9 eye/That] eyes/Which 52 ear-drum] ear-
drums 74 ogling] staring 80 visors] faces 83 Heavily veiled, seraphs
of heavy ore 89–114 *contracted to*: By the drums and flutes of its
volume. We watched them / Move like drugged victims as they
melted / Toward their sacrament – a consummation / Where only
one thing was certain: / The actual, sundering death. The rebirth /
Unknown, uncertain. Only that death 125–7 Peered from the
window, under the cobalt blaze, / Down onto Greenland's
unremoving corpse 129–34 The burden of the river, beyond
waking, / Numbed back into my marrow. While I recorded / The
King Salmon's eye. And the blood-mote mosquito. / And the stilt-
legged, one-rose rose *River (Faber edition, 1983)*.
Title: The Gulkana *text identical to River (Faber 1983), except for:*
melted / Toward their sacrament [89–114] *read* dissolved / Toward
their ecstasy *and for* seized [117] *read* seized on *LRB, 19 May 1983*

In the Dark Violin of the Valley 9 glassy] draughty *River*. 9 glassy]
steely 18 a grave] the grave *Grand Street, Autumn 1981*

Low Water 5 She lies back. She is tipsy and bored. *River*

A Rival 17 The river lies, mutilated. Face averted, *A Primer of Birds*

Performance *Title*: Last Act (performed by a male) 5 Her] A
19 Phaedra] A Phaedra 22 So frail and so sulphurous, *River. Title*:
Last Act 15 still in her] in her 17 crypt] core 18 Such a destiny, so
drugged a victim! 19–20 *omitted* 27 him] her 29 puppet-clown]
puppet-priestess 29 his] her *Quarto, Oct 1980*

Eighty, and Still Fishing for Salmon 21 Though] Now *River*

September *omitted from Three Books*

An Eel, I–II [*text*: NSP] *section II was not included in the text as
published in River or in Three Books; it was first included in CAP,
and the poem reprinted thus in NSP*

Riverwatcher *omitted from Three Books*

October Salmon 8 hardly a winter] a bare winter *SP 1982.*
18–19 The sea-going Aurora Borealis of his April fury, 25 already
dressed] dressed 26 regimentals] ceremonials 26 her badges]
badges 45 energy] elation *LRB, 16 April 1981*

Torridge *title*: The Woman in the Valley 16 December] November
*SP 1982 (where the poem was first published); omitted from Three
Books*

Salmon Eggs [*text*: NSP] 30 advent] coming *Three Books.*
2 Shuddering together, touching each other 3 Shedding]
Emptying 5 peel] curve 23 tidings] toilings 28 dislocated] burst
30 Earth's advent] the earth's tidings 31 Of raptures and
rendings. / Sanctus Sanctus / Swathes the blessed issue. Perpetual
mass 33 This is] It is *River.* 2 Shuddering together, caressing
each other 33 This is the swollen vent] It is the raw vent
*Grand Street, Autumn 1981 and SP 1982, where poem was first
collected*

UNCOLLECTED (1983–86)

The Mayfly *London Magazine, Oct 1983; phrases from the poem
contribute to 'Saint's Island' (p.716)*

The Pigeon's Wings *London Magazine, Oct 1983*

The Live-Bait *Outposts, Autumn 1983*

Waste *(ed.) David Harsent, Winter Poetry Supplement (PBS) 1983*

The Hare [*text*: NSP] *TLS, 30 March 1984. Collected in What Is
The Truth? (1984) and in NSP*

Waterlicked *TLS, 27 April 1984. Collected in CAP*

Familiar [*text*: Elmet] *first collected in Three Books.* **2** sip] take
3–4 Your friends are the Wesleyan vicar and the Catholic priest, /
One brings you flowers, one whisky. A lifted glass – **10** Sage] Owl
Three Books. **3–4** The Wesleyan Vicar had brought flowers. / The
Catholic Priest whisky. A lifted glass – **9–10** My father is hardly
four. You are forty, / Already an old salt of the dyer's vat.
13 Heirloom bit of ghost **20** boot] punt **30–6** Into such a blank
negative / Your burial left not a trace. / Even the grave's lost. // In
the sour, sodden, rubbly dirt / Of the Calder crevasse, you escaped
/ Granny's Victorian blacks, church blocks, the labour / Of the
valley conscience. / Yet I'm proof **37** reach] move **38** As I touch]
And now, as I touch **39–40** The phrases aside. Peer deeper / Into
my misty mirror of paper. *TLS, 18 May 1984*

Disarmament *Critical Quarterly, Spring/Summer 1984*

Mokomaki
'Thirteen etchings of shrunken & tattoed Maori heads by Leonard
Baskin & three poems by Ted Hughes', the Eremite Press, 1985 [no
date]. 50 copies.
Halfway Head *reprinted in Grand Street, Autumn 1986*
Aspiring Head *never reprinted.*
Landmark Head *untitled* **7** Where air is its lung, world is its
beauty **9** membrane] animal threads **13** fear] horror **16** And my
knowledge, and my emptiness *Aspect, 1978 [no date], where the
poem is described as from the projected sequence Caprichos (cf.
pp.352–4); in his correspondence Hughes described all three poems
as from the Caprichos sequence*

What's the First Thing You Think of? [*text*: Elmet] **9** Below] Just
below **9** above] by *Three Books. Title*: Three Voices *additional
opening line*: The first one mused: 'Funny things, memories. **1–2** My
brother bowed over his aeroplanes. / I crept out. But I'd left a blood-
splash **4–5** Off a twelve-bore cartridge. The knife that cut me / Had
a deer's foot. I found our black cat **7** the] my *additional line after 7*:
The second thought: 'Is it worth it?' Then aloud: **8–10** *omitted*
12 Flew past] Flew *additional lines after 14*: And smiled: 'Something
and nothing!' // Then the third: **15–16** 'A beeswax casque, a delicate
Viking prow / Lay there, from some sea **17** Wilder] Vaster
19–20 and for all the gaping/wound] and the/terror *Spectator, 2 Feb
1985. First collected in Three Books (Remains of Elmet)*

Conscripts *South West Review, Feb 1985*

The Best Worker in Europe *published as a leaflet, The Atlantic
Salmon Trust, 1985; the first three stanzas only were printed in The
Times, 18 March 1985*

Grouse Butts *Listener, 15 August 1985; an extensively revised
version of the poem of the same title in Remains of Elmet (p.471)*

Edith *Listener, 5 Sept 1985. Edith (Farrar), the poet's mother*

Rights *Arts Yorkshire, Oct/Nov 1985*

The Pike *Listener, 22 May 1986*

Mayday *Listener, 22 May 1986*

Sketching a Thatcher [*text*: NSP] **8** the] a **16** Cackling] Crowing *additional line after* **22**: A machine of mechanical merriment, hacking its iron *additional line after* **26**: Lean, quick face from the undergrowth, elvish warrior **27** the bird-stare] its weasel bone **28** The] And *additional lines after* **35**: With a hawk-fling of wild spirit. / Merry as a mink. Biologically merry. **38** *expanded to*: As his crusty roofs. And too quick-vertical / For spirit-sludge to collect and thicken in him / To puddling malaise. He ladder-dances *ed. Susan Hill, People: Essays and Poems, Sept 1983. Collected in Moon-Bells (1986) and in NSP, where it is retrospectively placed within the Moortown Diary sequence.*

Lamenting Head *Grand Street, Autumn 1986*

Reckless Head *Grand Street, Autumn 1986; first published as a broadside, Turret Bookshop, May 1993. Collected in NSP*

Sacrificed Head *Grand Street, Autumn 1986*

FLOWERS AND INSECTS

Published by Faber and Faber, October 1986, with watercolours by Leonard Baskin. The text is reproduced complete, with the following exceptions: 'An Almost Crownless Thorn' was reprinted in *Rain-Charm for the Duchy*, where it is placed in the present edition; 'Eclipse' was first published as a pamphlet, in 1976, and is here entered at its earlier date (p.347).
    Subtitle: Some Birds and a Pair of Spiders. *Dedication*: For Frieda and Lucretia

A Violet at Lough Aughresburg *title*: Violet **3** branch] tree-full **10** holds it all, a moment] protects it all *New Statesman, 9 Dec 1983. Collected in NSP*

Daffodils 1 patch] bit **4** A gilding] It was a gilding **5** kept] they kept on **15** Did not] I did not **19** rustlings] wrappers **20** I sold] And I sold **21** dark] green **24** their] the **26** their] the **28** scared, bright] bright, scared **29** a defter] gentler **29** So many] A thousand **31** Felt deep into her chilly fountain of blades − **36** Buckling] The buckling **42–3** *transposed* **45** Had taken refuge inside me − **61** so alive] alive **65** garden] grass **68** With a grisly awe **76** earth-weight] corpse-weight **78** my unlikely] with my unlikely *LRB, 1 March 1984. The poem was partially adapted for 'Daffodils' in Birthday Letters (cf. p.1125 and endnote)*

Two Tortoiseshell Butterflies 10 *expanded to*: Maywear of the lawn, brocade of Daisies, / Embroidery of Dandelions. **21** to flat]

then flat 30 Wobbles] Wobbling 33 She] As she 49 just like] like
London Magazine, Nov 1985. Collected in NSP

Where I Sit Writing My Letter 18 [...] Where? Where? Where now?
– and they're off *Listener, 13 June 1985. Collected in NSP*

Tern *dedication omitted* 8 By his] For his 14 triggered magnet]
powerful elastic 21 precarious] perilous 22 In] Hovering in 23 His
meaning has no margin] Priest of this place *A Primer of Birds.*
Title: A Tern 8 By his] For her 12 his] her 15 him] her 16 He] She
18 His] Her 20 His] Her 20 He] She 23 His meaning has no
margin] Priestess of this place 23 He] She 24 his] her 25 his] her
(ed.) William Scammell, Between Comets: For Norman Nicholson
at Seventy, Sept 1984. Collected in NSP

The Honey Bee *collected in NSP*

In the Likeness of a Grasshopper 5 flimsily] daintily 6 raspy-dry]
raspy, dry 8 A belly of life, pulsing sexual signals. 11 The nimble
trap *Literary Review, Oct 1986. Collected in NSP*

Sunstruck Foxglove 4 dress] gown *London Magazine, Nov 1985.*
Collected in NSP

Big Poppy *additional opening line*: Whiskery, animal shank!
Barbarous leaves! 17 And enter monastic afterlife 18 inwardly]
internally 19 maternal nectars] stupefying nectar 20 cradle] the
cradle *New Republic, 26 March 1984*

Nightjar *first collected in A Primer of Birds*

UNCOLLECTED (1987-89)

Devon Riviera *(ed.) Jonathan Barker, PBS Anthology 1986/87;*
reprinted in the Sunday Times, 5 July 1998, as the first of 'Two
Views of the Devon Riviera', the second of which continues: The
prisoners / Rush to the eyes, press their faces / To the light. //
They can hear the shoutings of freedom. // They rush to the lips,
race through the galleries / Of the tongue // They beat on the
throat / Beat on the bars of the chest // Crowd every stair, storm
downward / To the gate of the genitals // Pound and thunder and
scatter again // Search up and down the walls of the legs / Scrabble
at the floors of the hands // Lever at the crack under the fingernails
// Rush again to the eyes and stare out / Flinging their shouts
outward / Into the deafenings of freedom. // The jailor / Opens
another comic.

First Things First [*text*: ed. Jonathon Porritt, Save The Earth, Sept
1991] *additional lines after* 10: etc / etc / etc etc etc 11 Annual
Expansion] Expansion *additional stanzas after* 22: SECOND
TWIN: / The Sphinx is man's nobility. / The riddle – our own
story. / Bored, experimental beast. / Earth for laboratory. // BOTH

(singing): / The heady bubbles of the brain / Give men their giddy
legs O / So bang your skulls together boys / And drain it to the
dregs O 23 Man's] Our 23 I] we 24 his] our 25 He] We *additional
lines after* 26: BOTH (singing): / The heady bubbles of the brain
(*etc*) // SECOND: / Although the Bomb, that ended War, / Was
greatly to our tastes, / Who'd have thought the very globe / Would
shrivel with the wastes? // BOTH (singing): / The heady bubbles of
the brain (*etc*) // SECOND: / Yet who declared: 'No matter though
/ We atom-happy men / Rid Earth of Life, the Bugs of space / Will
start it up again'? // BOTH: / The heady bubbles of the brain (*etc*)
additional lines after 30: BOTH (singing): / The heady bubbles of
the brain (*etc*) *Times, 4 June 1987*

A Full House *(ed.) Charles Osborne, Poems for Shakespeare, July
1987. Section 5 ('King of Hearts') was reprinted in Sept 1998 as a
separate poem, entitled 'Shakespeare, drafting his will', omitting the
'Envoi' and adding a prose gloss (see p.1193)*

Birthday Greetings *(ed.) Harry Chambers, Causley at Seventy, Oct
1987*

Chinese History of Colden Water [*text*: Three Books] *a rewriting
of 'The Trance of Light' from Remains of Elmet (p.459).* 1 A
fallen immortal] An Immortal 2 Leafy conch] A conch 6 These
hushings] The sounds 6 missed] never noticed 7 toiling] coming
8 Asleep he heard the clink of fairy metal 9 To a] Under 12–13 He
awoke in a panic. Lay panting. / Blinked away 18 the waves] a tide
*(eds.) Maura Dooley and David Hunter, Singing Brink: An
Anthology of Poetry from Lumb Bank, 1987. Collected in Three
Books*

Kore *(ed.) Gillian Clarke, PBS Anthology 1987/88, Oct 1987*

Glimpse *LRB, 4 Feb 1988*

If [*text*: Three Books (River)] *title*: What the Serpent Said to Adam
3 which] that 11 your corrupted flesh] your flesh 14 get] find
15 Already – the drop] Already, look, the drop *Sunday
Correspondent, 17 Sept 1989. Collected in Three Books*

Mayday *(ed.) Christopher Reid, PBS Anthology 1989–90, Oct 1989;
a revised version of 'Cuckoo' in A Primer of Birds (p.599)*

Lines about Elias *PN Review, (16 ii:44) 1989. Collected in NSP*

WOLFWATCHING

Published by Faber and Faber, September 1989. Two of the poems
were previously collected in *A Primer of Birds* (1981); eight poems
were subsequently reprinted in *Elmet* (1994). The present edition
prints the complete text of *Wolfwatching*, with the exception of 'A
Dove' (placed at the end of *Collected Poems*, cf. endnote p.1303).

Text: *Wolfwatching*, but incorporating revisions from *Elmet* and *NSP*, as noted below. *Dedication*: For Hilda

A Sparrow Hawk 1 your] the 11 We find the earth-tied spurs, among ashes 12 you] we *A Primer of Birds*

Astrological Conundrums [*text*: NSP]. *Title*: 'Two Astrological Conundrums'. 1.1 just walking] walking 1.27 fear] terror *section* 11 *omitted (first published in NSP)* 111.4 So perfectly strung] Strung so perfectly *Wolfwatching*

Slump Sundays 15 The homegrown hallucinogen] decrepit mythology 22 Like a stone tipped from the overgrown quarry *TLS, 8 Mar 1985. Reprinted in Elmet (1994)*

Climbing into Heptonstall 7 weeps] drains 10 Congealed] Condensed 30 That] The 32 their one plenty. So] their sole plenty 41–4 *contracted to*: Of going without – of going without – ' 53 With a sweep of the arm, as if he'd heard nothing: *LRB, 19 June 1986. Reprinted in Elmet (1994), with an Epigraph*: 'Bout's bare, but it's easy' [Proverb]

Macaw *title*: A Macaw 8 cords] strings 18 that] your *LRB, 15 Nov 1984. Title*: The Macaw 1 How you hate it all! 4 With] And with 7 you weave you entangle] and weave and entangle 9 and trample] trample 10–15 Look at those eyes – embittered / By their sockets, in that sulphurous club-axe / He has to use for a face – // That helm, that black flint-cowl / Which is also his third foot! / And that flint cup-jaw, so crudely cut off. 16 Such a pale eye] His pale eyes 19 hauberk] armour 20 Nothing will help, you know] – and cannot help, / He knows 21 you come] he comes 22 dancing] smiling 25 Torture-instrument 27 your] his *A Primer of Birds*.

Dust As We Are *title*: 'Dust as we are' etc. 10 curtain] veil 10 deftly] briskly 22 Slithered] Tumbled 24 sprawled] lay 28 a silence like prayer] prayers 30 very] all 33 fragility] smallness 33 And I filled] I filled up 35 A] The 38 kind] sort *Listener, 2 Jan 1986*

Wolfwatching *first published as a pamphlet, Morrigu Press, July 1982. Title*: Wolf-Watching 8 Behind] Inside 49–50 His big limbs/ Are full] Big limbs/Full 60 *omitted* 61 resplays] and resplays 64 Dropped] Fallen 66–7 *omits*: But all the time / The awful thing is happening 75 gossip] the talk 75 forest] forests 76 panic] rustling 80 around] round 83 all this is] it's all 94 prodigious] immense 98 tangled] knotted 99 damaged his brain] knocked him unconscious 102 *expanded to*: Souring in his skin] Going sour in his skin. All that readiness / Rejected, reabsorbed. 106 A million] Ten thousand 107 Ten million] A million 113 tarot-card] tarot-dream *Morrigu Press*

Telegraph Wires 1 lonely] empty *Listener, 21 Nov 1985. Reprinted in Elmet, 1994*

Sacrifice 1–2 *expanded to*: Little One Too Many – / Born at the bottom of the heap. / The baby daughter's doll. / She trailed after the others, lugging him. // Little One Too Many grew up / With a strangely wrinkled brow – fold on fold 9 built] piled 11 His fateful] Little One Too Many's 13 Screwdriver, drill] Drill, screwdriver 17 jars] shakes 30 five-inch] four-inch 30 skylines] sky 31 to] then 34 of] in *LRB, 24 Jan 1985. Reprinted in Elmet, 1994*

For the Duration 19 appalling] astounding 34 marvel and laugh] laugh and marvel *Listener, 9 May 1985. Reprinted in Elmet, 1994*

Anthem for Doomed Youth [*text*: Elmet] 1 the morning star] the morning 30–1 [...] hold/In her broody fingers? *additional line after* 43: Exorcists of our own Annunciation – *Wolfwatching. Title*: Plenty Coups 1–4 *omitted* 5 9th, 10th, 11th of August, 9 the top towards] the tops to 10 Days heather] When heather 16 feather] husk 23 quiet-eyed] quiet-browed 30–1 *are identical to the later Elmet text, rather than the Wolfwatching version* 41 Dumb and deaf] Thin, wet, vicious 43–4 Dialogue with history, / Democratic, levelling – 47 *expanded to*: Incidental, big peonies / For Grandad's grave. (*ed.*) *David Harsent, New Poetry 7, Nov 1981. Reprinted in Elmet, 1994*

The Black Rhino *title:* On the Brink 1.1 This is the Black Rhino] Here he is 11.14 Child] Son [*in section* 111 *the Rhino is male and the White Egret female*] 111.20 between] beneath 111.27 bigshots] VIPs *additional section* 1v [*omitted in Wolfwatching*]: The Rhino's mask, a total wound – / The whole face a mouth opened / Uttering its heart-blood a cry – / Fails to deter a single fly. // His murderer hears the bloody mouth / Tell more than the horn is worth: / Glamour of the game, the poachers' wars, / Appease addicted ancestors. // The middleman, who folds the notes, / Deafened by the silenced throats / That feed mankind, yawns at blood / That curses man and cries to God. //And he who wears the Rhino's knife, / Hearing the cry, cannot believe / That this, his pride, is a global crime / For which the fine is global shame. *Daily Telegraph Weekend, 24 Oct 1987*

Leaf Mould [*text*: NSP] *reprinted in Three Books (1993) and in Elmet (1994), the poem is a much revised version of 'Hardcastle Crags' in Remains of Elmet (1979), p.456, and was first published in the TLS under the title 'Hardcastle Crags'; in Elmet the poem carries an epigraph (omitted from the NSP text) which quotes the opening line of the original 'Hardcastle Crags':* 'Think often of the silent valley, for the god lives there.' *Title*: Hardcastle Crags 15–16 And birches, and oaks, / And conifers – / The lightest air-stir 17–18 Released their love-whispers when that other / Walked beneath them weeping, dedicating 19 spectre-double] spirit-double 26 her whole] this whole 28 Now, wherever] Whenever 30–31 Leaf-loam. Warm leaf-loam. / Crumbly deafness. *TLS, 7 June 1985. ll.7–11: cf. endnote to 'For Billy Holt', p.1275*

Manchester Skytrain 1 The nightmare is that last straight into the camera 19 whirls] flings 32 Eased hot from the wreck] Salvaged from the crash 36 A dark horse] 'A dark horse' *LRB, 6 Mar 1986*

Walt, I–II 1. *'Under High Wood: cf. 'My Uncle's Wound',* *p.100.* I.35–6 'Here,' he hazarded. 'It was somewhere here. / This is where it happened. I got this far.' *(ed.) Lawrence Sail, First and Always: Poems for the Great Ormond Street Children's Hospital, Oct 1988.* II.29 And I almost] I can almost II.34 full-rigged] full-sailed II.38 *The Times* Index] *The Financial Times* II.40 'Why can't I die?' he'd cried, straightening, turning. II.69 reaching] turning *LRB, 15 Nov 1984. Reprinted (part I only) in Elmet*

Take What You Want But Pay For It 1.15 surrounding] primaeval 1.20 finished] sculpted II.11 the] his *LRB, 29 Sept 1988*

Little Whale Song 26 Earth-drama] world-drama 29 exquisite] delicate *Poems for Charles Causley, Enitharmon Press, Aug 1982*

CAPRICCIO

Published by the Gehenna Press, Spring 1990. 50 copies. With engravings by Leonard Baskin. There was no Faber edition of these twenty previously unpublished poems, eight of which were however subsequently collected in *NSP*, as noted below. Text: *Capriccio*, incorporating *NSP* revisions.

The Locket [*text*: NSP] 14–15 [...] secret, blueish,/Demonic flash] secret/Demonic flash 17 read] heard *Independent on Sunday, 7 June 1992.* 1 Song of Songs] Canticles 11 breasts!] breasts. 14–15 A secret, blueish,/Demonic flash] A demonic/Secret flash 22 How your death looked] What your death looked like *Capriccio. Collected in NSP*

Descent [*text*: NSP] 19 all you had] that you had 22 in] at *Capriccio. Collected in NSP*

Folktale [*text*: NSP] 1 cinders] the cinders 5 of Ein-Gedi] Ein-Gedi 17 Cabala] the Cabala 18 bag full] bagful *Capriccio. Collected in NSP*

Fanaticism *subsequently adapted to form part I of an uncollected poem entitled 'Two Views of the Sea', a contribution to A Garland for Stephen Spender (ed. Barry Humphries, May 1991), part II of which reads:* Where blown spray falls / We are the stones. // Of lands that burst / From sleep and bowed / Like animals / To quench their thirst / Where waters flowed / We are the bones.

Snow [*text*: NSP] 1 melted] fractured 5 the heather] heather 20 frozen again] frozen 29 I watched it, thinking of something else. 30 footprints] prints 31 *omitted Capriccio. Collected in NSP*

The Other [*text*: NSP] *title*: Rules of the Game *Capriccio*. *Title*: Laws of the Game *PBS Anthology 3, Oct 1992. Collected in NSP*

The Coat *reprinted in (eds.) Carmen Callil and Craig Raine, New Writing 7, 1998*

Shibboleth *collected in NSP*

The Error [*text*: NSP] **4** the] her **6** Accused, incriminated: demented **21** selflessly] fearlessly **25** mere] just **32** Drop] Escape **36** tarred and brimstone] tarred, brimstone *Capriccio. Collected in NSP*

Opus 131 *collected in NSP*

Flame **28** bit of paper] paper **35** open] rip *PBS Anthology 1 (New Series), Oct 1990*

RAIN-CHARM FOR THE DUCHY

Published by Faber and Faber, June 1992, in a limited edition simultaneous with a Faber trade edition. Most of these Poet Laureate poems first appeared in national newspapers, and there are many local variants between those texts and the texts as printed in *Rain-Charm*; these have not been recorded in the notes to the present edition, with the exception of 'An Almost Thornless Crown', an earlier text of which was published in *Flowers and Insects*. Hughes supplied a commentary on the poems, for both Faber editions, which is reproduced in Appendix One.

Solomon's Dream [*epigraph*] *this quatrain revises 'A Nation's a Soul', p.381*

A Birthday Masque, 2. An Almost Thornless Crown *subtitle*: Titania Choreographs a Ballet, Using Her Attendants **2** Over] Watching **4** She links] Let her link **7–10** Of dark nipples and full cup. / So she links / With a daffodil – one / Whose chill, scrubbed face, and cold throat / Looks utterly true and pure, **12** Let] And let **16** fling] throw **18** yet] but **20** Through to] Into **23** tall, September] and tall, autumnal **26** from] of **27** Dressed] Over-painted **27–8** *transposed* **30** more] find some **31** bowed stiffly] stiffly bowed **32** gravestones] the gravestones **34** Flint-raw] Flint-raw and steely **35** Touching] Who touch **36** Thinking] Who think **37** Or] Though sometimes **40** giddier] wilder **42** Away alongside scruffy rivers – **43** shiver their faces] shake their heads **48** An intricate, masterly Japanese brush **49** signature] identity signature **54** drugged] gentle **61** gently] kindly **63** Doubles as] Softens into **64–5** *contracted to*: And now an Arum lily, anorexic **66** *and* **68** *transposed* **70** nunnery] seminary **72** a last] one more **73** utterance] appeal **78** mid-air] breathless **81** And now the heavy part, a tumbling *etc* **83** Cored] Shadowed **86** hanging] left **89** A faint stipple of freckles darkening the fine tissue. **91** these] snowdrops **94–5** *transposed* **96** Their faces are so childish! *additional lines after* **99**: all Cordelias. / Or else all green-veined Gonerils / Under the empty frenzy of hoar-frost. // Or a little court, all Queens, / Listening for the Moon. *Flowers and Insects*

UNCOLLECTED (1992–97)

Lobby from Under the Carpet *Times, 9 Apr 1992; cf 'First Things First', p.730*

Three Poems for J.R.
[*text*: (eds.) Malcolm Bradbury and Andrew Motion, New Writing 2, 14 Jan 1993] *written i.m. Jennifer Rankin (1941–1979), Australian poet and dramatist*
Lovesick *first published in (ed.) Jonathan Barker, PBS Anthology 1986/87*
Atavist *title*: Remembering Jenny Rankin **10** dream lay moon open] moon-dream lay full open **26** provoked] Stirred **27** off] away *Rialto, Spring 1985*

Two Photographs of Top Withens [*text*: Elmet] *first published in Three Books (1993)* **32** that moment] a moment *Three Books. Cf. 'Wuthering Heights', in Birthday Letters, p.1080*

1984 on 'The Tarka Trail', I–II *first published in Three Books (River) (1993). Section II ('Nymet') incorporates and reorganizes an earlier uncollected poem entitled 'Nymet', first published LRB, 4 Dec 1980, and reprinted in Britain: A World By Itself, Reflections on the Landscape by Eminent British Writers (Nov 1984). 'The Tarka Trail' is a trail for walkers, along the twin rivers of north Devon – the Torridge and the Taw – as celebrated in Henry Williamson's classic animal story, Tarka the Otter 1927)*

Be a Dry-Fly Purist *first published in Three Books (River), 1993*

The Bear [*text*: Three Books] **59** gossip] love-lives **83** a scapegoat, an offering] an offering, a scapegoat *(ed.) Alan Tucker, Poems for Alan Hancox, March 1993. Collected in Three Books (River), 1993*

The Mayfly is Frail *first published in Three Books (River), 1993*

High Water *first published in Three Books (River), 1993*

Everything is on its Way to the River *first published in Three Books (River), 1993*

Why the '21st Child' Could Not Be Lifted *(eds.) Ken Smith and Judi Benson, Klaonica (Poems for Bosnia), Sept 1993*

The Last of the 1st/5th Lancashire Fusiliers [*text*: NSP] *title*: The Last of the 1st/5th Lancashire Fusiliers from the May 6th 1915 Landing **5** flutter] fluttering **9** wake] furrow *Guardian, 23 Nov 1993. Collected in NSP. cf. endnote to 'Mayday on Holderness, p.1243*

Snapshot *(eds.) Eugene England and Peter Makuck, An Open World: Essays on Leslie Norris (Columbia S.C. 1994)*

Playing with an Archetype *Spectator, 24 Sept 1994*

Epigraph *first published in Earth Dances: Poems by Ted Hughes, The Old Stile Press, Christmas 1994*

Old Oats *first published in NSP, 1995*

Anniversary *first published in NSP, 1995*

The Oak Tree *Daily Telegraph 4 Aug 1995; published on the occasion of the Queen Mother's 95th birthday*

A Trout? *(eds.) Joy Hendry and Allan Campbell, Norman MacCaig: A Celebration, 1995 [no date]*

Black Hair *Guardian, 10 Oct 1996; first published in the New Yorker, 5 Aug 1996*

Platform One [*text*: Sunday Times, 10 Nov 1996] *title*: The Freedom Fighter **7** Somebody, still bowed over something **17–18** [. . .] He's reading a letter – / Or is it the burial service? The raindrops **21** Sunk in his bronze] In his black bronze **24** remember us all] think of us all *additional final line, after* **24**: Just beside 'Lost Property', I notice. *Freedom: A Commemorative Anthology to Celebrate the 125th Birthday of the British Red Cross, 1995*

Comics *published as a pamphlet, Prospero Poets, 1997*

Mother-Tongue *Sunday Times, 12 Oct 1997*

6 September 1997 *The Guardian, 6 Sept 1997; published on the occasion of the funeral of Diana, Princess of Wales*

TALES FROM OVID

Published by Faber and Faber, May 1997 (simultaneously with a Faber limited edition). *Subtitle*: *Twenty-Four Passages from the Metamorphoses*. Four of the 'passages' were first published in (eds.) Michael Hofmann and James Lasdun, *After Ovid: New Metamorphoses* (Faber, November 1994), as noted below. Text: *Tales from Ovid*.

Creation; Four Ages; Flood; Lycaon 3 beings] powers **4** contrived] invented **5** The] These **13** moment] very moment **38** such] other **39** Began] Started **120** Alit] Settled **120** in] into **183** Magnified] Amplified **229–30** And not / To the blind opportunity of the moment. **234** Truth **235** Loyalty **338** a single] one **340** gesture] jerk **363** assemblies of heaven] divine assembly **395** I was still] Still I was **454** near] almost to **466** rabid] unappeasable **498** set] bent **525** Darkening] Deep **526** Two vast] Vast **538** Swept] Sweeping **538** topping] topped **542** To quench the

fury of Jove 546 the ocean] ocean 555 over] out over 582 halls]
avenues 591 Growing] Tiring 594 thunderbolt and lightning flash
transposed After Ovid

Venus and Adonis [and Atalanta] 5 forced] pried 16 thick-webbed]
smothering 29 Strained] Strains 41 Or his bow] Or if he had worn
one 41–2 subtlest of things, / Too swift] the subtlest thing, / Too
slight 56 by] with 310 slighted so] so slighted 360 scramble]
stumble 361 Bedded] Stabbed 362 strength] fury 363 hurtled him
aside, mangled] tossed him aside broken 371 gouged] tore 380 Into
the broken] Over the mangled 381 thickly] richly 384 packed]
crammed 386 fall] loosen *After Ovid*

Bacchus and Pentheus 3 Flared] Blazed 11–12 Of the corrector, are
nothing of the kind. / They are [...] 29 miscall] call 31 face] body
32 Will look like what it is not 33 mask] blanket 61 palazzo]
palace 104 its quiet] its roof-tree 141 Hungry] Greedy 143 to
liberate] will liberate 149 They will lift] To lift 281 In front of and
behind] On both sides of 284 Epopus] Epopeus 349 wicked – it is
stupid] wrong – it is foolhardy 396 Lycabus] Lycabas 399–400 in
the long smile of a dolphin *omitted* 410 dolphin tail] tail 411 That
had relaced his legs. 424 Now] Then 458 reverberating] resounding
473 stumbled] tripped 482–3 Pentheus bounded into it and halted –
/ Too astonished to take cover 501 claws] tries 521 Twists and
tears off the other. *additional line after* 526: Gazes a moment
527 And] Then 533 night-frost of the year] night-frost
535 Precariously attached *After Ovid*

Salmacis and Hermaphroditus 90 she laughed] she laughed to
nobody in particular 95 reach] grab 97 legs below] legs *After Ovid*

BIRTHDAY LETTERS

Published by Faber and Faber, 29 January 1998 (simultaneously
with a Faber limited edition). Twelve of the poems were serialised
in *The Times* between 17 January and 22 January 1998. Eight
poems in the volume were reprinted from *NSP* (1995), where they
were first published, or first collected, as noted below. *Dedication*:
for Frieda and Nicholas

The Tender Place *first published in NSP*

You Hated Spain *first published in (ed.) Douglas Dunn, Poetry
Supplement 1979, Dec 1979. Collected in SP 1982 and in NSP.*
16 So] When 20 fear. And the horn] fear – the horn *Ploughshares,
1980*

Chaucer *first published in NSP*

The Earthenware Head 1 your] the 2 Some American student
friend] An American friend 6 Unease] Comments 7 rite] ritual
12 Switch-horns, leafless] Leafless switch-horns 16–17 the socket of

a healed bole-wound, / A twiggy crotch] a twiggy crotch, the socket / Of a healed bole-wound **19** upright, firm] firm **29** We] You **30** ponder] nurse **31** much more] much **33** still there, representing] still representing **34** and happy] happy **37** – and shatter it?] (And shatter it?) **41–43** *contracted to*: Your head, made in a furnace, kisses God – *LRB, 21 Feb 1980. Collected in NSP*

Wuthering Heights *cf. the earlier poem 'Two Photographs of Top Withens', p.840*

Black Coat *first published in NSP*

Portraits *title*: An Icon **1** What happened / To Howard's portrait of you? **5–6** Calling "Howard! Howard!" – far off, / Fainter and fainter.' **7** started] tried **9** on its tripod] his fiery furnace **10** Session after session. **11–13** Yaddo Fall. Woodstoves. Tribal conflict / Of crows and their echoes. Rain, rain in the conifers. / You deepened – [...] **14–15** *omits*: looking at us / From that window of Howard's vision of you. **19–21** Out of the muddy, neglected, contrast background – / Who stood there behind you? A cowled **23–24** Howard smiled at it, surprised and watchful. / Ventured some more touches. 'I like it **26** Came from where?] From where? **27** Hungry rag-knot – eyeing the glaze wetness **29–36** *contracted to*: I didn't like it at all. Who was it / Edging up behind you in that cell / Of darkness and emptiness? You were pregnant. / What had Howard glimpsed? / We all watched **37** A small] An electric **45** *expanded to*: Because it's evil. It's evil, and that's why you like it. / Not because of anything else, but only / Because it's evil.' **46–53** Did you comment on it? / Barely a week before – / Entranced, gnawing your lips, / Counting on your fingers, and bowed low / In maternal care – you had enshrined / On your page the dead and immortal / Doppelganger of this. *Grand Street, Autumn 1981*

Stubbing Wharfe 31: My drunken grandad, dragged out of the canal, / Had sat in a sheet singing – *cf. 'Familiar', p.691*

Daffodils *cf. 'Daffodils', p.711, published in Flowers and Insects (1986); the later poem is extensively indebted to the earlier, specifically for ll.24–49*

The Rag Rug 50 dragged] dug and dragged *New Yorker, 5 August 1996*

Being Christlike *first published in the Spectator, 17/24 Dec 1994. Collected in NSP*

The Inscription *ll.20–26 largely reproduce ll.1-8 of 'The Laburnum', in Howls & Whispers, p.1176*

The God *first published in NSP*

The Dogs Are Eating Your Mother *first published in NSP*

Published in a limited edition by the Gehenna Press, Winter 1998 (dated Spring 1998). 110 copies. With etchings by Leonard Baskin. No trade edition was published.

The Laburnum *ll.1–8 largely reproduce ll.20–26 of 'The Inscription', in Birthday Letters, cf. p.1154*

The City 1 are a dark] are like a dark 2 Your novels, your stories, your journals] Your novels, your stories, your journals, your letters 23 or suddenly not to remember] or not to remember *Sunday Times, 26 Oct, 1997*

The Offers *printed in the Sunday Times, 18 Oct, 1998*

UNCOLLECTED (1997–98)

from **Sir Gawain and the Green Knight** *a translation of ll. 2160–2349, first published in (eds.) Seamus Heaney and Ted Hughes, The School Bag, 1997*

Some Pike for Nicholas *Waterlog, Dec 1997/Jan 1998*

Brother Peartree *(eds.) Carmen Callil and Craig Raine, New Writing 7, 1998. The poem addresses Hughes's older brother, Gerald, who had emigrated to Australia in December 1948 (cf. also 'A Solstice', p.381)*

Shakespeare, drafting his will *Sunday Times, 6 Sept 1998, where the following note accompanies the poem*: Shakespeare is imagined dividing his estate into three, like King Lear. One third goes to his wife Anne, 52 in 1606, and another to his daughter Judith, the twin of Hamnet who had died in 1596 aged 11. Hamnet would have been 21 in 1606. The third part goes to his eldest child Susanna, born in 1583. Both Susanna and Judith married: Susanna in 1607 (she bore Shakespeare his only grandchild, Elizabeth, in 1608), and Judith in 1616, two months before Shakespeare's death. The coat of arms mentioned in the last stanza was granted to Shakespeare's father in 1596. In 1606, the only heir to it was Edmund (or Edward), the illegitimate son of Shakespeare's youngest brother, Edmund – who died just before his father in 1607. *The poem was first published, with variants, under the title 'King of Hearts', as part 5 of the sequence 'A Full House', in July 1987, p.733*

The Prophet *The Telegraph, 9 Jan 1999; a version of Pushkin, based upon an annotated literal translation provided by Daniel Weissbort and Valentina Polukhina; one of the last poems written by Hughes*

A Dove *[text: NSP] first published in the Listener, 15 Mar 1979; anthologised in (ed.) D. J. Enright, the Oxford Book of*

Contemporary Verse (1980); collected in A Primer of Birds;
reprinted in Season Songs (1985); placed as the last poem in both
Wolfwatching and NSP. The Collected Poems follows NSP in
placing 'A Dove' as the final poem in the volume.
additional line after 1: Free **11** Porpoises] Dolphins **12** dove-lust]
blood-lust *Seasons Songs (1985)*. **7** Or] and (*l.11 reads* Porpoises,
l.12 reads dove-lust) *A Primer of Birds*

Individual poems, especially within Hughes's sequences, often employ first lines as titles, and it is sometimes uncertain as to whether a poem is untitled or whether its first line constitutes a title. The following Index of Titles broadly follows Hughes's mixed practice: it includes poems from *Adam and the Sacred Nine*, *Remains of Elmet*, *Moortown Diary* and *Earth-numb* as having titles; and it excludes poems from *Gaudete*, *Prometheus On His Crag* and *Orts* as untitled.

In cases where the title of a poem also functions unambiguously as
its first line, or as the opening of its first line, it is included in the
Index of First Lines as well as in the Index of Titles.

After a routing flood-storm, the river, 648
After Phaeton's disaster, 896
After the bloody dead-end, 133
After the brown harvest of rains, express lights, 339
After the fiesta, the beauty-contests, the drunken wrestling, 321
After the five-month drought, 803
After years of methodical, daily, 405
Against the rubber tongues of cows and the hoeing hands of men, 147
Aged Mother, Mary, even though – when that thing, 32
Air, 395
All darkness comes together, rounding an egg, 429
All day, 655
All night a music, 669
All night the river's twists, 594
All the dreary Sunday morning, 175
All things being done or undone, 59
All this time his cry, 444
All white is black as charcoal, 167
Always bad news from the Ouija board, 1076
Among ropes and dark heights, 72
Among smashed crockery rocks of jet, 589
Among those demi-gods, those perfect girls, 1021
An oak tree on the first day of April, 310
And everything had become so hideous, 421
And faces at the glutted shop-windows, 150
And finally he has fallen. And the great shattered wing, 178
And he is an owl, 178
And now Athene, daughter of Zeus, descended to change matters, 93
And Owl floats, 448
And suddenly you, 430
And the ashes gust, hands, faces, crumble, 192
And the Phoenix has come, 450
Angrier, angrier, suddenly the near-madman, 33
Applaud this scene, cheer, stamp, but do not, 12
Are a stage, 458
Are they children or senile, 565
As I lay under Bridestones, on that lovely bit of grass, 700
As if the eye and the head, 67
As if you descended in each night's sleep, 1135
As Mary bore, 736
As often as I affirm, 411
As to the limestone upland, 121
As we came through the gate to look at the few new lambs, 517
As you bend to touch, 723
At curious eyes, 380
At his begetting a Welsh adder, 126
At midnight in our rose garden a hyena laughed out loud, 10
At nightfall, as the sea darkens, 149
At some juncture the adult dies, 395
At the bottom of the Arctic Sea, they say, 573
At the end of the ritual, 440
At the top of my soul, 358
At your sixtieth birthday, in the cake's glow, 1166
Awake! said the flint-faced bird, Awake! Arise, 444
Away, Cuckoo, 741

Baby bawled for Mama – skull savaged it, 265
Bad-tempered bullying bunch, the horned cows, 504
Baled hay out in a field, 528
Barely prick the meniscus. Lightly caress, 845
Barley grain is like seeds of gold bullion, 497

Creation's hammer, 550
Crow, 336
Crow, feeling his brain slip, 232
Crow followed Ulysses till he turned, 240
Crow got impatient knocking on God's door, 270
Crow heard the maiden screaming – and here came the dragon, 203
Crow jeered at – only his own death, 272
Crow looked at the world, mountainously heaped, 221
Crow realised God loved him, 227
Crow saw the herded mountains, steaming in the morning, 220
Crow thought of a palace, 234
Crow was nimble but had to be careful, 253
Crow was so much blacker, 243
Crow who willed his children all, 814
Crueller than owl or eagle, 173
Crumbling, glanced into, 137
Cuckoo's first cry, in light April, 599
Curlews in April, 461

Daddy had come back to hear, 1158
'Dare you reach so high, girl, from the gutter of the street', 32
Dark voices, 460
Dawn – a smouldering fume of dry frost, 541
Dawn. The river thins, 658
Daylong this tomcat lies stretched flat, 66
Days are chucked out at night, 456
Dead eyes, blurred by hard rain, 128
Dead farms, dead leaves, 469
Dead, she became space-earth, 559
Dear Sir, 53
Death also is trying to be life, 553
Desire's a vicious separator in spite, 28
Destiny, not guilt, was enough, 937
Did music help him? Indeed it helped him, 742
Does it matter how long, 409
Down the black drain, and across the Black Lough, 1191
Dragonflower, 587
Drawing calmed you. Your poker infernal pen, 1071
Drip-tree stillness. Spring-feeling elation, 381

Each new moment of my eyes, 565
Earth heaved, splitting. Towers, 335
Earth is just unsettling, 644
Earth rolls, 587
Eighty four years dead, younger than I am, 691
Einstein bent the universe, 823
Empire has rotted back, 112
Enfolds you, as in arms, in winding waters, 430
Enter Hamlet, stabbed, no longer baffled, 585
Every creature in its own way, 631
Every day the world gets simply, 374
Eye went out to hunt you, 398

Face was necessary – I found face, 560
Faces lift out of the earth, 371
Fair choice? The appearance of the devil! Suave, 31
Fallen from heaven, lies across, 664
Famously home from sea, 673
Far thunder of the coming sun; ablaze, 8
Farmers in the fields, housewives behind steamed windows, 42
Fearful of the hare with the manners of a lady, 154